THE RUSSO-GERMAN WAR 1941-45

Other books by the Author

The Battle for Moscow 1941–42

The German Army 1933–45

The Soviet Army

The Fall of Fortress Europe 1943–45

Stalin as Military Commander

The Crimean War—A Russian Chronicle 1852–56

The Horsemen of the Steppes (The Cossacks)

The
Russo-German
War 1941-45

Albert Seaton

PRESIDIO

First published in the United States by Praeger Publishers, 1971

This edition published 1993 by Presidio Press
505 B San Marin Dr., Suite 300, Novato, CA 94945

Distributed in Great Britain by
Greenhill Books
Park House, 1 Russell Gardens
London NW11 9NN

Library of Congress Cataloging-in-Publication Data

Seaton, Albert, 1921–
  The Russo-German War, 1941–45.

  Includes bibliographical references.
  1. World War, 1939–1945—Campaigns—Eastern.
I.   Title.
D764.S377   1990   940.54'21   90-7191
ISBN 0-89141-491-6

Printed in the United States of America

Contents

CONTENTS

vi

CONTENTS

CONTENTS

CONTENTS

Maps

Acknowledgements

Gratitude is expressed to the authors, editors, publishers and agents concerned for permission to quote from the following books: *The Life of Neville Chamberlain* by K. Feiling – Macmillan and Co. Ltd; *Years Off My Life* by A. V. Gorbatov – Constable and Co. Ltd; *The New York Times* of 24 June 1941; *Generaloberst Halders Kriegstagebuch* – Verlag W. Kohlhammer GmbH; *Der Generalquartiermeister* by Elisabeth Wagner – Günter Olzog Verlag; *Hitlers Weisungen für die Kriegführung* edited by W. Hubatsch, and *Kriegstagebuch des Oberkommandos der Wehrmacht* edited by H-A. Jacobsen, A. Hillgruber, W. Hubatsch and P. E. Schramm – both published by Bernard u. Graefe Verlag: *Das Heer* by B. Mueller-Hillebrand – E. S. Mittler u. Sohn.

Notes on Sources and Style

The German sources used for this book have included unpublished documents, interviews and published material.

Of the official unpublished material, the most important and reliable sources of information giving the German order of battle are the *Schematische Kriegsgliederungen*, which were compiled by the *Oberkommando des Heeres* at frequent intervals throughout the whole course of the war. These are supported by the *Lage Ost* maps, which show in addition the German intelligence appreciation of the Soviet tactical deployment. The war diaries of army groups have been consulted and, less frequently, the war diaries of armies; little use has been made of the war diaries of corps or divisions, except on occasion to check details. Much use has been made of the surviving OKH files, particularly those of the *Fremde Heere Ost*. Other important unpublished sources have included Jodl's diary (which is in places little more than a collection of desk jottings) and the very full personal diaries of von Bock and von Weichs, together with the Speer interrogation reports, the Flensburg Collection of Speer's papers, and the minutes of the Naval *Führer* Conferences.

Of the published German documents the main sources have been the *Kriegstagebuch des Oberkommandos der Wehrmacht*, edited by Jacobsen, Hillgruber, Hubatsch and Schramm, Hubatsch's *Hitlers Weisungen für die Kriegführung*, Halder's *Kriegstagebuch* edited by Jacobsen, Jacobsen's *Der Zweite Weltkrieg in Chronik und Dokumenten*, *Nazi-Soviet Relations* and *Nazi Conspiracy and Aggression*. Other published documents and diaries used were Heiber's *Hitlers Lagebesprechungen*, Picker's *Hitlers Tischgespräche* and *Goebbels' Diary*.

Few German Generals have been asked for material or assistance, only because the surviving documents tell the story with greater accuracy than could be done by memory. An exception has, however, been made in the case of some aspects of operational and intelligence work, where former members of the OKH have been asked for comment

A large number of other German published works have been used, it is hoped with discrimination, in that preference has been given to the account by the participant or the witness. Guderian's *Panzer Leader* cannot be ignored; von Manstein's *Lost Victories*, Warlimont's *Inside Hitler's Headquarters* and Keitel's *Memoirs* are well known to English readers; although comparatively little material has been taken from these books, all have been used. Many other published accounts by German Generals have been referred to and used and these have included works by von Ahlfen, Chales de Beaulieu, von Choltitz, Deichmann, Doerr, Erfurth, Friessner, Fretter-Piro, Hoth, Heidkämper, Heim, Hümmelchen, Lange, Lasch, Morzik, von Mackensen, Niehoff, Philippi, Pickert, Plocher, Rendulic, Schwabedissen, von Vormann and others. Where these books have been available in English, the English language editions have been used; most, however, have not been translated from the German. In one case (von Choltitz), due to the non-availability of the German original, a French translation has been used. Frequent reference has been made also to the large number of excellent German divisional histories which have appeared since the war. The chroniclers of these histories, most of whom themselves served on the Eastern Front, motivated by the wish to honour the men who died, have made use of official and private records to provide a plain and unbiassed account of the war as it was seen by the German soldier.

For day to day reference work, constant use has been made of Burkhart Mueller-Hillebrand's *Das Heer*, Wolf Keilig's *Das Deutsche Heer*, Dr G. Tessin's *Verbände und Truppen der Deutschen Wehrmacht und Waffen SS* and Dr K. G. Klietmann's *Die Waffen SS*.

Whereas there is available a superfluity of unpublished and published German material on which to base a history, the problems in drawing on Soviet, that is to say Russian, sources are very different. Of archive material, which is the life-blood of history, none has been made available. In 1958, the military press of the Ministry of Defence in Moscow published Platonov's single volume *The Second World War* (*Vtoraya Mirovaya Voina*), a well produced work, which even today is in some respects superior to the fuller histories which were to follow. From 1961 onwards followed the six volumes of *The History of the Great Fatherland War of the Soviet Union* (*Istoriya Velikoi Otechestvennoi Voiny Sovetskovo Soyuza*), and an attempt was made to give this the appearance of a serious and objective historical study by including a number of footnotes on sources; since most of these refer to files in the archives of the Soviet Ministry of Defence, they signify nothing to the reader, inside or outside of the Soviet Union. In 1965 appeared *The Short History of the Great Fatherland War of the Soviet Union* (*Kratkaya Istoriya Velikaya Otechestvennaya Voina Sovetskovo Soyuza*), this being little more than a condensed form of the six volume work, although it does include some new detail. Two earlier books by Zhilin and Telpukhovsky are of only minor significance.

The six volume *Istoriya* and the single volume *Kratkaya Istoriya*, together with Platonov's *Vtoraya Mirovaya Voina*, are the only three Russian narratives covering the whole of the war; they have been used *faute de mieux* as the main sources to provide the framework on which the description of Soviet actions is based. Although much of the content of these Soviet histories is probably true, much of it can be proved to be false.

In the last ten years other Russian works written by official historians have appeared, covering certain aspects or operations of the war. In addition, a number of Soviet Generals including Timoshenko, Zhukov, Vasilevsky, Konev, Rokossovsky, Sokolovsky, Eremenko, Grechko, Lelyushenko, Golikov and Shtemenko, have written or have lent their names to books and articles. The books by Rokossovsky, Grechko and Sokolovsky are well produced and detailed military studies, which could, however, have been written equally well by a Soviet military historian. The accounts by Zhukov, Vasilevsky, Konev, Eremenko and Lelyushenko on the other hand are simpler, and include much interesting personal detail. The published books, whether written by Soviet Generals or by Soviet historians, do not, however, portray the whole truth or even necessarily what the writers believe to be the truth, since all the works bear evidence of official editing and censorship to ensure that they do not contradict previous accounts or deviate from the current Soviet Government and Party views. Soviet Generals, whether serving or retired, are servants of the USSR, and it is very doubtful whether they are permitted free expression of opinion or latitude to divulge information which has not been formally released. Unfortunately there are very few Soviet accounts of the war as seen through the eyes of the soldiers in the field comparable with the German divisional histories, and most of those in existence are written in a false-heroic propaganda style.

Notwithstanding these strictures, much information regarding the Second World War has become available in the last ten years through published Soviet works. The doubt remains as to its truth. This will never be verified until the Soviet Union throws open its archives to the public.

Only three Soviet books (those by Chuikov and Gorbatov) are available in the English language and these editions have been used as sources. All other Soviet published sources used are in Russian, except in a few cases where, due to difficulty in obtaining the Russian work, it proved necessary to use German translations. The language of the source is made clear by reference to the notes and the list of sources.

Whereas the books on the German Army by Keilig, Mueller-Hillebrand and Tessin are based almost in their entirety on German State Archive documents, and for this reason have been used freely for source material, no equivalent works exist on the Soviet Armed Forces or on the Red Army. The works on the Soviet Armed Forces published outside the USSR rely for sources on Russian publications; none of these non-Russian works has been used in the writing of this book, since it has been found preferable to draw direct from the Russian originals.

Some explanation is required here concerning orthography and the transliteration of Russian words. Geographical names are shown in accordance with *The Times Atlas* current between the two World Wars, even though this does not follow exactly the spelling used on modern Russian maps. The older form of spelling is, however, easily understandable. In transliterating Russian surnames and titles the Library of Congress method has been used, since this will be readily understood by all English speaking readers who know Russian. No use has, however, been made of the apostrophe for **ь**, which letter has been ignored. **й** has been shown as *i*, but **ий** at the end of surnames has been rendered by the more usual older English form of *y*; thus *Malinovsky* and not *Malinovskii*. At the risk of offending the purist, **Г** has been shown as *v* and not *g*, where *v* is its Russian pronunciation.

Generally, little use has been made of other histories of the Russo-German War. *Der Feldzug gegen Sowjetrussland* by Philippi and Heim and *Die Geschichte des Zweiten Weltkriegs* by von Tippelskirch have been read but have not been used for source material, except where their authors became principals in the actions they describe, and therefore primary sources. Reference has been made too, to the United States Department of Army publications, *The German Campaign in Poland 1939*, *The German Campaign in Russia – Planning and Operations 1940–1942*, *The German Northern Theater of Operations 1940–1945* and *Stalingrad to Berlin*; little source material has been taken from them, only because they are either unannotated or only partially annotated. Use has been made of the annotated works of Beloff, Butler, Dallin, Deutscher, Feis, Gwyer, Hillgruber, Janssen, Klink, Medlicott, Milward, Roskill, Woodward and others.

Surnames have been used throughout this book without initials (except where these are necessary to distinguish between two of the same name), and without titles or ranks. These can be found by reference to the index. The names of commanders have been shown down to the level of German corps and Soviet armies, since, until the latter stages of the war, these were roughly of the same size. The names of the political members and chiefs of staff of the Soviet armies have not been included, although they were of course of no less importance than the commanders, of whose military councils. they formed part and whose responsibilities they shared.

Any hint of dramatic effect has been studiously avoided, since the truth is drama enough. When the Deputy Commander of 25 Soviet Rifle Corps set out in pursuit of the leading regiment of 162 Rifle Division, a regiment which had run away in face of the enemy, it is his words which are used in describing the scene. When the 98 Franconian-Sudeten Infantry Division marched from the Ukraine on Moscow, one day following like another, the great chain of men moving forward in the slashing rain, obedient and silent, with nothing to be heard but the snorting of horses and the creak of the wagons, and the everlasting roar of the wind in the firs on either side of the track, this is the description by the divisional diarist and historian who marched with them.

Foreword

The subject of this book covers so vast a field that the work could not have been completed without the assistance of a large number of people. To all of them I express my gratitude.

I owe a very great debt to my readers: Professor Dr Hans-Adolf Jacobsen for reading the typescript, for his stimulating comment and advice on the contents and presentation of the book, and for his suggestions on the sources of new material, both German and Russian; Mr Malcolm Mackintosh for his helpful advice and for the systematic reading of the typescript and correction of errors; Professor Max Beloff who has read and commented on the early chapters of the typescript and who has given me valuable criticism and guidance; Mr Brian Melland who has read and commented on those chapters dealing with the German Armed Forces; General Adolf Heusinger who read extracts describing the personalities of Hitler, Jodl, Zeitzler and Paulus and the chapter covering the preparation of the *Barbarossa* operation; Captain Stephen Roskill who read and commented on the chapter on the war at sea and brought to my notice further sources; and General Burkhart Mueller-Hillebrand for his expert advice on the German Army.

I should like to express my gratitude to government departments, learned organizations, libraries and the many people in England, Germany and the United States who have given me assistance or advice in acquiring source material. In particular: Dr Friedrich-Christian Stahl and the staff of the Bundesarchiv-Militärarchiv and Professor Dr Andreas Hillgruber for their kindness and help during my visits to Freiburg; Dr Klaus-Jurgen Müller, Wissenschaftlicher-Direktor of the Stabsakademie in Hamburg and the family of Generalfeldmarschal Ritter von Leeb (for reference to the von Leeb diaries); Mrs N. Taylor and Mr W. Todhunter; Admiral Sir Geoffrey Miles and Commander A. Courtney; Mr J. D. Lawson of the Naval Historical Branch in London; the Foreign and Commonwealth Librarian and Keeper of the Papers; the Director General of the Imperial War Museum, the Archivists Dr L. J. Kahn and Miss A. Raspin of the Documents Section and Miss R. Coombs of the Imperial War Museum Library; the Librarian and staff of the Royal United Service Institution; the Librarian and staff of the Institute of Contemporary History and Wiener Library; the Director General and staff of the Meteorological Office; and the Hoover Institution, Stanford University, California.

FOREWORD

I am very grateful to Dr H. Schurer and the staff of the Library of the School of Slavonic and East European Studies, London University, for the loan of published Russian material and for help and advice on a number of Russian, Ukrainian and White Russian language queries.

My particular thanks are due to the Hon. Margaret Lambert for most helpful advice on the location of documents and to my wife who, over the years, has typed and retyped the script many times, and who has shared with me the arduous research of German material and indexing of Soviet military personnel.

Finally I would like to thank most warmheartedly Mr D. W. King, the Chief Librarian of the British Ministry of Defence Library (Central and Army) and Mr C. A. Potts, the Librarian in charge of the Library's Historical Section, for placing at my disposal a great store of English, German and Russian published material. Without their help and understanding this book could hardly have been written.

Introduction

When in 1940 Adolf Hitler decided to eliminate the Soviet Union as a political and military factor in Europe, he intended to destroy the USSR in a ten-week summer campaign. This campaign became one of the bloodiest and most pitiless of wars in modern times, developing rapidly from a European to a World War. Rarely can a war have been waged among civilized peoples with such savageness and such barbarous inhumanity.

This book is intended as a portrayal of war and not merely as a description of battles. More than anything else, it is about people.

The Russo-German War lasted four years and spread its battlefields over thousands of miles in breadth and depth, from the Arctic Ocean to the Caucasus, from the Caspian to the Elbe. Tens of millions of people died.

The subject of the war is so vast and so complex that it is impossible to cover all its aspects, even in outline, in a single volume; for this reason it is necessary to enumerate the subjects which are not discussed, or which are dealt with only cursorily in this book. German occupation policies in Russia had a great bearing on the outcome of the struggle and cannot be ignored; they are not, however, dealt with in detail here. Psychological warfare and the employment of partisans are most important aspects of modern war; but each is a study in itself, and for this reason could only be touched upon as part of the general narrative. Only one short chapter has been devoted to the naval war in the Baltic and the Black Sea, since the Soviet Union had no pretensions as a naval power and lacked the will, rather than the capability, to challenge German supremacy in these waters.

Since war is a political act, part of this book is necessarily devoted to a description of, and commentary on, the aims and foreign policies of the major powers, both before and during the Second World War. Economic and industrial potential and production provide the sinews of war; these subjects are discussed as a subsidiary of the main theme, although they are not examined in detail. Nor has it been possible, since space precludes it, to describe the operations in all of the many theatres of war on the Eastern Front; only two very short chapters have been allotted to the Finnish theatre; the fighting in front of Leningrad, bitter though it often was, is only touched upon from time to time. These omissions have been necessary in order to describe fully the decisive battles of the war, in Belorussia, West Russia, the Ukraine, on the Don, and in Rumania and Poland. It was in these theatres that the war was won and lost.

Errrata

P. xvii, line 25: "Generalfeldmarschal" should read "Generalfeldmarschall."

P. 4, footnote: "Volgagrad' should read "Volgograd."

P. 18, footnote 37: "1939" should read "1940."

P. 92, lines 34 and 35: change "independent tank regiment" to "independent tank brigade."

P. 145, footnote 47: "Morovaya" should read "Mirovaya."

P. 146, line 26: change "theatre chief of staff" to "chief of operations."

P. 198, line 36: change "Blaskowitz's" to "von Both's."

P. 243, line 18: change "Blaskowitz's" to "von Both's."

P. 276, line 10: "Konstantinovka' should read "Konstantinovska'
        footnote 29: both dates "1941" should read "1942."

P. 316, line 26: change "Colonel" to "Ivan."

P. 326, line 5: change "Vatutin" to "Eremenko."
        line 14: "Kalmuch" should read "Kalmyk."

P. 358, line 19: change "Mattenklott's" to "Dostler's."

P 360, footnote 24: change "38 Army Moskalenko (vice Chibisov)" to "38 Army Chibisov, 40 Army Moskalenko."

P. 435, footnote 6: "2 Belorussian" should read "1 Belorussian."

P. 515, line 14: *lishnyi* should read *lishnii.*

P. 560, line 32: "remined" should read "remained."

P. 581, footnote 41: change *OKH* to *OKW.*

P. 594, add entry after 50 Let: *"Voenno-Istoricheskii Zhurnal (V. Ist. Zh.)."*

P. 599, line 26: "1968" should read "1968–73."
        line 43: "Korowski" should read "Kurowski."

P. 600, line 2: should read "Vasilevsky, A. *Delo Vsei Zhizni.* Moscow 1974."

CHAPTER ONE

Duplicity and Guile

The Soviet Union, despite the attempts of its leaders to seal it from the outside world, was never a riddle or an enigma.

The political characteristics and aspirations of the Soviet Union in 1939 were the product of the history of Russia. Originally founded on a Slavonic people whom the Swedish Vikings conquered and to whom they gave their own name of Russ, the Russians became for ever segregated from the other Slav races. They were not destined to remain as a single people for long, however, for they were partitioned and kept in isolated subjugation for many centuries by the Tartars in the east and the Poles and Lithuanians in the west. From this period of partition was born Great Russia, first dominated by the Tartars and then by the growing power of Muscovy, and Little Russia, now known as the Ukraine, which, together with White Russia (Belorussia), formed part of the great Polish-Lithuanian Kingdom. The Great Russians, the Ukrainians and the White Russians became three distinct national groups speaking separate languages, each with their own culture. The history of Imperial Russia was bound up with the expansion of the Great Russians not only into Asia, but also into the Baltic and South-East Europe, in order to find an outlet to the seas and acquire land and peoples. The minority and nationalist problems which resulted, and in particular the efforts of the Great Russian to absorb and russify the Ukrainian, the White Russian, the Estonian, the Latvian, the Lithuanian, the Finn, the Pole and the many Asiatic nationalities, were the cause of much internal bitterness and bloodshed.

In 1917 the old Tsarist order was overthrown and in 1923 the Soviet Union came into being. The communist doctrine of universal brotherhood and the fact that many of the leaders of the movement such as Stalin, Trotsky and Kaganovich were not Russians, tended to some extent to conceal the racial antipathies of the nationalities within the new Union. The traditional expansionist policies of the Tsarist Empire were retained, however, without any great change, although there were some adaptations of method to conform to the newly injected communist thought. During the period from 1921 to 1941, the aims and the policies of the USSR remained consistent and logical.

1

Soviet foreign policy was founded on the basis of Marxism-Leninism which propounded that capitalist and communist systems and states were incompatible and could not permanently endure side by side, a collision between the two being inevitable and resulting in a final and complete victory for communism. The capitalist nations were to be hastened to destruction by subversion and propaganda intended to discredit their governments and social systems and sap the morale of their peoples. Differences between capitalist countries were to be accentuated and fomented in order to weaken their resistance and to establish communist states on their ruins. The Soviet Union was both the stronghold of communism and the springboard for the launching of world revolution and, as it later transpired, new foreign communist states as they emerged were to be subjected by Moscow to strict and rigid control over both foreign and domestic affairs.

In the early years following the revolution, the new Russian Communist State was weak economically and militarily, and was vulnerable to both external attack and internal insurrection. Lenin's aim at that time was to secure a respite against foreign intervention and to attract capital into the country, and for this reason he adopted an elastic and flexible foreign policy. By 1927, however, there were signs of a return to rigidity when Stalin, at the Fifteenth Party Congress, said that the period of peaceful coexistence between the Soviet and the capitalist states was coming to its end.[1] It was during Stalin's dictatorship that two very important aspects of the communist doctrine became apparent. The first was that the Soviet Union, as the foremost communist state and bastion of the movement, was to be kept strong and intact ready to overthrow tottering capitalism. For this reason a conflict with any power strong enough to endanger the Soviet régime was to be avoided. The second aspect was the confirmation of expansionist aims by subversion and the spread of communism, although the USSR was unlikely to embark on direct aggression if this involved any risk to itself. It was unable and unwilling to challenge France, Japan, Britain or even Poland in the post-war years, and with the re-emergence of Germany as a military force, the Kremlin took the greatest of pains not to be drawn into conflict with this power from which it had so much to fear.

The Soviet Union at this time was in the complete power of the dictator Joseph Stalin. A Georgian who had been expelled in his youth from a theological seminary, he became a revolutionary and an associate and disciple of Lenin. Having been appointed to the influential post of Secretary-General of the Communist Party, he concentrated power in his own hands and began after Lenin's death the removal and liquidation of the other members of the Politburo. Nationalism in the Ukraine had been put down in the post-war period with the greatest of barbarity, and this was to be followed by the collectivization of agriculture and the emergency measures against the *kulaks*,

[1] Deutscher, *Stalin*, p. 404.

2

EASTERN EUROPE
June 1941

the land-owning farmers and peasants. Millions were to die in the repressions and the famines.

In the thirties Stalin took a hand in the writing of the history of the revolution, in which he gave himself much credit, and in 1936 he instigated the great purges which destroyed nearly all in positions of authority, together with his former comrades who, because they were once close to Lenin, might one day have challenged his position. He, who had initiated the cult of Lenin, was to perpetuate the cult of Stalin. Zinoviev and Kamenev, once Stalin's main supporters after Lenin's death, met their end in the first of the 1936 public trials, and they were followed by nearly all the other members of the Politburo. The purge spread to every walk of life and became the terror which Stalin may have intended it to be. So-called confessions and denunciations followed arrests, and arrests followed denunciations, and so the purge spread like wildfire. Beatings, torture, transportation and shootings were the order of the times. Since in the Soviet Union relatives share with the accused the responsibility for political crimes, confessions were extorted by the threat that refusal would result in the arrest of whole families. Some of the accused underwent the formality of a trial, but many were never heard of again. The numbers purged are not known, but it is commonly assumed that they numbered millions and that nearly all were innocent of the crimes with which they were charged.

Millions of deaths apparently left Stalin unmoved. Even close members of his own family were casualties of the purge, some being shot, some sentenced to long terms of imprisonment from which they returned physical and mental wrecks. It is doubtful whether any autocratic Tsar ever had Stalin's power or wreaked such vengeance on his compatriots. His record in cruelty could only be matched by the Khans of the Golden Horde who ordered the vassal Russian princes to come to Sarai, the Tartar capital on the Volga, there to undergo public humiliation as token of their submission, or to answer denunciations made by their fellow Russians. The call to Sarai was often the last journey they ever made.[2] Their lands were laid waste and their peoples exterminated.

Stalin still remains a figure in the shadows and his character cannot yet be assessed with accuracy, since Soviet descriptions of the dictator are biassed and contradictory. Western observers who met him have recorded their impressions, and some additional light has been thrown on him by the writings of Milovan Djilas and Svetlana Alliluyeva. Many gaps remain, however. On the other hand there is no possible doubt that Stalin was in complete and undisputed control of the government within the Soviet Union and that he alone formulated all important policy, taking a close and personal interest in its execution. Such evidence as is available of Stalin's mentality and of the machinery which he used to control his subordinates indicates clearly that Stalin could not have remained long in ignorance of the actions of his ministers, should these have been contrary to his policy and interests.

[2] Sarai was on the Volga not far from modern Stalingrad (Volgagrad).

4

It is said that the dictator was deeply suspicious of any hint of opposition or challenge to his authority, this showing itself in a pathological persecution mania, to the extent that he saw conspiracy and enemies everywhere.[3] This particular aspect of his character enabled him to survive in the police state which Lenin and he had created, whereas the Old Guard Communists in whom this trait was less developed perished by the firing squad. Particularly skilful in assessing others and exploiting their weaknesses, pretence and deceit were said to be spontaneous in him, so that he could immediately adjust himself to the company he was in. What he said, he did not necessarily mean, and what he meant he did not necessarily say, which made for difficulties with his immediate circle where everyone hung on the dictator's words, avoiding any expression of opinion before Stalin had spoken, and then hastening to agree with him. He had brutal will-power and a lively, cunning, devious and dexterous mind. He was obstinate and malicious. Wit he certainly had, but of an ironic, taunting and cynical kind. His character appears to have been many-sided. Although motivated by a powerful will, he sometimes showed signs of a nervous, highly strung temperament and could be capricious and mercurial. His political knowledge and interests appear to have been wide although possibly uneven. When not engaged in fathoming another's brain, his speech could be blunt and to the point. Although his mind was apparently cramped by narrow dogmatism when he dealt with political, social and economic questions, he also gave evidence of having a great fund of realism and common sense. He could be very genial when it suited him. Yet in all, he was a monster amongst monsters, and his immediate circle apparently lived in great fear of him.[4]

In 1935 the rise of an anti-communist and Hitlerite Germany indirectly threatened the security of the Soviet Union which, already a member of the League of Nations, became a pressing advocate of collective security. There is evidence to suggest, however, that its intention was to use the League as a sounding-board for its own propaganda, while its concern in security did not extend beyond self-interest. It continued its policy of promoting strife between capitalist states and the first real opportunity occurred at the time of the Munich crisis in September 1938. It was here that the seeds of the Russo-German War were sown. According to the post-war account of Maisky, the Soviet Ambassador in London, Stalin encouraged Czech resistance to German demands by passing verbal communications to Prague through the renegade communist Gottwald (who was in due course to supplant Benes as President). This he may have done, but a state which is determined to stand by its treaty obligations does not make its intentions known by undercover word of mouth

---

[3] Svetlana Alliluyeva, *Twenty Letters to a Friend*, p. 207.

[4] Djilas, *Conversations with Stalin*, pp. 96–108 and 133–46. Stalin's close circle was always in danger of liquidation and others were admitted only to be executed. In 1949 Molotov's Jewish wife and Mikoyan's sons were arrested or transported, and Molotov and Voroshilov were themselves in danger shortly before Stalin's death. Deutscher, *Stalin*, p. 619.

messages through sources which can be readily repudiated.[5] The public promises of aid made by Litvinov, at that time Soviet Foreign Minister, were so vague and so couched in provisos as to be virtually worthless to the luckless Benes. In 1938 Czecho-Slovakia was separated from the USSR by Poland and Rumania, and both of these nations were adamant in their refusal to allow the passage of the Red Army through their territories. Offers of not too firm a nature could therefore be made by the Soviet Union in the knowledge that they could never be implemented. Meanwhile Moscow spurred on the reluctant Daladier and Chamberlain. To the British Prime Minister's disastrous illusions as to the honesty of Hitler's European policy were coupled deep-rooted mistrust of and aversion to Russia so that, regarding the Soviet Union's offers to have been made in bad faith, he virtually ignored them.[6] Maisky had for some time cultivated Winston Churchill who was still out of office and who, as a bitter antagonist of Fascism and Hitlerism, was more responsive to Moscow's arguments. The Soviet Ambassador used the impulsive and emotional Churchill unconsciously and indirectly to further the Soviet view.[7]

Whether or not Churchill was correct in his belief that a revolutionary and communist USSR would take up arms to protect a capitalist Czecho-Slovakia or whether he was guilty of the same misguided and ill-informed idealism which he condemned in Chamberlain, remains a matter of conjecture. The Soviet press, a reliable indicator of Moscow's intentions, at that time gave no hint of the possibility of war with Germany, and no mobilization measures were taken inside the Soviet Union.[8] The part played by Britain and France was an ignominious one, and it has been widely accepted that the Soviet Union was the only power ready to go to Czecho-Slovakia's aid. The failure of the two democracies to support a system of collective security disillusioned the USSR and obliged it to look elsewhere for safety. This was the argument subsequently used by Stalin when explaining his sudden *volte-face* of August 1939, and Churchill apparently believed him. Moscow propaganda has contrived to gain the maximum credit from the Munich affair, yet at the time there were other indications which threw doubt on the honesty of Soviet intentions. To counter a Polish threat against Czecho-Slovakia, Moscow informed Warsaw on 23 September that in the event of a Polish invasion, it would denounce the Soviet-Polish Non-Aggression Treaty. It committed itself to nothing stronger

---

[5] Maisky, *Who Helped Hitler*, p. 79. Benes made much of the closeness of the understanding which, he said, existed between Stalin and himself. See also Churchill, Vol. 1, *The Gathering Storm*, pp. 224–5; Schellenberg, *The Schellenberg Memoirs*, pp. 46–50.

[6] At this time Chamberlain was to write to his sister about the Soviet Union:
'I distrust her motives which seem to me to have little connection with our ideas of liberty, and to be concerned only with getting everyone else by the ears'.
Feiling, *The Life of Neville Chamberlain*, p. 403.

[7] Churchill, Vol. 1, *The Gathering Storm*, p. 242.

[8] See also Deutscher, *Stalin*, p. 426; Beloff, *The Foreign Policy of Soviet Russia*, Vol. 2, p. 163.

than a note. The next day when the Czecho-Slovak Government had already ordered general mobilization and it looked as though war were inevitable, the USSR withdrew rapidly from its exposed position, when it was stated in *Pravda* that the Czecho-Slovaks were trying to provoke Germany and that such provocation relieved the Soviet Union of any responsibility to come to their aid.[9] Less than six months later in March 1939, at the Eighteenth Party Congress in Moscow, Stalin spoke out clearly and unequivocally when he confirmed that at all costs he was not going to involve the USSR in war for the benefit of others.[10] This political line was taken up by the Soviet press which said even more explicitly that the USSR was not going to be dragged into a war against Germany by the machinations of Great Britain and France.[11] The idea of the Soviet Union going to war in such circumstances was certainly out of keeping with the accepted behaviour of communists and their tenets of faith. The history of the Soviet Union over the following years was to confirm this.

In March 1939 Lithuania, under pressure from Germany, returned the border strip of Memelland which it had seized in 1923, and in the same month Hitler annexed Czecho-Slovakia and established Slovakia as a separate puppet state. The British and French Governments, in an attempt to establish a *ne plus ultra* line as a bar to German aggression, guaranteed the territories of Poland and Rumania. Churchill, convinced that the Soviet Union was a potential ally of reliability which would fight Poland's battles in Eastern Europe, was exhorting the Chamberlain Government that the USSR should be brought into a military alliance with France and Britain and the Baltic States. With this in view, exploratory talks began in Moscow on 15 April between Sir William Seeds, the British Ambassador, and Litvinov; but almost immediately the Kremlin opened parallel secret negotiations with the German Foreign Ministry through the Soviet Embassy in Berlin. On 3 May the Jew Litvinov was replaced as Foreign Minister by Molotov, in order to smooth the path of negotiations with Hitler's rabidly anti-Semitic Germany, and on 30 May, after some preliminaries, the German Foreign Office confirmed its readiness to come to a settlement with the USSR. Meanwhile the talks continued in Moscow with the political and military envoys from Britain and France, until on 20 August Hitler brought matters to a head by his telegram proposing to dispatch his Foreign Minister, von Ribbentrop, to Moscow, with the fullest possible powers to conclude and sign a non-aggression pact and secret protocol. The announcement of the signing of the Nazi-Soviet agreement on 23 August came as a surprise to both the British and the French Governments.

[9] Wollenberg, *The Red Army*, p. 265.

[10] *Istoriya Velikoi Otechestvennoi Voiny Sovetskovo Soyuza*, (hereafter shown as *Istoriya*), Vol. 1, p. 164.

[11] *Pravda*, 6 April 1939. At about this time the tone and attitude of the German press towards the USSR changed, an indication that there was some activity behind the scenes.

In attempting to safeguard the territories of Poland and Rumania against aggression Britain was striving to achieve its aim by the use of the threat of Soviet arms. Poland and Rumania probably had a closer and more realistic understanding of the political factor when they refused to allow Red Army troops to cross their borders, even should these countries be attacked by Germany; some of the Baltic States went so far as to declare that any Soviet guarantee of their sovereignty would be regarded as an act of war. In the light of subsequent events, when their leaders, intelligentsia and part of their population were brutally done to death, often in the most bestial and barbaric fashion, or were transported to Siberia, such an attitude is understandable. It was somewhat indicative of Soviet aims that Marshal Voroshilov, the Minister of Defence and the leading Soviet representative at the Anglo-French talks, appeared to show more interest in the entry of the Soviet armed forces into the Baltic States, Poland and Rumania, whether these countries wanted them or not, rather than in fighting Germany.[12] Churchill echoed Moscow and blamed the Chamberlain Government for the failure of the negotiations in that it was suspicious of the Russians and, lacking any faith in the feasibility of agreement, sent empty-handed envoys to Moscow who were without status and without powers.[13]

In assessing the attitude of the Soviet Union at that time it is probable that Chamberlain was right and Churchill was wrong. It would have made little difference to the outcome of the negotiations whatever Britain's military strength and whatever the status of her mission. Britain and France offered the Soviet Union the prospect of a bloody war against a foe whom it had good reason to fear, an enemy who in the First World War had held the British and French off with one arm while it beat the Tsarist Empire into submission with the other. Even if Britain and France were to defeat Germany, it would be of little consolation to the Kremlin, since an invasion of Russia by German troops would jeopardize the security of the communist régime as it had that of the Tsar. For this gigantic stake the Soviet Union was to be offered nothing, not even the tiniest of the Baltic States. The proposal to fight such a war for a hostile and capitalist Poland was contrary to communist dogma and policy. Germany was linked to Japan by the 1936 Anti-Comintern Pact, and the Soviet Union was engaged in border fighting against the Japanese on the Khalkhin Gol river while the Moscow negotiations were actually going on. In no circumstances, so the Kremlin has subsequently said, would the USSR have conducted a war on two fronts by choice.[14] On the other hand, the signing of the Nazi-Soviet agreement served to exacerbate the strained relations between capitalist states and, although there is no proof that it was the Kremlin's

[12] Beloff, *The Foreign Policy of Soviet Russia*, Vol. 2, p. 267; and Maisky, *Who Helped Hitler*, pp. 173–4. For the Soviet version of the Voroshilov talks see Bezymensky, *Sonderakte Barbarossa*, pp. 47–127.

[13] Churchill, Vol. 1, *The Gathering Storm*, p. 303.

[14] *Istoriya*, Vol. 1, p. 176.

intention to instigate a war between Germany and the West, such a war, according to their Leninist faith, was the salvation of the Soviet Union and a necessary step in the direction of world communism.

Such was Hitler's anxiety to neutralize the USSR that he instructed von Ribbentrop to make any concessions he thought fit, even if it took the Russians to the gates of Constantinople. By the Non-Aggression Pact signed in Moscow late at night on 23 August and the hastily concluded and loosely worded secret protocol, Poland was once more partitioned between Germany and the Soviet Union, and Estonia, Latvia and Finland were declared to be within the sphere of interest of the USSR. As far as the Balkans were concerned, the wording of the protocol was to cause the *Führer* some surprise when ten months later he examined it more closely. It recognized the Soviet interest in Rumanian Bessarabia and stated that Germany had no political interest in these areas, these latter words referring, however, not to Bessarabia alone but to Bessarabia and the Balkans.[15] The exact position of Finland and the Baltic States in the Soviet sphere of interest was also far from clear. The Germans had not agreed to the incorporation of these territories into the Soviet Union without prior consultation, and it is certain that Hitler later came to resent the 1940 annexation of the Baltic States by the USSR. In addition to the pact and protocol, a trade agreement was signed, by which the Soviet Union was to deliver to Germany large quantities of food-stuffs and raw materials, including grain, oil, cattle, coal, lead and zinc, in exchange for manufactured articles. In all, the pact, protocol and agreement were highly satisfactory to the Kremlin which, at the cost of a little ink, gained the predominantly White Russian and Ukrainian regions of Poland, and an imprecisely defined free hand in the Baltic and the Balkans. In the event of war, Germany became an economic dependency of the Soviet Union, since a British blockade would cut off most of its sea-borne imports. The only stipulation for these gains was that the Soviet Union should not go to war. Meanwhile Stalin had high hopes that the fighting ability of the French Army, which he himself regarded highly, would reduce the German Army to a more manageable size, and he took advantage of the shock administered to the Japanese by the signing of the Nazi-Soviet Pact to patch up an agreement with Tokyo.

The stage was set for a German attack on Poland and a consequent Anglo-French declaration of war. Voroshilov and the Soviet Ambassador in Warsaw then assured the Poles of the Soviet Union's benevolent neutrality towards

<hr />

[15] *Nazi-Soviet Relations 1939–41*, pp. 78 and 157; and Beloff, *The Foreign Policy of Soviet Russia*, Vol. 2, p. 278, footnote 2. The English version given in *The Manchester Guardian* of 30 May 1946 and quoted by Professor Beloff was published before the full detail of the texts had become available and is not an exact translation. The text shows clearly that the German political disinterest refers both to South-East Europe and to Bessarabia. Von Ribbentrop confirmed this in his minute of 24 June 1940 to Hitler. The German text is: '*Hinsichtlich des Südosten Europas wird von sowjetischer Seite das Interesse an Bessarabien betont. Von deutscher Seite wird das völlige politische Desinteressement an diesen Gebieten erklärt*'. The Russian text is an exact translation of the German.

Poland in the event of war, and held out a promise of war supplies and equipment.[16] This duplicity may have been intended to ensure that Poland should not capitulate as Czecho-Slovakia had done without putting up some armed resistance, and that the Anglo-French should be forced into the war. On the Sunday night of 3 September, the same day that the United Kingdom and France declared war on Germany, von Ribbentrop invited the Soviet Union to take immediate armed action against Poland and to occupy those territories previously agreed as its sphere of interest. Molotov agreed, but the USSR did nothing for a fortnight in spite of frequent German promptings, the reasons for this tardiness being not entirely due to the need to prepare Soviet public opinion for armed intervention. It is probable that Stalin did not intend to enter Poland until he was certain that the French would not speedily overrun Germany from the west, at that time virtually unprotected, since he did not want to become involved in war with France and Britain. He had to wait too until his position in the Far East was secured. The truce with the Japanese was signed on 16 September, and on the very next day, after assuring the British and French that the USSR was neutral in their war against Germany, the Red Army was ordered across the Polish frontier. By a further secret agreement signed by Molotov and von Ribbentrop in Moscow on 28 September, the Soviet sphere of interest in Poland was moved eastwards, roughly from the line of the Vistula to the line of the Bug, in return for which Germany renounced its interest in Lithuania except for a small corner strip of Lithuanian territory in the south.[17]

In Western Europe in the first nine months of the Second World War, the Soviet Union continued to intrigue against the capitalist world. In Britain and in France the communists were active in weakening national resolution, and the Soviet Embassies in neutral countries conducted clandestine campaigns aimed at spreading the conflagration, some of this activity being directed against Germany.[18]

The partition of Poland was followed by the so-called pacts with the Baltic States, which were forced to allow the Soviet Union to establish naval and military bases on their territories. Similar demands made to Finland were rejected, and this led to the four months Winter War, after which the defeated Finns ceded the province of Viborg, the area to the north and west of Lake Ladoga, certain northern frontier districts and islands in the Gulf of Finland.

[16] *Polish-German and Polish-Soviet Relations 1933–39*, p. 183, No. 163; also Beloff, *The Foreign Policy of Soviet Russia*, Vol. 2, p. 273.

[17] *Nazi-Soviet Relations 1939–41*, p. 107. Molotov was to refer on 31 October 1939 to an independent Poland as an abortion. *Istoriya*, Vol. 1, p. 249. Soviet historians, to appease the post-war Poland, had to retract these words. In the Soviet history the German 1939 invasion of Poland is condemned as banditry, and in the section devoted to it no mention is made of Soviet participation. This is included elsewhere in a section describing measures taken by the USSR to protect the White Russians and Ukrainians of Poland.

[18] Berlin was obliged to protest in particular against the activity of Mme Kollontay the Soviet Ambassador in Stockholm.

10

Soviet claims on the strategically important Petsamo area on the Arctic coast, containing the nickel mines operated by a Canadian combine, were not pressed, presumably in case the British Navy should interfere, since it was significant that after the Germans occupied Norway and the nearby base of Kirkenes in the spring of 1940, the Finns came under renewed Soviet pressure to replace the foreign concessionaires by Soviet nominees. Meanwhile Soviet demands were made on Turkey for joint control of the Bosporus and Dardanelles Straits, but these were dropped for fear of British intervention from the Mediterranean. The Soviet Union let rest its outstanding claims in the Baltic and the Balkans until Germany attacked France in May 1940, when the surprising speed with which the campaign developed forced Moscow to take action before the victor should move his troops back into Central Europe. In mid June all the Baltic States were occupied, including that part of south-west Lithuania which had been allocated by the agreement of 28 September to Germany, and the new territories were incorporated into the Soviet Union. Before the end of the month an ultimatum was delivered to Rumania, and two days later the border areas of Bessarabia and North Bukovina were occupied, Bukovina not having been specified in the protocol to the Russo-German Pact of 23 August.

Although Molotov was to offer von der Schulenburg, the German Ambassador in Moscow, his warmest congratulations on the victory in France, the rapid collapse and defeat of the French came as an unpleasant surprise to Stalin.[19] Tension mounted in Moscow even as early as July 1940, and the realization became general that the USSR was in no little danger. In August, however, spirits were somewhat restored when it was obvious that the British, by then under the energetic leadership of Churchill, were not out of the war and could rely on material assistance from the United States. Meanwhile Moscow awaited the invasion of the United Kingdom taking what pleasure it could in the mounting German air losses. By then Hitler had time to devote to the political situation in Eastern Europe. There was no question of regretting the vague *carte blanche* protocol made by von Ribbentrop on the night of 23 August because in the *Reich*, once an agreement had served its purpose, it no longer existed. The *Führer*'s interest centred on Finnish exports of food, flax, timber, copper and nickel, and on the pressure being exerted by Moscow to acquire the control of the Finnish Petsamo nickel mines. There was yet another danger, since the USSR, from its new naval bases in the Baltic States, was in a position to cut off German sea-borne trade with Finland, and, much more important, the Baltic imports of iron ore from Sweden. Nor had Hitler ever really intended that the Soviet Union should have any hand in Balkan affairs. For two generations Bulgaria, in spite of its Slav affinity with Russia, had sought leadership and assistance from Germany. Rumania, failed by Britain,

---

[19] Compare Köstring's letter to von Tippelskirch 16 May 1940. '*Glückwünsche Anerkennung – alles war da, aber doch eine merkbare Zurückhaltung*'. Teske, *General Ernst Köstring*, p. 239.

could only look to Germany for security against Soviet demands. Germany needed Rumanian oil. So it came about that Hitler, having dispatched France, was soon to make his presence felt again in Eastern Europe and the Balkans. He deliberately misread the third item of the secret protocol of 23 August that Germany had no political interest in South-East Europe, as 'no interest in Bessarabia', and was later pointedly to misquote it to Molotov, who, however, made no comment.[20] Immediately after the campaign in France, he moved more than twenty divisions to the Lithuanian border to ensure payment of compensation by Moscow for the wrongful occupation of that south-west strip of territory which had been earmarked for Germany. He opened negotiations with Finland in August 1940, and in exchange for arms and other material assistance secured the right to move German troops through Finnish territory to and from Northern Norway, together with the necessary transit facilities. This eventually allowed him to quarter German troops in Finland and to keep the Red Army out of Petsamo.

In the Balkans the Germans lost no time in countering Soviet penetration and mischief-making. Hungary and Bulgaria both had territorial claims against Rumania, and the USSR sided against Rumania, concentrating troops on its border as earnest of its intention. Hitler, believing the Ploesti sources of German oil to be threatened, replied with a counter concentration of German troops in occupied Poland (the *General Gouvernement*); this was followed by an arbitration under von Ribbentrop's chairmanship, when, by the Vienna Award of 30 August, Hungary was persuaded to accept part of its original claim to Rumanian Transylvania, Bulgaria having previously agreed to be satisfied with only the southern part of Rumanian Dobrudja. In return for this cession of territory, Rumania was to be guaranteed by Germany against aggression from any quarter. German missions and troops were then moved into the country, ostensibly to reorganize and train the Rumanian Army. In this way the German oil supply was safeguarded and a Soviet instigated Balkan war was avoided. At no time was Moscow consulted or informed of the negotiations until the Award was made public, and the Soviet Union's sharp protests against the breach of the consultative clause of the Non-Aggression Pact of 23 August were given scant attention in Berlin. The USSR had a further snub when Germany signed the Tripartite Pact in September 1940 with Italy and Japan, Moscow rightly considering that the Pact was intended as a threat to her Far Eastern Territories. Meanwhile the return of manufactured German goods to the USSR so lagged behind the programme set by the August 1939 and the February 1940 Trade Agreements, that the Soviet Union was obliged to curtail deliveries of raw materials as a counter-measure, eventually threatening to suspend them altogether.

At this stage it does not appear that the Kremlin was unduly perturbed at the state of Nazi-Soviet relations. Germany had admittedly, much to the chagrin

[20] The translation of the words used by Hitler to Molotov is 'in the original agreement Germany was disinterested only in Bessarabia'. *Nazi-Soviet Relations 1939–41*, p. 235.

of the Soviet Union, come out of the French war victorious and unscathed. Hitler was competing with Stalin for the control of, or alliances with, Finland and the Balkans. This was to be expected. Diplomatic exchanges, political infiltration, stern notes and veiled menaces, the concentration and counter-concentration of troops in border areas, were part of the war nerve game which the communists knew so well. In the autumn of 1940 Moscow was not convinced that the Germans had won the war. The British Empire had been a bogey to Russia for a hundred and fifty years and, with its sea power and industrial resources, was still a force to be reckoned with. Even more important was the support which Britain could call on from the United States, and Stalin, unlike Hitler, never underestimated the wealth and power of that nation. Germany, blockaded from the west, was dependent on the economic help it got from the Soviet Union, which was even acting as Germany's agent in that it imported materials from abroad merely to re-export them. For this reason if for no other, it appeared in the Kremlin that Germany was unlikely to attack and cut off its source of supply. Although Stalin intended to avoid war at almost any cost, and was respectful but reserved towards Germany, he appears to have reasoned that a long war and a war on two fronts were entirely against German interests. He found some consolation too in the strength of the Red Army, notwithstanding its poor showing in the Finnish War; but he could not know that this last factor weighed little with Hitler and the German intelligence staff, who had a very inadequate understanding of the military and economic strength of the USSR.

By this logic Stalin considered in 1940 that his bargaining position was still stronger than that of Hitler, and he believed that the Germans would eventually be forced to come to terms with him. On 26 October the Red Army suddenly occupied some islands at the mouth of the Danube, in order to control the river traffic and put political pressure on Rumania and Bulgaria. Shortly afterwards Molotov arrived in Berlin in response to an invitation from von Ribbentrop, who was flirting with the idea of an extension of the Tripartite Pact to include the Soviet Union, and possibly Spain and Vichy France, as a continental bloc against the Anglo-Saxon Powers. On the 12 November Molotov, briefed by Stalin, listened to the German proposals without much enthusiasm, particularly when it became apparent that their object was to deflect Soviet attention away from the Balkans, southwards in the direction of the Persian Gulf and the Indian Ocean. He then subjected the meeting to a long monologue in which he repeated the well-known Soviet aspirations in Finland, Southern Bukovina and the Dardanelles Straits. Molotov wanted German troops out of Finland, and Japan to renounce her concession rights to coal and iron in North Sakhalin. He further proposed that the Soviet Union should issue a guarantee to Bulgaria, similar to that given by Germany to Rumania, with the additional right to set up bases capable of controlling movement through the Turkish Straits. In the air raid shelter talks with von Ribbentrop, Molotov revealed his secondary spheres of interest, which

13

included Greece, Yugo-Slavia, Hungary and Poland and the control of the outlet of the Baltic Sea.[21]

On 25 November the Soviet Union offered Bulgaria a pact, in return for which it promised to support Bulgaria's claim for the whole of Dobrudja and for access to the Aegean Sea through Greece. This offer was not accepted. By mid January Moscow had become aware of German troop movements towards the Balkans, and protested to Berlin against any proposed occupation of Bulgaria, Greece and the Dardanelles, saying that such a step was a violation of the security interests of the USSR. By then the Kremlin realized that Hitler was indifferent to Soviet threats, and in the warning delivered on 17 January to von Weizsäcker, the State Secretary of the German Foreign Office, Dekanozov, the new Soviet Ambassador in Berlin, dragged in the possibility of British intervention in the Balkans to give further weight to his note. From this time onwards the main initiative in Central and South-East Europe was in German hands, and Soviet diplomacy was reduced to a succession of protests. On 1 March Bulgaria adhered to the Tripartite Pact, following the lead of Hungary, Rumania and Slovakia, and German troops entered the country, this causing some uneasiness in Turkey. Greece was already fighting the Axis, and in South-East Europe only Turkey and Yugo-Slavia remained uncommitted. In order to involve these two nations in the war, Moscow pursued the same intrigue and diplomacy as it had done with Poland. The Soviet Union made known to Turkey its complete understanding and benevolent neutrality should Turkey be obliged to go to war with a third party, the third party being Germany. This offer to hold Turkey's coat was thankfully refused by Ankara.[22] Yugo-Slavia was forced by Germany to sign the Tripartite Pact at Vienna on 25 March. Two days later the Yugo-Slav Government was overthrown by an anti-German *coup d'état* and, in a final attempt to recruit a belligerent against Germany, the Soviet Union hastened to sign a Treaty of Friendship with Simovich, the leader of the new government. The usual promise was held out of military commitments and assistance in order to stiffen Yugo-Slav resistance to German demands, but on 5 April, as German troops concentrated on the Yugo-Slav frontier, the Kremlin resorted to its normal withdrawal tactic when Vishinsky, the Deputy Foreign Minister, told Gavrilovich, the Yugo-Slav Ambassador in Moscow, much to the latter's consternation, that there must have been some misunderstanding since a military convention or assistance had never been intended. Hitler, by way of reply, bombed Belgrade and invaded Yugo-Slavia the next day.[23]

There is strong evidence that the rapid overrunning of Yugo-Slavia and Greece and the ejection of the British subdued Stalin, and from this time onwards he abandoned his reserve and fawned on the German diplomatic staff in Moscow. This was duly noted by the German and the Turkish Ambassadors,

[21] *Ibid*, p. 252.
[22] Beloff, *The Foreign Policy of Soviet Russia*, Vol. 2, p. 365.
[23] *Ibid*, pp. 366–7.

and both put the same interpretation on it in their dispatches to their respective governments. The Turkish Ambassador went so far as to give an opinion that Stalin had hoped that the Yugo-Slavs would hold the Germans for at least two months, enough time to bring substantial Anglo-Saxon forces in to their aid.[24]

The USSR had been subdued, but was not yet fearful for its own safety. It earnestly desired to improve its relations with Germany and it switched to a policy of placation. In January 1941 Berlin had been paid compensation for the seizing of that Lithuanian strip of territory which had been allocated to Germany. At the same time a new trade agreement, very advantageous to Germany, had been concluded, and by April the Soviet deliveries of raw materials were being made at the full quota, no less than 200,000 tons of grain and 90,000 tons of petroleum being delivered in that month.[25] Stalin and Molotov continued to cold-shoulder Sir Stafford Cripps, the British Ambassador, having virtually nothing to do with him, and in May and June they expelled the Yugo-Slav, Belgian, Norwegian and Greek diplomats from Moscow, in order to demonstrate their solidarity with Germany's New Order. From April onwards, however, tension began to mount in the western military districts in Russia. Border violations were frequent and there were widespread rumours of an impending German attack.

On 20 March 1941, Golikov, the head of the GRU, the military intelligence directorate forming part of the General Staff, is said to have presented an intelligence appreciation, in which was set out the evidence of the apparent German intention to attack the USSR. That there was an increase of German military activity in the frontier area was known, and the Soviet Military Attaché in Berlin was said to have been informed by a German major of the intention to march against Russia. Golikov viewed the rumours and reports purporting to show the imminence of war as provocations originated by either British or German intelligence, and he came to the understandable conclusion that a German attack on the USSR was unlikely until Hitler had conquered or made peace with Great Britain. During April and May the German troop activity in Finland was closely noted, and on 5 May Golikov is said to have estimated that there were over 100 German divisions near the Soviet frontier. These appreciations and reports were seen by Stalin.[26]

[24] The change in Stalin's attitude was noted in von Tippelskirch's dispatch from Moscow of 16 April. *Nazi-Soviet Relations 1939–41*, p. 326. The Turkish Ambassador sent to Ankara a long appreciation dated 1 May on the foreign policy of the USSR but this, in that capital of intrigue and espionage, found its way to the German Ambassador von Papen's desk, from which it was dispatched to Berlin. *Documents on German Foreign Policy, Series D*, Vol. 12, p. 873.

[25] Soviet historical accounts are now silent concerning the economic aid which the USSR gave in this period, although Switzerland and Sweden come under attack for trading with Germany. On 1 August 1940 Molotov stressed in a speech that the German victory over France would not have been possible without Soviet help. Hillgruber, *Hitlers Strategie*, p. 105; and Degras, *Soviet Documents on Foreign Policy*, Vol. 3, p. 461.

[26] Zhukov, *Vospominaniya i Razmyshleniya*, pp. 233 and 248.

Although the Germans were at pains to delay bringing forward more than fifty per cent of the invading force until shortly before the campaign started, the build-up in the east could not be concealed. That there was some concentration of German troops was known in Washington and London as well as in Moscow. The Germans anticipated that they would receive Soviet queries as to the assembly of troops in the *General Gouvernement*, and they briefed Köstring, their Military Attaché in Moscow, on how such queries should be answered, the excuse being given that Poland offered good training grounds out of range of British air attack.[27] In addition Keitel, as head of the office of the Armed Forces High Command (OKW), had been entrusted with the fostering of a wide and involved counter-intelligence plan, which portrayed the concentration of troops in the east as a rehearsal for the invasion of England. Underwater-fording apparatus was fitted to a number of tanks, and the enemy was written in to the training exercises as British. The Crete airborne operation was described as a preparation and rehearsal for air landings on the United Kingdom, and there were deliberate leakages of information to the German and foreign press.[28]

The United States Commercial Attaché in Berlin received information in January concerning German intentions, which intelligence Washington referred to the Kremlin in the following March; the possibility of a German invasion was common table-talk among the diplomatic circle in Moscow during the spring and early summer.[29] On 24 April the German Naval Attaché complained of the rumours of war, which in his opinion were manifestly absurd, and reported that Cripps was predicting that the invasion would start on 22 June.[30] Churchill in his history has told how, acting as his own intelligence officer, he deduced at the beginning of April the imminence of a German attack on the Soviet Union, and infers that the failure of Cripps to hand an immediate communication to Stalin may have had an adverse effect on the opening stages of the war.[31] The information on which Churchill based his deduction was the rail movement of three German panzer divisions from Bucharest to Cracow. Three is a relatively small proportion of the nineteen panzer divisions then available to Germany in Central Europe, and in any case there was no reason why the Germans should not attack the Soviet Union from Rumania as well as from Poland. Churchill's deductions do not appear to have been entirely logical, and for this reason, amongst others, his intelli-

[27] *Nazi Conspiracy and Aggression*, Vol. 5, p. 574.
[28] *Nazi Conspiracy and Aggression*, Vol. 3, p. 635; von Lossberg, *Im Wehrmachtführungsstab*, pp. 116–8. It is doubtful whether this had much effect on the British, although if Zhukov is to be believed, it did bear some fruit in the USSR. Zhukov, *Vospominaniya i Razmyshleniya*, p. 241.
[29] Shirer, *Rise and Fall of the Third Reich*, p. 843 and footnote. Sumner Welles, *The Time for Decision*, p. 136.
[30] *Nazi-Soviet Relations 1939–41*, p. 334. The date of the invasion was not finally decided until 30 April 1941.
[31] Churchill, Vol. 3, *The Grand Alliance*, p. 319.

gence could have carried little weight in Moscow, while his motives would thereafter, in Stalin's opinion, have been even more highly suspect.[32] It is now known that Hitler had in fact intended to use these panzer formations as part of a thrust from Rumania into the Ukraine, but on 17 March he changed his mind and ordered the removal of all tanks from Rumania to the north wing of Army Group South in Poland. This was the movement noted by British intelligence.[33]

At the beginning of June the United States consul at Königsberg in East Prussia reported indications of war, and further intelligence of this type was received from United States sources in Bucharest and Stockholm. This information was handed to the Soviet Foreign Office by the United States Ambassador Steinhardt. On 10 June Sir Alexander Cadogan, the British Under Secretary for Foreign Affairs, gave to Maisky, the Soviet Ambassador in London, intelligence concerning the build-up in the east. On 12 and 13 June Maisky was again summoned, this time by Anthony Eden, the British Foreign Secretary, and given information which had persuaded the British Joint Intelligence Committee that a German offensive was imminent. The text of this British information was that 11 German Army had been identified in Rumania (where in fact it was) and that there was reliable evidence that a German army group headquarters was also established in that country (this latter was not true). It was also stated that Field-Marshal List's 12 Army had moved from Athens to Lublin (this too being false). Taken at its face value this intelligence, although of some weight, was in no way conclusive, even if it had been true, that an attack was imminent on the Soviet Union, since once again 11 and 12 Armies represented a comparatively minor proportion of the German troops in Central and South-East Europe.[34] The other indication noted by the British was increased *Luftwaffe* radio communication networks in Eastern Europe, but since there had been no apparent decrease of radio traffic on the networks in the west, this information was suggestive rather than conclusive.[35]

Some measures were taken within the USSR to prepare for war, although these were not of an extensive nature. In the spring of 1941 there was a special induction of reservists. According to Soviet figures, this increased the strength of the armed forces to 4,200,000 men but, as far as the Red Army was concerned, a considerable proportion of its other ranks lacked training, probably as much as twenty-five per cent of the strength having about eight months'

---

[32] For Stalin's reaction compare Zhukov, *Vospominaniya i Razmyshleniya*, pp. 243–4.

[33] Hitler's decision was noted in Halder's diary on 17 March and in the OKW War Diary on 18 March 1941. *Kriegstagebuch des Oberkommandos der Wehrmacht*, (hereafter shown as *Kriegstagebuch des OKW*), Vol. 1, p. 361; Halder, *Kriegstagebuch*, Vol. 2, p. 320, 'Panzer aus Rumänien möglichst bald heraus'.

[34] Maisky, *Memoirs of a Soviet Ambassador*, p. 148. For the detail of the intelligence given to Maisky see Gwyer, *Grand Strategy*, Vol. 3, Part 1, p. 83.

[35] *Ibid*, p. 83; and Kesselring, *Soldat bis zum letzten Tag*, p. 112.

service or less.[36] Concentration camps and prisons were combed for officers who had survived the purge, and some of these were speedily rehabilitated and returned to duty.[37] In March and April there was some movement of additional troops into the western border districts, four armies totalling twenty-eight divisions being moved from the interior.[38] The Kremlin appeared more interested, however, in making a demonstration of force rather than in safeguarding its security, and this was reflected in the pattern of the subsequent deployment. When Kirponos, the Commander of Kiev Military District, was ordered by Moscow to move some of his formations close to the border, he did so, but he was openly grieved and perplexed at what he regarded as a waste of reserves and 'passive defence'.[39] This curious deployment had been noted in Berlin, and there was a little speculation as to whether Red Army troops were closing up to the frontier preparatory to making a preventive attack. Halder, the Chief of German General Staff, thought the Soviet deployment could possibly signify a readiness to attack, but believed such a contingency quite improbable, and one of his principal intelligence officers, Kinzel of Foreign Armies East, made an accurate assessment when he dismissed the Soviet grouping as a political demonstration.[40]

In mid April the Soviet Union had signed a Treaty of Neutrality with Japan, and on 6 May there was an indication of the seriousness of the times when Stalin displaced Molotov as Chairman of the Council of Peoples Commissars, Molotov retaining his post as Foreign Minister. By openly filling the office of Premier in addition to his post of Secretary-General to the Communist Party, Stalin made it clear that he had assumed all powers.

[36] USSR Armed Forces strength 4,200,000 given in *Istoriya*, Vol. 1, pp. 460 and 475 and elsewhere, although Zhukov says the strength was five million. Zhukov, *Vospominaniya i Razmyshleniya*, p. 234. The field strength was said to be 303 divisions. *50 Let Vooruzhennykh Sil SSSR*, p. 235. There is a tendency to understate the true figure in order to put a more favourable light on the 1941 defeats, and since the figure includes the Red Fleet it appears low. Private soldiers served for two and non-commissioned officers for three years conscripted service. In September 1939 the conscription age was lowered from 21 to 19 years, the intake and release taking place in October and November of each year. By June 1941 therefore four annual intakes were with the colours. Nearly 1·5 million men reached the conscription age each year but a proportion would not be taken into the armed services because of economic, political or medical reasons, or because of service in the NKVD. Halder's rough estimate worked out on this basis gives the Soviet strength at about 4,700,000, but the OKH Secret Handbook '*Die Kriegswehrmacht der UdSSR*' (*OKH/Gen St d H/O Qu IV Abt Fremde Heere Ost (II) Nr 100/41g*) of 15 January 1941, page 16, put the Red Army mobilized strength at about 6,200,000.
[37] Rokossovsky had been released from a concentration camp as early as the beginning of 1939. Gorbatov was not released until March 1941.
[38] These armies were to become prominent in the subsequent fighting, Lukin's 16 Army from Baikal to the Ukraine, Konev's 19 Army from the Caucasus to the Ukraine, Efremov's 21 Army from the Volga to Gomel and Ershakov's 22 Army from the Urals to Velikiye Luki. Zhukov, *Vospominaniya i Razmyshleniya*, p. 236.
[39] Bagramyan (then chief of the operations department Kiev Military District), *Voenno Istoricheskii Zhurnal* No. 1, 1967.
[40] Halder, *Kriegstagebuch*, Vol. 2, pp. 351 and 353, 6 and 7 April. Kinzel's *Fremde Heere Ost* Appreciation of 20 May 1941.

It is believed that the USSR was well served by its own espionage organization. Moreover, even in Moscow overt indications were everywhere. The diplomatic corps talked of little else and the German Embassy, as Köstring, the Military Attaché, was to complain, was gripped by the fear of imminent war.[41] Even as early as the middle of May when Köstring had returned to Moscow from a long absence on sick leave, during which time Colonel Krebs had deputized for him, he noted that the members of the Embassy staff were sending back to Germany all their personal valuables, rugs, clothing, furs, silver and jewelry. Children and wives followed. Köstring railed bitterly to General Matzky, the Chief of Army Intelligence, in a weekly series of long demi-official letters, against the war-scare atmosphere and the behaviour of the German staffs in the USSR, and even his air and naval colleagues did not escape his censure. The Russians on the other hand, he said, were behaving perfectly normally, although they were quite aware of the panic measures being taken by German families.

On 11 June Köstring again reported that, after a short lull, the war-fever was increasing once more, with a resultant exodus of staff. In confidence, he retailed to Matzky the interesting and mysterious news that the Japanese Ambassador had just received a strange and laconic telegram from Berlin, presumably from General Oshima the Japanese Ambassador there, containing but two English words (sic) 'verry near'.[42]

There had been a thinning out of the German civilian naval architects in Leningrad, who had been reconstructing a cruiser for the Red Fleet. Their chief, the retired Admiral Feige, and all the women secretarial staff had left the country, and Köstring was to complain about the tactless way in which they were recalled.[43] There was no German shipping in Soviet ports and Soviet shipping was experiencing delays in being released from Germany, all kinds of difficulties being put in its way. The Soviet boundary commission had been expelled from the German side of the frontier in the previous March, and had not been allowed to return. A German aircraft which had made a forced landing at Rovno had been seized, and its maps and photographs showed unmistakably that it had been engaged in mapping the roads of West Russia.[44]

---

[41] Köstring had come from a Hanoverian family which settled in St Petersburg in the nineteenth century, and he was brought up in Russia from birth. He entered a German Uhlan Regiment in 1895. In 1931 he was appointed Military Attaché in Moscow as a colonel and was retired two years later. In 1933 he was reappointed Military Attaché to the Soviet Union and Lithuania as a major-general and he remained in that post until 1941 being promoted first to lieutenant-general and then to General of Cavalry. Krebs, who spoke Russian, had been employed with the Soviet-German boundary commission and had been sent to Moscow during Köstring's absence. Contrary to what has been said subsequent to the war, both Köstring and Krebs at that time had a low opinion of the Red Army.

[42] Letters to Matzky dated 14, 21 and 28 May, 4, 11, 14 and 18 June reproduced in full in Teske, *General Ernst Köstring*, pp. 304–319.

[43] Admiral Feige was employed under contract by a German civilian shipbuilder and the recall was authorized by Hitler. *Naval Führer Conferences*, 6 June 1941.

[44] *Nazi-Soviet Relations 1939–41*, p. 328.

Violations of the air space had been a daily occurrence for months past, yet Stalin had given categorical orders that German aircraft should not be fired upon, in case Berlin should treat such incidents as provocation. Armed parties of men, equipped with radio, had crossed the frontiers repeatedly and had been landed from the sea. Of these some were dressed as civilians and some as Red Army troops. Sometimes these infiltrators conducted an armed reconnaissance, engaging with fire any chance-encountered Soviet NKVD border troops, and sometimes, since they were nationals of the Baltic States or Ukrainians, they melted into the civil population of the Soviet occupied area.[45]

Totalitarian states, particularly when they are about to commit a surprise and unwarranted aggression, must keep the true facts of the case from their own people. On 14 June, barely a week before the day fixed by the Germans for the invasion, Molotov made use of a device to test Hitler's intentions when he issued a public statement to von der Schulenburg, the German Ambassador. This statement openly and frankly discussed the rumours of war and confirmed at some length the peaceful intentions of the Soviet Union. The test to be applied was to see whether Berlin would release it to the German press. The statement was never published.[46]

According to the account of the Soviet General Boldin, a German deserter arrived over the frontier on 18 June and gave what transpired to be the correct date for the intended invasion, the spontaneity of the German's actions and account apparently making a deep impression on General Rokossovsky.[47] By 20 June the Germans had been observed to be removing wire entanglements on their own side of the frontier. On the evening of 21 June at dusk, there was a marked increase of border-crossing activity by infiltrators from the German side.

The Stalin government at that time, although theoretically collective in form, was entirely subordinate to the will of the dictator. Stalin, cautious and doubtful, continued to appraise the situation coolly and logically. The mistake he made was to put himself mentally into Hitler's place and view the European and world situation through his own communist eyes, rather than to study the German dictator's mentality and appreciate what he, the *Führer*, was likely to do in a given set of circumstances. Stalin could not bring himself to believe

---

[45] The Soviet history complains of 152 air violations of the border in six months and blames the Chief of the NKVD Beria, whom it describes as a traitor, for ordering border troops not to open fire on German planes. *Istoriya*, Vol. 1, p. 479. The records of Kinzel's Foreign Armies East (OKH) show that refugee officer and NCO volunteers from the Baltic States were recruited by the Germans and segregated on airfields, ostensibly as aircraft fitters, and trained for line-crossing missions, being equipped with radio and Polish and Belgian arms. The Germans used Skirpa, the exiled Lithuanian Minister, as cover for this illegal organization so that Berlin might disclaim responsibility for these provocations.

[46] *TASS* dispatch 14 June 1941. *Nazi-Soviet Relations 1939–41*.

[47] Boldin, *Stranitsy Zhizni*, quoted by Werth, *Russia At War*, p. 147. This may not be true. The codeword 'Dortmund' for the invasion was sent out from Berlin just after midday on 21 June.

that the Germans would defy all reason and enter into a war on two fronts. He appreciated that all the indications of war were part of the war of nerves to frighten off the Soviet Union from the Baltic and Balkans, possibly presaging new German political or territorial demands. His communist logic told him that the obvious salvation of the British lay in provoking a war between Germany and the Soviet Union by intrigue and lies. He therefore dismissed the warnings of the British and their American friends as mischief. In all, these were the tactics which Stalin had himself used over the last three years, and it is understandable that he should credit the Germans and the British with trying to repay him in his own coin.[48]

On 13 June Marshal Timoshenko, the new Defence Minister, had wanted to bring the border military districts to war readiness because of Golikov's reports of increased German troop concentrations near the frontiers, but he failed to convince Stalin, and was told not to believe intelligence reports. On the afternoon of 21 June, Purkaev, the Chief of Staff of Kiev Military District, was said to have telephoned the Chief of General Staff, Zhukov, with the information that a German sergeant had deserted to the Red Army, bringing news of imminence of war. A clearly worried Stalin summoned Timoshenko, Zhukov and Vatutin, a deputy chief of staff, to the Kremlin.[49] Throughout the evening of Saturday 21 June, the Politburo met to discuss the likelihood of war, Timoshenko, Zhukov and Vatutin being present.[50] In the early evening a telegram was received from Maisky giving an account of a meeting that same afternoon with Cripps in London, in which Cripps, once again presumably by inspired guess-work, had forecast the invasion date as Sunday 22 June, or the next week-end. The alternative and later date must have much reduced the credibility of the intelligence.[51] At 9.30 p.m. that same night Molotov summoned von der Schulenburg for the last time and cross-examined him as to the possible demands likely to follow the threatening German military deployment. No answer was forthcoming. Von der Schulenburg was probably unaware of the imminence of war, and there is no conclusive evidence that his Military Attaché Köstring had been briefed on the coming invasion.[52] Whatever von der Schulenburg's demeanour, the Politburo

[48] According to Zhukov, Stalin said of the British 'You see how they try to scare us using the Germans, and frighten the Germans with the bogey of the Soviet Union, and so goad us on one against the other'. Zhukov, *Vospominaniya i Razmyshleniya*, p. 244.

[49] *Ibid*, p. 251.

[50] *Ibid*, pp. 251–4; also Budenny's account, Salisbury, *The Times*, 3 November 1967.

[51] Maisky, *Memoirs of a Soviet Ambassador*, p. 156. It is sometimes stated without any source substantiation that Cripps' intelligence was based on information given by the defecting Rudolf Hess, the Head of the Nazi Party Office and Deputy Leader (of the Party), who arrived in Scotland on 10 May 1941. The evidence available from the British Foreign Office is entirely to the contrary. Cripps was in fact anxious to hear of any revelation by Hess of 'positive German preparations for either direct attack on Russia or a political undermining of the present régime' but Hess had not imparted any such information.

[52] *Nazi-Soviet Relations 1939–41*, p. 355. Köstring, according to his post-war testimony, was briefed by Halder in August 1940. *Nazi Conspiracy and Aggression*, Vol. 5, p. 574. He was forbidden however to inform anyone, even his superior. This may have been the case,

obviously found no reassurance in this interview. Marshal Budenny was then appointed as Commander of the Reserve Armies, and the warning order was sent out shortly before midnight ordering the border military districts to a state of readiness. This order was not received by many of the field formations until after the invasion had taken place.[53]

---

but the probability is that he was consulted in hypothetical planning terms, and was in no way a party to the intention. Köstring's long letters to Matzky tend to confirm that the attaché had no idea of what was afoot in Germany. Teske, *General Ernst Köstring*, p. 306. On von der Schulenburg's ignorance. *Goebbels' Diaries*, p. 49. Von der Schulenburg, Köstring and the remainder of the diplomatic staffs were exchanged against Dekanozov and his staff in Turkey at the end of June.

[53] The account published during the time of Khrushchev's ascendancy blamed Stalin, Molotov, Timoshenko and Zhukov for the failure to take timely measures in the face of this evidence. *Istoriya*, Vol. 2, p. 10.

CHAPTER TWO

Enigmatic Paranoia

Adolf Hitler was the enigma, not the Soviet Union. In 1939 few outside his immediate circle realized the unlimited extent of his power and the arbitrariness and wilfulness of his character.

An Austrian of humble parentage, a wanderer and a misfit, he served during the First World War in a Bavarian infantry regiment for nearly six years as a private soldier and lance-corporal, and was later to look back with pride on this period, identifying himself with all that was German. After the war, a wave of communism and violence swept over Germany, and Hitler became in 1919 a civilian political agent in the German Army, part of his duties being the detection and countering of communist influences, so that he became in effect an anti-communist commissar. He then entered politics. Poorly educated and self-taught, his policy and aspirations were nothing more than a repetition, an extension of the past development of Germany, some of it rooted in the past two centuries, some of it stretching back for more than a thousand years. Hitler's mentality was a hotchpotch of ideas, many of them erroneous and some bordering on fantasy, borrowed from the writings of Houston Stewart Chamberlain, Gobineau and Nietzsche, and from the policies and achievements of Kaiser Wilhelm II, Bismarck, the Prussian Kings and Brandenburg Electors, the Teutonic Knights, and what he chose to consider the virtues and character of the early German warrior peoples.

The remarkable phenomenon in the history of the development of the German peoples has been their gradual movement, by a process of conquest and colonization, from what is now France and the Rhine Valley eastwards into Central and Eastern Europe. Great cities and towns such as Lübeck, Rostock, Stralsund, Stettin, Berlin and Frankfurt-on-Oder did not exist before the twelfth and thirteenth centuries and German settlers were used to found or reconstruct Posen, Cracow, Lublin, Warsaw, Vilna, Brest-Litovsk, Dorpat and Riga.[1] A resolute Poland resisted this eastward movement, and

[1] German peasants had been recruited by the crusading orders and warrior bishops to maintain their claims to conquered land. So effective were they as a stake that the Kings of Poland and Hungary themselves tried to attract the services of German settlers, whom they deployed against each other and against the encroachments of the German knightly orders from the west. In this way the German (*Volksdeutsch*) communities spread in large numbers into Central and Eastern Europe.

in the nineteenth century, after Poland had been partitioned between Russia, Prussia and Austria, the Germans were halted by the counter-pressure of the pan-Slavs in St Petersburg. In 1871 the German national state was born, and by the early twentieth century pan-Germans were advocating the conquest and annexation of territories which were Germanic or had in the past been developed by Germans. These included the Baltic States, Holland, Flemish Belgium and part of Switzerland. Jews and Slavs were to be deported to Poland and the Ukraine was to become part of Greater Germany. In 1918 the Ukraine was actually detached from Russia and became temporarily a puppet state dependent on Germany. In 1924, when he was serving a term of imprisonment in the fortress at Landsberg and writing *Mein Kampf*, Hitler first gave to the world his future design for the German nation and for Europe, a design impregnated with a hatred of Jews and Bolshevists and a contempt for all the Slav races. His ultimate aim was the conquest of those rich soils which would bring Germany grain, cattle, oil and ores.[2] In 1933 when he eventually came to power, he gave full rein to his anti-communist and anti-Soviet policies. In 1937 von Ribbentrop, then German Ambassador in London, outlined to Churchill what he said were the *Führer*'s territorial ambitions, which included Poland, White Russia and the Ukraine.[3] Even as late as August 1939, immediately before the signing of his Non-Aggression Pact with the USSR, Hitler blamed the statesmen of the western democracies for being so blind as not to understand that the bedrock of his foreign policy was the destruction of the Soviet Union.[4] Like Lenin and Stalin, Hitler was consistent in his aims. He differed from them in that, being governed by his emotions rather than by expediency, he was less predictable in his shorter term methods.

Hitler's character was a complexity of contradictions. Although poorly educated, he was both able and astute. An adventurer and an opportunist, like Stalin he had a keen eye for assessing the strength and frailties of others and could use both to his own advantage. His own brain was very quick but disorderly and his memory was extraordinarily retentive but clogged with useless trivia. On matters of minor importance he could quickly discern the essentials and could be logical and far-sighted. On the major decisions concerning the German *Reich* he was swayed by emotion and ideology and could be totally irrational. Much of the basis of his political faith was insane. Intensely interested in technicalities which were not his concern, too often he could not see the wood for the trees and saw the details but not the grand design. He was a gambler, convinced that boldness always paid; but his boldness had no basis on intelligence or sober estimate, but rather on sudden impulse. He was volatile and having given rein to impulse he was prone to bouts of nervousness and timidity from which he learned nothing, for having regained his composure he became both overbearing and over-confident and

[2] Hitler, *Mein Kampf*, Chapter 14.
[3] Churchill, Vol. 1, *The Gathering Storm*, p. 174.
[4] Hillgruber, *Hitlers Strategie*, p. 29.

rushed on to new excesses. When in difficulty he often refused to face up to threatening situations or unpopular decisions, and he pretended they did not exist. He was an untidy improviser and a man of snap decisions. He could become violently excited over unimportant matters, yet could hear out disasters with calm detachment.

He was entirely unscrupulous and ruthless and, like Stalin, despised anything but that which he judged as strength. Although he did not incite the same degree of terror among his associates as Stalin did in his Moscow circle, Hitler was mean and vindictive and his close associates feared him, for he had a long memory and did not fail to repay old scores. The people around him, and indeed the German nation, merely served as the instruments of his ambition and his will. His powers eventually became so complete that he was able to order arbitrarily, without any form of trial, removal from office and forfeiture of pension and property. Later were to be added incarceration in concentration camps, torture and execution. These punishments were sometimes visited not only upon those who had displeased him, but were extended to their families.

He was not always truthful. Some lies were told for effect. Some were self-delusion and wishful thinking. Some were for the furtherance of his Machiavellian schemes. He was secretive and kept the right hand in ignorance of the activities of the left. He believed in the dispersal and limitation of authority, all authority and knowledge being centralized in himself. According to his *Basic Order No. 1*, the need for security dictated that no one should know more than was necessary for the performance of his duties, and this meant that Hitler alone was the all powerful co-ordinator and director of the *Reich*. Collective rule by cabinet withered and the cabinet never met even for consultation, matters requiring decision being referred by ministers direct to Hitler. He was a paranoiac with a deep-rooted pathological distrust, and there were few who enjoyed his complete confidence for long; in his dark suspicious mind he saw everywhere conspirators intent on misleading or deceiving him. His own circle was very narrow and he disliked admitting new faces to it, possibly because he feared assassination. Urged on by his inordinate vanity, his restless ambition and his strength of will, he was determined on a path of conquest in his own short lifetime, and he was resolved to stop at nothing. This megalomaniac, particularly as the stress and strain of war took its toll of his nervous system, was to become increasingly immoderate and unbalanced.[5]

At some time subsequent to 1943 the dictator was to show symptoms of a nervous affliction or disease, which has been described variously as Parkinson's Disease, as a nervous breakdown brought on by strain and hysteria, or as a condition resulting from the administration of drugs. Since Hitler relied exclusively on the advice and drugs given to him by Dr Morell, his personal physician, and would not submit to other medical examination, the true nature

---

[5] See Schramm's introduction to Picker, *Hitlers Tischgespräche*; Schramm, *Hitler als militärischer Führer; inter alia*, accounts by Keitel, Jodl, Halder, Heusinger, Guderian, Zeitzler, Speer, Schellenberg and von Manstein.

of his disability has never been proved.[6] Consequently no deductions can be drawn as to the effect that his illness may have had on his mind. Until his death his mental powers seemed unimpaired. Rages were more frequent and his views became even more extreme, but these tendencies were strong in the days of his health. Before his death he certainly became divorced from reality but this phenomenon was common throughout the whole of the Nazi hierarchy.

Like Stalin, Hitler had an obverse side to his character. No dictator can indulge in a sense of humour at his own expense, and his wit was earthy and coarse and used others as its butt. Except to those who incurred his displeasure or distrust he made some attempts at courtesy. He could be gay, even charming, if he so wished, and to many who talked to him, even in his later days, he could give the impression of a rational being whose views were logical and moderate. Yet this same man was responsible for the murder of millions of innocents, the majority of whom were women and children.

In 1933 Hitler had been offered and had accepted the Chancellorship, although his party did not command a complete majority in the *Reichstag*. The *Reichstag* fire and the Enabling Bill allowed him to outlaw the substantial communist opposition and then force out the other political parties, so that he became a dictator at the head of a one party state. Any independence of the Federal States ended at this time, and the National Socialist Party was actually superimposed on the organs of the national and local government as part of the executive. So it came about that Göring, a former drug addict, became Prime Minister of Prussia, the Minister responsible for the Four Year Plan, Minister for Aviation and Commander-in-Chief of the German Air Force (the *Luftwaffe*) while the police and the security and espionage services became the empire of the bureaucrat Himmler with a staff largely recruited from the Party.[7] Party bosses, the *Gauleiter* and the *Kreisleiter*, began to usurp the authority of the local government bodies and many enriched themselves at the expense of the German State. In 1934 on the death of Hindenburg, the last President, Hitler adopted the title of *Führer* and Chancellor and Supreme Head of the Armed Forces. He had in fact taken over the office but not the title of the former President.

On 2 August 1934 all troops were ordered to take the oath of loyalty not to the constitution of the republic or to its elected government but to the person of Adolf Hitler. Hitler had formerly relied on the tacit support of the German Army while he purged, in a series of murders, the Nazi Party's strong-armed brownshirt *Sturmabteilung* bodyguard of those elements which appeared to threaten him. Since it was not in his interest to rely on the Generals to keep him in power, he began to extend his own influence inside the body of the armed forces and, at the same time, slowly but steadily increased the size of the SS,

---

[6] Also Trevor-Roper, *Last Days of Hitler*; Rechtenwald, *Woran hat Adolf Hitler gelitten?*; Rohr, *Hitlers Krankheit*; Bezymensky's account in *The Death of Hitler* throws no light on the subject.

[7] Military espionage and counter-espionage remained however the responsibility of Canaris' *Abwehr* in the Armed Forces High Command (OKW) until July 1944.

his own private army. In 1935 a secret defence law was passed in the *Reichstag*, conferring upon Hitler powers of emergency, mobilization and the declaration of war.[8] These developments had far-reaching effects on the High Command organization and on Germany's fortunes in the Second World War.

When Hitler became Chancellor, General von Blomberg was the Minister of Defence and *de facto* Commander-in-Chief of all the Armed Forces. This officer was an ardent supporter of the Nazi Party and had strong views in favour of a single High Command organization which would control both the Navy and the Army (the *Luftwaffe* being for a time an organic part of the German Army). This innovation was completely foreign to German tradition, which had hitherto relied on the Army and on the Army General Staff to undertake all war measures. The Armed Forces or *Wehrmacht* Office was brought into being at this time, its two principal staff officers being a Major-General Keitel and a Colonel Jodl. Hermann Göring, a Party henchman and crony of Hitler's, who had served in the First World War as a captain, was appointed in addition to his many other posts to command the newly founded *Luftwaffe* as a General. Von Blomberg had incurred Göring's enmity because of his earlier opposition to the establishing of the *Luftwaffe* as a separate service independent of the German Army, and Göring, moreover, coveted the appointment of Minister of War.[9] So when it came about that the widower von Blomberg married a woman who was subsequently alleged to have a police record as a delinquent, Göring saw to it that Hitler was speedily informed and used his influence in favour of von Blomberg's removal. This accorded well with Hitler's plans since von Blomberg had, in the *Führer*'s view, shown a weakness of nerve at the time of the reoccupation of the demilitarized zone of the Rhine. In any event Hitler had someone else in mind for the position of Commander-in-Chief. Von Blomberg was prevailed upon to resign and remove himself and his wife to Italy.

In February 1938 Hitler proclaimed himself as the actual (as distinct from the titular) Commander-in-Chief over all the Armed Forces. The War Ministry with its *Wehrmacht* Office was transformed into a single Armed Forces High Command *Oberkommando der Wehrmacht* (OKW) with Keitel at its head. Keitel, a Hanoverian artillery officer of no great ability, sometimes known among his fellows as the blockhead or the nodding ass, was an ardent Nazi supporter and, although named by Hitler as his deputy with the rank of Minister and the powers of the former War Minister, he was in fact to exercise no powers of command at all.[10] Nor was his position that of a chief of staff

[8] O'Neill, *The German Army and the Nazi Party*, p. 89.

[9] In 1935 the title of the Minister of Defence was changed to Minister of War.

[10] One of the few personalities on whom most were agreed was that of Keitel. Hitler, although praising him for his loyalty '*treu wie ein Hund*', said he had the brains of a cinema commissionaire, Göring, that he was the absolute zero, and Mussolini, that Keitel was a man who was pleased he was Keitel. Hitler found it useful to drag Keitel round in his retinue to impress foreign heads of state by his arrogant bearing. Keitel did, however, protect officers of his staff, one of them von Lossberg, from Hitler's spite.

since his opinions and advice counted for nothing, and his function was little more than that of Hitler's aide and administrator. The *Führer* had found the man he was seeking and a number of worthy General Officers unpleasing to the régime were retired. By then Hitler exercised direct control over the High Command of the Navy *Oberkommando der Kr. Marine* (OKM), the High Command of the *Luftwaffe Oberkommando der Luftwaffe* (OKL) and the High Command of the Army *Oberkommando des Heeres* (OKH). Even this did not entirely satisfy him, since it was the Army which he most earnestly desired closely and personally to control. Colonel-General von Fritsch, the Army Commander-in-Chief, and General Beck, the Chief of the Army General Staff, had opposed some of the *Führer*'s plans. By a conspiracy in which presumably Himmler and Göring had part, von Fritsch was wrongfully accused of homosexual practices and was suspended from duty. Before he was even tried on the charges, von Brauchitsch had been offered and had accepted the not yet vacant post as Commander-in-Chief of the German Army. Beck remained in office for a little time, vainly endeavouring to persuade von Brauchitsch to make a stand against Hitler's wild plans of aggression in Europe and tyranny in Germany, but von Brauchitsch was already Hitler's man and expressed the view that the German Army should be kept out of politics. At the end of August 1938 Beck resigned in protest and was retired, being replaced as the Chief of the General Staff by Halder.[11]

By the end of 1938 the command organization had been evolved which, except in one important particular, was to continue in being throughout the whole of the Second World War. By 1938 most of the principal actors had taken their places. At the head of the *Reich* stood Adolf Hitler, who as *Führer* and Chancellor took a directing and detailed interest in all affairs of state. In addition he was the Commander-in-Chief of all the Armed Forces. The Armed Forces High Command (OKW), nominally headed by Keitel, was nothing more than a secretariat, and, although it had a joint service staff, without Hitler's direction it had neither the authority nor the experience to issue orders of any weight to any of the three services. In consequence, therefore, on naval affairs Hitler dealt directly with Admiral Raeder of whom, at any rate until the middle of the war, he had a high opinion, and as he had no pretensions to being an expert on the war at sea, he avoided interfering in naval operations. With air matters it was very much the same story. Göring, as his Party confidant, enjoyed a special relationship and, in the early days of the war, a certain misplaced confidence. It was the Army which was destined to receive the major share of Hitler's attention.

Jodl was probably closer to Hitler than any other military officer, since he personally briefed the *Führer* daily on all OKW theatres of war and discussed at length plans and orders. It was thus that Jodl may have unconsciously served in the early days as a military tutor. Jodl was intelligent and very able, in spite of the fact that his views were narrow, in that his knowledge was

[11] Halder had been the equivalent of Director of Military Operations (*O Qu 1*) under Beck.

28

limited to military matters. Although ambitious, he was taciturn and reserved, and even his colleagues were unable to assess his character with any certainty. He was one of those who regarded the *Führer* as a genius; but it is not impossible that Hitler, who knew how to use subordinates, merely acquired ideas, with which Jodl not unnaturally found himself in complete agreement. At the critical time of the invasion of Norway in 1940, Jodl's nerves and judgement were sounder than those of Hitler; this the dictator readily recognized. From then onwards Jodl was obliged to sit next to the *Führer* at meals, which practice continued until Jodl fell from grace three years later when he sided with the recalcitrant List shortly before Stalingrad.

Jodl's reserved nature did not invite confidences or trust, and gave the impression to those who did not know him well that he was lacking in warmth, and it was partly for this reason that his relationship with other officers was not always good. His advocacy of the supremacy of the Armed Forces High Command (OKW) estranged him from many of his fellows, including the successive Chiefs of General Staff. He was, too, somewhat partisan in that, intent on bringing all theatres directly under the control of the Armed Forces High Command (OKW), he sometimes interfered in German Army matters which were not his concern. Yet the most serious flaw in his character was his inability or reluctance to judge and condemn the *Führer* for what he was, for, as Speer said, Jodl was as submissive to Hitler as was Keitel. He followed the *Führer* obediently right to the very end. He concerned himself with both strategic and tactical matters, but since he was merely Hitler's executive, his activity did not match his ability, and he was unable to rise above the level of routine. Jodl had no experience of command since the *Führer* refused to release him, and from 1938 onwards he was employed for seven years without a break in the offices of the OKW at the *Führer* Headquarters. It is doubtful whether he had more understanding than the *Führer* of the effect on the troops of some of the orders which he caused to be issued, and as Germany began to lose the war, Jodl's influence on Hitler, such as it was, became malignant, in that agreeing with his master in most matters, he added fuel to the flames and fortified Hitler's obstinacy. Jodl's influence was, however, very limited and he was not the only source of military knowledge.[12] Hitler picked up his ideas from many quarters.

Hitler's qualifications and experience in military matters were limited to his four years' service in the First World War on the Western Front, in which theatre he had served in no higher a capacity than that of company orderly

---

[12] Warlimont noted that Jodl was the only reliable source of information on Hitler's thoughts and intentions. Warlimont, *Inside Hitler's Headquarters*, p. 47; also Greiner, *Die Oberste Wehrmachtführung*, pp. 12–13; *Speer Interrogation Reports, F.D.C.1, Report 19*. Jodl's character is difficult to assess, particularly since some of the published descriptions are by authors who were in varying degrees hostile to him. On the other hand others, among them Heusinger, strongly maintain that, behind his reserve, Jodl was basically a decent man whose principal fault was his unreasoning loyalty to Hitler. This is true. Jodl's loyalty, however, was hardly to be distinguished from subservience.

in a rank something between that of first-class private and lance-corporal. He had during that war won the Iron Cross First and Second Class, an unusual award for one of his rank, and never ceased thereafter to impress on his Generals that he had been a front line soldier and knew what war meant.[13] That he had innate military ability there can be no doubt. Yet his previous service, commendable though it might have been, was certainly a very inadequate preparation for the post of Commander-in-Chief. But by attending military manoeuvres, exercises and presentations, he soon acquired the vocabulary, and by lending an attentive ear to the opinions and criticism of subordinate officers and disgruntled military specialists with *avant-garde* views, he soon had at his disposal a store of tactical and technical detail with which to confound his own military chiefs. With the egoism of the politician he reproduced this information as his own. This practice proved so effective in disconcerting opposition that he extended it to using as part of his arguments a great wealth of statistical and technical information which could not on the spot be refuted, since the subject matter was entirely outside his opponent's province. Nor indeed was he above fabricating evidence to win his point. In this way it was a relatively simple matter to manipulate the weaker of his General Officers, the more naïve of whom soon began to regard him as a genius. The *Führer* was quick, too, to sense any opposition or schism within the body of the German Army, and he was an expert in using one faction as a counter or check on the other.

Hitler's function as the Commander-in-Chief was very real and he did not hesitate to interfere with planning or the conduct of operations. Some of the higher ranks of the German officer corps were to prostitute themselves before this man in their scramble for advancement, power, grants of landed estates and even gifts of money from his privy purse. For this they plotted and intrigued against each other thereby earning the dictator's contempt, which as the war progressed, he did not bother to conceal. Even at the time of the occupation of Austria, he startled his staff by declaring that he would assume overall command of the operation himself. Having presumably been briefed by some disgruntled whisperer of mobile troops, he attacked Halder's plan for the employment of tanks in the occupation of Czecho-Slovakia.[14] Not content with confining himself to the general directions normally associated with the functions of a Supreme Commander, Hitler began to immerse himself in details of the conduct of operations. The invasion of Norway was originaily

[13] A story has since become current that Hitler's Iron Cross was inserted in the army records after he came to power. Although the Nazi régime was quite capable of such action there appears to be no evidence that this was the case. In 1932 Hitler brought a libel action, which he won, against a defendant who had cast doubts on the veracity of the meritorious service.

[14] Warlimont, *Inside Hitler's Headquarters*, p. 15; Keitel, *Memoirs*, pp. 67–9; Hitler at the Berghof subjected Halder, who had just taken up his new appointment, to a long and detailed lecture on the use of tanks, so that Halder, still quivering with indignation, was to ask Keitel in the vestibule afterwards 'What's he really after?' This was in 1938.

suggested by the German Navy, and was seized on by Hitler as his own project, it being mounted by a cell of the Armed Forces High Command (OKW), to the exclusion of von Brauchitsch and Halder, with very inadequate staff preparation.[15] Many of the *Führer*'s plans in the early days of the war were good, and the early German success in the campaign in France was due to Hitler and von Manstein. It is said that both produced, independently of each other, ideas on which the operational plans were subsequently based, and both proved themselves right in the face of earlier hostile criticism from German Army commanders and staff planners. Before and during the campaign in France, Hitler was to interfere frequently in both major and minor decisions, and Army leaders and staffs were apparently content to continue under these conditions without thought of resigning. Not only did Hitler, by encroaching on von Brauchitsch's prerogatives, become Commander-in-Chief of the Army in fact if not in name, but he was also the Commander-in-Chief of all the Armed Forces, as well as being Hitler the Head of State, Hitler the politician, Hitler the economist, Hitler the industrialist, Hitler the Party Leader, and, as the personal status of von Ribbentrop declined, Hitler the Foreign Minister. Not unnaturally, the demands and counter-demands of these many offices and the consequent confusion in priorities was to have a deleterious effect on Hitler's untrained and unstable mind, and this was to prove a contributory cause of failure as soon as Germany attacked the Soviet Union.

Hitler, the master improviser to whom established channels and organizations meant nothing, extended the extemporizing process, already common in government and industry, to the High Command. The campaigns in Poland, France and the Balkans were undertaken mainly by the High Command of the Army (OKH) supported by the *Luftwaffe* (OKL), both under Hitler's direction. The only Command with the experience and staff capable of mounting ground operations of this size was the Army (OKH), but it had arrived at the grotesque situation where it prepared its own campaign orders, and took them to Hitler and the OKW for concurrence. By the end of 1941 Hitler's authority was so paramount and his sphere of activity was so wide, that he personally controlled all foreign theatres through Jodl and the Armed Forces High Command (OKW). In December 1941 he was to dismiss Field-Marshal von Brauchitsch and take over the operational command of the Army in the East as well as elsewhere, so that he, as Supreme Commander, was giving orders to himself. He overcame this absurdity by using Halder and the Army High Command (OKH) as his own secretariat to control all operations in the east against the Soviet Union, while Jodl and the Armed Forces High Command (OKW) acted as his staff in controlling all other theatres. The Army (OKH) was thereby cut out of the responsibility and the communication channels for all theatres except Russia. Scandinavia (including Finland), France, the

[15] Jodl was complaining on 19 April that Hitler insisted on giving orders on every tactical detail. Warlimont, *Inside Hitler's Headquarters*, p. 78.

Balkans, Italy and Africa became known as OKW theatres and received their orders through an organization of the OKW headed by Jodl, known as the *Wehrmachtführungsstab*. In addition to the Navy (OKM) and *Luftwaffe* (OKL), the *Führer* therefore had two separate coequal staffs to assist him in fighting the war, one looking east and the other west. This was an inefficient and unsatisfactory method of high command, since neither understood what the other was about and both competed for army resources. The system was improvised and not planned and was a makeshift organization convenient to Hitler, according well with the dictator's mentality since he kept east and west in isolation and none could challenge his own personal authority and position.

Von Brauchitsch, the Commander-in-Chief of the German Army, was a Brandenburger and in some respects a typical Prussian. He was an able but by no means an outstanding soldier. Had it not been for von Fritsch's removal and the fact that von Brauchitsch was acceptable to Hitler to fill a post which the *Führer* intended should be that of an executive rather than that of a Commander-in-Chief, it is unlikely that von Brauchitsch would have even been considered for such an exalted position. Von Brauchitsch took up his appointment, which was not yet vacant, under an obligation to Hitler, in that he accepted the *Führer*'s assistance over the matter of his divorce. Halder, the Chief of General Staff, was an indefatigable, competent and cautious Bavarian. The relationship between von Brauchitsch and Halder was cool.

Back in 1938, however, Adolf Hitler was firmly in control of the state machine and armed forces for life. He offered the German people what appeared to be the only alternative to the unemployment, inflation and communist threat from which they had suffered in the post-war years. The proscribing and imprisonment of communists, trade unionists, freemasons and some clergy and socialists was to many a small price to pay, although presumably the national conscience had some qualms in reconciling itself to the treatment of its Jews. Organized violence in the streets, arbitrary arrests, beatings and concentration camps were already a feature of Nazi Germany. Generally speaking, the great mass of the people were united in their support of the National Socialist Party, and were to remain so until the very end, and for Hitler they showed a sickly adulation. Yet there is no doubt that the support was not entirely spontaneous. Much of it was indoctrinated by propaganda and some of it by fear. Schools were hotbeds of political education from the earliest age, and this was intensified even in infant organizations, the Hitler Youth, the compulsory Labour Service and finally in the armed services, where the swastika had been incorporated in the uniform, chaplains were few and the National Socialist newspaper, *Völkischer Beobachter*, was provided free out of *Reich* funds. All were encouraged to join the Party or one of its associate organizations, and towns and villages were divided into cells and blocks, where the civil police and Party officials kept a close check on the activities and views of each household.

32

By 1938 the Rhineland and Austria had already been occupied. Originally faltering, Hitler gained confidence with each step and his political and military advisers, whose forecasts had proved so often wrong, became more hesitant in restraining him. In September he precipitated the Munich crisis. It was believed by a substantial body of world opinion that the dictator's threats were both blackmail and bluff, and that a determined stand by Britain and France would have changed the course of history and averted the Second World War. In the light of subsequent evidence concerning Hitler's mentality, this is by no means certain. Hitler had already started on his career of conquest, and probably preferred war to a major political check which might have been fatal to his personal position. In August 1939 he was still sufficiently cautious to be opposed to making war on two fronts, but when von Ribbentrop's meeting in the Kremlin cleared all doubts, Poland's fate was sealed. The unexpected and rapid victory over the French and the reasonable terms imposed, encouraged the *Führer* to believe that the British would be more willing to enter into negotiations. When these offers were declined, Göring was empowered to make good his boast that Britain would be crippled by air attack, and the directives were issued for the invasion of the United Kingdom. These, however, came to nothing due to the failure of the *Luftwaffe* to gain air superiority over the British Isles and the German Navy's inability to safeguard the landings on a sufficiently wide frontage.

Even before the autumn of 1940 Hitler was in a quandary. The risks involved in the invasion of Britain had led to an indefinite postponement, but the longer the operation was deferred the less the likelihood that it would ever be undertaken. Hitler rightly reckoned that time was on the side of the British and Britain would, he knew, look for fresh allies. The United States, under the Roosevelt administration, was already overtly in Churchill's camp and would support the British with material aid, short of war. The German leader was parochial in his outlook and knowledge and he tended seriously to underestimate the resources and military potential of the United States.[16] He had no immediate reason to fear America as an enemy and he intended in any case to encourage Japan to divert the attention of the United States to the Pacific. On the other hand any suspicion of collaboration between the United Kingdom and the USSR was of immediate and close concern to him.

Cripps had been appointed as British Ambassador to Moscow with the express purpose of improving British-Soviet relations, since the British at that time believed, quite wrongly, that the more Marxian the Socialist the better his standing in the Kremlin. Stalin and Molotov were determined, however, not to become enmeshed in British intrigue, and Cripps was forced to deal,

---

[16] Hitler was to say that the USA was not so great a danger even if she entered the war. *Nazi Conspiracy and Aggression*, Vol. 6, p. 944. In his Chancellery speech to the army commanders on 17 March 1941, Hitler proclaimed himself the only judge capable of assessing national production figures. He considered that the armament production figures of the United States were pure humbug (*als reinen Humbug*). Von Lossberg, *Im Wehrmachtführungsstab*, p. 119.

at very infrequent intervals, with Vishinsky, the Deputy Foreign Minister. There is evidence that the British Ambassador's relationship with Vishinsky was of a restricted and formal nature and it is certain that his personal relationship with Molotov was decidedly unsatisfactory. On the occasion on which Molotov did receive Cripps he was deliberately offensive, making a demonstration of boredom and impatience, this being in marked contrast to the amiable and communicative fashion in which he treated von der Schulenburg.[17] Cripps, however, made some play among diplomatic circles in Moscow of the cordiality which, he inferred, existed between the Soviet leaders and himself. This he may have done with intent, in order to instil into the uncommitted nations the belief that German good fortune was shortly to change, but it is more likely that it was the natural result of injured pride and part of the process of sustaining his own morale. Whatever his intention, the effect was beneficial to Britain since the talk of the closeness of this relationship, although played down by von der Schulenburg, reached Hitler's ears through intercepted dispatches from the Turkish and Yugo-Slav Ambassadors to their respective Foreign Ministers. Any hint of British-Russian accord, even though ill-founded, served as an irritant and fed the *Führer's* suspicious mind. Gavrilovich, the Yugo-Slav Ambassador in Moscow, was himself on good terms with Molotov, since the two cultivated each other, and Gavrilovich's account of their cosy chats, which were decidedly anti-German in character, reached Hitler by the same intercepted channel. Amongst matters discussed were the more pertinent chapters of *Mein Kampf*, including German ambitions in the East and the treatment of Slav peoples. These literary criticisms found their way back to the author.[18]

Göring and von Ribbentrop were later to argue, when on trial for their lives at Nuremberg, that the actions of the Soviet Union in Central and South-East Europe precipitated the war between the USSR and Germany. It is certain that this was not the case. Soviet actions from June 1940 onwards not unnaturally displeased Hitler, but were not unexpected, particularly as Germany was the unbidden guest at the Soviet feast and was returning to territory in which, according to what von Ribbentrop had said in 1939, Germany had no political interest. Molotov's November visit revealed nothing to Hitler which he did not already know. The Simovich April 1941 Treaty of Friendship between Yugo-Slavia and the Soviet Union was seized upon by Hitler to justify to himself and to others the serious step he was about to take. The truth of the matter was that Hitler, no less than the Soviet Union, was convinced of the incompatibility of the capitalist and communist states and had never for one moment altered his political beliefs, which saw

[17] Woodward, *British Foreign Policy*, pp. 147–8.

[18] A memorandum of the Cripps conversation with Stalin had been handed by Molotov to von der Schulenburg on 13 July 1940. *Nazi-Soviet Relations 1939–41*, p. 166. There was some discrepancy between this and the tones of the Gavrilovich-Kalinin and Gavrilovich-Molotov conversations. Halder, *Kriegstagebuch*, Vol. 2, p. 34, 22 July 1940; also *Documents on German Foreign Policy* 270 (1), Vol. 5, 796 dispatches of 5 and 26 July 1940.

Germany's future prosperity linked with expansion in the east and in particular in the USSR. Hitler understood Bolshevism better than did the Anglo-American leaders at that time, and there is little doubt that in the long term his estimate of Soviet intentions was correct. If Germany were to become heavily engaged in a war elsewhere, the USSR would, if it could safely do so, extend its hold on Central Europe, the Baltic and the Balkans. At such a time it might cut off the delivery of supplies, without which Germany could not wage war. If Germany were ever near collapse the Red Army would occupy the whole of South-East and Central Europe and seize what it could of German soil. Not without reason therefore did he regard the USSR as a threat. Yet it is certain that, whatever the attitude of the Soviet Union, Hitler intended to destroy it, come what may, firstly because he coveted its territories and secondly because it was communist. The first of these reasons was cause enough. With the disintegration of the French Army the way lay open for him, except that he was still at war with Britain.

The oft repeated basis of Hitler's political and military policy was that he would never repeat the mistakes of the First World War and fight simultaneously on two fronts. Britain's air power and naval supremacy made a German invasion a very grave risk, even if a potentially hostile Soviet Union had not been in Germany's rear. Although Hitler had ordered the disbandment of German divisions in order to concentrate more resources on the *Luftwaffe* and German Navy, there was little likelihood that the German armament production could ever make up the deficiencies in naval equipment, or that the Germans could outpace the rapidly expanding air and naval forces of the British which were backed by the industrial potential of the whole Anglo-Saxon bloc. Hitler tended, too, to make the Soviet Union the scapegoat for his inability to concentrate all his air forces against England. Each incident and each irritant was used as confirmation to justify the course he had already set himself, and to persuade others of the correctness of his views. Although he exaggerated and dramatized the danger from the Soviet Union – it was in fact no immediate danger provided that Germany was strong – to Hitler the simplifier the issues were clear cut. In the east the enemy could be speedily cut down by the might of the German Army, the finest that the world had ever seen and then at the peak of efficiency. In the west this fine army availed him nothing and would go stale watching the beaches.[19] Delay might be fatal in that he would be faced with a strong Britain, backed by the United States, ready to re-enter the war on the mainland of Europe. Meanwhile he showed himself not unwilling, if only for the sake of form, to make some examination of the alternative strategy suggested by his commanders and staffs. These alternatives would have led the Germans into Spain, the Mediterranean and the Middle East.

[19] At this time Hitler said to Keitel that he was not going to have the German Army rot for the rest of the war, and that the war would not come to an end of its own accord. An invasion of Britain he admitted would not be practicable. Keitel, *Memoirs*, p. 122.

On Sunday 30 June 1940, hardly a matter of days after the French had laid down their arms, Halder noted in his diary Hitler's views passed on by von Weizsäcker. Amongst the cryptic headings were the jottings 'eyes must be fixed on the east' and 'the surrender of England will leave our backs free for the east'. In consequence, when three weeks later, von Brauchitsch was instructed to study the problem of a campaign against the Soviet Union, both he and his chief of staff had already given the problem some preliminary thought. In his diary entry for 22 July Halder gave the first outline of the scope of such a campaign.

It was estimated at that time that between eighty and one hundred German divisions would be needed, and that the necessary forces could be concentrated in about four to six weeks. In laying down his design for the war, Hitler saw the campaign as a repetition of that which he had just concluded in the west, an even vaster *blitzkrieg*, which, due to the severity of the Russian winter and the difficulty in carrying out any large scale movement between November and April, would have to be concluded in the short summer season. After the glorious victory over France none of his senior Generals appeared to have had doubt, according to the contemporary evidence, whatever they may have said subsequent to the war, that such a rapid campaign was militarily possible, and for the last time Hitler was in general agreement with his High Command. Such was the spirit of Hitler's buoyant optimism that consideration was even given to the possibility of mounting and executing a lightning decisive war in the autumn of 1940.[20]

On 29 July Jodl was already quoting Hitler as having said that he had decided on a preventive war and two days later Hitler said that Russia must be finished in one blow next spring, as it was insupportable to have it on the Baltic shore. The previous reductions ordered in the German Army were countermanded, and the strength was increased again by the thirty-five divisions it had lost, to which were added a further ten panzer and ten motorized divisions. The *Führer's* ideas had been so far clarified that he could see the attack being made in two main thrusts, one on Kiev and one on Moscow, but his aim, this time given by him as destroying Russia's strength (*Lebenskraft*), remained generalized and obscure.[21] From this time onwards planning proceeded steadily without interruption or check.

On 9 August 1940 the OKW issued the directive for *Otto*, the build up in the east, covering the setting up of administrative installations and training areas and the improvement of the road and rail network in the *General Gouvernement* of Poland.

By the autumn and winter a number of Germans were having second thoughts, not as to the military difficulties of the new war but rather as to the necessity to go to war at all. Halder told von Brauchitsch that the new war did

---

[20] Halder, *Kriegstagebuch*, Vol. 2, p. 49, note 14.

[21] Warlimont, *Inside Hitler's Headquarters*, p. 111; Halder, *Kriegstagebuch*, Vol. 2, pp. 49–50, 31 July 1940.

not help Germany in any way with its fight against England and could only lead to a worsening of the German economy. For himself he did not under-estimate the danger in the west (from Britain) and regarded Italy's entry into the war on Germany's side with misgiving since, if matters went wrong, Germany could become bogged down in the Mediterranean trying to extricate its Axis partner. If war with the Soviet Union was inevitable, the war must be total, with a strengthening of the German Army in men and materials.[22] Nor was Halder alone in entertaining reservations of this nature. Raeder, the Commander-in-Chief of the German Navy, was convinced that a war against the Soviet Union would not bring Germany a step nearer its immediate and true aim of defeating Great Britain and its Commonwealth and Empire, and he spoke out constantly and steadfastly against it. A war against the Soviet Union, he said, would involve too great an expenditure of German strength and it was impossible to tell where it would end.[23] As it had proved impossible to invade the United Kingdom, he would have preferred, as an immediate alternative, the destruction of British interests in the Mediterranean and Middle East by seizing Gibraltar, Egypt and Palestine. Von Brauchitsch, Halder and Göring added their support in favour of this proposal, and planning staffs had been at work examining this possibility. Even the German Foreign Office disapproved of a new war. Von Weizsäcker opposed the invasion plan on the grounds of logic and economics. Germany's stocks of strategic war materials, in particular rubber, oil, copper, platinum, zinc, asbestos, jute and tungsten, were so low that an interruption in Soviet supplies might cause serious diffi-culties. In a memorandum to von Ribbentrop on 28 April 1941 von Weiz-säcker said that if every destroyed Russian town were as important to Germany as every sunk British warship, then he, Weizsäcker, would be in favour of the new war, but as it was, he foresaw military victories but economic losses. The Soviet Union, he thought, would never willingly be an ally of Great Britain.[24] Von Ribbentrop was still mulling over the idea that the Soviet Union might be brought into the war against Britain.

At the end of October Mussolini, without consulting the Germans, had attacked Greece, the territorial integrity of which had been guaranteed by Britain, but he had made no headway in the face of determined Greek resis-tance. In November Molotov was already putting pressure on Bulgaria and seeking bases to control the Dardanelles, and in the following month the small British Army of the Nile destroyed the very much larger Italian Army of Libya. Hitler, fearing both Soviet and British intervention in the Balkan States and being uncertain of the attitude of Turkey, decided to secure his right flank in the Balkans before invading the USSR. In November and December a number of decisions had been made in determining the strategy and priorities for 1941. Further planning for Operation *Felix*, the attack against Gibraltar, was can-

[22] Halder, *Kriegstagebuch*, Vol. 2, pp. 45–6 and note 15, and p. 261, 30 July 1940 and 28 January 1941.

[23] *Naval Führer Conferences* 14 November, 26 September and 27 December 1941.

[24] Hillgruber, *Hitlers Strategie*, p. 512.

37

celled, as Franco was demanding too high a price for his assistance. A German attack, Operation *Marita*, was to be made on Greece from Rumania and Bulgaria, and this involved the adherence of Bulgaria to the Tripartite Pact so that German troops might enter its territories. The air offensive against the British was to be stepped up in the Eastern Mediterranean, but Hitler was unwilling to be drawn into a land offensive against the Middle East by an attack along the North African littoral or through Turkey and Syria, in spite of the urging of his naval staff, and he would do no more than allot German troops to Tripoli to bolster the retreating Italians.

On 27 March came the Yugo-Slav *coup d'état* and the negotiations between the Soviet Union and the new government of General Simovich. This posed a further threat to the German flank, and Yugo-Slavia had to be eliminated by force of arms. A new campaign, Operation 25, was immediately planned, involving the thrusts by German and Italian formations from Austria and Trieste, and by German and Hungarian troops across the Danube. The right wing of *Marita* was diverted westwards and additional German divisions were withdrawn from the troops concentrating against the USSR. By then it was obvious that the Balkan operations could not be brought to a successful conclusion by mid May, in time for the divisions to be returned to take part in the opening stages of the invasion of Russia, and Hitler found that he had stretched his resources too far. He was unwilling to thin out the many divisions occupying Norway and Western Europe because of his exaggerated fears of a British landing, and so, on 7 April, he found that he had no alternative but to postpone the invasion date for about five weeks from the original planning date of 15 May.

Some German apologists regard the Balkan situation as irrelevant to the delay, since they maintain that the late spring in 1941 and the consequent flooding by the thaw and spring rains would, in any case, have delayed the onset of the invasion. The Polish rivers had subsided, however, by the beginning of June, so that in any event, even on the central front, flooding could only have delayed the invasion date by two or maybe three weeks. The argument that the weather would have caused the delay is beside the point, as the need to secure the Balkan flank imposed a delay of five weeks irrespective of weather conditions.

Measured against the short campaigning season in Central Russia from June to October, when autumn mud brings movement to a temporary halt, or June to the onset of winter in the beginning of December, the delay of five weeks in the invasion date was of great importance. Yet this delay was no longer than the delay which occurred later that summer when Army Group Centre sat on its heels while Hitler wrangled almost interminably with von Brauchitsch and Halder. Even the time wasted by both of these delays was not the only cause of German failure in 1941 and must be measured against the other principal causes, the confusion of political and military aims, an inadequate High Command, poor intelligence and insufficiency of resources.

38

Hitler was in need of allies and he turned firstly to those two countries, Rumania and Finland, which had suffered from Soviet aggression. Rumania was willing to go to war, but its war aims did not extend beyond its real interests, the return of Bessarabia and North Bukovina and the acquisition of the part of the Ukraine between the Dniester and the Bug. Since Rumania depended so heavily on Germany, however, Rumanian wishes were to take second place and it was to be caught up in the advance to the Volga. Finland, continually menaced by the Soviet Union, allowed itself to be drawn into the preparations for war, but its position was to become a special one, not really comparable with that of Rumania. Admittedly, Finland was to allow the German Army of Norway to put an expeditionary force into Finnish Lapland and Central Finland, and was to add a Finnish corps to the German command, the whole force being designed to secure the nickel area of Petsamo and to cut the Murmansk railway. On the main southern front north of Leningrad about Lake Ladoga and the Karelian Isthmus, however, the Finns would not tolerate German interference. Whereas the Germans would have liked Finnish troops to seize Leningrad from the north, the war aims of the Finns were limited to the recapture of the territories lost to the Soviet Union in the Winter War. Thereafter Finland was content to do nothing and await developments. The Finnish Commander-in-Chief, Mannerheim, far from welcoming any participation by German troops in the south, was later to return the single Brandenburg division loaned to him, and he refused to take any further German formations under his command; nor would he subordinate himself militarily to German war direction.[25]

Italy and the puppet state of Slovakia were both to send troops against the Soviet Union. In Hungary there was some goodwill towards Britain. For this reason and because, as a former citizen of the Austro-Hungarian Empire, Hitler had some antipathy towards Hungarians, the Hungarians were to be excluded from all planning and preparations. Hitler intended, however, that Hungary should be brought into the war at the very last moment.

Hitler's remarkable successes against Poland, France, Yugo-Slavia and Greece were not entirely due to the numerical or qualitative superiority of German troops. The German economy was already geared to war and there was available a ready stock of armaments of all types. The German war preparations had a four year advantage over those of Britain and its Commonwealth and Empire, and between 1939 and 1941 Germany was able to defeat its neighbours, all of which were inferior in industrial and economic power.

As a consequence of the setting up of a dictatorship and the introduction of the 1936 Four Year Plan designed to make Germany economically independent, it was commonly assumed abroad, particularly in London, that Germany in 1941 was a powerful, monolithic, highly efficient industrial and economic machine, prepared for a long and exhausting world war. This assumption was

[25] The Finns did not regard themselves as allies of Germany but only as brothers-in-arms, maintaining that they were fighting their own war.

in fact far from the truth. Some action had been taken to decrease Germany's dependency on imported iron ores by exploiting domestic low grade ore, but even so, large quantities continued to be imported from Sweden and France. By 1942 the rubber shortage was to be overcome by the manufacture of the synthetic buna, and remarkable results were achieved in producing synthetic benzine, petroleum and oil products. Yet Germany was in 1941 to fight on two fronts and embark on the biggest war in its history on an annual oil allocation which was hardly seventy per cent of the domestic consumption of the United Kingdom before the war.[26] Tin and copper reserves had been used up in 1939 and Germany produced no tungsten and no chrome or nickel required for the manufacture of steel. In 1941 it still relied heavily on imports of oil, bauxite, tin, copper, lead and zinc.

The German war industry lacked centralized direction and was in the hands of competing groups. Göring, with his Four Year Plan Office, had succeeded Schacht as economic dictator, but the Ministry of Economics continued in being. In March 1940 Todt, who was also responsible for the Labour Service, had become the first *Reichsminister* for Armaments and Munitions, and to add to this threefold organization it had been decreed that the policy and priorities for the production of all military armaments was the responsibility of the *Wehrmacht*. These duties, although theoretically performed by Keitel in the Armed Forces High Command, were delegated to Thomas, who headed the War Economy and Armaments Branch *Wehrwirtschaft und Rüstungsamt* (*Wi Rü Amt*) in the OKW and who was responsible for the policy and co-ordination of the production of army equipment. Branches of the OKL and OKM were responsible for the policy for the production of air and naval armament. The whole of the German war industrial organization was extemporized and makeshift, without clearly delineated responsibilities. There was no systematic use o direction of labour and little restriction on the production of consumer goods. War plant was being worked on a single shift basis and, since there was a lack of a consistent and centralized direction, production priorities were continually subject to change with a consequent loss of efficiency. After the fall of France there had been a reversal in the emphasis on the production of armour and army equipment, and eighteen divisions had been given ticket of leave to enter the air and naval armament industry in preparation for the campaign against Great Britain. A further seventeen divisions were disbanded. The production of army equipment was throttled back. When Hitler turned his eyes eastwards, the men were recalled to the colours and the *Luftwaffe* and German Navy were relegated to second priority in armament production.[27]

The German armament industry was organized in breadth but not in depth

---

[26] In 1942 the estimated German oil requirement was 15 million tons, and of this Germany received less than 10 million tons. United Kingdom pre-war consumption was 13 million tons.

[27] Milward, *The German Economy at War*, pp. 5–13 and 19–46.

and in 1941 was quite unfitted for mass production or for a protracted war of attrition.[28] The four years start and the readily available stocks of good equipment enabled Germany to undertake its *blitzkrieg* campaigns against its weaker enemies, but by 1941 the British war production alone was rapidly overtaking the German.[29] Because of this economic weakness Germany could play the role of a first class military power for only a very short period of time, and thereafter was reliant on the ores and grains of occupied Europe and frightened neutral states. The shortage of oil and mechanized transport Germany never overcame.

Meanwhile Hitler dreamed his dreams. In February 1941 he was seriously discussing with Jodl the invasion of India through Iran or Afghanistan, and before the middle of the year was drafting further directives which foresaw Germany and Italy, after the destruction of the Soviet Union, controlling the whole of Europe, subjugating Turkey, if necessary by force of arms. Gibraltar, Egypt and Palestine were to be taken and the death blow dealt to the United Kingdom.[30]

The build-up continued in East Prussia and the *General Gouvernement* of Poland, and at the end of March there were between forty and fifty German divisions in the east. By the end of May the figure had increased to eighty and a fortnight later a further forty were added.[31] Most of the formations were concentrated well back from the frontier west of a line Radom-Warsaw-Neidenburg and not before the last week in May did the infantry formations begin their movement towards the frontier in a series of night marches. Assaulting panzer and motorized divisions were the last to move and came forward by night only a few days before the attack. On 22 June some infantry formations of 11 Army in Rumania together with the GHQ reserve were still on the march or on rail from the Balkans and Western Europe.

Up to the beginning of April these concentrations of troops could be partly explained by the subsidiary operations against Yugo-Slavia and Greece. The so-called preparations for the invasion of England were said to be progressing and these were discreetly publicized by a deliberate leakage of information, this being intended to draw the attention of the USSR and the rest of the world away from the eastern frontier of Germany. The German troops who were massing against the Russian border were conversely told

[28] *Ibid*, pp. 1–5. Medlicott, *The Economic Blockade*, Vol. 1, pp. 25–36, Vol. 2, pp. 1–26. Janssen, *Das Ministerium Speer*, pp. 13–29.

[29] By 1940 British aircraft production had already exceeded that of Germany.

[30] *Kriegstagebuch des OKW*, Vol. 1, p. 328.

[31] Build-up of German divisions summarized from the *OKH Gen St d H (Abt III) Schematische Kriegsgliederungen* (henceforth known as *OKH Kriegsgliederungen*), of the following dates.

1941	East	Balkans
12 March	34	15
23 April	59	27
5 June	100	13
22 June	124	7

that the concentrations were part of a gigantic bluff designed to draw the attention of the British away from the preparations for the sea landing. Eventually, however, the concentration and movement could not be concealed from the Polish population and it was assumed, and later confirmed by intelligence indicators, that the Russians knew what was afoot. On 10 April Moscow ordered some minor precautionary measures and there had been further reinforcing of the Red Army troops on the frontier. In the Baltic States particularly, the occupying Soviet forces appeared nervous and from the night of 13 June onwards there were mass arrests of all elements of the civilian population likely to prefer a German to a Soviet occupation. About 50,000 citizens were deported.

CHAPTER THREE

A Little Knowledge

In peace or in war, the intelligence service, however efficient, rarely has a really clear picture of its target; for, as von Clausewitz said, the greater part of the information obtained in war is contradictory, a still greater part is false, and by far the greatest part is of a doubtful character.

Whereas during the period between the two World Wars the Soviet Union had been the primary intelligence target for many of the major military powers, German intelligence interest had been directed mainly westwards. In consequence, in 1941, the comprehensiveness of German military intelligence on the Soviet Union compared unfavourably with the intelligence picture of the USSR collated by other nations, and, in particular, with that produced by the British military intelligence service.

The German military intelligence staff organization (*O Qu IV*) within the Army High Command (OKH) was headed by Major-General Matzky, who, on returning from the post of Military Attaché in Tokyo, had recently replaced von Tippelskirch as Director of Army Intelligence. *O Qu IV* was subdivided into two main sections, Foreign Armies West and Foreign Armies East. Foreign Armies West under a Lieutenant-Colonel Liss dealt with the armies of Western Europe, which since June 1940 centred on those of Britain and its Commonwealth and Empire. Foreign Armies East was under a Lieutenant-Colonel Kinzel and covered the armies of the Scandinavian and some Balkan countries, the USSR, China and Japan and, until December 1941, the armies of the New World, including that of the United States. This allocation of duties was indicative of the relative importance attached by the Germans to Britain and the Soviet Union as intelligence targets. Since the USSR had not been designated as a primary target, little time or money had been devoted to the collection or evaluation of material on the Red Army; during 1939 and 1940 Hitler had even forbidden such activity. Moreover, intelligence on the USSR was only a minor part of Kinzel's responsibilities. Kinzel was an infantry officer of the General Staff who had held his appointment since the end of 1938. He had no particular knowledge of the Soviet Union or the Red Army nor was he a specialist intelligence officer. He could not speak Russian.[1]

[1] It was the practice in the German Army at that time to regard the main intelligence appointments as normal General Staff posts to be filled by officers without specialist intelli-

Originally, in the days of the *Reichswehr*, there had been a fairly close liaison between the German General Staff and the Red Army, but this ceased abruptly after 1933 when Hitler came to power. From 1934 onwards there was an exchange of information with Poland which, with its White Russian and Ukrainian population, had some sources of information on the border regions, but this interchange was discontinued in the spring of 1939 when Hitler renounced the Polish-German Non-Aggression Pact. The Red Army troops which invaded East Poland in September 1939 did not impress the German Army by their bearing or efficiency, yet it is significant that German military intelligence failed to identify correctly the army headquarters in the invading force.[2] Thereafter some information was gleaned from refugee sources in the Baltic States and East Poland, but this was of a very localized nature. It was to prove very difficult to collect military or economic information or intelligence from the interior of the Soviet Union because all frontier areas were occupied and controlled by NKVD border guards, who had received a long and specialized training designed to discourage border crossing by illegal entrants or by defectors and deserters. The Soviet system of the registration of the population by both the police and the Party and the carrying of identity documents and labour books made it difficult to introduce agents into the country. The most effective bar to the collection of any information, even of an overt nature, was the attitude of the Soviet population. Encouraged by the régime so to be, they were unfriendly to and suspicious of both strangers and foreigners. Foreigners of any status were rarely allowed to travel inside the Soviet Union, and, on the rare occasions when official permission was given, they travelled by defined routes and at specified times under the close supervision of the NKVD, the journey being made as difficult and often as uncomfortable as possible. The badges and insignia of Red Army men at that time, unless they were Cossacks, showed only rank and arm of service and gave no indication of their formation or unit. Foreign embassies and missions, even from states allied or friendly to the USSR, were given no information of value.

The Germans relied for their order of battle intelligence on agents and border-crossers and on information acquired from Finland, Hungary,

gence experience or training. Kinzel's experience of the Red Army was confined to a period of three months when in 1929 he had been appointed as a conducting officer to a party of Soviet officers visiting Germany; thereafter Kinzel was attached to the Military Attaché Warsaw where he learned some Polish. On leaving Foreign Armies East Kinzel subsequently had a distinguished career as a staff officer, being Chief of Staff firstly to 29 Corps and later to Army Group North and Army Group Vistula. He was a signatory of the surrender document signed at Field-Marshal Montgomery's headquarters on Lüneburg Heath. Kinzel then committed suicide.

[2] *OKH O Qu IV, Abt Fremde Heere Ost Nr. L 55/39 geh* and *Nr. L 63/39 geh.* According to Foreign Armies East the invading forces were:

Belorussian Front	(Kovalev)	3 and 11 Armies
Ukrainian Front	(Timoshenko)	1 and 10 Armies

See also Kennedy, *The German Campaign in Poland* (D of A No. 20–255), pp. 124 and 125. According to the Soviet account however Kovalev's Front consisted of 3, 4, 10 and 11 Armies while Timoshenko's Front consisted of 5, 6 and 12 Armies. *Istoriya*, Vol. 1, p. 246.

Rumania and Japan. Some information too was gained by radio intercept and radio direction finders, but this was restricted by range and by the fact that the Red Army, being deficient in reliable radio equipment, preferred to use telephone or telegraph cable links. In consequence the Germans produced a reasonably good intelligence picture as to the Soviet dispositions in the border areas but had no idea at all as to what was to be found in the hinterland, even in European Russia. Topographical intelligence was poor, for although the Germans had campaigned in the First World War almost as far east as Leningrad, Kiev and Rostov, they had no experience of the effects of ground and climate on the operation of radio, aircraft, tanks and motor vehicles, or of the complex problems involved in mechanized warfare in such an inhospitable land. Soviet maps were difficult to acquire and the maps which the German Army reproduced were so poor and out of date that much reliance had to be placed on air photographs.

The German Military Attaché to the Soviet Union, General Köstring, had been born in Moscow, and in 1941 was sixty-five years of age. He spoke Russian, was a Russophile, and had held the same appointment for the last ten years. In spite of his long service in the country, Köstring's knowledge about the current development of the Red Army and Soviet industry was limited, because, in company with the remainder of the diplomatic corps, his movements and activities were severely restricted.[3] During October 1940 Foreign Armies East compiled an appreciation, based on a collation of Köstring's reports, coming to the general conclusion that the Red Army was a factor to be reckoned with and would be a serious opponent in defence, but that it was not capable of mobile warfare on the grand scale. It was estimated that the Red Army would still be inferior in effectiveness to the German Army, even if it had a numerical superiority of two or three to one, but a warning was added that the Red Army's best allies were time and space, the lack of roads and the bad weather. These factors, according to Köstring, needed to be experienced in order to understand their importance in a war inside Russia.[4] There was of course much truth in this appreciation, and what Köstring said was by and large correct, but the report dealt with the general rather than the particular and the conclusions could equally well have applied to the Tsarist Army in 1914 or even to that of 1812. Nor can it be disguised that Köstring and his deputy Krebs both had a low opinion of the effectiveness of the Red Army. Köstring, in his post-war testimony, said that he had been consulted during the planning for the invasion of the USSR and had given as his opinion that the Red Army's powers of improvisation should not be underestimated, and that the seizure of Moscow was not of paramount

[3] On 3 September 1940 Köstring told Halder that the Red Army would need another four years to reach its pre-purge efficiency, and he complained to Halder of the difficulty in getting information because of the supervision of the (sic) GPU. (The GPU/OGPU had in fact been replaced by the NKVD in 1934). Halder, *Kriegstagebuch*, Vol. 2, p. 86.

[4] *Fremde Heere Ost 20/001/geh Ausl. XXIb.* dated 17 October 1940. These views are repeated in Köstring's correspondence with von Tippelskirch during 1940.

C

importance because the larger part of Soviet heavy industry had already been withdrawn to beyond the Urals. He may in fact have given this opinion in 1940 although its emphasis hardly accords with the tenor of the collated official reports or of his personal correspondence.[5]

The German High Command had no means of knowing the number of tanks and aircraft in the Soviet Union, and the numbers quoted in German intelligence reports were guesses rather than estimates since the figures could not be based on accurately established facts. Nor had it any reliable information on the number of divisions which the Red Army had in peace or could form in war, its intelligence estimates being arrived at by rough-and-ready rule-of-thumb methods based on population strength and estimated industrial potential. It knew little of the Soviet High Command or of the leading General Officers of the Red Army.[6] The German official secret Handbook on the Armed Forces of the USSR published by Kinzel's department on 1 January 1941 was an illuminating document in that it indicated the extent of the great gaps in the German intelligence picture. It candidly admitted that information about the order of battle of the Russian Army was almost entirely deficient and that a firm basis was also lacking for knowing the number of fronts (army groups) and armies in existence.[7] Not having any knowledge of the detailed organization of Soviet formations, the handbook was reduced to making obvious statements that an army *presumably* consisted of a headquarters, a number of rifle corps, army troops with heavy artillery and air detachments and supply services. The attachment of army cavalry or motorized troops was, it thought, also possible.[8]

Not unexpectedly, the conclusions drawn in the official secret handbook were to be proved erroneous. One of the general and more sweeping of these was that the Red Army was not fit for modern war and could not match a boldly led and modern enemy. The remedies being applied by the Soviet Government would not have any success for years, maybe for decades.[9] On the industrial capacity of the USSR the handbook relied on information supplied by Thomas in the Economic and Armament Office of the OKW, but this merely cast doubts on Soviet resources and stated that the ability of Soviet industry to provide weapons, clothing and vehicles sufficient in kind or in quantities for a long war was questionable.[10]

[5] For Köstring's post-war testimony, see *German Campaign in Russia Planning and Operations 1940–2* (D of A No. 20–261a), p. 12; compare this with Halder, *Kriegstagebuch*, Vol. 2, p. 86, and footnote 2. Jacobsen makes the comment that if this was Köstring's opinion in 1940 he does not appear to have given it to Halder. Halder subsequently told Jacobsen that he had no recollection of this briefing by Köstring.

[6] The only Soviet officers noted by Halder and Foreign Armies East as having any great ability appeared to be Timoshenko and Shaposhnikov.

[7] *Die Kriegswehrmacht der UdSSR, OKH Gen Std H O Qu IV Abt, Fremde Heere Ost (II) Nr. 100/41g* of 15 January 1941, p. 13.

[8] *Ibid*, p. 14.

[9] *Ibid*, pp. 61 and 72.

[10] *Ibid*, p. 66.

Although German tactical intelligence was generally good and was to improve enormously once the war had started, the OKH had no exact information of the identity of all the Red Army formations which were on the frontier on 21 June. The presence of 9 Army and 26 Army in the Ukraine was not confirmed until 17 July, although these two formations had been in the fighting almost from the beginning of the campaign.[11] On Soviet strategic reserves the Germans were to remain poorly informed throughout the war.

The German assessment of the fighting value of the Red Army was of course influenced by the knowledge that its more able and experienced commanders had been purged in 1937 and by its inadequate performance in the Winter War against the Finns. Many of the German conclusions arising from this campaign were, however, false, and many of the others, although true at the beginning of 1940, no longer applied in mid 1941. Few realized for example that Finland, taking its size and resources into account, was prepared for war, and that the Finn, when fighting in his own forested swampland, was superior to both Russian and German. Red Army troops had admittedly made poor showing there, but on the Soviet side intelligence had been at fault, so that Moscow had underestimated its task and used formations unsuitable for forest fighting. The winter had been unusually severe and the Red Army, lacking ski troops, had become bogged down because of supply and transport deficiencies.

The German economic intelligence appreciation on the Soviet Union was erroneous, but the actual margin of error cannot be assessed in the form of statistics, since no statistics were produced. Much of the detail of the actual Soviet industrial production at that time has still not been released, although the location of Soviet heavy industry in 1941 is now known. In addition to the great industrial areas around Leningrad, Moscow, in the Ukraine and the Donets Basin, there were other industrial belts in the Urals and in Asia. In the Urals the industrial area stretched for hundreds of miles in all directions about Perm, Sverdlovsk and Magnitogorsk, while other large complexes were to be found along the Trans-Siberian railway in a belt near Omsk, Novosibirsk, Tomsk, Krasnoyarsk, Bratsk and on to Irkutsk near Lake Baikal. Further heavy industry was established in the areas of Ashkhabad, Samarkand, Tashkent and Alma Ata near the Afghan and Chinese frontiers.[12] In 1941, however, this detail was not known to the western world. It was of course generally understood that the centre of gravity of Soviet heavy industry was being moved eastwards and that this process had been going on since 1928.

Thomas, the head of the OKW Economic and Armament Office (*Wi Rü Amt*), produced for Göring an economic intelligence appreciation at the end of 1940, apparently compiled largely by estimate from out-of-date information, the only information which was available to him, in which he stated that the occupation of European regions of the USSR (without the Urals) would

[11] *OKH Lage Ost* daily battle situation maps from 21 June to 17 July 1941.
[12] *Istoriya*, Vol. 1, p. 408.

secure for Germany about seventy-five per cent of all the Soviet armament industry and nearly 100 per cent of the optical and precision tool industry, and this appears to have formed the basis for German economic strategic planning.[13] Even in the second year of the war Hitler continued to believe that the loss of the Ukraine and the Donets Basin and the cutting of the oil routes from the Caucasus would cripple, if not destroy, the Soviet economy. Stalin himself, when talking to Roosevelt's emissary Hopkins after the war had started, and when demanding early material aid, said that seventy-five per cent of the Soviet armament industry was concentrated in the area of Leningrad, Moscow and Kiev and that a 150 mile advance to the east of these areas *might* cripple the USSR.[14] It has since transpired that he was talking for effect in order to create the required sense of urgency in Washington, because as the war progressed it was eventually realized that the Soviet Union was still capable of resistance even if deprived of Moscow, Tula, Kursk, Kharkov and the entire steel, iron and coal resources of the south. Before the end of 1941 Thomas had entirely changed his views when, in an appreciation dated 2 October, he maintained that even if Gorki and Baku were lost, the Soviet position would still not be catastrophic. Only when the Urals were taken, he thought, would the USSR begin to break up.[15]

Only two months after the start of the war Hitler was to blame German intelligence for its failure.[16] That German political, economic and strategic intelligence was poor there can be no doubt. Yet the fault lay with Hitler and with the German High Command, since it was an act of folly to enter into such a war without wide and good intelligence and adequate preparation. In the days when the German General Staff was at the height of its power, five to ten years intelligence preparation would have been considered necessary before any worthwhile operational planning could have been started. Halder, von Manstein, Guderian, Köstring and others were subsequently to blame Hitler for underrating the Soviet Union. Yet the responsibility was not entirely his. Although many voices spoke out against the war on the grounds of expediency, and many were averse to a war on two fronts, there appears to be little evidence that any doubted the ability of the German Army and the *Luftwaffe* to knock out the USSR in a lightning campaign, whatever they may have said

---

[13] Birkenfeld, *Geschichte der deutschen Wehr- und Rüstungswirtschaft (1918–45)*, p. 268.

[14] Sherwood, *The White House Papers*, Vol. 1, p. 339.

[15] Birkenfeld, *Geschichte der deutschen Wehr- und Rüstungswirtschaft (1918–45)*, p. 270. All these areas except Gorki and Baku were lost to the Soviet Union during 1942. Although the evacuation eastwards was accelerated from 1941 onwards the emergency evacuation would not have accounted for the industrial reserves in the interior.

[16] *Ciano Papers*, p. 448. According to von Kleist, the German Army 'which was kept well informed by Köstring' did not underrate the Red Army. Liddell Hart, *The Other Side of the Hill*, p. 257. Guderian said much the same. A rather different post-war view is that of Rendulic who, as a divisional commander and lieutenant-general in June 1941, said that at that time he met no one in his particular circle who was not convinced that the *Reich* Government knew what it was about and would take all the necessary steps to gain victory. Rendulic, *Gekämpft Gesiegt Geschlagen*, p. 22.

after the war.[17] Indeed the documentary evidence of 1940 and 1941 is to the contrary.

The question remains as to whether Hitler would have gone to war if he had known the true industrial and economic strength of the Soviet Union. When Germany's fortunes were already sinking, he said that he would not have done so.[18] That, however, was being wise after the event. If German intelligence had produced good evidence of the true strength of the USSR at the end of 1940, it is highly probable that Hitler would have rejected it as an imbecilic fabrication, just as he did that given to him by Gehlen later in the war.[19] A man who could purge von Blomberg, von Fritsch and Beck for hesitancy and doubt was hardly likely to be deterred from attaining his destiny by the alarmist scribblings of a colonel in Foreign Armies East.

[17] Professor Jacobsen has pointed out that after the unexpectedly swift victory against France, nothing appeared impossible to the German High Command. From the experience of the First World War, the fighting stamina of the French Army was rated higher by the Germans than that of the Russian Army.

[18] Guderian, *Panzer Leader*, p. 190.

[19] Gehlen succeeded Kinzel as head of Foreign Armies East in the spring of 1942. Hitler was alleged to have called a Gehlen intelligence estimate the greatest imposture since Ghenghis Khan. On another occasion he was reported to have said that the author of these reports should be shut up in a lunatic asylum. Guderian, *Panzer Leader*, pp. 383 and 387.

CHAPTER FOUR

Führer Strategy

War is of course a political act, and political, military and economic action are interdependent. The military aim in war, although usually associated with the destruction of fighting forces, has in fact a much wider application in that it includes the seizure or destruction of the enemy's military potential, that is to say his reserves of manpower and his industrial and economic strength, the occupation of his territory and the reconciliation of his people. Political or economic aims may have priority over military ones, but in the final outcome war cannot be won without the destruction of the enemy's military power. More than a century earlier, von Clausewitz had written that in disarming a nation there were three general aims, military power, the country, and the will of the people. Military power must be destroyed, he said, and the country conquered, for out of the country a new military force might be formed. Even when this was achieved the war was not at an end, as long as the will of the enemy was not subdued.[1] Hitler was unable to clarify his aims in this manner or order his conflicting political, economic and military priorities.

By 1941 the German Army High Command (OKH) was no longer capable of independent politico-military thought and was merely the tool of the dictator. Von Brauchitsch, the Commander-in-Chief of the Army, although professionally competent, was a weak man who lost composure and nerve when in Hitler's presence and who was completely dominated by him. Halder, the Chief of the General Staff, a much more stubborn character than von Brauchitsch, was apparently impervious to the oppressive atmosphere of the *Führer*'s presence. The extent of his activities was very wide; he was efficient, a meticulous master of detail and had earned the professional respect of the Army. Yet, until late in 1941, his diary showed him as a loyal, hardworking executive, and if he disapproved of many of the *Führer*'s views, he rarely recorded it. It was only when operations started to go wrong in Russia that the bitter animosity grew between the two.

On 21 July 1940 von Brauchitsch had a discussion with Hitler on the

[1] Von Clausewitz, *On War*, Book 1, Chapter 2.

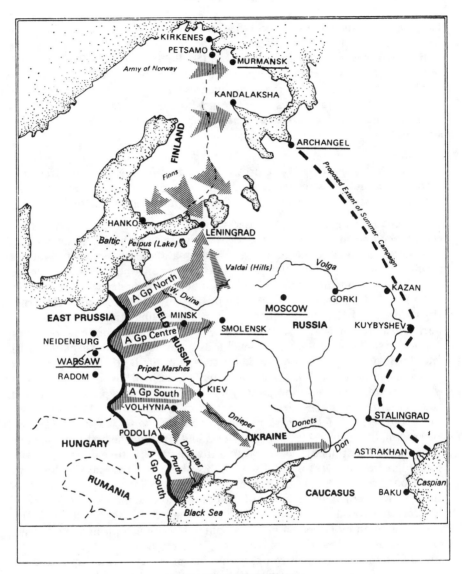

OPERATION BARBAROSSA

German war aims in the East, and these were noted by Halder in his diary the next day. The political aims listed were the enlargement of Finland and the setting up of new political states, the Ukraine, Belorussia and a Baltic Federation, all to be dependent on Germany. These were not in fact political aims at all, but merely some of the consequences of the dismemberment of the Soviet Union. The military aim of the new war as recorded by Halder was imprecise and contained no fewer than three aims, each capable of conflicting with the other. It read:

> To defeat the Russian Army or at least (*oder wenigstens*) to occupy as much Russian soil as is necessary to protect Berlin and the Silesian industrial area from air attack. It is desired to establish our own positions so far to the east that our own air force can destroy the most important areas of Russia.[2]

This vague mission was to be carried forward in various forms in directives and orders, and to it, at Hitler's instigation, were to be added other political and economic aims. Less than three months after Germany had launched itself eastwards in the greatest war of its existence, operations were to be brought to a standstill because of fierce disputes as to the true aim of the war.

On 19 July Marcks, the Chief of Staff of 18 Army, was attached to the Army High Command (OKH) in order to direct the preliminary planning for the war. When briefing Marcks as to his task, Halder opposed, on the grounds of political instability, the use of Rumania as a springboard for a main thrust into the Soviet Union, and regarded the seizure of the Baltic States as of only secondary importance. On 5 August Marcks presented his views, aspects of which were of significance in that they had a bearing on the production of the final plan with which the Germans went to war. His aim was to defeat the Red Army and seize all territory west of a line North Dvina, Middle Volga and lower Don, that is to say Archangel, Gorki and Rostov (the first time this line came to be mentioned), in order to safeguard German soil from Soviet bombing.[3] He then went on to discuss in his objectives material which was to prove both controversial and dangerous to the subsequent operations. This material, which included mention of the political and economic importance of Moscow, the Ukraine, the Donets Basin and the Leningrad industrial centre, was seized upon by Hitler as the main politico-economic objective of the war, so that weightier aims, those of destroying military power and occupying the Soviet Union, were lost. There were other inconsistencies which appeared for the first time in the Marcks' plan and which were carried into the final directive. At this time was born the erroneous belief that the Soviet Union would hold

[2] Halder, *Kriegstagebuch*, Vol. 2, pp. 32–3, 22 July 1940.
[3] The aim of the Marcks plan was 'to defeat (*schlagen*) the Soviet armed forces and to make impossible Russia's re-emergence as an enemy of Germany in the foreseeable future'. Marcks went on in his preamble to define the area of the Soviet Union's economic and industrial power as the Ukraine, the Donets Basin, Moscow and Leningrad. The industrial area in the east he said, was of no consequence (*noch nicht leistungsfähig genug*). General-major Marcks, *Operationsentwurf Ost*, 5 August 1940.

on to the Baltic States and that the forces there constituted a threat to the flank of a German thrust on Moscow.

It was intended that the Soviet Union should be defeated by the overrunning of a thousand miles of its territory as far east as Gorki, yet the USSR stretched for several thousand miles beyond that point. The significance of this arbitrary Archangel-Rostov (later Archangel-Astrakhan) line is difficult to determine. The effectiveness of the Soviet long range bombing force was much exaggerated and could in fact have been disregarded entirely, although admittedly Germany was not to know this at the time. If the USSR had really been defeated, it is not easy to understand why German power should have stopped at such a line and not have extended to the Pacific. On the other hand an undefeated Soviet Union east of the Volga was hardly likely to be liquidated by the not very significant bombing power of the German *Luftwaffe*.[4] In any case, Hitler had said that he would destroy Bolshevik power and this aim would not be achieved by permitting the continued existence of the Soviet Empire. Von Bock, the Commander-in-Chief of Army Group Centre, voiced similar doubts when on 2 February he asked Hitler the action to be taken should the German Army arrive at the line and should the Soviet Government still be in existence. The *Führer* gave an evasive answer, assuring von Bock that by then the communists would have asked for terms, adding for good measure that if they had not done so the Germans would advance to the Urals. Hitler said that he was determined to fight and he refused to consider the alternative of some form of settlement with the USSR instead of war.[5]

Hitler had a good understanding of communism and of the aims and working of the Bolshevik government, and he was not ignorant of the political and ethnic complexity of the peoples which formed the population of the Soviet Union. He rightly reasoned that because of the diversity of the races and the deep schisms within the Soviet peoples the USSR lacked solidity, and this gave rise to his belief that one good kick would bring the tottering and rotten structure down. His argument had both validity and weight. But not to have enlisted the support of all the multi-racial Soviet peoples, including the Great Russians, would have been therefore a grave political and military error. Hitler did even worse; his brain was teeming with insane doctrinaire and ideological obsessions so that, far from calling in the Soviet peoples to his aid, he determined that this Slav vermin, as he once had called them, should be kept in their proper station at the disposal of the master race. For this reason he ordered the economic despoliation of the conquered territories, the liquidation of the Jews and communist intelligentsia and the virtual enslave-

[4] Except for a few early raids on Moscow, the *Luftwaffe* was too weak to undertake the systematic bombing of strategic targets or of Soviet industry.

[5] Von Bock, *Tagebuch*, 2 February 1941. '*Ein Nachgeben lehnt der Führer scharf ab, ohne dass ich ihn angedeutet hätte*'. According to von Lossberg, who had been set to work by Jodl at the end of July 1940 preparing campaign material and plans for Jodl's own information, the *Führer* believed that the sixty million inhabitants beyond the Volga would be no danger to Germany. Von Lossberg, *Im Wehrmachtführungsstab*, pp. 105 and 113.

ment of the population by the direct rule of *Reich* Commissioners. The Great Russians in particular were to be subjected to the most brutal force.[6] On 30 March 1941, at a meeting in the *Reich* Chancellery, the *Führer* addressed the more senior commanders in a long diatribe on the waging of *a race war without pity*, which, according to the later testimony of the audience, occasioned resentment and dissent. This was not, however, voiced to Hitler.[7] Thereafter followed orders which indemnified members of the German armed forces against the legal consequences of crimes against the Soviet population, and the notorious order by which the commissars were denied the treatment normally accorded to prisoners of war, in that they were to be handed over to the special field detachments of the security service to be shot.[8] Only two days before the invasion, Alfred Rosenberg, a Baltic German recently appointed as General Commissioner for the East European Region, said that no Russian State must ever be allowed to exist again, even in a Germanized form. The responsibility for the occupied territories was to be handed to the SS, and order was to be maintained by the deliberate spreading of terror. This was to be achieved by mass murder, torture, deportations and confiscations irrespective of sex or age. In these circumstances it was no wonder that Russia and the Ukraine, after the first few months of German occupation, recoiled into the arms of the Soviet Union and became the breeding ground for spies and partisans.[9]

Hitler was determined not merely to annihilate the Soviet Union and the Bolshevist system but also to destroy the coherence of any Russian State, the Russians being reduced to the level of slaves.[10] In his speech to his

[6] Halder, *Kriegstagebuch*, Vol. 2, p. 320.

[7] The dissent was voiced to von Brauchitsch who took no action. For details of address see Halder, *Kriegstagebuch*, Vol. 2, pp. 335–8; Warlimont, *Inside Hitler's Headquarters*, pp. 160–1; von Lossberg, *Im Wehrmachtführungsstab*, pp. 118–9; *Tagebuch* von Bock and others.

[8] It was originally intended that the German Army should shoot the commissars on capture and it appears that the OKH framed a draft on the *Führer*'s order. Halder, according to his diary on 6 May, seems to have been briefed on the drafting of such orders by the Judge Advocate's Department. A draft order was sent from OKH to OKW for concurrence. Later an attempt was made to withdraw the order, it being understood that the SD (*Sicherheitsdienst*) would carry out the executions.

[9] The combat zone and certain rear areas were administered by the German Army through a network of town majors or military commandants. Behind this line enemy areas were handed over to Rosenberg's civil administration. Rosenberg, the Minister for the Occupied Eastern Territories, had two *Reich* Commissioners, Koch for the Ukraine and Lohse for *Ostland* (the Baltic States and White Russia). By Keitel's Directive of 13 March 1941, however, the SS was made responsible for all security and police duties and for anti-partisan warfare in rear areas. The occupied territories, therefore, had two, sometimes three, masters greedy for power and loot, for the German Foreign Office was not disinterested in these territories; the staff of *Oldenburg* (*Wirtschaftsstab Ost*), intent on economic despoliation, appeared to be independent of both the military and civil administrations. See also Dallin, *German Rule in Russia*, Chapters 2 and 5.

[10] Hitler said that the first duty of the Russians was to serve Germans and that the main object was the removal from occupied Russia of everything which could aid the German economy. Picker, *Hitlers Tischgespräche*, p. 270.

Generals on 30 March the *Führer's* intention was to prepare his commanders psychologically for the new pattern of the radical ideological war, complete in its totality, a war which would be fought by both sides without compassion or mercy, without honour or decency, and he quoted as examples the terrible atrocities already perpetrated on the inhabitants of the Baltic States, by those whom he mistakenly called the commissars.[11]

The liquidation of the commissars, communist intelligentsia, gypsies, Jews and civilian hostages in the early stages of the war was to be followed by *Führerbefehle*, forbidding the acceptance of the surrender of Leningrad and Moscow, and ordering the encircled cities to be razed to the ground by shell fire and bombing. The female population of Stalingrad was to be transported and the males destroyed.[12] The Soviet High Command and Red Army troops were of course equally guilty of similar barbarities. Never in modern times was a war to be waged so pitilessly.

The Russo-German frontier in 1941 ran from just north of the Memel on the Baltic, roughly along the line of the old East Prussian-Lithuanian frontier and then curved westwards into Poland in a great bend known as the Bialystok salient, before moving eastwards to Brest-Litovsk. It then continued southwards towards the Hungarian border where it ended. In all, this Russo-German frontier extended about 700 miles in length. The Ukrainian-Rumanian border ran for about 450 miles along the line of the river Pruth to the Black Sea. Since the attitude of Hungary was not yet known, there was a 200 mile gap between the German eastern front and that of its Rumanian ally.

In the centre of West European Russia, immediately to the south-east of the frontier at Brest-Litovsk, lay a vast area of swampland about 150 miles in width from north to south and over 300 miles in depth. This area, known as the Pripet Marshes, was interlaced with numerous sluggish streams which fed the Pripet, the Dnieper and the Berezina. Except for one or two highways built up on causeways, few tracks crossed the area which was in parts heavily wooded, and because of this the swamp was an effective barrier to tanks and motor vehicles, so dividing the whole front into a northern and southern theatre. The southern theatre comprised the partially wooded areas of Galicia and the Volyn-Podolian Uplands, and the Ukraine, a vast treeless black earth steppe which stretched from Bessarabia eastwards to the Donets and beyond, an area which, in spite of its lack of roads, was particularly suitable for armoured warfare except that it was crossed by a number of river barriers such as the Pruth, the Dniester, the Bug and the Dnieper, all running from north to south. Kiev, the capital of the Ukraine, lay less than 350 miles in a direct line from the Russo-German border.

In the Belorussian area immediately to the north of the Pripet Marshes was the direct route to Minsk, Orsha, Smolensk and Moscow. The country along

[11] Hitler's account of the NKVD atrocities was in the main correct, as the Germans were to find when they entered the Baltic States.
[12] Halder, *Kriegstagebuch*, Vol. 3, p. 514.

this route between Orsha and Moscow, being both open and free from water obstacles, was known as the Orsha landbridge, since it ran along the watershed between the rivers running north into the Baltic and those which flowed south to the Black Sea. The Orsha landbridge was the gateway to Moscow and it formed the gap between the two major water obstacles, the West Dvina and the Dnieper. Before the Germans could arrive at this landbridge they had to cross heavily wooded forest belts, fifty miles or more in depth, by way of roads. These forest roads would have the effect of funnelling movement and stringing out formations in great depth. Moscow lay about 700 miles in a direct line from the frontier.

In the Baltic area there were a few indifferent roads from East Prussia which ran through the Baltic States to Leningrad. The only rivers of importance were the Niemen, the West Dvina and the Velikaya Narva,· but there were other formidable obstacles in the many swamps and thick forest belts. The area between Leningrad and Moscow about the Valdai Hills was heavily forested and marshy and was unsuitable for the use of armoured formations. Leningrad was over 500 miles from East Prussia.

Topography and political geography therefore restricted the frontage on which the campaign could be launched to three main areas. The first of these was in the north across the frontier which ran from the Baltic to Brest-Litovsk and could be used for thrusts either into the Baltic States towards Leningrad or into Belorussia and Central European Russia towards Moscow. The second was in the more restricted area between the Pripet Marshes and the Hungarian frontier which gave entry through Galicia into the Ukraine. The third was from Rumanian territory across the Pruth into Bessarabia and the Ukraine.

A few days after the Army High Command (OKH) had been told to study the problems of a campaign against the Soviet Union, its operations division produced the first draft of a plan in which the main German effort was to be placed south of the Pripet Marshes. Halder, who was already convinced that the primary thrust should be made in the north towards Moscow, rejected it. The Marcks' plan had envisaged the main attack being made north of the Pripet on to the Orsha landbridge and Moscow, together with a subsidiary attack on the Baltic States and Leningrad, as a wing of the main thrust. Marcks had proposed that a further additional thrust should be made to the south on Kiev and the Dnieper, extending thereafter to Baku in the Caucasus.

Von Brauchitsch and Halder were cool towards Jodl and left him out of plans which, in their view, did not concern him. Jodl, however, was not to be excluded. He instructed his principal staff officer Warlimont to produce an OKW plan of campaign, in order that Jodl might be in a position to comment on the OKH plans worked out by von Brauchitsch and Halder.[13] This OKW plan undoubtedly had much effect on Hitler's thinking and a direct bearing on

---

[13] Warlimont was head of Department L (*Landesverteidigung*), a joint service department of the OKW, and acted as Jodl's principal staff officer. Von Lossberg headed the army section inside Department L.

the main directive which was to be issued at the end of the year. Jodl's draft, which was completed in September 1940, envisaged three army groups being used for the attack, two to the north of the Pripet Marshes and one to the south, but his main stipulation, which was frequently to be repeated by Hitler, was that the continuation of the offensive on Moscow beyond the Orsha landbridge-Smolensk area should be dependent on the progress made in clearing the Baltic States.[14] On 29 October Paulus, the new Assistant Chief of Staff (Operations) in the OKH, submitted to Halder his own views on the strategic aspects of the proposed campaign. This survey was presumably to Halder's taste since it fitted his own early conceptions. Two German army groups (known as north and centre) were to be used north of the Pripet Marshes and one to the south. The plan laid more stress on the German Army's immediate interest in gaining military victory by destroying the enemy rather than in acquiring economic advantages, and emphasized the need to prevent a withdrawal of the Red Army into the interior. It attached minor significance to the forces in the Baltic States, which were estimated at only thirty divisions compared with sixty divisions in Belorussia and seventy in the Ukraine, and deduced that a thrust direct on Moscow would offer the best chance of success. The rest of the survey dealt with the well known but little understood problems of time and distance in the Soviet Union, the indifferent leadership of the Red Army, the difficulty in assessing the fighting value of the Red Army soldier, and the lack of unity among the many races which form the Soviet peoples. For the first time too the question of the Soviet preponderance of manpower was raised. Although he made no comment in his diary, Halder appears to have accepted the Paulus survey and he was later to re-echo some of the doubts expressed in it.[15]

Between 28 November and 3 December a series of war games were played, mainly presentations and map exercises under the direction of Paulus, in order to complete an examination of the main problems, before a formal discussion took place with Hitler on 5 December. The chiefs of staff of the three army groups which were to undertake the campaign examined the strategic problems independently of one another, and they were all much impressed by the difficulties of space and manpower. They pointed out that the funnel shape of the hinterland was such that the deeper one penetrated the wider became the frontage, and that what was initially a front of 1,300 miles would rapidly

[14] According to Warlimont, the OKW draft was the work of von Lossberg. Warlimont, *Inside Hitler's Headquarters*, p. 136. Compare also Greiner, *Die Oberste Wehrmachtführung*, p. 295; *The German Campaign in Russia Planning and Operations 1940–2* (D of A No. 20–261a), p. 13. Bezymensky, in *Sonderakte Barbarossa*, pp. 307–13, has reproduced what the Soviet Union claims to be *die Lossberg Studie WF. St/Op H 905* of 15 September 1940. From this document can be traced the source of a number of the *Führer's* fixed ideas, which later caused him to turn away from taking Moscow in August 1941, in particular the switching of forces from Army Group Centre to Army Group North, once the Dvina had been crossed.

[15] *The German Campaign in Russia Planning and Operations 1940–2* (D of A No. 20–261a), p. 14.

extend to 2,000 and even 2,500 miles. Unless the Red Army was to be destroyed close to the frontier west of a line Peipus-Minsk-Kiev, there would not be enough German troops to hold any form of continuous front deeper in the hinterland. Other problems were ventilated, including the difficulties of maintaining a force of three million men and half a million horses in a vast country where there were few roads and where the railway could not be used for through running, since the track was wider than that used in Germany and Central Europe.[16] The Commander-in-Chief Replacement Army, Fromm, had already emphasized that there were only sufficient reinforcements available, just under half a million, to replace the wastage for a summer campaign. There was too an acute shortage of motor vehicles, although it was hoped that this might be made good by purchase from the French civilian output. The vehicle fuel position was very tight indeed, there being no more than three months' reserves of petrol and one month's diesel in Germany. Tyres were a problem because of the lack of pure and synthetic rubber, so that consideration was being given to equipping lighter vehicles with steel-shod wheels.[17] German armour production at the beginning of 1941 was less than 250 tanks and armoured assault guns a month.[18] German industry was still capable of enormous expansion but its basis at this time lacked depth and it was dependent on imported raw materials from the USSR and elsewhere.

By then both von Brauchitsch and Halder had some doubts as to the direction of the *Führer*'s world-wide strategy. If war against the USSR was in fact necessary, they had become convinced that the destruction of the Red Army was the overriding aim and that no economic considerations could take priority. A thrust at Moscow would draw on it the main enemy forces; the seizing of the Moscow area would not only inflict on the Soviet Union loss of control and communications but would tear a great hole in any form of continuous Red Army front.

At the meeting on 5 December von Brauchitsch gave Hitler some indication of the trend of his thoughts when he expressed his doubts as to whether the *Luftwaffe* was strong enough to carry on the war against both Britain and the Soviet Union, but discontinued this approach on being told tartly by Hitler that it could wage war on two fronts provided the Soviet campaign was not prolonged. Halder continued to emphasize the importance of the main thrust on Moscow to be made by Army Group Centre, the wings of which were to be so strong in armour that they could, if need be, deal with flank attacks from the Baltic or the Ukraine. Hitler, however, would have none of it and retorted with contrary views, some his own and some of which might be attributable to his talks with Göring and Jodl. He repeated once more the need

[16] The railway track in the Soviet Union, Finland and the Baltic States (except for Lithuania) was 5 feet broad gauge. The Central European gauge (Germany, Poland and Rumania) was 4 feet 8½ inches.

[17] Halder, *Kriegstagebuch*, Vol. 2, pp. 257–60.

[18] In 1941 2,800 tanks and assault guns were produced. *FD 2690/45 Vol. 10 (Flensburg Collection) Statistische Schnellberichte zu Kriegsproduktion.*

to protect the territory of the *Reich* from air attack; distance and depth were wanted. Economic objectives too were of great importance and could not be lightly disregarded. He believed that the Kremlin would hold on tightly to the Baltic and the Ukraine because of their seaports and economic importance and would give ground freely in the centre. The seizure of Moscow by the Germans after all 'was not so very important'. The strong armoured wings of Army Group Centre should be ready to turn north to the Baltic or south to the Ukraine; the Baltic States in particular interested him. At this point von Brauchitsch came to the support of Halder, stressing the importance in the Soviet mind of the old Smolensk-Moscow route, only to be crushed by the scoff that only ossified brains could think of such an antiquated idea! So it was left that the initial planning should take Army Group Centre as far as the Smolensk-Orsha landbridge and thereafter the *Führer* did not want to commit himself as to further operations.[19] In this lacuna lay one of the causes of German failure in 1941.

The German Army High Command (OKH) was obviously at fault in not insisting on clarity of the aim and execution of the campaign. Hitler, however, was in undisputed control of the whole German war machine and like his precursor, the man of destiny, was convinced of his star. The OKH was content therefore to let the matter rest, trusting that the future would take care of itself and that Hitler's latest fancies, if undisturbed, would pass. Meanwhile it strengthened the forces of Army Group North in the hope that it would make as rapid progress through the Baltic States as Army Group Centre to Smolensk, and thus obviate the necessity for a standstill before Moscow. Directive 21 presented to Hitler for signature on 17 December took insufficient account of the *Führer*'s latest directions. This did not escape his eagle eye or retentive memory and he thereupon altered the draft, clearly stating that priority would be given to the clearing of the Baltic States and the capture of Leningrad and Kronstadt, and that strong armoured forces would be detached northwards from Army Group Centre for this purpose. Only then would offensive operations be resumed towards Moscow. The operation, formerly known as *Fritz*, was renamed on Hitler's order *Barbarossa*, after Frederick Hohenstaufen, the twelfth century Holy Roman Emperor who died in the Orient; the new name was to give the war the nature of a crusade. Directive 21, *Fall Barbarossa*, was signed on 18 December 1940 by Hitler as the Commander-in-Chief of the Armed Forces.[20]

The directive was rambling and indecisive in its aims, its language and its form. The aim given in the opening lines was to crush Soviet Russia in a rapid campaign. Under the general intention heading, however, it was stated that the final aim of the operation was to form a barrier against Asiatic Russia on the general line Archangel-Volga. In the main body of the directive could

[19] Halder, *Kriegstagebuch*, Vol. 2, pp. 211–4; Halder, *Hitler as War Lord*, p. 41.
[20] The draft of Directive 21 was put before Hitler by Jodl and Hitler's redrafting was accepted by Jodl and the OKH in silence. Warlimont, *Inside Hitler's Headquarters*, p. 138.

be traced the hand of Hitler, wearing in turn his many hats, that of industrialist and economist, of commander-in-chief, of commander of army formations down to corps (he discussed the detail of using two or three divisions in the Rovaniemi area), and even of Hitler the airman as he instructed the *Luftwaffe* on how to secure the river crossings. Industrial areas were to be wiped out by the *Luftwaffe* and the Red Army was to be routed and sometimes pursued. The Donets Basin, important because of its armament industry, was to be taken 'as part of the pursuit operations' as was Moscow, the capture of which represented 'a decisive economic and political success'. The directive thus contained a large number of disconnected objectives, with priority given to none. Hitler was about to send the German Army into the Soviet Union on a four year will-o'-the-wisp chase after seaports, cities, oil, corn, coal, nickel, manganese and iron ore.

After 5 December, preliminary orders were given to army groups. On 31 January 1941 full OKH orders were signed by von Brauchitsch.[21] These were clear and to the point, but they covered nothing more than the launching of the three army groups into the Soviet Union and the opening phase of the campaign, it being the intention to prevent the enemy from establishing a firm front either on the new or the old frontier fortifications or on the river line West Dvina-Dnieper. Von Brauchitsch echoed Hitler's false assumptions that the Kremlin would make determined efforts to hold the Baltic bases and Black Sea areas, and gave emphasis to Hitler's orders that Army Group Centre, as soon as it reached Smolensk, should detach armoured forces towards Leningrad. Only when the Baltic States and North Russia had been cleared would the question arise of a thrust on Moscow.

On 3 February there was a long presentation by Halder of the army directive for the campaign, and this passed without incident except that Hitler declined to entertain any thought of raising further formations.[22] He was by then emphasizing the economic importance of the Baltic States and the Ukraine, both to the Soviet Union and to Germany.

In May 1941 the Germans credited the Red Army with having the equivalent of 121 rifle divisions and twenty-one cavalry divisions available in the first instance to withstand the German attack. About Soviet armour they were more vague, but believed that the Red Army had about five tank divisions and thirty-three mechanized brigades in the west. It was estimated that a further twenty-five divisions were deployed against the Finnish and Turkish borders and that as many as thirty divisions might be in the Far East.[23] The total Red Air Force strength was believed to be over 4,000 first line aircraft and the

---

[21] *Aufmarschanweisung Barbarossa. OKH Gen St d H Op Abt (I), Nr. 050/41 g. Kdos Chefs* 31 January 1941.

[22] *WF St 44089/41 g. Kdos Chefs* of 3 February 1941.

[23] Kinzel's *Fremde Heere Ost* Appreciation dated 20 May 1941. Also Halder, *Kriegstagebuch*, Vol. 2, p. 266. By the eve of war on 21 June this estimate had increased slightly, so that for the whole of European Russia the totals were 154 rifle, ten tank and twenty-five cavalry divisions, and thirty-seven mechanized brigades. Halder, *Kriegstagebuch*, Vol. 2,

Soviet tank strength 10,000. Aircraft and tanks were correctly considered to be qualitatively inferior to those of the Germans.[24]

The German invasion was to be made by the three army groups, each supported by an air fleet. Army Group North, commanded by Field-Marshal von Leeb, was the smallest of the army groups, consisting of a panzer group and two armies, totalling twenty-six divisions, of which three were panzer and three motorized.[25] Army Group North was to attack from East Prussia through the Baltic States to Leningrad. The largest army group, Army Group Centre, commanded by Field-Marshal von Bock, consisted of two panzer groups and two armies, in all fifty divisions of which nine were panzer and six motorized. It was to make a widely separated two-pronged attack north and south of the Bialystok salient, the northern panzer group and army attacking from the area of Suwalki through the Vilna gap to Vitebsk and Smolensk, while the southern prong moved from Brest-Litovsk along the north edge of the Pripet Marshes to Bobruisk and Smolensk. These prongs were to form the strongly armoured wings which guarded the flanks of the army group and were to be ready to turn outwards to the north into the Baltic or south into the Ukraine, should such a movement be ordered by Hitler. Army Group South, commanded by Field-Marshal von Rundstedt, was to attack on two separate wings, one from southern Poland and one from Rumania. In Poland a panzer group and an army were to strike from the Lublin area south of the Pripet Marshes to the general area of Kiev and the Dnieper, while another army to its right attacked towards Lvov (Lemberg) and Vinnitsa. In Rumania a single German army, including some panzer and motorized troops, together with Rumanian forces was to attack across the Pruth into Bessarabia and the Ukraine. Von Rundstedt's force totalled forty-one German divisions of which five were panzer and three motorized. The equivalent of fourteen Rumanian divisions were also under his command.

---

p. 461. According to Zhukov the Soviet strength in the border districts facing Germany, Hungary and Rumania stood at 150 divisions deployed as follows:

	Rifle	Tank	Divisions Mech.	Cav.	Total
Baltic	19	4	2	—	25
W	24	12	6	2	44
SW	32	16	8	3	59
Odessa	13	4	2	3	22
Total	88	36	18	8	150

Zhukov, Vospominaniya i Razmyshleniya, p. 250. A further twenty were deployed against Finland and a further 133 in the interior and Far East. 50 Let Vooruzhennykh Sil SSSR, p. 235.

[24] The Luftwaffe estimate in May 1941 was 7,300 aircraft of all types in the west including training, intercommunication and reconnaissance planes. Halder, Kriegstagebuch, Vol. 2, p. 267. It was afterwards conceded that these air and tank estimates were far too low.

[25] Details of all German army groups are given at Appendix B to this book. All divisional totals are from OKH Kriegsgliederung dated 18 June 1941.

In addition to the divisions making up the three army groups, there were twenty-eight German divisions, of which two were panzer and two motorized, kept back as the High Command (OKH) Reserve.[26] About eight German divisions were to be committed in Finland. In all the German Army in the East, not including the troops in Finland, was to total 145 divisions, of which nineteen were panzer and fourteen motorized, while Germany's allies were to contribute the equivalent of a further forty divisions.[27] The German panzer divisions totalled about 3,300 tanks, only 800 more than had been used against France. To this figure of 3,300 tanks must be added about 250 tracked armoured assault guns.[28] The number of low category field divisions left in Western Europe was possibly higher than needed, taking into account the fact that the British Army at that time was incapable of providing many divisions fit for an amphibious offensive and had few landing craft to carry them. Thirty-eight German divisions were in occupied France and Flanders, one in Denmark and seven in Norway, a further seven in the Balkans and two in North Africa. The *Luftwaffe* forces in the east totalled a little more than 2,000 first line combat aircraft of which fewer than 800 were fighters. More than 1,500 aircraft were retained in the west for home defence and action against Britain.[29]

Planning and briefing continued during the last few months before the invasion date. In March the *Führer* had second thoughts about launching an armoured offensive from Rumania. Each of the rivers running diagonally across the front was a formidable tank obstacle, but he was particularly fearful in case Soviet attention should be drawn to this area and a Red Army counter-offensive put the German oil supplies at Ploesti in danger. All panzer and motorized divisions were thereupon transferred from 11 German Army in Rumania to 1 Panzer Group in South Poland, on the left wing of Army Group South. 11 Army was given the role of bolstering the Rumanians in what was no more than a pinning action, as they made a slow advance into Bessarabia. The rifle corps of 11 Army were to be widely dispersed across the

---

[26] This reserve was committed in the first few weeks of the fighting and no sizeable reserve was held again for the rest of the war.

[27] The German personnel strength was 3,200,000 men. Soviet sources greatly exaggerate the Axis force. For example, Telpukhovsky, *Die Sowjetische Geschichte des Grossen Vaterländischen Krieges*, p. 40, quotes the invading troops at 5,000,000 men and more than 9,000 tanks and 5,000 aircraft.

[28] The assault gun strength in June 1941 was only eleven battalions (the *Abteilung* at that time numbering only eighteen fighting vehicles).

[29] Approximate *Luftwaffe* strength in the east (first line combat aircraft only).

Army Group	Air Fleet	Number of aircraft
North	1	430
Centre	2	910
South	4	600
Finland	5	60
Total		2,000

Compare Deichmann, *German Air Force Operations in Support of the Army*, p. 158.

whole Moldavian front, sandwiched between Rumanian formations.[30]

The difficulties brought out in the series of exercises and discussions were to be solved in a variety of ways. Intelligence showed that the identified bulk of the Red Army was deployed well forward to the west and it seemed likely that it would defend ground near the frontier rather than rely on any form of mobile elastic defence.[31] It was therefore intended that the German panzer groups should penetrate deep into the enemy rear in wide enveloping and encircling movements and cut all withdrawal routes. The German armies, which were made up almost entirely of rifle divisions, the mobility of which was governed by the march endurance of its infantry, could not match the speed of the motorized panzer groups, and close co-ordination of movement between the two was impossible. The rifle armies were to operate independently, destroying and mopping up the encircled forces in the course of their steady advance. The panzer groups would, however, need some assistance initially in breaking through the Red Army defensive crust, assistance which only infantry could give, and for this reason an infantry corps was detached and put under the command of each panzer group. The task of these infantry corps was to make a rapid breach in the Soviet defences, through which would pour the armoured formations of the panzer groups. The infantry corps would then revert to the command of their own armies.[32]

There was some apprehension regarding the control of the entrances and exits of the roads which traversed the deep forest belts on the Army Group Centre front, and it was originally intended to secure these by the use of airborne forces. However, many of these woods were very deep in the enemy rear and for this reason it was unlikely that airborne detachments would be speedily relieved. Moreover, since the German airborne forces had recently suffered heavy casualties in Crete, they were not yet ready to take on such a commitment. So the project was dropped.

The supply of the advancing German troops over enormous distances in a vast war of movement was to prove particularly difficult. In the first instance no reliance could be placed on the railway system at all since it had to be converted from the broad to the standard gauge. Little air transport was available and almost exclusive reliance had to be placed on the use of motor transport, supplemented by such local resources as were available. Inadequate provision had been made for winter clothing, this being for only one-third of the troops since it was intended that the campaign should be completed by the autumn.

---

[30] Hitler was also to justify the removal of tanks from the right wing by the excuse that he wanted the Red Army pinned in the South Ukraine and Bessarabia, not driven back across the Dnieper. The argument was really a second thought. The absence of tanks in the South Ukraine was later regretted.

[31] Kinzel's *Fremde Heere Ost* (*OKH*) Appreciation of 20 May 1941 which concluded that a preventive war by the USSR was improbable and that the Red Army, if attacked, was unlikely to withdraw.

[32] An infantry corps was not used in the break-in on the left flank of Army Group South.

In outline, the *Barbarossa* strategy was based on achieving tactical surprise and encircling and destroying the Red Army formations which were close to the German and Rumanian frontiers before the enemy could withdraw. Army Group North was to encircle and destroy the enemy in the Baltic States and, together with the Finns, take Leningrad and clear North Russia. Army Group Centre was to encircle and destroy the enemy in Belorussia by a bold rush forward to Minsk and the Orsha landbridge. It was then to detach about half its armoured formations to assist Army Group North in the clearing of the Baltic and Leningrad, while the other half was to be held in readiness to be sent into the Ukraine. In the Ukraine, Army Group South was to break through rapidly to Kiev and the Dnieper crossing places in order to cut off the enemy withdrawal.

What was to happen thereafter none knew, least of all Hitler. In itself this might not necessarily have been of serious moment, except that no one knew what forces the Soviet Union held or could raise in Central European Russia or in Asia. No German knew in fact even what these regions looked like, and the invading troops were to find great industrial cities where twenty years before there were hamlets, and fertile cultivated prairieland where formerly had been barren steppe.[33]

[33] The inadequacy of German maps of Russia is stressed in numerous personal and divisional diaries from the first day of the war. In the far north Dietl's corps attack along the Murmansk coast failed after the first few days because the roads between the Titovka River and Motovka and from Motovka to the Bolshaya Zapadnaya Litsa shown on the maps did not exist. Guderian complained that the Glinka-Klimiatino road, marked 'good' on German maps, did not exist at all. *Panzer Leader*, p. 180. 98 Divisional road and axis marked as a broad red route ended after a few miles in marshy fields. Gareis, *Kampf und Ende der 98 Division*, p. 82. In the Bialystok battles the infantry of 35 Division found the maps so unreliable that it was safer to ask the way from the local inhabitants. *Die 35 Infanterie-Division*, p. 75. Of the Nogaisk Steppe in the South Ukraine, von Choltitz was to say 'where our maps indicated desert, were numerous new villages, immense cotton and melon fields and huge rubber plantations'. *Un Soldat parmi des Soldats*, p. 115. Meyer complained that Kherson, a great sprawling industrial city, was shown on German maps as a small municipality. *Panzergrenadiere*, p. 100. It must be remembered, however, that in the Soviet Union all maps are secret.

CHAPTER FIVE

Japan and Finland

The Japanese had been firm allies of the British from 1902 to 1919, but Britain's refusal to renew the Anglo-Japanese Treaty and her alignment with the United States had caused lasting resentment in Tokyo. From 1931 onwards, Manchuria and China were invaded by the Japanese; in 1936 Japan signed the Anti-Comintern Pact with Germany and within three years Japanese troops were engaged in fighting against Red Army formations on the borders of the Soviet Far East Maritime Provinces. In 1940 Japan became a signatory to Hitler's Tripartite Pact, by which it was bound to enter the war on the side of the Axis if the United States should enter on the side of Britain. Japan then endeavoured to safeguard the position on its Manchurian northern flank by trying to improve its relations with Moscow.

The German attitude towards Japan was one of friendly reserve, devoid of mutual trust or co-operation. When the Japanese Foreign Minister Matsuoka visited Berlin at the end of March 1941, von Ribbentrop had said that real co-operation with the Soviet Union was impossible and had made friendly recommendations that Matsuoka should keep clear of political discussions with the Soviet Union during his coming visit to Moscow. Von Ribbentrop committed himself only so far as to reveal that war between Germany and the USSR was 'possible', and went on to promise German assistance, should the Soviet Union attack Japan. Matsuoka, in taking note of von Ribbentrop's assurances, was non-committal as to Japan's probable course of action, but replied that he intended to discuss a non-aggression pact in Moscow. On 4 April Matsuoka saw Hitler who, being that day in an extravagant state of mind, said that he had made preparations so that no American soldier could land in Europe, and promised assistance in the event of a Japanese war with the United States. This verbal undertaking, loose though it was in its wording, appeared to have been made without provisos or without insisting on any form of *quid pro quo*, the Germans being intent only that the Japanese should attack Singapore.[1] On the other hand there was some nervousness in Tokyo that Japan was bound under the Tripartite Pact to come to Germany's aid, whereas Germany was not reciprocally bound to assist Japan where the Soviet

[1] *Nazi-Soviet Relations 1939–41*, pp. 298–315; also Hubatsch, *Hitlers Weisungen für die Kriegführung 1939–45, Weisung Nr. 24 über Zusammenarbeit mit Japan*, pp. 103–5.

Union was concerned.[2] On 13 April Matsuoka signed in Moscow the Soviet-Japanese Non-Aggression Pact which, although not received with enthusiasm in Berlin, was regarded as being compatible with the Tripartite Pact. Five weeks later Oshima, the Japanese Ambassador in Berlin, well aware that the possibility of a German attack on the Soviet Union was being freely discussed among the diplomatic corps, asked in vain for information from von Weizsäcker.[3] Kinzel, in the Foreign Armies East Department of the OKH, noted in an appreciation on 20 May that the signing of the Soviet-Japanese Pact had not caused any thinning out of the Red Army troops in the Far East, while four days later the German Military Attaché in Tokyo went so far as to surmise that if the United States were forced into the war as a result of a Russo-German conflict, Japan might attack Vladivostok.[4]

When Hitler attacked the Soviet Union, Japan had been given no prior intelligence as to the intention. The German relationship with Finland was very different.

In the autumn of 1939 after the signing of the August Russo-German Pact in Moscow, the Soviet Union had made the first of its demands on Finland and the rejection had led to the four months' Winter War, following which Finland lost more than one-tenth of its best territory and resources to the Soviet Union, nearly half a million of its population being displaced and made homeless. Thereafter, between March 1940 and June 1941, Finland lived under a threat of occupation and destruction. The Soviet Union was pressing for the Petsamo nickel mines concession and for compensation for private and public property which, it was alleged, had been destroyed in, or removed from, the ceded territories. Moscow interfered with the internal affairs and foreign relations of its tiny neighbour by making strong recommendations on the presidential election and on cabinet nominations and by restricting Finland's right to take part in any form of Scandinavian defensive alliance, and it appeared that the USSR was awaiting a suitable pretext to annex Finland, being deterred only by Hitler's newly awakened interest in the Baltic. In September 1940 the Finns had to allow military rail facilities over Finnish territory for the Soviet garrison at Hanko.[5]

In October 1940, the German Military Attaché in Helsinki hinted to the Finns about the possibility of a clash between Germany and the Soviet Union, and it became apparent that the Germans were anxious to cultivate under various pretexts a liaison with Finnish military circles. Hitler himself had formerly a low opinion of the value of Finnish troops and was surprised when he heard how highly they were regarded by the German Military Attachés. In mid

[2] Beloff, *The Foreign Policy of Soviet Russia*, Vol. 2, p. 373.
[3] *Nazi-Soviet Relations 1939–41*, p. 342.
[4] *Nazi Conspiracy and Aggression*, Vol. 4, p. 100.
[5] A few weeks later Finland permitted the transit of leave and sick parties of German troops between Norway and the Baltic. Travel began in December 1940 and although originally restricted to only 750 men at any one time in each direction it was the first step towards closer collaboration and the build-up of German troops in Finland.

December the Finnish General Talvela was invited to Germany and the next month the Chief of the Finnish General Staff, Lieutenant-General Heinrichs, gave a lecture on the Winter War to the German Staff College in Berlin. Halder and his staff used these opportunities to glean what information they could on Finnish operational matters.[6] Meanwhile Buschenhagen, the Chief of Staff of the Army of Norway, was a frequent visitor to Finland, ostensibly to discuss transportation questions.[7] On 26 May 1941 Hitler had sent Schnurre as a special envoy to President Ryti of Finland to explain that, although a peaceful solution could be found to the differences between Germany and the USSR, the possibility that the Soviet Union might attack Finland could not be ignored. It is said that Ryti expressed unwillingness that Finland should be drawn into a war between the Great Powers, but derived some consolation from Schnurre's assurance that a Soviet attack on Finland would be regarded in Berlin as an act of war against Germany. In response to Hitler's invitation, Heinrichs was sent with a small staff to conduct talks with Keitel and Jodl at Salzburg on 25 May, and the next day with Halder in Berlin. Jodl, who described himself as no optimist, said that the war in the West was already over and that a campaign in the East would certainly not last many months; he asked that, in the event of war, Finland should tie down the Red Army formations on her frontiers and assist the Germans in operations against Leningrad, Murmansk and Salla.[8] At this stage the Finns, who had lived so long on the brink of war and destruction, hastened to take what protection Germany would afford. German arms began to flow to Finland during the later summer of 1940, and Dietl's mountain corps in North Norway had been ordered to plan the securing of the Petsamo area. In December and in the following January von Falkenhorst's Army of Norway was ordered to undertake a study known as *Silver Fox* to formulate plans by which German and Finnish troops would take the port of Kandalaksha and the Kola Peninsula, so cutting the Murmansk railway, and at the same time advance south-eastwards in the area of Lakes Ladoga and Onega.

The original basis for the planning for *Silver Fox*, which involved the movement of strong German forces from Northern Norway into South-East Finland, was found to be impracticable for a number of reasons. The only railway from the Barents Sea to Ladoga was that from Murmansk which was in Soviet hands. The Soviet Northern Fleet had its base near Murmansk and, as the British Navy was both active and strong in the area and the Army of Norway had little air support, there could be no question of taking Murmansk

[6] Halder, *Kriegstagebuch*, Vol. 2, p. 264, 30 January 1941.

[7] Mannerheim, *Memoirs*, p. 405.

[8] *Ibid*, pp. 406–8; Keitel, *Memoirs*, p. 156; Halder, *Kriegstagebuch*, Vol. 2, p. 428, 26 May 1941. According to Erfurth, however, Jodl asked Finland only to pin the Soviet troops which were against its border in June 1941. Erfurth, *Der Finnische Krieg 1941–1944*, pp. 30–1. This is in accordance with Hitler's statement on 17 March that Finnish troops were only expected to attack Hanko and prevent the movement of the Soviet fleet into the Baltic. Halder, *Kriegstagebuch*, Vol. 2, p. 319.

from the sea. Very few road vehicles were available to the Army of Norway and it was impossible to move troops rapidly across Finland from north to south by the overland route. Moreover, the Swedes showed reluctance to allow the movement of a great number of troops across their territory.

Hitler had laid down in his original *Barbarossa* directive that the Army of Norway should secure the Petsamo nickel mines against attack and should cut the Soviet Murmansk railway link with the outside world, Murmansk being the only Soviet port which was ice free throughout the year.[9] Since the Finns showed little interest in operations in the northern area and welcomed the German initiative there, it was decided that the attack on the Murmansk railway should be made mainly with German troops; but for some unexplained reason Hitler directed that three very widely separated thrusts be made, none of which was to prove strong enough to achieve its purpose. In the northern coastal strip Dietl's mountain corps of two divisions was to move from Norway into the Finnish area of Petsamo and advance along the Barents Sea coast to the port of Murmansk. Nearly 200 miles to the south Feige's 36 Corps, with the equivalent of two German infantry divisions and one Finnish infantry division, was to move east from the area of Rovaniemi, cutting the railway near the White Sea port of Kandalaksha. The Finnish 3 Corps, commanded by Siilasvuo, consisting of little more than a division, was to make a subsidiary thrust yet a further hundred miles to the south, towards Ukhta and Kem parallel to the 36 Corps attack. The whole operation was commanded by von Falkenhorst, the Commander of the German Army of Norway, who was to establish a forward headquarters in Finland in addition to his own headquarters in Norway. Von Falkenhorst was responsible to the Armed Forces High Command (OKW) and not to von Brauchitsch and the OKH.

It remained to draw the Finns into the planning, which in its early stages was described as meeting a hypothetical situation. On 3 June further talks took place with the Finnish General Staff, the Germans being represented by Buschenhagen, from the Army of Norway answering for the OKW, and Kinzel, from Foreign Armies East representing the OKH. The Finns agreed that they would be responsible for operations in South-East Finland and be ready to attack east and west of Lake Ladoga at five days notice, initially using six divisions with a further seven to follow, but there was a noted Finnish reluctance to cross the Svir.[10] All troops in the south-east were to be under the Finnish Commander-in-Chief Mannerheim, a Finn of Swedish stock who had served with distinction as a General in the Imperial Tsarist Army and later in the war of independence against the Bolsheviks. The detail of the command arrangements over the Finnish theatre and the co-ordination between Mannerheim and von Falkenhorst were left imprecise and undetermined. The Finns began to mobilize secretly on 17 June, after they had extracted a promise from

---

[9] Hubatsch, *Hitlers Weisungen für die Kriegführung 1939–1945, Weisung 21*, p. 86.
[10] *Fremde Heere Ost, Chef, Protokoll über die Besprechungen in Finnland vom 3–6 Juni*; Erfurth, *Der Finnische Krieg 1941–1944*, p. 33.

68

Berlin that Germany was going to guarantee Finland's independence and a restoration of its earlier frontiers. The Finns knew that war was imminent even if they did not know its date, and there is some evidence that Helsinki had asked Berlin that it should not be involved in operations until several days after the start of *Barbarossa*, in order to create the impression that Finland had been drawn unwillingly into war.[11] For this reason Finland declared its neutrality on 22 June 1941. In expectation of a short war, half a million men, nearly sixteen per cent of the population, had been mobilized.

The difficulty in the supply and movement of troops particularly in North and Central Finland was to prove the key to the war in the north. The surest and safest way to get supplies and troops into Finland was by the Baltic Sea route, but this could not be used in winter due to freezing and it was in any case restricted by the lack of German shipping. The northern sea route from the Atlantic ran the gauntlet of British surface vessels and submarines, and there was only one road from Norway to the Kirkenes on the Norwegian-Finnish frontier, this being unusable in bad weather. The only other entry was by one road and one railway through Sweden. Inside Finland there were very few roads and only one single track railway which served the German troops in the centre but not in the north. This had very little rolling stock and, as the wide Russian gauge was used, this deficiency could not be made good by the *Reichsbahn*, nor could trains be run through over the Swedish frontier.

---

[11] *Erfurth an OKH Attache Abteilung für Gen Std H Op. Abt.* 16 June 1941 reproduced from Ziemke, *The German Northern Theater of Operations*, p. 136.

CHAPTER SIX

Arms and the Man

Before 1870 the French were regarded as the foremost military thinkers and the most competent soldiers in the world, and Napoleon Bonaparte's staff and army organization was to serve as a model for the other military powers, including Prussia, Russia, Japan and the United States. After the Franco-Prussian War, world military interest became focused on Prussia and the new Imperial German Army, and from then on followed the German lead. So it came about that the methods, organizations and tactics of the armies of all the great powers were similar in outline and bore the Continental stamp. The basic field formation devised by the French and still in use over a century and a half later, was the division, an all arms grouping of troops made up principally of infantry, artillery and engineers. The division was said to be basic because it was designed to be capable of operating in isolation and was self-contained and self-supporting, and the military might of a nation was reckoned in the number of divisions which it could muster. The numerical strength of a division varied from as few as ten thousand to as many as seventeen thousand men, but its fighting effectiveness depended not merely on its numbers but rather on its fire power and mobility and on its tactical handling. There was no hard and fast rule for the grouping of divisions into higher formations. Several divisions usually made up a corps, several corps made up an army and several armies were formed into an army group, known in Russian as a front.[1] Army groups were usually directly controlled by a General Headquarters or High Command, although on occasions early in the war the Red Army was to group two or more fronts under a theatre headquarters, which was itself subordinate to the High Command.[2]

[1] The corps and the army consisted predominantly of infantry formations and were sometimes known as rifle corps or rifle armies. Even though the adjective might be absent in the designation, the term corps or army usually denoted a basic infantry formation. Tank corps or tank armies on the other hand were always referred to by their full titles. Rifle corps or rifle armies always had supporting arms, artillery, engineers and signals, and sometimes tanks as well. In the Red Army rifle formations were sometimes known as 'integrated' or 'combined arms' armies. The detail of German army groups and Soviet fronts is given in Appendices B and C to this book.

[2] The Russian term is 'direction' which in British or United States military terminology makes little sense. The nearest translation is 'theatre'.

The German successes in Poland, France and the Balkans were due largely to good equipment, a high standard of tactical training and field leadership, and the revolutionary use made of tanks and air power. Originally tanks had a role something between that of artillery and of engineers, in that they were intended to assist infantry to fight and to move by providing fire power and by overcoming obstacles, but the military theorists. between the two world wars began to envisage the use of large numbers of tanks, supported by infantry and other arms, outflanking and encircling the slow moving infantry armies of the enemy. In such a role tanks became coequal with infantry, a main arm rather than a supporting arm. Except in Germany, most of these theorists were without position or influence.

By 1941 German armour was grouped into panzer (tank) divisions each consisting of a panzer regiment and a motorized infantry brigade. The panzer regiment had three panzer battalions and totalled in all about 160 tanks. The motorized infantry brigade had two infantry regiments each of two battalions which were either armoured or motorized, the difference being that the armoured infantrymen accompanied the tanks into battle in armoured half-track vehicles and could give immediate support, if necessary fighting from their armoured carriers, whereas the motorized infantry, who were carried in lorries, had to dismount and went into action on their feet.[3] The other German armoured formation was the motorized infantry division known from May 1943 onwards as the panzer grenadier division, consisting of two motorized infantry regiments, each of three battalions, these motorized battalions numbering somewhat less than 600 men and being carried in trucks although, as the war progressed, a number were remounted in armoured half-track vehicles. In addition, the motorized infantry division normally had either a panzer or an assault gun battalion of from thirty to fifty armoured fighting vehicles.[4] The two armoured divisions varied only in the proportion of tanks to infantry, the panzer division having from four to six battalions of infantry to about 160 tanks while the motorized infantry division had six battalions of

[3] German Army field establishments were by no means uniform. The 1939 panzer division had a panzer brigade of two panzer regiments totalling in all about 330 tanks, with one motorized infantry brigade of one (sometimes two) infantry regiments. By 1941 one panzer regiment had been removed from each division in order to form new divisions and these were not replaced. The 1941 division establishment totalled 190 tanks although it rarely had this number. The brigade organization was eventually abolished, all infantry were redesignated grenadier and all motorized infantry became panzer grenadier, and finally all panzer divisions had one panzer and two panzer grenadier regiments. After 1944 there was a further reduction in divisional strength from 165 to 54 tanks by the removal of a tank battalion and the reduction of equipment holdings. See also Keilig, *Das Deutsche Heer*, p. 103; Guderian (1 Panzer Division only), *Panzer Leader*, pp. 519–20; Mueller-Hillebrand, *Das Heer*, Vol. 1, pp. 72 and 163, Vol. 2, pp. 182–3.

[4] The motorized infantry division was in 1940 a three regiment infantry division carried in trucks, having motor instead of horse transport. By 1941 the third infantry regiment had been given up to form new divisions, although the SS divisions normally retained three regiments. The tank element was added from 1942 onwards (but was not always present) and consisted either of a tank battalion (usually in SS divisions) or an armoured self-propelled assault gun battalion.

infantry to about fifty tanks. These armoured formations, known in German as mobile troops, were originally grouped into panzer corps, each of two panzer divisions and one motorized infantry division, the panzer divisions providing the shock action while the motorized infantry division formed the supporting element and pivot. Two or three panzer corps formed a panzer group later known as a panzer army, which might consist of up to 800 tanks together with armoured and motorized infantry and supporting arms.

The successes up to 1941 were in part due to this use of tanks in mass and the emphasis on mobility and bold handling. The Germans had a clear appreciation of the interdependability of tanks and infantry and had provided the infantry and supporting arms with suitable equipment to move and fight at tank speed. The motorized infantry divisions in particular were ambidextrous since their equipment and organization enabled them to fight as panzer or infantry formations and consolidate the gains of the spearhead panzer divisions. On the other hand there was rarely any question of restricting the mobility of the panzer corps to the speed of the great mass of marching infantry divisions coming up behind, and the risks of wide gaps and of dangerously exposed flanks were generally accepted. Fire support was provided not so much by artillery but by ground attack aircraft, by tanks and by tracked armoured assault guns. Until the Soviet T 34 tank appeared, German tanks were the best in the world, and the German superiority in tank radio and optical equipment remained unchallenged throughout the war. The main German armoured strength in 1941 was to be found in the 22 ton Mark III and the 23 ton Mark IV tanks.[5]

German infantry relied on the armoured assault gun probably more than they did on the tank, and towards the end of the war more assault guns than tanks were being manufactured. The early armoured assault gun was a turretless, open-topped, tracked and armoured tank chassis mounting a gun in the hull. It was originally designed to provide close fire support for infantry and it did this by the direct fire of the gun. The vehicles had a low silhouette and, since the early models were open, the crews could hear and see the battle around them and did not experience the same difficulty as tank crews in orienting themselves and identifying targets. Although the guns had little traverse and the whole vehicle had in fact to be aimed in the direction of the

[5] The 22 ton Mark III had an excellently designed hull with 50 mm frontal armour, and to later models a furthei 20 mm spaced armour was added. Its main armament was a 50 mm high velocity gun of 42 or 60 calibres in length. The Mark IV had 60 mm frontal armour and originally had a short barrelled low velocity 75 mm gun of 24 calibres, being intended primarily to support infantry. In 1942 it was rearmed with high velocity 43 and 48 calibre guns to enable it to engage enemy tanks, and eventually it had a 70 calibre 75 mm weapon. The thickness of plate is only partly relevant to tank armour unless slope, design and type of plate are taken into account. A 30 mm plate sloped at 60 degrees gives better protection than 60 mm at the vertical. Protection can be improved by the use of face hardened or homogeneous hard armour, by spaced armour or by skirting plates. The anti-tank efficiency of a gun depends not only on calibre but also on the design of the shot and the muzzle velocity at which it leaves the barrel. Muzzle velocity varies largely on the barrel design and the length of the bore (which is measured in calibres).

target, the assault gun could engage to a flank as quickly as a tank with a rotating turret, provided that the ground was firm and free from obstruction. The assault gun had other advantages over a tank in that it was easier to produce and could carry heavier frontal armour and a heavier gun. It was manned by the artillery arm and not by panzer troops and was organized in battalions (*Abteilungen*) of eighteen fighting vehicles, these later being increased to thirty-one and then redesignated as assault gun brigades. Towards the end of the war assault artillery brigades of forty-five assault guns and a small integrated infantry element came into being.

These assault gun battalions, which formed a most important part of the German order of battle, had no counterpart in America or Britain, and are not to be confused with self-propelled artillery, in which the tracked and armoured chassis merely forms a mobile platform from which the gun engages the target by indirect fire. The assault gun, like the tank, was a fighting vehicle designed to engage the enemy at close quarters, and the earlier types had not even the necessary equipment to allow them to use indirect fire.

The 1940 and 1941 assault gun models were usually mounted on Mark III tank chassis and carried a low velocity short twenty-four calibre L24 75 mm gun or a low velocity 105 mm howitzer designed to engage pin point targets, infantry or gun crews, with high explosive shell. In order to provide a more effective counter to enemy tanks, however, the low velocity guns and howitzers were gradually replaced by the long high velocity L43 and L48 75 mm gun which was used both for engaging tanks with solid shot and for supporting infantry with high explosive shell. So it came about that, although manned by German artillery, the role of the assault gun battalion was little different from that of a panzer battalion, with which in fact it was interchangeable. Its anti-tank performance was truly formidable and by early 1944 the assault artillery arm claimed to have destroyed 20,000 enemy tanks.[6] So successful were they, that the Red Army introduced its own version, known as the SU, which was employed tactically in exactly the same way as its German counterpart.

The responsibilities of the panzer and anti-tank arm on the one side, and the artillery on the other, were not, however, clear cut in the German Army, and, as the war progressed, it became more difficult to define them. Although one of the two main roles of the assault gun was that of a tank killer, tank destroyers manned by the anti-tank arm were brought into use. The lightest of these was a L48 75 mm gun on either a Mark IV or a 16 ton Czech tank chassis (*Hetzer*) and these could be used for the same dual roles as the assault gun. The true tank destroyers came later in the war in 1943 and 1944 when 88 mm guns were mounted on the Mark V *Jagdpanther* and the Mark VI Tiger in the form of the *Hornisse*, which was later known as the *Nashorn*, and the *Ferdinand*, afterwards called the *Elefant*. To add to the complexity of the

[6] See also Munzel, *Die Deutschen Gepanzerten Truppen bis 1945*, pp. 113–34; Tornau und Kurowski, *Sturmartillerie*, pp. 13–29. Assault guns were also used by the panzer arm.

picture, before the end of the war the Germans added to the many direct fire armoured vehicles manned by panzer, assault gun and anti-tank units, by introducing tracked and armoured self-propelled field and medium artillery, which engaged targets by indirect fire, the 105 mm howitzer *Wespe* on a Mark II or French tank chassis and the 150 mm howitzers *Brummbär* and *Hummel* on Mark III and IV chassis.

Although the Germans owed so many of their earlier successes to their expert use of the tank arm, they entered Russia with only nineteen panzer and fourteen motorized infantry divisions, the other one hundred and twelve German divisions being divisions of marching infantry.[7] The reason for this was to be found in the limited German tank and vehicle production and the shortage of motor fuels. There can be no doubt that there was a need for many more armoured divisions of both types, and yet, after the first flush of victories, there was also to be an acute lack of infantry formations which was to last throughout the course of the whole war. Although armoured formations filled a very spectacular role, they suffered from serious limitations. Tanks could not normally fight by night and were sensitive to ground and of limited use in the great forest belts and many swamps. Armoured formations were often crippled too by the autumn and spring mud, and even when tracked vehicles could keep moving they were finally brought to a halt because the wheeled supply and fuel trucks had already become bogged down. Nor could tanks actually hold ground against heavy infantry attack for any length of time.

The main fighting element of the German Army was the infantry division, and its organization set a pattern for many of the armies of the world, particularly those of the Soviet Union and Japan. The basic unit was the infantry regiment, three regiments to the division, and the regiment comprised three infantry battalions, each of three rifle companies and a support company of medium machine-guns and mortars.[8] The regiment had its own anti-tank company and an infantry gun company equipped with short range 75 mm and

---

[7] *OKH Kriegsgliederung* 18 June 1941. The total of 145 divisions does not include the equivalent of a further eight infantry divisions in Finland. The total German Army and SS strength in Europe and Africa in 1941 stood at:

> 163 infantry divisions including four light and six mountain divisions
> 1 cavalry division
> 9 security divisions
> 14 motorized infantry divisions (including four SS)
> 21 panzer divisions
> ───
> 208 divisions
> ───

Of these only 167 divisions, of which 131 were infantry, light or mountain, were at full battle organization and strength. The remainder were security divisions or on low mobilization categories (Wave 13, 14 or 15), see note 8 below.

[8] Mountain divisions and light divisions known after June 1942 as *Jägerdivisionen* had only two infantry regiments each. A number of the more recently formed infantry divisions known as 'Wave 13, 14 or 15 formations' had only two regiments and few supporting arms, and the security divisions often had only one regiment. For this reason the total of German

150 mm guns.[9] Among the divisional troops was an anti-tank battalion and a single artillery regiment of forty-eight guns, mainly 105 mm gun howitzers and a few 150 mm howitzers. German equipment was simple but of very good quality, most of it of new design and recent manufacture. The old pattern bolt-operated 1898 rifle was still the personal weapon, but fully automatic machine-carbine pistols and the gas-operated self-loading 41 rifles were already in use. The principal infantry armament, however, was the light and medium 34 machine-gun and the mortar.[10]

The main characteristic of artillery has always been the mobility and flexibility of its fire, and to exploit this it was necessary to keep artillery under a single commander at the highest possible level and not allocate it to lower formations or units, since this was generally wasteful. This is understood and practised by artillerymen all the world over, and yet this principle was often ignored by the German Army in the Second World War. German artillery fire was not as effective as it might have been, since it lacked concentration, and the artillery arm had been somewhat neglected because the High Command came to rely on aircraft, tanks and armoured assault guns to provide much of the close support.[11]

The favoured position which Göring occupied in the Nazi hierarchy established the *Luftwaffe* as an independent force, theoretically coequal with the Army. The main task of the *Luftwaffe* in its early days was to have been the support of ground operations and this was reflected in the design of the bomber force, which consisted of light twin engined aircraft with limited range and bomb load, such as the Junker 88, the Dornier 17 and the Heinkel 111. These were intended for tactical support and were not suitable for a strategic bombing role, so that they were unable to take the battle into the depth of the enemy rear or homeland. Between 1943 and 1945 the air war with the Anglo-Americans rarely ceased by day or by night, and Western long range fighter strength and the heavy strategic bombing attacks made on the homeland of Germany caused the Germans to concentrate on fighter production and convert some of their twin engined bombers to fighters. The bomber force was neglected and gradually withered and, as the air power of its enemies grew, the *Luftwaffe* was forced to go on the defensive, being unable to undertake

---

divisions by itself therefore is apt to give a misleading picture of the strength. Infantry divisions relied on about 3,000 to 4,700 horses for movement. Mueller-Hillebrand, *Das Heer*, Vol. 2, p. 100.

[9] Regimental artillery consisted of eight infantry guns with a maximum range of only 5,000 yards. The gunners were infantrymen and the guns were normally used for direct (aimed on line of sight) fire.

[10] The 34 MG was soon to be replaced by the pattern 42. On a bipod, this was the rifle section light machine-gun. On the tripod it became the longer range medium machine-gun.

[11] The Germans frequently made successful use of *ad hoc* tactical groupings of all arms, but this led to the further decentralization of artillery which only too frequently was put under command of such groups.

offensive operations or to provide the German Army with adequate tactical air support.[12]

German combat aircraft were of excellent design and these were restricted to a few types which were easily modified to undertake widely differing roles. To maintain the output of new planes the Germans relied on these modifications and improvements rather than creating entirely new models. The standard single engined fighter was the Messerschmitt (Me) 109, with a maximum speed of about 400 mph at 20,000 feet, which was for long to remain one of the best aircraft in the world. The twin engined fighter bomber was the Me 110 which had a far greater radius of action than the Me 109 but a maximum speed of only 360 mph at 20,000 feet. The principal ground attack aircraft, the Junker 87 dive bomber or *Stuka*, was a single engined aircraft with a distinctive inverted gull or crank shaped wing, but its speed was cut by exterior bomb racks and by a non-retractable undercarriage to a maximum of only 250 mph; except in very favourable conditions it could not operate without a fighter escort. The standard transport plane was the Junker 52, a three-engined low winged monoplane used as a civil aircraft before the war.

The scope of the activities of the *Luftwaffe* was far wider than one would normally associate with a military air force. It was of course entrusted with the fighter defence of the German homeland and the occupied territories, but to this was added other air defence roles such as air raid precautions and the manning of searchlights and anti-aircraft guns over 20 mm in calibre. Whereas in other armies gun crews are part of army artillery, until 1942 German anti-aircraft belonged to the *Luftwaffe* and was allotted to army formations for air defence, many of the guns, in particular the 88 mm high velocity mobile anti-aircraft guns, being used as anti-tank guns or as ground to ground field artillery. Parachute formations were part of the *Luftwaffe* but airborne formations were part of the Army. During the course of the war, however, the German Army needed manpower, and the *Luftwaffe* was ordered to find a large number of men for ground combat duties in the field; but since Göring objected to the transfer of his officers and men for retraining and use as reinforcements to the German Army, Hitler approved that the *Luftwaffe* should raise its own infantry divisions commanded by its own *Luftwaffe* Generals and officers. In all, twenty-two of these divisions were raised. Their fighting value was low and could not be compared with that of the Army or the

---

[12] The *Luftwaffe* air organization was flexible and was usually based on the air fleet (*Luftflotte*) consisting of one or more air corps, known as *Fliegerkorps* or *Jagdkorps* (if the formation was exclusively fighter). The air corps comprised a number of air divisions, each of a number of air groups called *Geschwader*, commanded by colonels and each holding about a hundred aircraft. The air group had three or more wings (*Gruppen*), the *Gruppe* being the basic combat unit for both operational and administrative purposes. It was usually housed on a single airfield. The *Gruppe* had three squadrons (*Staffeln*) of about ten or twelve aircraft each. For tactical purposes the squadron flew in half squadrons (*Schwärme*), in flights (*Ketten*) or in pairs of aircraft (*Rotten*). A German air division might consist of several hundred aircraft. A Soviet air division was no more than sixty to ninety aircraft.

Armed SS, because they were formed too rapidly and were without professional leadership and training.[13]

The National Socialist Party's SS organization was to play a prominent part in the war in the East and on public life in Germany. It consisted of two main branches, the General SS and the Armed SS. The General SS was uniformed but not armed, and except for cadre staff, its members were part time and unpaid, the cost of the organization being borne by membership subscription and Party funds and not by the German State. It had no military significance. The Armed SS, known before the war as the *Verfügungstruppe*, was originally raised as a full time para-military armed mobile reserve at the disposal of Hitler. It lived in barracks and its cost was borne by the German taxpayer, regular full time service in its ranks being a bar to conscription into the armed forces. As a corollary it would not normally accept recruits who had formerly served in the Army, Navy or the *Luftwaffe*.

The strength of the *Verfügungstruppe* was originally very small and even by the outbreak of war was no higher than four regiments.[14] It is doubtful whether it was Hitler's intention to form a very large number of SS divisions to serve as a political counter to the German Army, since the SS was meant to be nothing more than Hitler's own Praetorian Guard and armed political police. When the war came, however, many of its number thirsted for action and it was believed to be in the interests of the Party that they should take a prominent, or at least a well publicized, part in the fighting. The *Verfügungstruppe* began to expand rapidly and was redesignated as the Armed SS. A number of army officers had sought re-employment with the *Verfügungstruppe* from its earliest days.[15] Like that of the German Army, other rank recruiting was governed by racial standards, but originally no recruit was accepted for the SS unless he was of Nordic race and a firm adherent to National Socialist political thought, and its members in consequence were usually political extremists or fanatics, sometimes of criminal tendencies. Later, the field of

[13] The German armed forces were not necessarily organized according to military logic. Conservatism, prejudice, political dogma, jealousy, vested interest and Hitler's improvisations came into play. Both the *Luftwaffe* and the Army had airborne forces and eventually both manned anti-aircraft guns of all calibres. The *Luftwaffe* and SS also manned tanks and field artillery in *Luftwaffe* and SS formations. The manning of armoured assault guns by artillery was bitterly opposed by the mobile (panzer) troops. The infantry, however, preferred the support of the assault gun to the tank battalion since the largest assault gun formation, the battalion/brigade, was rarely removed from infantry formations and could be relied upon to be at hand when needed, which was not always the case with tank units. Göring, when ordered to find men as reinforcements for ground combat duty, objected, so it is said, to the diminishing of his personal empire, on the political grounds that he was not going to give up his National Socialist boys to the Army, where some General would send them to church.

[14] Divisions were formed from 1939 onwards. Klietmann, *Die Waffen* SS, pp. 32 and 72.

[15] Amongst these were Hausser, retired as a *Reichswehr* lieutenant-general in 1932, who became Inspector of the *SS Verfügungstruppe* in 1936 and who subsequently commanded the SS division *Das Reich*, 2 SS Panzer Corps, 7 German Army and Army Group G. Steiner, Keppler, Gille, Ostendorff, Kleinheisterkamp, Bittrich and Demelhuber were other former army officers who served with the SS almost from its inception.

D

recruiting was widened to include firstly the *Volksdeutsch* and those of Germanic race, and then finally most other nationalities. Its military organization was close to that of the German Army but it had different titles for its ranks and organization. In the field it wore army uniform and used army equipment, providing its own tank and artillery regiments and training its own officers and NCOs, and in due course it was to have priority over the German Army in the allocation of equipment and personnel.[16] Officers and men were not normally interchangeable between the SS and the Army although SS formations did serve under Army command as part of a higher formation. Very occasionally SS officers were put in command of German Army formations and towards the end of the war some German Army staff officers were transferred and recruits inducted compulsorily into the SS.[17]

Not every SS soldier was guilty of war crimes, but the Armed SS did contain a substantial proportion of such criminals and former concentration camp guards. In any case, even the Armed SS field formations were called upon to find troops for the guarding of concentration camps and the carrying out of punitive measures, including the liquidation of Jews, communists, suspected partisans and innocent hostages. These liquidation operations were additional to those carried out by the *SS Einsatzgruppen* and *SS Einsatzkommandos* made up of teams recruited and controlled by Heydrich's security service *Sicherheitsdienst* (SD) and security police (*Sipo*).[18]

Hitler was the Supreme Commander of the Armed SS, but this command was exercised through Himmler, the *Reichsführer SS*. No SS formation or unit could be disbanded or carry out strategic movement without the authority of Himmler, and SS commanders had the right of access to Himmler through the normal SS channels. In this way SS formations and units were independent of any superior German Army headquarters in that they could always exercise their right of appeal. For military operations the Armed SS were placed at the disposal of the German Army, although wherever possible they were given independent tasks. Special emphasis was placed on their propaganda value and many spectacular missions were given to them, but their military efficiency and importance were sometimes exaggerated. Their morale was normally very good but their tactical handling was often at fault, and, in the view of the German Army, which tended at times to be patronizing towards them, their

[16] The SS had its own distinctive collar patches and shoulder straps and wore the *Hoheitsabzeichen* on the left sleeve.

[17] The Death's Head SS was yet a third branch of the SS, originally enlisted for the guarding of concentration camps. In April 1941 it had been amalgamated with the Armed SS. 3 SS *Totenkopf* Division owed its name to the fact that it was raised in 1939 from reinforcements and men transferred from the Death's Head SS. See Klietmann, *Die Waffen SS*, p. 107.

[18] The security police was an amalgam of the Gestapo and the Criminal Police (*Kripo*). The war diary entry of 1 SS Motorized Infantry Brigade on 30 July 1941 reported the shooting of 'about 800 Jews and Jewesses from sixteen to sixty years old' in the previous three days. A *Sonderkommando* raided the Jewish ghetto at Slonim in Belorussia on 27 June 1942. Its war diary reported 'about 4,000 Jews were put down'.

casualties were disproportionately high when measured against their achievements. In all, the fighting value of the German Armed SS was certainly no less than that of the German Army, because its professional deficiencies were compensated by its wealth of equipment and its fanaticism. Towards the end of the war the SS fought desperately, believing that the tell-tale tattoo mark which each of them bore would probably spell death if they fell into the hands of the enemy or the local population. In all, thirty-eight SS divisions and a number of brigades were raised. Many of the foreign SS had no fighting value.

Originally there were no separate political organs within the German Army comparable with the Soviet commissar system but, as the reverses mounted later in the war, special National Socialist Leadership or Guidance Officers were appointed to serve on the staffs of all higher commanders in an effort to instil political awareness and determination. The Armed SS eventually formed an effective counterweight to the German Army and there is no doubt that it would have readily taken up its arms against the Army in defence of Hitler and the Nazi régime. The SS was connected through the person and officers of Himmler to the whole of the German police organization and, after 1943, to the *Reich* and Prussian Ministry of the Interior, and in this Himmler's SS empire was a parallel to that of Beria's NKVD. Under Himmler, as the Chief of the German Police, came all branches of the civil police, both uniformed and plain clothes, the frontier police, the secret state police or *Gestapo*, the security police and the security service (SD). The SD, headed by Heydrich, a former officer who had been forced to leave the German Navy, was originally the Nazi Party intelligence service for use against Germans of other political persuasion, and this was superimposed on the civil police organization. The tasks of the SD included political and military espionage, its activity overlapping that of the *Abwehr*, the intelligence organization of the High Command of the Armed Forces (OKW), the head of which was Admiral Canaris. The political and military organization of Hitler's Germany had many similarities to that of Stalin's Communist Empire.

In June 1941 the Soviet High Command was patterned on German military thought as it had been in 1933, when the military liaison between the USSR and Germany was interrupted by Hitler's accession to power. Its defence system was based on separate Commissariats or Ministries for the Red Army and Navy, since the Red Air Force was not a separate armed service but was part of the Red Army. The organization of the Soviet High Command (NKO) was otherwise similar to that of other major military powers, consisting of military and naval councils, the General Staff branches, inspectorates and directorates for all the main arms. The Defence Ministry had, as part of the General Staff, its own military intelligence organization, the GRU, which had world-wide espionage networks, but which was not responsible for counter-intelligence. The Soviet High Command and military system differed radically from that of the outside world, however, in that it incorporated organic commissar and secret police organizations.

The system of military commissars originated at the time of the revolution when trustworthy communists were recruited to keep under surveillance the suspect Tsarist officers re-employed in the Red Army as military specialists. To each officer at all levels of command from battalion upwards was appointed a political commissar of equivalent rank and authority, who was made responsible for the political reliability and military effectiveness of officers and men. This political officer had very wide powers, including that of veto of the military commander's orders. The status and power of the commissar *vis-à-vis* the military commander was later to vary according to the political situation inside the Soviet Union. By 1934 there was some relaxation of political tension and the military officer had been restored to full command. Then followed the great purges when millions of prominent citizens in all walks of life, including the armed forces, were liquidated or imprisoned, and the status of the commissar was raised again to equality with that of the military commander, this probably leading to a deterioration in military efficiency. In 1940 as a result of the débâcle in Finland, the commissar's powers were reduced once more to those of a political deputy divorced from command affairs, whose task it was to assist with military administration and welfare and be responsible for political instruction and propaganda. This was the position in June 1941. Although the commissar no longer had the original power of veto which enabled him to interfere with the officer's function and powers of command, he could still report on the military commander's efficiency through his own political channels. Commissars were the Communist Party's representatives with the Red Army. They wore army officers' uniform with badges and insignia of the arm to which they were accredited, their true identity being apparent only by a red star with a hammer and sickle emblem worn on the sleeve. At times the title of commissar and the post of company political leader were officially though temporarily abolished, but the commissar organization was always in existence even if its powers had been restricted and even if it was called by another name.[19]

The commissar was usually the best informed man in the formation or unit because, in addition to his staff of political leaders, he had a propaganda network of trusted and zealous Party members and Komsomols, junior non-commissioned officers or private soldiers trained as activists and agitators to spread the official line of propaganda by lectures and barrack room talk. They could also be relied upon to report any deviationists or free thinkers. There was some interchangeability between combatant officers and commissars since most commissars had spent their adult lives in the Red Army

[19] The commissars' ranks were: political and senior political instructor (*politruk*); battalion and senior battalion commissar; regimental, brigade, divisional, corps and army commissar (first and second grade). The description was that of a rank and not of a function, so that a battalion commissar was often found with a regiment or division, while a brigade commissar could be appointed to an army or a front. After October 1942 all commissars were given army ranks. See *Kratkaya Istoriya Velikaya Otechestvennaya Voina* (hereafter known as *Kratkaya Istoriya*), p. 61 and footnote.

and were often as capable as the officers on military matters. In battle many took over command when the military commanders became casualties, and during the course of the war many elected, or were selected, for transfer from the corps of commissars to military command appointments. Nor was it unknown for combatant officers of political education and reliability to be appointed to senior political appointments. The exact relationship between the officer and commissar varied largely on their personalities, and it was sometimes very good, but much depended also on the political climate at the time. If repression or purge were imminent no man could trust his neighbour, and at such times the commissars, in self preservation, would work hand in glove with the feared special department or special sections of the NKVD secret police, and would themselves become the object of hatred.

At the higher levels of command, the military district in peace, and front and army headquarters in war, all operational orders of any consequence were invalid, unless signed jointly by a military council or *sovet* consisting of the commander, his chief of staff and the political member. The political member could be the formation senior political officer (commissar), but was usually a civilian communist party official or commissar nominated by Moscow. After October 1942 these civilian officials were given military ranks. Above the level of corps therefore, the command responsibility was shared by the *sovet*, the commander and political member being the senior partners in the *triumvirate*. In this way the Kremlin hoped to safeguard itself against military insurrection or *coup d'état*.[20]

The secret police organization was entirely separate and distinct from that of the political officer and commissar. Internal security in the Soviet Union was the province of the Ministry of the Interior, known as the NKVD, which had responsibilities for the maintenance of law and order, the police, the fire service, prisons and public records. The main difference between the NKVD and the Ministries of the Interior or Home Offices of the democracies lay in the fact that the NKVD maintained a very large military force of internal security troops, organized into divisions with tanks and artillery, concentration camp guards and convoy troops and border guards. These troops, although they wore the usual khaki army uniform, had distinctive badges and headdress and were in no way part of the Army, and since they were recruited from politically reliable conscripts of the annual intake, they formed a political and military counterweight to the Red Army. In some respects the military NKVD had close similarities with the German Armed SS and many of its members, even by the Red Army standards of the time, were particularly brutalized. In emergency NKVD formations would be put under Red Army command and a number of NKVD Generals were to be found in command of

---

[20] A military council often included other co-opted members, but its decisions and orders were not valid unless all members of the *triumvirate* were present. Military councils have never existed below army level, where corps and divisional commanders were responsible for their own actions. Petrov, *Partiinoe Stroitelstvo v Sovetskoi Armii i Flote*, Chapter 2.

Army formations. Unlike the German Armed SS, NKVD troops were not normally used in the forefront of battle, but formed the garrison of vital centres or were held back to round up stragglers or threaten Red Army units which were in danger of breaking. They also provided escorts. In addition to this paramilitary responsibility, the NKVD in 1941 included the GUGB or Main Directorate of State Security, which was in effect the state secret police and the forerunner of the KGB. The responsibilities of the secret police included all forms of political and military intelligence abroad and counter-intelligence both at home and abroad, its espionage systems being independent of, and duplicating, those of the military intelligence of the GRU. Secret police organs existed in every walk of life, in embassies and trade and cultural missions abroad, in the armed services, in industry, agriculture, sport, music and in the Communist Party itself. In the Red Army, secret police representatives, forming what were known as special sections, were to be found at all levels of command down to division. They ranked as officers and wore the uniform and insignia of the troops to which they were attached. Secret police officers were often detached to regiments and sometimes to battalions. Their true identities could not of course be concealed from Red Army officers, but the networks they operated were clandestine, the informers, recruited by fear or hope of gain, reporting on their superiors and their fellows. The secret police had their own channels of communication and their intelligence targets included officers and men, the commissars and fellow members of the secret police. During the purges the secret police itself had suffered a high proportion of the liquidation and transportation casualties.[21]

In 1941 the Soviet Navy was neither large nor efficient and it was to play a very minor part in the course of the war. Control over the Black Sea was soon wrested from it by the *Luftwaffe*, and German and Rumanian shipping used the coastal waters in safety. The Soviet Navy did in addition operate a number of river gun boat flotillas on the main rivers and canals as far inland as the Pripet Marshes. In the Baltic the Soviet Navy was to be curiously passive, for although it had material resources enough at least to challenge German naval supremacy there, the Baltic Red Fleet remained port-ridden in Leningrad and Kronstadt, contained by mine barriers and German air and naval power. In general, the Baltic and Black Sea Fleets were regarded

---

[21] NKVD officers received the same form of military training as army officers in their own NKVD schools. NKVD border guards wore green and blue caps and green shoulder straps, NKVD internal troops wore red and blue caps and red shoulder straps. The NKVD secret policemen wore army insignia of the formation to which they were attached and not that of the NKVD. Before June 1941 German intelligence staffs, although fully understanding the commissar system, appear to have been ignorant that NKVD secret police existed inside the Red Army; mention was omitted from the German Secret Handbook '*Die Kriegswehrmacht der UdSSR*' dated 1 January 1941, but it was given great prominence in the second edition twelve months later. On 8 December 1941 Halder noted with surprise the existence of an NKVD organization in Soviet divisional headquarters, this intelligence having been picked up by radio intercept. Halder, *Kriegstagebuch*, Vol. 3, p. 334.

as a reserve of manpower to provide infantry brigades of sailors for the land fighting. In the Arctic, activity was limited to operations in coastal waters and submarine forays.

Immediately after the outbreak of war with Germany the Soviet military command was reorganized. No special field accommodation had been prepared for the High Command and it remained in its peace-time buildings throughout the whole war. Stalin was the *de facto* Supreme Commander and he stayed in his rooms at the Kremlin; through his own adjoining signal centre and secretariat under Poskrebyshev he was in constant communication with the commanders in the field by high frequency radio or by telegraph. Within the first two weeks of war a new command organization had been evolved, based on two committees. The first of these was the State Committee of Defence (GKO) and was the superior in that it was responsible for all the wider aspects of the conduct of war, political, economic and military. Stalin was its chairman and its first members were Molotov, Malenkov, Voroshilov and Beria, the head of the NKVD. Other members of the Politburo were co-opted as required. The second committee, known as the *Stavka*, was mainly military and was responsible for the direction of all land, sea and air operations. Stalin was chairman and its original members were Molotov, Timoshenko, Voroshilov, Budenny, Shaposhnikov, Zhukov and N. G. Kuznetsov. [22] Other military representatives, including heads of staff branches and supporting arms, were ordered to attend when needed, and members of the GKO or Politburo sometimes took part in the *Stavka* proceedings. Stalin was the centre of all activity and the meetings took place either in his office and rooms in the Kremlin or in his *dacha* just outside Moscow. Although Timoshenko gave up the appointment of Minister of Defence, this in effect being held by Stalin, the Defence Ministry remained, the General Staff and arms branches acting as the executive of the *Stavka*. [23] The *Stavka* soon had at its disposal a pool of senior officers, either members or co-opted to supervise all planning, and these included Vatutin, Vasilevsky, Antonov, Voronov, Shtemenko, Fedorenko, Golovanov and Novikov. Some were staff officers or arms specialists, others were field commanders, and it became the practice to detach many of them to command or co-ordinate fronts during the course of

---

[22] Timoshenko was nominally the head of the *Stavka* for about two weeks from 23 June. *Istoriya*, Vol. 2, p. 21. Voroshilov and Budenny were old cronies of Stalin's from the days of the Civil War. Voroshilov had been Minister of Defence but after the Winter War with Finland had been replaced by Timoshenko. Budenny was in command of the Reserve Armies. Shaposhnikov was on fairly close terms with Stalin and had been Chief of General Staff from 1937 to 1940, but, being in poor health, he was relieved by Meretskov and became Deputy Defence Minister for Fortifications. Meretskov held the post of Chief of General Staff only for a few months being replaced in February 1941 by Zhukov. Admiral N. G. Kuznetsov was the Naval Minister.

[23] Also Zhukov, *Vospominaniya i Razmyshleniya*, pp. 301–3; Shtemenko, *Generalnyi Shtab v Gody Voiny*, p. 29. Shtemenko refers to the 'permanent college of military advisers' at the service of the *Stavka*, the members of which he names as Shaposhnikov, Meretskov, Vatutin, Voronov, Zhdanov and others.

critical operations.[24] All of·these officers, except for Budenny, were men of some ability. The Commander of the Soviet Navy also formed part of the *Stavka*, together with representatives from the Red Air Force.

Stalin's position in the GKO and the *Stavka* was theoretically that of *primus inter pares* in that he was a participant and the chairman, but the fiasco resulting from the invasion of 22 June apparently brought home to the dictator the realization of the fallibility of his judgement since he withdrew for some little time from prominence in the public eye. It is certain, however, that he did not relax for one moment his iron grip on the affairs of state, and he began from this time to immerse himself in military affairs. He took the leading part in the direction of the war and he alone had the final word in all political and military decisions of importance. Of military experience he had none, save for that as a commissar during the revolution and the short war against Poland, and he probably had much less natural aptitude than did Hitler. A taciturn and guarded Konev, when cross-examined in 1944 by Djilas about the capabilities of the war leaders, gave a critical appraisal of Voroshilov, Budenny and Shaposhnikov. Of Stalin he said that the dictator was brilliantly able to see the war as a whole and for this reason was able to direct it so successfully.[25] He made no other comment.

Having made due allowance for the fact that Konev was bound to make some form of favourable remark, what he said and, even more important, what he did not say, probably gave some indication of what he really thought. There is no doubt that as a politician and head of state Stalin was well able to judge and act on the larger strategic and economic issues of the war. Yet as a Generalissimo he in fact personally and closely controlled military operations with directness and menace.[26] There is evidence also that, like Hitler, he had no sense of what was practicable and for this his lack of military education and experience was responsible.[27] Many of his military views were erroneous, and originally he was more obsessed with holding ground than in saving his armies, and for this reason he probably bore the major share of the responsibility for the enormous losses in the Ukraine in the first year of the war.[28] His early commanders were unlucky and found wanting. Some like Pavlov, the Com-

[24] Vatutin at this time was first deputy chief of staff. Vasilevsky headed the operations department of the General Staff and later became the Chief of General Staff, although he was to fill this appointment only nominally, his duties during his long absences at the front being performed by Antonov, his deputy. Shtemenko later headed the operations department of the General Staff. Voronov was from the artillery inspectorate but was to function in a command capacity, and Novikov and Golovanov were from the Red Air Force.

[25] Djilas, *Conversations with Stalin*, p. 54.

[26] Vasilevsky, twenty years after the event, still spoke of the radio telephone conversation he had from Stalingrad with Stalin in Moscow on 24 August 1942, when the Germans had broken through to the Volga. The unpleasant conversation, he said, would remain for ever in his memory. *Voenno Istoricheskii Zhurnal*, No. 10, 1965.

[27] Compare Konev, *Sorok Pyatyi God, Novyi Mir*, May–July 1965; According to Konev Stalin had little idea of the time factor and the confusion which would be caused in the transfer of a tank army already committed to battle near Berlin from one front to another.

[28] For Stalin's erroneous views compare Sherwood, *The White House Papers*, pp. 336–41.

mander of West Front, he liquidated. To others like F. I. Kuznetsov, the Commander of North-West Front in the Baltic States, he gave a second and a third chance. Budenny he withdrew from circulation. Yet he was already, even in the first few months of war, collecting around him able and talented senior officers in his *Stavka*. These became a source of strength to the Soviet High Command. Due to his separate NKVD and commissar communication networks, Stalin was more quickly and better informed of battle developments than were his front commanders.

When all opposition is stifled and when counsellors fear to advise in case their views should be contrary to those of the dictator, good government must suffer, and this was as true of a communist as of a fascist régime. The picture drawn by the Soviet marshals subsequent to the war of Stalin consulting each of the GKO and *Stavka* members in turn, weighing their views and advice, and finally coming to a decision, may be a true one.[29] Yet the menace was never absent, and the careers, freedom and the lives of these senior officers were entirely in Stalin's hands. The memories of the purges were still fresh in their minds and some of their number had Hitler, not Stalin, to thank for the imminence of a war which had forced their rehabilitation and release from the brutalities of the concentration camp. The Soviet High Command did make errors, some of them grievous ones, and continued to do so throughout much of the war, and many of these were probably due to Stalin's dominance of the *Stavka*. Yet in spite of these mistakes, the war direction of the GKO and the *Stavka* was in many ways superior to that of the German OKW and OKH.

The GKO had complete powers, and the military *Stavka* organization was joint service and centralized. Strategic moves were made after detailed staff preparation and planning and not as the result of intuition or snap decision. In this respect the Soviet High Command was the antithesis of Hitler's makeshift war direction and strategy. However, whereas Germany's strength lay in the well developed tactical sense of its field leaders from the corps commander downwards, Soviet war leadership in 1941 and 1942 was generally better than the German at the top, but deteriorated rapidly through the lower echelons of command, so that in the corps and divisions Soviet commanders lacked initiative, experience and training. In the early part of the war the outcome of these phenomena was that the Kremlin's best laid plans availed it little because the Red Army was not the trained field force to carry them out, while the brilliant tactical victories of the Germans were made nugatory by the absence of a cohesive and logical strategy.

Military thought in the Soviet Union had few roots and little of any real value had been bequeathed by the heritage of the Imperial Tsarist Army,

---

[29] See Zhukov, *Vospominaniya i Razmyshleniya*, pp. 304 and 566–76; Virta, *The Stalingrad Battle*, pp. 230–1, quoted by Deutscher, *Stalin*, p. 496, footnote 1; also Konev, *Sorok Pyatyi God*, *Novyi Mir* 1965, on the procedure when Konev was recalled to Moscow; Eremenko, *Stalingrad*, pp. 31–9, on his meeting with Stalin; Vasilevsky, *Voenno Istoricheskii Zhurnal* No. 10, 1965.

except possibly the strong bias in favour of the artillery.[30] Before 1933, when there had been some liaison between the Red Army and the German *Reichswehr*, the Red Army had been organized closely on the German model. After that time the Soviet High Command, as it so disarmingly admits, was left floundering and was forced to pick up information where it could, and copy foreign armies. From its experience in Spain it culled a number of false lessons which included the breaking up of its large armoured formations and the decentralization of many of its tanks to infantry divisions.[31]

The Soviet Union had originally created the nucleus of a strategic force of heavy four engined bombers, but the German example, followed by experience in Spain, caused a reversal of this policy, and priority was given to the production of fighters, ground attack aircraft and light bombers suitable for the close support of ground operations. The heavy obsolete bombers were retained within a single command for troop transport and supply missions. The Red Army aviator, it must be emphasized, was a soldier, whose main task, together with the artillery, was to provide fire support for the ground forces. He was under army command and he was uninterested in the destruction of the enemy's economy or in strategic bombing. He wore army uniform and could only be distinguished from an artillery or infantry soldier by the light blue colour of his arm of service gorget patch. Shortly before the war flying formations had been reorganized to enable them to fit more easily into the ground army organization, and by 1941 the air brigades had been reformed into air corps, air divisions, air regiments, squadrons and flights. Air divisions, which might be bomber, fighter or mixed, were placed under the command of front or army headquarters.[32]

In 1941 the Red Army Air Force was large in numbers but over eighty per cent of its first line strength was obsolete and by German standards often of very crude design. The standard fighters were the I15 and the I153, a biplane with a maximum speed of only 230 mph, and the I16, a low wing single radial engined monoplane known as the *Rata*, which although very manoeuvrable

---

[30] Much has been made of the fact that Shaposhnikov, the Chief of General Staff 1937–40 and again 1941–2, was a former colonel of the Tsarist Army. It appears that Shaposhnikov was an efficient staff officer and little else and he certainly did not attempt to perpetuate the imperial heritage. This idea appears to have been propagated by German intelligence. In August 1941 it was even assumed that Shaposhnikov was the Soviet Front Commander in the Ukraine, so successfully had the withdrawal been conducted. *OKH Gen St d H O Qu IV Abt Fremde Heere Ost Nr. 284/41 g. Kdos Chefs* dated 10 August 1941.

[31] *Istoriya*, Vol. 1, p. 439.

[32] The Red Air Force organization changed frequently both before and after the war and it was not modelled on that of the *Luftwaffe*. The air 'park' of an air regiment in June 1941 consisted of sixty aircraft, but these included reserves and replacements. In July 1941 because of the heavy losses and lack of reserves the park for a regiment was reduced to thirty aircraft, the regiment was reduced from three squadrons to two and the air corps disappeared temporarily as a formation. At the end of 1942 fighter and bomber regiments had the third squadron restored and the fighting strength of a fighter regiment was given at thirty-two aircraft. *Istoriya*, Vol. 2, p. 62 and Vol. 3, p. 217; Sokolovsky, *Military Strategy*, p. 162. 50 Let Vooruzhennykh Sil SSSR, p. 238.

had a maximum air speed of about 285 mph and was outpaced by the German medium bombers.[33] The TB1 and TB2 heavy bombers had top speeds of not much above 130 mph, while the fastest bombers were the medium SB1 and SB2 with maximum air speeds of 220 and 260 mph. Although 1,700 new fighters are said to have been taken into use by June 1941, mainly Yak 1, Lagg 3 and Mig 3, all of which were inferior to the Me 109, only nineteen air regiments had been completely re-equipped.[34] The new *Stormovik* Il 2 single engined ground attack fighter with an armoured rear was just entering the service and this, although admirable as a tactical support aircraft, with a top speed of 280 mph hardly ranked as a fighter. The Pe 2 twin engined fighter bomber, somewhat similar in appearance to the German Me 110, with a speed of about 340 mph, was also becoming available in small numbers, and this aircraft was to give a creditable performance and good service as a long range fighter and light bomber. A two seater biplane known as the Po2 or the U2, first designed in 1927, was used throughout the whole war on reconnaissance, intercommunication and even bombing tasks. It had a top speed of only 100 mph.

Aircraft auxiliary equipment was either of poor quality or entirely lacking, and radar and direction and locating aids were non-existent. In 1941 the Soviet radio industry was unable to cover the requirements of the armed services and in the Red Air Force only squadron commanders had radio, this being of so uncertain a quality that it was frequently unusable. There was no intercommunication equipment inside the aircraft and planes could not communicate by radio with each other, with the base airfield, or with the troops on the ground. Pilots were for this reason obliged to use signal flare and flight manoeuvre signals.[35] The ground signal communication system between air formations was limited to telephone and cable telegraph, such radio as did exist being so primitive that commanders generally refused to rely on it.

The Soviet Union succeeded later in the war in producing aircraft of very

[33] Soviet air design was controlled by a Central Aero Institute and the only users of the state manufactured aircraft were the Red Air Force and *Aeroflot*, the state airline. Before 1940 military aircraft were designated according to their function, the prefix DI signifying twin seater fighter, I single seater fighter, TB heavy bomber, DB long range bomber and SB medium bomber. After 1940 aircraft were named according to the designer, ANT for Tupolev, Il for Ilyushin, La for Lavochkin, Pe for Petlyakov, Su for Sukhoi and Yak for Yakovlev. Lagg was a joint enterprise by Lavochkin, Gorbunov and Gudkov and Mig by Mikoyan and Gurects.

[34] *Istoriya*, Vol. 1, p. 458. Although ready to admit that their early fighter aircraft were of very inferior design, Soviet accounts exaggerate the performance of the planes produced in the war years. The Yak 3 and the Mig 3 are given speeds of over 400 mph at 20,000 feet and were said to be better than the current Me 109. Kolganov, *Razvitie Taktiki Sovetskoi Armii v Gody Velikoi Otechestvennoi Voiny*, pp. 61–6. It is doubtful whether the Yak 3 at that time had a maximum speed of over 350 mph. Similarly when Soviet accounts quoted aircraft strengths, with the fascination for large numbers, all aircraft were included, even the ubiquitous 100 mph U2 biplane being classed as a bomber.

[35] *Istoriya*, Vol. 1, p. 454 This is largely borne out by Western observers. Navigation was primitive and pilots flew by the aid of a map and their own keen sight, often at tree-top height. Deane, *The Strange Alliance*, pp. 79–81.

much improved performance, but in spite of this, Red Army aircraft were inferior to those of the *Luftwaffe* in speed, range, manoeuvrability and rate of climb, so that the Germans were usually able to obtain local air superiority up to the last year of the war. Yet at no time, even in the earliest and darkest days, was the Red Air Force completely overwhelmed. In some sectors it was obliterated, yet in other parts of the theatres it was active even to the point of enjoying air superiority. The reasons for this included the vast extent of the fronts and hinterland and the limited resources of the *Luftwaffe*, a large part of which was to be tied down by the Anglo-American air offensives over Germany. A third reason lay in the large numbers of aircraft, though of inferior quality, which the Red Air Force kept in the air even in adverse weather conditions. In spite of the relatively low standard of their training, aviators and ground crews had great endurance and hardiness, being particularly clever at improvisation, and it was Soviet practice to keep on operations even obsolete aircraft of very doubtful value.[36]

The vastness of the theatres and the fact that both the *Luftwaffe* and Red Air Force tended to decentralize much of their air resources, in contrast to the Anglo-Americans who used their air power in highly concentrated and massive blows, meant that the intervention of air forces, except perhaps in the first few weeks on the central front and in the final stages of the war in Belorussia, Rumania and Galicia, by itself rarely had any decisive effect on the outcome of ground operations.[37]

In the Red Army before 1935 there was no saluting or rank system common to the other armies of the world, but by three decrees of 1935, 1939 and 1940, these were fully restored, introducing two additional ranks, that of major and of colonel-general, which were not in use in Tsarist times.[38] During the five years before the outbreak of war the standard of living, education and culture of the officer improved enormously, his pay being increased by as much as 300 per cent. In addition he was given excellent quarters and many privileges.

The Red Army was almost entirely a conscript force framed on a permanent cadre of regular officers and senior non-commissioned officers. The conscript served for only two years, unless he became a junior non-commissioned officer when his service was extended to three, but in the Air Force the length of conscript service for all ranks was three years and in the Navy it was for as long as five years. Non-commissioned officers were recruited from men in the ranks who had distinguished themselves by good service and attained a satis-

---

[36] According to Deane, maintenance in the Red Air Force was synonomous with replacing a component or aircraft when it no longer worked. *Ibid*, p. 79.

[37] Compare also von Mellenthin, *Panzer Battles*, p. 155.

[38] The rank systems in the German and Red Army were similar. Soldier, corporal, sergeant, sergeant-major, lieutenant, captain, major, lieutenant-colonel, colonel, major-general, lieutenant-general, thereafter, in the Red Army, colonel-general, general and marshal. In the German Army the positions of colonel-general and general were reversed, so that a colonel-general ranked above a general but below a field-marshal. The Soviet rank 'Marshal of the Soviet Union' introduced in 1935 was of course a rank unknown in former times.

factory standard of education, emphasis being laid on Party or Komsomol membership. The NKVD had priority in the selection of conscripts for its own border guards and internal security troops. Within the Red Army, conscripts were graded, the best being allocated to the air arm and the worst to the infantry. After the Air Force came the artillery, followed by the engineers and the tank arm.[39]

According to Soviet post-war descriptions and according to the published Soviet disciplinary and field service regulations in use at the time, the Red Army would appear to have been a highly efficient and disciplined force, and these published regulations are sometimes quoted by Western writers as evidence of the state of morale and training of the Soviet armed forces. The truth was, however, much otherwise and too often there was a wide gap between the regulation and its application. The people were at that time primitive, and the military system was often inefficient and sometimes corrupt. The code and practice of discipline too were very strange as seen through Western eyes. On occasions officers were unable to control their drunken men, while officers themselves could be sentenced summarily to periods of guard room arrest for drunkenness. Officers might be criticized publicly at political meetings by the meanest soldier, and the commander of an army could make personal vindictive attacks on his divisional commanders in widely distributed orders.[40] Standards of discipline and efficiency varied widely between units. Although they were given little time or opportunity to indulge them, the most common vices among the troops were drunkenness, apathy and absence. Whereas political unreliability often incurred draconian penalties, and punishments relating to misuse or loss of government property tended to be severe, military discipline was certainly not irksome and by German standards was decidedly lax.

Women served in the Red Army in peace and in war. A very high proportion of the army doctors and the medical orderlies in the field were female and the majority of the enlisted women carried out the many ancillary services, replacing men, even in field formations, as clerks, typists, telephonists and as cooks. Traffic police were often women. Women were sometimes given more spectacular and highly publicized propaganda roles as parachutists, snipers and partisans, and instances were to be recorded of German troops being fired on by armed women, the so-called *Flintenweiber*. On rare occasions women were to be found among tank crews, probably as radio operators, but instances were recorded of women acting as tank commanders.

Stress has been laid in German accounts on the cheapness of life in the Soviet Union, and this is apt to give a distorted picture of the Red Army

[39] See also Rendulic, *Gekämpft Gesiegt Geschlagen*, p. 126.
[40] In 1937 the commander of 7 Cavalry Corps and one of his divisional cavalry commanders received such treatment at Party meetings before being arrested. Public criticism was usually, but not always, an indication of the imminence of disgrace. In 1942, Gorbatov, still a divisional commander, was subjected to public persecution by the Commander of 38 Army. Gorbatov, *Gody i Voiny*, Novyi Mir, March–May 1964.

soldier. The German soldier in the Second World War was well looked after in privileges, pay and home leave. The Red Army soldier had poor pay and no home leave and accepted deprivation without demur, because he could not do otherwise. Within his unit he was well equipped, well clothed and, when conditions allowed, well fed. The relationship between the soldier and the officer was generally close and good, and between the soldier and the commissar, except sometimes in times of stress, not always as bad as was depicted in German descriptions.[41] There was little brutality within the Army unless the soldier was in arrest. On the other hand a political suspect was far more badly treated than a criminal, and the soldier arrested by the NKVD for a political offence had no rights at all, his life not being worth a kopeck. The Soviet soldier might have been careless of the lives of prisoners of war or even of those of the population of occupied territories, but there is no doubt that he valued his own.

It was Stalin and the members of the government organ of the Soviet Union who viewed life so cheaply. Millions of Russian and Soviet lives had been sacrificed during the Civil War and at the times of the enforcement of collective agriculture, merely in order to achieve a political aim. In 1940 following the serious defeats suffered during the Finnish Winter War, Red Army officers and commissars were empowered to shoot cowards on the spot. Although it was unlikely that this would happen in peace, the time was to come in war when these powers were to be needed and used. Nor was this fate to be meted out only to cowards. It was to include the incompetent, the unlucky and the unsuccessful, irrespective of rank. Expendable punishment battalions made up of failed former commissioned and non-commissioned officers came into being. The Soviet Union was not a signatory to the Geneva Convention and Red Cross and its attitude towards prisoners of war was based entirely on utility. German, Rumanian and Italian prisoners found their way to the labour camps, indispensable to the Soviet economy, from which, for the majority of them, death could be their only release. Moscow was entirely uninterested in the fate of the Soviet prisoners of war in German hands, making a public declaration that such persons were traitors; those that were repatriated usually changed one prison camp for another. Not content with taking vengeance on the returned prisoner of war, vengeance which was in any event an insufficient safeguard against desertion or surrender in battle, the régime used the same methods as it had done in the Civil War, in that it held the soldier's family as hostage for his conduct in battle. The relatives of those taken prisoner could be, and in many cases were, sentenced to long terms of imprisonment.[42]

The Red Army differed from the German Army in that its organization was based on logic and common sense with clearly defined responsibilities and

[41] The good relationship between Red Army officer and man was noted both by German intelligence and was also commented upon by Rendulic. Even in the first year of war, few prisoners of war would speak against their own officers. The commissar came off somewhat worse and when captured was often denounced by his men.
[42] Orders No. 356 of 1940 and No. 274 of 1941.

without overlapping of functions. Like the German Army, the Red Army's main strength lay in its rifle divisions. Except that most of these included a tank battalion of thirty armoured cars and tanks, the detail of divisional organization was almost exactly the same as the German, three rifle regiments, each of three battalions of three rifle companies and a machine-gun and mortar support company. Even the weapons are comparable, the Red Army using a bolt-action Moissim Nagant M91/30 rifle to which were added gas-operated Tokarev and Simonov self-loading rifles and the Shpagin PPSh41 machine-carbine. The light and medium machine-guns were the Degtyarev and Maxim, and the regimental close support artillery group had 37 mm or 45 mm anti-tank guns (the 37 mm being an exact replica of the German weapon), and 76 mm guns and 120 mm mortars, which had the same function as the German infantry guns. The divisions had one or sometimes two artillery regiments, but the total of guns by types was usually the same as that of the German, forty-eight guns consisting of 76 mm guns, 122 mm howitzers and 152 mm gun howitzers. The quality of small arms equipment was comparable and that of mortars and guns generally superior to their German equivalent. Unlike the German, the command arrangements and signal equipment in the rifle divisions were poor. The guns and transport of the Soviet rifle divisions were mainly horse drawn.[43]

Soviet artillery was probably the most efficient of all arms, in spite of its deficiencies in good radio equipment. Although Halder the Bavarian artillerist, ill-informed by his intelligence department Foreign Armies East, rated Soviet equipment as inferior to that of the German, Soviet guns were of excellent design and performance, and Soviet artillery, because it was to retain the more conservative methods of control and handling, was often more effective than the German.[44] Unlike the Germans, the Red Army created and maintained very substantial reserves of artillery, both organic to higher formations, and as part of the pool of regiments, divisions and corps, which formed the reserve artillery of the High Command.[45]

[43] *Istoriya*, Vol. 1, pp. 456–7. The standard infantry division in June 1941 had 14,500 men, seventy-eight field guns (including the infantry guns), fifty-four anti-tank guns, twelve anti-aircraft guns, sixty-six mortars, sixteen tanks, thirteen armoured cars and 3,000 horses. *50 Let Vooruzhennykh Sil SSSR*, p. 235.

[44] Halder, *Kriegstagebuch*, Vol. 2, p. 214, 5 December 1940.

[45] During 1941 and 1942 the Red Army made extensive use of heavy mortar regiments, these replacing much of the field artillery lost to the Germans. In 1941 there came into use BM8 and BM13 truck-mounted batteries of multiple rail-launched free-flight rockets known as *Katyusha* (Little Kate, a popular song of that time by Isakovsky) which were capable of laying heavy area fire at a range of about 7,000 yards. Reloading, however, was a slow process. These equipments were also known as Guards mortars, although they were not in fact mortars at all. Their equivalent in the German Army was the *Nebelwerfer* and the *Wurfrahmen* and *Wurfgerät*. During 1943 the Red Army was equipped with the *samokhodnaya ustanovka* or SU, (also known as the *samokhodno-artilleriiskaya ustanovka* or SAU) a direct fire tank gun mounted on a tracked armoured turretless tank chassis, the Soviet version of the German armoured assault gun. There is evidence that the SU was originally manned by Red Army artillery, but eventually the responsibility was taken over by tank troops. At no time did the Red Army introduce self-propelled artillery.

The Soviet Union in the years immediately preceding the war had organized its heavier tanks into tank brigades of three or four tank battalions of thirty tanks each without any infantry support element. Medium and light tanks on the other hand were formed into mechanized or motor mechanized brigades each of two or three tank battalions and one or two battalions of lorried infantry. These brigades were sometimes grouped into mechanized corps.[46] In 1939 most of the mechanized corps were disbanded and tank battalions were distributed to cavalry and rifle divisions in accordance with the French and British pattern at that time. During this period the Soviet High Command appeared to have a childlike faith in the efficacy of tanks and these were used in numbers to support any action, irrespective of the need for that support or the suitability of the terrain for tanks. Some lip service was paid to the use of tanks in a deep penetration role, and tanks were classified as being either long range or supporting, but the roles envisaged for the long range tanks were no more than short tactical envelopments aimed at destroying headquarters and reserves. The rapid defeat of the French by massed German armour caused a reversal of this policy and the Ministry of Defence decided to build up large groupings of armour, additional to the tanks already decentralized to rifle divisions, these new armoured formations being a replica of German panzer corps.[47] The new 1941 Soviet mechanized corps consisted of two tank divisions and one motorized rifle division, the tank division having two tank regiments and one motor rifle regiment while the motor rifle division had one tank regiment and two motor rifle regiments. Unlike the earlier Soviet armoured formations, these divisions had their own artillery regiments and supporting arms. This reorganization had been partially completed in all the border military districts when the Germans attacked in June, but elsewhere tanks were to be found in various groupings, in old type mechanized corps, in tank brigades and mechanized brigades and in the tank battalions of rifle divisions. The reorganization of tanks on a divisional basis was not continued after the outbreak of war, and there was a reversion to the corps and brigade establishment, a tank corps consisting of two tank brigades each of three tank battalions and a motor rifle brigade, in all about 140 tanks and 7,000 men. A tank corps was very roughly the equivalent of a German panzer division. A Soviet mechanized corps was a good deal larger, having an independent tank regiment and three mechanized brigades each with its organic tank component, in all about 200 tanks and twelve motor battalions, a total of 17,000 men.[48]

Soviet tanks had originally been copied from those of the United States,

[46] Martel, *The Russian Outlook*, pp. 14 and 15.

[47] The Soviet frenzied reorganization in 1940–1 was based on the lessons deduced from the war in France, from which it was learned that 2,600 German tanks in mass defeated about 3,000 French tanks, of which 2,000 were decentralized to infantry formations.

[48] *Istoriya*, Vol. 1, p. 457. Tank and personnel figures have been extracted from German intelligence files but see *Das Gesetz des Handelns Zitadelle*, pp. 345–7; also Konev, who speaks of tank corps of three tank brigades, a tank brigade consisting of seventy tanks, an artillery battery and a motorized battalion. Konev, *Sorok Pyatyi God, Novyi Mir* 1965.

Britain and France, but by 1939 the Red Army was equipped with a large variety of models and, like the Red Air Force, was already paying the penalty for over-production in that its tanks were mainly obsolete. Because of its faith in the overwhelming power of numbers it could not bring itself to withdraw obsolete tanks from service, and the old equipment was either converted to another role or farmed out to formations which had no use for it. Most of the tanks in use at the beginning of the war were entirely outclassed by the German Mark III and Mark IV, although some of the Soviet tanks had a good 45 mm high velocity gun, sometimes additional to a 76 mm close support gun. Not until the Soviet T34 and the KV1, the KV85 and the KV2 tanks were produced in numbers, could this inferiority be rectified.[49] The fighting efficiency of a tank unit depends not only on its armament and armour, however, but also on its optical and power equipment and on its intercommunication and radio system. Soviet tank units suffered in the same way as the Red Air Force in that they were woefully deficient of ancillary equipment, and even at the end of the war many T34 tank battalions relied mainly on intercommunication by flag signal. By mid 1941 the T34 medium and KV1 heavy tanks were already in production but, according to the Soviet account, less than 1,000 T34 and 500 KV1 had been received by units.

In June 1941 nearly all Soviet formations were in the process of reorganization and re-equipment. The Soviet High Command policy was to give everyone something, probably to facilitate training, and thereby no one received enough and few units were battleworthy. The tank state as at 15 June was said to have shown twenty-nine per cent of all tanks under heavy repair, forty-four per cent undergoing or in need of medium repair, while only twenty-seven per cent were fully serviceable.[50] The interrupted reorganization resulted in the Red Army going to war with incomplete and untried armoured formations on various establishments.

In addition to its armoured and rifle formations, the Red Army had at this time no fewer than thirty cavalry divisions, some of which were organized into cavalry corps, and a number of independent cavalry brigades. A cavalry division numbered only 7,000 men and consisted of three or four horsed cavalry regiments, sometimes a mechanized cavalry regiment equipped with

---

[49] Among the 1940 Soviet tanks the T26, T27, T37 and T60 models were light tanks of no great significance. The T28, T32, T35 and M2 tanks mounted a short barrelled close support 76 mm gun with limited anti-tank capability, except where this was additional to a high velocity 45 mm gun. The lauded BT or fast tank series was an 11 ton tank on American Christie suspension and had little value except that it served as the forerunner of the T34. The T34 weighed about 28 tons with well sloped 60 degree frontal armour of 45 mm thickness, mounting either a short or long barrelled 76 mm gun. Eventually in 1944 it carried an 85 mm gun. The front turret armour was 100 mm thick and its width of track gave it a much superior tactical mobility to any German model. The KV was a heavier tank of about 48 tons mounting either a 76 mm or 85 mm high velocity gun, or a 152 mm gun howitzer. Its frontal armour was 105 mm thick. Kolganov, *Razvitie Taktiki Sovetskoi Armii v Gody Velikoi Otechestvennoi Voiny*, pp. 53–7.

[50] *Istoriya*, Vol. 1, p. 475.

tanks, a horsed artillery regiment and supporting arms.[51] The Soviet Union was the only great power to retain a large force of horsed cavalry, since it visualized that these would form a mobile striking force capable of operating in any type of terrain, particularly in winter warfare. Its mobility was in fact to prove of value in exploiting a breakthrough.

Germany had begun the war united and strong, engaging enemies who were badly led and militarily ill-prepared. Nothing succeeds like success and success is in itself a great fillip to morale. Germany's early fortunes, brought about largely by excellent equipment, sound training and tactics, and good leadership in the field, reinforced in the German mind the National Socialist teaching concerning the superiority of race and the invincibility of the German soldier, and the nation as a whole undoubtedly drew strength and comfort from this illusion. Although the legend of invincibility may be dismissed as a myth, since the inadequate performance of the *Luftwaffe* infantry divisions alone proved that German success was to be associated not with race but with leadership and training, the German was by common assent acknowledged as a redoubtable warrior, in adversity as well as in good fortune. The relationship between the German Army officer and man was excellent.

In 1941 there was some variation in the military aptitude of German stock, although this was in the main so slight as to be negligible, since it could be counterbalanced by other factors, particularly leadership and experience. An East Prussian and a Pomeranian, thanks to their admixture of Polish or Sorbish blood, were usually livelier than a Westphalian, quick in the attack and, because of their long association with Prussia, took readily to the profession of arms. A Westphalian and an Oldenburger on the other hand were often more stolid and steady than a Rhinelander or a Bavarian. All had different characteristics but all made good soldiers. Only the Saxons might perhaps be considered to be less martial. The standards of the Germanic Austrian were usually somewhat lower than those of the German because he was slacker and less disciplined. German troops gained much strength in that they were homogeneous and united in speaking a common tongue, and the fact that the regional variations were so slight made all Germans dependable and reliable in almost all circumstances. The situation with Germany's allies were otherwise.

The Finn was the finest warrior on the side of the Axis and for winter and forest warfare he was inferior to none. The Finn population numbered only four million, however, and the Finns were determined not to become German pawns. The Rumanians were Germany's most faithful yet unwilling allies. Rumanian troops could not of course be compared with German, being poorly equipped and relying mainly on captured and obsolete French equipment. Their officers were untrained and ill-suited to their responsibilities and a

[51] During the war the strength of cavalry divisions was often as low as 3,000 and that of infantry divisions about 8,000. This figure did not however reflect the real strength as all the administrative troops did not count against the divisional totals.

trained cadre of non-commissioned officers did not exist. A large proportion of the rank and file were illiterate and tended to regard the fighting capabilities of the German and the Russian with exaggerated respect. Yet the Rumanian peasant was brave, tough and obstinate, and he had much in common with his Russian enemy, being patient, stoical and inured to hardship. The Italian, like the Rumanian, did not lack courage, but he too suffered from poor equipment and ill-trained leaders. The Hungarians, a race with a long history of war, were no better, having more interest in keeping an eye on their real enemies the Rumanians, than in fighting for Hitler. The best Hungarian formations were kept at home.

There was no reason why, given the officers and the equipment, the Rumanians, Italians and Hungarians should not have made very good soldiers, since the men themselves had stamina enough. They were, however, little interested in fighting what they regarded as Germany's battles, and for this the Germans bore much of the blame. In 1941, the German Government and diplomatic corps, the armed forces and probably a large part of the German population, drunk with heady success, were arrogant and unbridled. Under Hitler's New Order all foreigners took second place to German citizens, so that the Germans, in Horthy's words, were regarded as an unbearable, tactless and boorish people. In April 1942 it was sardonically noted in Rome that the Germans who had devastated half of Europe wept about the brutality of the British, and the next month the Italian journalist Sorrentino returned from Russia with horrific tales of the German massacring of entire populations, raping, and the killing of children.[52] Nazi Germany had become feared, but also hated and despised by its allies, and the high-handed and contemptuous way in which some German commanders and troops treated their allies in the field caused deep and bitter resentment. Only in Finland were the roles reversed. There the Finn tended to regard sceptically the efforts of his German brother-in-arms.

The population of the USSR in 1941, including that of the newly occupied territories, was about 190 million. It was made up of over 170 different races, speaking 140 different tongues, but many of the races were very small since fourteen of them made up ninety-four per cent of the population and only twenty races had populations in excess of half a million. The Great Russians totalled more than ninety million, the Ukrainians about forty million and the White Russians slightly less than ten million. The Cossacks were not an ethnic group, being of both Great Russian and Ukrainian stock.[53]

The process of russification, that is to say the superimposing of the Great

---

[52] *Ciano's Diaries*, pp. 423, 463 and 473.

[53] The 1939 Census showed the population of the Soviet Union as about 170 million, but in 1941 were added the populations of the areas conquered from Poland and Finland, the Baltic States and Bessarabia and Bukovina. In 1941 the population by areas, and not by ethnic groups, was as follows: Russia 70 m, Ukraine 32 m, Belorussia 5 m, East Poland 17 m, Bessarabia and North Bukovina 4 m, Baltic States 5 m, Asia 54 m. Total 187 million. The population of Germany in 1939 was 78 million.

Russian language and standards on those of the racial minorities, had been going on since the beginning of the nineteenth century and had been intensified under the communists. A good knowledge of Russian was essential before a minority national could take part in government or party business or obtain any form of higher education. In the armed forces Russian was the only recognized language. It was therefore usual, when discussing the characteristics of the Red Army soldier, to equate them with those of the Great Russian, since in any case the Great Russian represented the largest single element and, in the conditions which existed in 1941, was probably the most dependable fighting man of the numerous races of the Soviet Union. Other minorities in the USSR could produce more formidable warriors, but they were relatively few in number and, unless fired by a fervent belief in communism, they lacked the patriotic instincts of the Great Russian. Often too there still existed among minorities resentment against the loss of independence and the process of enforced russification. Experience was to prove that the fighting capabilities of the Asiatic races were little different from those of the Great Russian.

The other main element in the population was the Ukrainian. His national characteristics resembled those of the Pole, being intelligent, quick-witted, courageous and merry, having *panache* and *élan*. He lacked, however, the stolidity of the Great Russian. The White Russian was usually inferior as a soldier to both the Ukrainian and the Great Russian. Even in 1941, notwithstanding the supra-national pretensions of communism, bitter animosity still existed between the White Russian and Ukrainian on the one hand and the Great Russian on the other.[54]

The outstanding characteristics of the Great Russian were obstinacy, cunning and stamina and these qualities had been bred into him by the harshness of his climate, the barrenness of his soil, the invasions of the Asiatics, the overlordship of the Tartars and possibly by the copious admixture of Finnish blood into his stock.[55] The Great Russian soldier was not lacking in courage, he was tenacious, and irrespective of whether or not he was a true communist, he was usually patriotic with a strong love for his native land.[56] He was gullible and was easily swayed by the propaganda of his commissars, although this was true of most Red Army soldiers, irrespective of race. He had no great love for the life of a soldier, which he endured with patient stoicism, and unless dragooned by his officers and commissars, his military efficiency

[54] Great Russian is the accepted language known as Russian both inside and outside the Soviet Union. Ukrainian and White Russian are not dialects of Great Russian but are distinct national languages not very much more akin to each other than English is to Dutch or Dutch to German. The White Russians have tended to look towards Lithuania and Poland, and the Ukrainians towards Germany and Poland for their culture. Some Ukrainians and White Russians were Roman Catholics or members of the Uniate Church, the head of which was the Pope.

[55] Finnish tribes and settlements were to be found throughout North and Central Russia and parts of Siberia, and still exist today.

[56] Stalin in his hour of need exploited this sentiment by appealing to all sections of the population nationalists, conservatives, communists, Slavs, atheists, Jews and Christians.

was poor and he became dirty, indisciplined and unruly or apathetic. All Russians tended to be unpredictable and subject to violent changes in moods and this characteristic was to show itself in the pattern of the fighting in the Second World War. On occasions formations fought to the death with the greatest tenacity. Sometimes they gave themselves up *en masse* or ran away. Generally they were better in defence than in the attack, but they tended to be slow-witted, slow-moving, ponderous and cautious, and they suffered from the age-old curse of passivity and the lack of originality and initiative. This was to show itself in the terrible defeats suffered at the hands of insignificant numbers of Finns in the Winter War of 1939–40, and again in the summer campaign of 1941.

In the days of the Tsars the Russian was not a bad soldier and the Great Russian had more innate soldierly qualities than the other Slav nations of southern and eastern Europe, with the exception of the Pole. It is doubtful whether he was the superior of the Anatolian Turk and he was inferior to the Finn, the Finnish Swede and the German. This assessment was based entirely on personal qualities and took no account of the effects of leadership, training and equipment. It took no account either of the draconian threat hanging over the heads of the soldier's family, or of the galvanizing effect of the commissar's pistol, a political instrument guaranteed to dispel both apathy and mood and to infuse a surprising measure of energy and efficiency.[57]

[57] Order No. 356 of 1940 ordered commanders to use their weapons on their own men should such compulsion be necessary. Order No. 274 of 1941 declared that all prisoners of war were traitors to their country. Stalin's eldest son Yakov, an artillery captain, was taken prisoner in Belorussia in 1941. Stalin, presumably motivated by spite, had his daughter-in-law imprisoned under the statute which provided for the punishment of the relatives of prisoners of war. Svetlana Alliluyeva, *Twenty Letters to a Friend*, pp. 172 and 196.

CHAPTER SEVEN

The Outbreak of War and The Baltic

German troops were due to cross the frontier at first light on the Sunday morning of 22 June, and just before that time artillery began to shell NKVD and Red Army barracks and headquarters. Heavy air raids took place on airfields, marshalling yards and ports as far afield as Kronstadt near Leningrad, Ismail in Bessarabia and Sevastopol in the Crimea. Between 3.00 and 3.30 a.m. the frontier was crossed at numerous places from the Baltic to Hungary, sometimes in the face of a spirited defence by the NKVD border guards who turned out to man the strong points. Swarms of saboteurs and diversionists, many of them Lithuanians and Ukrainians, crossed the border with the German troops, having been given the tasks of destroying telephone lines and signal centres and laying ambushes on roads and tracks.

On the Soviet side of the frontier the scene was one of the greatest confusion. More than sixty airfields in the border districts had been bombed repeatedly and intensively, and before midday the *Luftwaffe* claimed to have destroyed 800 aircraft against a loss of ten.[1] The Red Army divisions on the frontier were away from any defensive positions and had been engaged in normal peace time routine duties; some commanders were absent, and many divisional artillery regiments and signal battalions had been sent away to firing camps or arms centres to carry out specialized arms training.[2] German aircraft had almost undisputed air superiority and made Red Army road movement almost impossible, while the control and communication system in the forward areas broke down completely, paralysing the Soviet formations there. Resistance was uncoordinated and insignificant. The Politburo itself, dazed by events and still hoping to stop the war even in the thirteenth hour, at 7.15 a.m. issued a directive ordering the Red Army to keep out of Germany and restricting air activity to a limit of ninety miles within enemy territory. Meanwhile it kept open the radio link with the German Foreign Ministry and asked Japan to mediate.[3] By the afternoon the higher Red Army headquarters and the

---

[1] Halder, *Kriegstagebuch*, Vol. 3, p. 4, 22 June 1941. *Istoriya*, Vol. 2, p. 20, admits the loss of 1,200 aircraft by midday 22 June, 800 of which had been destroyed on the ground.

[2] *Ibid*, Vol. 2, p. 16.

[3] Halder, *Kriegstagebuch*, Vol. 3, p. 4. *Istoriya*, Vol. 2, p. 17.

Kremlin were already divorced from the reality of the situation, and for this the breakdown in signal communications was primarily responsible. Commanders lost touch with their troops and with each other and many formations and units became leaderless. Too often Soviet Generals were both unwilling and afraid to admit to their superiors that the true situation was unknown to them and beyond their control, so that within hours of the outbreak of war the military districts and the Ministry of Defence were already in the position where they not only imagined that they understood the true situation, but also believed that the counter-offensives which they had ordered were in fact taking place. By 10 p.m. that day, the battle position was said to be regarded by the• Chief of the General Staff in Moscow as being relatively favourable, 'the enemy having been thrown back'.[4] Some counter-bombing raids were ordered against Ploesti, Bucharest, Warsaw and Danzig, but since the bombers flew without fighter escorts these achieved little at the cost of heavy casualties.[5]

During the first days of war there was an immediate reorganization of the Soviet Higher Command and Red Army to bring them on to a war footing. Fourteen annual classes from the years 05 to 18 were mobilized. Timoshenko, formerly the Defence Minister, was temporarily appointed to the post of Commander-in-Chief. Leningrad Military District, under M.M. Popov, became North Front; Baltic Military District commanded by F. I. Kuznetsov, of 8 and 11 Armies, took to the field as North-West Front; West Military District commanded by Pavlov, of 3, 10 and 4 Armies in Belorussia to the north of the Pripet Marshes, became West Front; the Kiev Military District commanded by Kirponos, of 5, 6, 26 and 12 Armies, became South-West Front.[6] Odessa Military District was reformed as 9 Army, which afterwards became part of the newly formed South Front covering Bessarabia. The North-West, the West and the South-West Fronts were to take the brunt of the invasion.

In the Baltic area German Army Group North commanded by Field-Marshal von Leeb had been given the task of destroying the enemy in the

[4] *Ibid*, Vol. 2, p. 29. Zhukov in his apologia has said that the counter offensive (Directive 3 dated 22 June) was issued over his name in his absence and contrary to his wishes. Zhukov, *Vospominaniya i Razmyshleniya*, pp. 259–60.

[5] Red Air Force bomber crews usually showed a blind and dogged determination. Fighter pilots on the other hand often lacked initiative and a spirit of aggression when opposed by German aircraft. Kesselring, *Soldat bis zum letzten Tag*, p. 120.

[6] The details of the Soviet fronts are given at Appendix C to this book. The military councils were as follows, the second and third named being political member and chief of staff respectively: North Front, Popov, Klementev and Nikishev; North-West Front, F. I. Kuznetsov, Dibrova and Klenov; West Front, Pavlov, Fominykh and Klimovskikh; South-West Front, Kirponos, Rykov and Purkaev; South Front, Tyulenev, Zaporozhets and Shishenin. Pavlov was a general and Kuznetsov and Kirponos colonel-generals. The rank of general had only recently been reintroduced into the Red Army and armies were commanded by relatively low ranking lieutenant-generals or major-generals. Before the end of the war army commanders were generals, and sometimes even marshals.

THE BALTIC OFFENSIVE
June–December 1941

Baltic States and of joining up with the Finns, and its final objective was Leningrad 500 miles away. Army Group North consisted of 18 Army commanded by von Küchler, and 16 Army commanded by Busch, and had a total of twenty infantry divisions of which one was held back in army group reserve. Three security divisions were later added. In addition, its 4 Panzer Group commanded by Hoepner, consisted of two panzer corps, 41 Panzer under Reinhardt and 56 Panzer under von Manstein, and had three panzer and three motorized infantry divisions. Army Group North was supported by 1 Air Fleet of about 400 aircraft commanded by Keller.[7]

The country in the Baltic States resembled that of East Prussia, being flat with occasional uplands, in parts covered with thick forests, sandy moorlands and numerous lakes and swamps. Only the coastal region was fertile pasture land. The further to the north-east one travelled the more desolate and heavily wooded the terrain became. There were few good roads, and most were narrow and in poor repair, being made unusable by the frequent summer rains. Two rivers, flowing from east to west into the Baltic, lay like barriers across the German axis of advance. The first of these was the Niemen lying about forty miles beyond the German start line, except where its lower reaches entered East Prussia as the Memel. The second more formidable obstacle was the West Dvina running through Vitebsk to Riga, about 200 miles from the East Prussian frontier. The seizure of this river would prevent its use by the enemy as a defensive line and cut off the Red Army formations to the south of it.

The forward Red Army dispositions were known to the Germans. F. I. Kuznetsov commanding the Baltic Military District, which on the outbreak of war became North-West Front, had only two armies, and these were believed to be fairly close to the frontier, with Sobennikov's 8 Army on the right nearest the coast and Morozov's 11 Army on the left. These armies were correctly estimated to have a strength of about twenty divisions and two mechanized corps, but this total included a number of divisions of the old Lithuanian, Latvian and Estonian Armies which had been incorporated into the Red Army a year earlier. These, the Germans believed, would be unlikely to give a good account of themselves.[8] Von Leeb's frontage of attack was comparatively narrow and fell on the entire 8 Soviet Army but only on part of 11 Soviet Army, the southern wing of 11 Army having been included in the assault

---

[7] Telpukhovsky and Zhilin both exaggerate the German Army Group North strength to forty-three divisions (of which, they say, seven were panzer and six motorized), 1,500 tanks and 1,200 aircraft. Telpukhovsky, *Die Sowjetische Geschichte des Grossen Vaterländischen Krieges*, p. 56, and Zhilin, *Die Wichtigsten Operationen des Grossen Vaterländischen Krieges*, p. 56.

[8] The armies of the former three Baltic States were formed into three separate rifle corps of the Red Army, originally keeping their own uniforms but adding Red Army insignia. They had been completely purged and russified with Russian commanders and commissars, and their own officers had been executed, dismissed, or transported, often with their families. North-West Front, according to Zhukov, consisted of nineteen rifle divisions, two motorized divisions and four tank divisions. Zhukov, *Vospominaniya i Razmyshleniya*, p. 270; also Pavlov, *Leningrad 1941*, p. 3.

boundaries of the neighbouring German Army Group Centre. Von Leeb intended that 4 Panzer Group should make the main attack along the centre line of the German army group, with 18 German Army on its left and 16 German Army on its right following along behind. 4 Panzer Group's right was formed by von Manstein's 56 Panzer Corps, which, attacking on a very narrow front, had only one fair road for its three divisions.[9] Von Manstein had to move 200 miles direct to the Dvina at Daugavpils (Dünaburg). Reinhardt's 41 Panzer Corps, which had two panzer divisions as against von Manstein's one, was to move on the left on a much broader front ready to engage 3 and 12 Soviet Mechanized Corps which were believed to be on the left flank, before advancing on the Dvina near Krustpils (Jacobstadt).

The tactical grouping of the German formations was not ideal. 4 Panzer Group had only two panzer corps and both were forward side by side with nothing in reserve, and after the Dvina was reached the movement of one was to become dependent on the progress of the other. The two infantry armies were to be fully committed side by side and von Leeb held only a single infantry division under his own hand as an army group reserve. It was, as the Chief of Staff of 4 Panzer Group was to say, the solution of a poor man.[10] Of the two infantry armies on the right and left of 4 Panzer Group, one was to clear the coastal area while the other took Kaunas (Kovno) and then moved up to Daugavpils.

4 Panzer Group was launched from 18 Army area in the narrow strip of land between the lower Memel and the frontier, the panzer divisions entering the bridgehead on the night of 21 June by the Tilsit roadbridge and by two pontoon bridges which were put into place after dusk. Infantry formations had been allotted from 18 Army to assist the two panzer corps through the heavily wooded area on the frontier, and at 3.05 a.m. infantry and tanks, supported by the fire of about 600 guns, crossed the frontier and plunged down the forest tracks. Resistance was almost negligible but this increased later in the day, particularly in the forested areas, although the fighting was sporadic and the action of small groups rather than that of a co-ordinated defence. The weather was fine and dry, yet bad routes and narrow sandy tracks winding through the forested ravines and gullies limited the rate of German progress. On the Soviet side, some 80,000 Soviet citizens of non-Baltic origin, soldiers' families, airfield and port construction workers, police and administrators who had been engaged in sovietizing and russifying the new territories, flooded the few roads back to the Soviet Union, impeding the movement of

[9] A division normally needed at least one road for movement in European terrain. The more roads it was given the faster its rate of movement.

[10] Chales de Beaulieu, *Der Vorstoss der Panzer Gruppe 4 auf Leningrad*, p. 20. 4 Panzer Group worked on lines or axes of advance and not on boundaries, and the two infantry armies were responsible for the maintenance and supply of all panzer and motorized troops operating in their areas. The panzer group was not subordinate to the infantry armies but operated directly under Army Group North.

Red Army reserves.[11] These would-be colonizers suffered many casualties from German air attack and were sped on their way by the incursions of armed Lithuanians and Latvians.

By the morning of 23 June the infantry of 18 German Army on the left flank near the Baltic coast, although suffering from the heat, had already marched more than forty miles through Lithuania and had entered Latvia. Nearer the right flank, von Manstein's 56 Panzer Corps had moved forward boldly and cut the main Daugavpils-Kaunas highway about eighty miles to the south of the Dvina, and along this highway a few Red Army tank units and artillery batteries put up a stubborn resistance to cover the withdrawal, losing about seventy tanks and numerous guns before von Manstein broke off the action on 26 June a short distance from the river. Two captured Red Army lorries were then loaded with Germans and Lithuanians from the *Abwehr*-trained *Brandenburg Lehr Regiment* disguised as wounded Red Army troops, and were sent forward to join the columns of enemy transport crossing the Daugavpils roadbridge. On reaching the Dvina they drove off the Soviet guards and demolition parties and held the crossing places until the arrival of 56 Panzer Corps, part of which crossed the river and formed a bridgehead to the north of the town.[12] The first of the crossing places had thus been secured.

In the first big two-day tank battle of the war, starting on the evening of 23 June, Reinhardt's 41 Panzer Corps, to the left of von Manstein, was engaged in heavy fighting at a small hamlet called Raseiniai (Rossieny), by about 300 enemy tanks of three tank divisions of 3 and 12 Mechanized Corps supported by cavalry and guns, the Soviet force attacking frontally in waves, impetuously and without skill. The attack was held by one panzer division while the second panzer division counter-attacked from the flank forcing the Soviet troops back into a bog, thereby destroying 180 tanks and over a hundred guns.[13] Reinhardt followed up, moving over the marshy ground on a broad front towards Krustpils and nearby Lievenhof on the Dvina. Meanwhile the marching infantry of 18 and 16 Armies continued to make good progress, taking Kaunas and numerous airfields and ports, for the most part being welcomed by the local population. Some serious fighting occurred at the port of Leepaja (Libau) where the Red Army garrison fought desperately, attempting to break out from the ring which 291 Infantry Division threw round the town. In Riga there were heavy casualties suffered by the regimental group Lasch, the same Lasch who four years later was to be the last defender of Königsberg. Else-

---

[11] Pavlov, *Leningrad 1941*, p. 4.

[12] The *coup de main* party was trained for this mission by the *Abwehr*, the designation *Brandenburg Lehr* being merely a cover name. Leverkuehn, *German Military Intelligence*, p. 163; Chales de Beaulieu, *Der Vorstoss der Panzer Gruppe 4 auf Leningrad*, p. 50.

[13] The German troops were horrified to meet heavy Soviet tanks which were proof against both anti-tank guns and a 150 mm howitzer at 300 yards. Chales de Beaulieu calls them Stalin 1 and 2. They cannot be identified but were possibly the KV 1 and 2. Chales de Beaulieu, *Der Vorstoss der Panzer Gruppe 4 auf Leningrad*, p. 31; Platonov, *Vtoraya Mirovaya Voina*, p. 184; and Zhilin, *Die Wichtigsten Operationen des Grossen Vaterländischen Krieges*, p. 59.

where Soviet resistance was stiffening but was still uncoordinated and the worst threat came from the bands of armed troops who had taken to the woods. These waylaid single vehicles and ambulances and murdered the wounded.

From the Soviet side, the battle had gone badly; yet Sobennikov's 8 Soviet Army had suffered heavy equipment losses but it was still capable of an ordered withdrawal from Riga. Morozov's 11 Army astride the German army group right boundary had come under heavy attack from both Army Group North and Army Group Centre, and fell back so rapidly that it left a gap between 8 Army and the flanking 3 Army on the north wing of the West Front. Although by 28 June over 400 armoured fighting vehicles, 200 guns, several hundred aircraft and a number of warships had fallen into von Leeb's hands, only 6,000 prisoners had been claimed by Army Group North.

Soviet pre-war strategy had envisaged the enemy being held while the reserve group of armies should come forward to aid the troops fighting on the borders. After the first few days of fighting the Soviet High Command rightly appreciated that the intervention of the reserve armies could not take place near the frontier, and part of the reserves were used in an effort to stabilize the position and extricate the fighting troops.[14] On 25 June Kuznetsov was still intent on holding the line of the Dvina and he was given Berzarin's 27 Army from the reserve to assist him in delaying von Leeb's advance. Berzarin was sent hurriedly forward to plug the gap left by the retreating 11 Army and, together with Lelyushenko's 21 Mechanized Corps, newly arrived from Opochka, bar the progress of 4 Panzer Group from the area of Daugavpils.[15] Lelyushenko's corps, which according to his own account totalled no more than about seventy tanks, began to counter-attack the 56 Panzer Corps bridgehead, where von Manstein was holding his ground and awaiting further orders.[16]

On 27 June Hitler, elated by von Manstein's rapid success in seizing the Daugavpils crossing, first began to take a hand in the tactics of the battle. Using Keitel as his telephonist, he instructed Halder to alter 41 Panzer Corps axis of advance and put all armoured formations across the Dvina behind von Manstein.[17] To this order he added more precise instructions as to how the Krustpils crossing was to be seized for the use of the infantry armies.

From this period onwards the tactical handling of the German forces was bedevilled by uncertainty at all levels and by frequent change and interference

[14] There were six reserve armies in all.

[15] A further army (13 Army) had been given to Pavlov's West Front, and the remaining four (19, 20, 21 and 22), forming the Reserve Front under Budenny, dug in behind North-West and West Fronts on a new defensive line from Nevel, Vitebsk and Orsha to the Dnieper. *Istoriya*, Vol. 2, p. 35.

[16] Lelyushenko, *Zarya Pobedy*, pp. 7–18.

[17] Von Leeb, by accident or design, assured Halder that it was his intention to change the axis of 41 Panzer Corps. This was not done, however. An attempt by the *Brandenburg Lehr Regiment* to seize the Krustpils bridge by a *coup de main* failed. Halder, *Kriegstagebuch*, Vol. 3, p. 20.

from above. The mission given to von Leeb, according to Hitler's Directive 21, was to destroy the enemy in the Baltic area, a task *to be followed by* the occupation of Leningrad. The OKH directive, however, was not so specific as to the relative priorities of the two tasks, and in this lay the seed of the subsequent dissension and recrimination.[18] On 27 June Hoepner flew up in his light aircraft to the Dvina bridgehead near Daugavpils to see von Manstein, who has subsequently said that he was surprised that the Group leader appeared to be uninformed as to what was to happen next.[19] Four days later von Leeb arrived at Utena, the tactical headquarters of 4 Panzer Group, to give Hoepner the outline of his plans. Von Leeb, who had been retired as a colonel-general in 1938 and recalled in August 1939, was Catholic in his religion, cautious and conservative in his outlook, calm and detached in his manner, and critical of the Nazi régime. Although very competent, he was, like many other more senior German Generals, without a wide understanding of the characteristics or capabilities of tank formations. Hoepner on the other hand was an outspoken, bold, somewhat impetuous cavalry officer, and an able leader of armour. Because of their personalities and military backgrounds, differences in opinion arose between them almost immediately, both as to the objectives and the methods by which these objectives might be attained, and von Leeb was soon to find himself between the lower millstone represented by Hoepner, whose tactical ideas were sound but who was prone to rashness, and the upper in the form of a daily list of *Führer* worries, telephoned or telegraphed from the Army High Command (OKH) in East Prussia.

Von Leeb proposed that 16 Army should seal off the Baltic States from Russia while 4 Panzer Group should cover the exposed eastern flank and form what von Leeb called a cornerstone, by moving in a north-easterly direction to Lake Ilmen through an area devoid of roads and covered by swamp and forest. Hoepner, dismayed at this abuse of armour, objected that von Küchler's and Busch's infantry armies would not be effective for another fourteen days, since many of their infantry divisions were still strung out all over the Baltic States, and he protested that the tank thrusts should be made between the Peipus and the Ilmen Lakes on the direct route to Leningrad.

[18] The wording of Directive 21 is not imprecise in this particular and it is definitely implied that the occupation of Leningrad should *follow* the destruction of the forces in the Baltic. The actual wording was '*feindliche Kräfte zu vernichten . . . diese Aufgabe, welcher die Besetzung von Leningrad und Kronstadt folgen muss*'. Hubatsch, *Hitlers Weisungen für die Kriegführung 1939–1945*, p. 86. The OKH directive is less clear. It gives Army Group North the task to destroy the enemy in the Baltic *and* to occupy Leningrad, Kronstadt and the Baltic ports. No priority is stated. *Aufmarschanweisung Barbarossa, OKH Gen St d H, Op Abt (1), Nr. 050/41 g. Kdos, Chefs*, 31 January 1941, para. 4c.

[19] Hoepner had been instructed in the *Aufmarschanweisung Barbarossa* to advance to the area north-east of Opochka, preparatory to moving north (to seal the Baltic escape route) or north-east (in the direction of Leningrad). This possibly was not known by all due to the restriction of Hitler's Basic Order No. 1. Von Manstein made a curious statement when he speculated as to whether his final objective was to be Leningrad or Moscow. Von Manstein, *Lost Victories*, p. 185; see also Chales de Beaulieu, *Der Vorstoss der Panzer Gruppe 4 auf Leningrad*, p. 144.

Hoepner was surprised too that there could be any doubt as to the next objective.[20] Von Leeb then ordered a compromise, which was neither one plan nor the other, in that von Manstein's 56 Panzer Corps was to thrust on Novorzhev in the direction of Lake Ilmen, while Reinhardt's 41 Panzer Corps was to move to Ostrov in the direction of Leningrad. The next day a dissatisfied Hoepner sent his OKH liaison officer, a Major Golling, to Halder to inform him of the differences of opinion which had arisen about the objectives of further operations. In recording this interview Halder made a telling entry in his diary that 'the objectives were of course dependent on the directives which we (the High Command) had not yet issued, but which were certainly overdue'.[21] All that emerged from this meeting was the revelation that Halder, von Leeb and Hoepner appeared to be in doubt about the priorities of the various aims and that there existed diametrically opposed views on the methods by which the objectives were to be secured. There, for the moment, the matter was left until the *Führer* should clarify his priorities. Five days later von Brauchitsch returned from a visit to Army Group North, content that all was in order; but not until 9 July were any firm orders issued by the Army High Command (OKH).

On 3 July the heavy rain which had recently restricted all air support gave way to fine weather again and the advance of 41 Panzer Corps from Krustpils made good progress against a relatively weak enemy, who was defending only the main routes. Ostrov was taken on 4 July. The new commander of the Soviet North-West Front, Sobennikov, in accordance with orders issued to him on 29 June, was frantically trying to build a new defensive line on the River Velikaya, to the south of Lake Peipus, using 1 Mechanized Corps and a further two reserve rifle corps which had been allotted to him by the High Command; but this did not prevent 41 Panzer Corps from taking Pskov on Lake Peipus on 8 July in the face of determined resistance by Soviet armour.[22] Red Army tank losses continued to be heavy and included a train-load of factory-new tanks captured by the Germans in the Pskov sidings. Meanwhile further to the right von Manstein's 56 Panzer Corps moved out of its Daugavpils bridgehead, driving off to the east the hastily assembled enemy 27 Army and 21 Mechanized Corps. In accordance with von Leeb's orders, von Manstein advanced north-east towards Opochka and Novorzhev along narrow

---

[20] Chales de Beaulieu, *Der Vorstoss der Panzer Gruppe 4 auf Leningrad*, p. 45; von Manstein, *Lost Victories*, p. 187. Hoepner and his chief of staff Chales de Beaulieu thought that the immediate objective of 4 Panzer Group should be Leningrad. Von Leeb was more concerned with the destruction of the enemy in the Baltic States.

[21] Halder, *Kriegstagebuch*, Vol. 3, pp. 35–6. Halder recorded his own personal view that 4 Panzer Group's task was to seal the old Soviet-Estonian border while the infantry corps should guard its open right flank and also clear the Baltic States. This aim was the same as that of von Leeb but the method was more orthodox.

[22] F. I. Kuznetsov was replaced by Sobennikov (the Commander of 8 Army) on 30 June, Bogatkin replacing Dibrova as political member at the same time. The new Commander of 8 Army was F. S. Ivanov. On 23 August Sobennikov was replaced by Kurochkin as front commander.

tracks through swamps and forests, eventually coming to a standstill when the pathways petered out or were found to be impassably jammed with mile upon mile of abandoned Red Army tanks, guns and vehicles. An attempt to build corduroy log roads through the marshes was given up and Hoepner was then obliged to withdraw 56 Panzer Corps from this non-existent axis and send it hurrying northwards to Ostrov, following the route used by 41 Panzer Corps. The Lake Ilmen objective was still maintained, however, and 56 Panzer Corps, with only one panzer and one motorized division, was sent eastwards once again from Ostrov towards Novgorod and Chudovo into yet more forest and swampland.[23]

Hoepner, on 7 July, was still intent on a bold armoured stroke on Leningrad, with von Manstein's 56 Panzer Corps approaching it from the east while Reinhardt's 41 Panzer Corps took the direct road to Leningrad through the town of Luga. Von Brauchitsch, who was visiting Army Group North on that day, approved Hoepner's plans.[24] 41 Panzer Corps axis through Luga was on one main road which ran through marsh and forest, where the undergrowth was so dense that visibility was restricted to a few yards and it was impossible to get vehicles off the roads. The advance started on 10 July against Red Army rearguard action but progress was less than seven miles a day, since each enemy strong point and each tank covering each bend in the road had to be destroyed in turn. The Germans suffered from lack of infantry and the close country prevented them from bringing their superior armoured mobility and fire power into play. New Red Army identifications were frequently noted. Two days later Hoepner and Reinhardt, with von Leeb's agreement, decided to break off the 41 Panzer Corps thrust on the Luga axis and to move it north along the east coast of the Peipus Lake to the Narva and then attack Leningrad from the west over the more open country on the Baltic shore.[25] When 41 Panzer Corps was moved to the north the axes of the two panzer corps became separated by over a hundred miles of difficult wooded swamp, impenetrable for armoured vehicles except by one or two roads and tracks, and there was no longer any question of one corps being able to support the other. The German infantry divisions were still many miles behind. Von Manstein's corps, moving slowly towards Dno and Lake Ilmen, was dangerously exposed, with an unprotected right flank facing a Soviet build-up of newly arrived formations to the south of Staraya Russa and Lake Ilmen.

Back in his East Prussian Supreme Headquarters in Rastenburg, the *Führer* kept in close touch with the course of operations and busied himself with details which were the concern of his subordinates. Hoepner's movement forward in the direction of Leningrad had been noted and at midday on 11 July Keitel telephoned Halder with the daily list of *Führer* worries in which he

[23] Von Manstein blames 4 Panzer Group. *Lost Victories*, p. 193. The responsibility appears to be much wider and the fault that of the High Command for not laying down clear aims and priorities.

[24] Chales de Beaulieu, *Der Vorstoss der Panzer Gruppe 4 auf Leningrad*, p. 58.

[25] *Ibid*, p. 64.

expressed anxiety in case Hoepner should race off madly to Leningrad and lose touch with the infantry armies.[26] This particular worry was well founded because such was Hoepner's intention, sanctioned by von Brauchitsch four days earlier. On 14 July, Halder noted with disapproval the great gap which had appeared between von Manstein and Reinhardt; nor had this escaped the eye of the *Führer*, who had worked himself into a nervous and excited state, particularly as von Manstein had already come under attack from elements of Morozov's 11 Army on his right flank, and at one time was completely cut off between Dno and Lake Ilmen.[27] Army Group North was told to stop Reinhardt moving on Leningrad. Brennecke, the Chief of Staff of Army Group North, explained to Halder's satisfaction that the terrain alone had forced the change of 41 Panzer Corps axis from Luga to Lake Peipus, but Halder was obviously not prepared to enter into a further argument with Hitler, particularly since von Brauchitsch had the previous night been subjected to a long-drawn-out and acrimonious examination by the *Führer* as to the conduct of operations in this sector. For this reason Brennecke was instructed by Halder to commit his reasons to a paper to be laid before Hitler. Halder went on to complain bitterly in his diary that the everlasting interference of the *Führer* in matters about which he was not fully informed was growing like the plague and was becoming unbearable.[28] This was after only three weeks of war.

The forced marches of 18 German and 16 German Armies had brought numerous difficulties. Because of the funnel-like shape of European Russia the further the progress made towards the east, the wider the frontage became, and in consequence the axes of the moving infantry divisions spread out like the ribs of a fan, becoming so wide apart that gaps appeared between formations. Moreover, whereas Army Group North was moving north-east in the direction of Leningrad, its neighbour Army Group Centre was advancing due east towards Smolensk and it was becoming impossible for the two army groups to keep in touch with each other on the flanks. 18 Army on the left of Army Group North, with eight infantry divisions, had to secure the seaports and the many islands and clear the Baltic States and, at the same time, give infantry support to the left flank of 4 Panzer Group. Von Leeb was subjected to frequent interference from Hitler through the Army High Command (OKH), requiring him to move more divisions from 18 Army westwards away from 4 Panzer Group in order to hasten the clearing of the Baltic ports.[29] Meanwhile in front of von Küchler's 18 Army, F. S. Ivanov's 8 Soviet Army, still hugging the coast, withdrew northwards to establish a defensive line from Parnu to Tartu in North Estonia with the Gulf of Riga on one flank and Lake Peipus

---

[26] Halder, *Kriegstagebuch*, Vol. 3, p. 65.
[27] *Ibid*, pp. 73 and 76.
[28] *Ibid*, pp. 78–9.
[29] On 30 June the *Führer*'s worries and priorities were all economic ones and included the Ukraine industry and foodstuffs and Swedish iron ore. The capture of the Baltic seaports on this day was an overriding priority. Again on 9 July 18 Army was being pressed to turn its strength towards Dorpat and the north. Halder, *Kriegstagebuch*, Vol. 3, pp. 29 and 59.

on the other. The Soviet High Command, in spite of the threat to Leningrad and the danger that its troops in Estonia might be cut off, reinforced 8 Army by adding to it a third rifle corps. In doing this it purchased additional time for the defence of Leningrad, because by then Hitler had no intention of attacking that city until the Baltic States had been cleared of all enemy troops. Morozov's 11 and Berzarin's 27 Soviet Armies, cut off from 8 Army by Lake Peipus, withdrew north-eastwards.

On the right flank of Army Group North the problem of over-extended frontages and lack of troops was aggravated even further, particularly since a new formation, Ershakov's 22 Soviet Army, had made its appearance west of Nevel. As the battle developed Hitler required, come what may, not only that Army Group North should keep close contact with Army Group Centre, but that Busch's 16 Army, which consisted of twelve infantry divisions, should be so strong on its right south flank that it could support the adjoining Army Group Centre. For this reason he ordered infantry formations to be moved away from the centre line of Army Group North to the south-east flank in Belorussia and Schubert's 23 Infantry Corps was actually transferred from 16 Army to Army Group Centre; nearly sixty per cent of Busch's strength was committed to this south flank.[30] This gave rise to a great vacuum to the south of Lake Ilmen in the centre of von Leeb's front, and the flanks of 4 Panzer Group were left virtually unsupported and exposed to the counter-probing by Morozov's 11, Berzarin's 27 and later Kachanov's 34 Soviet Armies.

A fundamental weakness of the *Führer*'s mentality was his failure to allot and maintain priorities, and in his own hurried indisciplined fashion he wanted everything to be done, with insufficient resources. Hoepner's armoured thrust in the centre was unable to get forward either to seal off the Baltic States or to reach Leningrad, because of the lack of infantry support, which, at Hitler's insistence, had been diverted out to the far flanks, to the Baltic coast and into the Belorussian forests.

The fighting ability of the Red Army had not been put seriously to the test in the first weeks of this Baltic campaign. The sudden shock of the invasion had caused a partial collapse of Soviet formations in that many of the troops fled or retreated with more than necessary alacrity. When the shock had passed the stragglers emerged from the woods to attack German supply columns, ambulances and rear installations. Some of these attacks were made by organized bodies of men, even tanks being used on occasions. Because of the hostility of the local Baltic population, this activity was not prolonged. Elsewhere stragglers and defeated Red Army units retreated, were rallied, reformed and committed to battle again. Although in general they did not

[30] On 28 June two divisions were reserved by OKH from Army Group North for the fighting north of Vilna (Army Group Centre). On 2 July Schubert's 23 Corps from Army Group North was put at Army Group Centre's disposal. On 7 July Halder was bothered about the possible enemy threat near Nevel at the junction between the army groups. Two days later the right wing of 16 Army was given the task of covering 3 Panzer Group. *Ibid*, pp. 21, 34, 49 and 55.

E

fight well, sometimes their lack of initiative and skill was compensated by a display of obstinacy and toughness which was to surprise all but those German officers who had served on the Eastern Front in the First World War.[31] Soviet troops fought best in those areas where they were not threatened by tanks or assault guns and this was usually in the forest and swamp, but even there the Red Army man showed himself to be unpredictable. German prisoners and wounded falling into Soviet hands were commonly killed, sometimes in the most brutal and appalling fashion.

The Germans were apt to condemn the enemy as subhuman, bestial and treacherous, but this judgement was not entirely true. After the first few days of fighting all commissars and Jews knew the fate in store for them if they fell into German hands, and determined that neither they nor their comrades should surrender. It was impressed on all that any captured Red Army soldier would probably be tortured and undoubtedly be killed by the Germans. Atrocity stories were circulated, many of them fabrications but some of them true. The Red Army soldier believed what he was told and his emotions were an easy target for the race hatred preached by the commissar. Many of the troops were primitive and some were barbaric, and chivalry or the niceties of established rules of war meant nothing to them. In consequence they determined in revenge to repay the German in what they imagined to be his own treatment. For this the Germans' senseless attitude of race was partly to blame.[32]

Before battle there was always an intensification of Soviet political indoctrination and the effect of this was usually shown in the strange behaviour of the troops on the battlefield. The Red Army soldier, often fearful and in action for the first time, remained at his post until the close approach of the enemy. Political indoctrination and a sense of duty enabled him to shoot down the first German to show himself, after which his courage often deserted him and he stood up and surrendered. Alternatively, he lost his nerve before he could fire the first shot and surrendered on the spot, only to be filled with immediate remorse at having failed in his duty, or with fear for the consequences to his family, this causing him to pick up his weapon and shoot a Fascist in the back. Sometimes from his cover in the undergrowth he shot down an approaching German and then doubled a hundred yards to the rear, there to repeat the performance. Whatever the sequence of the shooting, such tactics caused the Germans mounting casualties and great delays, particularly in the closely

[31] Blumentritt, *The Fatal Decisions*, pp. 38–9. In 11 Infantry Division, the determination of the NKVD border guards was rated as much higher than that of Russian infantry in the First World War. Werner-Buxa, *11. Division*, pp. 10–12.

[32] Even if the Germans had entered the USSR on a genuine crusade to rid the Soviet peoples of the yoke of communism and had treated Soviet prisoners and the population of the occupied territories with justice and compassion, the Kremlin would still have preached race hatred and would have relied on the fabrication of evidence of atrocities to achieve its aims. Circumstances being what they were however, National Socialist doctrine played into the hands of the communists.

wooded areas. The temper, even of those German troops who would normally conduct themselves fairly, was not improved by what was regarded as enemy cunning and treachery, and, as his comrades fell about him, there was always the danger that the infuriated *Landser* might use his bayonet on the surrendering enemy rather than risk a bullet between the shoulder-blades. Such cases, where they occurred, reinforced the determination of other Soviet soldiers to fight to the end.

By the last week in July, the Soviet position in the Baltic looked very serious, particularly since the Finns had begun to exert pressure to the east and west of Lake Ladoga on the North Front. This North Front consisted of Pshennikov's 23 Soviet Army north of Leningrad on the Karelian Isthmus and Gorelenko's 7 Army between Lakes Ladoga and Onega. Both of these armies were to be forced back about eighty miles in the first six weeks of the war.

By a Soviet directive of 29 June, the gravest measures were announced against rumour-mongers, panic-spreaders and cowards, and it was ordered that all civilian offenders should be handed over to military courts for trial and punishment.[33] Political discipline was tightened and the commissars' powers were increased to parity with those of the military commanders.[34] The loss of weapons became a most serious offence. Special field general courts martial, consisting of military and NKVD officers and commissars, were set up on the withdrawal routes throughout the rear areas to make short work of offenders, and, although it was impossible to take disciplinary action against the hordes of men retreating without orders, an attempt was made to single out from their numbers officers and commissars, and soldiers without personal arms. Particular suspicion was attached to any soldier without tunic and papers, because this often denoted a panic-stricken commissar who, threatened by capture, had rid himself of the tell-tale evidence of the stitched star on the sleeve.[35]

By 10 July Stalin, at the head of the new Defence Committee (GKO), had assumed overall command in the place of Timoshenko, and there was a further high command reorganization when three new theatres were established. The first was North-West Theatre, under Voroshilov with Zhdanov as the political member of the military council, consisting of both Popov's North and Sobennikov's North-West Fronts together with the Baltic and Northern Fleets. The second was the West Theatre under Timoshenko with Bulganin as the political member, consisting of only the West Front and the naval Pinsk Flotilla. The third was the South-West Theatre under Budenny, Khrushchev being the political member, consisting of the South-West and the South Fronts and the Black Sea Fleet. A new post was created of Commander-in-Chief Air Forces, in order to centralize the reorganization of the badly

---

[33] *Istoriya*, Vol. 2, p. 53.
[34] *Ibid*, p. 63.
[35] For a description of these courts compare Konstantin Simonov's *The Living and the Dead*.

shattered air arm, this post being given to Zhigarev.[36] Because of the difficulty in finding sufficient numbers of trained staff officers, corps headquarters were cut out from the air force and army channel of command, divisions being placed directly under army headquarters.[37] The corps was to be reintroduced later in the war.

On 10 July Popov's North Front was ordered to take over the responsibility for the defence of the approaches to Leningrad from the south, and man all the defences on the line of the River Luga.[38] The North-West Front with 11 and 27 Armies fell back eastwards to the area of Lake Ilmen, 8 Army remaining in North Estonia. The North-West Front had been heavily defeated in the Baltic and yet, in truth, even by the end of the third week of the war, von Leeb's Army Group North had already failed to carry out its mission, in spite of its spectacular performance in the rapid overrunning of most of the Baltic States. In this time 4 Panzer Group had advanced in the face of many difficulties about 430 miles and was less than eighty miles from Leningrad. 16 and 18 Armies had cleared most of the Baltic States but had failed to encircle or destroy 8 and 11 Soviet Armies and had not made a junction with the Finns. Nor were the Germans to reach Leningrad.

The campaign began well for the Germans with the successful tank battle at Raseiniai and the capture of the main crossing places over the Dvina by 4 Panzer Group. The German infantry had already been left too far behind, however, and in the broken and heavily wooded country it was impossible for an armoured force to prevent the Soviet troops withdrawing to the north of the Dvina under cover of the forests and darkness. The seizing of the crossing places did no more than force the retreating Red Army to jettison its vehicles and heavy equipment. Nor did the seizing by Hoepner's panzer troops of Pskov and Ostrov and the line of the Velikaya River, together with the old Soviet frontier defences, have greater success in cutting off the enemy in the Baltic. Only infantry could have held him, and in view of the closely wooded country, far greater numbers of German infantry divisions would have been required than were available. For this reason the larger part of 8, 11 and 27 Armies escaped. On 10 July North-West Front had lost none of its formations and still numbered thirty divisions, of which five were complete and up to strength, although admittedly many of the others had suffered so grievously in equipment losses and stragglers that the Soviet High Command was to estimate the superiority of the German Army Group North as a whole on this day at two to one in infantry, four to one in artillery, but little or no advantage

[36] *Istoriya*, Vol. 2, p. 62. Zhigarev's functions were similar to those of the head of the Main Artillery Administration (Director of Artillery). The chiefs of staff of the new theatres were: North-West M. V. Zakharov (from 4 August Tsvetkov); West, Malandin (from 21 July Shaposhnikov and from 30 July Sokolovsky); South-West Pokrovsky.

[37] The corps organization was rarely used by the Red Army for the first two years of war and armies commanded from three to six divisions. The corps was reintroduced from mid 1943 onwards.

[38] On 23 August Popov's North Front was split into the Leningrad and Karelian Fronts.

in numbers of tanks.[39] Yet the German strength was still very widely dispersed, much of it at the end of a 400-mile line of communication and bogged down in most difficult country. North-West Front on the other hand had fallen back on a military and industrial base with short and secure lines of communication. For these reasons the relative strengths in front of Leningrad were more favourable to the Soviet Union than its figures admit. In the circumstances the North-West Front did well to retreat, even if it did so in disorder. To have stood and fought near the border would have spelt disaster.[40]

The failure of the lightning blow in the Baltic was caused by the defects in the German High Command. German military intelligence was inadequate. If 8 and 11 Soviet Armies had been totally destroyed in the Baltic, the Soviet Union could have protected Leningrad by a number of other armies, the existence of which was unknown to Kinzel's Foreign Armies East Department of the Army High Command (OKH). Even 8 and 11 Armies were deployed in greater depth than was generally realized. For the German disregard of topographical intelligence there was less excuse. Forests and lakes on the approaches to Leningrad were easily identifiable from the air and large numbers of repatriated *Volksdeutsch* and Baltic refugees were available to give detailed information about the Baltic States. Many German officers, including von Küchler, the Commander of 18 Army, had served in the Baltic States after the First World War and a clandestine Baltic organization called the Forest Brotherhood operated in the rear of the Red Army and was in radio communication with the Germans. Much of the Baltic States and all the approaches to Leningrad were unsuitable for the use of tank formations and yet this was not acknowledged until 4 Panzer Group had come to a standstill in the forested marshes near Lake Ilmen. On 26 July Paulus, as Halder's representative, visited a disgruntled von Manstein, who told him that the best thing to do would be to withdraw all the tanks from the Army Group North area, where any rapid advance was out of the question. Reinhardt and Hoepner were of the same opinion, and regarded the whole of the Peipus and Ilmen area as entirely unsuitable for armour, so that, that same night, having received Paulus' report, Halder was to comment sadly that the only alternative would be the use of infantry with a consequent slowing up of operations.[41] Although still superior as tacticians to the soldiers of all other nations, the Germans were not the complete tank masters they were generally assumed to be. Hitler, the High Command and many of the more senior field commanders were ignorant of the characteristics and capabilities of the armoured arm. The use of tanks in mass had served the Germans well on the plains of Poland, the fields of France and the mountainous but open country in the Balkans, and in conse-

[39] *Istoriya*, Vol. 2, p. 79. Zhilin, *Die Wichtigsten Operationen des Grossen Vaterländischen Krieges*, p. 61, says that three divisions were lost.

[40] According to Zhukov no clear report was received from North-West Front as to the dispositions of its own troops until the eighteenth day of war. Zhukov, *Vospominaniya i Razmyshleniya*, p. 283.

[41] Von Manstein, *Lost Victories*, p. 198; Halder, *Kriegstagebuch*, Vol. 3, p. 124.

quence it came to be assumed that tanks were the answer to all tactical situations; terrain was not taken into account. Too much was asked of the panzer arm, and its planning, which consisted of little more than drawing lines across a map and calling them axes, was done for it by Hitler and the High Command. Military operations had left the realms of the practicable and were based on ill-founded optimism.[42]

The German political appreciation had been equally at fault, since the Soviet Union had no intention of holding on to the Baltic States, come what may.[43]

The resources of Army Group North were inadequate for the mission. The population of Leningrad numbered about three million and during this summer nearly half a million people were employed daily in building fortifications covering the southern approaches to the city. With this great reserve of manpower, the supply of reinforcements presented no problem and by mid July new Home Guard workers' divisions were being formed, a number of which went into action with the Red Army. Even if 4 Panzer Group had penetrated into Leningrad, it is very doubtful that it could have cleared the built-up and industrial area without heavy infantry support, or having cleared it, held it against Soviet counter-attack or infiltration. The handful of divisions of the panzer group in the forests outside Leningrad was, as its chief of staff was to admit, merely a drop in the ocean, and its average rate of progress, which before 10 July was seventeen miles a day, dropped during August to a little more than a mile a day.[44]

Present day Soviet accounts are usually silent on the effects of terrain and space on German movement and attribute the German failure to the success of Soviet arms. In the very early days Red Army resistance was weak but it stiffened when the fighting took place on Russian soil, and it goes without saying that without this resistance von Leeb would have reached Leningrad and joined with the Finns. On the other hand had it not been for the forests and the marshes, North-West Front would have been totally destroyed, however desperately it had fought.

The German campaign in the Baltic was ill-conceived and poorly planned. Halder, who in these early halcyon days, appears to have been in accord with the *Führer*'s general war aims, on 3 July recorded that, as soon as the Dvina and Dnieper had been crossed, the war would entail not so much the destruction of the enemy armed forces but rather the seizing of his industrial and production areas.[45] On 8 July he recorded 'a new thought' of Hitler's, stressing the necessity for cutting off Leningrad in the south-east by von Manstein's ill-fated thrust through the Lake Ilmen forests, and added his own comment that the *Führer*'s thought 'was quite right'. On that day Hitler had decided that

[42] Chales de Beaulieu, *Der Vorstoss der Panzer Gruppe 4 auf Leningrad*, p. 143.
[43] The political unreliability of 'class enemy' Balts is emphasized by Zhilin, *Die Wichtigsten Operationen des Grossen Vaterländischen Krieges*, p. 58.
[44] '*Ein kleiner Haufen in diesem weiten Gebiet*'. Chales de Beaulieu, *Der Vorstoss der Panzer Gruppe 4 auf Leningrad*, p. 59.
[45] Halder, *Kriegstagebuch*, Vol. 3, pp. 38-9.

tank forces should not be committed in the assault on Leningrad, but had come to the remarkable conclusion that the city, together with Moscow, should be bombed out of existence by the *Luftwaffe* and razed to the ground.[46] The absence of a coherent strategy led to lack of confidence and mutual suspicion among the commanders in the field and the incessant interfering in tactical detail was eventually to result in disorder. The *Führer's* impatient brain wanted everything, everywhere, all at once. The careful and detailed planning formerly associated with the German General Staff had given way to the whim, the intuition, the new thought and the afterthought.

[46] *Ibid*, p. 53. '*Als neuer Gedanke kommt dabei die Betonung der Notwendigkeit, den Bereich um Leningrad im Südosten und Osten durch starken rechten Flügel der Gruppe Hoepner abzusperren. Der Gedanke ist richtig*'. Until 8 July it had been Hitler's intention to occupy Leningrad. The order to destroy Leningrad was later extended to cover Moscow, it being specifically stated that no surrender was to be accepted. *Wehrmachtführungstab Befehl No. 41 1675/41* of 7 October.

CHAPTER EIGHT

Belorussia

The mission given to Field-Marshal von Bock's Army Group Centre was to encircle and destroy the enemy in Belorussia. Two deep thrusts were to be made, one in the north from the area of Suwalki in East Prussia and one to the south from the area of Brest-Litovsk along the northern edge of the Pripet Marshes. The northern thrust was to be made by 9 Army, under Strauss, of twelve infantry divisions together with Hoth's 3 Panzer Group of four panzer and three motorized infantry divisions. The thrust to the south consisted of Field-Marshal von Kluge's 4 Army of twenty-one infantry divisions and Guderian's 2 Panzer Group of five panzer and three motorized infantry divisions and one cavalry division. Hoth's panzer group had two, Guderian's had three panzer corps, and both groups were under the command of the infantry armies.

The task of the two panzer groups was to drive deep wedges in the form of pincers into the enemy rear, the arms of the pincers joining in a double envelopment movement at Minsk, the capital of Belorussia, 250 miles deep inside Soviet territory. Part of the marching infantry divisions was to follow the panzer groups to Minsk in order to prevent the encircled enemy from escaping, and part was to make two shorter enveloping thrusts to the north and south of the Bialystok salient, aimed at a point on the Bialystok-Minsk road about 100 miles from the Russo-German frontier. The two great pockets formed by the encircled enemy, one inside the other, were to be destroyed before the advance was resumed on the Orsha landbridge to Smolensk. Mobile operations would then cease temporarily at Smolensk on Army Group Centre front, as the panzer formations were to be removed to assist Army Group North in the final attack on Leningrad.[1] Army Group Centre had the support of the largest of the air forces, Field-Marshal Kesselring's 2 Air Fleet, with a strength of nearly a thousand aircraft.[2]

Von Bock had disagreed with the orders issued to him at the end of January 1941, being sure that his first objective should have been Smolensk and not Minsk, and he had pressed von Brauchitsch for a change of plan. On 27

---

[1] *Aufmarschanweisung Barbarossa OKH Gen St d H Op Abt (1) Nr. 050/41 g, Kdos. Chefs*, dated 31 January 1941, para 4b.
[2] 2 Air Fleet of Loerzer's 2 and von Richthofen's 8 Air Corps and Axthelm's 1 Flak Corps.

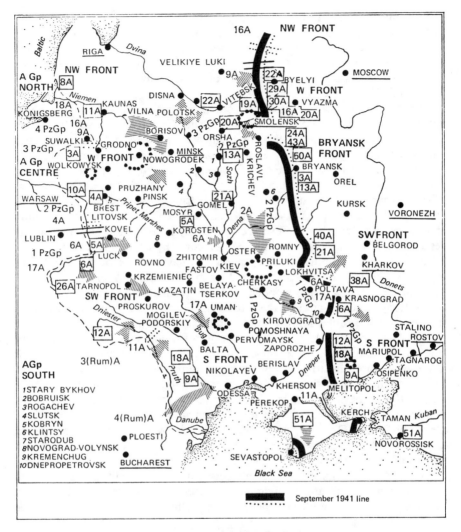

OPERATIONS OF ARMY GROUPS CENTRE AND SOUTH
June–September 1941

March he recorded that the OKH only busied itself with trivialities and complained that he could still get no clear-cut answer as to whether the cauldron was to be closed at Minsk or Smolensk. This doubt remained even after the war had started, and von Bock, Guderian and Hoth were still in ignorance as to their objectives on the third day of the war.[3]

[3] Von Bock, *Tagebuch*, 27 March 1941; also Guderian, *Panzer Leader*, pp. 158–66. Halder on the other hand, according to his diary entry on 23 June 1941, appears satisfied that the objective was Minsk.

117

The initial German attack was to fall on the left flank of Morozov's 11 Soviet Army belonging to North-West Front and on the whole of the Soviet West Front in Belorussia commanded by General Pavlov. This front had 3, 10 and 4 Armies deployed against the frontier, each of these armies having its own mechanized corps under command. Further mechanized and a cavalry corps were held in front reserve.

Hoth's 3 Panzer Group attacked from East Prussia into Lithuania side by side with Hoepner's 4 Panzer Group of Army Group North, and it experienced the same difficulties in crossing the heavily wooded and almost trackless sandy terrain. Enemy resistance was more determined than in the north. Some of the NKVD border troops, although without any artillery support, fought to the very end, and the Lithuanian corps, which barred the progress of the panzer group, put up an unexpectedly tough resistance.[4] The few roads running from west to east were little more than narrow sandy woodland tracks, many of which had never been used by a vehicle before, and enemy resistance, however light, could not be overcome by deployment off the road. In consequence columns were repeatedly halted and the many forest fires added to the confusion. Any bogged or broken down vehicle completely blocked the route, and the wooden bridges over the network of streams had to be strengthened to convert them to vehicle carrying. At von Brauchitsch's insistence, some routes had been allocated to infantry formations, but there were in fact too few routes for either armour or infantry. A marching infantry division allotted the use of a single route occupied twenty-two miles of track and took a whole day to pass a point, and when in danger of being left too far behind by the panzer formations, infantry horse-drawn transport and guns frequently disobeyed orders and left the allotted route to join the axes of the panzer troops, where they often blocked or slowed down motorized movement. 19 Panzer Division was halted for hours by a column of nearly two thousand Luftwaffe lorries, many of them loaded with telegraph poles, which had ignored the vehicle march table, and 9 Army, forgetful of its own orders, began to drive the infantry divisions forward, urging them to form mobile detachments by centralizing their limited number of motor vehicles. These motorized elements took to the panzer axes as there were no other fast routes available to them.

In the face of these many difficulties, the advance of Rudolf Schmidt's 39 and Kuntzen's 57 Panzer Corps at first made slow progress, not reaching the road bridges over the Niemen, about thirty to forty miles beyond the East Prussian border, until midday on 23 June. In accordance with their normal practice, the Soviet commanders had held back their armoured mechanized corps ready to use them against the flanks of the German thrusts, but they were unable to commit all their mechanized troops in a co-ordinated counter-

---

[4] An indication of the effect, however temporary, which the presence of commissars can have even on foreign troops not well disposed to the Soviet régime.

offensive because of the chaotic conditions resulting from poor communications and the German air offensive. On 23 June, as 7 Panzer Division was advancing from the Niemen roadbridge, it met its first serious opposition when it was attacked by Red Army armour coming from the nearby tank training ground at Varena. These tank units, believed to be 5 Soviet Tank Division, attacked with great determination, so that the commander of the panzer regiment, who had formerly fought in France, was to report that the battle was the most spirited in which he had yet been engaged.[5] Within a matter of hours, however, the Soviet tank troops had been destroyed due to their inferior training and leadership.

On the Soviet side of the frontier the confusion was at its greatest. Kesselring's air fleet had cleared the skies of Red Air Force planes and was carrying out a sustained and intensive bombing of all ground movement. Hordes of refugees, amongst them civil administrators and soldiers' families, were trying to move out of the battle area; elements of the White Russian and Ukrainian population became openly hostile to the Soviet colonizers and the Red Army and the feeling of insecurity and distrust was accentuated by the activity, much of it exaggerated, of the nationalists and German recruited armed bands which roamed the countryside.[6] Bridges were being blown to the rear of the Red Army by these diversionists, and railway lines and telephone wires were cut. Red Army units themselves were often dazed and apparently leaderless and many of them took to the woods to avoid the bombing. The tank and cavalry formations, however, were still capable of some offensive action.

Pavlov's West Front had in fact been deployed close to the frontier almost wholly in the great Bialystok salient where it was in great danger of being rapidly encircled by the double thrusts from Suwalki and Brest-Litovsk. All three armies were forward side by side inside the gaping German mouth, and with the snapping of the jaws nearly all of Pavlov's formations would be destroyed, for, as Kinzel had rightly observed, the Soviet deployment was neither offensive nor defensive. Hoth's 3 Panzer Group attack had been made due east against Morozov's 11 Army of North-West Front, but the thrust was aimed not at Morozov but at Pavlov's rear in order to encircle West Front. To the left of Morozov and inside the Bialystok salient lay V. I. Kuznetsov's 3 Army about Grodno, then Golubev's 10 Army forward of the town of Bialystok and in the south of the salient Korobkov's 4 Army, each army having its affiliated mechanized corps forward in its own area. On 22 June, Pavlov had only a mechanized and a cavalry corps in reserve although his West Front is said to have consisted of six mechanized corps, a cavalry corps and twenty-four rifle divisions.[7] On 24 June began a two day armoured and cavalry counter-offensive made by part of 6 and 11 Mechanized Corps under Boldin,

---

[5] Hoth, *Panzeroperationen*, p. 56.

[6] Compare Werth, *Russia at War*, p. 145.

[7] According to Zhukov, West Front had twenty-four rifle, two cavalry, six motorized and twelve tank divisions. Zhukov, *Vospominaniya i Razmyshleniya*, p. 270. The six mechanized corps were 6, 11, 13, 14, 17 and 20, some of them in the process of formation.

the Deputy Commander of West Front, from the area of Grodno to the north-east of Bialystok, against those infantry divisions of 9 Army which were moving south-east in the short envelopment movement.[8] This was made without air or artillery support and was beaten off with ease by the German infantry and anti-tank gunners, the Soviet losses being very heavy.[9] Meanwhile Hoth's 3 Panzer Group began to make more rapid progress to the east and north-east, Vilna falling to 7 Panzer Division on 24 June.

At this point Pavlov made the decision which was to confirm the destruction of West Front when, observing the forward elements of his 3 and 10 Armies in the Bialystok salient threatened by the shorter double envelopment move-ment of the marching German infantry divisions and presumably being unaware that Hoth's and Guderian's armoured thrusts were to close deep in his rear in the longer double envelopment, he ordered all army and front reserves forward.[10] By doing this, he left a vacuum in the vital Minsk area and made the German task even easier by sending his remaining troops west into what was to become the Nowogrodek pocket.

To the south of the Bialystok salient von Kluge's 4 German Army and Guderian's 2 Panzer Group had been making progress against 4 Soviet Army, as'the southern arms of the pincers. In the early morning of 22 June an infantry corps of 4 Army had attacked into the town of Brest-Litovsk while von Schweppenburg's 24 Panzer Corps crossed the river to the south of the town and Lemelsen's 47 Panzer Corps to the north, some of the tanks fording the thirteen feet deep river Bug by underwater wading.[11] The fighting inside Brest-Litovsk was particularly severe, the NKVD border guards and part of 6 and 42 Soviet Rifle Divisions in the Citadel area holding out until 29 June and causing heavy casualties to the assaulting 45 German Infantry Division.[12] Elsewhere the German advance went as planned, the only serious resistance encountered being that of 14 Mechanized Corps, the armoured reserve of 4 Soviet Army, which engaged 18 Panzer Division of the left flanking 47 Panzer Corps in a tank battle near Pruzhany. The difficult wooded swampland of the edge of the Pripet Marshes on the extreme right flank was covered by the

---

[8] The mechanized corps had been removed from the command of 3 and 10 Armies.

[9] Zhilin, *Die Wichtigsten Operationen des Grossen Vaterländischen Krieges*, p. 86.

[10] *Ibid*, p. 86. Since Pavlov had little or no air reconnaissance and his communications were interrupted, intelligence on the deep German panzer thrust was denied him.

[11] The tanks had all openings sealed and were equipped with air intake and exhaust snorkel pipes. The device was developed for the invasion of Britain and was used later in the war by Soviet tank units.

[12] The Soviet account of the Brest battle has been developed for propaganda purposes into an epic of *six weeks* heroic fighting until 20 July and is false. Platonov, *Vtoraya Miro-vaya Voina*, p. 187; *Istoriya*, Vol. 2, p. 18. German war diaries, divisional histories and eye-witness accounts, including those of von Bock, Guderian and Rendulic who were on the spot, agree that the bitter fighting ceased on 29 June. *45. Infanterie Division an AOK 4 30 Juni 1941 Anlagenband 3 zum KTB d. 45. Div (1a) 14875/15 (47)*; Guderian, *Panzer Leader*, p. 154; Rendulic, *Gekämpft Gesiegt Geschlagen*, p. 23; von Bock, *Tagebuch*, 4 July 1941; Gschöpf, *Mein Weg mit der 45. Infanterie-Division*, p. 158; Halder, *Kriegstagebuch*, Vol. 3, p. 22.

advance of 1 Cavalry Division, the only mounted formation in the German Army. Except in this marshland sector, the country was better suited to armoured warfare than that used by 3 and 4 Panzer Groups, and Guderian's rate of advance in the first few days was spectacular. By 26 June Slutsk, about sixty miles due south of Minsk, had been taken by the right-hand 24 Panzer Corps, but the left flank of the panzer group was coming under repeated attack from Soviet formations which were trying to break out to the south from the Bialystok and Nowogrodek areas in order to escape from the encirclement.

Notwithstanding its enormous losses the Red Air Force, after the first few days of war, became active again, causing numerous casualties to the horses of 1 Cavalry Division. This division, which was operating as mounted infantry rather than as cavalry, moved through the marshlands to Kobryn and Pinsk skirmishing and advancing 300 miles in seven days at a cost of less than 500 casualties. It was surprised at the excellence of Soviet artillery and at the poverty of the Red Army infantry which, instead of defending the close country and causing the Germans heavy casualties as was done in the Baltic and in the Ukraine, counter-attacked repeatedly in waves without co-ordinated covering fire, losing very heavily as it did so. In the divisional record the Red Army infantry was described as being poorly trained and of low morale and the fact that it could be induced to attack at all indicated the firm hold exercised by officers and commissars over their troops, and this in itself was surprising so early in the war. The German cavalry suffered from a lack of artillery ammunition and the difficulty, in the close country of the Pripet Marshes, of finding suitable artillery observation posts.[13] Low cloud and the more important operations to the north deprived 1 Cavalry Division of air support and the battle might have gone badly for it, had not the enemy offered himself as an easy target to the cavalry carbine and machine-gun.

By midday 26 June Hoth's 3 Panzer Group was only eighteen miles to the north of Minsk, and that same afternoon Guderian, who was still thrusting eastwards, was ordered by Army Group Centre to turn the greater part of his group northwards and close the enemy pocket by joining Hoth in Minsk. Guderian's right flanking 24 Panzer Corps, however, was to be permitted to continue its eastwards advance towards Bobruisk on the Berezina and towards Rogachev on the Dnieper. Guderian and Hoth obeyed reluctantly since both opposed this order and wanted to penetrate 200 miles deeper into the enemy rear and close the north and south pincers near Smolensk.[14]

In Rastenburg tensions and disagreements were mounting between Hitler, the Army High Command (OKH) and Army Group Centre. The original OKH order of 31 January was clear that the panzer double envelopment in depth should be directed on Minsk. Field-Marshal von Bock, however, had always favoured the much deeper envelopment on Smolensk, and again on

[13] Von Senger und Etterlin, *1. Kavallerie-Division*, p. 56.
[14] Guderian, *Panzer Leader*, pp. 158–66; Hoth, *Panzeroperationen*, pp. 51 and 62.

23 June had tried, without success, to have his orders varied.[15] Hitler, on the other hand, was fretting that the panzer groups should not overreach themselves by thrusting too deeply eastwards, and was concerned in case the very large numbers of Soviet troops, estimated at twenty divisions, about to be trapped in the Bialystok-Nowogrodek pocket, should break out. On 25 June Hitler's aide, Schmundt, arrived at Army Group Centre Headquarters posthaste from the *Führer*, who was nervously suggesting that the cauldron be closed much short of Minsk at Nowogrodek, and this proposal von Bock resisted with all the eloquence at his command.[16] On 26 June Army Group Centre was told that Guderian must continue to drive eastwards to the Berezina at Bobruisk, but at the same time should move the greater part of his force northwards to close the gaps in the pocket between Baranovichi and Minsk. Three days later Halder was bitterly complaining that, due to the *Führer*'s nervousness and interference, von Brauchitsch was forced to forbid a bold thrust further to the east and for this reason the probe on Bobruisk could only be regarded as a reconnaissance in force. Halder expressed the hope that Guderian would do the correct thing and cross the Dnieper at Mogilev and Rogachev in spite of the lack of orders which the OKH dare not issue for fear of the *Führer*.[17]

This unusual method of war direction sowed confusion and distrust among the higher echelons of the German command organization. Hoth and Guderian were convinced that their primary duty was to secure the Vitebsk-Orsha-Smolensk triangle and landbridge and prevent the enemy from creating a defence line on the Dnieper. Von Bock, the Army Group Commander, a strategist rather than a tactician, who had entered the Kaiser's Foot Guards in 1898 and who was a particularly difficult officer with both superiors and subordinates, agreed with them, and after his telephone conversation of 23 June with von Brauchitsch, who was ordering one thing but hoping that von Bock would do another, he not unnaturally insisted thereafter that the OKH should give him his orders in writing.[18]

On the first day of the war Stalin had sent Zhukov, the Chief of General Staff, as the *Stavka* representative to Kirponos with the South-West Front, while two of the four marshals of the Red Army, Shaposhnikov and Kulik, were sent on the same mission to Pavlov's West Front. Kulik, like Voroshilov and Budenny, had been promoted to this highest rank because of Stalin's

---

[15] Von Bock, *Tagebuch*.

[16] *Ibid*, 25 June; Halder, *Kriegstagebuch*, Vol. 3, pp. 8 and 10, 25 June 1941.

[17] *Ibid*, p. 25. '*Es ist zu hoffen, dass die mittlere Truppenführung auch ohne ausdrückliche Befehle, die wir wegen der Willensäusserung des Führers an ObdH nicht geben dürfen, von selbst das Richtige tut*'.

[18] *Ibid*, p. 14. On good terms with Halder, von Bock reserved his sarcasm for von Brauchitsch. When on 26 June the effusive Commander-in-Chief arrived to congratulate him on the Minsk encirclement, von Bock was deliberately cold and remarked acidly that he doubted whether any enemy would be left in the pocket. Von Bock, *Tagebuch*, 26 June.

favour rather than military ability.[19] Shaposhnikov soon became ill again under the strain of war, and Kulik, after visiting Boldin, set off to reach 3 Army and thereafter disappeared for nearly a week. Meanwhile Stalin fretted with worry and rage. On 26 June he sent a message to Zhukov in Galicia saying that Shaposhnikov was sick, Kulik lost and that it was absolutely incomprehensible what Pavlov was about.[20] Zhukov was ordered to return to Moscow.

Inside the great seething cauldron between Bialystok and Minsk more than twenty Soviet divisions were almost encircled. Some Soviet accounts blame Pavlov for his second major error when he delayed until after 25 June the order to 3 and 10 Armies for a general withdrawal, since by then there was only a corridor less than forty miles wide through which they could retire, the very few routes being under air and artillery attack.[21] On the evening of 25 June the principal and shortest route from Bialystok to the east was cut by Lemelsen's 47 Panzer Corps between Wolkowysk and Slonim. Pavlov had been allotted an additional army, Filatov's 13 Army, to hold the area of Minsk and assist in extricating 3 and 10 Armies from the pocket and it was on this army that the double blows of Guderian's 2 and Hoth's 3 Panzer Groups fell when they joined up near Minsk on 27 June, one coming in from the south and the other from the north. Three of 13 Army's four rifle divisions were themselves entrapped in the pocket. By nightfall on 28 June the marching infantry of Strauss' 9 and von Kluge's 4 German Armies had joined up in the shorter encirclement and completely cut off the Bialystok pocket from the larger Nowogrodek pocket to the east.

Pavlov himself at this time was unaware of the catastrophe which had overwhelmed his armies. On 30 June Stalin and Timoshenko first knew of the encirclement from the German wireless, and when Zhukov spoke that day on the radio to Pavlov it was to ask him whether there was any truth in the German claim that two armies had been encircled east of Bialystok. Pavlov replied that he thought there was a great deal of truth in it.[22] Pavlov, his chief of staff Klimovskikh and some of his principal arms advisers were recalled to Moscow the same day, arrested, tried and shot. Fominykh, the political

[19] Kulik had been a Deputy Minister for Defence heading the Main Artillery Administration. In this post he had been responsible together with his deputy, Voronov, for the development and provision not only of artillery equipment and ammunition but of all types of weapons for all arms of the Red Army. (This was an artillery responsibility in the Soviet forces.) He came under criticism, probably unjustly, for failing in this duty. Compare *Istoriya*, Vol. 2, pp. 29 and 49. There appears to be no doubt, however, that he had little ability. He commanded 54 Army in 1941 and 1942 and 4 Guards Army for a short time in 1943, from which command he was dismissed. Zhukov, *Vospominaniya i Razmyshleniya*, p. 515.

[20] Boldin, *Stranitsy Zhizni*; and Zhukov, *Vospominaniya i Razmyshleniya*, pp. 268 and 276.

[21] Zhilin's account (p. 88) appears to imply that the fault was Pavlov's. The more recent history says that the order to withdraw came from Moscow on 25 June and was retransmitted the same day. *Istoriya*, Vol. 2, p. 34.

[22] Zhukov, *Vospominaniya i Razmyshleniya*, p. 280. Zhukov's account, which is pro-Stalin in undertone, makes no mention of Pavlov's and Klimovskikh's fate beyond the court martial.

member, escaped punishment. Pavlov had held the command for only six days of war, and in the circumstances there was little that he or any other Soviet commander could have done, since the bulk of his formations were right forward in the Bialystok pocket, already partially encircled by the Germans before a shot had been fired.[23] The complete and rapid German victory was due firstly to the overwhelming concentration and superiority of the *Luftwaffe* in Belorussia, and secondly to the achieving of strategic and tactical surprise. The third reason lay in the decisive superiority of German tactical leadership, training and battle experience, both on the ground and in the air. The battle was to show, for the first of many times during the war, that the destruction of large enemy forces usually rested on the double envelopment in depth, that is to say encircling the enemy by two flanking pincers which met deep in the enemy rear. A single flanking pincer was inadequate for the purpose, as it was slow, and the enemy usually contrived to escape it. The opening stage of the Belorussian campaign was a resounding success, while the thrusts into the Baltic and the Ukraine, both of which were based on pinning the Soviet enemy against the sea by the use of a single enveloping arm, failed in their strategic object.

Hitler had always intended that the deep encirclement should be directed on Minsk. Von Bock, Guderian and Hoth wanted to close on Smolensk about 400 miles from their start line, and in this they obviously had some support from von Brauchitsch and Halder. Whether they were right and Hitler wrong was of no great moment to the outcome of the 1941 campaign, since a Smolensk encirclement would in all probability have added only 19 and 20 Soviet Armies to the formations already encircled.[24] The marching German infantry divisions would, of course, have been left even further behind and it is very doubtful whether Army Group Centre had sufficient formations to seal off such an enormous enemy pocket. As it was, a number of Soviet troops escaped from the small Bialystok pocket into the larger Nowogrodek one and then, using the cover of woods and darkness, made their way to the Dnieper. Only when the encircled Soviet formations had been sufficiently broken up would the *Führer* agree to the continuation of the offensive to the Dnieper and Smolensk.

Meanwhile the relationship between the German Generals became exacerbated even further when at the end of June, after only eight days of war, a new 4 Panzer Army was formed out of 4 Army Headquarters to take 2 and 3 Panzer Groups under command, with Field-Marshal von Kluge at its head.[25] Von Kluge, an energetic commander intolerant of half measures or compromise, soon clashed with both panzer group commanders and in particular with Guderian, because of the surreptitious filtering off of panzer formations

---

[23] The injustice has been subsequently admitted. *Kratkaya Istoriya*, p. 68.

[24] At the time these armies were in the areas of Vitebsk and Orsha.

[25] Headquarters 4 Army became Headquarters 4 Panzer Army. Headquarters 2 Army (von Weichs), which had been without formations and held in reserve, took over the command of the infantry divisions of 4 Army.

from the Nowogrodek pocket away to the chase to the Dnieper.[26] Guderian blamed personalities, von Kluge finding no favour in his eyes, but Hoth was more objective and more accurate when, subsequent to the war, he censured the High Command for so lightly undertaking a war without written plans on the basic strategy, all moves being made as a consequence of day to day conversations between Hitler and his staff.[27] Headquarters 4 German Army was relieved by a new headquarters, Headquarters 2 Army under von Weichs, which together with 9 Army began to destroy and clear the encircled Red Army troops. By 3 July the enemy in the Bialystok area had surrendered and by 8 July the count of prisoners was 290,000 including several corps and divisional commanders, 2,500 captured or knocked out tanks and 1,500 guns. The Germans estimated that twenty-two rifle divisions and the equivalent of seven tank divisions and six mechanized brigades had been destroyed.[28] The Red Army troops encircled were 3 and 10 Armies, some elements of the flanking 4 and 11 Armies and the larger part of the reinforcing 13 Army.[29]

The first of the Belorussian battles, concluded in a space of two weeks, was a remarkable victory even by the German standards of that time. The Red Army troops had been well equipped and in numbers were as strong as their attackers, and in aircraft and tanks, although qualitatively inferior, they were numerically superior.

Von Kluge's 4 Panzer Army, closely supported by Strauss' 9 Army on the left, resumed the advance eastwards towards the upper Dvina and upper Dnieper with 2 and 3 Panzer Groups, both of which had left some divisions cordoning the Minsk pocket. The new command arrangement was not a good one, because both panzer group commanders were in some doubt as to the higher intention. Both believed that, having taken the river line, the next strategic objective would be Moscow. Neither of them appears to have been ordered in so many words to make a double envelopment on Smolensk in order to encircle and destroy the Soviet troops which were by then pouring into the area between Orsha and Smolensk. There was friction between von Kluge and his two subordinates, and yet the control exercised by von Kluge appears to have been loose. Guderian, because he had received no other orders, assumed that his objective remained the Dnieper and the general area Smolensk-Elnya-Roslavl and he therefore advanced eastwards with all three panzer corps forward on a very broad front, and, as he was obsessed with the open flank to the south, he kept extending to his right.[30] Hoth, who had only

[26] 17 Panzer and 14 Motorized Divisions. See Guderian, *Panzer Leader*, p. 162; Halder, *Kriegstagebuch*, Vol. 3, p. 46, 6 July 1941.

[27] Hoth, *Panzeroperationen*, p. 25.

[28] Halder, *Kriegstagebuch*, Vol. 3, p. 56, 9 July 1941; von Bock, *Tagebuch*, 8 July 1941.

[29] The Soviet account admits that 3 and 10 Armies were cut off and that 13 Army lost three divisions, in all 'eleven divisions and parts of others'. On the actual casualties including loss of prisoners it is silent. *Istoriya*, Vol. 2, p. 37. According to Biryuzov, *Surovye Gody*, p. 24, Filatov, the Commander of 13 Army, received fatal wounds in the fighting. He was replaced by Remezov.

[30] Guderian, *Panzer Leader*, p. 166.

two panzer corps, was obliged to direct Kuntzen's 57 Panzer Corps far to the north on Polotsk and Nevel, because of the *Führer*'s preoccupation with the enemy build-up in the area of Nevel-Velikiye Luki on the boundary between Army Groups North and Centre, the same concentration which had caused him to transfer von Leeb's infantry over to the flank.[31] Rudolf Schmidt's 39 Panzer Corps moved on Vitebsk. So it came about that the five panzer corps of 4 Panzer Army moved forward on an extended frontage of over 200 miles with nothing in reserve, so that their armoured thrusts lacked momentum, as Hoth said, like the fingers of an outspread hand rather than a clenched fist. An error was also made in exerting pressure on the Orsha-Smolensk axis, since this merely drove the enemy eastwards.[32] Heavy summer rain had begun to fall and the roads and tracks turned overnight from deep sand and dust to seemingly bottomless rivers of mud, and in consequence the German armoured columns slowed down and became strung out. The enemy's resistance was steadily stiffening; the Red Air Force was active once more and his sappers had time enough to destroy all the bridges.

On 2 July Timoshenko took over command of the Soviet West Front. Budenny's Reserve Front, which had consisted of 19, 20, 21 and 22 Armies and which had been digging in on the line of the upper Dvina and upper Dnieper, was incorporated into Timoshenko's command.[33] West Front still had nearly 1,000 tanks at its disposal, although these were almost entirely of obsolete pattern, and under the martinet Timoshenko's direction there was to be a further stiffening of Soviet resistance. Nehring's 18 Panzer Division, part of Guderian's left flank, advancing along the Orsha-Smolensk motorway against 20 Army and the remnants of 13 Army, had come under fierce counterattacks near the banks of the Berezina by elements of the Borisov tank school under Divisional Commissar Susaikov and Kreizer's 1 Moscow Motor Rifle Division equipped with the new T34 tanks.[34] Kuntzen's 57 Panzer Corps of 3 Panzer Group on 6 July succeeded in bridging the Dvina at Disna in the face of air attack, but came under pressure from Ershakov's 22 Soviet Army, while Rudolf Schmidt's 39 Panzer Corps on the right was held short of Vitebsk on 5 and 6 July by heavy flank attacks made by Kurochkin's 20 Army together with 5 and 7 Soviet Mechanized Corps. Vitebsk, already in flames, fell on 9 July, having been encircled from the north by Stumpff's 20 Panzer Division, but fierce fighting continued until 10 July to the south-west near Syenno, in the area held by Red Army mechanized troops.

[31] These troop concentrations were in fact no more than Ershakov's 22 Soviet Army digging in on the right flank of West Front and the presence of large numbers of stragglers and disorganized units of Sobennikov's North-West Front which were being reformed in the marshalling and assembly areas near Velikiye Luki. *Istoriya*, Vol. 2, Map 21.

[32] Hoth was subsequently to describe this broad front advance as a showpiece as to how armoured warfare should not be conducted. Hoth, *Panzeroperationen*, p. 78.

[33] Pavlov was replaced temporarily by Eremenko who had just arrived from the Far East. Eremenko and Budenny became deputy commanders under Timoshenko. *Istoriya*, Vol. 2, p. 38.

[34] *Ibid*, p. 39.

Timoshenko's West Front, which a few days later became the West Theatre, at this time consisted of seven armies, from north to south, Ershakov's 22 Army north of Vitebsk, Konev's 19 Army in reserve east of Vitebsk, Kurochkin's 20 Army near Orsha, Remezov's 13 Army on the Dnieper about Mogilev, Gerasimenko's (later V. I. Kuznetsov's) 21 Army on the south wing, with Lukin's 16 Army in reserve and 4 Army still retreating before the German thrust in the south through Bobruisk. The West Front strength actually deployed forward on the Orsha triangle and on the Dnieper was said to total only twenty-four divisions, many of the armies being little stronger than rifle corps. Although the troops lacked depth and, after the Vitebsk-Orsha battles, the tank fighting strength was said to have dropped to less than 200, the Soviet resources here were still far greater than the Germans imagined them to be. Further reinforcing formations were arriving daily and another group of Soviet armies was being formed in the rear, east of Smolensk.[35] The Soviet position on this front was critical and was yet to grow worse, particularly since the morale of the Red Army had been temporarily shattered and numbers of its troops were deserting. Some of the Soviet post-war propaganda descriptions of the mass heroism and fearlessness of the Soviet troops ill accord with the situation on the ground at that time.

Gorbatov, a former non-commissioned officer of the Tsarist cavalry, an experienced and distinguished soldier and a confirmed communist, was in July 1941 the Deputy Commander of 25 Rifle Corps, which had arrived near Vitebsk from the area of Kiev, with Konev's 19 Army. The corps had been deployed piecemeal and had hurriedly dug a defensive position. As soon as a few scattered shells dropped among the forward elements of 162 Rifle Division forming part of the corps, the leading regiment, which was probably about 1,500 strong, together with its officers and commissars, took to its heels and streamed off the field *en masse*. Gorbatov, by his own example, managed to rally and to reform the regiment and, as it was impossible to return it to its earlier line, made it dig in on a new position to the rear. Later that day, when the earthworks of these new localities were coming under enemy artillery fire, he observed with satisfaction by the lack of stragglers that the regiment appeared to have regained its nerve and was stoically sitting out the bombardment; but when he went forward to congratulate and encourage it, he found to his horror that the position had long before been deserted. Only the regimental commander, a Lieutenant-Colonel Kostevich, remained with his small headquarters. Kostevich reported that the regiment had made off as soon as the bombardment had begun, and made some excuses to the effect that he had not been able to force his regiment to obey his orders. Gorbatov left him where he was and set off in pursuit of the fleeing men.

He had no difficulty in following the trail, because the men had left a great broad flattened track through the thick and high grass as they ran. He caught up with groups of them eastward bound for the villages of

[35] *Ibid*, p. 65.

Lesno and Rudnya. Others were sitting round bonfires drying out their socks. Some had left their weapons behind. He stopped them, shamed them and cursed them, and having ordered them to return, watched them as they unwillingly set off, until they were out of sight. He then went on to catch the next lot.

To Gorbatov, newly back in the Red Army from a concentration camp, this all seemed an evil dream. He could not believe his eyes.[36]

On the German side, particularly in Army Group Centre, there was unbounded confidence and this was notably strong in the marching infantry formations. Success at this time was measured by stamina and marching ability. 52 Infantry Division, marching hard on Guderian's heels, came upon an organized and armed formation of several thousand Red Army men, together with its headquarters, hidden in the woods near Bobruisk, but taking good care not to disturb it, hurried past and on to the Dnieper. As the long marching days stretched into weeks the men became harder and fitter and less tired, but not so the horses which, unstirred by patriotism and careless of the impetus of victory, grew resentful at the loss of the weekly rest day. Thirty miles a day were frequently covered, sometimes more, the troops marching through thick clouds of dust which rose as high as a house, hanging over the forested march routes in the hot windless air, since the high trees on either side of the tracks were like walls, cutting off any breath of wind. Even the trees were grey, there being no trace of green to be seen anywhere. Faces were covered with a thick grey mask. Men and clothing were sweaty and filthy with no time or opportunity for bathing or washing. The marching infantry, but not its transport, greeted the occasional thunderstorms and torrential rains with delight, as a relief from the insufferable heat and all-pervading dust.[37] News was difficult to come by and the infantrymen relied for their account of breath-taking German victories largely on the word of mouth of the long distance motor transport driver, who at this time was one of the best informed and most welcome soldiers in the German Army.

The German tank men, who had been fighting continuously since the first day of war and whose effectiveness and lives were linked with their vehicles, took yet another view. When Schmundt, the *Führer*'s personal aide, visited Hoth near Vitebsk on 13 July, Hoth told him that the casualties suffered by his panzer group were in no way heavier than those suffered by the formation in the fighting in France. The terrain and climate, however, were far more wearing on tanks and men than they had been in the west, and the nature of the enemy and the monotony of the landscape tended to have a depressing effect on the German troops. The hate and bitterness of the Red Army soldier was a factor too which had not been reckoned with. Hoth was little impressed

[36] Gorbatov, *Gody i Voiny*, *Novyi Mir*, May 1964, translated as *Years off My Life*, pp. 163-5.
[37] Rendulic, *Gekämpft Gesiegt Geschlagen*, pp. 25-6.

by Red Army leadership in the field, except that 'only in Polotsk sat an able man' (*ein tüchtiger Mann*). This presumably was a reference to Ershakov, the Commander of 22 Army.[38]

The situation on Timoshenko's West Front continued to deteriorate. Ershakov's 22 Army on the extreme right flank, which had for so long been a thorn in the *Führer*'s side, was in an isolated and exposed position, since it was coming under attack by both Army Groups North and Centre. Polotsk and Nevel were taken by Kuntzen's panzer corps, which was to advance as far as Velikiye Luki. The corner-stone of both the North-West and West Fronts was thus knocked away. On the south flank Guderian's 2 Panzer Group, which had already closed up to the Dnieper, crossed the river on 10 and 11 July and secured bridgeheads south of Orsha and to the north of Novy Bykhov, and started moving rapidly eastwards in the direction of Smolensk and Krichev, driving Remezov's 13 Army before it, encircling four rifle divisions and part of 20 Mechanized Corps near Mogilev. A Soviet counter-offensive by Gerasimenko's 21 Army against Guderian's south flank in the area of Bobruisk made little headway.

Hoth, using Rudolf Schmidt's 39 Panzer Corps, the only corps available to him since 57 Corps had been deflected to Velikiye Luki, moved eastwards from Vitebsk and encircled Smolensk from the north, his spearhead arriving near Yartsevo east of the town on 15 July. The next day Guderian's 29 Motorized Infantry Division took the town of Smolensk from the south and a huge pocket of Red Army troops between Orsha and Smolensk was almost encircled. Between Yartsevo and Smolensk, however, there was a gap to the south of the main Moscow highway, a gap which Guderian could not close, in spite of Hoth's urging, because the bulk of his troops were spread far to the south and were coming under counter-attacks which were particularly heavy in the Elnya salient.[39] Von Kluge appears to have exerted little influence as a co-ordinator of these operations.

The bulk of Lukin's 16 and Kurochkin's 20 Armies, estimated by German sources to have a strength of between ten and fifteen divisions, together with great numbers of detachments and stragglers, were entrapped in the Smolensk pocket. Vehicles lay four deep along the main Smolensk highway, all facing east, while officers and commissars tried feverishly to marshal and form units. The counter-attacks made against Hoth to the north lacked co-ordination. The Soviet High Command then made desperate attempts to relieve its encircled troops and at the same time cover the approaches to Moscow. On 14 July steps had already been taken to build up another reserve front, covering a new line from Lake Ilmen in the north to Bryansk in the south, and this, under the new Reserve Front commander, I. A. Bogdanov, consisted of the new 29, 30, 24, 28 and 31 Armies. Behind these, a further front

[38] Hoth, *Panzeroperationen*, p. 92.
[39] *Ibid*, pp. 97. Hoth closed the gap about 27 July using 20 Motorized Division, one of his own divisions.

covering Moscow was brought into existence from 32, 33 and 34 Armies under Artemev, the Commander of Moscow District.[40]

In order to lighten Timoshenko's heavy responsibility and to enable him to concentrate on relieving the encircled troops, the southern wing consisting of 13 and 21 Armies was detached from West Front and formed into a new Central Front under F. I. Kuznetsov, the former commander of the North-West Baltic Front. Sixteen rifle divisions and four tank divisions were sent forward from Bogdanov's Reserve Front and formed into temporary tactical formations known as groups, one of which was commanded by Rokossovsky, and these counter-attacked in the direction of Smolensk from Byelyi, Yartsevo and Roslavl in order to break in to the encircled troops.[41] Further attacks were made by 30, 19 and 24 Armies of West Front to the north of Smolensk and on Elnya to divert German attention. These counter-attacks, forming part of what is known in the Soviet Union as the Battle of Smolensk, lasted throughout July and August.

By then the German front extended in a great salient from Stary Bykhov in the south to Roslavl, jutting out at Elnya and Byelyi, and then back in the north near Velikiye Luki. The two panzer groups and part of Strauss's 9 German Army had to withstand the attacks made by Timoshenko's West Front and at the same time prevent the encircled enemy from breaking out. Soviet pressure, particularly to the east of Smolensk, was heavy in places and yet the issue was not in doubt as soon as the marching German infantry formations began to arrive. The Soviet thrust by Kachalov's 28 Army in the south from the important communication centre of Roslavl made some progress until it was countered by a grouping of von Schweppenburg's 24 Panzer Corps and Fahrmbacher's 7 Infantry Corps under Guderian, who contrived to encircle the relieving Red Army force. On 5 August the last Soviet resistance ceased inside the Smolensk pocket with a loss of about 300,000 prisoners and over 3,000 tanks.[42] Three days later the Roslavl pocket, consisting mainly of 28 Soviet Army, was cleared by Guderian with the capture of a further 38,000 prisoners and 200 tanks.[43] 24 Panzer Corps was then dispatched further to the south against the rear of F. I. Kuznetsov's new Central Front to the west and north of Gomel. These attacks made by 24 Panzer Corps on Klintsy from the north, and by von Weichs's 2 German Army eastwards from Bobruisk, virtually destroyed the Central Front, and by 24 August lost the Red Army a further 78,000 prisoners. In all, from the conclusion of the Minsk battle on 8 July to the beginning of September, when the West Front attacks died down, the Red Army lost to Army Group Centre about 400,000 prisoners and over 3,300 tanks destroyed or captured. Soviet accounts maintain that Group

---

[40] *Istoriya*, Vol. 2, p. 70.

[41] The other commanders were Maslennikov, Kalinin, Kachalov and Khomenko.

[42] 309,110 prisoners, 3,205 destroyed or captured tanks, 3,000 guns. Von Bock, *Tagebuch*, 5 August 1941.

[43] Guderian, *Panzer Leader*, p. 186.

Rokossovsky effected an entry on 4 and 5 August into the Smolensk pocket enabling the main part of the encircled Soviet troops to escape.[44] This is untrue.

Army Group Centre had carried out its allotted task and had destroyed most of the Soviet forces in Belorussia, taking about 600,000 prisoners and destroying or capturing over 5,000 tanks. It had advanced over 500 miles to Smolensk, well beyond the line of the Dvina-Dnieper, and was about 250 miles from Moscow. On 3 July Halder had jubilantly noted in his diary that the campaign against Russia was almost won; and yet in September elements of no fewer than twenty-seven Soviet armies were still deployed against the Germans in the forward areas, from Leningrad to the Black Sea.[45]

Many of the German Generals were subsequently critical of Hitler's tactical direction and interference. Hitler was in favour of deep thrusts to the east, but was disinclined to accept the risks involved, and wanted security and a firmly held cordon round the enemy pockets. The panzer group leaders on the other hand were primarily concerned with the bold seizure of deep tactical or strategic objectives such as Smolensk and Moscow rather than with the destruction of the enemy. Guderian's logic in particular was based on the assumption that boldness always paid, and it might be considered that his advocacy of daring thrusts represented a concept of mobility which, although it gave quick and spectacular returns, was unrelated to a strategic master plan. He blamed the OKH and Hitler for the selection of Minsk rather than Smolensk as the objective of the first double envelopment and for holding him back during the cordoning of the Nowogrodek pocket. As it transpired, Hitler's caution probably brought a much higher net of prisoners, since fewer escaped from the Bialystok-Nowogrodek pockets, whilst in the meantime five new Soviet armies were drawn forward to the Vitebsk-Mogilev line. Many of these Red Army troops were destroyed in the second series of envelopments. Guderian tended to be uncompromising and narrow in his views and at this time, like many of his fellow commanders, was unaware of the wider aspects of the campaign and what was going on behind the scenes in the German High Command.

On the Soviet side there has been an attempt to build up the Smolensk battle

[44] Moscow admits the loss of only 32,000 men and 680 tanks in the Smolensk fighting. *Istoriya*, Vol. 2, p. 72. The 1965 edition of the *Kratkaya Istoriya*, p. 76, admits no losses but says that 16 and 20 Armies broke out. Some Soviet troops did in fact escape through the Dorogobuzh gap before Hoth closed it, and a cavalry corps of three divisions broke out to the south. On 2 August another gap was opened up to the east and the *Luftwaffe* reported that the enemy was pouring through as if over a bridge. Von Bock, *Tagebuch* 2 August. Infiltration went on through the German ring all the time. On the other hand, the OKW war records describe the Soviet attacks to break in as relatively weak and uncoordinated; all resistance in the pocket had ceased by 5 August. *Kriegstagebuch des OKW*, Vol. 1, pp. 451–4. Even between 10–21 July Army Group Centre recorded the capture of 100,000 prisoners and 1,000 guns. Halder, *Kriegstagebuch*, Vol. 3, pp. 98, 128 and 150. In spite of the escape of large numbers of Red Army troops, there appears little doubt that 309,000 remained in the pocket and went into captivity.

[45] *Istoriya*, Vol. 2, Map 1.

to the proportions of a victory.[46] The Kremlin was convinced that the seizure of Moscow was the Germans' immediate and main objective and were astonished when Army Group Centre did not attempt to advance beyond Smolensk. In consequence it has construed its own version of events for which there is no supporting evidence. Within the Soviet Union it is said that the resistance of Red Army troops before Smolensk was the decisive factor in forcing Hitler and the Germans to alter their original plans and cancel the attack on Moscow.[47] Although the Soviet counter-attacks were at times desperate, and although in the main the Red Army fought with determination, its strength could not in truth have held the Germans if it had been Hitler's intention to advance directly on Moscow. Nor is the Soviet claim true that Hitler broke off the attacks on Moscow because of the danger of Soviet flank attacks from the north and south.[48] In accordance with Hitler's orders, the *Barbarossa* Directive and the subsequent plans were based on the premise that when Smolensk was reached, the main German effort would be switched to Leningrad and possibly to the Ukraine.

[46] Zhukov even goes so far as to say that 'according to the accounts of the German Generals, the Hitlerite forces lost in the Smolensk battle 250,000 men and on 30 July it was decided to order Army Group Centre to go over to the defence'. He makes no mention of the Soviet losses in the Smolensk encirclement. Zhukov, *Vospominaniya i Razmyshleniya*, p. 297. Compare also Platonov, *Vtoraya Mirovaya Voina*, p. 212; Vasilevsky, *Bitva za Moskvy*, p. 12; Vorobev and Kravtsov, *Pobedy Sovetskikh Vooruzhennykh Sil v Velikoi Otechestvennoi Voine* 1941–45, p. 92.

[47] *Istoriya*, Vol. 2, p. 76.

[48] *Ibid*, p. 70.

CHAPTER NINE

The Führer Vacillates

Field-Marshal von Rundstedt's Army Group South consisted of 1 Panzer Group and 6 and 17 Armies in Poland, and was separated by Hungarian territory from its right wing in Rumania, made up of 11 German Army and 3 and 4 Rumanian Armies. The armies in Poland were to attack eastwards to the south of the Pripet Marshes into the Ukraine, while the Rumanian-German force moved north-east through Moldavia-Bessarabia to join them. Hungary was to join the war against the Soviet Union and put into the field a number of brigades forming the connecting link between the Polish and Rumanian fronts. Von Rundstedt had a total of about fourteen Rumanian and forty-one German divisions, of which only five were panzer and three motorized.[1]

It had originally been intended to use the tactics of the double envelopment, one armoured pincer from Poland joining up with another from Rumania in the area of Kiev on the Dnieper. Three months before the opening of the campaign, however, Hitler had changed his mind in favour of a single envelopment from Poland, and had given as his reason the fact that the rivers Pruth and Dniester were formidable obstacles across the axis from Rumania. This was only a half-truth, since part of the cause lay in his nervousness regarding the safety of the Ploesti oilfields, because he feared that an energetic thrust across the Rumanian frontier might provoke a Soviet counter-offensive into Rumanian territory.[2]

For this reason the main Army Group South thrust was to be made by 6 Army under Field-Marshal von Reichenau and by 1 Panzer Group under Colonel-General von Kleist, the total strength of von Reichenau's command being twenty divisions, of which five were panzer and three motorized infantry. Von Reichenau was to drive vigorously eastwards from the area south-east of Lublin, 6 Army having a special responsibility for the left flank protection towards the Pripet Marshes, while 1 Panzer Group had as its objective the general area of Kiev on the Dnieper. The panzer group and the marching infantry divisions of 6 Army following in its wake were then to turn south-east

---

[1] All details of order of battle are from *OKH Kriegsgliederung* dated 18 June 1941.

[2] Hitler remarked 'The Pruth and Dniester are rivers which must block any attack. Why drive the Russian away from where we want him to stay. Leave in Rumania only what is needed for security'. Halder, *Kriegstagebuch*, Vol. 2, pp. 319–20.

along the banks of the river towards the Black Sea in order to secure the Dnieper crossings and prevent the enemy withdrawing eastwards. 17 Army under von Stülpnagel, with a total of thirteen infantry divisions, was to move on von Reichenau's right through Lvov and Vinnitsa.[3] The forces in Rumania consisted of von Schobert's 11 German Army, of seven German infantry divisions, and 3 and 4 Rumanian Armies totalling the equivalent of about fourteen Rumanian divisions. 11 German Army formed the centre between the two Rumanian armies but had detached one corps to 4 Rumanian Army, one infantry division to safeguard Ploesti, and some further small groupings had been allotted to Rumanian formations. The task of 11 German and 3 Rumanian Armies was merely to safeguard Rumanian territory by remaining passive until seven days after the start of the war, by which time it was hoped that the Red Army in the Ukraine would be either encircled or withdrawing. 11 and 3 Armies would then advance by way of Kamenets Podolskiy and Mogilev Podolskiy into the Ukraine in an attempt to pin the Soviet forces there, while 4 Rumanian Army was to move on Odessa.[4] Army Group South had the support of 4 Air Fleet, consisting of about 600 aircraft.[5]

Although Stalin, like Golikov, considered a German attack upon the Soviet Union to be most unlikely until Germany conquered or made peace with Great Britain, he had given as his opinion that when war did come, the Germans would make their main thrust into the Ukraine in order to seize Ukrainian grain, Donets coal and Caucasian oil.[6] This assumption was certainly reflected in the Soviet defensive deployment in June 1941, in that the greater part of the Red Army was to be found in the Ukraine, the forces there being greater than the combined strength of Pavlov's West and Kuznetsov's North-West Fronts. The Soviet troops in Galicia and Bessarabia covering the Ukraine were organized into the South-West and South Fronts. The South-West Front was commanded by Kirponos and consisted from north to south of Potapov's 5 Army, Muzychenko's 6 Army, Kostenko's 26 Army and Ponedelin's 12 Army stretching roughly from the area of the Pripet Marshes to the northern edge of the frontier with Rumania. After the first week of war the Rumanian frontier was covered by a newly formed South Front under Tyulenev consisting of A. K. Smirnov's 18 Army and Cherevichenko's 9 Army.[7] South-West Front had a strength of thirty-two infantry and three cavalry divisions and eight mechanized corps, most of the mechanized corps being concentrated in 5 and 6 Army areas against the Russo-German frontier.[8] Tyulenev's South Front

---

[3] *Aufmarschanweisung Barbarossa, OKH Gen St d H Op Abt (I) Nr. 050/41 g. Kdos Chefs* of 31 January 1941, paragraph 4a.

[4] Of Army Group South's total of forty-one divisions three were security divisions and five were mountain or light divisions consisting of only two regiments.

[5] Loehr's 4 Air Fleet of Greim's 5 and Pflugbeil's 6 Air Corps and a flak corps, in all six bomber and three fighter wings, with other fighter, bomber and reconnaissance elements.

[6] Zhukov, *Vospominaniya i Razmyshleniya*, p. 228.

[7] Formed from Odessa Military District.

[8] The tank forces included 4, 8, 9, 15, 16, 19, 22 and 24 Mechanized Corps.

was weak in infantry divisions but had no fewer than two mechanized corps deployed against the Rumanian border.[9]

Kirponos not only had more troops and tanks than his fellow commanders to the north of the Pripet, but he was also better prepared for battle. According to Zhukov, Kirponos was already at his battle headquarters at Tarnopol by midnight on 21 June when he spoke to Moscow giving news of the arrival of a second German deserter bringing information of the imminence of war. This incident may possibly have happened, although the regiment and division from which Zhukov said the deserter came are not to be found in the German Army lists.[10] Whether such a desertion took place or not, Kirponos was the only front commander who recovered immediately from the shock of the German invasion and he conducted his defence with great skill. In this he was aided by the nature of the country, the broken swampland to the south of the Pripet and the woodlands of Galicia and the West Ukraine. Tyulenev's South Front on the Moldavian uplands of Bessarabia was not brought into action until the end of June and there, with its strong tank and mechanized force, it had the German marching infantry and Rumanian horsed cavalry at a disadvantage. The battle might, however, have gone very differently if, instead of being passive, the Germans had used a right enveloping armoured pincer from Rumania on the very first day of the war.[11] In the North-West Ukraine, von Rundstedt's Army Group South had almost undisputed air superiority, and diversionists were particularly active in the Red Army rear cutting telephone and rail communications so that there was some confusion and loss of control on the Soviet side of the frontier.[12] Von Kleist's 1 Panzer Group therefore broke through without much difficulty on a thirty-mile gap along the boundary of Potapov's 5 and Muzychenko's 6 Soviet Armies in the direction of Rovno; this axis lay across the concentration areas of some of the Soviet mechanized

[9] *Istoriya*, Vol. 2, p. 98; Zhukov, *Vospominaniya i Razmyshleniya*, p. 250. According to Zhukov South-West and South Fronts together totalled forty-five rifle, twenty tank, ten mechanized and six cavalry divisions. See also *50 Let Vooruzhennykh Sil SSSR*, pp. 251–2.

[10] Neither 222 Infantry Regiment nor 74 Infantry Division existed in the German Army order of battle. Zhukov, *Vospominaniya i Razmyshleniya*, p. 254. Compare also Mueller-Hillebrand, *Das Heer*, Vol. 2, pp. 194–200; Keilig, *Das Deutsche Heer*, Vol. 1, Sect. 34, pp. 29–39; and *OKH Kriegsgliederung* for 18 June 1941.

[11] In spite of the two major rivers, the rolling open steppe of the South-West Ukraine was excellent for the rapid movement of tanks, and an armoured attack through Bessarabia might have been very successful. Red Army tank forces were to experience no difficulty crossing this area in 1944.

[12] The Germans used more native born diversionists in the Ukraine than elsewhere. Canaris of the *Abwehr* sponsored a Ukrainian nationalist organization known as *Bergbauernhilfe*, composed mainly of Ukrainian Galicians, Stephen Bandera being one of its leaders. A number of armed units were raised, including the notorious Nightingale battalion, which in addition to being anti-communist, also settled a number of private and personal scores when they took the law into their own hands against Russians, Poles and Jews. There were a number of civil uprisings in the Red Army rear particularly in the area of Lvov, these being suppressed by the Red Army and NKVD with the greatest barbarity. Compare also Dallin, *German Rule in Russia*, pp. 114–22; Teske, *Die Silbernen Spiegel*, p. 116.

corps. On 23 June began a series of tank engagements between Luck and Rovno as 22, 9 and 19 Mechanized Corps were drawn into the fighting, and until 28 June 1 Panzer Group was fighting its way slowly forward in a series of local tactical battles instead of racing away, as had been hoped, towards deep tactical or strategic objectives.[13] There was, however, some lack of co-ordination between 5 and 6 Soviet Armies, Potapov's 5 Army falling back to the north-east on the Pripet Marshes where it was to live to fight – most successfully – another day, while Muzychenko's 6 Army recoiled to the south.[14] By 1 July the Germans had reached the area of Rovno, Dubno and Krze-mieniec.

On 1 July 11 German Army and the Rumanians started to cross the Pruth in their advance towards the Dniester, against Red Army troops who were ready for battle and were well equipped with tanks. Von Schobert's divisions were of marching infantry and Rumanian cavalry with little or no air support and, as they marched steadily forward, they covered no more than an average of about eight miles a day because of the aggressiveness and mobility of the Soviet armoured rearguards, which, in the open terrain so ideally suited to tanks, forced the invading columns to deploy several times a day. Red Air Force bombers and fighters carried out harassing raids, and the frequent and sudden cloudbursts churned the rich black soil into liquid glue, bringing all wheeled movement to a halt for hours. Even field guns drawn by six pairs of horses came to a standstill.[15]

Von Choltitz, the regimental commander of 16 Oldenburg Airborne Infantry Regiment, and Malaparte, the Italian Alpine captain attached to the German troops as a liaison officer and observer, are agreed in their accounts of the fighting on this sector. After the Germans had crossed the Dniester and the so-called Stalin line on the old Soviet frontier, which consisted of nothing but a few deserted and isolated earthworks, Red Army resistance grew much stronger, the rearguards falling back skilfully and leaving behind them neither wounded nor dead. Soviet armoured counter-attacks were made with vigour and the Germans found that the infantry pattern 37 mm anti-tank gun had no effect on the heavier Soviet tanks, even though these tanks were of obsolete pattern. Soon the wooded and hilly country of Moldavia-Bessarabia gave way to the flat steppe of the Ukraine, covered with corn and sunflowers, and the only occasional features on the landscape were the little rows of peasant huts sheltered by acacias. The livestock and poultry were still in the fields and only the horses and the men had gone. The broad, featureless horizons emphasized the loneliness and emptiness of the great land, with its sense of vastness and the infinite. It took 11 German Army no less than two months to skirmish and march the 400 miles to the Dnieper, regiments marching entirely on their own, accompanied by their own small artillery and anti-aircraft detachments, as von

[13] Zhukov was present with Kirponos from 22–26 June.
[14] Zhukov, *Vospominaniya i Razmyshleniya*, pp. 260–2.
[15] Malaparte, *The Volga Rises in Europe*, pp. 52–5 and 157–9.

Choltitz has said, like tiny vessels lost on a vast ocean of waving corn. There was no reconnaissance in depth and no liaison to the flanks. For weeks the Oldenburg Regiment saw no other troops except for occasional Red Army men, and often they were out of radio touch with their divisional headquarters for days. They never saw a German tank or a single German aircraft. Once or twice they crossed the tracks of Rumanian troops, and once they saw an Italian motorized formation which looked as though it was out on a holiday. For the most part the war there was heat, dust and daily rain, incessant marching and the engagement with the enemy. Ammunition had to be conserved, and this meant that mortars and guns were used sparingly, reliance being placed on the light machine-gun. All harboured the nagging anxiety in case they should be wounded, for the seriously wounded went away into the emptiness in a horse-drawn ambulance. Meanwhile the ranks were slowly but steadily thinned by the daily casualties, the march being marked by the tiny collection of graves left behind along the route.[16]

The deep thrust of 1 Panzer Group put Muzychenko's 6, Kostenko's 26 and Ponedelin's 12 Soviet Armies in the forward Lvov salient in danger of being cut off, and the gravity of their position was emphasized when von Schobert's 11 German Army began its advance across the Pruth at the end of June. On 30 June, two days after the Minsk encirclement, Kirponos was told by Moscow to order a general withdrawal to the line from Korosten to Novograd-Volynsk and Proskurov nearly 150 miles to the rear, roughly in the area of the 1938 Soviet frontier, and the speed with which Red Army troops were to escape encirclement and withdraw, after jettisoning their heavy equipment, caused Kinzel's intelligence department to trace, quite erroneously, here as on other fronts, the influence of the British Military Mission in Moscow.[17] By 8 July, however, this rearward line had been pierced by the German advance; Berdichev fell and the next day Zhitomir, less than ninety miles from Kiev, was taken, despite strong counter-attacks by elements of 15, 4 and 16 Mechanized Corps. On 10 July Potapov's 5 Army made its presence felt again, when, reappearing from the southern edge of the Pripet Marshes, together with parts of 9, 19 and 22 Mechanized Corps, it attacked the rear flank of 1 Panzer Group from the direction of Korosten, cutting the main supply route; the intervention of von Reichenau's 6 German Army was required to drive Potapov back to the north into the marshes. Thereafter 5 Soviet Army was to be a constant danger and irritation to the German flank and was to draw 6 German Army away from its dual task of supporting von Kleist's armour and consolidating its gains. Muzychenko's 6 and Ponedelin's 12 Soviet Armies fell back eastwards.

[16] Von Choltitz, *Un Soldat parmi des Soldats*, pp. 98–110.

[17] Halder, *Kriegstagebuch*, Vol. 3, p. 164. The British Mission had no function at all in Moscow except as a provider of equipment. It is probable that the unsettled political situation in Galicia and the West Ukraine and the resounding defeat at Minsk caused Stalin on 30 June to sanction the withdrawal of South-West Front to the old USSR borders. Compare Platonov, *Vtoraya Mirovaya Voina*, p. 193.

The fighting to the south of the Pripet, in Galicia and the North-West Ukraine, was entirely different from that experienced by the Germans and Rumanians in Bessarabia and the South-West Ukraine. The country was more like that of Belorussia, partly cultivated but largely covered with woods and heathland. German air activity was heavy and tanks and vehicles, both German and Soviet, were to be found everywhere. Fighting, which was both confused and bitter, continued in pockets over the whole area a hundred miles behind the German spearheads, since numerous Red Army formations had not been able to withdraw in time. The roads were lined with abandoned Red Army vehicles of all types, the cornfields were full of enemy infantry and the woods rumbled with the clatter of the tracks of Soviet tanks. At night Soviet trucks sometimes made the fatal error of joining German transport columns. When Red Army soldiers had time to orient and prepare themselves, they often fought with great determination and bitterness, even though they were isolated. When they were surprised or threatened by armour they surrendered in large numbers, often plaintively crying 'Ukrainian' as they did so.[18]

On the marshland sector of Potapov's 5 Soviet Army near Korosten the pattern of the fighting was different yet again. Potapov, a General of Tank Troops, using the shelter of the Pripet, had kept his formations together and put up a determined, cohesive and properly co-ordinated defence against the attacks of von Reichenau's 6 German Army, using concentrated artillery with great effect. 98 German Infantry Division, arriving in the town of Malin, near the fringe of the Pripet, was astounded at the frightening picture of rubble, destroyed houses and torn up roads which was a witness to the fierceness of the fighting. Moving forward to their forming up places for the attack, they themselves came under heavy and accurate Soviet artillery fire which was to drive them off the road into the marsh. The shouts for stretcher bearers were to be heard everywhere. When the attack was eventually launched it had to be made through standing corn and scrub, and although the infantry was supported by armoured tracked assault guns, casualties were not light. Even when the objective was taken, Red Army sharpshooters from the scrub continued to be troublesome, and the enemy was found to be systematically seeking out and bayoneting German wounded who were lying helpless in the high corn. By then the Germans, most of them in action for the first time, were becoming infuriated and when the attack was resumed the fighting was of the bitterest, no quarter being given by either side. At the end of less than two days of fighting III battalion of 282 Infantry Regiment had lost 170 men dead and wounded, more than a quarter of its strength.[19]

The German salient of Zhitomir-Berdichev to the south of Korosten menaced Kiev and for this reason came under heavy counter-attack from 5

[18] Meyer, *Panzergrenadiere*, pp. 79–82.
[19] Gareis, *Kampf und Ende der Fränkisch-Sudetendeutschen 98. Division*, pp. 86–104. In eleven days the division lost 78 officers and 2,300 men. Its morale was unaffected, but the trained leaders and specialists could not be replaced.

Soviet Army to its north and 6 Army to its south and from elements of 26 Army which had been withdrawing from the Carpathians. It was only after several days fighting that von Reichenau's 6 German Army and von Kleist's 1 Panzer Group were able to make further progress to the east. Although it seemed possible that 1 Panzer Group could have taken Kiev in a bold thrust, Hitler on 10 July forbade any armoured formation to enter the city.[20] Von Rundstedt then varied his plan, directing only von Mackensen's 3 Panzer Corps with part of 6 German Army towards the Dnieper while the greater part of 1 Panzer Group, consisting of von Wietersheim's 14 and Kempf's 48 Panzer Corps, moved from Berdichev in a south-easterly direction through Kazatin and Belaya Tserkov to Pervomaysk and Pomoshnaya, enveloping 6, 12 and part of 18 Soviet Armies in a flanking movement. In choosing this deep encirclement von Rundstedt disregarded Hitler's prompting for an armoured axis from Berdichev to Vinnitsa, since the Red Army was already in full retreat and would have escaped such a short envelopment.[21] Meanwhile von Stülpnagel's 17 German Army, together with some Hungarian mobile brigades from the Carpathians, was to continue its eastwards advance through Vinnitsa and drive 6 and 12 Soviet Armies against 1 Panzer Group, which by then would be straddling their line of withdrawal. Von Schobert's 11 German Army and 3 Rumanian Army were marching hard towards Pervomaysk and driving A. K. Smirnov's 18 Army before them, to form the third side of the triangle to entrap the Soviet troops.

In the second week in July Budenny had taken up his new appointment as the Commander-in-Chief of South-West Theatre, commanding both the South-West and the South Fronts, with Khrushchev as the political member of his military council. Thereafter, by misjudgement or mischance, fortune began to desert Kirponos' South-West and Tyulenev's South Front. Within a week or so of assuming command Budenny transferred two of the principal armies in the centre, Muzychenko's 6 Army and Ponedelin's 12 Army, from the command of Kirponos to that of Tyulenev, by moving the inter-front boundary to the north. The reason for this is not entirely clear but it is probable that von Kleist's thrust was threatening to bisect the South-West Front and

---

[20] Halder, *Kriegstagebuch*, Vol. 3, p. 60. On 12 July 3 Panzer Corps stood with two panzer divisions on the Irpen River close to Kiev and Philippi has commented on Hitler's failure to take Kiev by a bold 'raid'. Philippi und Heim, *Der Feldzug gegen Sowjetrussland 1941–45*, p. 62. It is doubtful whether the Germans could have held Kiev at that time, even if they had succeeded in taking it, unless they were to forgo the Uman operation. Soviet accounts on the other hand exaggerate the defence of Kiev, which was covered by Vlasov's 37 Army, and infer that the Germans were deflected to the south because they could not take the city. Zhilin, *Die Wichtigsten Operationen des Grossen Vaterländischen Krieges*, pp. 116–7; Vorobev and Kravtsov, *Pobedy Sovetskikh Vooruzhennykh Sil v Velikoi Otechestvennoi Voine*, p. 98; *Kratkaya Istoriya*, p. 88.

[21] Von Brauchitsch, who happened to be with von Rundstedt at the time, convinced the Führer (through Halder) that the encirclement ought to be made much further to the east. See also Röhricht, *Probleme der Kesselschlacht*, p. 52; and Halder, *Kriegstagebuch*, Vol. 3, p. 60, 10 July 1941.

Tyulenev was therefore made responsible for the defence of the Ukraine on the right bank of the Dnieper (and to the south of the 1 Panzer Group wedge) while Kirponos was to concentrate on the defence of Kiev and be responsible for opèrations against von Kleist's left flank.[22] This caused some confusion and disorganization in control. Twice Budenny was permitted by Moscow to withdraw to the east, but the permission appears to have been given grudgingly, since the extent of the withdrawal was merely tactical and did not meet the dangers of the situation.[23] As soon as the true German intention became clear, Kirponos mounted strong attacks on the north flank of 1 Panzer Group, using a reformed 26 Soviet Army under Kostenko, across the Dnieper from the area between Kiev and Cherkasy. These attacks were fended off by a group of infantry divisions under von Schwedler, the Commander of 4 Corps, and did not halt von Kleist's panzer advance towards Pervomaysk. On 2 August Pervomaysk was taken and a large part of 6 and 12 Armies and some elements of 18 Army, the equivalent of about twenty divisions, were cut off from the east in a large pocket near Uman. Soviet resistance continued until 8 August when 103,000 prisoners passed into German captivity, among them the two army commanders and seven corps headquarters. Over 300 tanks and 800 guns were captured.[24] The remainder of Tyulenev's Soviet South Front which stretched forward in a great salient along the edge of the Black Sea coast was by then in danger of being completely cut off by a thrust from the north, and it fell back rapidly eastwards, leaving behind a number of troops to garrison Odessa as an independent coastal army under Sofronov.[25] The Red Army in the Ukraine had been routed, although at some cost in casualties to the Germans, and by the end of the month the Soviet forces had lost their last foothold west of the Dnieper at Kherson, Berislav and Dnepropetrovsk.

Some German commanders have subsequently speculated whether better results might have been obtained if von Kleist's armour had struck further to the south-east or even crossed the Dnieper and made the encirclement down the left bank of the river, leaving the clearing of the South Ukraine to the

[22] Platonov, *Vtoraya Mirovaya Voina*, p. 216; and Zhilin, *Die Wichtigsten Operationen des Grossen Vaterländischen Krieges*, p. 119.

[23] According to Platonov, South Front had been authorized at the end of July to fall back on the line Ternovka-Balta. This was of no assistance as it was still far to the west of Uman. Zhilin on the other hand said that the front commander had decided to fall back on the River Ingul, more than a hundred miles to the east of Uman. In any event he did not.

[24] Halder, *Kriegstagebuch*, Vol. 3, p. 163. Ponedelin and Muzychenko were taken prisoner. Soviet accounts admit the loss of part of 6 and 12 Armies without giving further details. *Istoriya*, Vol. 2, p. 102. Platonov, *Vtoraya Mirovaya Voina*, p. 217. In technical terms Uman was a battle from a reversed front against an enemy already withdrawing. It was a double envelopment, but only one of the enveloping arms was of armoured troops, the other arm (11 Army) and the pinning troops in the centre (17 Army) being entirely of marching infantry.

[25] Tyulenev was replaced during August as Commander-in-Chief South Front by Ryabyshev. Ryabyshev's new chief of staff was Antonov, Zaporozhets remaining as political member.

infantry armies.[26] Such a bold move might have brought success. On the other hand, the victory at Uman would not have been possible without the presence of 1 Panzer Group close in the Red Army rear, and it is doubtful in any case whether the German infantry divisions could have outmarched the Soviet forces, since the marching stamina and mobility of Red Army troops, even over the most difficult country, was quite remarkable. The Soviet enemy was unimpeded by heavy equipment, most of which he had abandoned. The route further to the south-east was long and circuitous, and Kirponos to the north was still strong. Moreover, it is unlikely that von Kleist could have prevented large numbers of Soviet troops from withdrawing across the whole extent of the Dnieper.

During this period the Soviet High Command had been frantically engaged in throwing together new formations. South-West Front had received ten and South Front twelve newly formed divisions, and three new or reformed armies, 26, 37 and 38 Armies, had appeared on the Dnieper from the interior. A new 6 Army under Malinovsky was already defending the Dnieper north of Dnepropetrovsk.[27]

By then the German Army on the East Front had carried out the first part of its mission, in spite of some failures. Leningrad had not been taken, a junction had not been made with the Finns and many of the enemy had escaped from the Baltic and the Ukraine. But German troops had taken the Orsha-Smolensk landbridge, had crossed the Dvina, and were on or over the Dnieper. They now awaited the *Führer*'s further orders.

Hitler had always intended that Leningrad should be taken before Moscow and very early on he came to regard the seizure of the whole of the Ukraine, the Donets basin and even Caucasia as having priority over an eastwards advance from Smolensk. On 30 June he had emphasized the economic importance of the Ukraine and that of the Baltic.[28] A week later he had proposed that Hoth's 3 Panzer Group should move away from Smolensk to the north-east as flank protection for von Leeb's Army Group North, while Guderian's 2 Panzer Group should move south-east into the Ukraine.[29] His attention was riveted on the Crimea which he came to regard as a Soviet aircraft carrier for use to bomb the Ploesti oilfields, and the occupation of the Crimea would, he thought, enable German troops to invade the Caucasus by the shorter route

[26] The movement of 1 Panzer Group down the east bank of the Dnieper was discussed with Hitler on 23 July. Halder, *Kriegstagebuch*, Vol. 3, p. 108. Von Brauchitsch opposed it on the grounds of supply and maintenance difficulties.

[27] *Istoriya*, Vol. 2, p. 102. As soon as a Soviet army was destroyed a new formation appeared, bearing the same designation. This was to be German practice later in the war.

[28] Halder, *Kriegstagebuch*, Vol. 3, p. 29. Hitler was again stressing the value of Swedish iron ore and Ukrainian industry and grain.

[29] *Ibid*, p. 53; also Keitel, *Memoirs*, pp. 150–1; Warlimont, *Inside Hitler's Headquarters*, pp. 181–3. Hitler (and Jodl was apparently echoing him) was to say that the decision to turn north or south would probably be the most difficult of the whole war. By 27 July, however, Jodl was to give his opinion to the *Führer* that the main offensive should be made on Moscow.

F

across the Straits of Kerch.[30] On 19 July he issued Directive 33 ordering Army Group Centre to advance on Moscow, using only its infantry formations, since its panzer troops were to be transferred to the north and the south.[31] Four days later, on 23 July, Keitel, at the *Führer's* order, issued a very optimistic supplement to Directive 33, ordering Hoth's 3 Panzer Group to be transferred to the Baltic for the outflanking of Leningrad, after which it would be returned to Army Group Centre ready for the advance as far as the Volga, while Hoepner's 4 Panzer Group, together with other troops, would be withdrawn to Germany.[32] Guderian's 2 Panzer Group was to join von Kleist's 1 Panzer Group in the Ukraine.[33]

At meetings held on 23 and 26 July Halder emphasized the need for a final autumn thrust to be made on Moscow, since he himself considered Hitler's Leningrad and Ukraine objectives to be of secondary importance, believing that in the final outcome the *Führer's* plan would bog the German forces down to position warfare. Halder himself was having belated doubts as to the purpose and direction of the war.[34] Hitler had had second thoughts, but only insofar as he would permit von Bock's Army Group Centre to go over to the defensive after its armour was removed instead of using its infantry to fight its way to Moscow. Meanwhile 2 and 3 Panzer Groups were to be withdrawn temporarily for refit and rest.[35] Von Bock had been pressing that Army Group Centre should retain its panzer groups and make an early advance on Moscow, and in this view he had been supported most strongly by Guderian and Hoth. Between 4 and 6 August the *Führer* visited the Headquarters of both Army Groups Centre and South in order to hear the views of the army group and panzer commanders, all of whom advised the immediate resumption of the offensive towards Moscow.[36] This advice was not in accordance with Hitler's views and he rejected it, submitting his Generals to a lecture on the economic aspects of war.[37] Halder then attempted to pin Jodl with the direct question as to whether the *Führer's* immediate aims were military conquest or economic exploitation, and received the reply that the *Führer* considered both to be war

[30] Guderian, *Panzer Leader*, p. 190; Halder, *Kriegstagebuch*, Vol. 3, pp. 191–2.

[31] Hubatsch, *Hitlers Weisungen für die Kriegführung*, p. 141.

[32] *Ibid*, p. 143.

[33] On 21 July when visiting von Leeb in Army Group North, Hitler said that Moscow was 'merely a geographical idea'. Warlimont, *Inside Hitler's Headquarters*, p. 186. Hitler was also convinced that Leningrad would have to be destroyed as it was a naval base and the seat of communism, and he told von Leeb that the capture of this symbol of Bolshevism might lead to a collapse of the Soviet regime. Von Leeb, *Tagebuch*, 21 July; *Kriegstagebuch des OKW*, Vol. 1, pp. 1029–31.

[34] Halder, *Kriegstagebuch*, Vol. 3, pp. 107 and 103 footnote 21, '*Wir laufen in die Breite, haben schliesslich keinen Schwerpunkt mehr*'.

[35] Directive 34 of 30 July. Hubatsch, *Hitlers Weisungen für die Kriegführung*, p. 145. Von Kluge's 4 Panzer Army Headquarters gave up the command of the two panzer groups after the Smolensk operation and reverted to its former designation of 4 Army.

[36] Von Bock recorded in his diary on 4 August that it was obvious that the *Führer* was not clear what he was going to do next.

[37] Warlimont, *Inside Hitler's Headquarters*, p. 186; Guderian, *Panzer Leader*, p. 190.

aims of equal importance and priority.[38] On 12 August Keitel signed a supplement to Directive 34 confirming the intention of moving the armour from Army Group Centre and attacking towards Leningrad, the Crimea, Kharkov, the Donets basin and the Caucasus, after destroying the heavy concentrations of enemy troops which had formed on the flanks of Army Group Centre.[39] The enemy concentration in the Pripet to the north of Kiev, which was always referred to as 5 Soviet Army but which in fact consisted of other Soviet armies as well, was singled out for destruction.[40]

On 18 August von Brauchitsch and Halder struck their final blow in support of the direct offensive on Moscow, when they addressed a memorandum to Hitler setting out their arguments.[41] Three days later he rejected it in a counter-memorandum which reproached von Brauchitsch for not really commanding the German Army, but being far too much influenced by the views of the army group commanders. An indignant Halder then proposed to von Brauchitsch that they should both resign, but this suggestion was received with little enthusiasm by the Commander-in-Chief.[42]

On the Army Group Centre front von Schweppenburg's 24 Panzer Corps of Guderian's 2 Panzer Group was already engaged on the southern flank, together with von Weichs's 2 German Army, in the destruction of the two armies of F. I. Kuznetsov's Central Front in the area of Gomel, nearly half-way between Smolensk and Kiev.[43] Guderian coming down from the north was in fact already approaching the rear of Kirponos's South-West Front, which was menacing von Rundstedt's flank from the Pripet, and Hitler intended that 2 Panzer Group should continue south into the Ukraine. On 23 August Guderian was summoned to Army Group Centre Headquarters to meet Halder for consultation. Guderian voiced his doubts as to the ability of his equipment or men to mount a campaign in the East Ukraine and then return to the area of Smolensk in time to undertake an advance on Moscow before the onset of

[38] Halder, *Kriegstagebuch*, Vol. 3, p. 159; Warlimont, *Inside Hitler's Headquarters*, p. 186.

[39] Hubatsch, *Hitlers Weisungen für die Kriegführung*, pp. 148–9.

[40] By then the concentration consisted of a large part of Kirponos' South-West Front, including Potapov's 5, Vlasov's 37 and Kostenko's 26 Armies.

[41] The memorandum was initiated by Heusinger and was addressed to von Brauchitsch. It was posted on to the *Führer*. Heusinger discussed its contents with Jodl who agreed with them but warned Heusinger that he expected to have the greatest of difficulty in persuading the *Führer*. Two days later Jodl was sent by Hitler to the OKH with orders to win over von Brauchitsch and Halder to the *Führer*'s opposite views, and this, Jodl, being himself convinced that Hitler was wrong, failed to do. Warlimont, *Inside Hitler's Headquarters*, pp. 188–90; Heusinger's verbal account.

[42] Hitler sent both a *Führerweisung* drafted by Jodl, and a personal memorandum to von Brauchitsch, full of reproaches that the OKH was not carrying out the operation as he (the *Führer*) wanted it and comparing von Brauchitsch unfavourably with Göring. *WF St L Nr. 441412/41* of 21 August 1941 (*Kriegstagebuch des OKW*, Vol. 1, p. 1062); Halder, *Kriegstagebuch*, Vol. 3, p. 192. Halder, whom von Bock described as absolutely beside himself (*ausser sich*), appeared at Army Group Centre on 23 August with Hitler's signed memorandum in his hand. Von Bock, *Tagebuch*.

[43] F. I. Kuznetsov's Central Front consisted of 13 and 21 Armies. Efremov was in command at the time of Guderian's attack on 8 August.

winter, and this was the music which Halder wanted to hear. This was also von Bock's view and, at the army group commander's suggestion, Guderian returned by air to Rastenburg with Halder to give these views personally to the *Führer*. According to Guderian's account of the meeting, which took place in the presence of Keitel, Jodl and Schmundt, he was overruled by the combined efforts of Hitler and his entourage and says he was astounded and hurt by the unexpected outburst of anger with which Halder heard his report the next day. Halder's diary account written on that evening of Sunday 24 August read somewhat differently, when he noted that Guderian had been completely convinced by Hitler's arguments and had agreed with them, being resolved to show the *Führer* that he (Guderian) was the man to accomplish the seemingly impossible. It was apparently this sudden change of face which occasioned Halder's wrath. So Hitler triumphed once again over Halder and the OKH by sowing dissension and using Guderian as his tool, and the German striking strength was turned northwards and southwards instead of to the east and Moscow.[44]

Meanwhile in Moscow Stalin, too, was having differences of opinion with some of his leading Generals. Vatutin had quitted his appointment as first deputy to the Chief of General Staff and had become Chief of Staff North-West Front, being replaced by Vasilevsky. On 29 July at a meeting attended by Mekhlis, the Head of the Central Political Directorate, Zhukov, according to his own account, advised the withdrawal of Kirponos's South-West Front from the line of the Dnieper, even at the cost of giving up Kiev. This occasioned an angry outburst from Stalin and cries of 'rubbish'. Zhukov's offer to give up his post of Chief of General Staff was eagerly seized upon with the retort that Stalin could easily get along without him (Zhukov) even if it meant taking back and bolstering the ailing Shaposhnikov.[45] So Zhukov departed for the Reserve Front while Shaposhnikov returned from West Theatre to become Chief of General Staff yet again.[46] Zhukov remained, however, a member of the *Stavka*.

The movement of von Schweppenburg's 24 Panzer Corps to the area of Starodub and Gomel and the destruction and dispersal of the divisions of

---

[44] Halder, *Kriegstagebuch*, Vol. 3, pp. 194–5. '*Ich habe ihm darauf erklärt, dass ich für einen solchen plötzlichen Umschlag ins Gegenteil kein Verständnis hätte*'; also Guderian, *Panzer Leader*, p. 202. The main opposition to the *Führer* plan came from Halder and von Bock, since von Brauchitsch appears to have already given up the argument. Guderian said that von Brauchitsch was against him and Guderian did in fact report to von Bock on 24 August that von Brauchitsch had met him with the words 'the *Führer* has decided and there is no point in bleating (*herummeckern ist zwecklos*)'.

[45] Zhukov, *Vospominaniya i Razmyshleniya*, pp. 309–12. Zhukov says that even on 29 July he forecast the move of 2 Panzer Group to the south instead of the continuation of the thrust on Moscow, this at a time when the Smolensk encirclement battle was still being fought. The reason he gave for appreciating that von Bock would break off his attack was the heavy casualties Army Group Centre was believed to have suffered. This part of his story is not convincing.

[46] Shaposhnikov was chief of staff to Timoshenko's West Theatre.

Kuznetsov's Central Front were regarded by the Kremlin as an effort to out-flank from the south Timoshenko's West Front and the Reserve Front, both of which lay one behind the other covering the western approaches to Moscow.[47] The Soviet High Command was hardly at fault for its failure to appreciate the illogical thought processes by which the *Führer* had sent his panzer troops off at tangents to the obvious and shortest axis to Moscow.[48] A new Bryansk Front under Eremenko had been hastily raised on 14 August of M. P. Petrov's 50 and Golubev's 13 Soviet Armies, taking under command the remnants of the destroyed Central Front, to cover the open Bryansk flank of the Moscow defences, and meanwhile, as Guderian's 2 Panzer Group, then consisting of von Schweppenburg's 24 and Lemelsen's 47 Panzer Corps, continued its march southwards, Bryansk Front and 43 Army of the Reserve Front were ordered at the end of August to prepare to attack Guderian's eastern flank by thrusting towards Roslavl and Starodub.

On 7 and 8 September Halder was at Headquarters Army Group South agreeing the details of the joint plan, the aim of which was to capture Kiev and destroy the enemy in the Kiev-Dnieper-Desna bend. Both Army Groups South and Centre were to take part. Guderian's 2 Panzer Group was to continue its southward thrust from Starodub to Romny and Priluki, while von Weichs's 2 Army from Army Group Centre moved southwards from Gomel covering Guderian's right flank. In Army Group South, von Stülpnagel's 17 Army would pin the Soviet forces on the lower Dnieper below Cherkasy and secure a bridgehead across the river near Kremenchug, from which von Kleist's 1 Panzer Group would drive northwards to meet Guderian's spearheads in the area of Romny and Lokhvitsa, these panzer thrusts cutting off about six Soviet armies to their west in the great bend of the river. Meanwhile von Reichenau's 6 German Army would move eastwards across the Dnieper and Desna into Kiev and commence the destruction of the great pocket of encircled troops.

On 19 August Potapov's 5 Soviet Army had already fallen back from Korosten to the Dnieper under heavy pressure from von Reichenau's 6 German Army, and the Soviet High Command ordered that Kiev and the line of the Dnieper be held at all costs.[49] Guderian's 2 Panzer Group and von Weichs's 2 German Army, thrusting southwards, had already crossed the Desna from the north, however, and gaps had appeared between V.I. Kuznetsov's 21 and Podlas's 40 Soviet Armies which could no longer hold the Ger-

---

[47] *Istoriya*, Vol. 2, p. 104, and *Kratkaya Istoriya*, p. 77, say that the Germans were expected to outflank the Soviet defences and then turn north-east towards Bryansk. The earlier *Vtoraya Morovaya Voina* by Platonov, p. 218, says that the possibility of an attack on Kirponos had been taken into account.

[48] Subsequent Soviet propaganda accounts explain that the reason for the German strategy had nothing to do with the vagaries of Hitler's political or economic aims, but was simply due to the German defeat suffered at Smolensk. Compare *Istoriya*, Vol. 2, p. 73.

[49] *Ibid*, p. 104.

[50] 40 Army had been formed by the transfer of formations from 26 and 37 Armies.

mans back.[50] 6 German Army, moving eastwards, crossed firstly the Dnieper and then the Desna at Oster and pinned Potapov's 5 and Vlasov's 37 Soviet Armies from the west. Eremenko had confidently assured Stalin that he would hold Guderian, but his Bryansk Front counter-offensive made by ten rifle divisions and tanks on the flank of 2 Panzer Group came to nothing, and its assaulting 13 Army under Golubev retreated eastwards with such speed that it lost contact with 40 and 21 Armies.[51] 21 Army, a reformed remnant from the old Central Front, was transferred from the Bryansk to the South-West Front.

By 9 September the execution of the German plans had already made good progress. Von Stülpnagel's 17 Army was across the Dnieper and von Kleist was preparing to move northwards to meet Guderian at a point in the Soviet rear nearly 150 miles to the east of Kiev. At Headquarters Soviet South-West Theatre, Budenny and Khrushchev at this time became aware of their danger. According to what is virtually the Khrushchev account of the events, South-West Theatre on 11 September asked Moscow for permission to withdraw eastwards from the Kiev bend and this request was categorically refused by Stalin. On 13 September Budenny was removed from his post but Khrushchev was permitted to remain, this in itself being a possible indicator that Khrushchev may not have been so loud or insistent in his requests for a withdrawal as he subsequently claimed. Timoshenko, rushed from one emergency to another, left his dual appointment as Commander-in-Chief West Theatre and West Front to replace Budenny as Commander-in-Chief South-West Theatre. Shaposhnikov, as Chief of Staff in Moscow, was apparently deaf to all warnings as to the impending catastrophe, and Khrushchev adds that on his (Khrushchev's) own responsibility on 16 September he sent Bagramyan, the theatre chief of staff, to Kirponos of South-West Front proposing what was in effect a withdrawal without orders. Kirponos declined Khrushchev's initiative and referred the matter direct to Moscow; but Shaposhnikov – and that meant Stalin – did not agree until 17 September that the Soviet troops should disengage and move off to the east, by which time it was already more than twenty-four hours too late, since Guderian and von Kleist had already joined forces at Lokhvitsa on 16 September, well in the Soviet rear.[52] If Timoshenko had in fact joined the South-West Theatre by this time, Khrushchev's story is unlikely to be entirely true, although there is evidence to suggest that Kirponos had already ordered a general withdrawal, only to have his order countermanded by higher authority, by either South-West Theatre or the Supreme Headquarters.[53]

[51] *Voenno Istoricheskii Zhurnal*, June 1965; Zhukov, *Vospominaniya i Razmyshleniya*, p. 319.

[52] The war diary entry for Army Group South on 16 September reads: *Die Einkesselung hat den Gegner zweifelsohne völlig überrascht, sodass er einen richtigen Führungsentschluss noch nicht gefasst hat. Kriegstagebuch Heeresgruppe Süd, II Teil, Band 4.*

[53] Platonov hints that Kirponos did not handle his troops well after they were encircled and Zhilin says that the withdrawal from the Dnieper was begun too late and was not well carried out. Only Khrushchev has amplified the story. *Istoriya*, Vol. 2, pp. 106–10. Potapov,

Between 16 and 26 September the encircled troops in what came to be called the great Kiev cauldron, originally about 130 miles in width and in depth, were broken up by the infantry of 2 and 6 German Armies. Kiev was taken on 20 September. 450,000 prisoners passed into German hands; 5, 21, 37 and 26 Armies were largely destroyed together with part of 40 and 38 Armies.[54] There is doubt as to the fate of Kirponos and his staff, particularly since it was the Soviet practice at that time to rescue high ranking commanders from encircled pockets, these officers being in effect ordered to desert their luckless troops. As it was, Kirponos, his chief of staff Tupikov, and the political member of the military council Burmistenko, were reported killed, presumably in attempting to escape German capture.[55]

The South-West Theatre was disbanded and a new South-West Front was formed under Timoshenko with Khrushchev as the political member. Originally this front commanded only elements of 40, 21 and 38 Armies and the new 6 Army transferred from South Front, to cover the huge hole torn in the defences in front of Kursk and Kharkov. Yet by throwing in remnants the Soviet Command made some form of continuous defensive line, so that when von Stülpnagel's 17 German Army began to advance again against Malinovsky's 6 Army, which had suffered comparatively little in the recent defeats, it was brought to a standstill near Poltava and Krasnograd.

On the Black Sea coast 11 German Army prepared both to take the Crimea and to drive the Soviet South Front eastwards. Von Schobert, the Commander of 11 German Army, had been killed when his light aircraft landed on a mine-field, and von Manstein, his replacement, deployed only E. Hansen's 54 Corps against the Crimea while the rest of his force, in company with 3 Rumanian Army, moved eastwards across the Dnieper along the shores of the Sea of Azov in pursuit of the withdrawing Soviet South Front. The Crimea was held by 51 Soviet Independent Army under the former Commander of the Baltic

---

the Commander of 5 Soviet Army, when a prisoner, told Guderian that Kirponos had given orders to withdraw from the Kiev bend, but that these orders were countermanded after the withdrawal had actually begun. *Panzer Leader*, p. 225. Zhukov has written his own version in which he has reproduced what are purported to be verbatim radio conversations between Stalin and Kirponos. It differs much from the Khrushchev account but Stalin still appears to be largely to blame, in that withdrawal was left too late. Zhukov, *Vospominaniya i Razmyshleniya*, pp. 317 and 321–3. Other very different accounts will undoubtedly appear in time.

[54] *Kriegstagebuch des OKW*, Vol. 1, p. 661, 26 September 1941. The count of prisoners and booty during the whole of the joint operation of Army Groups Centre and South from about the beginning of September amounted to 665,000 prisoners, 824 tanks, 3,018 guns and 418 anti-tank guns. According to *Kratkaya Istoriya*, p. 90, the South-West Front had 677,000 men before the Kiev operation, of which 150,500 escaped encirclement. Many others, it claims, broke out. Shtemenko on the other hand says that only one-third of the troops were encircled.

[55] It was once believed that Kirponos committed suicide. Compare Leonid Volynsky and Werth, *Russia at War*, p. 210. Current accounts say that he was killed by a shell. Potapov, so long a thorn in the German side (Shtemenko, *Generalnyi Shtab v Gody Voiny*, p. 32) survived German captivity and was eventually restored to rank and position.

North-West Front and the Central Front, F. I. Kuznetsov. The Perekop Isthmus, which was only five miles wide and gave entry into the Crimea, was defended by Red Army troops in great depth, use being made of the forty feet deep Tartar ditch, the many wadis and the Tartar Moslem graves, both as obstacles and observation posts. Elsewhere the terrain was devoid of cover, the Lazy Sea to the east of the isthmus being a brackish salt marsh difficult to wade and too shallow for stormboats. On this narrow front the German 54 Corps attack on 24 September failed for lack of strength. Von Manstein was unable to reinforce this corps, however, as the remainder of 11 Army and 3 Rumanian Army were making very slow progress further to the east against the Soviet South Front, which on 26 September had mounted a vigorous, although limited, counter-offensive against part of 3 Rumanian Army. The Rumanians were in danger of disintegration and had to be buttressed by detachments of German mountain troops and the *SS Leibstandarte*.

Von Kleist's 1 Panzer Group, designated on 6 October 1 Panzer Army, fresh from its Kiev victory, was directed southwards into the rear of the Soviet South Front, which on 5 October came under a new commander, Cherevichenko, and which then consisted of 12, 18 and 9 Armies.[56] From his concentration area in Dnepropetrovsk, von Kleist crossed the Samara River and moved southwards behind Cherevichenko's troops, joining up on 6 October with 11 Army near Osipenko on the Black Sea coast. Part of 18 and 9 Armies was encircled and the Germans took no fewer than 106,000 prisoners. Among the dead was A. K. Smirnov the Commander of 18 Army.[57] 1 Panzer Army then turned eastwards and advanced rapidly almost unopposed along the coast of the Azov Sea in the direction of Rostov, the gateway to the Caucasus, while the German 17 and 6 Armies moved up on its left between Stalino and Kharkov.

The fighting in the South and East Ukraine took a different form from that described earlier in the West Ukraine by von Choltitz and Malaparte. In the East Ukraine the Germans had a number of motorized formations and the advantage of superior mobility, and the Red Army troops were so low in morale that on the open steppe great numbers surrendered without a fight. The German units, however, were weakened by casualties and were hardly fit for sustained combat. Even the devout and staunch supporters of National Socialism in the *SS Leibstandarte* began to ponder the strategic aims of the war, noting that they could drive for hours without ever seeing a German soldier, and the vastness and emptiness of the land had a depressing and lowering effect on even the most hardbitten of the troops. Their leaders were weighed down by tiredness and the fact that they could see no end to the task.[58]

[56] Cherevichenko, formerly of 9 Army, replaced Ryabyshev as Commander of South Front. Zaporozhets and Antonov remaining as political member and chief of staff. The commanders of 12, 18 and 9 Armies were Koroteev, A. K. Smirnov and Kharitonov.

[57] *Kriegstagebuch des OKW*, Vol. 1, p. 693, 11 October 1941.

[58] This even reached von Brauchitsch's ears, Halder, *Kriegstagebuch*, Vol. 3, p. 191, 21 August 1941. '*Übermüdet, belastet von der Unendlichkeit der Aufgabe*'. Compare also Meyer, *Panzergrenadiere*, pp. 135 and 145.

After the victory near Osipenko, von Manstein's 11 Army, together with a Rumanian mountain corps, returned to the Perekop Isthmus leading into the Crimea where, at the end of October, it mounted a deliberate attack to overcome the stubborn defence of F. I. Kuznetsov's 51 Independent Army, which was being heavily reinforced by troops removed from Odessa.[59] On 22 October the Soviet High Command had set up a unified joint service Crimea Command under Vice-Admiral Levchenko, with Lieutenant-General Batov as his deputy, but this last minute reorganization was too late to have any effect on the course of operations, and may indeed have complicated control. 51 Army fought none the worse, however, since the terrain and fighting were of a type in which the Russians excelled.[60]

The Red Army defenders of the open and flat Perekop Isthmus occupied all prominent ground, which was both heavily mined and wired, and covered all the flat and bare approaches with well directed machine-gun and artillery fire. Delayed action mines were used, together with wooden box mines designed to escape the German electronic detectors, and the defences were thickened up by remote controlled flame throwers, turreted emplacements and dug-in tanks. The Red Air Force dominated the air space and, as von Manstein had no tanks, he relied on armoured assault guns to support his infantry. The fire fight was so intense that all German guns, horses and vehicles had to be dug into the marshy, waterlogged ground. In these unfavourable conditions E. Hansen's 54 Corps was called upon to attack once more, while von Salmuth's 30 Corps was held in reserve ready to exploit a breakthrough. The attacks were carried out in persistent October rain which turned the ground into a sea of mud. Sometimes there was fog which lasted for days. The fighting was of the bitterest. There seemed to be no end to the Soviet earthworks, many of which had been constructed by civilian labour, and even electrically detonated sea mines had been built in the defences.[61] The German divisions were at the end of their tether and at least one divisional commander asked for the engagement to be broken off. Encouraged and driven on by the determined von Manstein, however, after a ten-day battle in which it took over 100,000 prisoners and 700 guns, 11 Army broke its way into the Crimean Peninsula on 28 October, only to become bogged down on a two-sided front before Sevastopol in the west, and the Kerch Peninsula in the east.[62] Since the Soviet forces had command of the sea and the air, it appeared that the Red Army might hold out indefinitely.

Von Manstein noted with some alarm the rapidity with which the German fighting strength was ebbing.[63] Von Choltitz, still at the head of his Oldenburg

---

[59] Odessa had been evacuated on 16 October and its 80,000 troops and many of its 350,000 civilians had been transported by sea to assist in the defence of the Crimea.

[60] A Soviet Army was designated independent only when it came directly under the Soviet High Command.

[61] Von Metzsch, *Die Geschichte der 22. Infanterie-Division*, pp. 29–31.

[62] *Kriegstagebuch des OKW*, Vol. 1, pp. 737 and 742, 1 and 5 November 1941.

[63] Von Manstein, *Lost Victories*, pp. 217–21; also von Choltitz, *Un Soldat parmi des Soldats*, pp. 116–20,

regiment, said that for the first time in the war he was having problems with the new reinforcements, whose training was quite inadequate for battle. For this, quite rightly, he blamed the reinforcement and forwarding system.[64] Orders were no longer carried out automatically as a drill, or in response to a word or a look, and it was even difficult to get some of his men out of cover when under fire.

On the Leningrad Front the Germans were to have less success than in the Ukraine. The Finns had driven Gerasimov's 23 Army on the Karelian Isthmus north of Leningrad, back to the old 1939 Soviet-Finnish border. In the Karelo-Finnish region between Lakes Ladoga and Onega the Soviet 7 Army, commanded first by Gorelenko and later by Meretskov, although supported by the Ladoga naval flotilla, was forced back to the line of the river Svir, where the front was stabilized until 1944.

By the autumn the Germans were still deployed on the line of the River Luga with von Küchler's 18 German Army stretching from the area of Narva near the Baltic to Lake Ilmen, roughly in the position reached by Hoepner and von Manstein in July, while Busch's 16 German Army covered the area due south from Lake Ilmen along the line of the River Lovat. Against the German 18 Army, M. M. Popov's North Front was responsible for the defence of the approaches to Leningrad between the Baltic and Lake Ilmen, while the Soviet North-West Front held the sector south of Lake Ilmen opposite 16 German Army. On 23 August there came yet another of the frequent Soviet reorganizations of the higher echelons of command, when Voroshilov's North-West Theatre was disbanded and Popov's North Front was split into the Leningrad Front (Popov remaining as its Commander-in-Chief with Zhdanov as his political member) and the Karelian Front under Frolov. Kurochkin took over the North-West Front from Sobennikov. The Leningrad, Karelian and North-West Fronts were made directly responsible to the High Command in Moscow.[65] From 11 September to 8 October the command of Leningrad Front was assumed temporarily by Zhukov, an indication of the situation of crisis which existed at that time.[66]

Von Leeb then attempted to cut off Leningrad from the east and join with the Finns on the Svir. From the middle of August, von Küchler's 18 Army, reinforced by Rudolf Schmidt's 39 Panzer Corps and von Richthofen's 8 Air Corps, both of which, in accordance with Hitler's orders, had been removed from Army Group Centre, drove back Akimov's 48 Soviet Army to the north of Lake Ilmen. Novgorod was taken, and then on 25 August Chudovo, from whence the right wing of 18 Army crossed the Volkhov and started to fight its

[64] *Ibid*, pp. 124–5.

[65] *Istoriya*, Vol. 2, p. 89.

[66] Voroshilov relieved Popov temporarily before Zhukov's arrival. After a short stay in Moscow he returned to become the head of the War Council for the defence of Leningrad. The Leningrad Front military council on 12 September 1941 consisted of Zhukov, Zhdanov (political member), A. A. Kuznetsov (political member and Secretary of the Leningrad Party), Admiral Isakov and Khozin (chief of staff).

way forward towards Tikhvin, across difficult wooded and marshy country against stiffening resistance, a further two Soviet armies, Klykov's 52 and Marshal Kulik's 54, having been added to Yakovlev's 4 and Akimov's 48 Armies already deployed in the area.[67] On the extreme left flank Estonia was finally cleared of 8 Soviet Army by 4 September and the whole of the southern coast of the Gulf of Finland was occupied by the Germans, except for the small bridgehead at Oranienbaum opposite Kronstadt. Von Leeb's most promising success came, however, in the centre, where by mid September the Germans were almost at the outskirts of Leningrad, reaching the shore of Lake Ladoga near Schlüsselburg, and so cutting all road and rail communication between Leningrad and the Soviet Union.

Meanwhile Busch's 16 Army, reinforced by 57 Panzer Corps from Hoth's 3 Panzer Group, attacked the Red Army concentration of troops to the south of Lake Ilmen, consisting of 2, 34 and 27 Soviet Armies lying between Staraya Russa and Kholm, and advanced in the direction of the Valdai Hills to the lakeland areas between Demyansk and Ostashkov. Demyansk fell on 8 September.

The Germans had taken Smolensk on the direct road to Moscow by 17 July and the Smolensk pocket was cleared by 6 August. Not until 23 August were the final and firm orders issued as to the next phase of the campaign. On 5 September, just thirteen days after taking this decision, which had sent the tired and worn armoured formations over 400 miles to the north and south, Hitler decided that the aim was already achieved in Leningrad, which, as he said, could henceforth remain as a secondary theatre. The main task now, the *Führer* reasoned, was to go straight for Moscow, destroying the Soviet West Front before the onset of the bad weather. The attacking forces were to be concentrated and ready 'in the next eight to ten days'. Army Group North was to be ordered to give up its panzer formations, that is to say Hoth's 3 and part of Hoepner's 4 Panzer Groups, and von Richthofen's 8 Air Corps. Guderian's 2 Panzer Group and von Weichs's 2 Army were to be returned from the Ukraine to join in the destruction of the Soviet West Front covering Moscow.[68]

When Hitler took the earlier decision to disperse his forces over an area from the Baltic to the Black Sea, a thousand miles in extent, the reason he gave was that Leningrad, the Crimea, the Ukraine, the Donets Basin and the Caucasian oil all had priority over Moscow and the destruction of the Red Army troops covering the capital. By 5 September, however, when he changed his mind again, the redeployed German troops had hardly commenced the fight for their far-flung objectives in the north and the south. On 5 September

[67] Marshal Kulik was relieved by Fedyuninsky and degraded in rank.

[68] Halder, *Kriegstagebuch*, Vol. 3, p. 215, 5 September 1941. Halder wrote the word 'impossible' against the eight- to ten-day warning order, and having discussed the matter with Paulus and Heusinger, decided that no offensive could be made against Moscow before the end of September. According to Hitler's plan 16 Army was also to take part in the offensive from the area of the Valdai Hills. Halder commented 'the affair is completely unclear'.

Kiev and most of East and Central Ukraine was still in Red Army hands and the Guderian–von Kleist envelopment of the Kiev river bend had not yet begun. The Crimea and the Caucasus had not even been threatened by German troops. In the north the movement on Demyansk and Tikhvin was only just gaining in momentum and the decision to remove the fire power of the air corps and the panzer troops from Army Group North was to result in operations being brought to a halt at a time when they had hardly yet begun.

It is impossible to analyse the process of reason in Hitler's mind. That he dispersed the German effort against the advice of Halder and von Bock is known. The strategic advantages of cutting off Leningrad and of effecting a junction with the Finns were questionable, nor could any great success be expected in committing panzer formations to the wooded marshlands in the area of Lake Ilmen.[69] In the open steppe in the Ukraine, Guderian's 2 Panzer Group was to play a major part in the destruction of the Red Army forces in the Kiev bend, but was then too far to the south to be recalled in time to fill a fitting role in the advance on Moscow. Hitler had shown himself to be opposed to the daring deep tactical or strategic panzer thrusts, and preferred closer objectives, advancing uniformly by bounds across European Russia with a north-south line devoid of salients or exposed flanks. As it was, he over-exaggerated the importance of the Red Army troops on the flanks of Army Group Centre, troops which were in any event hardly mobile, and, as Halder said, altered his strategy merely to counter the tactics of the enemy. The strategic and economic importance of the Crimea, the Donets Basin and the Caucasus was irrelevant to the argument for or against advancing on Moscow, since these areas were still in Soviet hands when the Germans turned back to the Smolensk-Moscow road. Hitler believed in July that the war was almost won, but even this false assumption was unlikely to have any bearing on the failure to attack Timoshenko's West Front during July or August. Whatever the motive in the *Führer*'s logic, the effect was that Army Group Centre had remained virtually passive within two hundred miles of Moscow from the beginning of August to the first week in October.[70]

[69] The Baltic remained a German lake, controlled by the *Luftwaffe* and German Navy until the end of the war in spite of the fact that the naval bases at Leningrad and Kronstadt had not been eliminated.

[70] Some of the German infantry divisions on the Smolensk sector, to their own amazement, had actually been taken out of the line to assist collecting in the harvest. Compare Baumann, *Die 35. Infanterie-Division im Zweiten Weltkrieg*, pp. 100–2.

CHAPTER TEN

Finland

When the Russo-German war began, von Falkenhorst's headquarters had been at Rovaniemi in Central Finland since 15 June, and German divisions had taken up their positions two weeks before. The USSR chose to disregard the affirmation of Finnish neutrality, and attacked Finland by bombing raids on Helsinki and Turku and other towns in the south. Thereupon the Finnish Government declared war on the Soviet Union.

In the Far North Dietl's mountain corps had occupied the area of Petsamo and begun its thrust towards Murmansk only sixty miles away, which was covered by only two rifle divisions of Frolov's 14 Soviet Army. Dietl's advance was unattended by success. The Soviet Northern Fleet was active and landed Red Army troops in the German rear. German photographic reconnaissance had been inadequate and the German maps were of so little use that one of the charted tracks earmarked as the main movement and supply route was found to be non-existent. The inhospitable terrain was difficult and even the most experienced of the mountain troops could cover no more than half a mile an hour, and guns and ammunition had to be brought up by pack animal. German air support was not available. The first battle encounters had a sobering effect on Dietl's troops, since all the advantages lay with the Red Army, which had strong artillery and plentiful supplies of ammunition, air superiority and good road and sea communications. Defence from well prepared positions was the type of fighting for which Red Army troops had been trained and for which at that time they were best suited. Lacking fire power, Dietl was unable to dislodge them. A third Soviet division, thrown together from sailors and locally conscripted civilians, soon appeared and Dietl's advance, which had covered only fifteen miles, came to a final halt.[1]

On 1 July Feige's 36 German Corps began its thrust from near Salla towards Kandalaksha over rough and wooded country with one Finnish and two German divisions and a few tanks. Forest fires were widespread and the troops made very little progress, the *SS Brigade Nord* showing itself to be

---

[1] Hess, *Eismeerfront 1941*, pp. 111–8; also Erfurth, *Der Finnische Krieg 1941–1944*, pp. 48–50.

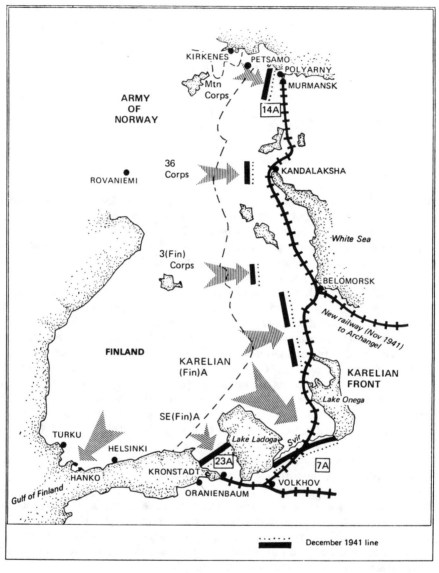

OPERATIONS IN FINLAND
June–December 1941

inexperienced and unsteady.[2] On the other hand 6 Finnish Division, although it had very little artillery, appeared unimpressed by the tough resistance put up by the two divisions of 42 Soviet Rifle Corps. On 16 July when von Falkenhorst appeared at 36 Corps Headquarters to know the reason for the lack of progress, a staff officer making the presentation explained that the Finns and Russians were superior to the German soldier who had lost his instinct for forest fighting, and it is said that this stung von Falkenhorst to ask whether he was to tell the *Führer* that 36 Corps could not attack because it was degenerate (*entartet*).[3] Two days later Buschenhagen visited Siilasvuo's 3 Finnish Corps sector further to the south and was astonished at the rate of progress. The Finns, operating in regimental groups, had broken into the Red Army rear and, advancing forty miles, had built a road behind them. In spite of the vigorous performance of the Finnish troops it became obvious that the Murmansk railway was not going to be reached, particularly since Frolov's 14 Soviet Army was making good use of its lateral rail and sea communications to rush reinforcements to Kandalaksha. On 25 August Siilasvuo informed von Falkenhorst that he would not be able to reach his objectives and he asked for reinforcements, specifying that he required a fresh Finnish division accustomed to forest warfare. The whole of the *SS Brigade Nord* was eventually transferred to Siilasvuo, who wanted to use it not as a formation but as a number of detached groups under the command of his Finnish regimental colonels, since he believed that the SS troops were inadequately trained to operate on their own, and he had his first disagreement with von Falkenhorst who insisted that the German troops should be used as a formation. Siilasvuo found that the SS were at this time unable to hold Soviet attacks without Finnish help. In spite of these difficulties, by 27 August two Soviet divisions were defeated near Kairala.

The relationship between von Falkenhorst, on the one side, and Mannerheim and Siilasvuo on the other, did not improve throughout the summer. Von Falkenhorst asked repeatedly for Finns to undertake tasks which would have been difficult for German troops and the request he made in October was abruptly refused. In the Finnish view the Germans were asking too much and giving too little and the *Luftwaffe* in particular had not always lived up to its promises. At the beginning of November Finnish troops had achieved further successes on the 3 Corps sector, but 3 Finnish Division, in carrying out a German planned attack near Kiestinki, lost a third of its officers.[4] Thereafter Siilasvuo declined to make any further move and this was to be the pattern of operations in Finland throughout the whole war, the Finns undertaking such operations as suited them.

[2] Halder, *Kriegstagebuch*, Vol. 3, p. 45, 5 July 1941. *SS Kampfgruppe Nord* was shortly afterwards expanded into a division.

[3] *Kriegstagebuch, 36 Corps, No. 3 22102, 3*, pp. 110–1. In addition 36 Corps was to complain of the difficulty in using tanks and artillery in the forest, although in fact the Russians used both.

[4] Erfurth, *Der Finnische Krieg 1941–1944*, pp. 73–4.

German strategy in North Finland, like that in Western Russia and the Ukraine, lacked purposeful direction. Hitler's concern with the defence of the Petsamo mine area was justifiable but, taking into account the resources available, the correctness of the decision to cut the Murmansk railway was open to doubt since war supplies could also be imported through Archangel, a summer port which could be operated throughout the winter provided that ice breakers were used. As it was, Hitler attempted to cover Petsamo and the thin waist of Finland around Salla, at the same time launching three widely separated thrusts eastwards. All three failed, whereas one might have been successful. Moreover the relevance of the campaign in North Finland to the war as a whole was questionable.

Finland was an Armed Forces High Command (OKW) theatre for which Jodl was responsible to the *Führer*. Operations south of Leningrad and the River Svir were the direct concern of Halder and von Brauchitsch and the Army High Command (OKH). Von Falkenhorst commanded the troops in Norway as well as in Finland, but he did not command his supporting 5 Air Fleet, which had its strength dissipated by orders of Göring's OKL on numerous tasks unconnected with the war against the Soviet Union. Nor did von Falkenhorst really exercise complete control over the Finnish corps and divisions which had been allocated to him, since their commanders were in close touch with Mannerheim and, when faced with action which was believed to be contrary to Finland's interests, Finnish troops ceased to march. Nor were the Germans necessarily given the true reasons for the lack of co-operation. A joint operation in Finland was found to be a very different matter from that in the Ukraine where the Rumanian could be commanded, sometimes with arrogance, and always carried out German orders. Elsewhere German troops had been used to buttress their allies, but in North and Central Finland Finnish troops were used to bolster German formations and, chastening as this was, the Germans were soon made to realize it. The Finnish Army and the civilian population had hoped that Germany would overcome the USSR in a lightning war and they were to feel disillusionment with the German performance.[5] In the south-east, Mannerheim was later to return 163 Brandenburg Division to German command rather than hand over Finnish troops, because he felt that the Brandenburgers' capabilities were not up to the demands of the theatre.[6] Yet the German troops were probably in no way inferior to their compatriots who had astounded the world as they swept across Russia; but they were defeated by the peculiar conditions of the theatre, the long hours of daylight and the difficulty with sleep, the rough primitive country with its lakes and swamps and swarming mosquitoes, the endless dark and melancholy forests, which had a cumulative frightening and depressing effect on all who stayed in them for any length of time.[7] The Finns, however,

[5] *Ibid*, p. 81.
[6] Mannerheim, *Memoirs*, pp. 429, 443 and 448.
[7] Erfurth, *Der Finnische Krieg 1941–1944*, pp. 48 and 61.

appeared impervious to this atmosphere, as to a lesser extent were the North Russian and Siberian troops who opposed them. Few tanks were used and in the forest areas where there was little visibility air power and artillery were of relatively minor importance, and transport and baggage were a hindrance. Much of the success went to the fleet-footed and daring infantrymen.

An offer was made from Berlin to give the overall command of all German troops in Finland to Mannerheim but this was refused, since the Finnish Commander-in-Chief was disinclined to put himself in a position where he would in effect be receiving through Jodl the orders of the *Führer*.[8] The position of Finland was a difficult and anomalous one, since it strove to remain independent of Germany by insisting that its war with the Soviet Union was its own concern, and for this reason it declined to join any form of coalition with Germany. It succeeded to the extent that it was spared occupation and was able before the end of the war to negotiate its own peace terms with the USSR; but its insistence on being known as Germany's brother-in-arms rather than its ally was a pretence, since the unfortunate little nation, which numbered no more than four million, was forced to depend on Germany for the supply of arms and equipment and for the import of grain.

It has already been explained how, at the outbreak of war, Leningrad Military District had become the North Front, commanded by Lieutenant-General M. M. Popov. Popov had only three field armies, 14 Army commanded by Frolov in the far north in the Kola Peninsula between Murmansk and Belomorsk, 7 Army commanded by Gorelenko in Ladogan Karelia roughly between Lakes Ladoga and Onega, and 23 Army, commanded firstly by Pshennikov and then by Gerasimov, in the Karelian Isthmus north of Leningrad. On 10 July North Front was coupled to Sobennikov's North-West Front, which was falling back from the Baltic States towards Leningrad, as part of the North-West Theatre under Voroshilov.[9] Six weeks later on 23 August North-West Theatre ceased to exist, although the North-West Front continued in being to the south-east of Leningrad in the area of the Volkhov and Lake Ilmen. North Front was split into Popov's Leningrad Front and Frolov's Karelian Front, the latter covering the area from Murmansk to Lake Onega. Popov was responsible for the defence of Leningrad and the Karelian Isthmus between the Gulf of Finland and Lake Ladoga, and had 23 Army facing the Finns to the north and three armies to the south engaging the German Army Group North. In addition 7 Army (later to become 7 Independent Army) was to the east of Lake Ladoga. On 5 September Popov relinquished the Leningrad Front to Voroshilov, who was succeeded temporarily from 11 September to 8 October by Zhukov.[10]

The main Finnish forces were in the south-east under Mannerheim, deployed in two main armies, the Finnish Karelian Army under Heinrichs, the former

[8] Mannerheim, *Memoirs*, pp. 422–3.
[9] *Istoriya*, Vol. 2, p. 62.
[10] *Ibid*, Vol. 2, pp. 89, 210 and 212.

Chief of Staff, of Talvela's 6 and Hägglund's 7 Corps with the equivalent of about six divisions, and what was sometimes known as the Finnish South-East Army made up of Laatikainen's 2 and Oesch's 4 Corps of eight divisions. Part of 163 German Infantry Division was in reserve. The Red Army troops opposing the Finns consisted of six rifle divisions of 23 Army and four of 7 Army, and were therefore outnumbered by nearly two to one. On 10 July Heinrichs attacked Gorelenko's 7 Army north-east of Lake Ladoga and drove it back, advancing over sixty miles in a week. Although fighting was very heavy in places Gorelenko appears to have been prepared to give ground as he leap-frogged his divisions back. In August Heinrichs went over to the defensive, having regained and crossed the 1939 Finnish frontier. Meanwhile 7 Soviet Army had been reinforced from 23 Army and its command was taken over by Meretskov. On 31 July Gerasimov's 23 Army was attacked in its turn west of Lake Ladoga, and during the second half of August a full offensive developed so that in less than three weeks Finnish troops retook all of the former Finnish territory held in 1939. Since the Finns were less than thirty miles from the outskirts of Leningrad, Keitel, at Hitler's direction, wrote to Mannerheim on 22 August asking him to continue the advance on both land isthmuses to the east and west of Lake Ladoga, requesting that the Finns should cross the Svir, so linking up with von Leeb in the area between that river and Tikhvin.

By then, however, Mannerheim and his Finnish commanders were showing a distinct lack of enthusiasm. Casualties had not been light. The strength of the Finnish armed forces could not be sustained by the economy and population, and Mannerheim intended to release some of his troops back to civilian life. There was, moreover, a distinct undercurrent of opinion in some Finnish quarters that the Finnish troops had done their share of the fighting and that they would welcome seeing the Germans take a hand.[11] Although politically and economically dependent on Germany, militarily the Finns were impervious to German pressures. One of Mannerheim's replies to German urging to join up with von Leeb was that he could not do so before 163 German Infantry Division took Suvilakhti. Since this division had made heavy weather of every offensive operation it had undertaken and was by then thoroughly bogged down, the Germans had to curb their impatience. Mannerheim eventually advanced to the Svir but there he remained, not more than eighty miles from Tikhvin, and no persuasion or urging would make him move further to the south.

In November 1941 the German command was reorganized, and the control of the German forces in Northern and Central Finland was taken over by a newly formed Army of Lapland under Dietl, a Bavarian popular with German and Finn alike, who enjoyed the confidence of Hitler.[12] In June 1942 the Army of Lapland was to be redesignated as 20 Mountain Army.

[11] Erfurth, *Der Finnische Krieg 1941–1944*, pp. 73 and 74.
[12] Hubatsch, *Hitlers Weisungen für die Kriegführung*, p. 167, *Durchführungsbestimmungen Nr. 2 zur Weisung 37*.

Dietl was to note the Finnish attitude and was to cast doubt on the reliability of the Finnish Army. While readily admitting that the Finn was an excellent soldier in forest fighting and in mountain warfare, he thought that the Finn underestimated the Russian. Dietl criticized the Finn for avoiding pitched battles and gave his view that in the event of a determined Soviet offensive the Finn's mentality and training were such that he would not be able to hold. Although this last opinion was quite erroneous, Dietl was correct in his view that the Finns were going to considerable lengths to avoid the spilling of Finnish blood. About German blood they had less qualms, and the German liaison officer with 3 Finnish Corps was to report that the German troops were being allotted more than their share of the major attacks. Although the relationship between German and Finnish troops was good, there was some tension between commanders and the Germans found their brothers-in-arms not a little difficult. The Finns complained that the Germans held on to Finnish troops and would not return them. The sturdy Siilasvuo went his own way, largely independent of the Army of Lapland. On 23 May 1942 Dietl was to try, rather tactlessly, to limit Siilasvuo's authority over his own corps, in that he was instructed not to withdraw troops from the line at will. Siilasvuo thereupon the very next day ordered all Finnish battalions out of the German sector of the front, and peremptorily told the Germans to return within seventy-two hours all Finnish horses and wagons on loan. If this had been done all German formations would have been stranded. Only Dietl's personal pleading caused Siilasvuo to reverse his decision.[13]

From 1942 onwards the Finnish theatre of war stagnated. In April of that year 14 Soviet Army attacked towards Petsamo with naval support but the offensive came to nothing and thereafter, although fighting flared up from time to time, the activity was of a local character and the battle lines were little changed.

The entry of Finland into the war was an embarrassment to both the USSR and to Britain. Finland could not be disregarded by the Soviet Union since it threatened Leningrad and tied down Red Army troops. There was a great fund of goodwill towards Finland in Britain and in the United States, and the entry of Finland into the war was regarded with dismay by both, since they were engaged in trying to support the Soviet Union which was reeling under the German invasion. Von Ribbentrop put pressure on the Finns to break diplomatic relations with the British and they did so, and at the end of July the British bombed German-occupied but Finnish-owned Petsamo. In August the Soviet Union expressed through the United States a willingness to make peace with Finland, even to the extent of offering territorial concessions, but this fell on deaf ears in Helsinki where it was expected that the USSR would soon be knocked out of the war. In September and October 1941 both Britain and the United States warned Finland against advancing beyond its 1939

---

[13] *Kriegstagebuch, AOK Lappland, Band 1*, 22–25 May 1942, pp. 2–3.

borders, the United States in particular being concerned in case the Murmansk railway should be cut by the Finns.[14] Finland declared itself indifferent to the warnings, but did not in fact advance far beyond her 1939 borders. This Finnish diplomatic activity with the United States caused von Ribbentrop some uneasiness, and he put pressure on Helsinki to become a signatory on 25 November to the Anti-Comintern Pact, in exchange for economic assistance. The signing of the Pact was given great prominence by the Germans for its propaganda and political value, and this stung Stalin in his turn to put pressure on Churchill to make Britain's attitude clear towards Finland. The British Government informed the Finns that unless they ceased operations and withdrew from all active participation in the war by 5 December Britain would declare war on Finland. No reply was received by that date and war was declared on 6 December.[15]

[14] The Finns had in fact already cut the Murmansk–Volkhov railway in August but Soviet railway engineers were at work building a new loop line connecting Murmansk with Archangel and Moscow. This was opened in November.

[15] Churchill, Vol. 3, The Grand Alliance, pp. 465, 467–74; Mannerheim, Memoirs, pp. 434–8.

CHAPTER ELEVEN

Mainly Political

On the evening of 22 June 1941, the day the Soviet Union was attacked, Churchill had broadcast from London a speech in which he foresaw the war against the USSR as a prelude to the attempted invasion of the British Isles and he identified Britain's cause with that of the Soviet Union.[1] Parts of this broadcast were republished in *Pravda* and, although there was no official Soviet response to Churchill, the speech was received with satisfaction by both the Soviet Government and its peoples.[2] Overnight Cripps was raised to a position of favour and at the Soviet suggestion a joint Anglo-Soviet declaration was signed on 12 July pledging mutual aid and no separate terms with the common enemy. A week after the invasion a British military mission, with General Macfarlane at its head, arrived in Moscow.

In the United States, Roosevelt and Cordell Hull, the Secretary of State, took much the same view as Churchill and were eager to assist the USSR. This readiness was by no means general among the officials of the State Department, or among the United States' politicians and public, where the Soviet Union was regarded as the anti-religious oppressor of the Finns, the Balts, the Poles and the Rumanians. The new war did not necessarily wash away the sins of the men in the Kremlin, and the USSR continued to be viewed with great distrust by the United States population of East European stock; to this distrust was to be added the hostility of a large number of citizens of German origin. Many of those Americans who were not influenced by European ties believed that communism was insidious and dangerous, and that the Soviet Union was the enemy of capitalism and of all religious and political freedom. These feelings were adequately expressed by Harry S. Truman and others who, although determined enemies of Fascism, believed that no trust could be placed in the pledged word not only of Hitlerite Germany but also of Stalin's Soviet Union. Subsequent events were to bear out the correctness of their views.[3]

---

[1] Churchill, Vol. 3, *The Grand Alliance*, p. 331.
[2] Compare Werth, who was in Moscow at the time. Werth, *Russia at War*, p. 161.
[3] These critics took a much more realistic view of Stalin and of the aims and methods of communism than did Roosevelt and many members of his administration.

As there was no reaction from Stalin to the BBC broadcast, after a long and what Churchill called an oppressive silence, the British Prime Minister was forced to take the next step in a personal communication to the dictator dated 7 July. Stalin, who had for the past two years been a loyal ally and supporter of Hitler, affording even port facilities from which German naval raiders might destroy British shipping, suffered from none of the shyness attributed to him by Churchill, when he suggested in his reply that the British should create immediately a second front in Northern France and Norway.[4] Within weeks these suggestions became abrupt demands, later to be coupled with insults, Stalin becoming convinced by degrees that the Soviet Union was fighting in defence of the British Isles, rather than for its own existence and the safety of the men who lived in the Kremlin.[5] From the beginning of the alliance Anglo-Soviet relations were anything but good. Stalin, who respected both force and guile, regarded generosity and truth as evidence of weakness. Churchill's Government and the British Foreign Office at that time adopted a policy of tolerant understanding not far removed from appeasement in their day to day dealings with the USSR. Nor were they always helped by the partisan attitude of the British Ambassador in Moscow.[6] Churchill's actions were, of course, largely governed by fear in case the Soviet Union should drop out of the war and, acting in what he believed to be the interest of the nation and the free world, he tolerated insult and calumny and made available to the Soviet Union war supplies which were badly needed in Britain.

On 26 June Sumner Welles had announced that the Neutrality Act would not be invoked against the USSR. The Soviet reaction was immediate when on 8 July, Oumansky, the Soviet Ambassador in Washington, submitted to the State Department a list of material requirements, staggering in its size and costing almost two billion dollars, including as a single item 3,000 fighter and 3,000 bomber aircraft.[7] There was some reluctance in Washington to commit

---

[4] Churchill, Vol. 3, *The Grand Alliance*, p. 342. The naval facilities near Murmansk were given up when the Germans occupied Norway. *Nazi-Soviet Relations 1939–41*, p. 185.

[5] Churchill, Vol. 3, *The Grand Alliance*, p. 347. On 15 September 1941 as Guderian's and von Kleist's panzer groups closed behind South-West Front, Stalin proposed that the British should land twenty-five divisions at Archangel or in the Ukraine. That he should have invited foreign troops to fight on Russian soil was out of keeping with accepted Soviet policy and can only be attributed to the sense of crisis and fright which must have existed in Moscow at that time.

[6] *Ibid*, p. 410. Golikov, the Head of the Soviet Military Missions in London and Washington was to be given every facility and courtesy by the British, yet Macfarlane in Moscow was given the shabby treatment reserved for all foreign attachés and was told and shown little. Martel, who headed the Mission in 1943, condemns the diffident, appeasing approach advised by the British Foreign Office, and tells of the vigorous, blunt and heated talk he used when faced by evasion from Malinovsky. Martel, *The Russian Outlook*, pp. 46–8. Churchill, when speaking of Martel's difficulties, was to write 'they (the Russians) treat all our people like dogs'. Churchill, Vol. 5, *Closing the Ring*, p. 620.

[7] Feis, *Churchill, Roosevelt, Stalin*, pp. 10–11.

the United States to an immense aid programme in case the Soviet Union should be quickly defeated and the material fall into German hands, and it was felt that the political and military situation inside the Soviet Union needed to be investigated since, in the opinion of the United States Secretaries of War and of the Navy, the USSR was unlikely to stave off defeat for more than three months.[8] The intelligence appreciations and reports received in Washington were contradictory and conflicting. The United States Military Attaché in Moscow, Major Ivan Yeaton, was critical of the Red Army and pessimistic of its chances of survival and the British Chiefs of Staff in London considered that the Germans would be in Moscow in six weeks.[9] On the other hand Cripps, Macfarlane and the United States Ambassador Steinhardt were more optimistic, although, as Steinhardt admitted at the time, it was very difficult for any foreigner in Moscow to get any idea of what was going on in the Soviet Union.[10] Moreover it was impossible to obtain any information as to Soviet plans or resources or to get any picture of what had already happened. To attempt to clarify the situation Roosevelt decided to send his own personal representative in Britain, Harry Hopkins, on from London to Moscow in order to discuss these matters with Stalin.

In the course of these conversations with Hopkins in the Kremlin on 29 and 30 July, Stalin, using all the friendliness and gruff bonhomie at his command, gave all the appearance of frankness and honesty. Hopkins was to learn that Stalin was the fountainhead of all information and authority and that his staff feared to discuss even trivial matters in his absence. Stalin was at some pains at this first meeting to court the President's representative, an attitude which was to change when United States materials were found to be readily available and the danger of defeat receded. He was under no illusions as to the industrial and latent military power of the United States and he pressed Hopkins that America should enter the war. The mere declaration of war, he thought, would be enough. The might of Germany was such that it would be very difficult for Britain and Russia combined to overcome it and he went so far as to say that he would welcome American troops on Soviet soil. He gave the number of Red Army divisions deployed at the front on the outbreak of war as 180 of which sixty were tank divisions, and this total had been increased in July to 260. By May 1942 Stalin expected to have 350 divisions in the field. Stalin said that at the beginning of the war the Soviet Union had 24,000 tanks and a tank production figure of one thousand tanks a month. His fighter aircraft force, according to him, had a strength greater than 7,000 and his aircraft production was about 1,800 warplanes a month.[11]

Stalin was, of course, talking for effect and for a purpose. He was a man who rarely gave interviews or used words unnecessarily, and at this particular time

[8] *Ibid*, p. 10.
[9] Woodward, *British Foreign Policy*, p. 150 and footnote.
[10] Sherwood, *The White House Papers*, Vol. 1, p. 328.
[11] *Ibid*, pp. 328–43.

he desperately wanted United States economic and military help. Yet subsequent events and intelligence have tended to confirm that in revealing these Soviet figures Stalin was probably speaking the truth. On other matters, however, his statements, particularly those relating to the German forces, were inaccurate. He much exaggerated the enemy strength, crediting the Germans with seventy tank and motorized divisions, and he made many other assertions which were equally untrue. This exaggeration may have been deliberate, in order to stress the need for help, or it may have been based on guesswork to cover the great gap caused by the breakdown of the Red Army tactical intelligence organization. Whatever he said, and whatever the accuracy of his statements, Stalin much impressed Hopkins, and through him convinced Roosevelt that the Soviet Union would not suffer an early defeat.

By the early autumn United States intelligence agencies were inclined to the view that the Soviet Union was likely to remain in the war for the foreseeable future, although no prediction could be made as to the outcome of the struggle. Following the Hopkins visit, Roosevelt and Churchill sent a joint supply mission to Moscow in order to discuss Soviet needs, Averell Harriman, who was then in charge of war assistance affairs in London, representing the Americans, and Lord Beaverbrook being Churchill's nominee. The method by which the Kremlin conducted this meeting was to come as a surprise and a shock to the Western delegation, although it was in fact in accordance with an established communist pattern. At the first meeting on 28 September there was some cordiality. Stalin gave a general review of the military situation at the battle front, which told the visitors little and was somewhat misleading, since the dictator glossed over the real cause of the Soviet defeat by pretending that it was entirely due to the strength of German armour.[12] On the second day of the meeting the atmosphere had changed completely and the visitors were made to sense the pervading suspicion and hostility. Nothing was achieved, Stalin showing little interest in the proceedings except insultingly to infer that the Soviet Union was bearing the whole of the burden of the war, and that the proffered aid was of little consequence. The next day Stalin performed the Pavlovian *volte face*, which was to be the common feature of many meetings with foreign statesmen and their envoys. He was all smiles, geniality and co-operation, and agreement was speedily reached.[13] Hospitality followed, so

---

[12] Stalin greatly exaggerated the panzer strength but much underestimated the offensive power of German infantry. Other arguments he used were sound, if not new, and included the well-known factors of time and space and his belief that the Germans had not enough troops to carry on a successful offensive war and at the same time guard their extended lines of communication.

[13] According to Sherwood, Beaverbrook returned from Russia a vociferous advocate of the Second Front in the West, and was to describe Stalin as a kindly man: Sherwood, *The White House Papers*, Vol. 1, pp. 389–92. See also Gwyer, *Grand Strategy*, Vol. 3, pp. 155–61; and Churchill, Vol. 3, *The Grand Alliance*, pp. 415–7. The British and American delegation had apparently hoped to get a full picture of Soviet production and future requirements.

that the envoys went off in an aura of goodwill and vodka, tolerably satisfied with themselves in that they had achieved any sort of agreement at all, even though this represented hardly more than readiness by the Kremlin to accept assistance.[14] This meeting was to demonstrate that the Kremlin made a practice of demanding, but rarely gave in exchange, and that anything given to the USSR was accepted as its right and its due. Up to then the United States had always insisted on justification or evidence of need before supplying war materials, but Stalin made it clear that such information would not be forthcoming. The Western democracies were later to find that they would be responsible for transporting these war materials and supplies to Soviet ports at their risk. The sudden change of face exhibited at the meetings probably had a double purpose, in that it tended to confuse and weaken the resolution of the foreign participants and, at the same time, sent them off in good humour, the better to deny the propaganda reports being put out at that time by the Berlin radio to the effect that the talks had broken down. The meeting had some appearances of an exercise in blackmail, in that it gave the dictator an indication of what the West was prepared to pay him as the price for his alliance.

Another significant aspect of Soviet diplomacy was the emphasis placed by Moscow on European post-war frontiers and on the demarcation of power and interest, this at a time when its armies had been destroyed in Belorussia and the Ukraine, and the Germans were about to advance on Moscow. Britain, still a power of the first rank with enormous resources at its disposal, had taken the place of Germany as the only European state likely in the post-war world to challenge the Soviet Union's ambitions on the Continent. Moscow began to press London to recognize its 1941 frontiers, which included its ill-gotten gains in Bessarabia, North Bukovina, the Baltic States, and part of Finland and Poland.[15] On the question of the National Polish State, Stalin was forced to change his ground. Regarding the formation of a new Poland as a matter of vital interest to the USSR, he offered the London Polish Government-in-Exile a home on Soviet territory, presumably in order, as later events were to show,

---

No information of any value was received. Churchill had included in the British delegation General Ismay 'with authority to discuss any (strategic) plans which the Russians might put forward', but the only words offered by Stalin to Ismay were by way of advice that the time had come for Great Britain to maintain in peace time a large army as well as a navy. With that particular pearl Churchill had to be satisfied.

[14] Feis, *Churchill, Roosevelt, Stalin*, p. 16. Werth was present at the time of the dispersal of the meeting and noted the gratified expressions of the Western delegation. *Russia at War*, pp. 290–1.

[15] In the autumn Stalin was pressing for a visit by Generals Wavell and Paget to discuss 'war aims and post-war policies' and was putting heavy pressure on Cripps for the same purpose. Eden, *The Reckoning*, pp. 281–2; see also Stalin's reproach to Churchill of 8 November 1941, Churchill, Vol. 3, *The Grand Alliance*, p. 469; The Baltic States and Finland, Vol. 4, *The Hinge of Fate*, pp. 292–4.

that he might curb, or if necessary, stifle it.[16] In 1941 he was already planning the disposal of the territories of Eastern Germany and the securing of the Soviet position in Central Europe, and he wanted to strike some form of bargain with Churchill by an agreement and secret protocol dividing Europe into spheres of influence, exactly as he had done with Germany in August 1939.[17] United States views on Europe he tended to regard as interference, but the fact that Churchill was unwilling to act without first consulting Washington was not lost on him.[18] Churchill, haunted by a fear, since proved baseless, that Stalin's pressure for recognition of his territorial gains was the price for carrying on the war, was tempted to come to some agreement with him, but Roosevelt and Hull were resolutely opposed to making Stalin what was in effect payment in advance. Throughout the war Roosevelt declined to become enmeshed in European problems, firmly believing that political frontiers and kindred problems should be resolved at the peace conferences after the war.[19]

In the early stages of the war the wide gap between the Soviet and the Anglo-American war aims had already become apparent. Churchill, who prided himself on being an anti-Bolshevist, had at this time an optimistic view of the aims of Stalin and his Kremlin associates. Although he had denied that he was bowing down in the House of Rimmon in allying himself with the Soviet Union, he had added the telling words, that he had only one purpose, the destruction of Hitler.[20] This laudable intent developed, however, into an oversimplified aim. Stalin and his government were no less determined on the destruction of Hitler and Fascism, but even in the first few months of the struggle they had already projected themselves into a post-war Europe in order to win not only the war, but the peace which was to follow. To Churchill, the only enemy was at Calais, and the Russians were far away. Whether at this time he ever seriously envisaged a post-war Europe where one evil megalomaniac, the dictator of a mighty and menacing state, would be replaced by another, is open to doubt.[21] Roosevelt's attitudes and policies were somewhat contradictory. His determination in the early part of the war not to pay

[16] Feis, *Churchill, Roosevelt, Stalin*, p. 31; Eden, *The Reckoning*, pp. 271–3. A Polish-Soviet agreement was signed on 30 July 1941 whereby Polish formations were to be raised on Soviet soil from Polish prisoners of war in Soviet hands. Many of these were equipped by the British and under General Anders were removed to the British command in Palestine and Italy. The other contingent under General Berling was armed and equipped by the Soviet Union and was eventually to appear in Belorussia and Poland.

[17] Feis, *Churchill, Roosevelt, Stalin*, p. 26; Eden, *The Reckoning*, p. 289. Stalin wanted his 1941 frontiers assured, the Polish frontier to be roughly on the Curzon line, with Soviet bases in Rumania and Finland. These were modest proposals in comparison with what he eventually acquired. In return, he said, he would not object to British bases in Norway and Denmark.

[18] Eden, *The Reckoning*, p. 300.

[19] Feis, *Churchill, Roosevelt, Stalin*, p. 62.

[20] Churchill, Vol. 3, *The Grand Alliance*, p. 331.

[21] Whether Churchill at this time understood the true nature of Stalin's Soviet Union appears doubtful, as Churchill's earlier attitude towards Moscow in 1938 and 1939 tend to illustrate.

Stalin with the territories of others did him credit, but he and his Secretary of State had no distinct policy with regard to Central and Eastern Europe, and in basing his design for post-war Europe on the trust that Stalin would vacate occupied territories in deference to the decisions or wishes of a peace conference, he misjudged Stalin and the aims and methods of the Soviet Union. Roosevelt appeared to have lacked an understanding of the close relationship and interdependence of foreign policy and military strategy, and he was inclined to abdicate his political responsibilities in waging war to his chiefs of staff and commanders in the field. Bold and far-sighted in his measures to combat Nazi Germany, and a constant advocate of the basic freedoms, he saw nothing incongruous in the Soviet Union being a founder member of the organization which was to become the United Nations. The idea of royalty was distasteful to him and he was inclined to be prejudiced against any state which did not call itself a republic. He disliked imperialism and colonialism, at least of the West European type, and he was very sensitive to any charge that he was using United States resources to buttress the British Empire. Like all great men, Roosevelt was an egotist with great faith in his own powers of personality and persuasion to win over a hostile Stalin, a faith which was in the event misplaced.

Stalin was to put heavy pressure on the British to declare war on Finland, Rumania and Hungary, although Britain had no quarrel with these countries, and a declaration of war could in any event have had little effect on the course of operations, except in so far as it would further isolate Finland.[22] On the other hand, no Soviet declaration of war against Japan was to follow the Japanese attack against Britain in the Pacific at the end of the year. Eden, the British Foreign Minister, was to arrive in Moscow at that time in order, amongst other things, to take up this very point. The meetings took the usual play-acting pattern. On 16 December, the first day, Stalin tried to press Eden for discussions on post-war Europe, including the detail of the frontiers of the USSR and the dismemberment of Germany. Little progress was made but the atmosphere was friendly. On the second day Eden was due for the customary shock. Stalin was irritable and entirely unreasonable, while Molotov was at his most unhelpful, and the whole atmosphere was tense and frigid. On 19 December, the third day of the talks, the usual Third Act was played out, and to Eden's surprise he was faced by a much more genial dictator.[23] During the course of the talks on this last evening Eden raised the matter of the

[22] Germany, Finland, Italy, Hungary, Slovakia and Rumania were of course at war with the Soviet Union. Spain, although not at war, was to provide a single formation, the Blue Division, for service in North Russia. Other foreign elements were recruited, usually by the SS, from France, the Netherlands and occupied Scandinavia for service against the USSR. Their numbers and importance were very minor.

[23] Eden has suggested that his deliberately outspoken comments made in the so-called privacy of his quarters (and presumably relayed by microphone through the NKVD) may have been responsible for the sudden change of Soviet attitude. This is possible but doubtful, since Cripps continued to get a gruelling time from Molotov on this third day. Eden, *The Reckoning*, pp. 297-9.

Soviet Union's participation in the war against Japan in the coming spring, but Stalin merely begged to be excused for the moment on the grounds that the feelings of the Soviet people would be against such a war.[24] The Eden talks were completed by the usual last minute lavish hospitality.

In Rastenburg the *Führer*, not without good cause, was convinced that no collaboration was possible between the Anglo-Americans and the Soviet Union, since he regarded their systems to be diametrically opposed, and believed that the long term aim of the Kremlin was the overthrow of capitalism, wherever it might exist. He confidently awaited the breakdown of the coalition and expected to profit from it. Great Britain and the United States, for their part, were determined that their alliance with the Soviet Union should not be undermined by German propaganda, or by Soviet mistrust and provocation.

When Germany invaded the Soviet Union Japan had been given no hint of the intention, and when the Japanese naval bombers attacked the United States base at Pearl Harbour, Hitler was as greatly surprised as the Americans. When von Ribbentrop and the *Führer* had talked to Matsuoka earlier in the year, they were intent on concentrating Japanese energies and ambitions against the British in the Pacific and the Far East, and it must be assumed that their assurances of help in the event of interference by the United States or the Soviet Union were meant to remove fears or misgivings in Tokyo. They had no wish that the Japanese should attack the USSR or the United States. Shortly after the outbreak of the Russo-German War, however, von Ribbentrop and the Army High Command (OKH) appear to have become interested in drawing the Japanese into an attack against the Soviet Union's maritime provinces in the Far East. On 10 July Ott, the German Ambassador in Tokyo, was told by von Ribbentrop to promote such a design, and the Japanese seemed to have given the matter some consideration. The day before, on 9 July, Halder had talked to Matzky, the Director of Military Intelligence, and had noted briefly that the intention with regard to Japan was still not clear, in that 'after having been urged by us to go for Singapore, just recently it has been incited against Russia'.[25]

On 4 August the Japanese Military Attaché in Berlin, Lieutenant-General Banzai, visited Matzky and it was noted in Kinzel's records that Banzai mentioned the possibility that Japan, notwithstanding difficulties and other commitments, 'might adhere to the Tripartite Pact and attack Russia'. In the event of such an attack by the Kwantung Army from Manchukuo, a minimum of sixteen divisions would be used, organized into four armies.[26] Thereafter

---

[24] *Ibid*, p. 301.

[25] Halder, *Kriegstagebuch*, Vol. 3, p. 56 and footnote 2. The words used by Halder were '*Japans Absicht immer noch unklar. Nachdem Japan zunächst von uns auf Singapur eingestellt war, ist es nun neuerdings gegen Russland angeheizt worden*'. It is not evident whether Halder meant (as written) 'Japan's intention is not clear' or more likely, in view of von Ribbentrop's activity and the sentence which follows 'Intention with regard to Japan is not clear'.

[26] *OKH Gen St d H O Qu IV Nr. 275/41 g. Kdos Chef* of 5 August 1941.

the matter seems to have been dropped, according to Warlimont because the confidence of the Germans was such, that when Japan was thought to have made a mention of assistance the offer was rejected.[27] On 19 August, General Ott was informed by the Japanese that Japan had no immediate intention of entering the war.

This was not known, however, in the Kremlin, and after it had been attacked by Germany the Soviet Union had good reason to fear Japanese intervention. On 23 June the Soviet Ambassador in Tokyo asked the Japanese Foreign Minister whether Japan intended to observe its Neutrality Agreement and the reply he received was imprecise. The Soviet Union continued to feel itself menaced by the Kwantung Army and feared to reduce its forces there until after the United States had entered the war in December 1941, although some thinning out did occur at the time of the battle for Moscow. In August 1941 there was some apprehension that Japan might make difficulties over the shipping of United States supplies to the Soviet Union through Vladivostok, through which it was planned to import 220,000 tons a month of foodstuffs, transported mainly in American shipping. When Japan did enter the war against the United States in December this supply channel was not cut, however, due to the fact that 120 United States Pacific freighters were transferred to the Soviet flag.[28]

There can be little profit in detailed speculation as to the likely effects of an attack on the Soviet Union by Japan. Japan at that time was a first class military power. Since Japanese army and naval aircraft were of a greatly superior quality to those of the Red Air Force, Soviet air power in the Far East would have been rapidly destroyed. On the other hand, the Japanese tank arm was relatively weak and sixteen infantry divisions hardly constituted a sufficiently strong force with which to have advanced far overland into Siberia. At the worst, an intervention of this sort might have lost the Soviet Union North Sakhalin, Vladivostok, the industrialized maritime provinces in the Far East and half the imports of Western aid. If, on the other hand, Japan had directed all its efforts against the USSR rather than against the United States and Britain, and if it had entered the war in the summer as a close ally of Germany,

[27] Warlimont, *Inside Hitler's Headquarters*, p. 45. A German reaction to Japanese help according to Warlimont was 'We don't need anyone just to strip the corpses'.

[28] The only other routes by which Western aid could reach the USSR were through the ports of Murmansk or Archangel in the Arctic. Of these two, only Murmansk was ice-free throughout the year; but it and its railway were threatened by German forces in Finland. Archangel, the main northern port, with an estimated handling capacity of 270,000 tons a month, was kept open by ice-breakers throughout the winter. In August 1941 a pro-German Iran had been jointly occupied by British and Red Army troops in order to combat the activities of the German community, which appeared to threaten the rear of the Caucasus and the oil producing areas of the British occupied Middle East. The Iran overland route into the Soviet Union was yet to be developed by United States engineers from very modest beginnings, until eventually it became as important as the North Atlantic sea route. The Pacific imports through Vladivostok in the end totalled 47 per cent of the whole of Western aid received by the Soviet Union.

it is probable that the whole of the Soviet Union would have been speedily overrun. Japan's power, however, was limited without the import of certain strategic materials and in particular oil which could only be obtained from the Americas, the Netherlands East Indies, Burma or the British Middle East. Japan could not have entered into a full scale war against the USSR without first ensuring the benevolent neutrality of Washington, since it relied on the Pacific waterways for survival. It is inconceivable that the American conscience, already in sympathy with the desperate struggles of China, would have aided Japan in this way. Economically and militarily the fate of Japan was to be decided by the United States of America.

CHAPTER TWELVE

Vyazma and the Autumn Mud

When the Germans went to war in the East only 400,000 reinforcements were held by Fromm's Replacement Army, and fuel reserves were limited to two to three months supply. Of the twenty-eight divisions originally held as a reserve by the Army High Command, all but three had been committed to the fighting in the summer. Although only fractional of those suffered by the Red Army, German casualties had been far from light and in the ten weeks fighting up to 26 August totalled 440,000, of which 94,000 had been killed.[1] By the end of August only 217,000 men had been allotted as reinforcements, but there was inevitably a time lag before these reached their units, since many of them had to make their own way forward of the railhead by march route. Except in the Baltic area where sea transport could be used, fuel replenishment was to grow increasingly difficult because the shortage of captured Soviet railway stock, particularly of bulk fuel tankers, meant that little use could be made of the railway until it had been converted from the broad to the standard European gauge. German tank strength had been reduced by casualties and breakdown to less than fifty per cent of establishment and there was difficulty in providing replacement vehicle assemblies to make good the heavy engine wear caused by dust, sand and long mileage. Motor vehicles, too, had been overtaxed and there was a shortage of about thirty per cent of establishment.[2] The overall position regarding the supply of tanks and motor vehicles was made even more critical by Hitler's decision to give priority in equipment to the raising of new divisions rather than in providing replacement material to existing formations.[3]

However difficult the shortages, quoted in round figures, appeared to von Brauchitsch or to the commanders of the German army groups, the position on the ground, particularly in the marching infantry formations, was in

---

[1] Halder, *Kriegstagebuch*, Vol. 3, p. 220. On 1 September Halder had noted that the necessary reinforcements could only be found if twelve divisions were disbanded, and on 15 August he estimated that nearly 200 officers were becoming casualties each day and that 16,000 replacements would be needed to take the East Front through to the end of the year. 5,000 only were available.

[2] *Ibid*, pp. 202–3.

[3] Guderian, *Panzer Leader*, p. 190.

reality much worse, since the wear and tear on men, horses and equipment could not be measured in statistical returns. Shortages and a lowering of standards gave some indication of the future change in Germany's fortunes. At the end of August Guderian was complaining of the exhaustion of the panzer troops and their limited combat strength, giving the example of Munzel's 6 Panzer Regiment which, he said, was temporarily reduced on 14 September to a strength of ten battleworthy tanks out of an establishment of about one hundred and fifty. Tank crew losses had been light so far, but motorized infantry companies had been reduced to fifty men each and the lack of combat experience and toughness of the replacements had already been noted. There was no winter clothing, and there was a shortage of boots, socks and shirts. Bread was becoming an irregular ration issue and there was no anti-freeze for vehicle radiators.[4] This was the condition of the favoured and well-supplied panzer and motorized troops. The marching infantry fared far worse.[5]

22 Infantry Division was not the only formation to note that difficulties were arising in battle with the infantry replacements, that all ranks were no longer part of a team, and that their action was no longer intuitive, all contingencies having to be covered by orders. The experiences of 98 Franconian-Sudeten Infantry Division were similar. When commenting upon the fanatical Field-Marshal von Reichenau's order that every junior leader should write above his mapboard 'pursuit without rest', their divisional commander, who was also their historian and diarist, noted the ominous signs. Long rows of motor vehicles were unable to move in the mud, the infantry were exhausted, and dozens of horses were dying every day in harness. The general service horse wagons with their rubber tyres and ball-bearing mounted wheels broke up, so unsuited were they to the abominable tracks. The locally impressed *panje* carts were apparently indestructible. Good German, Hungarian and Irish horses died from fatigue and lack of fodder, but the scrubby native Russian ponies survived, eating anything, even birch twigs and the thatched roofs of the farm huts. Signallers and dispatch riders started to go missing in the woods and a rest period for the infantry was synonymous with a new task, the combing of forest scrub for the hidden enemy. The division was frequently and ruefully to recall, as a gift to the partisans, the hundred tons of ammuni-

---

[4] *Ibid*, pp. 219, 227 and 230.

[5] At the beginning of September personnel deficiencies were as follows:

In fourteen divisions	more than 4,000
In forty divisions	more than 3,000
In thirty divisions	more than 2,000
In fifty-eight divisions	less than 2,000

The tank fighting strength (as a percentage of establishment) stood at:

	End August	End September
1 Panzer Group	53	70–80
2 Panzer Group	25	50
3 Panzer Group	41	70–80
4 Panzer Group	70	100

Mueller-Hillebrand, *Das Heer*, Vol. 3, Chapter 10.

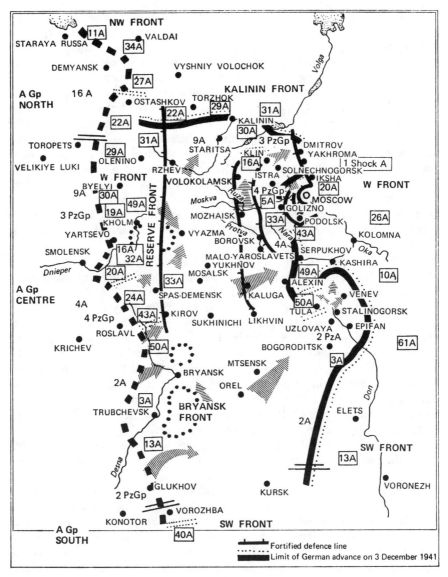

THE ADVANCE ON MOSCOW
October–December 1941

G

tion which it handed over for safe keeping to a Russian elder at Novy Glybov, since no transport was available to move it. Rifle companies had only thirty to forty of the original men left and from 31 July to 10 August a single infantry regiment lost thirty-seven officers and 1,200 men.[6] The division was 3,800 men under strength on 27 September when the first reinforcements arrived, and of these one battalion received thirty-seven men and reported the replacement as a drop in the ocean. A Coburg artillery battery received sixteen men and drily noted 'apparently no more men left in Coburg'.[7] A regimental commander wrote in his diary on 13 September that in this boundless country there was enough land to be conquered. The simple infantryman took a different view, however, from that of the motorized troops since every mile behind him had been covered by his own personal effort. This could be understood only by the marching infantry, long weeks of muck, rain, heat and cold, poorly and irregularly fed, attacking through heavy artillery fire, tired and lousy, with no protection but his own skin and no motive power other than his own courage and will.[8]

On 14 September 98 Infantry Division was off again, leaving the Pripet Marshes and von Reichenau's 6 Army of Army Group South behind it, on its long march north-east following in Guderian's wake to Army Group Centre, ready for the thrust on Moscow. At first the men were relieved to be away from the mud and the marshes, and the sight of a motor vehicle actually moving made them feel quite European again. Their elation was moderated, however, by the twenty-five mile a day marches over the deep sandy tracks, the difficulty of which defied description, and the sobering sight of the many foundering horses and the frequent jettisoning of vehicle loads. It was still only September, but soon there was incessant rain and a cold north-east wind, and any night shelter, squalid and bug-ridden though it usually was, had all been occupied by motorized troops before the worn-out infantry arrived. Anything during the day was bearable provided a night's shelter and warmth was to be had, but when this was denied, the troops plumbed the depths of wretchedness. Gradually the most simple necessities were missing, razor blades, soap, tooth paste, shoe materials, needles and thread. On 23 September came the first hoar frost. The rain, cold and lack of rest increased the sickness, which in normal events would have admitted the men to hospital. With the lack of transport all, even the sick, had to march and there could be no question of leaving anyone behind as the area was notorious for banditry. One day followed like another and the great chain of men moved forward in the slashing rain, obedient and silent with nothing to be heard but the snorting of horses and the creak of the wagons and the everlasting roar of the wind in the firs on either side of the track.[9]

[6] Gareis, *Kampf und Ende der 98. Infanterie-Division*, p. 125.
[7] *Ibid*, p. 128.
[8] *Ibid*., p. 126.
[9] *Ibid*, pp. 127–30.

Nor did the SS, the darling of the Party, fare any better. The reconnaissance battalion of the *Leibstandarte Adolf Hitler* received on 17 September six officers and ninety-five men as reinforcements. During the whole of the autumn twenty-six officers, forty-two non-commissioned officers and 450 men became casualties and the replacement figure totalled eleven officers and 186 men of which only one was a non-commissioned officer. The sickness rate mounted, due to dysentery, jaundice and diphtheria, so that before long, without official authority or cognizance, the battalion started to recruit Kuban Cossacks to fill its depleted ranks.[10] SS casualties, even under the heaviest of Soviet artillery bombardments, were negligible the SS commander was to report caustically, so thin were the troops on the ground.

The extended front and the lack of mobile German reserves resulted in the commitment of troops, particularly infantry, holding ground against steadily increasing enemy pressure. At the end of August the Red Army had its first local successes, when several divisions broke into 16 German Army area to the south of Lake Ilmen; further to the south, on 5 September, the Germans were forced to give up the tiny Elnya salient and fall back in order to straighten the line and save casualties.[11] During the course of the rest of the month of September the Soviet enemy showed himself to be increasingly active against Army Groups North and Centre. His air force became more aggressive and the Red Army appeared to have no lack of artillery or tanks, the T34 causing the Germans anxiety since the 37 mm anti-tank gun was ineffective against it. Nowhere was there any sign of the promised Soviet collapse. By 26 September the German casualty figures had risen to 534,000, about fifteen per cent of the total German establishment on the East Front.[12] As usual, the infantry bore the greatest casualties. However, except in 2 Panzer Group, the German tank availability had improved and had risen to seventy per cent of establishment.[13] The delay in mounting the offensive against Moscow had brought other administrative advantages, slight though these were, since the conversion of gauge of the railway line had proceeded from Gomel to Roslavl, from Minsk to Smolensk and through Vitebsk to Toropets and had brought some improvement in the supply position. These advantages had to be weighed against the drain of German strength through casualties caused by holding ground, and the great expenditure of artillery and mortar ammunition which defensive battles always entailed.

These field deficiencies in men and equipment were, however, only sympto-

[10] Meyer, *Panzergrenadiere*, pp. 119, 135 and 145–51. Long before this date all formations, again without authority, had started to recruit *Hiwis*, Soviet volunteers, usually from prisoners of war, to undertake B echelon and baggage work as labour, transport drivers and grooms.

[11] On 28 August von Bock told Halder that if the Soviet enemy kept up his attacks Army Group Centre (which had lost most of its panzer formations to north and south) could no longer hold its positions. Halder, *Kriegstagebuch*, Vol. 3, p. 202.

[12] *Ibid*, p. 260.

[13] *Ibid*, p. 262.

matic of Germany's economic *malaise*. On 9 October Wagner, the Quarter-master-General, outlined to Halder the main supply deficiencies, which were food, manpower and vehicle fuels. All theatres needed 90,000 tons of vehicle fuel a month for day to day maintenance, without covering special operations or training, and Wagner was 3,000 tons deficient of this figure. Stocks of rubber were expected to be exhausted by the following March.[14] Experience at Kiev had shown that a German division was needed for every 20,000 Soviet prisoners for guard, sorting and transporting duties, and although the enemy had left enormous stocks of good quality arms and equipment on the battlefield, it was impossible to find German labour to arrange and supervise the collection.[15]

Having, as he thought, safeguarded his flanks by the clearing operations in the areas of Kiev, Velikiye Luki, Staraya Russa and Demyansk, Hitler issued on 6 September the order for the thrust on Moscow in Directive 35, which operation was later to be known as *Typhoon*.[16] In Central European Russia the weather usually broke in late September or early October, the heavy rains slowing down or stopping all movement until the ground was hardened by the frosts of October and November. The first snow to settle usually fell at the beginning of December. Short periods of thaw might occur at any time during the winter and these turned the ground and tracks into a sea of slush and mud. For this reason the mounting and completion of the Moscow operation had become a race against time.

The main planning for *Typhoon* was done between the Army High Command (OKH) and von Bock's Army Group Centre, all plans being subjected to Hitler's approval. The German intelligence appreciation of the Soviet troop dispositions before Moscow had much improved in its accuracy, but was still imperfect, and believed that the Red Army order of battle consisted of Timoshenko's West Front of seven armies deployed forward and Eremenko's Bryansk Front of two armies to its south.[17] Nothing was known of the Soviet armies in the rear, and the strength of West Front was estimated variously as between seventy and one hundred divisions, in the event this estimate being not very far from the actual Soviet strength. The hurriedly constructed lines of defences right back to the capital were easily identifiable from the air.

Von Bock's task was to destroy the Soviet forces before advancing on Moscow, and the basis of the German plan was an attack in the centre on a general line Smolensk-Moscow with a double panzer envelopment, the pincers meeting at Vyazma about eighty miles in the Red Army rear, a repetition in outline of the pincer movement formerly carried out at Minsk. The northern pincer was to consist of the combination of Strauss's 9 Army with

---

[14] This particular shortage was overcome by synthetic buna, the production of which by 1942 was sufficient for both civilian and military needs.

[15] Halder, *Kriegstagebuch*, Vol. 3, p. 276.

[16] Hubatsch, *Hitlers Weisungen für die Kriegführung*, pp. 150–3. The OKH order *Typhoon* was issued on 19 September.

[17] Compare maps in *Istoriya*, Vol. 2, pp. 72 and 232 with the *OKH Lage Ost* Map of 25 August 1941.

Hoth's 3 Panzer Group under command, the same grouping which had before formed the northern thrust on Minsk and Smolensk.[18] It comprised twenty-three divisions of which three were panzer and two motorized. The southern enveloping pincer was formed by von Kluge's 4 Army and, since Guderian was still far to the south, Hoepner's 4 Panzer Group which, together with all but one of the panzer corps, had been removed from Army Group North. 4 Army had 4 Panzer Group under its command and consisted of twenty-two divisions, of which five were panzer and two motorized.[19] Once the Vyazma pocket had been closed 9 Army and 3 Panzer Group were to move north-east so that their main axis lay on the line Byelyi-Rzhev-Kalinin, so encircling Moscow from the north and cutting Soviet communications to the North-West Front and the Leningrad area. 4 German Army with 4 Panzer Group was to move from Roslavl to a line Vyazma-Yukhnov and Moscow.

Guderian's 2 Panzer Group, shortly to be redesignated as 2 Panzer Army, had been recalled to the north with von Weichs's 2 Army from the Ukraine, but time would not permit the concentration of this force in the vital area of Smolensk. It was decided for this reason that Guderian's force consisting of three panzer and two infantry corps, in all fifteen and a half divisions of which five were panzer and four motorized infantry, should attack from the area of Glukhov in a north-easterly direction on Orel and Tula to the south of Moscow. As part of the northwards movement, Guderian's left flank was to curl round behind Eremenko's Bryansk Front. On Guderian's left, von Weichs's 2 Army of eight divisions formed the link between 2 Panzer Army and 4 Army, and was to move eastwards to join Guderian's left flank at Bryansk and complete the envelopment of the three armies of Eremenko's Bryansk Front.[20] Guderian was to start the offensive on 30 September and this was to be taken up by the other armies two days later.

Hoepner had taken over a panzer corps near Roslavl formerly belonging to Guderian, who had been given in exchange a panzer corps removed from von Kleist's 1 Panzer Group. In all, von Rundstedt's Army Group South gave up to von Bock's Army Group Centre nine divisions, of which two were panzer and two motorized, and was to regret the loss of these troops when it came under heavy Soviet counter-offensives only eight weeks later. Von Leeb's Army Group North had been obliged to release five panzer and two motorized divisions together with von Richthofen's 8 Air Corps, and was thereafter to lose the initiative near Leningrad and in the north-east.[21] These

[18] Hoth was relieved by Reinhardt as Commander of 3 Panzer Group on 8 October while the Vyazma battle was in progress. Hoth replaced von Stülpnagel as Commander of 17 Army.

[19] All order of battle details from *OKH Kriegsgliederung* 2 October 1941.

[20] Eremenko had in fact three armies and not two as the Germans supposed.

[21] The interchange of corps and divisions was confusing and can only have led to a loss of efficiency. Hoth had already lost both his original corps, 39 and 57 Panzer Corps (with the exception of two divisions kept in 9 Army Reserve) to Army Group North. For the thrust on Vyazma he eventually received Hoepner's two corps, 41 and 56 Panzer, brought down from the north. Guderian's 2 Panzer Group (on 6 October redesignated 2 Panzer Army) was to

formation losses were not compensated by the promised reinforcement of an infantry division from France, the Spanish Blue Division and two parachute regiments.[22] Von Leeb's protests at the removal of his troops before their tasks were completed were brushed aside, since the Army High Command (OKH) appeared to be convinced that the thrust on Moscow would relieve all enemy pressure in the area of Army Group North; in fact the Army Group Centre offensive increased this Soviet pressure against von Leeb, since the Kremlin made frantic efforts to save Moscow by mounting counter-offensives in the north as well as in the Ukraine.

Once again the success of the new German offensive hung by a thread. By thinning out Army Groups North and South, the strength of von Bock's Army Group Centre had been raised to seventy divisions, of which fourteen were panzer and eight were motorized infantry. Air support was to be provided by Kesselring's 2 Air Fleet of 2 and 8 Air Corps, made up of thirty-two air groups, in all about 1,000 of the 2,400 aircraft then available to the East Front. The Soviet strength covering Moscow was estimated by German intelligence at the end of September to be as high as eighty infantry divisions, eleven tank formations, either divisions or brigades, and nine cavalry divisions. The total Red Army Air Force on the Russo-German front was put at only 1,100 aircraft. The Army Group Centre frontage extended over 400 miles and von Bock held less than two divisions as his own army group reserve. The Army High Command (OKH) held no reserve at all.

Moscow had suffered its first air attack on the night of 22 July and this was repeated on the two subsequent nights. The Germans had by then reached Smolensk and at that time the Kremlin lived in daily expectation of the final thrust on Moscow. The Soviet Government had made frantic efforts to build two great linear earthwork systems west of Moscow using civil labour, more than three-quarters of which was female. The forward of these defensive lines, known as the Vyazma line, ran from an area about thirty miles east of Ostashkov near the Valdai Hills in the north, forward of Vyazma to beyond Kirov in the south, being about 200 miles in length. The rearward Mozhaisk line was about eighty miles to the west of Moscow and ran from Volokolamsk to Likhvin and was about 160 miles in extent. A further four semicircular defence lines ringed Moscow from the west. The defence of the approaches

---

consist of 48 Panzer Corps (taken over from von Kleist's 1 Panzer Group) and 24 and 47 Panzer Corps. Since Guderian was too far to the south to form the south pincer of the attack on Vyazma, Hoepner's Headquarters 4 Panzer Group was brought to the south of Hoth to take over a concentration of armour near Roslavl, this including 46 Panzer Corps (taken over from Guderian), 57 and 40 Panzer Corps. The detail of the movement of the divisions within the corps was even more complicated. Of it Hoth was to say that it really was most difficult to make head or tail of all this going to and fro. Hoth, *Panzeroperationen*, p. 131.

[22] Army Group North retained 39 Panzer Corps and Army Group South kept 3 and 14 Panzer Corps.

to Moscow was entrusted to West Theatre, with Marshal Timoshenko as its Commander-in-Chief until mid September, when he was removed to the Ukraine. West Theatre stretched from its boundary with North-West Front at Ostashkov in the north, to Vorozhba at the junction with South-West Front in the south, having a frontage of about 450 miles from north to south, and being made up of three separate fronts. Of these the principal was West Front, commanded by Konev, deployed sixty miles to the west of Vyazma and stretching from the Ostashkov Lakes to Elnya, about forty miles south-east of Smolensk. West Front consisted of six Soviet armies.[23] The Reserve Front, which was temporarily once again under the command of Budenny, who had recently been removed from South-West Theatre, consisted of a further six armies and was echeloned in depth behind Konev's West Front roughly on the Vyazma line, from the source of the Volga near Ostashkov in the north, to Elnya in the south.[24] The Reserve Front was not in contact with the enemy except on the extreme left where two of its formations, Rakutin's 24 and Sobennikov's 43 Armies, formed the link between the West and the Bryansk Fronts. Budenny was not long to be entrusted with an active command and at the first indications of battle he was to find himself superseded.

To the south of the Reserve Front beyond the Roslavl-Kirov railway line ran Eremenko's Bryansk Front, then consisting of M. P. Petrov's 50, Kreizer's 3 and Gorodnyansky's 13 Armies, with the Ermakov Group covering the far left flank.[25] West Theatre is said to have numbered eighty-three divisions, nine cavalry divisions and thirteen tank brigades, in all 800,000 men, 770 tanks and 360 aircraft.[26]

Until late in September the West Theatre was unaware that a major German offensive was to be launched against it and for this the *Führer's* uncertain strategy was again mainly responsible. Even as late as the third week in September the Germans were still dispersed, having just completed the Kiev encirclement, and there was heavy fighting still going on to the north of Lake

[23] Konev's West Front consisted of Yushkevich's 22 Army, Maslennikov's 29 Army, Khomenko's 30 Army, Lukin's 19 Army, Rokossovsky's 16 Army and Ershakov's 20 Army.

[24] Reserve Front consisted of Dolmatov's 31 Army, Zakharkin's 49 Army, Vishnevsky's 32 Army, Onuprienko's 33 Army, Rakutin's 24 Army and Sobennikov's (later Akimov's) 43 Army.

[25] The military councils were: of the Bryansk Front, Eremenko, Mazepov and Makarov (both ranking as divisional commissars and political members) and G. F. Zahkarov; of the Reserve Front, Budenny, Kruglov and G. M. Popov (both political members) and Anisov; of the West Front, Konev, Bulganin, Lestev and Kholkhov (both political members) and Sokolovsky; the last named in each council being the chief of staff.

[26] Sokolovsky, *Razgrom Nemetsko-Fashistskikh Voisk pod Moskvoi*, p. 30; Zhukov, *Vospominaniya i Razmyshleniya*, p. 346. Forty per cent of troops and artillery and thirty-five per cent of all tanks and aircraft of the whole Red Army were said to be in front of Moscow in the West, Reserve and Bryansk Fronts. *Istoriya*, Vol. 2, p. 234. The strength of West Theatre is difficult to reconcile with the German claim in booty and prisoners for the Vyazma and Bryansk encirclements. *Voenno Istorichiskii Zhurnal* 1967, No. 3, pp. 70–2 says, however, that West Theatre was 1,252,000 strong.

Ilmen.[27] The initial blow of the Moscow offensive, launched on the last day of September, caught the Soviet High Command by surprise. As soon as the German intentions were confirmed, there was a cessation of all Red Army attacks, these being in any event only local engagements with limited objectives, and all troops went over to the defensive and hurriedly prepared to meet the onslaught. Reserves were scraped up at all levels for counter-attacks and defence in depth, and a central theatre reserve was formed under Boldin, still a front deputy commander, from elements withdrawn from 19, 20, 24 and 32 Armies. Any form of mobile defence was forbidden and troops were ordered to fight where they stood.[28]

On 30 September Guderian's 2 Panzer Group attacked Ermakov's flank group with three panzer corps forward, but all concentrated on a fairly narrow front, and in fine weather advanced over fifty miles during that first day, in the face of scattered bombing raids by the Red Air Force. The marching German infantry formations provided the flank protection and mopped up pockets of resistance. By 2 October Gorodnyansky's 13 Soviet Army had been driven off to the north when it attempted to close the breach made by the German armour and the next day Orel, about 130 miles in the Soviet rear, fell into German hands. Meanwhile Lemelsen's 47 Panzer Corps on the left flank had changed direction sharply to the north in order to envelop the troops of Eremenko's Bryansk Front from the rear.[29] These German successes had been achieved at the cost of light casualties but when the Soviet commanders had recovered from their surprise, resistance stiffened and Zakharkin's 49 Soviet Army, which was in reserve and west of Tula, was ordered to go forward from the Mozhaisk line in the rear and retake Orel. Events outran this order.

On 1 October, when the danger of Guderian's attack had become apparent, Stalin had sent for Lelyushenko, the commander designate of 1 Special Guards Rifle Corps, a commander without troops since the corps had not yet been assembled, and dispatched him to undertake the defence of Mtsensk and Orel. He left Moscow, accompanied by a motor cycle regiment, the only troops readily available, and at Tula, according to his own account, picked up some guns from the artillery school which were towed by Tula municipal buses. He was, however, in constant telephonic communication with the friendly and fatherly Shaposhnikov, who began to route to him by road and rail part-formations and detachments, offering Lelyushenko *Katyusha* batteries, provided that there was no risk of losing them to the enemy.[30] Among the first

[27] The rapidity of German movement, taking into consideration the weather and the ground, was no less remarkable than that of the Red Army, but whereas Soviet troops made much use of the railways, the Germans were unable to do so because of lack of rolling stock and the slow conversion of the track gauge. Track conversion was concentrated on east-west lines and not on north-south laterals. German infantry divisions therefore usually marched from one army group to another.

[28] *Istoriya*, Vol. 2, pp. 235–6.

[29] Compare Biryuzov, *Surovye Gody*, pp. 64–73.

[30] 'Take care of them, dear fellow (*golubchik*), otherwise you will answer for it with your head. So says the Supreme Commander.' Lelyushenko, *Zarya Pobedy*, p. 43.

troops to arrive from Leningrad at Mtsensk station was part of Katukov's 1 Tank Brigade, equipped mainly with KV and T34 tanks, and these, with infantry support, on 6 October ran headlong into von Schweppenburg's 24 Panzer Corps on Guderian's right flank on the Tula road near Mtsensk. Heavy fighting followed.[31] On the left of Guderian's 2 Panzer Army, 17 Panzer Division had already taken the town of Bryansk, so freeing the German road and rail supply line from Roslavl to Orel. That night the first snow of the winter fell on the Army Group Centre front.

The German envelopment of the Bryansk Front made very satisfactory progress as the infantry formations of von Weichs's 2 Army in the west made their way steadily towards the Desna, working closely with the left flank of 2 Panzer Army, and completing the encirclement of part of Kreizer's 3 and Gorodnyansky's 13 Soviet Armies to the south, and elements of Petrov's 50 Soviet Army to the north, of Bryansk. On 10 October Guderian received fresh orders from Army Group Centre, these detailing numerous tasks including the mopping up of the enemy in the two pockets to the north and south of Bryansk, the seizure of Kursk about fifty miles away to the south-east, and a resumption of the advance on Tula, all to be carried out immediately. Guderian sensed, probably rightly, that these orders emanated from some headquarters above Army Group Centre and was given no reply when he asked for priorities to be allotted to the missions.[32] As it transpired, mobile operations were by then out of the question since the snow continued to fall, but did not settle, and the ground and roads were soon churned into deep mud. Vehicle columns once more became stationary, and aircraft were used to drop bales of rope to isolated units in order that they might use their tracked vehicles to tow themselves free.

Since 6 October, Eremenko with the Bryansk Front had lost all communication with the Soviet High Command in Moscow, and on the night of 8 October he ordered the withdrawal by night of his already encircled forces. Many of his troops did succeed in breaking out. On 17 October that part of 50 Soviet Army in the pocket to the north of Bryansk surrendered, but resistance to the south of the town lasted until 25 October. 3, 13 and 50 Armies lost very heavily in stragglers and yielded about 50,000 prisoners; Petrov the Commander of 50 Army was killed.

By 15 October 2 Panzer Army, still bogged down by the weather, had not advanced beyond Mtsensk.[33] There was only one good route from Orel to Tula and this had broken up under the weight of the heavy traffic and bad weather; Red Army sappers had mined the road verges and demolished the bridges, and the Germans had to lay corduroy roads of tree trunks for miles on end. Vehicle fuel was in very short supply and this further restricted mobility. Red Army troops were already falling back fast in this sector,

[31] Livshits, *Pervaya Gvardeiskaya Tankovaya Brigada v Boyakh za Moskvu*, pp. 34–68.
[32] Guderian, *Panzer Leader*, p. 237.
[33] *Ibid*, p. 240. *Kriegstagebuch des OKW*, Vol. 1, pp. 702, 704, 706 and 713.

however, Eremenko being ordered on 24 October to withdraw as best he might to the line Tula-Elets covering the southern flank of Moscow. Although not admitted by Soviet sources, Eremenko's front had been virtually destroyed.[34]

1 German Cavalry Division near Trubchevsk was covering Guderian's left flank and it closed in on the cauldron to the south of Bryansk. Heavy rain and scattered snow had begun to fall on the night of 9 October and thereafter the rain fell incessantly. Swamps appeared everywhere and great torrents of water rushed through the woods cutting up the ground into gullies and ditches. The conditions of the tracks became, in the words of the divisional historian, simply catastrophic. Motor vehicles could not be moved without heavy tractors, horses were up to their bellies in slime and even the lightest cart needed a team of draught animals. The supply of fuel, rations and fodder broke down. Of shelter there was none and the East Prussian cavalry watched, without any surprise, a German higher formation headquarters trying to shelter itself in a verminous one-roomed house together with pigs and poultry. The clearing of the Bryansk pocket was no easy task since the forests, unlike those of the Fatherland, were unthinned and untended, full of primeval marsh, thicket and undergrowth, and combing the Red Army men out could be a costly and dangerous business. Prisoners said that the Headquarters of 3 Soviet Army was somewhere in the vicinity, but 1 Cavalry Division was unable to find it.[35]

A little further to the north-east 52 German Infantry Division, on the right flank of von Kluge's 4 Army, had moved from Sukhinichi to Kaluga, leaving the forest belt behind it, when on 13 October the rains began in earnest. The remaining general service army carts were ditched since they were slung too low, and Russian farm vehicles were seized from the fields. Everything was unloaded and left behind, except for two light guns in each battery and two limbers, each piece being pulled by ten horses, while unharnessed teams of spare horses brought up the rear. Within two days the horses had lost their shoes, but in the soft going could manage without them. The same could not be said for the unfortunate infantrymen whose calf boots were frequently sucked from their legs as they waded on, knee deep in mud. Their boots began to fall to pieces. After the first day's march the horse-drawn baggage, light though it was, could not keep up, and the troops went rationless, except for tea and potatoes looted from the farms. The troops, foolishly and unwittingly, longed for the coming of the frost and the winter.[36]

Meanwhile much further to the north on the Smolensk-Vyazma axis the Soviet position appeared disastrous. The weather had been particularly fine

[34] See, however, Sokolovsky, *Razgrom Nemetsko-Fashistskikh Voisk pod Moskvoi*, pp. 63 footnote and 77.

[35] Senger und Etterlin, *Die 1. Kavallerie-Division*, pp. 61–3.

[36] Rendulic, *Gekämpft Gesiegt Geschlagen*, pp. 74–6.

when 9 and 4 German Armies first launched their main attack towards Moscow and by the end of the first day of the attack, on 2 October, Strauss's 9 Army and Hoth's 3 Panzer Group had already broken through at the junction between Khomenko's 30 and Lukin's 19 Soviet Armies. Hoth had a total of only three panzer divisions but he attacked with his two panzer corps forward, Schaal's 56 Panzer on Kholm (on the Dnieper) and Vyazma, while Reinhardt's 41 Panzer Corps moved east to north-east in the direction of Rzhev on the upper Volga. Resistance was much weaker than had been anticipated, except for a single counter-attack by a Soviet tank brigade south-west of Kholm. With the fine weather, the hard ground and the excellent tactical air support of 8 Air Corps, the tanks were soon over the upper Dnieper and on to Vyazma. 35 German Infantry Division which followed up Hoth's panzer group through Kholm on the northern axis to Vyazma, said that although the enemy defences which had been prepared over the last two months were strong, the Red Army had been taken completely by surprise and, except for three days heavy fighting before 7 October, the resistance was weak. In the ten days' advance the division took 8,500 prisoners.[37]

To the south of the Smolensk-Vyazma axis Rakutin's 24 and Sobennikov's 43 Armies of Budenny's Reserve Front bore the brunt of the attack by von Kluge's 4 German Army and Hoepner's 4 Panzer Group, and broke under the strain. In less than two days Hoepner's Group was through the so-called Vyazma line, taking Spas-Demensk and Kirov on 4 October and Yukhnov and Mosalsk the next day. That same night Budenny reported the overall situation as very serious, since Hoepner had got behind him and was rolling up the defence line from south to north. Any intention to stand and fight could only have led to the destruction of the West and Reserve Fronts and both were ordered to carry out a general withdrawal to the east of the Vyazma line on the night of 6 October, covered by Boldin's force and 31 and 32 Armies from the Reserve Front. At this crucial moment the Soviet Command, instead of retaining the simple and established methods of control, became involved in another complicated regrouping. 30 Army was relieved by 31 Army and the divisions of 16 Army were transferred to 20 Army. Rokossovsky's 16 Army Headquarters was to have taken over command of all troops in the Vyazma area, then threatened by the junction of the pincers of 3 and 4 Panzer Groups. Events once more outran orders and all communications and control broke down within both the West and the Reserve Fronts.[38] Boldin's miscellaneous reserve force and 31 Army were overcome and by 7 October the greater part of 19, 20, 24 and 32 Armies and Boldin's Group had been encircled by 3 and 4 Panzer Groups in the area to the west of Vyazma. The encircled troops continued to resist, thereby contributing to the defence of Moscow, yet the defence was neither very determined nor protracted, since it lasted barely a week and

---

[37] Baumann, *Die 35. Infanterie-Division*, p. 113.
[38] *Istoriya*, Vol. 2, pp. 238–9.

yielded to the Germans no fewer than 650,000 prisoners. It is estimated that at least forty-five divisions were destroyed.[39]

There was a general panic in Moscow, resulting in the big exodus of 16 October. Refugees were blocking the roads as they streamed back. In the capital itself, although Stalin, the GKO and the *Stavka* remained, many departments of government and the diplomatic corps were ordered to move to the city of Kuybyshev in the interior. A large number of officials and their families, with or without permission, joined in the flight. Looting was widespread, the British Embassy being pillaged, and on 19 October a state of siege was declared.[40]

On 5 and 6 October Stalin had telephoned Leningrad to order the return of Zhukov. Zhukov, not for the last time, was having difficulties with Marshal Kulik; but leaving Fedyuninsky temporarily in command on the Leningrad Front and detaching Khozin, the chief of staff, to the errant Kulik, he returned by air to Moscow on 7 October. Communications with Konev's West and Budenny's Reserve Front had largely broken down and Stalin, who was suffering badly from influenza, was unable to obtain a picture of what was happening. Zhukov left hurriedly by vehicle for the west. That night he found Konev's headquarters without much difficulty and heard the details of the encirclement. Eremenko's Front had put up uneven resistance and nothing was known of Budenny. Having telephoned Stalin in the early hours of the morning of 8 October he set off again looking for Budenny who was believed to be near Maloyaroslavets. After much difficulty and cross-examining of soldiers, he came upon the Reserve Front Headquarters, presided over by Anisov, the chief of staff, and Mekhlis, the *Stavka* representative. From the surly Mekhlis came the question 'and what brings you to us', but of the position of their own troops or of those of the enemy the pair knew little, nor did they know of the whereabouts of Budenny, whom they feared lost with 43 Army. From Konev nothing had been heard for two days. Zhukov left them busy giving orders for the netting and reforming of detachments and stragglers, and set off in search of Budenny.[41]

There was never any question of undertaking the relief of the troops encircled in the great Vyazma pocket since, as Zhukov has said, there were no forces available for the purpose, and it was decided to put every formation or detachment which could be mustered on the Mozhaisk line in front of

[39] Compare Hoth, *Panzeroperationen*, p. 136; *Kriegstagebuch des OKW*, Vol. 1, p. 702. By 15 October 558,000 prisoners, 1,000 tanks and 4,000 guns had been taken and more was yet to come. On 19 October von Bock recorded the count as 673,000. Von Bock, *Tagebuch*, 19 October 1941. Lukin, the Commander of 19 Army, was among the prisoners. The Soviet account admits the loss of formations of 19, 20, 24 and 32 Armies and Boldin's group as a heavy disaster, but is silent on the number of personnel losses.

[40] On 12 October, 450,000 Muscovites had been mobilized for emergency work, and of these 75 per cent were women. *Kratkaya Istoriya*, p. 115. For comment on what Werth calls the big skedaddle, see Werth, *Russia at War*, pp. 236–8; also Eden. The *Reckoning*, p. 302; Samsonov, *Die Grosse Schlacht vor Moskau*, p. 70.

[41] Zhukov, *Vospominaniya i Razmyshleniya*, pp. 344–52.

Moscow.[42] These were to total no more than fourteen rifle divisions, sixteen tank brigades and forty rifle regiments, in all 90,000 men, and these began to concentrate on 14 October under the Headquarters of Rokossovsky's 16 Army, Golubev's 43 Army, Zakharkin's 49 Army and Lelyushenko's (later Govorov's) newly formed 5 Army, all of which were regrouping on the Mozhaisk defence line, where S. I. Bogdanov had been entrusted with the preparation and co-ordination of fortifications.[43] Further armies were, however, being drawn into the area. Some thinning out of the troops in the Far East began at about this time, and Kurochkin's North-West and Timoshenko's South-West Fronts transferred some formations to the Moscow area. On 10 October Zhukov took over the command firstly of the Reserve Front and then the West Front, the two fronts being fused into one command. Konev, the former Commander of West Front, was reappointed as Zhukov's deputy commander, and Sokolovsky as his chief of staff, Bulganin being the political member of the military council. Konev was not to remain long in this post, however, because of a new crisis which had arisen to the north-west of Moscow, where 3 Panzer Group, by then under the command of Reinhardt, was moving north-east, entering Kalinin on 14 October in the rear of 22, 29 and 31 Soviet Armies and causing the precipitate withdrawal of these formations. A new Kalinin Front was then formed on 17 October under Konev, consisting of Vostrukhov's 22, Maslennikov's 29 and Khomenko's 30 Armies and an operational group under Vatutin, this new front stretching at right angles to West Front from the area of the town of Kalinin in the east to the Ostashkov Lakes in the west.[44]

Zhukov was made responsible for the defence of all of the approaches to Moscow and commanded all troops on the defence lines. Artemev, the Commander of Moscow Military District, was entrusted with the defence of the city under Zhukov. On 18 October tanks of Stumme's 40 Panzer Corps had already entered Mozhaisk on the second defence line about sixty miles from Moscow, after some fierce fighting against three tank brigades near Borodino, and the Mozhaisk defence line had already been breached by Kuntzen's 57 Panzer Corps near Maloyaroslavets and Borovsk, and by Felber's 13 Corps near Kaluga. A threat existed to the Naro-Fominsk and Podolsk areas to the south of Moscow and the communications between Moscow and Tula were in danger of being cut. To meet this situation a new army, 33 Army under Efremov, was formed in this area and Golubev's 43 Army was reinforced. The three Moscow defence rings were strengthened by barricades, strong points and anti-tank obstacles and three workers divisions were hurriedly formed from volunteers and conscripted civilians. Special orders were enacted to strengthen the political and military control over the civilian population and

[42] *Ibid*, p. 355.
[43] *Istoriya*, Vol. 2, p. 241. Govorov succeeded the wounded Lelyushenko and Golubev had replaced Akimov.
[44] *Ibid*, p. 245.

these included the setting up of military tribunals and, where necessary, the shooting of offenders on the spot.[45]

By the middle of the month of October when the weather finally broke up, the advance as shown by the daily situation maps in von Brauchitsch's headquarters was very satisfactory, but did not reflect the true position. It was known that Guderian's force was failing to make any further progress and appeared to be bogged down near Mtsensk, but it was not realized that the weather was shortly to halt movement everywhere. On 14 October von Brauchitsch issued an OKH order, which was of course a Hitler order, outlining the further development of operations by Army Group Centre. Moscow was to be surrounded but not occupied and any offer of capitulation was to be rejected.[46] The military orders which followed this curious premise were no less impracticable, and involved the complete dispersal of the force which had been concentrated for the destruction of West Front and the seizure of Moscow. Von Weichs's 2 German Army was to move from Kursk to Voronezh while Guderian's 2 Panzer Army was to take Tula and encircle Moscow from the south-east. Von Kluge's 4 Army was to pin the Red Army forces to the west of Moscow while Reinhardt's 3 and Hoepner's 4 Panzer Groups were to encircle the capital from the north-east. Strauss's 9 Army was to move directly north from the line Kalinin-Staritsa to Vyshniy Volochok in the area of the Valdai Hills to assist Army Group North. These operations would have spread Army Group Centre over a frontage of about 600 miles; von Brauchitsch's plan brought a protest from von Bock who wanted to attack Moscow by the shortest and most direct route.[47]

From mid October onwards the worsening weather conditions had slowed down the rate of the German advance in front of Moscow, just as it had done that of Guderian's 2 Panzer Army in the area of Mtsensk, where the winter had broken ten days earlier. The same scenes were enacted. The main Smolensk-Moscow motorway started to break up and all wheeled traffic came to a standstill in the vast seas of mud. Only tracked vehicles and *panje* wagons were capable of any movement at all. Whole divisions came to a halt, the stationary units and detachments being scattered over hundreds of miles. Thousands of horses died through over-exertion and lack of fodder, and guns and heavy equipment remained stuck in the glue-like morass. Anti-tank guns could not be got forward to combat the enemy tanks which were numerous once more, and many signal vehicles were to remain separated from their headquarters. The supply system broke down and there was insufficient air transport to cope with anything but emergency supply dropping operations. Even when it was possible to get wheeled motor vehicles moving with the assistance of tracked prime movers, the abominable going conditions quickly

[45] *Ibid*, pp. 247–8.

[46] Teleprint *OKH Gen St d H Op Abt (IM) Nr. 1571/41 g. Kdos Chefs* of 12 October 1941.

[47] In particular von Bock disagreed with the dispatch of his panzer force to the north of Moscow. Von Bock, *Tagebuch*, 7 October 1941.

used up the limited stocks of fuel. Stranded detachments were in danger of starving.

Von Kluge's 4 Army, with a strength of about thirty-six divisions on the River Nara to the west of Moscow, had made little progress and instead of pinning the Soviet forces, was itself pinned. The condition of the German troops here gave rise for concern. 98 Franconian Sudeten Division, after its long 600-mile march through the Ukraine, had joined 4 Army just after the Vyazma battle and had fought its way forward from Maloyaroslavets, a point only sixty miles from Moscow, taking over the pursuit in the muddy October period when 17 Panzer Division came to a halt beyond the Protva. There was heavy low cloud with continual rain and snow showers but, since the panzer formations had been left behind, the infantry enjoyed the nightly warmth of the miserable little hovels, while the armoured troops, stuck in the mud, wintered it out. It was weeks before some of these motorized troops got on the move again and meanwhile they had frequent fights with stragglers and partisans. Supply columns could only move with the help of captured Soviet tractors. The Red Army rearguards in this sector fought with skill and left numerous stay-behind detachments in wood and bush. On the Nara Soviet resistance began to stiffen again, many Mongols and Kalmucks being taken among the prisoners, and there were rumours of peace-time Siberian and parachute formations being committed to the battle. With companies hardly of platoon strength, 289 Regiment took the Chernishay heights, but an immediate enemy counter-attack threw it off. This was unheard of in the earlier days, when German infantry could not be prised loose from its objective. 290 Regiment, with the help of assault guns, retook the objective but became separated from its armour and was immediately counter-attacked by swarms of hurrahing Bolsheviks who drove it off. The Germans suffered through enemy mortar and rocket fire, although the poor splinter effect of the rocket projectiles saved many a German life; but the Soviet superiority in artillery and automatics caused heavy losses. 98 Division rue-fully noted that the Soviet enemy at least had no difficulties with ammunition supply.

The T34 tanks made a lasting impression on the German infantry. An attack on the boundary between 289 and 290 Regiments caused some of the men to panic, and it was only the personal intervention and presence of the regi-mental colonel which persuaded the troops to return to their positions. Only when the German armour and 88 mm flak guns began to pick off the T34s did the infantry start to breathe again. Even so, Soviet tanks continued to break into the German positions but, since they were rarely accompanied by their own infantry, they milled about the area achieving little until they were destroyed or forced to withdraw by German fire. German regimental staffs, clerks, signallers, sappers and anti-tank gunners were all used as infantrymen. Infantry companies, twenty men strong, led by second-lieutenants or sergeants, were bearded and filthy, not having bathed or changed their clothes for months. Tormented by lice, they lay all day cramped and stiff in the narrow weapon pits filled with water, their feet so cold that they had lost all feeling. Sickness and cold caused more casualties than enemy action. Rain fell incessantly and the *Luftwaffe* seemed unable to cope with the Red Air Force fighters and bombers which dropped out of the low cloud, bombing and machine gunning. One officer was to write that only forty-five miles from Moscow the troops still had confidence, because they could not believe that everyone else was in such a wretched state as they. On 2 November a regimental commander had reported that without rest and refitting his troops had no further fighting value, and on 5 November Field-Marshal von Kluge arrived at the division personally to investigate its weakness; but this made no difference to the intention to use the division in the final offensive, since its condition was in fact little worse than that of many other infantry formations.[48]

35 German Infantry Division was the right flanking division of 5 Corps, the southernmost corps of 9 Army, as it started to move towards the area north of Moscow; but on 19 October the rain and thaw brought most of this division to a standstill. The infantry, however, although many of its rifle companies were down to little more than thirty men, trudged on to the east through knee-deep mud. All motor vehicles, wireless stations, heavy artillery and baggage were left behind between Klushino and Sereda. A few light guns were got forward, each piece and limber being dragged slowly and laboriously by no fewer than twenty-four horses. Surgeons with field surgical teams were loaded into *panje* carts and sent forward with the infantry, and an attempt was made to establish a supply chain from Gzhatsk, using pack animals and carts. By 20 October the infantry were over the Ruza against light resistance, the enemy having only a few guns but no shortage of ammunition. Between 24 and 26 October it appeared that the Soviet defence was collapsing and on 27 October Volokolamsk was taken. Four days later 35 Infantry Division, although reduced to two regiments and very much under strength, had taken 1,800 prisoners and covered sixteen miles of the most difficult waterlogged terrain in five days. On 31 October a fortnight's pause was ordered, while more guns and ammunition were brought up.[49]

During the rest of the month of October von Bock's Army Group Centre worked its way slowly forward in accordance with its orders. Von Kluge's 4 Army had reached the River Nara on the line Serpukhov-Volokolamsk, while Strauss's 9 Army, after heavy fighting, secured the area north of Rzhev on the approaches to Kalinin. Guderian's 2 Panzer Army, further to the south, finally took Mtsensk on 24 October; but since the fuel shortage would not allow the whole of 24 Panzer Corps to advance on Tula, such fuel as was held was pooled in order to get some tanks forward and an improvised panzer brigade was sent under Eberbach to seize the town by a *coup de main*. The

[48] Gareis, *Kampf und Ende der 98. Division*, pp. 142–60.
[49] Baumann, *Die 35. Infanterie-Division*, pp. 114–17.

attack against Ermakov's 50 Army, which was holding Tula, failed and the German tank losses were heavy.[50]

The breaking of the weather caused an almost complete falling off in violence of the German attacks and gave the Red Army much needed relief. Already by the end of October the Soviet High Command regarded the position as stabilized and began to withdraw some troops to reserve for rest and retraining. A feverish race began to make good the enormous losses suffered in the first two weeks in October at Vyazma and Bryansk, and to prepare to withstand the next German onslaught.

It was expected that the German offensive, when it came, would follow the same pattern as the preceding attacks and would be made by strong panzer forces on each flank. Counter-action was to be taken by attacking these flanking panzer forces before they could be organized for an offensive. One tank and five cavalry divisions from the area near Volokolamsk were to thrust against the flank and rear of Reinhardt's 3 Panzer Group. South of Stalinogorsk one cavalry and two tank divisions began to infiltrate into the rear of Guderian's 2 Panzer Army. West Front received reinforcements and new formations in addition to numerous anti-tank and mortar regiments from Eremenko's Bryansk Front which had been broken up on 10 November.[51] Much more important was the organizing and training of a further nine armies during October and November, these being deployed on a line Lake Onega, Yaroslavl, Gorki, Saratov, Stalingrad and Astrakhan. Two complete armies and elements of another three were to reach the Moscow area by the end of November.[52] Some of the divisions in these armies were raised from newly inducted recruits, but some of the formations were well trained and equipped and had been withdrawn from the military districts in Central Russia and Siberia. In order to move and concentrate these troops behind West Front the whole of the railway network was given up to the Red Army, and on 24 October the Moscow railway complex was put entirely under military control. According to the Soviet account large numbers of military trains ran from Tomsk, Omsk, Sverdlovsk and Kuybyshev without stopping to change locomotives or crews, covering between 500 and 600 miles a day.[53] In October and November extensive administrative preparations were made by the Soviet High Command for the final defensive battle before Moscow and large numbers of pack and animal truck and sledge companies were formed, as a pony had far greater mobility in mud or soft snow than a wheeled motor vehicle. However, as the problems caused by the shortage of transport, the weather and the terrain were readily recognized, seven days' rations, six refills

[50] 50 Army had in fact been virtually destroyed in the encirclement north of Bryansk, but it was resurrected and fought again north of Mtsensk and in Tula.

[51] 50 Army went to West Front. The remnants of 3 and 13 Armies to Timoshenko's South-West Front.

[52] *Istoriya*, Vol. 2, p. 257.

[53] *Ibid*, p. 274.

of vehicle fuels and three first lines of ammunition were dumped with the forward troops.

German movement for the very first time during the Second World War had been brought to a standstill, and it was halted during the second and the third weeks in October by rain and by mud. Soviet historians tend to scoff at what they describe as German excuses and maintain that von Bock was halted by the valour and skill of the Red Army.[54]

Red Army resistance stiffened in late October, and to the west and south of Moscow it was bitter. Yet an examination of the evidence shows without doubt that the German advance, which at first promised to be as rapid and spectacular as any of those of the late summer, abruptly petered out because of the weather and the terrain. In the first fortnight of the *Typhoon* offensive Army Group Centre destroyed nearly 700,000 of the Soviet defenders at comparatively little cost to itself, and with another three weeks' dry, mild and clear weather, it would inevitably have been in Moscow. The German successes which had been so outstanding over the Poles, the French, the British and the Red Army up to this time had been brought about by the much superior mobility and firepower made possible by the massing of tanks and the concentration of tactical air forces, good communications and bold leadership. Once this mobility was removed, firepower was also lost and the German tactical concept of the *blitzkrieg* foundered. The almost unbelievably difficult conditions in Russia and the seas of mud brought all wheels to a halt and destroyed the horses. Tracked vehicles could keep going, but only at very reduced efficiency with a prohibitively increased fuel consumption, and since the fuel supply had also ceased, tracks soon came to a standstill. Little air transport was available and the low cloud and poor visibility made difficult any form of sustained air offensive or air transport support.[55] The German infantry continued to go forward, knee-deep and sometimes even waist-deep in mud and water, but it was no longer part of a well co-ordinated and powerful fighting machine. Without tanks or air support and with little artillery or mortar fire at its disposal, even the anti-tank guns sometimes having been left behind, it moved at the best a few laborious miles a day. It lacked fire support and ammunition, equipment and food, clothing and warmth, shelter and medical care, because even necessities could not be got forward to it. Suddenly, almost overnight, the Germans were to depend for success in their thrust on Moscow on the efforts of a number of unsupported, tired and understrength spearhead infantry battalions, while the rest of the German Army and *Luftwaffe*, immobilized and powerless, stood idle and looked on.

Soviet resistance, as always, was uneven. In front of Tula and on the Nara where new formations were arriving, it was most determined and tough. Near

---

[54] *Ibid*, p. 252; also *inter alia* Samsonov, *Die Grosse Schlacht vor Moskau*, p. 80. The German case is not examined and demolished by rational argument, but merely denounced as a lie.

[55] Kesselring, *Soldat bis zum letzten Tag*, p. 129.

Volokolamsk it was insignificant, many of the Caucasian cavalry there giving themselves up. From mid October onwards the Red Army was being engaged by only part of the German strength. It is true that the Red Army suffered the same movement problems as did the Germans, but Army Group Centre was at the end of a thousand mile long line of communication, while the defenders were barely forty miles from their main base; any conditions which inhibit movement must favour the defence.

It would be entirely wrong, of course, to ascribe the German failure solely to the weather or to misfortune. The main failure was that of misjudgement and mistiming, since *Typhoon* was mounted too late in the year, at a season when the weather was due to break up. A secondary cause was the lack of understanding of the special effects on mobile operations of the weather and the terrain in Russia, and the third was the ever present problem of the inadequacy of resources. Since the offensive was mounted so late in the year some other form of transport was needed to replace or supplement the wheels. The only alternative method at that time would have been air transport, if the air transport and air supply resources had been available, which they were not.[56] Too much had been asked of German troops, and in particular from the infantry, and strengths had been allowed to drop too low. In a paper prepared on 6 November 1941, which if anything understated the seriousness of the position, the 101 infantry divisions in the East (outside Finland) were reckoned to have a fighting effectiveness no greater than that of sixty-five divisions at near establishment strength. The seventeen panzer divisions had been reduced to the effectiveness of six. In all the German Army in the East, which numbered 136 divisions on its order of battle, had a fighting strength equivalent to only eighty-three divisions.[57]

---

[56] Motor load carriers of special design, either tracked or wheeled, could have negotiated the Russian mud. No steps had been taken, however, to design or provide them and since they would have been needed in large numbers it is certain that the German motor industry at that time could not have produced them. The alternative could have been provided by air transport, if an air transport and supply organization of sufficient size had been in existence. This, however, had been neglected in the *Luftwaffe*. Morzik und Hümmelchen, *Die Deutschen Transportflieger in Zweiten Weltkrieg*, pp. 23–5. Halder, *Kriegstagebuch*, Vol. 3, p. 283.

[57] *Gen St d H Org Abt (I) Nr. 731/41 g. Kdos* of 6 November 1941. (*Kriegstagebuch des OKW*, Vol. 2, pp. 1074–5.)

CHAPTER THIRTEEN

Rostov, Tikhvin and Moscow

In the Ukraine von Rundstedt's weakened Army Group South continued its advance eastwards into the Donets Basin and towards the Caucasus. After its loss of formations to Army Group Centre and to other theatres its strength had been reduced to about forty German divisions, of which only three were panzer and two motorized, together with a number of Rumanian, Italian, Hungarian and Slovak formations.[1] The supply and fuel situation was steadily worsening due to the lack of motor transport and the demolition of the railway bridges over the Dnieper, and hard fighting had locked von Manstein's 11 Army and part of 3 Rumanian Army in the Crimea.[2] Von Kleist's 1 Panzer Group, by then redesignated 1 Panzer Army, after the successful encirclement battle between Zaporozhe and Osipenko, centralized and pooled its reserves of motor fuel and moved on Rostov.[3] On 1 Panzer Army's north flank 17 Army under its new commander Hoth, was moving towards Voroshilovgrad (Lugansk) and the North Donets River, while on Hoth's left, on the extreme north flank of Army Group South, von Reichenau's 6 Army, still trying to keep in touch with von Weichs's 2 Army on the right flank of Army Group Centre, took Sumy on 10 October and then advanced on Belgorod and Kharkov.[4]

Hitler, interfering repeatedly with operations, was to direct that both 17 and 6 Armies should move in a south-easterly direction in order to support and keep in close contact with von Kleist's 1 Panzer Army, in spite of the fact that Halder did warn him at the time that this would leave the right flank of Army Group Centre in the air and give rise to a gap between 6 and 2 Armies.[5] The German armies were in fact moving on divergent rather than on parallel

[1] Army Group South had three panzer, two motorized and thirty-six German infantry divisions, an Italian motorized corps of three divisions, six Rumanian and three Hungarian formations of about brigade strength and two Slovak divisions. *OKH Kriegsgliederung* of 2 October 1941.

[2] The other part of 3 Rumanian Army was guarding the Black Sea coast.

[3] Von Kleist had von Mackensen's 3 and von Wietersheim's 14 Panzer Corps under command.

[4] Von Stülpnagel, the Commander of 17 Army, had apparently incurred von Brauchitsch's displeasure and reported sick on 5 October.

[5] Halder, *Kriegstagebuch*, Vol. 3, p. 295.

axes and gaps were bound to appear between them. Von Weichs's 2 Army in its turn was to be continually drawn to the south-east and east, in order to keep in touch with 6 Army to its south, and in consequence was unable to give any support to Guderian to its north. Guderian's 2 Panzer Army was moving in a north-easterly direction towards Moscow, with a dangerously exposed right flank which von Weichs could not cover.

The weather had been bad from about 6 October and Halder noted two days later that it was slowing von Rundstedt's rate of advance. On 11 October it finally broke and both 17 and 6 German Armies came to a standstill in the mud. The bad weather had not reached the Black Sea coast and von Kleist continued to move forward, having reached the River Mius north-west of Taganrog on 11 October, where tough enemy resistance delayed him for several days until he was finally brought to a standstill by the rain storms on 14 October.

The Donets Basin is known as the coal-scuttle of the Soviet Union and in 1941 it was producing sixty per cent of the coal and seventy-five per cent of the coke of the USSR, in addition to thirty per cent of the total output of iron and twenty per cent of the steel production.[6] The slowing down of the German movement gave sufficient time to the Soviet teams to dismantle much of the industrial equipment and make the Donets and Kharkov area of little economic value to the Germans for some time to come.

The German advance was opposed by Timoshenko's South-West Front consisting of 40, 21, 38 and 6 Armies and Cherevichenko's South Front of 12, 18 and 9 Armies.[7] The fighting in front of Pavlograd and Kharkov caused heavy Red Army casualties and the Soviet High Command ordered the two fronts to fall back to straighten and shorten their line and so create a reserve. The line chosen ran along the railway from Kastornoye to Staryy Oskol, Liman, Gorlovka and the Mius, and the reserves were created into a new army, 37 Army under Lopatin, concentrated in the area of the south-east of Voroshilovgrad.[8] On 17 October Taganrog fell and by the end of the month the Germans had reached Kharkov, part of the Donets Basin and the approaches to Rostov-on-Don, which formed the gateway to the Caucasus.

The falling back of the Red Army troops in the area of Kharkov and Voronezh was interpreted by Army Group South as a thinning out to reinforce the Moscow or the Rostov sectors, and von Rundstedt ordered a general pursuit. This was beyond the capability of the troops, however, as by day the snow, rain and mud made sustained movement impossible, and by night the

---

[6] *Istoriya*, Vol. 2, p. 219. The Ukraine and Donets Basin areas occupied by the Germans in November 1941 were said to produce the following percentages of the total USSR output: Coal 63; Iron 68; Steel 58; Aluminium 60. Platonov, *Vtoraya Mirovaya Voina*, p. 243.

[7] Army commanders were as follows: 40 Army Podlas; 21 Army V. I. Kuznetsov; 38 Army Maslov; 6 Army Malinovsky then Gorodnyansky; 12 Army Koroteev; 18 Army Kolpakchy; 9 Army Kharitonov.

[8] *Istoriya*, Vol. 2, p. 220.

heavy frosts froze the vehicles into the ground and robbed the tired troops of sleep. Von Reichenau's over-extended 6 Army had reached the Donets but was unable to cross it and pin the withdrawing enemy, von Reichenau declining to move further until the troops had closed up and the supply system had started to function again properly.[9] On von Reichenau's right 17 Army came to a halt near Artemovsk and Slavyansk. 1 Panzer Army made little progress from Taganrog to Rostov on account of the weather, the difficult fuel situation and the hardening Soviet resistance. At this time Wagner, the *General-quartiermeister*, was to comment that von Kleist's panzer columns had become *panje* columns, so great was the reliance on the horse.[10] On 5 November von Kleist launched a further attack against Kharitonov's reinforced 9 Soviet Army and after a three day battle drove it back twenty miles to the east and then, suddenly changing direction to the south, von Kleist attacked Remezov's 56 Independent Army which was covering Rostov and the lower Don.[11] On 16 November, in a temperature of nearly minus twenty degrees centigrade, the attack into Rostov began which, as the understrength and sobered German troops well knew, was to be a dangerous undertaking, many commanders giving as their opinion that Rostov could be taken but not held. The *Leibstandarte Adolf Hitler* attacked down one of the main roads into the town, the Sultan Saly Chaussee, and with a bitterness without equal had to fight for every foot of it, the counter-attacking T34s rolling flat the anti-tank guns of 60 Motorized Infantry Division as if they were scrap iron. Underfoot the ground was so hard that without explosives even shallow weapon pits could not be dug. German losses were heavy; but by 20 November Rostov had been taken with a loss of about 10,000 Red Army prisoners.

The fighting, far from ending, was just beginning. Remezov's 56 Independent Army counter-attacked on Rostov across the Don, trying to cut off Rostov from the west, and the German defenders were amazed to see Red Army troops, fortified by vodka, coming out of the evening dusk cheering and singing, in some cases even linking arms until fire or minefields forced them to break up. Many of the attackers fell in rows where they were hit by machine-gun fire, while others clambered over the heaps of dead and still went forward. So the fighting continued late into the night. The next morning after daylight when the sun momentarily broke through the heavy low cloud, it showed heaps of men lying on the frozen river. Here and there was some slow painful

---

[9] *Kriegstagebuch des Oberkommandos der Heeresgruppe Süd, II Teil, Band 5*, 27 October 1941. Halder noted on 4 November that 6 Army was stuck in the mud and had lost contact with the enemy, and von Brauchitsch chafed for the next fortnight at von Reichenau's lack of progress. Halder, *Kriegstagebuch*, Vol. 3, pp. 283 and 293; *Kriegstagebuch des OKW*, Vol. 1, pp. 715 and 720.

[10] Elisabeth Wagner, *Der Generalquartiermeister*, p. 212.

[11] 56 Independent Army had been hurriedly formed in the first half of November from the North Caucasus Military District. Platonov, *Vtoraya Mirovaya Voina*, p. 239.

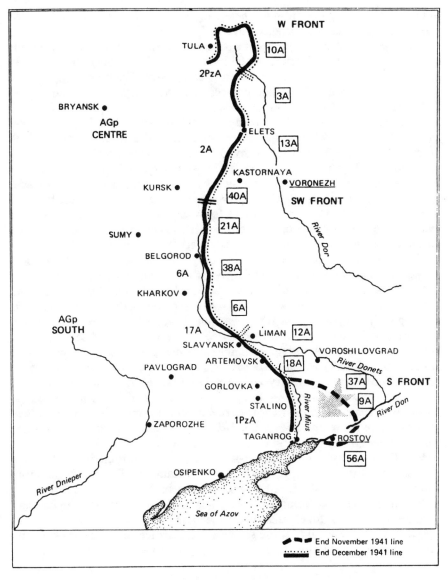

THE CHECK AT ROSTOV
December 1941

movement, but for the most the heaps lay still as the snow slowly covered them. Only riderless horses galloped madly about.[12]

The danger to von Rundstedt's troops came, however, not from the repeated counter-attacks made by 56 Independent Army, but from farther to the north. In the first week in November, South-West Front and South Front had been brought together again in a resuscitated South-West Theatre under Timoshenko.[13] A strategic counter-offensive plan had been approved in which the German enemy was to be pinned at Rostov by Remezov's 56 Independent Army while Cherevichenko's South Front launched a thrust from the flank to cut off 1 Panzer Army from Army Group South, this thrust being made by Lopatin's 37 Reserve Army supported by Kolpakchy's 18 and Kharitonov's 9 Armies on its flanks. The strength of the Soviet force was five tank brigades and thirty-one divisions, of which, however, nine were cavalry, while the German strength in this sector was about fourteen divisions of which three were panzer. The 37 Army counter-offensive was launched on 17 November, almost at the same time as 1 Panzer Army attacked Rostov, and the Soviet thrust gained over ten miles on the first day but only a mile or two on each subsequent day, as the Germans fought to hold open their supply and withdrawal route between the advancing enemy and the Sea of Azov. The key to the situation rested with von Reichenau, but as 6 Army could make no progress, the unsupported 17 Army to its south was unable to relieve the Soviet pressure on 1 Panzer Army, which stretched forward in a long exposed salient. To no avail Halder urged 6 Army forward, telling von Sodenstern, the Army Group South Chief of Staff, that his patience with 6 Army was exhausted.[14] Closer to Rostov 60 Motorized Infantry Division was attacked from north-east of the town and the Germans realized that they were fighting for dear life. A general withdrawal from the Don was ordered and the troops had already quitted Rostov on 28 November, when the *Führer*'s countermanding order hit them like a thunderbolt.[15]

Von Rundstedt, the Commander-in-Chief of Army Group South, had had a long and distinguished career under the Kaiser and in the *Reichsheer*. Entering 83 Infantry Regiment as a lieutenant in 1893, at first he rose only slowly in rank, not becoming a lieutenant-colonel until 1920. By 1938 he was a colonel-general and, together with von Leeb and many others, he was retired by Hitler in the removal of those senior officers unpleasing to the régime. Von Rundstedt was generally believed to be a strategist of ability and in the

---

[12] Meyer, *Panzergrenadiere*, p. 152.

[13] South Front was commanded by Cherevichenko until he took over the command of a newly formed Bryansk Front on 18 December, the command of South Front being then taken over by Malinovsky. Kostenko, Timoshenko's deputy, took over the command of South-West Front.

[14] Hitler was angered, wanting to know what 17 and 6 Armies were doing to take the pressure off von Kleist. Halder, *Kriegstagebuch*, Vol. 3, pp. 304 and 310.

[15] Meyer, *Panzergrenadiere*, p. 155.

opinion of some he was more fitted to be Commander-in-Chief of the German Army than von Brauchitsch.[16]

For some months past von Rundstedt had had no belief in the early collapse of the enemy and on 27 October had urged that operations should stop temporarily at Rostov, since the troops were exhausted and it was not possible to attain further objectives without reprovision and reorganization. On 3 November he had proposed without success that further objectives be postponed until the following spring.[17] When the Soviet South Front began to envelop 1 Panzer Army, von Rundstedt had ordered a general withdrawal to the line of the Mius in one bound, in order to break contact with the enemy, the Army High Command (OKH) endorsing his decision. On the night of 30 November, when Hitler issued his stand and fight order, von Rundstedt asked to be relieved of his command, and was replaced by a more pliant subordinate, Field-Marshal von Reichenau, the Commander of 6 Army.[18] A change in command could not alter the tactical situation and, with the retreating troops already on the march, the withdrawal had to be accepted by Hitler and von Reichenau. The *Führer* obstinately insisted, however, that von Kleist should occupy an intermediate position, which was in places only six miles forward of the Mius position. Von Reichenau, ardent in the support of the *Führer*, agreed with him.

Then followed a scene, repetitions of which were to become commonplace in the High Command throughout the whole war. On the ground, forward of the Mius, there was fearful confusion as all the motor transport which had arrived back in the position was turned about and sent back eastwards. At eleven o'clock on that morning of 1 December Halder discussed the position on the telephone with von Sodenstern, the Chief of Staff Army Group South, with von Reichenau butting in to say that the *Führer*'s decision was quite right and that he (von Reichenau) would take the necessary responsibility, even though von Kleist was of the opinion that he would be defeated if he fought in the intermediate position. An hour later Halder talked to von Kleist's Chief of Staff, Colonel Zeitzler, who gave a short and graphic description of the

[16] In the main von Rundstedt remained on good terms with Hitler throughout the war and in the Rostov affair he was to act with dignity and courage. It is doubtful, however, whether he was a really outstanding or a strong commander.

[17] Von Rundstedt proposed this to von Brauchitsch at Poltava on 3 November. Von Brauchitsch replied that the supply difficulties were well understood but that it was essential to reach the area of Maikop, Stalingrad and Voronezh as soon as possible. *Kriegstagebuch des Oberkommandos der Heeresgruppe Süd*, 3 November 1941.

[18] On 30 November the *Führer* was in an agitated state and forbade the withdrawal. At 1 p.m. he had a long one-sided conversation with von Brauchitsch, dispensing reproaches and impossible orders. Von Brauchitsch then issued an order to von Rundstedt (an order which of course emanated from Hitler) forbidding the withdrawal in one bound. Von Rundstedt, who feared that such a tactic would involve him in a running fight, asked that the order be rescinded. *Kriegstagebuch des Oberkommandos der Heeresgruppe Süd*, 30 November 1941. Halder commented 'These people (meaning the *Führer* and the OKW) have no idea of the condition of our troops and their thoughts are all in a vacuum'. Halder, *Kriegstagebuch*, Vol. 3, p. 319.

weakened condition of the three panzer divisions. In 13 Panzer Division, he said, the divisional commander and one excellent regimental commander were suffering nervous exhaustion. 1 Panzer Army regarded the intermediate position as useless and did not understand why the formation should be broken only six miles forward of a much better position. An hour later Halder discussed the matter again on the telephone with von Sodenstern who tried to win over von Reichenau. Von Reichenau refused to be convinced. At 2 p.m. Halder took the unusual step of bringing Jodl into the affair, asking him to talk to the *Führer*. At 3.30 p.m. von Brauchitsch went to see Hitler, and while he was actually present with him, von Reichenau telephoned Hitler direct to say that the Russians had broken through the *SS Leibstandarte* on the intermediate position and begged that he be allowed to fall back on the Mius. This permission was immediately given. So, commented a rueful Halder, 'we had arrived where we were yesterday evening. Meanwhile we had lost energy, time and von Rundstedt.'[19]

1 Panzer Army fell back to Taganrog and the frozen Mius where it could use its earlier positions, and dug itself in as best it might, the defences being prepared with the assistance of local civilians. There the German Army was to remain until the next summer. The retreat from Rostov was not in any way a major reverse but it was significant in that it was the first check suffered by German troops since the beginning of the Second World War and it was the first well conceived and efficiently executed counter-offensive attempted by the Red Army. The Rostov battle was both a tactical and a strategic setback, and failure was due to the fact that, taking the weather, the tiredness and the deficiencies of the troops into account, Army Group South had overreached itself and was too weak for its task. Von Manstein's 11 Army had been deployed in a secondary theatre in the Crimea, when it was in fact needed north of Rostov; but even if 11 Army had been brought forward to the Don, a deep penetration into the Caucasus in mid-winter with an ever-extending left flank would have been a very dangerous undertaking.

In the Leningrad area von Leeb's proposal that he should make use of any spells of fine weather during the autumn to extend his hold on the south bank of Lake Ladoga had been refused by Hitler, who ordered the move from Chudovo to secure the bauxite producing area of Tikhvin and to join with the Finns on the Svir. Tikhvin had been taken on 8 November by Busch's 16 German Army using Rudolf Schmidt's 39 Panzer and Blaskowitz's 1 Corps, the brunt of the attack falling on Yakovlev's 4 Soviet Army which began to disintegrate. Leningrad Front, to which 4 Soviet Army belonged, became out of touch with the situation on this flank. The German wedge was already threatening the rear of 7 Independent Soviet Army deployed against the Finns on the Svir, so that its uneasy commander, Meretskov, informed Stalin of the position by telephone. This dangerous situation was met by a typically Soviet

[19] *Ibid*, pp. 321–2.

command reorganization. Meretskov, who was well known to Stalin, having for a short time served as Chief of the General Staff, was ordered to hand over 7 Army to his deputy and himself take personal command of the dispersed 4 Army.[20] In addition he was to be responsible to the High Command for the control and co-ordination of 4, 7 and 52 Armies, Klykov's 52 Army being the only other army in the area. No other immediate reinforcements were available to him. Meretskov formed a reserve from a tank brigade, a rifle regiment and engineer and mortar units and, counter-attacking on 11 November, made some small gains into Tikhvin. On 25 November the Germans went over to the defensive and the next day a reorganized 4 Soviet Army began a series of counter-attacks, which were taken up by 52 Army to the south and Fedyuninsky's 54 Army from the Leningrad Front in the north, on the German Tikhvin salient which stretched for a distance of 230 miles from Mga to Novgorod. By then von Leeb had shot his bolt and no further advance was possible and, as the Finns would not advance from the Svir, it was apparent that the exposed salient could not endure. Besieged Leningrad was on a near starvation diet and the great stocks of meal collecting at Voybokalo railway station could not be ferried across Lake Ladoga by boat because of the icing. However on 18 November the lake finally froze over and four days later the first convoys of motor lorries moved across the ice into the city.[21] For this reason it was unlikely that Leningrad would succumb to starvation during the winter.

For the first time on the German side a feeling of crisis was becoming marked at the army group headquarters, since it was obvious that the Red Army, in spite of its very heavy losses, still had a good railway net, an efficient supply system and plentiful reinforcements and resources. Rostov, Tikhvin and Moscow were to be the sectors in which the 1941 campaign was to be decided.

Army Group Centre remained poised before Moscow bogged down by the weather and lack of all types of reserves. The choice was either to continue the attack on Moscow or retire, since there could be no question of staying in the present positions, exposed to both the weather and enemy attack. Fromm, the Commander of the Replacement Army, was tentatively and timidly to suggest to von Brauchitsch that the time had come to make peace proposals to Moscow.[22] Hitler, of course, was convinced that the Soviet enemy was at the end of his tether and his views were shared by von Brauchitsch and Halder, in spite of their reservations as to the *Führer*'s war direction. Halder, in a directive of 7 November, and again at a meeting at Orsha on 13 November, insisted on the continuation of the offensive since the enemy was considered to be no longer capable of holding a continuous line.[23] The Germans believed,

---

[20] *Istoriya*, Vol. 2, p. 213.

[21] Halder first heard of this from Radio Moscow and then not before 28 November.

[22] Compare Halder, *Kriegstagebuch*, Vol. 3, p. 309.

[23] Halder was chairman of a meeting at Orsha, attended by the chiefs of staff of all army groups and armies (except 1 Panzer and 2 Armies). Blumentritt, the Chief of Staff of 4 Army,

not without reason, that the Soviet High Command would place the greatest importance on the defence of the triangle Moscow-Vologda-Saratov, since the occupation of this area by the Germans would mean a complete loss of rail connection between the main theatres of operations, the Urals, the Caucasus and the incoming Anglo-Saxon aid.[24] The German intention, therefore, was to prevent the enemy withdrawing, to destroy him and reach the line running from Maikop through Stalingrad and Gorki to Vologda. The seizure of this area would in addition, it was believed, remove the enemy's industrial and armament support area and so prevent a re-equipping of his armed forces.[25] Hitler had no doubt as to the future success of the operation and, in order to ensure the full co-operation of the half-hearted, he expressly forbade the preparation of any rear defensive positions for use in case of failure. It is doubtful, however, whether the possibility of failure ever entered the heads of von Brauchitsch or Halder even at this late hour.[26] Of the army group commanders, von Rundstedt had for some time been doubtful about an early German victory, and von Leeb, who had been forced to undertake the Tikhvin operation against his own inclinations and judgement, was distinctly nervous about the vulnerable Tikhvin salient, but hoped that the resumption of the thrust towards Moscow would ease the pressure on his own sector.

Although the Chief of General Staff may have been confident of the success of the Moscow operation he certainly did not leave the *Führer* in ignorance as to the difficulties of the army groups. On 19 November Halder, in his notes for presentation to Hitler, told a long tale of gloom. Army Group South was said to be at a standstill because of the weather and the failure of supplies, and, as the Chief of General Staff moved round the East Front giving the details of the situation, the same words 'failure of supplies' and 'insufficient strength' were repeated. Of the half a million trucks, thirty per cent were off the road

said that Halder, von Bock and von Greiffenberg, the Chief of Staff of Army Group Centre, were all in favour of the continuance of the offensive. Westphal, *The Fatal Decisions*, Blumentritt, pp. 57 and 58; also Liddell Hart, *The Other Side of the Hill*, Blumentritt, pp. 284–6; Halder, *Kriegstagebuch*, Vol. 3, p. 288.

[24] The capture of this railway triangle would undoubtedly have destroyed the Soviet communication system and would have been an entirely different matter from the seizing of the Moscow nodal point. Saratov on the Volga, however, was almost as far distant as Stalingrad.

[25] On 19 November the *Führer* said that the secondary aim of the operations in the Moscow area was to reach the line Vologda-Rybinsk-Yaroslavl. Halder, *Kriegstagebuch*, Vol. 3, p. 295. Halder had put these ideas out to the chiefs of staff of army groups and armies in a written communication in which the minimum objectives were said to be Don-Tambov-Rybinsk and the maximum (spring objectives) the line Maikop-Stalingrad-Gorki-Vologda. These far-flung objectives were entirely unrealistic, as von Liebenstein and von Kluge were to point out. Guderian, *Panzer Leader*, p. 247; also Liddell Hart, *The Other Side of the Hill*, Blumentritt, p. 285; Warlimont, *Inside Hitler's Headquarters*, p. 194.

[26] Compare Halder's notes for his conference on 23 November. Halder appeared to believe that success was a matter of nerve and the final effort, as at the Marne, the last battalion weighing down the scales. Halder, *Kriegstagebuch*, Vol. 3, pp. 303 and 307, 22 November 1941.

and beyond repair and a further forty per cent awaited major repairs and over-haul. Only thirty per cent were still on the road. Army Group Centre needed a minimum of thirty-one trains a day for maintenance but only sixteen were being provided.[27]

6 Rhineland-Westphalian Division was on the left flank of 9 Army and lay about a hundred miles north-west of Moscow. Its casualties from the beginning of the war to 1 November, about 3,000 men, had been light, but like all other divisions, the arrival of the cold weather found it stretched out to the rear for a hundred miles or more. During October the supply system had failed entirely. The first line gun ammunition had been almost shot off and there was no barbed wire to be had. Of rations there were none, but, more fortunate than many, 6 Division had managed to live off the land. Local Russian horses were slaughtered and for nearly six weeks the troops ate little else but horse meat, although some potatoes were collected and thawed out. Bread was made, the troops threshing the rye themselves, and formations and units raised their own foraging commandos, searching for horses, food and fodder. With the freeze, supply and movement were gradually resumed and relay teams of horses brought *panje* supplies up from Sychevka to Ulitino, until fifteen tons a day were being delivered against a minimum requirement of thirty. By mid November the artillery ammunition was partially replenished, but all incoming vehicle fuel was needed to tank up the isolated and stranded vehicles miles to the rear. All the artillery could not be moved for lack of horses, as many as fourteen horses being needed to move a single gun, and the artillerymen were to compare their equipment unfavourably with that of the Red Army, which made use of gun-towing tractors.[28] It was noted, too, that although the Soviet enemy appeared to have lost most of his lighter field guns in the recent defeats, he still had a good number of medium and heavy guns, and had replaced his lost field guns with medium mortars.

The cold weather found the troops in their summer uniforms, although ten per cent of the divisional winter clothing arrived in Smolensk railway station at the beginning of November. The wounded suffered untold agonies, being evacuated across the rutted broken tracks in *panje* wagons filled with straw, with straw-built thatched roofs to keep off the frost.

The experiences of other divisions were very similar, although many of them were less fortunate than 6 Infantry Division. From the beginning of November the temperature in the Moscow area had dropped rapidly and the frozen ground had become firm. Time, however, was needed to bring up the artillery and the supply vehicles, which were still stranded far to the rear, these having been frozen in to their axles. There was a lack of motor vehicles and although the railway was in use as far forward as Bryansk, Vyazma and Rzhev, its capacity was low as track laying was still in progress.[29] The cold

---

[27] *Ibid*, pp. 296–9.
[28] Russian ponies were generally too light as artillery draught animals.
[29] Grossmann, *Geschichte der Rheinisch-Westfälischen 6. Infanterie-Division*, pp. 81–6.

weather brought with it both suffering and frustration. The frozen-in vehicles and guns had to be chipped out by hand with pickaxes, and many were damaged beyond repair in the attempts to tow them free. Unless muffled, vehicle engines iced up as they ran, and fires had to be lighted beneath trucks and tanks at rest. The oil in the recoil system of the guns became solidified and machine-guns and automatic rifles failed for the same reason. Only the mortar could be relied on. Optical gun sights and telescopic instruments gave off a bloom which made them useless. Without calks the tracked vehicles could not grip on the ice; and in the soft snow the narrow tracks of the German tanks gave them very poor tactical mobility.[30] Lack of a proper diet and the eating of frozen food gave rise to vomiting and stomach ailments. No camouflaged white smocks and no winter clothing had been received and many troops were even without underclothes and serviceable boots. No soldier could be left alone without a second man to watch him for the signs of frost-bite, and the wounded died where they fell, not from their wounds but from the shock and frost-bite occasioned by the loss of blood.[31]

On 7 November the decision had been taken to resume the offensive towards Moscow, but the immediate intention was to close in nearer to the city.[32] Von Kluge's 4 Army to the west of Moscow was to pin the Soviet defence along the line of the Nara and the Oka, between the Moskva River and Alexin, while Hoepner's 4 Panzer Group, which was under von Kluge's command, thrust on the left of the 4 Army sector in a north-easterly direction, enveloping Moscow from the north. Reinhardt's 3 Panzer Group was brought south from the area of Kalinin close alongside Hoepner's 4 Panzer Group, but was under command of Strauss's 9 Army which was itself responsible for the flank protection to the north. Guderian's 2 Panzer Army was to thrust north-east once more from the area of Tula to Kashira and Kolomna and the east of Moscow. Von Weichs's 2 Army, which was under the temporary command of Rudolf Schmidt, had only a minor part to play having been detailed for the security of the southern flank of 2 Panzer Army.

Zhukov was theoretically in sole command of the defence of Moscow and, according to his own post-war account, was confident of success. Why he should have been so sanguine, it is difficult to determine. Only once, on 14 November, was a counter-attack ordered by Stalin and Shaposhnikov and

[30] The mobility of a tank is expressed in nominal ground pressure, the lower the pressure the better the tank performance over soft ground. This pressure is the ratio between the weight of the tank and the area of track in contact with the ground. The German defect was one of insufficient track area rather than that of width and in subsequent winters it was to be overcome by adding a side extension to tracks. According to Brennecke, the Chief of Staff of Army Group North, no German tank could move in deep snow, while in the intense cold about one tank gun in five could fire. Halder, *Kriegstagebuch*, Vol. 3, pp. 328 and 331.

[31] Baumann, *Die 35. Infanterie-Division*, pp. 135–7.

[32] On 7 November in Moscow the traditional parade was taken by Budenny, the troops taking part in the parade, so it is said, being dispatched immediately afterwards to the battle front. According to the Soviet account no guns were available to take part in the parade and the deficiency was made good by withdrawing old guns from a museum.

this, mounted against Zhukov's wishes by Rokossovsky's 16 Army and Zakharkin's 49 Army on the German north and south flank in the areas of Volokolamsk and the lower Nara, achieved little except the pinning of part of von Kluge's force.[33] During the first fortnight in November, 100,000 troops, 2,000 guns and 300 tanks arrived at the West Front.[34]

The resumption of the German offensive was started on 15 November in clear and frosty weather.[35] Reinhardt's 3 Panzer Group and a part of 9 Army

[33] Zhukov, *Bitva za Moskvu*, p. 76.
[34] Zhukov, *Vospominaniya i Razmyshleniya*, pp. 362–6.
[35] Von Bock's Army Group Centre order of battle (not including 2 Army which was far to the south) is set out below.

		Pz.	Mot.	Inf.
3 Panzer Group	(Reinhardt)	3	2	3
9 Army	(Strauss)			10
4 Panzer Group	(Hoepner)	4	1	7
4 Army	(von Kluge)	2	1	12
2 Panzer Army	(Guderian)	4	3	6
		13	7	38 = 58

OKH Kriegsgliederung of 4 November.

The Soviet order of battle before Moscow in mid November was said to be as follows.

		Rifle	Tank brigades	Cavalry
West Front				
30 Army	(Lelyushenko)	2	1	
16 Army	(Rokossovsky)	4	4	6
5 Army	(Govorov)	5	5	
33 Army	(Efremov)	4	1	
49 Army	(Zakharkin)	7		
50 Army	(Boldin)	7	2	2
		29	13	8 = 50

		Rifle	Tank brigades	Cavalry
Kalinin Front				
22 Army	(Vostrukhov)	6		1
29 Army	(Maslennikov)	5		1
31 Army	(Dolmatov)	5 (?)		
Reserve		1	1	
		17	1	2 = 20

		Rifle	Tank brigades	Cavalry
South-West Front				
3 Army	(Kreizer)	5	3	2
13 Army	(Gorodnyansky)	9		2
		14	3	4 = 21

Formations before Moscow	60	17	14 = 91

Sokolovsky, *Razgrom Nemetsko-Fashistskikh Voisk pod Moskvoi*, pp. 67–78. Many of these formations were very much under strength. According, however, to the *Kratkaya Istoriya*, p. 122, by mid November the reinforced West Front already had more divisions than the attackers.

drove in Khomenko's 30 Army on the left wing of Konev's Kalinin Front in an attack towards Klin. On Stalin's order, Khomenko was immediately relieved of his command by Lelyushenko.[36] On the following day Hoepner's 4 Panzer Group attacked Rokossovsky's 16 Army on the right wing of Zhukov's West Front, thrusting towards Istra, and on 18 November Guderian's 2 Panzer Army took up the attack from the area of Tula. Meanwhile von Kluge's 4 German Army in the centre was itself attacked. 3 and 4 Panzer Group on the north flank had some success against 30 and 16 Soviet Armies, taking Klin on 24 and Solnechnogorsk on 25 November.[37] Three days later the panzer groups were immediately to the north of Moscow at Dmitrov and Yakhroma and had actually crossed the Moskva-Volga canal, being less than twenty-five miles from the north-west outskirts of the city.

At about this time occurred an incident which is indicative of the way in which Stalin conducted operations. Stalin telephoned Zhukov on 28 November to ask him whether he knew that the Germans had broken through Beloborodov's 9 Guards Rifle Division near the Istra and had taken Dedovsk. Zhukov did not know. He was told tartly by Stalin that it was the front commander's job to keep himself informed and that both he and Rokossovsky should proceed immediately to the threatened area and mount a counter-attack. A telephone call to Rokossovsky brought the information that Dedovsk had not fallen, but that the Germans had made some gains in Dedovo some distance away. This intelligence, when retailed to Stalin, apparently angered him, for he repeated his order, instructing that Govorov, an artilleryman (who had taken over 5 Army after the former commander Lelyushenko had been wounded when German tanks and infantry had overrun the command post) should accompany Zhukov and Rokossovsky to Dedovo 'in order to arrange the artillery support for the counter-attack'. A nonplussed Zhukov telephoned the order to Govorov, who being engaged in the thick of battle, did not quite see the point, since Rokossovsky had his own artillery commander. Govorov said so, but had to comply nevertheless. The front and the two army commanders proceeded to Dedovo, heard Beloborodov's appreciation of the situation, solemnly ordered him to mount a company counter-attack supported by two tanks on some German-occupied houses in the woods, and then returned to their more important duties.[38]

Zhukov had been urging that V. I. Kuznetsov's 1 Shock Army and Golikov's 10 Army should be allocated to him from the High Command Reserve and the command of these armies was transferred to him on 29 November.[39] The

[36] Lelyushenko, *Zarya Pobedy*, pp. 82, 88–9.
[37] According to *Istoriya*, Vol. 2, p. 260, Lelyushenko's 30 Army had only 20 tanks and 200 guns left. This may be true since it consisted of only a motor rifle and a rifle division, a tank brigade, a motor regiment and a reinforcement regiment. It is certain that many more Soviet tanks were available in the latter stages of the battle.
[38] Zhukov, *Vospominaniya i Razmyshleniya*, pp. 369–70.
[39] A shock army was a rifle army with greatly increased organic artillery.

armies were, however, very incomplete and most of the rank and file were hastily levied recruits who had never been in action before. The method by which 10 Army was raised is informative as to its readiness for war.

Golikov had been sent on 21 October to Kuznetsk in the Volga Military District to form 10 Army of nine rifle and cavalry divisions, without the aid of an army staff or headquarters, since this had not yet been formed. All the divisions were scattered as far apart as Moscow and Turkestan and most of them had to be recruited, trained and equipped. 10 Army consisted of 100,000 men, 11,000 each to the rifle and 3,000 to the cavalry divisions, but only a quarter of the rank and file were under thirty years of age, and quite a number were over forty. Ninety per cent were Russians and only four per cent Ukrainians, but what concerned Golikov and his military council particularly was that he had in 10 Army only 5,387 communist party members and 3,718 young communists. An appeal to the *Stavka* and to the Main Political Administration in Moscow brought a special dispatch of 700 party members to join the formation.

Golikov, according to his own account, was not so fortunate in the supply of equipment. Two of his cavalry divisions were without saddlery and one of his rifle divisions was deficient of 7,500 rifles. Three rifle and two cavalry divisions had not a radio set between them and the motor transport received varied in divisions from twelve to fifty-eight per cent of scale. There was a general shortage of artillery, heavy machine-guns, mortars and engineer equipment. On 24 November, a surprised Golikov, who had expected to receive three months to mobilize, was told by Shaposhnikov to be ready to move immediately.[40]

Further to the south-east Guderian's 2 Panzer Army was making very slow progress. On 13 November at the Orsha meeting at Army Group Centre, at which Halder was present, such far-flung objectives were discussed as the industrial city of Gorki (400 miles from Orel and 200 miles to the east of Moscow) much to the amazement and indignation of von Liebenstein, Guderian's chief of staff.[41] Guderian had become aware that Siberian formations were detraining at Ryazan and Kolomna on his exposed south-east flank and that one division had already arrived at Uzlovaya.[42] The weakened German infantry divisions could no longer cope with this fresh enemy and the Soviet counter-attacks supported by T34 tanks caused a wave of panic which spread as far back as Bogoroditsk. This, commented Guderian, was the first time that such a thing had occurred during the campaign.[43] 2 Panzer Army, made up of von Schweppenburg's 24 and Lemelsen's 47 Panzer Corps and two infantry corps, had a strength of only twelve divisions, half of which were of marching

---

[40] Golikov, *V Moskovskoi Bitve*, pp. 11–28.
[41] Guderian, *Panzer Leader*, p. 247.
[42] This was probably Golikov's 10 Army.
[43] Guderian, *Panzer Leader*, p. 249.

H

infantry.[44] On 21 November, however, Guderian took Uzlovaya and three days later 24 Panzer Corps, advancing northwards towards the Oka in the direction of Moscow, took Venev; 239 Siberian Rifle Division was encircled in the area of Stalinogorsk until several days later, when it broke out to the east abandoning its vehicles and equipment. On the afternoon of 23 November Guderian visited von Bock to stress the tired condition of his troops and said that von Bock referred by telephone to von Brauchitsch, Guderian listening in to the conversation, when it became quite obvious to both of them that the Commander-in-Chief was not allowed to make any decision. According to Guderian further representations to Halder, through the OKH liaison officer, were without avail.[45] Von Bock then gave up all hope of attaining the long range objectives which had been assigned to him and at the best intended to improve his position about Tula. Even this was denied him since 24 Panzer Corps and von Kluge's 4 Army were unable to co-ordinate their enveloping attack, a repetition of that made earlier on Bryansk, aimed at pinching out Boldin's 50 Soviet Army in the Tula area.

Hitherto von Bock had been driving his troops relentlessly on from his forward command post, but on 1 December it became evident that he considered success was no longer possible. He emphasized to von Brauchitsch and to Halder the weakness of his troops, who were by then having to attack well-prepared enemy positions frontally. Halder, by way of reply, could only stress that the difficulties were known but that it was the last reserves of strength which would count.[46]

In the area to the east of Moscow a further nine reserve Soviet Armies were in the process of being formed.[47]

Reinhardt's 3 and Hoepner's 4 Panzer Groups continued to make progress to the north of the city, but the newly arriving Soviet troops were fighting stubbornly. In vain did Hoepner telephone von Kluge day after day asking him to start his attack to the west of Moscow from the area of the Nara. For some unknown reason von Kluge was slow to act, as he repeatedly talked the

[44] Guderian had lost 48 Panzer Corps to 2 Army and this moved on Kursk. 2 Panzer Army received little flank protection from 2 Army since von Weichs was being pressed to advance due east in the direction of Voronezh near the Don. Before the offensive was launched it was believed, quite wrongly, that the Red Army was evacuating all territory to the west of the Don.

[45] Guderian, *Panzer Leader*, p. 252. On 23 November Halder recorded that von Bock had expressed doubt as to the feasibility of Army Group Centre objectives. That same day von Bock noted in his diary that Guderian still maintained that he could reach his operational objectives, this being at variance with Guderian's post-war account of his report that he could see no way of carrying his orders out. Von Bock wrote that he had warned both von Brauchitsch and Halder that it was already five minutes to twelve and not to exaggerate the strength of German troops. Von Bock, *Tagebuch*. Yet, even as late as 4 December, von Greiffenberg, the Chief of Staff Army Group Centre, saw no reason to call off Guderian's attack. Halder, *Kriegstagebuch*, Vol. 3, p. 326.

[46] *Ibid*, p. 322.

[47] *Istoriya*, Vol. 2, p. 271.

matter over with Blumentritt and von Bock.[48] Not before 1 December did he begin his attack.

3 Infantry Division, part of 57 Panzer Corps, was one of the divisions earmarked for the 4 Army offensive. It occupied a difficult area near Naro Fominsk, under observation from the Soviet positions. Red Army snipers were in the chimneys of buildings, and any daylight movement brought down heavy mortar fire. The German formations were too weak to cover the frontage; great gaps occurred and the enemy infiltrated deep into the rear. At night the temperature was down to minus thirty degrees centigrade and all soldiers had to be withdrawn after one hour in the open, for one hour in which to thaw out and restore the circulation. The divisional commander himself had some reservations as to the likelihood of success as he was opposed by fresh, well-equipped Siberian divisions with plenty of tanks and guns. 29 Infantry Regiment attacked with the support of a single armoured assault gun company and immediately started to lose heavily in casualties. A reinforced 5 Company of III battalion, a very strong company of seventy men, by evening had only twenty-eight left. The division came to a standstill because its task was too great for it. III battalion of 8 Motorized Regiment lost eighty men, a third of its strength, but of these eighty no fewer than fifty-eight were exhaustion or frost-bite casualties, caused by exposure. The co-ordination within corps and army was poor and 15 Infantry Division was brought up too late to exploit 3 Division's gains.[49]

The immediate threat to Moscow was the thrust of Reinhardt's 3 and Hoepner's 4 Panzer Groups to the north of the city, and to counter it Soviet troops were brought up rapidly from 24 and 60 Reserve Armies in the east; 7 and 8 Guards Divisions, the first two divisions to arrive in the northern outskirts, formed the nucleus of a new 20 Soviet Army commanded by Vlasov.[50] V. I. Kuznetsov's 1 Shock Army coming up from the area of Zagorsk, attacked between Dmitrov and the Iksha Lake and held the Germans on the line of the Moskva-Volga canal. Reinhardt's and Hoepner's panzer groups were halted by these two newly arrived armies together with elements of Lelyushenko's 30 and Rokossovsky's 16 Armies, only seventeen miles north-west of the city, and by 3 December these Red Army formations were already counter-attacking in strength. Guderian's offensive was brought to a standstill by the determined Soviet stand in Tula, Stalinogorsk and Venev which tied down troops, so that only one panzer division was available for the final attack on the Kashira bridges over the Oka. This attack, made by 17 Panzer Division, was repulsed by Boldin's 50 and Zakharkin's 49 Armies using tanks, cavalry and anti-aircraft guns in an anti-tank role. Meanwhile the new formations

[48] Halder, *Kriegstagebuch*, Vol. 3, p. 322; also Westphal, *The Fatal Decisions*, Blumentritt, p. 60.

[49] Dieckhoff, *Die 3. Infanterie-Division*, pp. 137–44.

[50] Because of his subsequent defection the name of Vlasov is rarely recorded in Soviet history and any credit is given to his deputy, Lizyuzov.

already noted by Guderian arriving to the east, 26 Army near Kolomna, Golikov's 10 Army in the Ryazan area, F. I. Kuznetsov's 61 Army behind South-West Front near Ryazsk, were approaching the 2 Panzer Army flank. 2 Panzer Army and 2 Army continued their pressure until 4 December but their attacks became progressively weaker, spread out as they were over a frontage of over 200 miles. Von Kluge's 4 Army offensive had its only noteworthy success when it breached the 33 Soviet Army line north of Naro Fominsk and tried to encircle Govorov's 5 Soviet Army to the north. This thrust was the last German effort of the campaign and it was brought to a halt by the reserves of Efremov's 33 and Golubev's 43 Soviet Armies near the railway town of Golizno on 2 and 3 December. It was in any event too late to assist Hoepner.

On 3 December von Kluge on his own responsibility ordered the withdrawal of 258 Infantry Division since he could no longer be answerable for its safety, and he reported that the bloody losses were quite colossal.[51] That day von Bock telephoned Jodl to ensure that the *Führer* was in possession of full information as to the situation on the ground. By 4 December the Germans were forced to fall back to the Nara for fear of being encircled. The next day von Bock with the acquiescence of the Army High Command called off the offensive, and von Brauchitsch decided that he was going to give up his appointment and leave the Army.[52]

On 6 December the *Führer* held a meeting to discuss future action. In reality, Hitler himself was at bay. The ideas he expressed and his decisions at this time were to set a pattern for the rest of the war and were to destroy three successive Chiefs of General Staff. The *Führer*'s head was teeming with figures, some of which were entirely inaccurate. He quoted German losses as half a million, whereas they were in fact over 800,000, and Soviet losses as between eight and ten million.[53] He persuaded himself that all the advantages lay with the Germans and proposed a number of makeshift schemes to release German manpower to the Eastern Front. These included the raising of fighting formations from motor vehicle drivers, now idle because of the great number of trucks derelict or awaiting repairs, the combing out of rear services and the replacement of German civil labour by prisoners of war. Under no circumstances would he permit any thinning out of troops from Scandinavia or Western Europe. The Russian had held on to the ground in front of Moscow

---

[51] *Kriegstagebuch des Oberkommandos der Heeresgruppe Mitte*, 3 December 1941, pp. 886–9.

[52] Von Brauchitsch was in poor health having already suffered from a heart attack and being on the verge of a nervous breakdown. Halder, *Kriegstagebuch*, Vol. 3, p. 328; Keitel, *Memoirs*, p. 163.

[53] It is probable that Soviet losses at that time were at least five to six million. Stalin in his 6 November speech did not give the figure for Red Army wounded and admitted the loss of only 350,000 dead and 375,000 prisoners. By 31 December 1941 Army Group Centre alone claimed 1,912,376 Soviet prisoners. (*Heeresgruppe Mitte H 3/158 Gefangene und Beutemeldung* of 4 January 1942), and the overall count of prisoners exceeded three million.

and so would the German. Although he was to change his views later, the *Führer* was not opposed in principle to shortening the defensive line, but there could be no question of pulling out before the rearward positions were prepared. He still had his eyes on Donets coal and Maikop oil, nor had he written off the likelihood of the recapture of Rostov during that winter.[54]

The next day the *Führer* was making difficulties about any withdrawals, however small, and Halder was to bemoan the depths to which the German Army leadership had sunk. He noted that von Brauchitsch, the Commander-in-Chief, was nothing but the *Führer*'s postman and Hitler now dealt direct with the army groups. The worst aspect was that no one in the Supreme Command (and by this Halder meant Hitler) understood the true condition of the troops. There, in the OKW, it was believed that the position could be restored by a little patching here and a little cobbling there, whereas in fact some far-reaching and grave decisions were required. One of these, in Halder's view, was the withdrawal of Army Group Centre back to the line of Ostashkov and the River Ruza.[55] Halder's criticism and his proposed remedy were justified and sound, yet it must be remembered that Hitler alone was not responsible for driving Army Group Centre on into a dangerously exposed, almost desperate; position, and it seems that von Brauchitsch, Halder and von Bock had been no less determined to get to Moscow so late in the season.

On 8 December the *Führer* grudgingly agreed to abandon the offensive and issued Directive 39 which laid the blame on 'the surprisingly early severe winter weather'.[56]

From this time onwards the German position on the East Front was critically dangerous and for the next few months German troops were on the defensive, sometimes retreating, and always fighting to stave off disaster. The Soviet counter-offensive did not start on 6 December when the German attacks petered out but had been gradually building up to a crescendo for some weeks before. The concentration of troops had been started in late October, and in November the Meretskov Group, the Leningrad Front and Timoshenko's South-West Front had been ordered to go over to the offensive in order to relieve the German pressure on Moscow and to ensure that no German formations would be moved from the flanks to reinforce Army Group Centre. Field-Marshal von Leeb, anxiously noting the failure of the thrust on Moscow, his own troops being under heavy Soviet attack, at last persuaded Hitler on 8 December to agree to the withdrawal from Tikhvin. However, whereas von Leeb wanted to withdraw about twenty miles or so to the south-west, the *Führer* continued to insist that the Tikhvin road and railway should be kept within the range of artillery.[57] Nearer Moscow, Konev's Kalinin Front began to thrust on the German flank from about 27 November onwards, and

[54] Halder, *Kriegstagebuch*, Vol. 3, pp. 329–31.
[55] *Ibid*, pp. 332–3.
[56] Hubatsch, *Hitlers Weisungen für die Kriegführung*, p. 171.
[57] Halder, *Kriegstagebuch*, Vol. 3, pp. 329 and 332.

towards the end of November the whole of Zhukov's West Front was gradually taking the initiative, its main thrust coming from the newly arrived V. I. Kuznetsov's 1 Shock Army and Vlasov's 20 Army to the north of Moscow. In addition, further heavy thrusts were made in the centre by Golikov's 10 Army, and Boldin's heavily reinforced 50 Army. In the south, the flank of Timoshenko's South-West Front was exerting increased pressure against 2 German Army and 2 Panzer Army.

At the first of Germany's defeats at Rostov the *Führer* had flown into a rage and, accepting von Rundstedt's offer of resignation, had ordered his replacement by von Reichenau. In company with Schmundt, his military aide, he flew to Mariupol to see his Party crony Sepp Dietrich, the divisional commander of the *SS Leibstandarte*, to hear what he hoped was the truth about the situation. He was disappointed, because the SS were convinced that they themselves would not have survived if they had remained in the forward positions. So Hitler returned, his mind inflamed instead against his former friend and supporter von Reichenau who had, surprisingly, apparently incurred displeasure by criticizing von Brauchitsch and von Rundstedt.[58] The Commander-in-Chief, von Brauchitsch, was to be the next casualty. According to Keitel, the *Führer* had for long realized, however he might try to conceal it from his staff, that military catastrophe was near and was searching for scapegoats; but the evidence inclines more to the view that Hitler was convinced that his senior commanders lacked the fanaticism, will-power and even the expertise to overcome their manifold difficulties. Some of them were guilty of the graver fault of beginning to doubt the *Führer*'s intuition and genius, and these were marked down for elimination. From the beginning of December onwards von Brauchitsch's position became increasingly untenable. Under the pressure of events and Hitler's bullying, he became sick and on 15 December he returned from a visit to Army Group Centre, very dejected in spirits, since he could see no way in which the troops could be extricated from their difficult position.[59] For some time past the *Führer*'s attitude to the Army High Command had been tinged with contempt, and at the time of von Rundstedt's dismissal and replacement, Hitler did not even consult his Commander-in-Chief.[60] On 16 December he sent his aide, Schmundt, to Army Group Centre to obtain a briefing on the situation, and Schmundt was told by von Bock that the *Führer* would have to make a choice. He could resume the attack towards Moscow, risking the danger that in doing so he would beat his own troops to pieces, or he could remain on the defensive. If he chose to defend, he should remember that no defensive works had been prepared either in the present positions or in the rear, and it was in any case doubtful whether the German troops could hold. Von Bock quoted as an example 267 Division which had

[58] Keitel, *Memoirs*, pp. 161–2.
[59] Halder, *Kriegstagebuch*, Vol. 3, p. 348.
[60] Warlimont, *Inside Hitler's Headquarters*, p. 194. According to Goebbels, Hitler spoke of von Brauchitsch as a vain cowardly wretch and a nincompoop. *Goebbels' Diary*, p. 92, 20 March 1942.

been forced to withdraw that very day, at the cost of leaving all its artillery behind.[61] As usual, the clear-sighted von Bock could ably appreciate and state the situation, without, however, coming to a firm conclusion as to the necessary action to be taken. From von Bock's views was born the fanatical stand and fight order of 20 December.[62]

The Army Group Centre war diary at this fateful time noted that the offensive spirit of the Red Army enemy was not at all well developed, and that the German failure was to be attributed firstly to the physical and moral condition of the German troops, whose strength had been grossly overtaxed, secondly to the troops' fear of capture by the Russians, thirdly to the reduced fighting strengths, fourthly to the lack of vehicle fuels and supplies, and fifthly, to the severe shortage of good horses.[63] Von Bock put the position more succinctly when on 7 December he recorded in his own personal diary that there were three main causes for the defeat, mud, the failure of the railway system and the underestimating of the enemy.[64]

On 19 December after a last acrimonious meeting, von Brauchitsch was dismissed and retired, and Hitler took over the function of Army Commander-in-Chief. The previous day Field-Marshal von Bock, the Commander-in-Chief of Army Group Centre, who had long suffered from a stomach ailment aggravated by strain and worry, had reported himself sick and had been replaced by Field-Marshal von Kluge, formerly the Commander of 4 Army.

Halder was sent for by Hitler on 19 December and was informed of the change with the words that this little affair of operational command was something anybody could do.[65] What was wanted was political awareness and determination. He was told that the *Führer* had decided on a policy of no withdrawal, irrespective of any threat to the flanks, and he had to listen to the usual reproaches in which the German Army was compared to its disadvantage with the *Luftwaffe*. The German Army had not, Hitler said, made sufficient provision against the weather, and the Chief of General Staff could forget any talk of withdrawing as there were not any rearward positions to fall back on, and they could not in any event be constructed on account of the cold. Halder would, in the circumstances, have been wiser to have taken the option of resigning rather than continuing in office. He may have felt himself as responsible as Hitler and von Brauchitsch that the German Army in the East had arrived in such straits, and it is said he was urged by von Brauchitsch to remain at his post, since only he was capable of extricating the troops from their dangerously exposed position.[66]

[61] *Kriegstagebuch des Oberkommandos der Heeresgruppe Mitte*, 16 December 1941, p. 999.

[62] *OKH Gen St d H. Op Abt (I) Nr. 32061/41 g. Kdos* of 20 December 1941.

[63] *Kriegstagebuch des Oberkommandos der Heeresgruppe Mitte*, p. 1008.

[64] Von Bock, *Tagebuch*, 7 December 1941.

[65] Halder, *Hitler as War Lord*, p. 51.

[66] Halder, *Kriegstagebuch*, Vol. 3, p. 354, note 2.

From the beginning of the war against the Soviet Union, the German Army Commander-in-Chief's operational responsibilities had been confined to the Eastern Front, not including Finland. All other fronts became OKW theatres, in that they were controlled by the *Führer* through Jodl and the *Wehrmacht-führungstab*. This direct control by Hitler applied, however, only to the German Army in the OKW theatres, since all formations and units of the *Luftwaffe* and Navy, whether in the East or the West, came directly under their own Commanders-in-Chief. The OKH therefore, unlike the OKL and OKM, had already suffered a serious diminishing of its operational authority. When Hitler stated his intention of taking over the post of Commander-in-Chief of the German Army, he sought direct operational, even tactical, control over the commanders of the army groups in the East.[67] In von Brauchitsch's many other important duties Hitler had no interest, and these he transferred to Keitel, the Head of the OKW. Thereafter Halder and the succeeding Chiefs of General Staff had little or no responsibility for staff branches outside the General Staff, and the real control over armament, equipment, administration and the Replacement Army passed to Keitel. The Chief of General Staff was in this way separated from other branches of the OKH, while Keitel, in addition to being Chief of the OKW, acted for Hitler on general affairs pertaining to the German Army.[68] Halder became merely Hitler's executive for the East Front and he and the later Chiefs of General Staff were at times to suffer interference from both Keitel and Jodl even on operational matters in Russia. This meddling was condoned by Hitler, who used Keitel and Jodl to counter unwelcome advice proffered to him by the Chief of General Staff.

The Army Personnel Office (*Heerespersonalamt*) headed by the younger (Bodewin) Keitel, who had formerly been responsible to von Brauchitsch for all army promotions and appointments, came directly under the *Führer*, and in the autumn this most important department was put under Schmundt, the *Führer*'s military aide.

The German Army, unlike the other two armed services, was in reality without a Commander-in-Chief.

---

[67] The operative art is difficult to define but at the risk of over-simplification it might be said that according to German and Russian military terminology the waging of war at corps level and below is known as tactics; at army group (front) and army level it is called operations; above army group level it becomes strategy. In British or United States terminology there is no equivalent for this use of the word operations (or the operative art).

[68] Compare Mueller-Hillebrand, *Das Heer*, Vol. 3, Chapter 10.

CHAPTER FOURTEEN

A Record of Folly and Error

On 8 December Japan, much to the *Führer*'s surprise, attacked the United States Pacific Fleet in Pearl Harbour, as well as the British Crown Colony in Hong Kong.[1] Originally the Germans had no wish to bring the United States into the war, but on 29 November General Oshima, the Japanese Ambassador in Berlin, telegraphed to Tokyo that the German attitude towards the United States had stiffened considerably. In the preceding spring Hitler had assured Matsuoka, the Japanese Foreign Minister, that should Japan become engaged in a war against the United States, Germany would join the war immediately, and this promise was repeated by von Ribbentrop to Oshima at the end of November. During the previous six months Tokyo had steadfastly refused to join Germany in the war against the Soviet Union, yet on Monday, 8 December, Oshima was already pressing von Ribbentrop that Germany should honour its verbal agreement and enter into war against the United States. Except for the verbal undertaking made by Hitler and von Ribbentrop neither Germany nor Italy was in any way bound to assist Japan, since the terms of the Tripartite Pact did not require the other two Powers to support Japan's aggression against the United States, and Japan had not consulted either before it made the attack on Pearl Harbour. It might be assumed that Hitler would have declared war on the United States only if Japan had agreed to enter the war against the USSR. Surprisingly enough the dictator appeared to have had no reservations and made no conditions.

Tokyo went to war because it was faced with United States counter-pressure to Japanese expansion in Indo-China and China, and because of economic sanctions imposed on Japan by the United States, Britain and the Netherlands East Indies.[2] Tokyo wanted oil and intended to fulfil its political and territorial ambitions in South-East Asia, and the Tojo Cabinet made a disastrous intelligence appreciation when it overestimated the military and economic power of Germany and grossly underestimated that of the United States.

---

[1] 7 December United States and Hawaiian time, 8 December Japanese and Hong Kong time.

[2] In answer to the Japanese aggression in Indo-China in July 1941, the three countries had placed an embargo on exports to Japan and Japanese assets in the United States had been frozen.

Japan's strategic war aims amounted to nothing more than the seizing of oil in the Netherlands East Indies and Burma, and the securing of its conquests in South-East Asia and the Pacific.[3] It had no intention of invading India or Australia and had no plan for overcoming the United States or Britain. Japanese strategy was short-termed and opportunist and was based on a misplaced confidence in German might. When the Japanese aircraft carriers sailed from Japanese home waters, it appeared that Moscow was about to fall.

The underlying logic of the *Führer*'s policy towards the United States defies analysis. Hitler was a European and it is doubtful whether before 1941 he gave much thought to the New World. He was certainly unimpressed by the American military establishment in peace. Yet during 1940 and 1941 he had exercised great restraint in the face of a United States which was rapidly moving towards belligerency, and he had strongly resisted Raeder's urging for a freer hand against the United States Navy and mercantile marine, for fear of worsening German-American relations.

Hitler made an error fatal for Germany when he underestimated the potential of the United States. He regarded Japan as the strongest naval power in the world and, counselled by Raeder, wanted Japan to intervene against the British in the Pacific, and so tie down the attention and energy of the United States to that distant theatre. The aim of Raeder's arguments was not, however, to bring the United States into the war. Hitler could reason, as he did, that the United States was implacably hostile to Germany. It was a major supplier of arms, equipment and raw materials to Germany's enemies, providing warships to convoy British vessels across the Atlantic and troops to garrison Iceland. It was bound to enter the war sooner or later. Yet it was an irrational act on the *Führer*'s part to have precipitated the event. Except for its submarine fleet, the German Navy was a negligible factor outside the Baltic. The German Army and *Luftwaffe* were already fully extended, and the United States was far beyond the range of German air power. For this reason Germany was powerless to wage any war against the United States. It is possible that Hitler expected a United States declaration of war against Germany, although there appears to be no evidence on which he could have based such an assumption, and was determined for reasons of prestige to get his blow in first. Like many other Germans, Hitler was elated by the Japanese successes in the first days of the war. Whatever the reason, he incorporated his declaration of war on the United States in his speech to the *Reichstag* on 11 December.

By that declaration of war Germany lost finally and irrevocably all hope of winning the war against the Soviet Union.

In the last seven months of 1941 the character of the struggle had changed from that of a European to a World War. In May, Germany had been the undisputed master of Europe, and the USSR hastened to do its bidding.

[3] Japan could produce only about ten per cent of its own oil requirements.

214

Britain, with its great resources and with its rapidly expanding air force and navy and the promise of United States material aid, might have remained at war almost indefinitely; yet its efforts to become a land power lacked conviction, since it appeared unwilling or unable to raise a large number of army field formations. Germany was not to be defeated by naval blockade or aerial bombardment, and until the German Army was destroyed on the mainland of Europe the *Reich* would apparently endure for ever.

When he attacked the Soviet Union Hitler broke his earlier promises to the German armed forces and nation by entering into a war on two fronts. Such was his exaggerated respect for British military power and so fearful was he of the effect of any reverse, however local, on his reputation, that he left fifty-four divisions to hold Western Europe and the Balkans.[4] In addition about forty per cent of the German first line combat aircraft remained in the West for the defence of the *Reich* and occupied Europe against attacks by the Royal Air Force. Whereas the *Führer* overestimated British potential at that time, he seriously underrated that of the Soviet Union. His attack on the USSR was to be a short prelude to the more serious business of putting the British Commonwealth and Empire out of the war and in this scaling of values he appears to have had the acquiescence or support of most of the senior German Army commanders. When the territory into which he had so light-heartedly entered bogged down his panzers and soaked up the blood of the German infantry, what was to have been an easily won summer campaign became instead firstly a major war and then an embittered struggle, an all-consuming crusade against the Bolshevik, pursued with ever-increasing fanatical fury, which made Hitler blind to any other considerations. This fury made him fly in the face of reason, so that, aping Napoleon to whom he liked to hear himself compared, he exchanged his role of Head of the German State for that of a war lord and field commander.[5]

At the outbreak of the war the British Chiefs of Staff, even though they rated the effectiveness of the Red Army more highly than did Kinzel's Foreign Armies East, considered that the Germans were capable of reaching Moscow within six weeks of the start of the war. Von Bock took Smolensk, not 200 miles from Moscow, on the twenty-third day and there appears to have been no reason why Army Group Centre should not have taken Moscow by the beginning of September, since it is certain that the Red Army at that time could not have barred its progress. On the other hand, the loss of the capital, however damaging it might have been from a political and a morale point of view, would not have put the Soviet Union out of the war, since much of

[4] Eight divisions were in Norway, thirty-eight in Western Europe, seven in the Balkans and one in Germany. Of these, however, only twenty-two were first class three-regiment divisions, the remaining field divisions being either two-regiment divisions or on lower establishments for equipment and personnel. Of the infantry divisions used against the Soviet Union in June 1941, only nineteen were two-regiment or lower category divisions. Mueller-Hillebrand, *Das Heer*, Vol. 2, p. 111.

[5] Halder, *Hitler as War Lord*, p. 39.

Soviet industry had its basis in the Urals and Siberia, and the loss of the Moscow industrial complex would not have robbed the USSR of its main source of armaments. Moscow was, of course, a nodal point for most of the Central Russian railway system, and on this account its loss would have been serious to the Soviet Union, but, even so, the railways from the Urals were still connected with Vologda, Archangel and the Finnish Front, the Western Front, the Caspian and the Donets Basin.[6] Nor should the Soviet powers of improvisation be lightly disregarded.[7] There is no reason to suppose that Stalin would have made peace with the Germans if Moscow had been lost, and there was perhaps even less likelihood that Hitler would have treated with him. Defeat for the Soviet Union would have meant complete submission to Hitler and in all probability the overthrow and liquidation of Stalin and his communist hierarchy. In such circumstances there can be little doubt that Stalin would have continued the war whatever his territorial losses, particularly when he had been assured of the support of the United States.[8]

Hitler has been blamed by his own High Command and General Staff for turning away from Moscow and squandering time and troops in separate offensives into the Ukraine and on to Leningrad.[9] The move into the Leningrad-Demyansk-Tikhvin area was abortive due to the closely wooded and marshy nature of the country. The advance into the Ukraine resulted in the great victory of the Kiev bend with the destruction of several armies and the taking of 600,000 prisoners; but if German success was to be measured by the destruction of Soviet armies, similar results at less cost in time and effort might have been obtained by adopting von Brauchitsch's plan and attacking Timoshenko's West Front in front of Moscow in July and August. If Hitler had done this, he would have taken Moscow, and Timoshenko's West Front would have been largely if not completely destroyed. On the other hand

[6] The railways radiated north, west and south of Moscow with the capital as the hub. To the east of the city, however, there were five main separate lines, all going to the Urals or Siberia; Vologda-Kirov, Gorki-Kirov, Moscow-Kazan, Ryazan-Kuybyshev, Ryazan-Saratov.

[7] Soviet railway construction was effective but very primitive. The track bed was of sand covered with a layer of stone to prevent erosion, but in emergency the bed would be dispensed with entirely. Sleepers were of untreated pine and light in weight, and numbered only 1,440 to the kilometre (compared with 2,000 in the USA). Chairs, sole or bedding plates were rarely used, and the rail was nailed direct to the sleeper. Pottgiesser, *Die Reichsbahn im Ostfeldzug*, p. 27.

[8] Stalin is said to have told Cripps that if the worst came he proposed to withdraw and fight from the territory beyond the Volga, believing that he could continue to wage war, but that it would take many years before he could strike back. Compare Deutscher, *Stalin*, p. 465.

[9] In October 1941 Halder and von Bock were critical of the *Führer's* strategy, but it is doubtful whether many other officers in the High Command had similar reservations at that time. Wagner, the Quartermaster-General, writing to his wife on 5 October, said that time and time again he marvelled at the *Führer's* military judgement. The *Führer* had interfered decisively in the conduct of operations and up to then he had always been right. The great victory in the south (i.e. the Ukraine), said Wagner, was the *Führer's* idea. Elisabeth Wagner, *Der Generalquartiermeister*, p. 206.

Budenny's South-West Theatre and Kirponos's South-West Front might have survived. For this reason the plan put forward by von Brauchitsch and Halder was superior to the *Führer*'s only in so far as it would have given marginally greater successes. It would certainly not have put the Soviet Union out of the war before the onset of winter.

Hitler's war direction aimed at too many scattered objectives. The loss of the Leningrad area and the Donets Basin would not have had a decisive and immediate effect on Soviet morale or economy. The possession of the Donets Basin was to prove of limited value to Germany. In the circumstances, it might have been preferable at the outset of the war to have adopted a strategy whereby Army Group North would have advanced directly eastwards towards Kalinin on the left flank of Army Group Centre, as part of a broad advance on Moscow, avoiding both Leningrad and the area of the North Baltic. Similarly Army Group South might have kept close to the right flank of Army Group Centre and, in the first instance, ignored the Crimea and the Transcaucasus oil region. If Kiev had been taken by the *coup de main* in the middle of July and the three army groups kept concentrated and more compact, the German thrust in the centre might have reached well beyond Moscow to the line of the Volga, from Vologda to Gorki and even to Saratov. Although the Red Army at this time lacked offensive mobility, the German flanks would still, however, have been vulnerable in some degree to Soviet counter-offensives from the South-East Ukraine and Leningrad, and whether the Germans could have held such a great salient during the winter months is questionable. Alternatively, the whole of the German effort could have been directed into the easier country of the Ukraine and the Donets Basin even as far as the Caucasian oilfields, as Stalin expected it would be; but the effect of the occupation would not have been immediate, and to derive any advantage the area would have had to be held for a year or more.

The truth was that, whatever strategy it had adopted, Germany entered the war in the East with inadequate resources. Fifty divisions and 1,500 aircraft had been left behind and in November, as the first warning of the danger inherent in fighting on two fronts, Kesselring's 2 Air Fleet Headquarters with one air corps was withdrawn to the Mediterranean, where Rommel was already in some difficulty in the face of a very modest British counter-offensive in North Africa. The Germans were entirely without troop reserves, and before autumn began the process of shuffling formations from one threatened sector to another, from theatre to theatre and finally, from 1942 onwards, from east to west and back again. The wide frontages, which increased in extent the further east one advanced, the depth of the penetration, and Hitler's insistence that formations should keep in close touch with their flanking neighbours, meant that the invading troops had neither depth nor reserves and eventually lost momentum. *Luftwaffe* air cover and tactical air support, except in the selected main sectors of operations, were sparse for precisely the same reason. No strategic bombing and little interdiction in depth were attempted. The

217

geography and climate of the USSR were to emphasize the German inadequacy, and the overrunning of a territory so vast as the Soviet Union did not necessarily imply that it could be held.

The German reserves of air transport were limited and little reliance could be placed on the Soviet railway system. In the early part of the campaign all loads had to be transferred from one railway to the other at the Soviet border because of the different width of track gauge. This, together with the lack of captured Soviet rolling stock, reduced capacity and made it imperative to re-lay the tracks to the standard European gauge. Except in some areas in the Ukraine where the Red Army had systematically ploughed up the track and railway bed, good progress was made in the conversion, but even so the capacity of the re-laid track was usually poor. Many of the main lines had only one track converted and the efficiency of a double track was limited until sidings, turntables and repair sheds had been similarly retracked. In the Ukraine the lack of timber hindered the work. All locomotives and rolling stock had to be provided by the *Reichsbahn* from German or West European sources, and German locomotives proved unsuitable for use in Russia since they could only operate on German fuel or a mixture of German and Donets coal, and were not designed to withstand the low winter temperatures. At one time during that hard winter eighty per cent of the German locomotives were out of action.[10] Because of the destruction of the rail bridges over the Dnieper all loads had to be off-loaded, and ferried over the river by the road bridges or by boat, and reloaded on the other bank, and winter brought only one advantage in that the frozen Dnieper served as a bed for a temporary railway track across the ice. By the end of the year there was evidence of partisan activity and one of the primary targets was the destruction of the German railway track and supply trains.[11]

Not only did Germany enter Russia with inadequate air and railway transport support, but it lacked sufficient numbers of motor vehicles, and those it had were of a most unsuitable type.[12] It had vehicle fuel reserves for

[10] Pottgiesser, *Die Reichsbahn im Ostfeldzug*, pp. 33–40. Only the motor transport organization prevented the whole supply system from collapse. The railway performance was so near disastrous that a committee of investigation, with the *Führer* himself in the chair, removed the responsibility for the railway from the Military Transport Officer-in-Chief to the *Reichsbahn* (the *Reich* Transport Minister Dorpmüller) as far forward as the army railhead, the responsibility being defined in a letter signed by Hitler *OKW/WFStb/Qu* (*Verw*) *Nr. 8/42* dated 4 January 1942. See also Keitel, *Memoirs*, pp. 176–7.

[11] This early partisan activity was much exaggerated in Soviet accounts. In January and February 1942 there were fewer than twenty attacks a month over the whole railway system. By May the attacks had risen to 170 and by September (the peak month of the year) to 730. In 1942 there were 400 attacks in January and 490 in February and by September and October they rose to over 1,900 in each of those months. Pottgiesser, *Die Reichsbahn im Ostfeldzug*, p. 85.

[12] Many of the motor vehicles were captured or of German or French civilian pattern. Hoth was to comment with acidity that motorized infantry company commanders motored into Russia, leading their troops in little civilian cars. Hoth, *Panzeroperationen*, p. 45.

three months and tyre stocks for only two months.[13] Even its horses and general service army wagons foundered and broke up under the weather conditions and the strain of the corrugated pot-holed tracks. Nearly seventy per cent of the German fighting strength advanced across Russia on its feet. In contrast to the Red Army, where winter uniform consisted of felt boots, fur caps and quilted garments, no winter clothing had reached the German troops in spite of the fact that by December the temperature by day had dropped to minus twenty-five degrees centigrade.[14] The *Führer*'s intention to complete the war in a single campaign and withdraw all but sixty divisions to Germany, in his view made a hundred per cent issue of winter clothing unnecessary, and it is said that he had even forbidden any mention to be made of a general issue in case this should cause disquiet among the troops.[15] The matter of winter clothing and accommodation had been raised by Halder as early as July, and planning and provision action was taken during August and September. Some stocks were eventually dispatched to the troops by rail, but these came to a halt in the provinces of Western Russia, unable to move forwards or backwards because of the catastrophic rail situation. The Nazi Party then undertook the collection of winter clothing from the German civilian population, this resulting in the Party receiving some gratuitous acclaim and the German troops a motley collection of garments which included women's fur coats and muffs.[16]

Whereas German success could be ascribed to the skilful use of the tank and the aeroplane, German failure to achieve its aim in a single lightning blow was due to poor political, economic, geographical and military intelligence,

---

[13] Halder, *Kriegstagebuch*, Vol. 2, p. 256.

[14] The autumn and winter of 1941 was particularly cold. Temperatures of minus 20 and minus 25 degrees centigrade were common in daytime and minus 30, even minus 40, by night.

[15] The responsibility for the failure to provide winter clothing to the troops remains unclear. Eckstein, the *OQu* of Army Group Centre, has said that to his knowledge a *Führer* order was in existence instructing that winter clothing should not be discussed as this would cause disquiet to the troops, and that in any event the war would be over before winter. Elisabeth Wagner, *Der Generalquartiermeister*, p. 289. On July 9 Halder discussed in general terms with Heusinger the provision of winter items in connection with the organization of the troops which were to be left in Russia after the defeat of the Soviet Union. On 25 July the matter was discussed again, probably with von Brauchitsch. Four days later Halder seemed satisfied that all was in hand. On 2 August the position appeared to be not so satisfactory and the difficulty of transport presented itself. Halder discussed the question repeatedly thereafter but on 10 November the conclusion was reached that the troops were unlikely to see the winter clothing and equipment before January. On 19 December Hitler blamed the Army for its own misfortunes in this respect. Halder, *Kriegstagebuch*, Vol. 3, pp. 58, 111, 130, 143, 286 and 354. On 20 December, according to Guderian, Hitler believed that winter clothing had already been issued. Guderian, *Panzer Leader*, p. 266. The scale of provision and the type of clothing ordered was quite inadequate, and could not be compared with the clothing of the Red Army.

[16] Little of the material was received by the troops that winter. The issue, where it was made, gave rise to the Soviet cartoon of Winter Fritz, with icicled nose, wearing a woman's fur coat with his head and neck encircled with a boa.

and in consequence the lack of a logical and realistic political and military plan. German resources and preparation were inadequate for the task.

The Soviet success in weathering the 1941 campaign was due in the main to the vastness of its territory and the bitterness of its winter.[17] When Stalin made the not very profound comment that no other country could have lost so much territory and still remained in the war, it called for the obvious retort that no other country had so much territory to lose. Later the Soviet Union was frequently to compare in disparaging terms the resistance of the French Army in 1940 with that of the Red Army in 1941. But the fact remains, that if the USSR, like France, had all its population, industries and economic wealth concentrated in a strip of territory only 500 miles deep with the sea behind it, nothing could have saved it from a rapid and complete defeat. Not its advantage in strength of population, its industrial power and economic wealth, nor its great reserve stocks of artillery and small arms, nor Stalin's brutal determination, nor the doggedness of the Red Army, nor any assistance from the United States or Britain, could have prevented Fascist Germany from utterly destroying the Soviet Union as a communist state. Both Britain and the Soviet Union owed their survival primarily to geography and to climate, only secondarily to their own endeavours.

Stalin's domination and the effect of the role played by the Communist Party and the communist organs should not, however, be underestimated. For Stalin and his associates no price was too great to pay in terms of lives and resources to ensure victory and the continued existence of communism, and in this their interest was by no means entirely motivated by idealism, since failure meant the liquidation both of Party and of self. Stalin in these times of stress was to ally and identify himself with any section of the population which could be used to advantage. The people became his brothers and his sisters. The Orthodox Church, formerly a despised and almost superfluous minor organ of the Communist Party, was used to appeal to any lingering religious susceptibilities of the middle-aged and elderly, while the support of the patriot and the Russian was enlisted by holding up as an example the earlier Russian heroes and warlike tsars.[18] Many of the inmates of the concentration camps and the prisons were released and, hoping for better times, were willingly to fight for their communist masters, whom they had had good reason to hate. The Communist Party played its part too in holding together the armed forces. Although many members of the Red Army fought bravely out of pride, patriotism or duty, its cohesion in the final outcome was tightly bound by the fear instilled by the communist system. The price for failure for the officer and commissar might mean loss of rank and status, or imprison-

---

[17] On 14 October 1941 Radio Moscow broadcast 'Snow is falling on fields covered with blood . . . Hitler cannot get through our winter . . . time is our ally.' The broadcast was of course aimed at encouraging resistance, but its content was true nevertheless. Feis, *Churchill, Roosevelt, Stalin*, p. 18.

[18] Stalin, War Speeches, pp. 25–6, quoted by Deutscher, *Stalin*, p. 468. *Istoriya*, Vol. 2, p. 254. The Church was not brought in until later in 1942.

ment or execution. For the commissar capture might mean death at German hands. His own survival was closely linked with success and for this reason if for no other he ensured that his men held out until the very end and gave no quarter. The Red Army man taken prisoner by the German, whatever the circumstances of his capture, wounded or unwounded, was no longer regarded as a Soviet citizen and for him the end of the war usually meant confinement in a concentration camp where he might atone for his guilt. Worse still was the Soviet practice of incarcerating the family or dependants of captured soldiers for the space of years, for no other reason than that they were relatives of a prisoner of war. In these circumstances there was little reason for wonder that the Soviet soldier, apathetic or fatalistic, and often fortified by several hundred grammes of vodka, climbed over the heaps of the dead and dying and with apparent indifference strode forward to certain death.

The part played by the Red Army in 1941 in halting the enemy advance has been exaggerated by Soviet historians. Success was due mainly to geography and climate and thereafter to Stalin's determination. Material resources in men and stockpiled equipment, and the earlier redeployment of industry to the Urals and Siberia, all played a part in stopping the German. The resistance of the Soviet armed forces was probably of only subsidiary importance. At that time men of the Red Army were not regarded highly as soldiers, either by their own kin or by the Germans, and although the truth of the defeats was kept from the Soviet people, there could be no disguising that the Red Army was no match for its enemy, and this gave rise to bewilderment and distress at home.[19] Yet, in spite of the many incidents of poor morale and the mass surrenders, the larger part of the Soviet troops fought on, often badly, but sometimes with the greatest determination and obstinacy, as the mounting German casualty rate was beginning to show.

The Communist Party's disregard for life and its contempt for any form of humanity and decency was one of the decisive factors in the recruiting and control of the partisan movement.[20] In the early part of the war the indigenous

[19] 10 Motorized Infantry Division apparently captured a Stalin order issued to the troops in the late autumn of 1941 reproaching the Red Army for its performance and telling it to learn to fight as the Germans fought. Schmidt, *Geschichte der 10. Division*, p. 113; 3 Infantry Division, even as late as November in front of Moscow on the Nara, reported that the enemy in front of it had no morale or fighting spirit and that enemy troops were throwing away their weapons and were willingly coming over as prisoners. The adjutant of II battalion of 8 Infantry Regiment together with a sergeant collected over a hundred such Red Army men and made them drag their heavy weapons with them into captivity. Dieckhoff, *Die 3. Infanterie-Division*, p. 135.

[20] The activity of Red Army stragglers or units cut off in the woods behind the German lines was distinct from that of the partisan movement which, although controlled by Moscow or the subordinate fronts, received the bulk of its recruits and support from the local indigenous population. Whereas the partisan movement was negligible during 1941, the uncoordinated hostile activity of military detachments in the German rear was widespread and took the form of attacks on convoys and installations. Eventually these detachments were destroyed or made their way back to the Soviet lines. Sometimes weapons and uniforms were thrown away and the soldiers hid themselves among the civilian population, a few of them to re-emerge as partisans later in the war.

population was not hostile to the Germans, and some White Russian, Ukrainian, Tartar and Cossack elements welcomed them. During the summer the German treatment of the population of the occupied territories lost them much popularity, but it did not follow that the inhabitants necessarily favoured a return to communist rule. During the autumn, however, small partisan elements in radio touch with Moscow became firmly established in the German rear areas, and these increased in size and influence by terrorizing the local population or making the Germans do their work for them. Failure to co-operate with the partisans meant death, sometimes of a most terrible kind, or reprisals against relatives who were living in the Soviet Union.[21] It soon became obvious that the Germans were unable to guarantee the safety of the population in the rear areas, and in the early days they were reluctant to arm it in order that it might rid itself of the guerrillas. The partisans sometimes perpetrated atrocities against the occupying power, apparently for no other reason than to attract German reprisals on to the heads of the innocent local population. In this they were only too successful as the German occupation authority, with its inborn arrogance that might was right, followed readily the orders of the High Command and Security Service that the discipline of the local population should be maintained by terror.[22] Mass arrests of innocent people and the shooting of hostages followed the partisan attacks, so that many of the unfortunate population, threatened by both sides, found it easier and safer either to take to the woods with the insurgents, or to work for the partisans while in the employment of the Germans. In 1941 partisan activity was of only minor significance; but in 1942, when it became apparent that the USSR would not be rapidly defeated and that Soviet strength was growing, so important was it to be on the winning side that more and more people flocked to join the movement.

It was probable that Hitlerite Germany was strong enough in 1941, even without allies, to have destroyed the Soviet Union, but the margin in their relative strengths was not great. The overthrow of the USSR would have required the mobilization of the whole of the German economy and of all of Germany's reserves, and there could have been no question of dissipating forces in Africa, the Balkans, Scandinavia and Western Europe, or of fighting Britain in a bitter air and sea war. Adding the United States to its enemies was the final senseless act. To have waged a successful war against the Soviet Union would in any event have entailed long preparation, and would in all probability have been bloody and costly. Even if it had concentrated all its strength against the USSR, Germany alone could not have won the war in a single summer and autumn campaign, because of its lack of mechanized forces and reserves. Victory might, of course, have been won before the end of the

[21] Many partisans in the autumn of 1941, having been briefed for an assignment, gave themselves up to the Germans as soon as they had crossed the line.

[22] The German civilian administrators of the *Ostministerium*, because of their strutting arrogance and brown uniforms, were known as the golden pheasants. To the German troops on the other hand they were known as brown partisans.

year if Japan could have been induced to take up arms against the Soviet Union in June, instead of attacking the United States and Britain at the end of the year; but assistance from Japan would have been conditional on the attitude of the United States.

The German record in 1941 was a history of costly blunders and misjudgements, and for these Hitler was mainly, but not wholly, to blame. Yet the most serious error was the German failure to follow the precepts of von Clausewitz concerning Russia and understand that Russia could only be conquered from within. To destroy communism permanently it was essential that the Germans should have offered all Russian and Soviet peoples freedom from the criminal oppression of the communist régime and independence from Germany. The latter of course was certainly not Hitler's intention. The Soviet peoples should have been encouraged to take up arms against their government, and the Red Army formations invited to join the Germans in their liberating crusade. At the start of the war, Kinzel in the Department of Foreign Armies East, presided over a meeting of *émigré* Russians, who included some former General Officers of the Imperialist Tsarist Army, to discuss the provision of Russian speaking interpreters for German units.[23] These émigrés went beyond their terms of reference when they urged that all Soviet citizens should be treated by the occupying German forces with courtesy and tact, and that efforts should be made to win over Red Army prisoners of war to the German cause. The commissars, the *émigrés* thought, should be treated with particular care, as they were worth cultivating, 'being not such bad fellows and often much cleverer than the officers'. Many of the commissars, the *émigrés* believed, were not dyed in the wool communists, but just went along with the régime the same as everyone else. Kinzel, beyond taking note of their views, made no comment, since he probably knew of the treatment to be reserved for the commissars. The words of wisdom spoken by the *émigrés* went unheeded.

[23] One of these Generals, by nature an optimist, claimed that he should have as pay for his interpreter duties the same rate of pay as a German General of equivalent rank.

CHAPTER FIFTEEN

Retreat from Moscow

On the night of 5 December began the first of a series of Soviet attacks made solely with the aim of saving Moscow, since the Kremlin did not at that time know that the Germans were exhausted and temporarily incapable of further effort.[1] Konev's Kalinin Front was the first to begin the offensive and, crossing the frozen upper Volga, it met everywhere with fierce German resistance, except on the sector allotted to Yushkevich's 31 Army. Much to the Soviet surprise, this formation advanced rapidly, penetrating 9 Army's right flank and reaching Turginovo, about twenty miles in the German rear. The following day the right flank of Zhukov's West Front, supported by 700 aircraft, took up the attack in order to prevent Reinhardt's and Hoepner's 3 and 4 Panzer Groups outflanking Moscow to the north-east of the city. The German troops gave ground, quickly falling back about fifteen miles to the west, and V. I. Kuznetsov's 1 Shock Army, Rokossovsky's 16 Army and Lelyushenko's 30 Army, recently reinforced by six Siberian and Ural divisions, began to move across the Moscow-Kalinin railway. To the south near Tula, Guderian's 2 Panzer Army had already begun to withdraw towards the upper Don, closely followed by Golikov's 10 Army which had been ordered to take Stalinogorsk and Epifan.[2] Further to the south, shock formations of tanks, cavalry and infantry had been formed by Gorodnyansky's 13 Soviet Army on the right of Timoshenko's South-West Theatre, for deep penetration tasks in 2 German Army rear.[3] These thrusts, beginning on 13 December, blocked the main withdrawal route from Elets to Livny and encircled and dispersed part of 45 German Infantry Division and caused severe losses to the withdrawing 95 and 134 Infantry Divisions.[4] For the first time in the war substantial quantities of German booty fell into Soviet hands, much of it broken down or

---

[1] Compare also Vasilevsky, *Bitva za Moskvu*, p. 24.

[2] *Istoriya*, Vol. 2, p. 280.

[3] Timoshenko in *Bitva za Moskvu*, p. 97, describes his command as a front and Kostenko as the deputy commander. Other works, including *Istoriya* (cf. Vol. 2, p. 222) refer to Timoshenko's command from November onwards as a theatre.

[4] Guderian, *Panzer Leader*, p. 262. The Red Army claimed to have captured 220 guns of 34 Corps in this sector. Halder admitted that 134 and 45 Divisions were no longer fit for battle for lack of supplies on 12 December, the day before the Soviet attack. Halder, *Kriegstagebuch*, Vol. 3, p. 340.

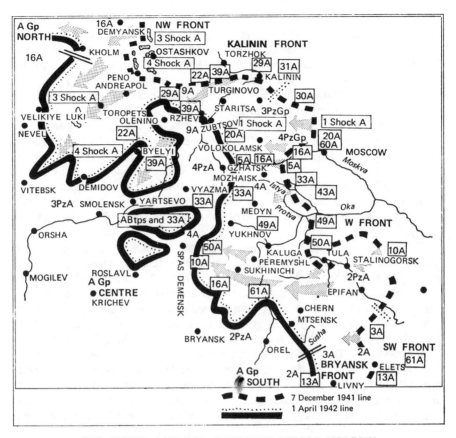

THE SOVIET COUNTER-OFFENSIVE BEFORE MOSCOW
December 1941–April 1942

bogged in the deep snow, and this included many guns and motor vehicles. By 12 December Halder was grimly and glumly noting the critical situation of 2 Army and what he called the bankrupt leadership between Tula and Kursk, presumably meaning that of Guderian, since Rudolf Schmidt had only just taken over the temporary command of 2 Army in place of von Weichs who was ill.

Von Brauchitsch, who a week earlier had submitted his resignation to Hitler, had met von Bock in Smolensk on 13 December. Von Bock was certain that his troops could no longer hold their positions and believed that to attempt to do so would invite destruction. Army Group Centre with sixty-seven exhausted and under-strength divisions was covering a 600-mile front, much of which was made up of exposed salients.[5] As usual, there were no German formations in reserve, and the lines of communication were guarded by only four security divisions. The Red Army strength facing Army Group Centre, according to the German intelligence estimate on 6 December, stood at twelve armies made up of eighty-eight rifle and fifteen cavalry divisions and twenty-four tank brigades.[6] Army Group Centre was already being closely pressed and was faced with the difficulty of disengaging from the enemy without losing control of its troops. Von Brauchitsch thought a withdrawal was unavoidable and sketched out on the map a so-called Winter Line to which the troops should be withdrawn, a north-south roadway about ninety miles to the rear, which ran just to the east of Vyazma through Zubtsov, Gzhatsk and Yukhnov. In order to make for easier co-ordination and control over the extended front-ages, Reinhardt's 3 Panzer Group was put under command of Hoepner's 4 Panzer Group and Schmidt's 2 Army was put under Guderian's 2 Panzer Army.

When the extent of the German weakness became apparent, the Soviet High Command changed its plan to a counter-offensive, based on a double envelopment from the flanks, rather than on a frontal attack made by Zhukov's West Front. The sector of the new Soviet counter-offensive was to cover a width of 600 miles and no fewer than sixteen armies were to take part. Army Group Centre was to be destroyed by an attack on each shoulder of the German salient, one thrust being made by Konev's Kalinin Front from the area Kalinin and Torzhok towards Smolensk, while the left flank of Zhukov's West Front, together with the newly reformed Bryansk Front under Chere-vichenko, which was already pressing hard against Guderian, drove in a great arc from the south from Stalinogorsk to Sukhinichi, and then on to Vyazma and Smolensk.[7] Kurochkin's North-West Front was ordered to make a secon-

---

[5] *OKH Kriegsgliederung* of 4 December 1941.

[6] *OKH Lage Ost* Map, 6 December 1941. The tactical detail was mainly accurate except that 1 Shock Army and 20 Army were not shown. Of the existence of the reserve armies in the rear, the OKH was ignorant. The actual Red Army strength according to Sokolovsky, *Razgrom Nemetsko-Fashistskikh Voisk pod Moskvoi*, pp. 169, 170–2, and Timoshenko, *Bitva za Moskvu*, p. 103, was as follows:

Front	Armies	Divisions Rifle	Tank	Cavalry	Brigades Rifle	Tank
Kalinin	3	15		1		
West	10	51	3	15	18	15
South-West	3	12		6	1	2
	16	78	3	22	19	17

The force was said to include 720 tanks and 1,170 aircraft.

[7] 3 and 13 Armies were removed from the right wing of Kostenko's South-West Front on 17 December and formed into the new Bryansk Front for ease of tactical grouping. 61 Army was added later. The Bryansk Front military council consisted of Cherevichenko, Kolo-byakov and Shabalin (both political members), and Kolpakchy (from mid January M. I. Kazakov) as chief of staff.

dary and yet deeper right encircling thrust to the west of that made by Konev, from the area Demyansk-Ostashkov roughly along the boundary between German Army Groups Centre and North. The whole counter-offensive was designed to encircle a great German pocket, nearly 200 miles in depth, stretching almost from Moscow to Smolensk, with one left arm and two right arms, one outside the other. Meanwhile, the right flank of West Front in the Moscow area was to continue its westward pressure and attempt to pin the Germans and prevent them from withdrawing. On 15 December, such was the optimism in Moscow, and so sure was the Politburo that the capital was no longer in danger, that the Central Committee and the main organs of government were ordered to return from Kuybyshev.[8]

In the moment of German crisis, on that same day, Hitler had overruled von Brauchitsch. Any withdrawal was forbidden and on 16 December German troops were ordered to put up a fanatical resistance in their positions, without regard to the enemy on the flanks or in the rear.[9] Von Brauchitsch, browbeaten and tired, by then being referred to by the *Führer* as strawhead, was on the verge of nervous collapse and without further ceremony was packed off to retirement, the retirement being opportune for Hitler and the Party since it could be implied that von Brauchitsch was wholly responsible for the set-back before Rostov and Moscow. Amongst Germany's allies, however, the news of the retirement came as an unpleasant surprise.[10]

Whether Hitler was right in insisting on a rigid defence in front of Moscow, none can be sure. A withdrawal made under heavy enemy pressure, particularly in the terrible winter conditions then experienced, could easily have deteriorated into a rout, ending with the destruction of Army Group Centre. Yet it is certain that this military factor carried less weight with the *Führer* than considerations of prestige and loss of countenance. Many, probably the majority, of the German commanders were of opinion that Hitler was right in ordering a standstill, and in this way saved Germany a heavy defeat. On the other hand there was a strong case for breaking contact with the Red Army at the most favourable moment and withdrawing as rapidly as possible, abandoning guns and vehicles which could not be moved, even if it meant falling back as far as Vyazma or Smolensk. Failure to hold, or to break contact successfully and withdraw, could only lead to a running fight, a very costly and dangerous act of war, and this is exactly what happened.[11] In spite

[8] From 17 October the General Staff had been split into two echelons, one in Moscow under Vasilevsky and the other outside the capital under Shaposhnikov. Shtemenko, *Generalnyi Shtab v Gody Voiny*, p. 40. The echelons were reunited after 16 December.

[9] '*Die 4. Armee geht keinen Schritt zurück*'. *Op Abt (IM) Nr. 1725/41 g. Kdos Chefs* of 16 December (*Chef OKW/WF St/L Nr. 442174/4/g. Kdos C*) and '*ist die Truppe zum fanatischen Widerstand in ihren Stellungen zu zwingen*' *OKH Gen St d H Op Abt (III) Nr. 1736/41 g. Kdos Chefs* of 18 December 1941; also *Op Abt (I) Nr. 32061/41 g. Kdos* of 20 December 1941.

[10] *Ciano's Diary, 1939–43*, p. 413.

[11] Many German divisional histories stress this point. For example the Commander and historian of the Franconian-Sudeten 98. Division, who although he agreed wholeheartedly

of its desperate defence, Army Group Centre hardly held any of its positions for more than a few days and was to be forced back everywhere in the next five weeks between 100 and 200 miles. Large numbers of guns and vehicles were to be lost, and exposure rather than fighting was to bring quite heavy casualties. For the Germans at this time equipment losses were easier to bear than those in men.[12]

Von Bock's battle line curved in a great extended salient and since neither the German Army High Command (OKH) nor Army Group Centre held any reserves to meet the Soviet counter-offensive, these could only have been found

with Hitler's order to stand and fight, related how the division, within two or three days of the standstill order, began a series of piecemeal withdrawals over the course of the next two months. The Rhine Westphalian 6 Division was very sceptical about the whole business. Its own proposal to withdraw in one bound was not approved by higher authority, and it was ordered to fall back in short bounds (*in kleinen Etappen*) only three miles at a time, so that, as it complained, contact could never be broken. Grossman, *Geschichte der Rheinisch-Westfälischen 6. Infanterie-Division*, pp. 92, 94 and 99.

[12] Halder gave a contemporary and comprehensive picture of German losses in the winter in a presentation to Hitler on 21 April 1942.

(a) Losses

	Period	Loss (all causes)	Replacement
Motor vehicles	1 October to 15 March	74,000	7,400
AFVs (all types)	1 October to 15 March	2,300	1,800
Officers and men	1 November to 1 April	900,000	450,000
Horses	15 October to 15 March	180,000	20,000

(b) Deficiency

The deficiency on the East Front in April 1942 stood at:

Personnel	625,000
Rifles	28,000
Machine guns	14,000
Anti-tank guns	7,000
Guns	1,900

(c) Casualty Breakdown

	Killed or missing	Wounded	Average sick figure
22 June–26 November (approximately five months)	187,000	555,000	16,000
4 February 1942			61,000
10 March 1942 (based on 2 per cent sick and including 10,000 typhus cases)			64,000
27 November–31 March (approximately four months)	108,000	268,000	

The average daily battle casualty figure for the period from 30 November to 1 April was consistent, varying from about 2,800 to 3,500 with a slightly greater loss (3,700) in the period from 31 December to 10 January. These figures indicate that the German battle casualties were not particularly high during the winter withdrawal. In addition to the 376,000 battle casualties during the winter period there were however over 500,000 sickness casualties, of which 228,000 were frostbite cases, making a total of about 900,000. Halder, *Kriegstagebuch*, Vol. 3, pp. 430–2. On the other hand Mueller-Hillebrand, quoting as authority *Sämtliche Angaben nach Abt WVW des OKW*, gives the total army and SS loss for the three months from December to February as 127,000 dead and 24,000 missing. *Das Heer*, Vol. 3, Table 65.

by a withdrawal to a shorter defensive line. There was yet another and even more cogent argument in favour of a rapid strategic withdrawal. The Germans failed to take Moscow for the principal reason that they were unable to overcome the problems of space and movement. The German formations, ill-supplied and completely exhausted at the end of a long and uncertain line of communication, without shelter or winter clothing, met well clothed and adequately fed Red Army men, abundantly provided with materials and munitions, whose base was only twenty miles or so to the rear. In addition, ample stocks of ammunition and food had been dumped with the Red Army troops.[13] In such circumstances, once it was obvious that they were not going to take Moscow, it would appear to have been unwise on the German part not to have fallen back rapidly on Vyazma or Smolensk. The Red Army soldier, hardy and used to the climatic conditions though he certainly was, was scarcely more able than the German to fight a successful major battle at the end of a 200-mile pursuit. He too lacked transport and for much of his mobility he relied on cavalry and the sledge. Deep snow and mud was as troublesome to him as it was to the German and, separated from his base and dumped munitions, the Soviet soldier, like the German, rapidly lost efficiency. The Soviet official historian goes to great lengths to deride German accounts which attribute Army Group Centre's failure to take Moscow largely to climatic conditions, mud and snow, and the supply difficulties caused by a long and insecure line of communications, and in denying this, Moscow emphasizes that the German defeat was due to the superiority of the Soviet soldier and the communist system. When the Soviet winter counter-offensive was finally brought to a standstill in front of Vitebsk, Smolensk and Vyazma, however, the same official historian explains, with logic and truth, but without embarrassment, that the Red Army was halted not by the Germans, but by exhaustion, lack of transport, climatic conditions, mud and snow, and the supply difficulties caused by a long and uncertain line of communications.[14]

Whether Hitler was right or wrong in insisting on a rigid defence, the Nazi Party propaganda machine and organization soon saw to it that the German Army and public firmly believed that the *Führer* was the saviour of the Army. This in itself did great and permanent damage to the German war direction. Hitler was even more convinced of his own military genius and became certain that any crisis could be weathered by will-power and rigidity; he was throughout the course of the whole war to quote what he believed to be his success before Moscow as a justification for his obdurate and often senseless attitude towards German withdrawals. This was to be one of the main factors which subsequently brought such heavy defeats to German arms at Stalingrad and in the Ukraine, in the Crimea and in the Baltic, in Africa and in France.

The battles before Moscow had yet another deleterious effect on the

[13] *Istoriya*, Vol. 2, p. 275.
[14] *Istoriya*, Vol. 2, pp. 252 and 331.

organization of the German High Command. In his arrogance and conceit Hitler, amid the acclaim of the whole German nation, took over the personal command of the German Army. He had previously been the *de facto* commander, but had kept himself in the background, so that as *Führer* he tended to take the credit for the German Army successes, whereas von Brauchitsch, particularly during the autumn, had collected a measure of opprobrium and blame for faults which were primarily Hitler's. The German Head of State, as von Manstein was later to explain, could not afford to permit himself to be identified with a subordinate post like that of German Army Commander-in-Chief.[15] Whereas it was a relatively easy matter to replace a senior General, the failure of a head of state in a subordinate and technical capacity put him in an invidious and almost ludicrous position. Henceforth Hitler was to view himself first and foremost as a soldier, and any army failure, however trivial, tended to be regarded as a personal affront. He was suspicious of and disliked the officer corps, particularly, as he called them, the gentlemen of the General Staff, and when von Rundstedt, von Brauchitsch, von Bock, von Leeb, Guderian, Hoepner and Strauss could not or would not obey his orders or asked to be relieved of their duties, he determined to keep his subordinate military commanders under very tight restraint. From December 1941 onwards the *Führer's* control in operations was paramount and he began to interfere in the most trivial detail, his mistrust of his personal military staff assuming such proportions that he was eventually to keep his own set of battle situation maps locked in his drawers and insist that stenographers should make a short-hand and typescript record of all his conversations.[16] Halder, the Chief of the General Staff, elected to remain in his post, but he was not to be suffered for very long, since he presumed from time to time to disagree with the *Führer's* views. This appointment, once occupied by von Moltke, was to become a subordinate executive post of no account, little different from that occupied by Keitel or Jodl, the occupant becoming the *Führer's* mouthpiece. The Chiefs of Staff who followed Halder were ambitious officers, often lacking status, seniority and experience, selected by Hitler because he believed them to be men whom he could bend to his will.[17]

During December the two great arms of the Soviet envelopment had started to encircle the German formations immediately to the west of Moscow. The men of 98 Franconian Sudeten Infantry Division on the Nara in 4 Army sector, still fighting without relief or rest, could plainly see the searchlight beams and the shell bursts of anti-aircraft fire above Moscow, when finally on 10 December the order reached them to go over to the defensive. On 13

[15] Von Manstein, *Lost Victories*, p. 287.

[16] Warlimont, *Inside Hitler's Headquarters*, p. 199; also Gilbert, *Hitler Directs His War*, p. XXI. Because of an argument between Hitler and Halder about what was really said between them, the *Führer* introduced stenographers to record all meetings and conferences.

[17] Zeitzler lacked seniority, status and experience. Guderian was unsuited to the appointment and was less effective than Zeitzler. Krebs was of little account. All three were originally enthusiastic supporters of National Socialism.

December a secret order, originated by von Brauchitsch, had been distributed to commanders, instructing them to break contact and withdraw to a line ninety miles away to the west. The next day the *Führer* order arrived countermanding the order of the previous day. Then information was received that 4 German Army was in danger of being outflanked from the rear, and elements of the division were sent back behind the Protva to prepare new positions. On 17 December these were turned round and sent back again. The repeated changes of orders led to a grave disquiet and for the first time confidence was shaken in the higher command. Three times in one day the engineers were ordered to complete the circuit and insert the charges to demolish a bridge and three times they were ordered to stand down. Not before the evening of 19 December was it finally ordered that troops should remain in their positions without withdrawing, and all commanders and troops began to breathe again in relief at having received clear and firm orders at last. The divisional commander, writing after the event, was of the opinion that the deep snow had made any large scale movement impossible, while a withdrawal under the eyes and guns of the enemy was unthinkable. Field-Marshal von Brauchitsch had gone and Hitler had taken over the personal command of the German Army; faith in the *Führer* was boundless and a new wave of optimism spread throughout the troops. The division continued to dig itself in with renewed energy, although constantly harried from the air, and in the next two days heavy fighting took place on its flanks. Immediately to the north, a Soviet tank attack made a penetration about six miles deep, just beyond the main Moscow motorway, while two to three enemy divisions broke in on its right flanking formation. Bad news ran up and down the front. On 23 December, only four days after the standstill order, 98 Division, like its neighbours, was forced to begin its long withdrawal. On 24 December it arrived at the field of Borodino on the banks of the frozen Istya, which afforded neither an obstacle nor a defensive position, and at seven that night, on Christmas Eve, the troops moved back again, some talking and even more thinking of 1812 and the Russian monument at Tarutino.[18]

292 Infantry Division, also on the Nara, felt relief when it heard the standstill order, because it considered that it would not have had the strength to carry out a long withdrawal. But in spite of this, it did have to fall back, and on New Year's night was holding a divisional sector about eight miles wide with rifle companies which, although down to only thirty men, were still stronger than those of its neighbours. On that night a Russian officer was killed in the divisional rear area, who had been busy listening in to German telephone conversations with a tapping device; but what impressed the unshaven, filthy and verminous German troops most, was the cleanliness of the Red Army man's clothing and the whiteness of his linen.[19]

To the north of Moscow Ruoff's 5 Corps, forming part of Hoepner's 4

[18] Gareis, *Kampf und Ende der 98. Division*, pp. 169–77.
[19] Nitz, *292. Infanterie-Division*, p. 78.

231

Panzer Group, was falling back from Moscow, covering from seven to fifteen miles a day in temperatures of up to minus thirty degrees centigrade. For three weeks the troops went without sleep, never knowing whether there would be any shelter for the night or whether the Russian would already be sitting waiting for them in the next village. The strength of the corps was diminishing rapidly day by day, but no help could be expected from appeals to neighbours or to higher headquarters. Everyone said that he was himself threatened and was fighting for his life.[20] Between Christmas and the New Year the corps commander and staff were juggling with little groups of men and single artillery pieces trying to plug gaps, cajoling, threatening and court-martialling officers. Battalions were down to a strength of fifty men without any anti-tank weapons, except the few artillery howitzers capable of engaging the attacking T34s. Battalions supported by a single field gun were being sacrificed to the enemy in order to gain a few more days for the corps. Men, including officers, had become so exhausted and apathetic that one dared not let them rest in the open, where they would gladly have slept and been frozen to death. In the six weeks following Hitler's standstill order, 35 Infantry Division, a division which had been in the war since June, lost over 2,500 men, more than one third of its casualties over the whole of the war.[21] The division had only two 50 mm anti-tank guns left and six field howitzers. 23 Potsdam Division, already without its divisional commander, whose health could not stand up to the rigours of the climate and campaign, had reformed its nine battalions to three on account of losses, and had hardly a thousand infantry left; its divisional artillery had been reduced to one 50 mm anti-tank gun and three howitzers. 106 Westphalian Rhineland Division, once a first class formation, had hardly any of its original leaders and disposed of only 500 infantrymen.[22]

In spite of the difficulties and danger, there were no cases of refusal to obey orders and certainly no hint of mutiny among the men of 5 Corps. By then, however, the German troops had a deep-rooted fear of tanks and had become distrustful and scornful of those orders and situation reports from higher headquarters which stressed the inferiority of the Red Army. Rudolf Schmidt, a friend and former colleague of Ruoff, the Commander of 5 Corps at that time, noted on 27 January that the troops still had trust in the High Command even if one began to hear the voices of critics. For himself, he had forbidden any defeatist talk or speculation as to who was responsible for so lightheartedly ordering the advance on Moscow and so reducing the troops to these straits.

6 Rhine-Westphalian Division was on the northern periphery near Kalinin, on the line of the River Tma in the area of Staritsa, when it began to fall back to the south-west. Its first equipment to be lost was its heavy howitzer battery

[20] From a letter by Rudolf Schmidt dated 27 January 1942.

[21] This figure by Schmidt is supported by the detail of the divisional history. Baumann, *Die 35. Infanterie-Division*, p. 143. It is important to note, however, that of these 2,500 casualties over 1,000 were due to severe frost-bite.

[22] Many of the infantry battalions were by then being reinforced by artillerymen and troops of the administrative services. Dieckhoff, *Die 3. Infanterie-Division*, p. 149.

as there were no horses to drag the guns, and the companies of III Battalion of 18 Infantry Regiment were down to five machine-guns, one mortar and seven rifles each. The wooded and thicket country was difficult to defend and whereas nearly all Red Army attacks were very heavily supported by guns and mortars, the remaining German guns could not fire for lack of ammunition.[23] Christmas Day had passed without celebration, except that an enemy attack was repulsed quite close to the divisional headquarters near Vasilevskoye, the enemy, apparently drunk, coming forward cheering and linked arm in arm. On New Year's Day the divisional headquarters was in a tiny village called Koledino, where the fifty officers and men took possession of two single-roomed houses and all got under cover. There they dictated orders, radioed, telephoned, wrote, typed, ate, deloused and slept. Typhus was proving a problem, but there were only sufficient medical supplies to inoculate those soldiers *over fifty years of age*. Outside, Russian women, for payment in tea and food, kept the tracks free of snowdrifts. The *Führer* order, that all houses and other shelter should be burned before retreating, was ignored, partly because the German commanders were convinced that the Red Army man could spend the night in the open without ill-effects, but more particularly since the first sign of smoke brought the Russian down on their heads.[24]

The *Luftwaffe* was to play a minor part in these battles, particularly since its activity was hampered by lack of visibility. Kesselring's 2 Air Fleet and one air corps had already been removed from the theatre, and only von Richthofen's 8 Air Corps remained for the support of Army Group Centre. This corps was to provide the only mobile support still available to the German commanders. A few army formations were brought up from Western Europe or from Germany but these arrived too late and were committed to battle piecemeal and had little effect on the fighting.[25] For the most, von Kluge had to rely on the troops already deployed, and his reinforcements had to be found by combing out headquarters and supply troops, and organizing alarm units from engineers, *Luftwaffe* ground staffs and security troops.

The Soviet inner right encircling pincer provided by Konev's Kalinin Front was based on Maslennikov's 39 Reserve Army, a force of six rifle and two cavalry divisions, supported on its right and left by Vostrukhov's 22 and Shvetsov's 29 Armies.[26] This flanking arm moved from the areas of Kalinin

[23] This division was to note that the intermediate withdrawal lines were entirely unsuitable for defence and had no tactical significance, having been obviously drawn by someone miles away in a much higher headquarters in the comfort of a map room. '*Man hatte den Eindruck eines Befehls von obersten grünen Tisch*'. Other divisions were similarly to complain of this interference in operations by 'the rarefied higher headquarters swine'.

[24] Grossmann, *Geschichte der Rheinish-Westfälishen 6. Infanterie-Division*, pp. 92–108.

[25] Six infantry divisions were moved from Western Europe to the Eastern Front in November and December. Between January and March a further seventeen divisions arrived against an exchange of burned-out divisions.

[26] On 21 December the Kalinin Front consisted of twenty-four rifle and five cavalry divisions and three tank brigades. Sokolovsky, *Razgrom Nemetsko-Fashistskikh Voisk pod Moskvoi*, p. 261.

and Torzhok towards Rzhev, a town about 120 miles due west of Moscow. Soviet progress in this sector was steady but slow, as the German 9 Army fell back fighting desperately and sowing mines as it went.

To the south near Tula, Guderian was showing some nervousness about the steadiness of 2 German Army to his rear, where detachments of Gorodnyansky's 13 Soviet Army had managed to install themselves near Livny.[27] Guderian's relationship with Halder and von Bock was by no means good and he had attempted to bypass both and bring his plight and views to the *Führer's* attention by sending written reports by way of the younger Keitel and Schmundt.[28] Von Brauchitsch, only three days before his dismissal, had met Guderian in Roslavl and had given him permission to fall back to the rivers Susha and Oka, nearly eighty miles behind the upper Don. Hitler countermanded the withdrawal order when the retreat had already begun, and promised 500 reinforcements by air to stop the advance of what was in effect six Soviet armies and a cavalry corps. Guderian flew to Rastenburg, confident that his persuasiveness and the *Führer's* reason would speedily resolve the misunderstanding, but he was doomed to disappointment, since Hitler was obdurate that the troops should hold in their positions. On Christmas Eve the position became critical when von Kluge, newly in command of Army Group Centre, accused Guderian of disobeying both his and the *Führer's* orders by continuing to retreat, von Kluge maintaining that Guderian had of his own volition evacuated Chern, in consequence causing a gap between 43 Corps and the main body of 2 Panzer Army.[29] Whatever the cause, a twenty-five mile gap had appeared between the formations and through this gap the Red Army poured into the German rear and advanced rapidly in the direction of Smolensk and Vyazma. For this, on the day after Christmas, Guderian was placed on the retired list, being replaced as commander of 2 Panzer Army by Rudolf Schmidt, the temporary commander of 2 Army and the former commander of 39 Panzer Corps.[30]

29 Motorized Division, which was part of Guderian's force, had fallen back steadily from the night of 6 December. The fact that the German offensive had been unsuccessful and that they were in retreat did not cause any significant loss of morale or efficiency in the troops. They were, however, contin-

---

[27] In December Gorodnyansky gave up his command to Pukhov and went to 6 Army.

[28] Guderian, *Panzer Leader*, pp. 261–3. Schmundt, as personal army adjutant to Hitler, rose in rank between 1938 and 1944 from lieutenant-colonel to General of Infantry and, acting as the *Führer's* eyes and ears, he was a more powerful man than either von Brauchitsch or Halder. Bodewin Keitel, the younger brother of Field-Marshal Wilhelm Keitel, was head of the Army Personnel Office from 1939 to 1942. He had little or no influence on Hitler and it is assumed that Guderian wrote to him, hoping that the letter would be passed on to Hitler through the elder brother.

[29] Von Kluge had replaced von Bock in mid December and had given up command of 4 Army to Kübler.

[30] Guderian, *Panzer Leader*, p. 270. Von Kluge entered in the war diary the words 'I am basically in agreement with Guderian but he must obey orders'. *Kriegstagebuch des Oberkommandos der Heeresgruppe Mitte*, p. 1075.

ually haunted by the fear that the bitter cold should bring them to a standstill, so leaving them pitted against superior numbers of Red Army forces, which were growing in strength almost hourly. By 12 December the division had withdrawn successfully and concentrated on Mtsensk, having lost heavily in equipment. Germany's declaration of war on the United States on 11 December had little effect on the men, so preoccupied were they with their own problems of survival.[31]

In the Tula area where 2 Panzer Army had been breached the Red Army advance was rapid and the Red Air Force was very active.[32] 1 Guards Cavalry Corps spearheaded the advance together with Boldin's 50 Army and Golikov's 10 Army, later to be joined in their movement westwards by Rokossovsky's 16, Zakharkin's 49 and Efremov's 33 Armies. Peremyshl was taken on Christmas Day and Kaluga on 30 December and 1 Guards Cavalry Corps continued its thrust towards Yukhnov, not seventy miles from Vyazma, butchering German wounded and stragglers as it went. However, by the New Year the Red Army formations were beginning to complain of the effect on operations of the heavy frosts and of the great difficulties in supply. The German strong points, too, were troublesome, particularly along the main railways.[33] In general, however, from the Soviet High Command point of view, the progress of the left enveloping thrust from the Tula area was very satisfactory, and it ordered Kurochkin's North-West Front to begin its deep encirclement on the right, from Ostashkov to Vitebsk, this being the outer right flanking pincer over 200 miles deep into the German rear, which was to support both Konev's Kalinin Front and the right wing of Zhukov's West Front.[34] On 9 January Purkaev's 3 Shock Army and Eremenko's 4 Shock Army, both of North-West Front, began their offensive from the area of the Ostashkov Lakes, making very little progress until the town of Peno was taken. 3 Shock Army then moved westwards on Kholm and Velikiye Luki while Eremenko advanced to the south-west towards Vitebsk. The country was heavily wooded with few tracks and, as the armies were moving on divergent axes, great gaps appeared between them and Vostrukhov's 22 Soviet Army on their left. Control and supply became difficult. In spite of this, Andreapol was reached on 15 January, and by the end of the month Red Army troops were near Velikiye Luki, Vitebsk and Demidov, having accomplished a largely unopposed advance of nearly 200 miles over very difficult terrain. Kholm, which was within the boundaries of German Army Group North, could not be taken in view of its desperate defence by 281 German Security

[31] Lemelsen, *29. Division*, pp. 169–71.
[32] In a twenty-day period at the beginning of December the Red Air Force flew 10,000 sorties in this area. Of these 50 per cent were in tactical close support of the ground forces, 26 per cent were reconnaissance and only 10 per cent were on interdiction or rear area targets. Sokolovsky, *Razgrom Nemetsko-Fashistskikh Voisk pod Moskvoi*, p. 415.
[33] *Istoriya*, Vol. 2, p. 319.
[34] The military council of North-West Front was Kurochkin, Bogatkin (political member) and Vatutin.

Division. The outer right arm of the Soviet enveloping movement was by then already in place, but the gap between the right and left pincer arms between Demidov and Spas-Demensk was still over 100 miles wide.[35]

Meanwhile there had been other casualties to the senior German field commanders. Strauss, commanding 9 Army, had become sick and had been replaced in mid January by Model, the former Commander of 41 Panzer Corps. Kübler, the newly appointed Commander of 4 Army, had felt that the post was not the one for him and had told the *Führer* this, so that he was replaced on 20 January by Heinrici, the former Commander of 43 Corps. On 8 January the Soviet enemy appeared to be on the point of breaking through near Sukhinichi, and von Kluge was demanding from Halder that the stand-still order be rescinded and that he, as Army Group Commander, be given freedom of action to move his troops as he thought fit. Halder could only refer the matter to the *Führer*; but then it was learned that Hoepner, the Commander of 4 Panzer Army, had taken the *Führer*'s law into his own hands and had begun to withdraw in order to escape encirclement.[36] This was to result in the immediate dismissal of Hoepner, whom Hitler at first wanted to cashier without trial. Wiser counsels prevailed however and Hoepner continued to receive full pay and retired pay.[37] Hoepner was replaced by Ruoff, formerly in command of 5 Corps.

Meanwhile deep in the centre of the pocket made by the Soviet double envelopment a specially reinforced 20 Army under the command of Vlasov, together with V. I. Kuznetsov's 1 Shock Army and 2 Guards Cavalry Corps, broke through on 13 January near Volokolamsk and moved eastwards. Maslennikov's 39 and Shvetsov's 29 Soviet Armies supported by 22 Army, all of which formed Konev's inner right pincer, had finally reached the area of Rzhev. By the end of January the German position was serious. Far from holding the original defensive line ordered by Hitler, the formations of von Kluge's Army Group Centre had been driven back between 100 and 150 miles to the south-west. Model's 9 German Army and Ruoff's 4 Panzer Army were

[35] By early January the Kalinin Front formations had been increased to thirty-one rifle and five cavalry divisions and two tank brigades. West Front stood at forty-two rifle and eleven cavalry divisions, twenty-six rifle and thirteen tank brigades. Sokolovsky, *Razgrom Nemetsko-Fashistskikh Voisk pod Moskvoi*, p. 311.

[36] 3 and 4 Panzer Groups were known as panzer armies from 1 January. 1 and 2 Panzer Groups had become panzer armies on 6 October 1941.

[37] At the time of his dismissal Hoepner said that he felt that he had a duty to the German soldier and that, although he knew it would result in the end of his military career, he had no hesitation in disobeying the order of the *Führer*. Hitler at first wanted to cashier Hoepner without trial, the cashiering to result in loss of rank, status and retired pay, and it was announced that this was to be Hoepner's fate. This did not happen, however, possibly due to the intervention of Schmundt, and Hoepner was retired in the following June and continued to live in the official residence of the Commander of 16 Corps in Grunewald-Berlin. See *Kriegstagebuch des OKW*, Vol. 2, p. 204; Halder, *Kriegstagebuch*, Vol. 3, pp. 366–7; Chales de Beaulieu, *Generaloberst Erich Hoepner*, p. 253. The State archives confirm that Hoepner received full pay until June and retired pay thereafter. His widow received a pension after his death.

deep in the almost closed pocket. 4 Army, under Heinrici, was holding open the entrance to the pocket, trying to delay the left enemy pincer which was slowly closing the gap from the south. 2 Panzer Army, commanded by Rudolf Schmidt, and 2 Army had escaped the envelopment and were to the south in the area of Orel.[38] The Soviet High Command then attempted to close the entrance of the cauldron by the use of airborne troops and partisans. 8 and 201 Soviet Airborne Brigades and other units of 4 Airborne Corps, in all about 4,000 men, were landed to the south-east and south-west of Vyazma, having the task of cutting the Smolensk-Vyazma railroad and closing the great gap at the mouth of the pocket. In Sukhinichi, to the south of the entrance of the cauldron, about 4,000 German troops remained by order of the *Führer*, and having been cut off on 3 January had to be supplied by air; in near-by Yukhnov a number of divisions were threatened with encirclement.[39] The Yukhnov-Roslavl road had been broken and the Smolensk-Vyazma road and railway were threatened, these being the main supply channels for 9 German Army and 3 and 4 Panzer Armies. Rokossovsky's 16 and M. M. Popov's 61 Soviet Armies were advancing further to the south against 2 Panzer Army between Bryansk and Orel and threatened the Roslavl-Bryansk-Orel railway, the communications link for both 2 Panzer Army and 2 Army.[40]

In the first week in January, Efremov's 33 Soviet Army had started to drive a wedge between 4 Panzer Army and 4 Army in the area of Medyn, and Hoepner had been dismissed for ordering a withdrawal to escape this encirclement. Ruoff, his successor, could not hold the line and on 13 January Hitler was forced to agree to what had already taken place. Meanwhile elements of 1 Guards Cavalry Corps and Efremov's 33 Soviet Army had succeeded in separating 4 Panzer Army in the north, from 4 Army to the south, and had thrust into the open neck of the pocket to the south of Vyazma, where they were to be joined by partisans and the airborne troops. A further threat to the Germans came from the north of the pocket where Shvetsov's 29 and Maslennikov's 39 Armies, together with 11 Cavalry Corps, had advanced rapidly south and south-westward from Rzhev towards Vyazma and Yartsevo right across the rear of 9 Army and 4 Panzer Army. The German situation appeared critical, since the entrance of the great pocket was nearly closed and the encircled formations were in the process of being cut up.

In mid February, however, the whole situation was once more suddenly

[38] Facing the Bryansk Front.

[39] Part of 216 Lower Saxon Division was moved hurriedly from France by rail to secure Sukhinichi, which was one of 4 German Army's main ammunition and supply bases. Only one and a half battalions of 396 Infantry Regiment and one battalion of 348 Infantry Regiment with the divisional headquarter company and band arrived before the area was surrounded. With other detachments and Russian volunteers the garrison numbered 5,000 men. Jenner, *Die 216/272 Niedersächsische Infanterie-Division*, pp. 47–53.

[40] Rokossovsky's 16 Army had been transferred towards the end of January from the sector due west of Moscow to the area of Sukhinichi in order to strengthen the left enveloping pincer which was trying to close the pocket from the south. M. M. Popov's 61 Army had been standing east of Tula as part of the High Command Reserve.

transformed. On 21 January the Soviet High Command had prematurely withdrawn V. I. Kuznetsov's 1 Shock and Rokossovsky's 16 Armies from the area to the west of Moscow in order to reinforce the north and south flanks, and this caused Vlasov's 20 Army offensive, which was attempting to roll up the German pocket from east to west, to peter out.[41] This relieved the eastwards pressure on 4 Panzer Army and 9 Army, both of which were inside the pocket. Efremov's 33 Army and 1 Guards Cavalry Corps which, together with the airborne troops and partisan units, were trying to seal the pocket between Yukhnov and Vyazma, were suddenly counter-attacked violently by Ruoff's 4 Panzer Army, which re-established contact with 4 German Army on the outside of the pocket on 3 February, and cut off the Soviet troops from their rear. On 5 February Model's 9 German Army, together with encircled German pockets near Olenino and Rzhev, attacked the encircling 29 Soviet Army under Shvetsov from east and west and separating it from its neighbours, encircled it in its turn and destroyed it. Only 5,000 survivors are said to have escaped to the south and joined 11 Cavalry Corps and 39 Soviet Army, by then themselves almost encircled.[42] Hitler had meanwhile been compelled to agree to a general withdrawal to the Winter Line and brought Reinhardt's 3 Panzer Army and elements of 9 Army out of the pocket to Vitebsk and Smolensk to form a reserve in depth. 3 Panzer Army soon contained the enemy thrusts towards Vitebsk and Demidov, all the more easily since Eremenko's 4 Shock Army, which was by then having great supply difficulties, was moving very slowly and with great uncertainty. A German division thrusting north-east from Smolensk reached Byelyi and separated 39 and 22 Soviet Armies. The encircled German garrison at Sukhinichi, with the Goslar bandsmen, had already been extricated on 25 January.

The key to the battle lay, however, in the area of Vyazma, in the mouth of the pocket. On 1 February Zhukov had become the Commander of West Theatre in addition to being the Commander of West Front, the new theatre including the West, the Kalinin and the Bryansk Fronts. By then the Red Army forces were too weak either to close the pocket or destroy the partially encircled enemy. 11 Cavalry Corps and part of 39 Soviet Army had been cut off by Model's 9 Army. A part of 33 Soviet Army together with 1 Guards Cavalry Corps, part of 4 Airborne Corps and partisan units, had been encircled in the mouth of the pocket when 4 Panzer Army and 4 Army re-established contact, and these Red Army troops were being supplied by air.[43] The desperate Soviet efforts to relieve them were without avail and none of the many other Soviet armies were in any condition to help or even move, since they were

---

[41] Zhukov said that he protested against the removal of 1 Shock Army and was told by Stalin to carry out his orders without further talk. Stalin hung up in the middle of the conversation. Zhukov, *Vospominaniya i Razmyshleniya*, p. 383.

[42] *Istoriya*, Vol. 2, p. 328.

[43] The encircled Red Army elements were not eventually cleared by the Germans until midsummer.

at the end of a 150-mile long line of communication and the bad weather and lack of transport made regular supply impossible. Moreover, the advance had outrun the range of the supporting fighter aircraft. In the circumstances, the only communist remedy available was to intensify the political indoctrination and awareness of the flagging supply and transport troops; but this measure failed to improve the position materially or convert itself into munitions and rations.[44] Meanwhile the encircled Soviet forces were slowly cut to pieces. During early March the fighting started to die down, with the Germans strongly and firmly entrenched with secure communications to Vyazma and Orel. On 20 March the Soviet High Command drove their troops forward in yet another offensive, the Kalinin Front being ordered once more to separate the Olenino from the Rzhev pocket while West Front was to attack eastwards with four armies along the Moscow-Vyazma railway. This offensive began at the end of March but was discontinued after a few days at the beginning of April, due to the exhaustion of the troops and supply and transport difficulties in the spring mud.[45] The Soviet winter counter-offensive before Moscow had spent itself.

The Soviet winter offensive against Army Group Centre was supported by other major offensives in the Leningrad and Lake Ilmen areas, in the Ukraine and in the Crimea. Only at Demyansk and Izyum was there any enduring success.

The Germans had overreached themselves when they set out without proper logistic preparation to take Moscow so late in the year. They failed because of the weather and because their resources were inadequate. The Soviet counter-offensive was launched in some strength but its momentum fell off rapidly the further westwards it progressed.

The Soviet High Command had overestimated the success of its winter defence and underestimated the strength, resilience and stamina of the German enemy. Elated by its success in saving Moscow and recalling Napoleon's defeat in 1812, it believed that the enemy could be destroyed in a winter campaign.[46] Offensives were ordered everywhere, and for this, Stalin was subsequently blamed.[47] These offensives, for which the Red Army had insufficient strength, led to a dispersal and dissipation of effort. Of the nine armies held in reserve at the beginning of the winter campaign, one each had been allotted to the North-West, Kalinin, Bryansk and South-West Fronts, two to the Volkhov Front and three to the West Front. This first Soviet offensive was without closely co-ordinated strategic direction, and was the natural consequence of the sudden change from a piecemeal and hasty defence to a general

---

[44] *Istoriya*, Vol. 2, pp. 327–8.

[45] *Ibid*, p. 331.

[46] *Kratkaya Istoriya*, p. 136.

[47] See Zhukov, *Vospominaniya i Razmyshleniya*, pp. 379–81. Stalin was said to have held a meeting on 5 January at which he stated his opinion that the time was opportune for a general counter-offensive everywhere. Other opinions were not wanted.

offensive, which was launched with little time for planning or preparation. If all energies and all reserves had been concentrated on the destruction of Army Group Centre, better results might have been obtained.[48]

In spite of this, the plans at the front levels, even if they were over-ambitious, were well conceived and were designed to be a double envelopment in great depth. They failed because of the weather conditions and because the Red Army lacked the grouped tank formations to execute them. The majority of the Soviet troops used in these enveloping movements were of marching infantry or horsed cavalry, supported by numerous tanks, and the distances they covered were remarkable. The performance and standard of training of the Red Army were inadequate, however, to carry out the strategic and higher tactical tasks allotted to it, the Soviet tactical deficiencies being those normally associated with untrained commanders and staffs. Troops were thrown into battle piecemeal without preparation, commanders being goaded and harried forward by their superiors. Reconnaissance was poor and artillery support uncoordinated with other arms. Tanks had been committed in small detachments rather than as complete brigades, and the use of airborne troops, both at Vyazma and Demyansk, was a failure since they were committed in too great a depth, their tasks not being in accordance with their capabilities. Even if the Soviet High Command had allotted nine instead of five reserve armies to West Theatre, it is probable that Zhukov would still have lacked the necessary strength to destroy Army Group Centre.

The Germans had suffered a significant defeat at the hands of Red Army troops before Moscow, but this reverse was not serious and the 376,000 German battle casualties which occurred during that winter on the Eastern Front were in no way excessive. The sickness casualty rate, due to exposure and typhus, increased this total, however, to about 900,000, and this was heavier than the German formations could afford.[49]

German accounts have tended to overstress the physical and mental qualities of the Soviet enemy and the lack of maintenance and administrative support to be found in the Red Army.[50] The Red Army soldier was hardy and had great stamina, and he was used to local weather conditions, but it is doubtful whether these qualities of endurance were superior to those found in German troops. If the Red Army soldier was not fed, he died, and if he was not clothed

---

[48] *Istoriya*, Vol. 2, pp. 359–60.

[49] For comparison of casualty figures, the British Commonwealth Armies in North Africa, engaged in what was in effect a minor theatre, suffered 102,000 battle casualties between November 1941 and August 1942. Red Army casualties for the winter offensive are not given in Soviet accounts but if the strength figures they quote for various formations are to be believed, they may have been heavy. The Soviet claim, repeated by Samsonov and Zhilin, that the Germans left 120,000 dead in front of Moscow alone between 6 and 27 December is untrue since according to Halder's contemporary record the German dead and missing from 27 November to 31 March on the whole Eastern Front did not amount to more than 108,000. Samsonov, *Die Grosse Schlacht vor Moskau*, p. 135; also *Kratkaya Istoriya*, p. 126.

[50] For example, the description by Blumentritt quoted by Westphal. *The Fatal Decisions*, pp. 37–9.

he succumbed to frost-bite. His rifle and his cannon needed ammunition and his horse had to have fodder. The Red Armyist felt the cold no less keenly than the German *Landser* and the difficulty in movement was not restricted to the German Army. The truth was that Soviet troops were much better clothed and equipped for winter warfare than the Germans, and administrative preparations, rough and ready though they undoubtedly were, went hand in hand with Soviet strategic and tactical planning. This was in contrast to the German practice of relying on luck and the fortunes of war.

CHAPTER SIXTEEN

The Flanks of the Russian Winter Offensive

The Soviet 1941 winter offensive against Army Group Centre was supported by other offensives in the Leningrad area, in the Ukraine and in the Crimea. In the area of the Baltic and Lake Ladoga von Leeb's Army Group North which consisted of one Spanish and thirty tired and depleted German divisions cover an extended front from Oranienbaum on the Baltic to the junction with Army Group Centre near Ostashkov.[1] Von Küchler's 18 Army was on the left, with 26 Corps enclosing the besieged defenders of the Oranienbaum bridgehead, while 28 and 50 Corps covered the southern approaches to Leningrad and the line of the Neva. Leningrad was still cut off by land, as the Germans held the narrow strip, barely ten miles wide, to the key fortress of Schlüsselburg on the southern bank of Lake Ladoga. The ice road across Lake Ladoga was open, however, and across this road nearly half a million of Leningrad's population were being evacuated. Further to the east, von Leeb had been forced out of Tikhvin on 9 December and had fallen back to the River Volkhov between Kirishi and Novgorod, a line held by 1 and 38 Corps. To the south of Lake Ilmen, Busch's 16 Army held the area between Staraya Russa and Ostashkov with 10 and 2 Corps and 39 Panzer Corps on the extreme right. Nothing was held in reserve.

On the Soviet side, the Oranienbaum bridgehead was commanded by a group headquarters known as a coastal command, while on the Leningrad Isthmus 23 Army faced the Finns to the north, and 42 and 55 Armies and the Neva Group stood opposite 18 German Army to the south. All these Soviet armies came under the Leningrad Front, which also commanded the detached 54 Soviet Army covering the area to the south of Lake Ladoga between Schlüsselburg and Kirishi on the Volkhov. On the line of the Volkhov from Kirishi to Novgorod, 4, 52, 59 and 2 Shock Armies had been regrouped on 17 December to form the Volkhov Front under Meretskov.[2] To the south of

[1] The Spanish Blue Division (250 Infantry Division) was Franco's contribution to the crusade against communism.

[2] Soviet commanders were as follows: 54 Army, Fedyuninsky; 4 Army, P. A. Ivanov; 52 Army, Klykov; 59 Army, Galanin; 2 Shock Army (the former 26 Army) first Sokolov and later Vlasov.

Lake Ilmen, Kurochkin's North-West Front with 11, 34 and 3 and 4 Shock Armies covered from Staraya Russa to Ostashkov, where it joined with Konev's Kalinin Front.[3]

On 7 January Meretskov's Volkhov Front mounted an offensive across the frozen river, immediately to the north of Novgorod, to cut through the communication zone of 18 German Army and move northwards towards Leningrad. Meretskov's offensive by Sokolov's 2 Shock Army, which consisted of six rifle divisions and six brigades, was supported on its flanks by Klykov's 52 and Galanin's 59 Armies, and started with probing attacks from 7 January; the main assault fell six days later on von Chappuis' 38 Corps between Gruzino and Novgorod. The fighting took place in swamp and forest in waist-deep snow under bitter conditions. Slowly 2 Shock Army moved forward and in the course of the next month penetrated to a depth of forty miles, until it had covered nearly half the distance to Leningrad. In the second week in March Fedyuninsky's 54 Soviet Army started to thrust from the area west of Kirishi in order to meet 2 Shock Army (by then under its new commander Vlasov) and actually reached a point not fifteen miles distant, placing Blaskowitz's 1 German Corps in imminent danger of being cut off.[4] 18 Army position was serious and its commander was forced to resort to a number of improvisations and patchwork moves. Battalions and companies hastily formed from returning leave personnel and SS, Latvian and Flemish volunteers were committed to plug gaps, and formations and units became almost inextricably mixed. 18 Army reversed the position, however, by counter-attacking the shoulders of the Soviet penetration with the 1 Corps SS Police Division from the north, and 38 Corps formations, including elements of 58 and 126 German and 250 (Spanish) Divisions from the south. These joined hands on 19 March and cut off Vlasov's force, which was estimated to have a strength of 130,000 men, in the Volkhov pocket. Meretskov succeeded at the end of March in driving a small corridor through the German envelopment, but this was too narrow and was open for too short a time to afford Vlasov any relief. Vlasov's 2 Shock Army remained in the deep forests until the following June, when the Germans routed it out, capturing Vlasov himself, 33,000 prisoners, 600 guns and 170 tanks.[5]

[3] North-West Front army commanders were as follows: 11 Army, Morozov; 34 Army, Berzarin; 3 Shock Army, Purkaev; 4 Shock Army, Eremenko. 3 and 4 Shock Armies were operating as the right outer encircling arm of the main Moscow counter-offensive and were transferred from Kurochkin's North-West Front to Konev's Kalinin Front on 22 January.

[4] Formerly a military adviser to Chiang Kai-shek, Vlasov, the Commander of 37 Army in the Ukraine and 20 Army west of Moscow, was a soldier of promise. Captured by the Germans, he was first used as an instrument of anti-Soviet propaganda and then, towards the end of the war, to raise formations from prisoner of war camps to fight in the German service.

[5] *Kriegstagebuch des OKW*, Vol. 2, p. 460. Soviet accounts are silent on the extent of the

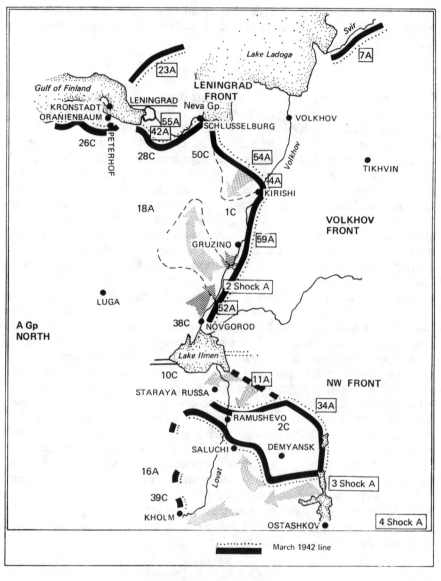

VOLKHOV AND DEMYANSK
January–March 1942

Further to the south between Lake Ilmen and Ostashkov North-West Front on 7 January began a large scale offensive, of which a part formed the outer pincer thrust on Vitebsk. Morozov's 11 Army attacked 16 German Army's 10 Corps under C. Hansen immediately to the south of Lake Ilmen and advanced rapidly on Staraya Russa, a number of ski battalions crossing the frozen surface of Lake Ilmen and penetrating the German rear to a depth of thirty miles. Berzarin's 34 Army attacked towards Demyansk to pin the Germans frontally, while elements of Purkaev's 3 Shock Army, later reinforced by V. I. Kuznetsov's 1 Shock Army removed from West Front, made an encircling thrust to the south aimed at cutting off most of the German 2 Corps between Lake Ilmen and Ostashkov and joining up with Morozov's 11 Army to the south of Staraya Russa. Part of 3 Shock Army was in addition diverted to take Kholm and Velikiye Luki. Eremenko's 4 Shock Army further to the south advanced on Vitebsk and Demidov. All Soviet attempts to take Staraya Russa and Kholm failed, the besieged Kholm holding out under Group Scherer for the next four months.[6] Elsewhere the Soviet offensive immediately to the south of Lake Ilmen made good progress and von Brockdorff-Ahlefeldt's 2 Corps front appeared in danger of breaking up, particularly where 123 Infantry Division was coming under heavy attack across the frozen lakes. On 9 January Busch told his formations that he had no reserves and that they must hold where they were.

In Rastenburg the *Führer* was attempting to cope with the very threatening situation in Army Group Centre where the Red Army was thrusting on Sukhinichi. Messages of importance were not left to Halder to relay, but were telephoned personally by Hitler to von Kluge. Von Kluge had begged in vain for permission to withdraw, Halder noting acidly that the *Führer* well understood the necessity for retirement but simply would not give a decision, and adding the comment that 'this sort of leadership will destroy the Army'.[7] On 12 January von Leeb had reported the plight of 2 Corps and wanted to withdraw immediately, proposing that all German troops should fall back behind the River Lovat. Long and repetitive telephone arguments followed. Hitler rejected this proposal and countered with the logic (which he had already explained the day before to von Kluge) that salients and encirclements tended to tie down more Soviet than German troops since the Red Army was on the periphery, whereas the Germans were fighting on interior lines.[8] Von Leeb, being unable to subscribe to this novel theory, asked to be relieved of his

---

loss of 2 Shock Army but emphasize that many troops infiltrated back to the Volkhov Front. On Vlasov, *Istoriya* says that 'for the unfavourable outcome of these operations the cowardly and supine Vlasov was responsible. He, fearing to answer for his defeat, defected'. Vol. 2, p. 555.

[6] Scherer, the Commander of 281 Security Division.

[7] Halder, *Kriegstagebuch*, Vol. 3, p. 385.

[8] *Ibid*, p. 381, also Note 23 by Jacobsen.

command and on 17 January was replaced by von Küchler.[9] Von Küchler's post as Commander of 18 Army was taken by Lindemann.[10]

On 8 February the left encircling arm of Purkaev's 3 Shock Army linked with the right pincer of Morozov's 11 Army near Saluchi and Ramushevo, and the Red Army achieved its first successful encirclement in depth, when it cut off 2 Corps and part of 10 Corps, in all between six and seven German divisions, a force of about 90,000 men, near Demyansk in an area about forty miles by twenty miles in size.[11] Demyansk was designated by the *Führer* not as a pocket, but as a fortress. On 15 February Soviet airborne units were dropped into the pocket in order to create diversions and panic in the rear areas and assist the attacking troops to break up the defences. This attempt failed. The encircled German troops were put on air supply but since at first only half of the maintenance needs could be flown in, due to the limited air transport available, rations and ammunition expenditure had to be drastically reduced. Demyansk was finally relieved by a specially created corps of five divisions under von Seydlitz-Kurzbach which, beginning its attack on 21 March from the area just to the south of Staraya Russa, fought its way forward through the twenty-five miles of Red Army occupied territory separating the encircled troops from 16 Army.[12] By 21 April von Seydlitz had cut a narrow corridor only a few miles wide into the pocket. Demyansk was then heavily reinforced by the Germans and held throughout the summer as a springboard to be used for reopening the offensive later in the year.[13]

The Demyansk air supply operation was of particular importance in that it convinced Göring and, through him, Hitler, that large numbers of encircled troops could be supplied by air by the *Luftwaffe*. This was to have disastrous

[9] On 15 January Halder's diary contained the cryptic entry 'Von Leeb asks to be relieved. Strauss is done for. Von Reichenau apoplectic fit'. In order to conceal the differences between Hitler and his commanders, sickness was henceforth to be given as the usual cause for removal from appointment. Von Leeb was recorded as being relieved at his own request for reasons of health. Compare *Kriegstagebuch des Oberkommandos der Heeresgruppe Nord*, 75128/50, p. 1810, 17 January 1942.

[10] Lindemann was the former Commander of 50 Corps. Brennecke, the Chief of Staff of Army Group North was replaced by Hasse, the Chief of Staff of 18 Army. Von Küchler soon came to hard words with Busch and within two weeks was asking Hitler for his removal.

[11] On 11 February Halder noted that as soon as the *Luftwaffe* had given an assurance that it could maintain the encircled troops in Demyansk by air, the order to remain was confirmed. This procedure was repeated, with different results, later in the year at Stalingrad.

[12] Von Seydlitz-Kurzbach was Commander of 12 Infantry Division, being rewarded for his services during the break-in by the command of 51 Corps. This took him into Stalingrad.

[13] German losses in the Valdai-Demyansk area from 28 November to 28 February are indicative of the proportion of sick to battle casualties.

Killed	6,300
Wounded	23,500
Frost-bite	2,400
Sick	31,400

Haupt, *Demjansk*, p. 211.

effects at the time of Stalingrad, later in the year. The Demyansk operation initially involved the supply of 90,000 men and these were encircled for a period of two and a half months. The garrison had, however, weathered the worst of the winter before the encirclement began and the hours of daylight necessary for air supply were already lengthening. Although the air supply operation was theoretically under the control of Keller, the Commander of 1 Air Fleet, in fact he had few resources and his fighters and bombers were already fully committed. For this reason most of the tactical control was exercised by the air transport command headquarters set up for the operation. No fighter aircraft were available to escort the transports or to protect the Demyansk landing ground and the Junker 52 transport aircraft flew in 'pulks', a *Luftwaffe* slang term for large formations, in this instance of twenty to thirty aircraft (presumably from *polk* the Russian word for a regiment). These closely knit transport formations defended themselves by the massed fire from their hull machine-guns, and this defence proved effective in keeping Soviet fighters at bay. In the occasional encounters more Red Air Force fighters were shot down than Junker 52 lost, and the Soviet aircraft restricted their activities to hit and run raids on the grounded aircraft on Demyansk airfield. Soviet anti-aircraft fire, as usual, was by far the greater menace and, as the Junker 52 flew at only 7,000 feet, this caused significant losses. Nearer Demyansk, aircraft landing or taking off were hotly engaged by any Red Army man with a rifle and one aircraft was actually brought down when its pilot was hit by a burst of submachine-gun fire.

At the beginning of the operation only 230 transport aircraft were assigned and of these only thirty per cent at any one time were available, due to repair, maintenance and weather difficulties. Since each sortie carried about two tons and the minimum maintenance requirement for the encircled force was 300 tons, 150 sorties had to be flown a day, but this minimum was not reached even though many of the aircraft flew two or three sorties. There were no night landing facilities at Demyansk and the supplying airfields were as far afield as Tylebiya (west of Staraya Russa), Pskov, Ostrov, Riga and Daugavpils. In the snow and muddy periods supplies were sometimes free or parachute dropped and not airlanded. The transport force was eventually raised to about 600 aircraft, and between 19 February and 18 May an average daily supply of 273 tons was delivered by air to Demyansk; 22,000 wounded were flown out and 15,000 reinforcements flown in.[14]

The Demyansk air operation was rightly regarded at the time as a notable achievement, but in retrospect even the *Luftwaffe* participants were to realize that it was a costly and pointless undertaking. That it was successful at all was due to the weakness of the Red Air Force and the lack of foresight and determination shown by the Soviet High Command in failing to concentrate all air resources against the German dispatch airfields. Not one of these air-

[14] Morzik und Hümmelchen, *Die Deutschen Transportflieger im Zweiten Weltkrieg*, pp. 121–46.

fields was to suffer an attack during the whole of the operation, and a single German fighter, even a Messerschmitt 110, was sufficient to make Red Army fighters turn tail. Even so, German air transport losses were not light, and 262 aircraft were lost during the period, mainly through crashes and anti-aircraft fire, and 383 crew became casualties. Worse still was the damage done to the structure and training organization of the air transport command, damage which could not be made good before it was called on later in the year to maintain the encircled 6 Army in Stalingrad and meet other demands in the Mediterranean. The holding of the Demyansk salient was unnecessary and von Leeb was correct when he proposed to withdraw 2 Corps as soon as it was threatened with encirclement.

At the end of December the situation in the Ukraine had temporarily stabilized itself after the German withdrawal to the line of the Mius. In January Field-Marshal von Reichenau, the new Commander-in-Chief of Army Group South, was suddenly taken ill with a stroke and died while being flown back to Germany. On 18 January Field-Marshal von Bock, the former Commander of Army Group Centre, having recovered from his stomach ailment, was called back to take von Reichenau's place. General Paulus, a staff officer and Halder's principal deputy, who, except for some months in command of an experimental motorized battalion, had in all his service commanded nothing larger than an infantry company, took over von Reichenau's old command of 6 Army.[15]

Army Group South was deployed with von Kleist's 1 Panzer Army against the Sea of Azov, while 17 Army, its northern neighbour, by then under the command of Hoth, covered the upper course of the North Donets. 6 Army under Paulus was deployed forward of the area of Kharkov, while 2 Army under von Weichs, which had been transferred from the command of Army Group Centre to that of Army Group South in mid January, lay between Orel and Kursk. The front from the Sea of Azov to Kursk stretched for over 400 miles and was held by thirty-seven German divisions and the equivalent of about seven divisions of Germany's allies.[16] The *Luftwaffe* 4 Air Fleet had about 300 aircraft, the greater proportion of which were bombers.

Facing Army Group South stood Timoshenko's South-West Theatre with Khrushchev as the political member of the military council.[17] South-West Theatre included Cherevichenko's Bryansk Front of three armies, Kostenko's South-West Front of four armies and Malinovsky's South Front of six

[15] Paulus' place as *O Qu 1* in the OKH was taken by Blumentritt, the former Chief of Staff of Army Group Centre.
[16] *OKH Kriegsgliederung* dated 2 January 1942.
[17] Chief of staff was Bagramyan.

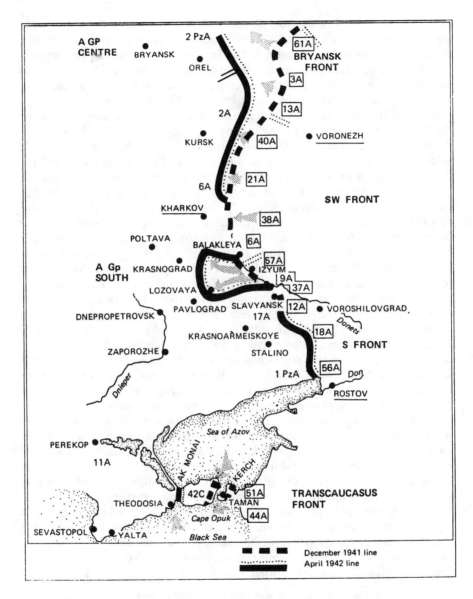

THE OFFENSIVES IN THE UKRAINE AND CRIMEA
January–April 1942

armies.[18] At the end of the year South-West Theatre was ordered to follow up the Moscow, Tula and Elets counter-offensives by two further consecutive offensives in January and February. The first attack was made by the Bryansk Front at the beginning of January together with 40 and 21 Armies, which formed the right wing of South-West Front, and was aimed against von Weichs's 2 German Army, the objectives being Orel and Kursk. This attack made only limited progress. On 18 January the main attack was taken up by the South-West Front and the right wing of South Front, when Maslov's 38 Army thrust towards Kharkov and Gorodnyansky's 6, Ryabyshev's 57, Kharitonov's 9 and Lopatin's 37 Armies attacked 17 German Army and the flank of 6 German Army across the upper Donets towards Krasnograd, Pavlograd, Dnepropetrovsk and Zaporozhe.[19] According to the German intelligence map of 28 January, twenty-one Soviet rifle and eleven cavalry divisions together with ten tank brigades were engaging seven German divisions.[20] The Soviet attack in this area soon achieved a breakthrough between Balakleya and Slavyansk about eighty miles in width, and by 26 January Soviet thrusts had reached a depth of sixty miles when the 17 Army main supply base at Lozovaya was captured. Soviet cavalry had penetrated even further to the south towards Krasnoarmeiskoye trying to cut the Dnepropetrovsk-Stalino railway, which was the main supply artery for 1 Panzer Army. At this critical time the exhausted 17 Army was placed by von Bock under von Kleist's command to form together with 1 Panzer Army Group von Kleist, and a Group von Mackensen was built around 3 Panzer Corps to hold the left wing of 17 Army. 1 Panzer Army was forced to divert the equivalent of six divisions to drive the enemy back from the railway over the Samara River. During the early part of February Soviet operations came to a standstill since the Red Army troops were once again exhausted, having supply and transport difficulties. The Soviet offensives had not been without success, however, some ground having been made towards Kursk and Kharkov. Even more successful had been the securing of the great Izyum bridgehead over the North Donets, a salient which bulged forward over fifty miles and threatened both Kharkov and the Dnieper crossings.

In the Crimea in the late autumn of 1941 von Manstein's 11 Army, after a ten day battle, had forced the Perekop Isthmus on 28 October. Alma had been taken on 31 October and the Soviet force had been split into two parts. The remnants of 51 Soviet Army had retreated eastwards along the Kerch Peninsula, while formations of what was to become the Independent Coastal

---

[18] The Bryansk Front had been south of Tula and had taken part in the Moscow counter-offensive; it consisted of 3, 13 and 61 Armies. The South-West Front was made up of 40, 21, 38 and 6 Armies. South Front had 57, 9, 37, 12, 18 and 56 Armies. The military councils of the fronts were: Bryansk; Cherevichenko, Kolobyakov and Kolpakchy. South-West; Kostenko, Gurov and Bodin. South; Malinovsky, Larin and Antonov.

[19] Gorodnyansky had just been recalled from the command of a mixed force based on 13 Army operating against 2 Panzer Army.

[20] *Lage Ost* Map, 28 January 1941.

Army fell back on the fortress of Sevastopol. 51 Soviet Army, pursued by the newly arrived 42 German Corps, had evacuated Kerch on 16 November and leaving its equipment behind, had crossed the seven miles of water to the safety of Taman and the Kuban. The *Führer* had originally intended that German troops should follow into the Kuban in order to meet up with von Kleist's autumn 1941 thrust through Rostov, but since the Soviet counter-offensive had made this impossible, it was intended to quell all Soviet resistance in the Crimea and take the fortress of Sevastopol preparatory to the resumption of a general offensive in the spring of 1942.

At the beginning of November 1941 a Soviet Sevastopol Defence Command was set up, the Commander-in-Chief being Vice-Admiral Oktyabrsky, who was also Commander of the Black Sea Fleet, with I. E. Petrov as his Army Deputy.[21] Sevastopol was ringed by three concentric defence lines, having a total depth of about ten miles, and the whole area was broken down into four defensive sectors for ease of control. The exact strength of the Sevastopol garrison at that time is not known, but according to Soviet statements by 10 November it amounted to 52,000 men, of which 21,000 were sailors organized into marine infantry brigades.[22] It is certain that a number of rifle divisions and marine brigades were subsequently shipped into the fortress from the Kuban. The defenders' artillery at the beginning of November numbered at least 170 guns, of which a number were mounted in concrete and steel emplacements.

During November several divisions of E. Hansen's 54 German Corps closed up to and probed the Sevastopol defences without success, and von Manstein in consequence prepared to reduce the fortress by heavily supported attacks made by two corps. The concentration of troops and equipment and the dumping of supplies was delayed by the heavy rain in the Crimea which washed away the roads, and by the winter conditions in the Ukraine which had put the railway locomotives out of action.[23] There was, moreover, a shortage of German troops for the task. The activity of Red Army stragglers in the hills to the north and north-east of Yalta was tying down Rumanian formations, and the defence of the Kerch Peninsula in the east had to be entrusted to 42 Corps with a single German infantry division. In the event, the preparations for the assault on Sevastopol were not completed until mid December. On 17 December the attack was launched by 22 and 132 Infantry Divisions down the Belbek Valley, westwards towards the coast on the north side of the town, this attack falling on 388 Soviet Rifle and 40 Cavalry Divisions and 7 Marine Brigade. Meanwhile 24 and 50 German Infantry Divisions further to the south moved westwards to secure the heights which looked down on the town of Sevastopol and its North Bay.

[21] *Istoriya*, Vol. 2, pp. 226–7.
[22] *Ibid*, p. 227.
[23] Throughout the winter the German railway system failed to function and even in February Halder was still calling the rail situation catastrophic.

22 Division had been awaiting the attack impatiently in the miserable Crimean winter weather. Storms were frequent and it rained almost incessantly. Many of the troops were in summer uniforms, without greatcoats, gloves or head protection. Although it was not very cold, many of the men were mentally and physically exhausted and had little resistance to illness or, when they were wounded, to death. The attack was eventually mounted, at first against very poor demoralized Red Army troops, who made little difficulty about running away or deserting. As the days passed, however, the influence of officer, commissar and the NKVD police re-established itself, and as newer enemy formations were committed to battle the fighting became bitter.[24] By Christmas von Choltitz was describing the resistance as desperate and his own losses as enormous.[25] The northern thrust made good progress against very stiff resistance, von Choltitz with 16 Infantry Regiment actually penetrating into 3 Sector close to the North Bay. 24 and 50 Infantry Divisions had less success, since they were fighting in fiercely defended scrubland covered by pillboxes.[26] The heavy fighting continued over Christmas until the New Year.

After the first few days of the German attack the position of the Sevastopol defenders appeared precarious and the Soviet High Command had yet another change of heart and reorganized its command channels once more. Vice-Admiral Oktyabrsky, who as Commander of the Black Sea Fleet was unfortunate enough to be 300 miles away at the Novorossisk naval base on the Taman Peninsula when the German offensive started, was peremptorily ordered by Stalin to return to Sevastopol, and on 20 December the responsibility for Sevastopol was transferred to Kozlov's Transcaucasus Front on the Kuban.[27] The next day a rifle division and marine brigade arrived in Sevastopol by sea, together with units of the Black Sea Fleet which were used to give fire support to the ground formations. The fate of the Sevastopol garrison, by then in the balance, was decided however by the intervention of Lvov's 51 and Chernyak's 44 Armies of the Transcaucasus Front in the far-away Kuban, which from 26 December made landings from the sea in the area of the Kerch Peninsula, supported by units of the Black Sea Fleet and the Azov Flotilla. The weather was stormy and the country where they disembarked was wild and open and without any cover, and specialized landing craft were not available. The Kerch Straits had already begun to freeze over. Small parachute troop detachments were dropped in the enemy rear but otherwise no air or artillery support was provided, as the landings took place mainly on a barren and deserted coastline. 51 Army landed 13,000 men on the north and east coast adjacent to Kerch, while 44 Army disembarked 3,000 troops at Cape Opuk. From 29 December a further 23,000 men were

[24] *Die Geschichte der 22. Infanterie-Division*, pp. 33–5.
[25] Von Choltitz, *Un Soldat parmi des Soldats*, pp. 130–1.
[26] Von Manstein, *Lost Victories*, p. 224.
[27] *Istoriya*, Vol. 2, p. 307.

landed in Theodosia Bay in order to occupy the port of Theodosia and the narrow neck of land behind the Germans at Ak Monai, so cutting the rear communications of 42 German Corps. Stormy weather and *Luftwaffe* air attacks caused the loss of a number of ships.[28]

42 German Corps, which consisted of only 46 German Infantry Division deployed in the area of Kerch, was commanded by Lieutenant-General von Sponeck, an officer who hitherto had had a distinguished career with airborne forces and was a former Commander of 22 Lower Saxon Division. Von Sponeck requested permission from von Manstein to evacuate the Kerch Peninsula and establish a defensive line behind the Ak Monai narrows where the 46 Division's front could be shortened.[29] The fact that the Kerch Straits were freezing over, so that within a few days Red Army troops were to cross over the ice, lent weight to his argument; but his proposal was rejected. On 29 December after Soviet landings had been made near Theodosia in the German rear, von Sponeck took the law into his own hands and ordered the withdrawal of the German troops out of the Kerch Peninsula, abandoning the guns and heavy mortars. Von Manstein's assistance to 42 Corps had been limited to the dispatch of a German infantry regimental group and some Rumanian troops on whose offensive capabilities he himself did not set great store, and none of these troops had in fact arrived with von Sponeck. Von Manstein's fears as to the reliability of the Rumanian mountain brigade were justified, when instead of attacking and retaking Theodosia it gave ground rapidly on coming into contact with Red Army troops.

The attack on Sevastopol was discontinued, although the fortress defences were crumbling fast, and 30 Corps, with 132 and 170 Infantry Divisions, was sent to the support of 42 Corps. 42 Corps, with its one German infantry division, the infantry regimental group and the Rumanians, had created a weakly held defensive line to the west of Ak Monai and Theodosia, all available German officers and men, including those from headquarters and rear units, having been attached to Rumanian units to stiffen their resolution and safeguard their heavy equipment. On 15 January von Manstein, apparently after some little soul searching, attacked with three and a half German divisions a force which he estimated to be eight Red Army divisions and captured the port of Theodosia together with about 10,000 prisoners and 170 guns. By then however the Red Army no longer required the use of Theodosia harbour, since formations had been arriving for some time in large numbers across the iced-over Kerch Straits. The unfortunate von Sponeck had been removed from his appointment and was later to be court-martialled and sentenced to death.[30] The precise nature of his crime it is difficult to

---

[28] *Ibid*, pp. 311–3.

[29] Von Manstein, *Lost Victories*, pp. 225–7; and Halder, *Kriegstagebuch*, Vol. 3, p. 369.

[30] Von Sponeck's sentence was commuted to one of imprisonment. Halder, *Kriegstagebuch*, Vol. 3, p. 401. After the 20 July 1944 bomb attempt on Hitler's life von Sponeck was shot without trial in Germersheim by the SS.

determine. He might have acted more aggressively and he might, in accordance with the spirit of the *Führer*'s latest orders, have held his ground at the eastern extremities of the Kerch Peninsula, but with the freezing of the Straits he could hardly have obeyed for long von Manstein's injunction to hurl the enemy back into the sea. The reinforcements dispatched to him were inadequate and unsuitable for the task. If 46 Division had held its ground near Kerch on a thirty mile front, it could not have prevented 51 and 44 Soviet Armies arriving across the ice and it would probably have been encircled. Three or more German divisions would probably have been required to halt the Soviet advance westwards and the attack on Sevastopol would in any event have had to be discontinued. Like Hoepner's, the fate of von Sponeck was meant as a warning to other German Generals not to give up one inch of territory unless the *Führer* should sanction it.

On 28 January Kozlov's Caucasus Front Headquarters, then in the Kerch Peninsula, was redesignated as the Crimea Front,[31] Stalin attached great importance to the relief of Sevastopol and the reoccupation of the Crimea, which he viewed as part of the Soviet counter-offensive from Leningrad to the Black Sea, and he sent to the Crimea Front as representative of the High Command Army Commissar Mekhlis, the head of the Main Political Administration of the Red Army, his presence being additional to that of the political member of the military council, Divisional Commissar Shamanin.

The Soviet offensive continued on 27 February both on the north part of the Kerch Peninsula and at Sevastopol, the heavy fighting dying out after six days. On 13 March began another mass attack from Kerch by eight rifle divisions and two tank brigades, the Soviet troops losing 130 tanks in the first three days of fighting. On 20 March von Manstein, who up to then had been without any tank formations, committed the newly arrived and inexperienced 22 Panzer Division in a counter-attack which proved a failure. On 26 March and again on 9 April the enemy Crimea Front mounted further offensives, the last being made by six rifle divisions and over 150 tanks. By then however its offensive capability was entirely spent.

Thus ended the Soviet 1941 winter offensives from the Baltic to the Black Sea. All of them were less successful than Zhukov's offensive west of Moscow, but they achieved their aim in that the *Führer*, far from being able to move troops from one army group to another, spent the first of several nerve-wracking and distressing winters, without reserves or resources, trying to hold ground and seal off gaps.

[31] Kozlov's Transcaucasus Front appears to have been redesignated as Caucasus Front at the end of 1941.

CHAPTER SEVENTEEN

German Preparation for the 1942 Summer Campaign

During the winter of 1941 Kinzel's OKH Department of Foreign Armies East had revised its opinions concerning the strength and capabilities of the Red Army. On 4 November Kinzel had issued an appreciation in which he said that he disagreed with the view once current in Thomas's *Rüstungsamt* that the Soviet economy would not be in a position to re-equip its own forces before the summer of 1942, and gave his own belief that by May the Red Army would be able to re-equip thirty cavalry and 150 rifle divisions 'together with a number of new tank formations using United States or English equipment'.[1] On 1 December the Soviet strength opposing the German forces was estimated at 200 rifle and thirty-five cavalry divisions and forty tank brigades, and the total Red Army strength was put at 265 rifle divisions, this estimate being in fact still much below the real Soviet strength.[2] At the beginning of 1942 Kinzel issued a rewrite of the German Army Handbook on the Soviet Armed forces, which bore little relationship in its content to that put out exactly a year before. The Red Army, it said, had been made into a fighting force, serviceable to a degree which had not been recognizable before the war. What was most surprising was not its numerical strength but rather the great stocks of available weapons, equipment, clothing, tanks and guns, stocks far exceeding those previously held anywhere else in the world. Generally, German intelligence was surprised how quickly the Soviet Command recognized and remedied its own weaknesses. The handbook admitted that it had seriously underestimated Soviet organizational powers and the ability of the Government, the High Command and the troops in the field to overcome their difficulties by improvisation.[3]

---

[1] *OKH Qu IV Abt Fremde Heere Ost* Appreciation of 4 November 1941.

[2] *Anlage 1 zu OKH Gen St d H Op Abt (1a) Nr. 1693/41 g. Kdos Chef.*

[3] Official Secret Handbook *Die Kriegswehrmacht der UdSSR OKH Gen St d H O Qu IV Abt Fremde Heere Ost (4) Nr. 100/41g.* of 1 January 1942, pp. 3-5. Page 9 included a detailed description of the NKVD within the Red Army (absent from the earlier issue) and page 130 onwards gave information (culled from the *Wi Rü Amt*) on Soviet armament production. Since this was given in round percentages it was of little value.

The position of Halder during these days is hard to define. Halder, like Zeitzler and Guderian, after the war denounced Hitler's military leadership and blamed him for being unable or unwilling to recognize facts and appreciate the enemy strength.[4] The *Führer* was bitterly criticized for disbelieving intelligence estimates and failing to match plans to German capabilities.[5] Yet on 17 January 1942 Halder signed a letter, partly drafted in his own handwriting, to be distributed down to German corps, in which he noted that the large number of new Red Army formations being identified was having a dispiriting effect on German leadership. Halder went on to say that it was intolerable that the leadership should fall a prey to the psychology of numbers and he reminded intelligence officers (*Ic*) of their responsibilities in this direction. He ended by saying that 'the tough and spirited German soldier shames the staff which meticulously tots up numbers'.[6]

On 31 March Halder decided that Kinzel no longer met his requirements and in early April Kinzel was replaced as Head of Foreign Armies East by Gehlen, one of Halder's General Staff officers who had formerly been his personal adjutant.[7] Gehlen was an able officer who had been the chief operations officer (*Ia*) of 213 Infantry Division early in the war, but like Kinzel he was a General Staff Officer and not an intelligence specialist. The 10 April intelligence estimate gave the view that the Red Army had mobilized all its manpower resources and was unable to raise any additional tank formations.[8] These views Halder passed on to Hitler.

The *Führer* at this time had gained enormously in self-confidence, since he was convinced that he and he alone had halted the Soviet counter-offensive and brought the German Army safely through the winter.[9] Previously it had been the practice of the German Army to rehearse plans for major offensives in the form of war games. With the dismissal of von Brauchitsch, this planning machinery was discarded, all plans henceforth emanating in outline and in detail from the *Führer*'s fertile brain.

On 5 April 1942 Hitler signed his Directive Number 41, another long and rambling discourse which set out the plans for the continuance of the war in

---

[4] There is no mention in December in Halder's diary of the entry of the United States into the war. This may be explained by the crisis on the Eastern Front.

[5] For example, Halder, *Hitler as War Lord*, pp. 42 and 57.

[6] Halder's draft letter of 16 January 1942 in *Fremde Heere Ost* files, issued as *Der Chef des Gen St d H Nr. 10/42 g. Kdos* dated 17 January 1942.

[7] Halder, *Kriegstagebuch*, Vol. 3, p. 422.

[8] Compare *The German Campaign in Russia Planning and Operations (1940–2)* (*D of A no. 20–261a*), pp. 124–5. Note however Gehlen's *Beurteilung der Gesamtfeindlage an der Ostfront of 1 May* (*Kriegestagebuch des OKW*, Vol. 2, p. 1273) which is cautious in tone.

[9] He described the defence as 'a success of unequalled magnitude'. Hubatsch, *Hitlers Weisungen für die Kriegführung*, p. 183.

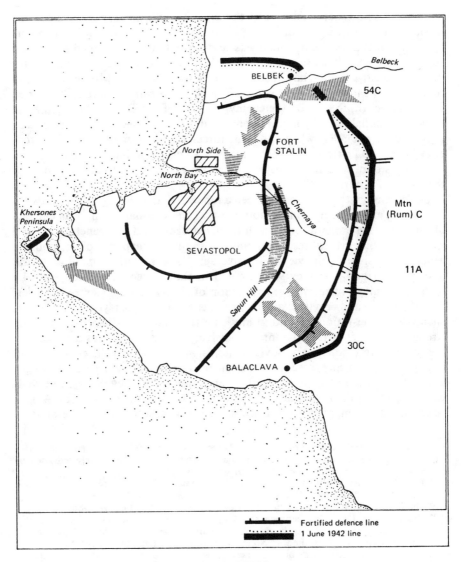

SEVASTOPOL
June–July 1942

257

the East.[10] The general mission of the directive was no longer to knock the Soviet Union out of the war in one blow, nor was any time limit set for the achieving of the next aim, which was to destroy the Soviet armed forces and separate the enemy 'as far as is possible' from their most important centres of war industry. Hitler had lost interest in the taking of Moscow and had reverted to his ideas of a year before. The main operations were to be carried out in the south, to destroy the enemy this side of the Don and to secure the Caucasian oilfields and passes.[11] Leningrad became a secondary theatre and it was to be encircled when sufficient forces could be made available from elsewhere. The first essential, however, was to clear the Kerch Peninsula and take Sevastopol and to destroy the threatening enemy salient at Izyum to the south of Kharkov.[12]

The coming of the summer had seen a renewal of the old arguments between the *Führer* and Halder. Halder doubted that the German Army was capable of any large scale operations which involved deep strategic penetration, and wanted to conserve its resources until it should be capable of resuming a general offensive. In his view, offensive actions were still permissible in the interim, provided that they were limited in their objectives. Once again he favoured limited offensives in the sector of Army Group Centre.[13] Hitler, on the other hand, revived all his arguments of the past year. The Soviet enemy was over-estimated and in any case the Red Army had dissipated its strength during its winter counter-offensive; Caucasian oil was a necessary, even a decisive factor in the Soviet Union's war effort, and the enemy would not spare himself in protecting these oil resources; German passivity might affect the attitude of the Fascist allies and even of Turkey.[14] To these well-worn arguments the *Führer* added yet another. In 1943 the threat of an Anglo-Saxon invasion might be very real and for this reason it was imperative to

[10] Clarity and decisiveness are lacking in Directive 41, probably explained by Scherff's statement that the section dealing with the main operation had been entirely redrafted by Hitler. *Ibid*, pp. 183–5; Warlimont, *Inside Hitler's Headquarters*, p. 231.

[11] The OKH (Army) directives covering the summer offensive bore the cover name *Siegfried*, afterwards changed to *Blau*.

[12] The Izyum salient stretched from Balakleya-Krasnopavlovsk-Lozovaya-Slavyansk.

[13] Halder's attitude varied between slight optimism and well justified pessimism. On 12 May he reported very sombrely on the strength of the German Army. The total of German divisions (excluding the thirty-one replacement divisions) had increased in the last nine months from 210 to 225 but the increase was not real since most of the infantry divisions were greatly understrength. The worst factor, however, was the great loss of motor vehicles which could not be replaced even by horses, and divisional reconnaissance battalions were beginning to appear on the field of battle on bicycles. Warlimont, according to his own account, prepared a similar paper dated 6 June. *Inside Hitler's Headquarters*, pp. 239–40. To reinforce Army Group South for the coming summer offensives meant that the other two army groups would be starved of men and equipment and so become vulnerable to Red Army attack.

[14] At this time when he had not a rifle to spare (much French, Czech and Russian equipment having been taken into use) Hitler was to offer the Turks 150 million marks worth of military equipment.

obtain a final decision in the East in 1942. To any suggestion that Army Groups North and Centre be permitted to withdraw from the two great salients at Demyansk and Rzhev-Vyazma, Hitler turned a deaf ear, and continued to maintain that a straightening of the line in these areas would release too many enemy troops.

Von Manstein's 11 Army, by replacing many of the German troops of 54 Corps round Sevastopol by Rumanians and making the Rumanians responsible for all coast defence, collected a force of six German and three Rumanian divisions for the attack on Kerch. Von Richthofen's 8 Air Corps had been removed from Army Group Centre to the Crimea to augment the special air headquarters attached to 11 Army and the air forces available totalled eleven bomber, three *Stuka* and seven fighter groups, a heavy weight of air power. Von Manstein's plan was a bold one and included landings by engineer storm boat in the enemy rear and a deep and rapid penetration as far as Kerch by motorized troops. The Soviet enemy in the Kerch Peninsula was several times the strength of the attacking troops; Kozlov's Crimea Front disposed of three armies, Chernyak's 44, Kolganov's 47 and Lvov's 51 Armies, but their defences lacked depth. On 8 May, after heavy *Luftwaffe* preparation, von Manstein broke through on a three mile front. By 12 May the battle had been decided and by 15 May the Germans were in the town of Kerch, the enemy having fled and abandoned his entire equipment. Against German casualties totalling only 7,500, the Crimea Front lost 170,000 in prisoners, 1,100 guns, 250 tanks and 3,800 motor vehicles and 300 aircraft. Very few men escaped across the Kerch Strait to the Taman Peninsula. The Sevastopol garrison was meanwhile passive.[15]

This lightning blow and telling defeat was to demonstrate once again the effect of air power and the continued superiority of German arms when good weather had restored their mobility. The Soviet account of the battle admits the total destruction of the Crimea Front and the loss of all the heavy equipment, much of which, the historian notes, was to be used against the defenders of Sevastopol. Silence is maintained on the loss of prisoners.[16] As was the custom, the senior Soviet commanders were removed from the theatre of operations in order that they might personally answer for their failure. Kozlov and the army commanders Chernyak and Kolganov were degraded in rank as were many others.[17] Mekhlis, the *Stavka* representative with the Crimea Front, was demoted to the rank of corps commissar.

The next preparatory clearing operation, known as *Fridericus I*, was to be undertaken in the Ukraine by Group von Kleist, consisting of his own 1 Panzer Army and Hoth's 17 Army, against the Balakleya-Lozovaya-Slavyansk

[15] Von Manstein, *Lost Victories*, pp. 236–8; Halder, *Kriegstagebuch*, Vol. 3, p. 444.
[16] *Istoriya*, Vol. 2, pp. 404–7.
[17] D. T. Kozlov, Chernyak and Kolganov appeared later in the war in lesser appointments. Shortly afterwards Mekhlis lost his appointment as the head of the Main Political Administration, being replaced by A. S. Shcherbakov, a member of the Politburo and a Secretary of the Central Committee of the Party.

(Izyum) salient, in conjunction with a southwards thrust made by Paulus' 6 Army.[18]

Only a few days before this German attack was due to be mounted, Timoshenko's South-West Theatre on 12 May began a Soviet offensive in the same area aimed against Kharkov.[19] The Soviet design of battle consisted of concentric attacks by Kostenko's South-West Front on 6 German Army; the thrusts were to be made by 28 Soviet Army under the command of Ryabyshev and formations of Gordov's 21 and Moskalenko's 38 Armies from the area of Volchansk attacking westwards, and Gorodnyansky's 6 Soviet Army and Group Bobkin thrusting northwards from the salient. Podlas' 57 and Kharitonov's 9 Army of Malinovsky's South Front on the southern edge of the salient had the task of protecting Gorodnyansky's and Bobkin's rear. The Soviet attack, made by twenty-three rifle divisions, two cavalry and two tank corps against the eleven divisions of Paulus' 6 Army, was pushed home with vigour and Paulus was forced to give ground and commit all his reserves, including the two divisions which had just arrived in Kharkov.[20] By 14 May the position of 6 German Army gave cause for some concern, but Kostenko's South-West Front, unsupported by Malinovsky's South Front which continued to be passive and worried by air reports of German tanks near Smiyev, failed to recognize that the time had come for the tank corps to be committed to battle. Group Bobkin, which contained a strong cavalry element, advanced north-west on Krasnograd and Poltava cutting the flank communication between 6 Army and Group von Kleist and causing von Bock such uneasiness that he proposed that he should postpone von Kleist's *Fridericus I* offensive, due to be launched on 18 May, and instead use two or three of the panzer divisions to aid Paulus's 6 German Army. This proposal was rejected by Hitler and Halder, although the advancing of the date of the offensive by one day was agreed, in order to take the pressure off Paulus.[21]

On the morning of 17 May von Kleist, with von Mackensen's 3 Panzer Corps of two panzer and one motorized divisions, eight German and four

[18] Hoth and Ruoff exchanged commands on 1 June 1942, Hoth taking command of 4 Panzer Army.

[19] Once again Platonov says that Timoshenko was commanding South-West Front. *Vtoraya Mirovaya Voina*, p. 293. *Istoriya*, Vol. 2, on the other hand says he was commanding South-West Theatre. It is assumed that, as was often the case, the Headquarters of South-West Front was an offshoot of that of South-West Theatre. Two separate command organizations appear to have been in existence each with its own military council. The military councils were: Timoshenko, Khrushchev and Bagramyan; and of South-West Front, Kostenko, Gurov and Bodin. Timoshenko also commanded the Bryansk Front, the military council of which was Cherevichenko (after the end of April, Golikov), Kolobyakov (later Susaikov) and Kolpakchy (later Kazakov), and South Front, the military council of which was Malinovsky, Larin and Antonov. In each council the second named was the political member and the third the chief of staff.

[20] Soviet strength figures from *Istoriya*, Vol. 2, p. 412.

[21] Halder, *Kriegstagebuch*, Vol. 3, p. 440. According to von Bock's diary neither he nor von Kleist held out any great hope of a successful outcome of the German offensive.

Rumanian infantry divisions and supported by 4 Air Corps, attacked the Soviet salient from the south. His attack fell on the troops of South Front, Podlas's 57 and Kharitonov's 9 Armies which, although they reacted vigorously, were soon swept aside, so that on the first day the Germans penetrated to a depth of twenty-five miles and the next day Izyum and Barvenkova were taken. An attempt by Timoshenko's South-West Theatre to mount a counter-offensive with 5 Cavalry Corps and other reserves failed and 9 Army fell back over the upper Donets. The danger that the salient was about to be cut off by the Germans was apparent to South-West Theatre, but any proposal to withdraw to the east was rejected by the Soviet High Command which insisted that 9 and 57 Armies should take more positive action against von Kleist and that the South-West Front offensive against 6 German Army should continue. Khrushchev, like Stalin, has attempted to have history rewritten and has asserted that he, as the political member of the military council, saw the real German design and protested in vain to the Kremlin.[22] By 19 May Kharitonov's 9 Soviet Army had already been defeated and a great fifty mile gap had been torn in the front, so that 6 Soviet Army, which was being attacked in its rear, had to turn about and fight without air or artillery support. The pressure fell off at once from Paulus's hardpressed troops; 8 German Corps of 6 Army was ordered to attack southwards to meet von Kleist, the two joining up on 22 May. Fighting continued until 29 May while the surrounded 6 and 57 Soviet Armies and part of 9 and 38 Armies and other elements were being cut to pieces. The Germans suffered a loss of 20,000 men. The Red Army loss in prisoners alone totalled 214,000 together with 1,200 tanks and 2,000 guns.[23] The forward tactical headquarters of South-West Theatre was taken inside the pocket and the Commander of South-West Front, Kostenko, and the Commanders of 6 and 57 Soviet Armies, Gorodnyansky and Podlas, were reported to have been among the killed. Although much of the credit for this success properly belonged to Hitler and Halder, Paulus received the Knight's Cross for his part in the victory, and the Nazi Party and the press began to publicize his abilities and activities.[24]

There appear to be some grounds for believing that Timoshenko's offensive was linked with a Soviet High Command strategic aim of destroying the German forces being concentrated for the summer offensive. At the end of March at a GKO meeting attended by Voroshilov, Shaposhnikov, Zhukov, Vasilevsky, Bagramyan and Timoshenko, Stalin demanded a pre-emptive general offensive in all theatres and condemned as a half measure Zhukov's

[22] *Istoriya*, Vol. 2, p. 414.

[23] *Kriegstagebuch des OKW*, Vol. 2, p. 391. Soviet sources are silent on Red Army losses.

[24] Paulus, like Rommel, represented the ideal National Socialist General. Although he had married into the Rumanian aristocracy, Paulus came from a lower middle-class background and was therefore free from the stigma of belonging to the traditional military class. He was an ardent admirer of Hitler and apparently considered that the *Führer*'s judgement at the time of Kharkov was much superior to his own.

suggestion that an attack be made against von Kluge in the area of Rzhev and Vyazma in order to pin the German enemy and disperse his reserves. Timoshenko and Voroshilov had supported Zhukov's idea of a pinning attack in the centre but had also hastened to agree with Stalin and other members who were in favour of attacking the enemy concentrations near Kharkov. The clever but careful Shaposhnikov, according to Zhukov, was silent when he should have spoken out.[25] So it was decided that the Soviet preventive offensive should be made in the Ukraine.

On 1 June Hitler flew to Army Group South at Poltava, Keitel, Heusinger and Wagner being present. The meeting was attended by von Richthofen, von Kleist, Ruoff, von Mackensen, von Weichs, Hoth and Paulus. Von Bock presented his plans for the summer offensive, with which the *Führer*, still in the best of spirits and in good health, concurred. According to Paulus' post-war testimony, Stalingrad itself was not mentioned as an objective but Hitler did say that 'if we don't get Maikop and Grozny, I shall have to pack in this war'.[26] Hitler, von Bock and Halder were agreed that mopping up operations should continue in the Volchansk area.

Later that month Reichel, the General Staff Officer (*Ia*) of 23 Panzer Division, disobeyed orders in taking plans for the opening attack by light plane and these fell into Soviet hands. In spite of this the *Führer* decided to take no action to alter the general plan of the offensive. Stumme, the Commander of 40 Corps, and his chief of staff were held responsible for the loss and were both sentenced to fortress imprisonment.[27]

Meanwhile a deception operation had been undertaken to mislead the Soviet High Command into believing that the main summer offensive would be made in the direction of Moscow. Goebbels was to organize a number of deliberate leakages to the foreign press, while von Kluge made overt preparations for an offensive apparently directed on the capital, known by the cover name of *Kremlin*.[28]

The stage was not yet set for the mighty thrust which was to take the Germans to Stalingrad and the Caucasus; it was still necessary to clear the Crimea and to force the enemy back in the small Volchansk salient and secure a bridgehead on the east bank of the Oskol, a tributary of the Donets. Two separate operations were mounted, one, known as *Wilhelm*, by 6 German Army against 28 Soviet Army in the Volchansk area, and a second, known as *Fridericus II*, by 1 Panzer Army and part of 6 Army from south-east of Kharkov against 38 and 9 Soviet Armies in the direction of Kupyansk. The first of these operations took place between 10 and 15 June and the second

[25] Zhukov, *Vospominaniya i Razmyshleniya*, pp. 396–7; Vasilevsky, *Voenno Istoricheskii Zhurnal* No. 8 August 1965.

[26] Goerlitz, *Paulus and Stalingrad*, p. 155.

[27] Stumme's sentence was commuted and he was sent to the Afrika Korps where he lost his life at Alamein.

[28] *Goebbels' Diary*, 23 May 1942, p. 170; *Heeresgruppe Kommando Mitte, Ia. Nr. 4350/42 g. Kdos Chefs* of 29 May 1942 (*Kriegstagebuch des OKW*, Vol. 2, pp. 1276–7).

between 22 and 26 June. The Soviet troops withdrew rapidly thirty miles to the east to avoid encirclement, but even so they lost another 40,000 prisoners. By then the South-West Theatre had lost all initiative and had been reduced to a shell.

In the Crimea 11 Army had entered into the final phase of its victorious campaign, the conquest of Sevastopol. Von Manstein had visited Hitler in mid April and discussed his plans for the coming attack, plans which were accepted by the *Führer* without demur. When Sevastopol was taken, it was intended that 11 Army should pass over the Kerch Straits and enter the Kuban to intercept the enemy forces falling back on the Caucasus from the lower Don.[29]

The Soviet garrison in Sevastopol totalled seven rifle divisions, three marine infantry brigades and other formations, and a further two rifle brigades were landed while the fighting was in progress, making in all a total of seventy battalions. In addition civilians for whom arms were available were pressed into service. According to the Soviet account the defending force mustered 600 guns but only forty tanks.[30] The German attack was made by E. Hansen's 54 Corps in the north, Fretter-Pico's 30 Corps in the south, and the Rumanian mountain brigade in the centre on the Yaila Heights, in all seven German and two Rumanian divisions supported by 700 guns, many of which were of heavy and medium calibre, and by heavy mortars. Except for some remote-controlled Goliath armoured tracked vehicles designed to carry high-explosive charges into the enemy's defensive system, von Manstein had no tanks but he did have a number of assault gun battalions. Von Richthofen's 8 Air Corps, with seven bomber, three *Stuka* and four fighter groups and seventeen flak batteries, was in support.

The Sevastopol perimeter had been reduced by the first German attack in the previous December to two-thirds of its former size, and stretched just to the north of the Belbek River to the village of Belbek, from whence the perimeter ran south over the mountains to the Black Sea near Balaclava. The defended area measured about sixteen miles across. Numerically the attacker and defenders were evenly matched, but the German still laid great store on his own superiority at arms when he accepted the great risk involved in attacking so strong an enemy in well prepared positions, over very difficult mountainous and broken country, much of it covered by thick scrub and defended by machine-gun nests built into the rock. The terrain in places proved too difficult for the passage of the armoured assault guns. In the air, however, 8 Air Corps had an overwhelming superiority.

The attack was launched on 7 June, heavily supported by artillery and aircraft. 54 Corps once again made good progress down the Belbek valley with von Choltitz taking Fort Stalin at the head of his Oldenburgers. 30 Corps took the forward positions of the Sapun fortifications. German casualties

[29] Von Manstein, *Lost Victories*, pp. 238–9.
[30] *Istoriya*, Vol. 2, p. 407.

were heavy, infantry regiments dwindling to the strength of hundreds while companies were down to the pitiful handfuls that they had been during the previous winter. It was then obvious that the main thrust should have been made on the left in 30 Corps sector, but since Halder warned 11 Army that any delay in the taking of the fortress would lead to the removal of 8 Air Corps which was needed for von Bock's offensive, there was no time for change and the attack had to be pressed home. 50 Infantry Division of 54 Corps crossed the Chernaya River and took Inkerman behind the Soviet Sapun defences, and on the night of 28 June, 22 and 24 Infantry Divisions crossed by assault boats the thousand yard wide North Bay in the enemy rear, immediately to the east of the town of Sevastopol. The Soviet defence then fell apart.

Fighting continued for several days. In places this was of the most desperate kind, particularly in the galleries of the gun positions and in the caves under the overhanging cliffs. There were cases where, rather than surrender, the commissars blew up themselves, the defenders and the attackers, and the women and children who had sheltered there. Many other units did not give up the struggle until their commissars had been killed or committed suicide. Von Manstein reported cases similar to those described by the *Leibstandarte* at Rostov the previous winter of masses of troops and civilians, with women and girls among them, linking arms so that none could hold back, rushing at the German lines. German losses had been heavy, about 24,000 men, and von Manstein declined to allow his troops to incur further casualties by clearing the built-up areas in the town and the port; these were subjected to bombing and artillery fire, during which many more civilians lost their lives.

German air superiority was so decisive that the Black Sea Fleet had been able to land reinforcements and supplies only by night. Eventually Sevastopol was closed to surface vessels, and supplies, in all about 4,000 tons, so Soviet historians claim, were brought in by submarine. Submarines removed also all Soviet high ranking officers, officials and functionaries before the Germans should capture them. The remnants of the Soviet Coast Army found their way to the Khersones Peninsula on the west side of Sevastopol in the vain hope of being picked up from the sea and there, on 4 July, 30,000 surrendered; in all over 90,000 prisoners were taken during the battle and 460 guns were captured. In this final attack on Sevastopol the Germans used 46,000 tons of ammunition and 20,000 tons of bombs.[31] In recognition of the victories at Kerch and Sevastopol von Manstein was promoted from colonel-general to field-marshal.

Von Manstein's victory at Sevastopol, a remarkable success when the difficulty of terrain, the determination of the defenders and the parity of the opposing ground forces are taken into account, fired the *Führer*'s imagination. He abandoned his earlier intention of putting 11 Army into the Kuban and decided that von Manstein and his victorious troops should undertake the

[31] *Ibid*, pp. 408–11; Von Manstein, *Lost Victories*, pp. 248–59; *Kriegstagebuch des OKW*, Vol. 2, p. 473.

reduction of Leningrad. Halder, by then rarely in agreement with Hitler, made it clear to the *Führer* and others that he was completely opposed to taking Leningrad and at the same time mounting the great offensive in the Ukraine and the Caucasus.[32] Most of the siege and heavy artillery which had supported the Sevastopol attack had been sent by rail to the Leningrad area. 11 Army followed, but not as a complete formation, since 42 Corps was left in the Crimea and only four of the infantry divisions accompanied 30 and 54 Corps to the north, the remainder of the divisions being dispersed as reinforcements to other formations between Smolensk and Crete. The loss of this complete army formation, which once totalled eight German divisions and which was the only formation with any experience of commanding and working with Rumanian troops, was to be sorely felt later in the year when 6 German Army was faced with crisis in Stalingrad and the German troops in the Caucasus were in danger of being cut off.

Further to the north, in Army Group Centre, 4 Army and 4 Panzer Army mounted operations against those elements of 33 Soviet Army, 1 Cavalry Corps and the airborne troops who remained in the Vyazma area, and these were steadily eliminated with a further gain of 20,000 prisoners. Not before 2 July was it possible to deal with the great Soviet salient between Byelyi and the area to the west of Sychevka, occupied by 39 Soviet Army and 22 Cavalry Corps in the rear of 9 Army. The removal of this salient shortened the German front by 130 miles and yielded a further 50,000 prisoners.

By then the launching of the great summer offensive in the south had already begun.

---

[32] Compare von Manstein, *Lost Victories*, p. 261. Halder made it clear that he disagreed with Hitler's intention to attack Leningrad before completing the offensive in the south. On the other hand, according to von Manstein, Halder believed that the presence of 11 Army was not needed in the Ukraine. For the sudden change of plan on the *Führer's* part see *Kriegstagebuch des OKW*, Vol. 2, p. 456; and Halder, *Kriegstagebuch*, Vol. 3, p. 485.

CHAPTER EIGHTEEN

Towards the Volga and the Caspian

Hitler had once more conjured up a picture which he described to Mussolini in a letter dated 22 June 1942 of German armies crossing the Caucasus and, together with the Axis force in Egypt, which at that time was hardly a hundred miles from Alexandria, occupying the whole of the British Middle East. Directive Number 41, which the *Führer* had himself drafted, was an untidy disarray of disconnected thoughts containing many asides and irrelevancies, a hotchpotch of strategy and tactics. It made no mention of the enemy strength, disposition and intentions and it was very confusing in its aims.

The general aim of the directive was to destroy the remaining Soviet defence strength (*Wehrkraft*) and to separate the Soviets from their sources of armament; but the word *Wehrkraft* was undefined and the location of the war industrial centres was not given. The particular and main aim of the operation was the destruction of the Soviet forces to the west of the Don, before seizing the Caucasus oilfields and the passes through the mountain range which opened into Turkey and Iran. The taking of Stalingrad or the reaching of the Volga formed no part of the general or particular aims.[1]

The seizing of the Caucasus passes, although necessary if the *Führer* proposed to occupy the Black Sea ports and the Middle East, had only minor relevance to the destruction of the Soviet State. The seizing of the Caucasus oilfields was of obvious advantage to Germany, and their loss would have been a most serious blow to the Soviet Union.[2]

The total Soviet oil output in 1940 amounted to 31,000,000 tons and by 1941 production rose to nearer 38,000,000 tons.[3] The main sources of crude

[1] Hubatsch, *Hitlers Weisungen für die Kriegführung* 1939–45, pp. 183–8.

[2] The area of the Caucasus was economically of great importance to the USSR because of oil, corn, manganese deposits and natural gas. *Voenno-Politicheskoe i Ekonomicheskoe Znachenie Kavkaza, Bitva za Kavkaz*, pp. 9–26.

[3] Soviet oil fuel production from Baransky, *Economic Geography of the USSR*, p. 23. (By 1960, according to Baransky, Soviet production stood at 135 million tons of which only forty per cent came from the Caucasus).

oil were the three great oilfields in the Caucasus, Maikop, Grozny and Baku, and of these Baku produced by far the largest share, believed by Western sources to be as much as eighty per cent of the total of Soviet output.[4] On the other hand it is known that these three oilfields were only part of the tapped oil resources available to the USSR in 1942, since oil was being produced in quantities in the areas of the Upper Volga and Kama (an area which since the Second World War has produced more oil than Baku), in the Urals, in the north near Ukhta, and to the east of the Caspian in the narrow belt across the whole south of the Soviet Union.[5] Of the total production in 1941 the Red Army and Air Force consumed less than 4,500,000 tons.[6]

The detail of the distribution and transportation of Soviet oil, where these were known, should of course have been a factor of importance in deciding German strategy in the east. In 1941 there were few oil pipelines in use and these were of limited length and capacity. The main pipeline which ran about 1,200 miles from Baku to the Black Sea port of Batum had been in existence since the First World War, and other shorter lengths ran from Grozny to Tuapse on the Black Sea, from Armavir to Rostov and Trudovuya, and from Guriev on the Caspian due north-east to Orsk. In addition, according to German estimates, about 9,000,000 tons of oil went up the Volga each year by river tanker and barge.[7] For the internal distribution of the bulk of the oil and oil products, the Soviet Union remained dependent, however, on the railways, the railnets having a total capacity of 29,000,000 metric tons.[8]

As Commander-in-Chief of the German Army Hitler had laid down binding and detailed orders as to the execution of the general directive. The campaign was to begin with three parallel thrusts, all made from west to east, each of the thrusts being made consecutively starting with the one furthest to the north. This first and most northerly thrust was to be an armoured and infantry break-through from the area near Kursk eastwards to the Don and Voronezh, Hitler stating specifically that the aim of this break-through was the capture of Voronezh (the city being about five miles beyond the Don). The armoured part of the force was then to turn south-eastwards and move rapidly down the west bank of the Don, rolling up the enemy from north to

---

[4] The actual figure in 1940 appears to have been 71·5 per cent, the other Caucasian oilfields producing 14·9 per cent. Kravchenko, *Voennaya Ekonomika SSSR 1941- 1945*, Chapter 2, Table 8.

[5] Said to total 14 per cent of the total output. *Ibid.* Table 8. On the other hand there is some evidence that Ural alternative oil resources were being hastily developed at this period. Compare for example Zhukov, *Vospominaniya i Razmyshleniya*, p. 524.

[6] Kravchenko, *Voennaya Ekonomika SSSR 1941–1945*, Chapter 6 and Table 17.

[7] Hitler's Munich speech of 8 November 1942, Jacobsen, *Der Zweite Weltkrieg in Chronik und Dokumenten*, p. 355. In fact in the first seven months of 1943 six million tons of oil products went up the Volga. *Istoriya*, Vol. 3, p. 434.

[8] This was the sum of the capacities of the following railnets, all in millions of metric tons: Central Asian, 2·3; Volga, 5·2; Urals, 1·2; Transcaucasus, 4·1; North Caucasus, 8·5. *Voprosy Ratsionalizatsii Perevozok Vazhneishikh Gruzov.*

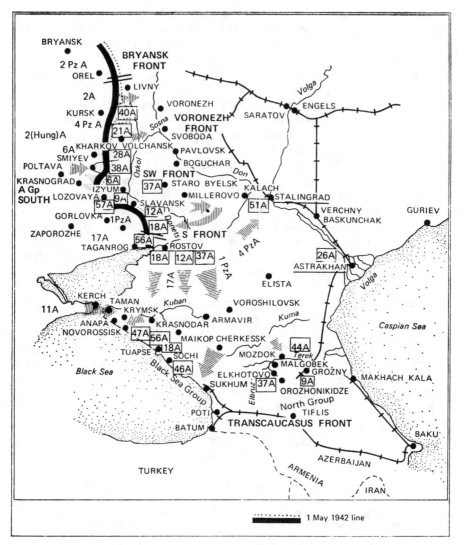

KHARKOV, THE VOLGA AND THE CAUCASUS
May–August 1942

south, in conjunction with the second parallel thrust made eastwards from the area of Kharkov, the object being to destroy the Red Army forces west of the river. The third parallel thrust was to be made in the south due eastwards from Taganrog, along the north bank of the lower Don to join in the area of Stalingrad with the German forces moving down the upper Don. Stalingrad was mentioned at this point in the execution paragraphs of the directive for the first time. The capture of the city was certainly not a part of the strategic aim, although the *Führer* insisted that every effort be made to reach Stalingrad 'or at least to control the area by the fire of heavy weapons' so that the enemy could no longer use it as an industrial or communications centre.[9]

Stalingrad was an industrial city on the Volga about forty miles east of the Don. Hitler's insistence on its seizure had little basis in reason, since its capture by the Germans did not assist in the destruction of the Red Army west of the Don or further the occupation of the Caucasus, and for this reason was to be opposed by Halder and von Bock. The holding of the landbridge between the Don and the Volga offered an advantage in that it gave some security to the northern flank, and the cutting of the Volga river traffic was of great importance as it interrupted the supply and oil channel to the north. There was, however, no reason why the landbridge should not have been seized to the south of Stalingrad or why the Volga should not have been cut further down stream nearer Verchny Baskunchak, since this would have had the additional advantage of cutting the Soviet Union's only remaining rail artery with Astrakhan. The cutting of the rail communication at Stalingrad was not of decisive importance, as Stalingrad could be by-passed by the rail link to Saratov.

It is probable that Hitler's insistence on the taking of Stalingrad was based partly on ideological grounds. Stalingrad, formerly Tsaritsyn, had been held for the Reds during part of 1918 by Voroshilov, Budenny and Stalin, all three claiming the victory when the Whites were repulsed. When Stalin came to power and history was rewritten, the defence of Tsaritsyn became a military legend, the entire credit accruing to Stalin. Five years after the event he had the city renamed as Stalingrad. Hitler appeared to have been attracted to the destruction of this city, since it bore Stalin's name and was connected with Stalin's early aspirations to political power and military fame.[10]

In outline, Hitler envisaged the main strategic thrust being made from the area of Kursk and Kharkov, first in an easterly and then in a south-easterly direction, in order to envelop and destroy the Red Army west of the Don. The south-easterly movement was to have the line of the upper Don as its left boundary. The further the progress to the south-east, the longer and more exposed the Don flank would become, and the Army Group South frontage which before the offensive stretched about 500 miles from Orel to Taganrog, was eventually to extend in a great salient from Orel to Stalingrad, then south

[9] Hubatsch, *Hitlers Weisungen für die Kriegführung*, Directive 41, IIC, p. 186.
[10] Halder, *Hitler as War Lord*, p. 56.

to the area of Grozny, and back again along the foothills of the Caucasus to the Sea of Azov, in all about 1,300 miles. Originally sixty-eight German divisions were available to Army Group South, of which only nine were panzer and seven motorized, and all but one-third of the infantry divisions had been reinforced to bring them up to eighty per cent of their personnel establishment, leaving fifteen only partially effective due to deficiencies in personnel and equipment.[11] During July this total of sixty-eight was reduced to fifty-two divisions. Ninety-six German divisions, many of them so under strength that they were little more than regiments, remained with Army Groups North and Centre; but as these were holding a 1,300 mile front no further thought was given to reducing their number in order to reinforce Army Group South.[12] Hitler had been forced to take some formations from Western Europe and the Balkans, but since he was unwilling to reduce the strength in the West below forty-three divisions, he was obliged to exert pressure on his Rumanian, Italian and Hungarian allies to increase their contingents with Army Group South to a total of twenty-eight field divisions.[13] Of this total the Rumanians found twelve, the Italians six and the Hungarians ten and it was intended that the total of the allied divisions should eventually be increased to forty-four. The introduction of this large number of non-Germanic formations was to undermine the security of the whole south-eastern front.

The Rumanians had not yet forgotten the loss of Rumanian territory to Hungary by the Vienna Award, and the two peoples were so bitterly antagonistic that the *Führer* found it necessary to order that Rumanian and Hungarian formations should not be brought into contact with each other. Both the Italians and the Hungarians were averse, on the grounds of national

[11] Compare also Mueller-Hillebrand, *Das Heer*, Vol. 3, Table 36.

[12] Halder, *Kriegstagebuch*, Vol. 3, p. 457, gives the following distribution of German divisions as at 16 June 1942.

East Front	North	36	Finland	5
	Centre	63	Norway	12
	South	68	France	26
			Balkans	5
			Germany	3
			Africa	3
		167		54

[13] The German distribution of army manpower with the field armies (and not including the Armed SS) was as follows.

	East	Other Theatres
22 June 1941	3,206,000	594,000
1 July 1942	2,847,000	971,000

The 971,000 in OKW theatres were distributed

Finland	150,000
Norway	166,000
West	520,000
North Africa	55,000
Balkans	80,000

Mueller-Hillebrand, *Das Heer*, Vol. 3, Table 38 *et seq.*

pride, to detaching subordinate formations to serve under German command or to admitting German detachments to stiffen their own troops. Such was Hitler's lack of men that he was forced to agree to his allies' conditions and the Italians, Hungarians and some of the Rumanians took part in the new offensive as national army formations. Hitler realized the limitations of his allies but hoped to use them in defensive tasks commensurate with their abilities, and the task personally selected for them by the *Führer* was the defence of the long and exposed north-east Don flank.[14]

Directive 41 was really intended to cover the destruction of the Red Army west of the Don by two great armoured pincers from Voronezh and Taganrog meeting near Stalingrad. Only then was the advance to be resumed into the Caucasus.[15] These priorities were not subsequently maintained, however, and the southern armoured pincer, instead of thrusting from the right flank, came to be launched from the centre.

Von Bock's Army Group South was entrusted with the preparations for the coming campaign and the opening stages of the actual attack, but there-after Army Group South was to be split into two new army groups, Army Groups A and B. Army Group B in the north under von Bock was to consist of 6 German Army and Group von Weichs. The new army group headquarters of Army Group A under Field-Marshal List, a new arrival to the theatre, was to command 1 Panzer Army, 17 German Army and 8 Italian Army.[16] Because the Soviet enemy was known to be in disorder after his defeats near Kharkov and his subsequent withdrawal over the Oskol, Hitler was pressing for an early start to the campaign in mid June, before in fact all the troops could be assembled, and for this reason it was decided to make the thrusts consecutively, each phase of the offensive being ordered as soon as the necessary troops could be mustered. Consecutive thrusts also gave the advantage that all air effort could be concentrated and switched in support of each successive attack. This air support was to be provided by von Richthofen's

[14] Directive 41, IIC last paragraph.

[15] The following mixed aims can be extracted from Directive 41.
'*mit dem Ziel, den Feind vorwärts des Don zu vernichten, um sodann die Ölgebiete . . . zu gewinnen*'. '*Ihr Ziel ist es – wie schon betont – zur Einnahme der Kaukasusfront die russischen Kräfte, die sich . . . westlich bezw. nordlich des Dons befinden, entscheidend zu schlagen und zu vernichten*'.

[16] 35 Italian Corps was already in position but 8 Italian Army had not yet arrived. The divisional strength of the armies of Army Group South on 4 July 1942 was as follows:

	German			Allied		
	Panzer	Motorized	Infantry	Hungarian	Rumanian	Italian
2 Army		1	4	2		
4 Panzer Army	3	1	6			
2 Hungarian Army				4		
6 Army	2	1	15			
1 Panzer Army	3	1	7		4	
17 Army	1	1	6		4	6

A further two German and six Allied divisions were in transit to the theatre. *OKH Kriegs-gliederung*, 4 July 1942.

4 Air Fleet consisting of 1 Flak Corps, 4 Air Corps and 8 Air Corps, as soon as the latter could be released from the assault on Sevastopol. 4 Air Fleet consisted in all of ten single engined fighter, eight long range fighter, sixteen bomber and five *Stuka* groups.

The first phase of the offensive known as Operation *Blue I* was to be launched in the north in the area of Kursk on 28 June by Group von Weichs, consisting of 2 Army (von Weichs), 2 Hungarian Army under Colonel-General Jany and Hoth's 4 Panzer Army, in all six Hungarian and seventeen German divisions of which three were panzer and two motorized infantry. On reaching the Don the infantry formations were to hold the northern and eastern flank on the line of the river, while Hoth's armour moved rapidly south. Two days later, as the second part of the same operation known as *Blue II*, Paulus's 6 Army of eighteen German divisions, of which two were panzer and one motorized, was to attack eastwards from the Kharkov area to the Don immediately to the south of von Weichs, and having encircled the Soviet troops in the area of Staryy Oskol, was then to move on south-eastwards on Hoth's right. The final thrust, *Blue III*, also known as *Clausewitz*, was to take place some days later and was to be made by Army Group A, von Kleist's 1 Panzer Army and Group Ruoff. Instead of directing this right enveloping arm from the area of Taganrog along the lower Don to Stalingrad, the main thrust was made nearly 150 miles to the north near Artemovsk, the reason for this change being that Army Group A lacked the offensive power to make such a wide sweep away from the flanking support of 6 Army and was deficient of bridging equipment needed to cross the broad stream of the North Donets so near its mouth. Tactical considerations greatly modified and in part nullified the strategic concept of Directive 41.[17]

In the modified plan von Kleist was to attack due east from Artemovsk-Izyum with four Rumanian and eleven German divisions, of which only three were panzer and one motorized infantry, while on the extreme right flank Group Ruoff, of 17 Army and Gariboldi's 8 Italian Army, had the subsidiary task of pinning the enemy in the area of the Sea of Azov since it was not powerful enough to form the right thrust towards Stalingrad. Instead of a large scale strategic envelopment the offensive plan had degenerated into a few small tactical encirclements.

Although the offensive was to be made in the height of summer, supply and transport difficulties were expected. The railway was still working at a very low capacity and reliance was placed on three west-east spurs with rail-heads at Kursk, Kharkov and in the Gorlovka-Stalino area. In the north the spur at Kursk ran eastwards to Voronezh, and in the south the railway continued to the east from the area of Gorlovka-Stalino to Stalingrad; both tracks were to require relaying before the Germans could use them. In the Kharkov area there was no rail track to the east, and the movement of 4

[17] Compare Doerr, *Der Feldzug nach Stalingrad*, p. 20; also Philippi und Heim, *Der Feldzug gegen Sowietrussland*, p. 132.

Panzer Army and 6 Army down the Don could not be supported by use of the Voronezh-Millerovo railway parallel to their axes, since part of the track between Voronezh and Svoboda was on the east bank of the Don and Hitler was expressly to forbid the securing of large bridgeheads east of the river. The only railway running into the Caucasus of value to the Germans crossed the Don bridge at Rostov. Since maintenance by rail was likely to prove difficult, reliance continued to be placed on the use of motor transport units, but the availability of vehicles and vehicle fuels was no better than it had been during the previous summer and in consequence the vehicle capacity was limited. All infantry divisions continued to advance at the speed of the walking horse.

German tactical intelligence of the enemy was good but strategic intelligence continued to be poor. In any case, the German plan had been drawn up without regard to Soviet strategy and likely intentions or to Red Army dispositions. Whether or not the Soviet forces west of the Don would be destroyed depended on the current defence policy of the Soviet High Command. If it insisted on holding fast, the Red Army forces were doomed. If, on the other hand, it had learned the lesson of the Kharkov defeat, a defeat as great as the Germans were yet to suffer at Stalingrad, it was possible that the Soviet troops might escape across the Don and become a menace on the German north flank. A few weeks before, between the Donets and Oskol, the Soviet forces had escaped encirclement by withdrawing with skill and great alacrity.

On the Soviet side, the Kharkov defeat had left Timoshenko's South-West Theatre weak and disorganized. Regrouping, and the inevitable Soviet reorganization of the higher echelons of command followed. South-West Theatre Headquarters was disbanded and Timoshenko reverted to the command of only the South-West Front, the Bryansk Front and the South Front coming directly under the control of the Soviet High Command. After the destruction of the Crimea Front a new front, the North Caucasus Front under the command of Budenny, was brought into being.[18] The imminence of the German offensive and the likelihood that the blow would fall initially on the Bryansk Front was known in Moscow, but the Soviet strategic intelligence appreciation regarded this attack as the preliminary to a major offensive to the north-east to outflank and encircle Moscow.[19] Such an appreciation was based on the probability of German intentions, and once again the Kremlin could not be censured for failing to follow the uncertainty of the Führer's strategy.[20] Golikov's Bryansk Front was reinforced by the Soviet

[18] *Istoriya*, Vol. 2, p. 419.

[19] Vasilevsky, *Voenno Istoricheskii Zhurnal* No. 8, August 1965.

[20] On 12 February Keitel had issued an intelligence directive for a cover plan to spread false information that the next German offensive was to be directed on Moscow. *German Campaign in Russia Planning and Operations (1940–2)*, p. 116; *Goebbels' Diary* and other references. It is believed that these were in the main successful. Yet on 3 July Hitler was already declaring that the German plan had been betrayed. Halder, *Kriegstagebuch*, Vol. 3, p. 471; Keitel was to blame a *Luftwaffe* officer for the leakage. Keitel, *Memoirs*, p. 178.

High Command with four tank corps, the equivalent of ten infantry divisions and four tank brigades, in order to meet the German offensive; but the German attack caught the Bryansk and South-West Fronts unprepared and off balance.

At 2.15 a.m. on 28 June, von Weichs, supported by a heavy weight of air support from 8 Air Corps, launched Hoth's 4 Panzer Army towards Voronezh, while 2 German Army covered its left flank. The attack fell on Pukhov's 13 and Parsegov's 40 Soviet Armies driving a great gap between them, and the Bryansk Front made the error of committing its tank corps piecemeal to battle. Two days later Paulus attacked Gordov's 21 and Ryabyshev's 28 Soviet Armies of South-West Front, forcing them apart. By 2 July von Weichs's troops met those of Paulus near Staryy Oskol and completed the first tactical envelopment, encircling part of 21 and 40 Soviet Armies and taking a number of prisoners. On 6 July Hoth's 4 Panzer Army was over the Don and seized Voronezh by an armoured thrust, the enemy having evacuated the city. The Soviet High Command, still believing that the German strategic objective was Moscow, then started to move a tank army and two further rifle armies from its reserves towards the Voronezh area east of the Don.

In the second week of the campaign the first of several differences of opinion arose between Hitler and von Bock. Hitler intended that the River Don should provide flank protection on the left, and that all the armoured formations should move rapidly southwards, leaving the river line to be held by the minimum of infantry divisions. In Directive 41 and in his order to Army Group South on 12 April, Hitler demanded the capture of the city of Voronezh, although this lay a few miles beyond the east bank of the Don. On 3 July, however, the *Führer* was vacillating and decided that it might not be necessary to seize Voronezh, and he left it to von Bock to take it or not as he pleased, provided that the taking of the city did not delay the movement of the armour to the south-east. The *Führer* soon began to fret and carp about von Bock's tardiness and although when he visited von Bock at this time all was sweet reasonableness, no sooner had he returned to Rastenburg than his suspicions and criticisms began to mount again.[21] Endless telephoning went on between the *Führer*, von Bock, von Sodenstern, Keitel and Halder, the worst part of it, according to Halder, being the endless and pointless chit-chat with Keitel.[22]

Von Bock was showing some nervousness about scattered enemy tank forces to his south and had in fact become temporarily bogged down on the east bank of the Don. In view of the considerable Red Army strength there, estimated at twenty rifle divisions with many tank formations, and the increasing pressure of the enemy in the Voronezh area, von Bock became

---

[21] In the middle of July the *Führer* Headquarters moved from Rastenburg to Vinnitsa in the West Ukraine.

[22] Halder, *Kriegstagebuch*, Vol. 3, pp. 470–6; Keitel, *Memoirs*, pp. 178–9.

reluctant to move his troops away to the south.[23] In consequence the one corps of 4 Panzer Army already dispatched to the south had insufficient momentum to envelop the elements of 21 and 28 Soviet Armies which were withdrawing rapidly eastwards under pressure from Paulus. By 8 July von Bock had released further armoured formations from Voronezh for the south, but within a day or so most panzer movement ceased near Tikhnaya Sosna, as the formations ran out of motor fuel. Not before 13 July did 4 Panzer Army reach Boguchar. In all von Weichs and Paulus took only 30,000 prisoners; this was nothing like the measure of success expected from such an offensive and it was obvious that the larger part of the Soviet forces was escaping over the Don.

The Army High Command (OKH) did not order the forward movement of Army Group A until 7 July, when it was already too late to destroy the Red Army forces west of the Don.[24] The Soviet South-West and South Fronts, aware of the danger of envelopment from the north, were already in full retreat, great columns of troops harried by the *Luftwaffe* crossing the Don at Kazansk and Yelansk.[25] 1 Panzer Army crossed the Donets on 8 July and three days later, having met only the action of rearguards, was near Starobyelsk on the Aidar. That same day Group Ruoff started to move forward against the Soviet South Front but made only slow progress in the face of widespread mining and spirited rearguard action, while near Taganrog on the Mius the Red Army enemy held fast, being determined to cover the approaches to Rostov; the German offensive was still not achieving its primary aim, the destruction of the enemy forces. Von Bock tended to be preoccupied with the protection of the left flank, and he was frequently halted by lack of petrol and cloudbursts. Group Ruoff was not strong enough to achieve anything of real value.

On 9 July an impatient *Führer* took a hand in the battle by interfering in tactical detail. Hoth with 4 Panzer Army Headquarters, still in the area of Voronezh, was told to quit and get down to the south immediately to the area of Kantemirovka and take over the command of 40 Panzer Corps (belonging to 6 Army) and use it in a short tactical encircling movement to meet up with von Kleist in the area of Kamensk, cutting off the enemy in the area of Millerovo.[26] When Hoth arrived at Kantemirovka, however, he found that von Bock had ordered the panzer corps eastwards down the Don towards Stalingrad and the tanks had already reached the Chir near Bokovskaya, when they were turned back to join hands with von Kleist. Only 14,000

---

[23] Von Weichs's diary shows that during July he advised the giving up of the Voronezh bridgehead but encountered opposition in the OKH, because, surmised von Weichs, of its possible use as a springboard on Moscow.

[24] List's Army Group A did not assume its command function until as late as 9 July in order to deceive the Soviet High Command as to German intentions.

[25] According to Doerr the river was so shallow there that in places it was fordable. Doerr, *Der Feldzug nach Stalingrad*, p. 21, footnote 8.

[26] Halder, *Kriegstagebuch*, Vol. 3, p. 477.

prisoners were taken in the Millerovo encirclement. The *Führer* was desperately seeking to destroy an elusive almost non-existent foe. High ranking Red Army officer prisoners had said that there were no Soviet forces of any consequence west of the Don and this was borne out by *Luftwaffe* air reconnaissance, but Hitler was certain that the Red Army must have withdrawn to the lower Don, north of Rostov. Disregarding his Stalingrad strategy and his previous orders, he then prepared what was to be a great encirclement battle to entrap the forces north of the mouth of the Don. On 13 July Hoth's 4 Panzer Army was transferred from von Bock's to List's command and was ordered to cross the lower Don at Konstantinovka and move westwards towards Rostov and the Sea of Azov. 1 Panzer Army was to right about turn, cross the Donets once again and move westwards along the northern bank of the lower Don. Meanwhile Army Group B had to protect the north flank of Army Group A. Both panzer armies started to move westwards away from Stalingrad, at times almost crippled by heavy rains and lack of motor fuel, when the resistance of the Soviet South Front to Group Ruoff suddenly ceased, the Red Army troops beginning to withdraw with some skill, having already evacuated much of their heavy equipment.

All orders were changed again on 18 July when the *Führer*, having the day before sneered at Halder's objection to the concentration of so much armour to so little purpose, and having rejected his Chief of General Staff's alternative that the lower Don should be crossed on a broad front, adopted that alternative as his own and ordered the continuance of the Army Group B advance on Stalingrad.[27]

Von Bock foresaw little success for an envelopment plan which was strong in the centre and weak on the flanks—this being a criticism of the OKH directive of 11 July which directed 1 and 4 Panzer Armies on to Kamensk and Millerovo.[28] Criticism of the OKH was criticism of the *Führer*, who had been railing for a week against von Bock for the delay at Voronezh. On the afternoon of 13 July Keitel telephoned von Bock to tell him that the *Führer* had decided, after a conversation with Halder and himself, to give the command of Army Group B to von Weichs and that he (Keitel) strongly advised von Bock to ask to be relieved of his appointment on account of sickness. When von Bock demanded to know the grounds for his dismissal he was told that Hitler was dissatisfied with the vehicle fuel supply arrangements in Army Group B, a particularly hollow reason, as both von Bock and von Weichs pointed out, since the *Generalquartiermeister* in the OKH alone was responsible for supply.[29] On 15 July von Weichs took over command of Army Group B, handing over his own 2 Army to von Salmuth. Von Bock went into retirement, worrying and fretting about his ill-usage, and was not re-employed.

---

[27] *Ibid*, pp. 484–5.
[28] Contained in an appreciation of the situation sent to the OKH on 13 July.
[29] Von Bock, *Tagebuch*, 13–15 July 1941; von Weichs, *Tagebuch*, 15 July 1941.

The opening stages of the campaign had not achieved their object. Yet notwithstanding the errors in executing the strategic plan and in spite of Hitler's continual interference, the real reason for German failure lay in the fact that the Soviet South-West Front was in no shape to stand and fight.[30] In consequence the attacking formations lacked the mobility to outpace the retreating Red Army troops, and this immobility was due to a lack of motorized troops and inadequate supply and transport resources.

By the middle of July Hitler had come to believe that the Red Army forces in the south had been virtually destroyed, so that Halder noted in his diary that the *Führer*'s underestimate of the enemy's potential was taking on such a grotesque form that serious planning for operations was no longer possible.[31] The *Führer*'s strategic and tactical direction was becoming increasingly uncertain and fumbling. When on 13 July he had decided against Halder's advice to concentrate all available armour against Rostov, Army Group B could no longer make ground towards Stalingrad. 2 German Army had been pinned in the north by the attacks of Golikov's Bryansk Front, and 2 Hungarian Army had taken over the defence of the Don between Voronezh and Pavlovsk, only Paulus's 6 German Army remaining to cover the long river line to the south of Pavlovsk and at the same time to advance into the Don bend. Even when 8 Italian Army arrived from the south to take over the Don sector to the south of the Hungarians, 6 Army position was not greatly improved. Halder disagreed with the *Führer*'s plans. By 19 July after days of argument, during which time the weather had broken and brought the armour to a standstill once more, a compromise was reached whereby two additional corps, one of them panzer, were allotted to 6 Army, and 1 Panzer and 4 Panzer Armies were to cross the lower Don between Rostov and Zimlyanskaya on a front about 125 miles wide.

More serious difficulties were yet to arise. On 11 July Hitler had signed Directive 43, in which von Manstein's 11 Army was ordered to cross the Kerch Straits into the Taman and Kuban and seize the Soviet Black Sea naval ports of Anapa and Novorossisk.[32] Only eight days later the *Führer* changed his mind and decided that only the Rumanian mountain divisions should cross into Taman, 11 Army and all the German divisions being used in other theatres.[33] On 23 July he issued Directive 45, for Operation *Brunswick*, covering the offensive into the Caucasus, in the preamble of which he stated that the aim of the offensive west of the Don *had already been achieved* and that only weak forces from Timoshenko's front had succeeded in reaching the further bank of the Don. The document was a muddled order rather than

---

[30] The *Stavka* is said to have ordered the withdrawal of the South-West Front and the right wing of South Front on 7 July, the movement to the left bank of the Don being completed by 24 July. *Kratkaya Istoriya*, pp. 164–5.

[31] Halder, *Kriegstagebuch*, Vol. 3, p. 489.

[32] Hubatsch, *Hitlers Weisungen für die Kriegführung*, (Operation *Blücher*), p. 192.

[33] Halder, *Kriegstagebuch*, Vol. 3, pp. 484–6.

a directive.[34] List's Army Group A was charged with the destruction of the enemy to the south and south-east of Rostov, after which its most important task was not, as might be expected, the seizure of the oilfields and the Caucasus passes, but the occupation of the entire eastern coastline of the Black Sea, thereby eliminating the ports and the bases for the enemy Black Sea Fleet. This was an entirely new strategic aim, carried forward from Directive 43. Although the occupation of the Black Sea coast was given as the most important task, this did not inhibit the Commander-in-Chief from ordering the seizure of Maikop and Grozny – to be carried out at the same time as the occupation of the Black Sea littoral – and a subsequent advance to Baku. Von Weichs's Army Group B was to seize Stalingrad and advance down the Volga to Astrakhan.

There was now a radical change and about turn once more in the deployment of German armour. Hoth's 4 Panzer Army was removed from the command of List's Army Group A and returned to von Weichs's Army Group B, but since it was concentrated on a narrow front beside 1 Panzer Army to the east of Rostov and had already secured bridgeheads over the lower Don at Zimlyanskaya and Nikolaevsk, it had to make a left-angled turn and move off north-east along the south bank of the Don towards Stalingrad. A great gap several hundred miles wide, the area of the Kalmuck Steppe, was to appear between Army Groups A and B as they advanced on their divergent axes, one moving south and the other north-east.

On 4 July Army Groups A and B disposed of sixty-four German divisions and twenty-six allied divisions.[35] Soviet losses in the two or three weeks of fighting had amounted to no more than 80,000 prisoners, an insignificant figure compared with the forces available to the USSR. According to Gehlen's Foreign Armies East estimate of the middle of August the Red Army strength over the whole of the East Front alone amounted to 254 rifle divisions, eighty-three rifle brigades and sixty-eight tank brigades of which total about a half were believed to be fit for battle. In addition, Gehlen estimated that there were another seventy-three rifle divisions, sixty-six rifle brigades and eighty-six tank brigades in reserve.[36]

From the Soviet point of view, however, the position was extremely serious. Golikov's Bryansk and Timoshenko's South-West Fronts had been broken open and a great gap nearly 200 miles wide had been driven into them. Malinovsky's South Front had maintained a continuous line against Group

[34] Hubatsch, *Hitlers Weisungen für die Kriegführung*, pp. 196–200.
[35] *OKH Kriegsgliederung*, 4 July 1942. This total includes nine German divisions of 11 Army not yet removed from the Crimea. By 5 August the number of allied divisions had risen to thirty-six.
[36] Greiner, *Die Oberste Wehrmachtführung*, p. 401. On 2 August Halder noted that Gehlen reported that fifty-four new rifle divisions and fifty-six new tank brigades had been identified in July. This entry is probably an error since it is at variance with the entry on 3 August of sixty rifle divisions, forty-six rifle brigades and seventeen tank brigades. Halder, *Kriegstagebuch*, Vol. 3, pp. 496–7.

Ruoff, but it had lost all contact with Timoshenko's South-West Front to its north since the night of 7 July. South-West Front Headquarters had fallen back to Kalach on the Don bend and was separated and out of touch with its formations, and the Soviet High Command had tried without success, due to difficult radio conditions, to transfer the command of the South-West Front formations to South Front.[37]

Golikov, the Commander of Bryansk Front, was dispatched by Moscow to the danger area of Voronezh leaving his deputy Chibisov in command. Vasilevsky, who had just taken over in midsummer as Chief of General Staff from Shaposhnikov, was attached by the *Stavka* to Chibisov's Bryansk Front, by then consisting of Zhmachenko's 3 and Pukhov's 13 Armies, Lizyukov's 5 Tank Army, 48 Army and two tank and a cavalry corps detached from the High Command Reserve. According to Vasilevsky the Bryansk Front at that time mustered 1,000 tanks, of which 800 were T34 or KV type, and had the necessary strength to have defeated the thrust by von Weichs and Hoth on Voronezh. For a number of reasons it failed to do so, however, although the pressure it exerted between Livny and Voronezh had the effect of pinning and keeping Hoth in the north, when in accordance with the *Führer*'s directive he should have been moving south-east down the right bank of the Don. On 5 July Vasilevsky was recalled to Moscow where Stalin and the *Stavka* decided on a command reorganization to meet the new threat.[38]

Meanwhile, on 7 July Golikov formed a new Voronezh Front from out of the Bryansk Front with himself as commander, consisting of 40, 3 and 6 Armies, together with three additional rifle and one tank corps; but seven days later he gave up his new command to Vatutin, who having returned from his staff appointment with North-West Front had become a deputy chief of General Staff once more.[39] On 12 July South-West Front Headquarters was reformed as the Stalingrad Front, still under the command of Timoshenko with Khrushchev as his political member, with three new armies drawn from the reserve and deployed to the north of the Don and in the Don bend. These were to become famous in the defence of Stalingrad, Kolpakchy's 62, V. I. Kuznetsov's 63 and Chuikov's 64 Armies, each having a strength of only six rifle divisions. To these were to be added Moskalenko's 38 and Kryuchenkin's 28 Armies, both about to be converted to tank armies, Tolbukhin's 57 Army and Danilov's 21 Army, these last four armies being survivors of South-West Front.[40] Timoshenko had suffered the successive defeats of Kharkov and the Donets, and on 23 July he was recalled to Moscow as a mark of

[37] *Istoriya*, Vol. 1, pp. 420–2.

[38] Vasilevsky, *Voenno Istoricheskii Zhurnal* No. 8, August 1965.

[39] When on 14 July Golikov gave up the command of Voronezh Front to Vatutin he was transferred to the Stalingrad area as a deputy front commander, his place at the Bryansk Front being taken by Rokossovsky. *Istoriya*, Vol. 2, p. 421; Platonov, *Vtoraya Mirovaya Voina*, p. 307; also Vasilevsky, *Voenno Istoricheskii Zhurnal* No. 8, August 1965.

[40] The military council of the Stalingrad (former South-West) Front remained Timoshenko, Khrushchev and Bodin.

Stalin's displeasure, and replaced as Stalingrad Front Commander by Gordov.[41] Although Timoshenko was to reappear later in the war as a *Stavka* representative and co-ordinator of fronts, his star was already on the wane and he was to be succeeded in positions of authority by younger and probably more able commanders.

Stalingrad itself was threatened and the same scenes were enacted as had taken place in the previous year in front of Leningrad and Moscow. Tens of thousands of workers built three lines of defensive works ringing the city from the west, the outer of which was nearly 300 miles in length. Over eighty home guard and workers battalions were already in existence and the number was steadily increased as battalions were successively brought into the line to receive their baptism of fire.

Although Rostov was lost on 23 July, Malinovsky's South Front had used to good advantage the wet weather, during which the German armour was partly immobilized, in order to pull back its troops behind the lower Don so that the front faced northwards. Immediately behind Malinovsky stood the troops of the North Caucasus Front.

Field-Marshal List, the Commander of Army Group A, had his two German armies and one Rumanian army organized in two tactical groupings. The first, known as Group Ruoff consisted of 17 Army of five infantry divisions and of Dumitrescu's 3 Rumanian Army of one infantry and three cavalry divisions, and the second grouping was von Kleist's 1 Panzer Army of three panzer, two motorized infantry, four infantry and one Slovak division.[42] The panzer army had, however, less than 400 tanks fit for battle. In accordance with Hitler's latest directive, Group Ruoff was to link up with 42 Corps, consisting mainly of Rumanian troops, which was to cross the Kerch Straits from the Crimea into the Kuban and clear the Black Sea coast. 1 Panzer Army was to move away from 17 Army on a divergent south-east axis towards Voroshilovsk, Grozny and Baku.

List was unenthusiastic about his assignment. A soldier of great ability and experience who had distinguished himself in the campaigns in Poland, France and the Balkans where fronts were narrow and German fire support overwhelming, he was already beset by difficulties. From Rostov to Baku was over 700 miles in a direct line, and the width of his frontage along the line of the Caucasus was over 800 miles. The Caucasus Range in places was up to 15,000 feet in height, and it could only be reached by first crossing the Don and the network of rivers which flowed in an east-westerly direction across his path. The flat plains immediately south of the Don were covered by vast cornfields, for long one of the main granaries of Old Russia, but these eventually gave way to a waterless and hot dry steppe. List had by then outrun his supplies and the mobility of the panzer and motorized formations had been severely

[41] Gordov, formerly Chief of Staff to and then Commander of 21 Army and for a short time Commander of 64 Army.
[42] *OKH Kriegsgliederung*, 5 August 1942.

restricted by the lack of vehicle fuels. The resistance of the enemy, it was true, was uncoordinated and weakening, but the Soviet commanders, whatever their orders, showed no intention of standing firm and fighting to the death. As was usual, however hard the Germans marched they could not overtake the fleeing Red Army man, accustomed as he was to local geography and conditions and unburdened by heavy equipment, most of which he had abandoned or evacuated. In the area of the lower Don the Red Air Force was both strong and aggressive and, as List's air support had been reduced to 4 Air Corps consisting of only two *Stuka* and three fighter groups, the Red Air Force had air superiority nearly everywhere, except in those very few areas where the *Luftwaffe* was concentrated.[43] Army Group A had already lost the SS *Leibstandarte* which had returned to France, and the infantry division *Grossdeutschland*, in reality a motorized division, was earmarked to follow.

The Soviet South Front, commanded by Malinovsky, although it continued to maintain a cohesive existence, was in a state of very great confusion. Some divisions were said to be down in strength to only a few hundred infantrymen and the communication and supply and transport services were almost entirely disrupted. To the south and east of the Don the roads and tracks were crammed with refugees, lorries, carts, agricultural machinery and herds of cattle, all moving away from the German advance. After the battle of Rostov Ryzhov's 56, Parkhomenko's 9 and Martsinkevich's 24 Armies had been taken to the hinterland to refit, and South Front had Kamkov's 18 and P. M. Kozlov's 37 Armies deployed south of the Don, together with Grechko's 12 Army and Trufanov's 51 Army from the North Caucasus Front deployed on the extreme right.[44] The North Caucasus Front, commanded by Budenny, to the rear in reserve disposed of only Kotov's 47 Army, 17 Cossack Cavalry Corps and some independent rifle corps.[45] On the Black Sea coast and along the Turkish and Iran frontier Tyulenev's Transcaucasus Front, which hitherto had been responsible for the security of the southern frontiers, was reinforced by the Soviet High Command and ordered back from the border in order to secure Grozny, Baku and Caucasus passes and prepare them for defence.[46]

On 25 July began the German attack from the three main bridgeheads over the Don. Malinovsky's South Front tried to hold its positions, because neither at this time nor at any other did the Soviet High Command ever adopt the defensive policy of drawing the enemy into the hinterland to destroy him.[47] The tired, disorganized troops of South Front were unable to take the strain

[43] Von Kleist was subsequently to ascribe his failure to lack of petrol and lack of air and flak support. Liddell Hart, *The Other Side of the Hill*, pp. 303–5.

[44] 51 Army was commanded by Kolomiets until 5 September during Trufanov's sickness. Grechko, *Bitva za Kavkaz*, p. 416.

[45] The military council of the North Caucasus Front consisted of Budenny, Seleznev and G. F. Zakharov (from August onwards Antonov).

[46] The military council of the Transcaucasus Front consisted of Tyulenev, Efimov and Subbotin (from late August Bodin).

[47] On 28 July Stalin issued his celebrated 'no step back' Order No. 227.

and P. M. Kozlov's 37 and Grechko's 12 Armies fell rapidly back away from the attacking 1 Panzer Army under von Kleist. 51 Army soon found itself in danger of being encircled from the west by Hoth's 4 Panzer Army, which had swung out from its bridgehead at Zimlyanskaya in its circuitous north-east march on Stalingrad, and Trufanov was driven eastwards until he eventually joined up with the Red Army troops of the Stalingrad Front. To the south of the Don 1 Panzer Army crossed the Sal River and Manych Canal, and the Soviet defences were breached to a depth of fifty miles on a hundred-mile front. Communications disintegrated and some of the Red Army troops took to their heels. Budenny's North Caucasus Front was absorbed on 28 July into the South Front, Budenny, because of his rank, being put in overall nominal command. This new front, which continued to be known as the North Caucasus Front, was split into two groups, the Don Group under Malinovsky, consisting of only 37 and 12 Armies, whose task it was to hold von Kleist's 1 Panzer Army thrust towards Grozny, and the Coast Group under Cherevichenko of Kamkov's 18, Ryzhov's 56 and Kotov's 47 Armies, together with 17 Cossack Cavalry Corps and a rifle corps. Each of these groups was allocated an air army in support.

The German advance had taken on the character of a pursuit, yet it was made in conditions of great hardship and privation. The marching infantry were once again being driven forward at the rate of thirty miles a day, each day and every day, across the flooded bed of the Manych River, sometimes through waist-high corn and sometimes across salt and barren steppe. The heat was suffocating, and men and animals were tortured by thirst and the stinging sand storms. Panzer and motorized formations were continually calling for an air supply of motor fuels and the momentum of the advance repeatedly died down when the demands could not be met.[48] Yet the advance was surprisingly fast and took the Soviet command unawares. At the beginning of August technicians began to remove oil equipment from Maikop, but the rapid German approach made evacuation impossible and the installations were handed over to the demolition teams and the fire raisers. On 5 August Voroshilovsk fell. The next day 1 Soviet Independent Rifle Corps broke in front of Armavir, and Cherevichenko's 18 and 12 Armies fell back south towards the mountains. The Germans pursued to the foothills, seizing the Maikop oilfields but little refined fuel, and the larger part of the railway system but virtually no rolling stock. Meanwhile 17 Army had taken Krasnodar and was closing in on the Taman Peninsula. Before the middle of August, however, The North Caucasus Front noted that the German momentum was falling off perceptibly.[49]

At the same time Soviet resistance was steadily increasing in its intensity.

[48] Motor fuels were said to be carried by pack camel. Liddell Hart, *The Other Side of the Hill*, p. 305.

[49] *Istoriya*, Vol. 2, p. 460. At about this time German intelligence showed a Soviet Krasnodar Front in its enemy order of battle, commanded by Marshal Kulik.

New national military formations were raised in Georgia, Azerbaijan and Armenia and reinforcements and supplies were brought in by rail and by sea through Astrakhan and Makhach Kala along the Caspian littoral, the only routes by which the Caucasus was still linked to the Soviet Union. Grozny, Makhach Kala and Baku were covered by numerous defence lines, mainly based on the mountain rivers, which were developed by military engineers and the civilian population. On the west coast Group Ruoff was having great difficulty in moving into the Taman Peninsula and advancing towards the big naval base at Novorossisk, which was defended by Kotov's 47 Soviet Army and marine infantry brigades. Fighting was particularly fierce near Krymsk and in the heavily wooded foothills. On 18 August began the battle for the passes, when two divisions of Konrad's 49 German Mountain Corps moving south from Cherkessk to the west of Elbruz, drove back 3 Rifle Corps of Sergatzkov's 46 Army and seized a number of passes hitherto regarded by the Transcaucasus Front as impregnable.[50] The German mountain troops could not advance further towards Sukhum on the coast because of supply difficulties and because the Soviet enemy was making good use of the very difficult country and mountain rivers so favourable to the defence. On 28 August Group Ruoff forced back Kotov's 47 Soviet Army and reached the Black Sea coast at Anapa, about thirty miles to the west of Novorossisk. List was still severely restricted by supply difficulties and the mineral oil brigades of oil specialists and engineers which had followed closely behind the troops to exploit the Soviet oilfields had found little that could be rapidly developed.[51]

By the end of August Tyulenev's Transcaucasus Front had taken over the responsibility for the defence of the mountain range. Cherevichenko's former Coast Group was renamed the Black Sea Group of the Transcaucasus Front, while the responsibilities of the former Don Group were taken over by Maslennikov's North Group of the Transcaucasus Front consisting of I. E. Petrov's 44, Koroteev's 9 and P. M. Kozlov's 37 Armies. The North Group stood on the Rivers Kuma and Terek, barring the progress of 1 Panzer Army to Grozny and Baku. The Red Air Force activity increased in intensity at this time, all the more successfully because Army Group A had to transfer a number of fighter groups to the area of Stalingrad.

In the south-east, von Kleist's 1 Panzer Army was still sixty miles from Grozny and 350 miles from Baku. An attempt had been made to close in on Astrakhan to the north by sending 16 Motorized Infantry Division across the Kalmuck Steppe to Elista, but, although some reconnaissance elements did in fact reach the Caspian, the division hardly came within a hundred miles of Astrakhan, which was in any event held by a newly formed 28 Soviet Army under Gerasimenko. The time had come for von Kleist to make his final main thrust towards Grozny and Ordzhonikidze. The two panzer corps of 1 Panzer

[50] Leselidze took command of 46 Army from Sergatzkov at the end of August.
[51] The oil brigades, which had an establishment of 10,000 men, were intended to restore the production of oil wells and refineries.

Army were already twenty-five miles east of Mozdok and had reached the Terek and Baksan Rivers. Enemy air activity, the fuel restrictions, and the unexpectedly bitter fighting on the Baksan were causing both delay and concern and on 25 August it was decided to cross the Terek on both sides of Mozdok, and from the bridgehead so formed thrust von Schweppenburg's 40 Panzer Corps with three panzer divisions due east on Grozny, while Ott's 52 Corps moved south into the Malgobek oilfields and Ordzhonikidze. Further to the south von Mackensen's 3 Panzer Corps which consisted of only a Rumanian mountain division and a German regimental group was to cut the Soviet military roads from Batum and Tiflis and prevent further reinforcements arriving from the south. Deserters and prisoners revealed that the Soviet North Group was being reinforced rapidly from the Transcaucasus, Iran and the Russian mainland and from this it was obvious that the German attack had to be mounted without delay.[52] Maslennikov's North Group standing in von Kleist's path was estimated to consist of about forty divisions and brigades. The attacking force stood at eight divisions.[53]

On 30 August 1 Panzer Army began to cross the River Terek, but the Soviet enemy was found to be so strong and his counter-attacks so violent that the weight of the German thrust was switched to the south towards Elkhotovo and Malgobek, in face of a bitter defence by Koroteev's 9 and Kozlov's 37 Soviet Armies. Fighting was heavy and costly to both sides. A further threat developed against the Germans in the north where on the open steppe flank 4 Kuban Guards Cavalry Corps tried to encircle Mozdok. By the end of September 1 Panzer Army could do no more and had to go over to the defensive until the *Führer* should make good his promise to make available panzer divisions from the Stalingrad area. On 25 October, however, yet one more effort was made against an enemy grouping of seven divisions of 37 Army near Nalchik, about seventy miles north-west of Ordzhonikidze. Two panzer divisions under von Mackensen's 3 Panzer Corps delivered a sharp and unexpected attack, supported by all available German aircraft of 4 Air Corps. Headquarters 37 Soviet Army itself came under heavy air attack and speedily lost control of operations. The appearance of tanks on this flank caused some consternation and within two days the Soviet divisions were routed.[54] The German armour was then turned towards Ordzhonikidze and by 2 November reached a point only five miles from the town.[55] Snow was already falling, and there von Kleist came to a standstill at the most easterly point ever to be reached by German troops.

[52] In 1941 the connection between Astrakhan and the North Caucasus was by Caspian steamer. During the latter part of 1942 however a railway was laid over 200 miles of steppe between Astrakhan and Grozny. Compare von Kleist, Liddell Hart, *The Other Side of the Hill*, p. 304.

[53] *OKH Kriegsgliederung* 2 September 1942.

[54] Grechko, *Bitva za Kavkaz*, pp. 173–9.

[55] 3 Panzer Corps in the fighting from 25 October to 12 November claimed to have taken 16,100 prisoners and 249 guns and destroyed 188 tanks. Von Mackensen, *Vom Bug zum Kaukasus*, p. 106.

In the West Caucasus and on the Black Sea Front Ruoff's 17 Army made slow progress against bitter Soviet resistance. Ruoff's objectives remained unaltered, the occupation of the Taman Peninsula and the Black Sea ports of Novorossisk, Tuapse and Sukhum. At the end of August Rumanian cavalry had already occupied the coast town of Anapa and at the beginning of September the Taman Peninsula was cleared of the Soviet enemy. On 6 September German troops took the naval port of Novorossisk and part of the town, before being forced to a standstill by marine brigades and Kotov's 47 Soviet Army consisting of a mountain and a rifle division. Meanwhile one German and five Rumanian divisions had crossed the Kerch Straits into Taman, their passage being covered by German Navy U boats and motor torpedo boats which had entered the Black Sea from the Elbe via the Danube.[56] On 23 September Ruoff mounted a heavy attack by two corps, amounting in all to seven divisions, against Ryzhov's 56 and Kamkov's 18 Soviet Armies covering Tuapse and after a week had advanced seven miles against very determined resistance. By 7 October Cherevichenko managed to stabilize the position, but a week later the Germans resumed the attack and the situation deteriorated once more. Cherevichenko was removed from his command and was succeeded as the Commander of the Black Sea Group by Petrov, and the German attack was brought to a halt only a few miles from the town of Tuapse.

The *Führer* was urging List to reach the coast in strength so that he could move down the Black Sea littoral to Batum and the Turkish border. This strategy would have split Army Group A on both sides of the Caucasus without, however, any provision being made for its supply.[57] Konrad's 49 Mountain Corps had already taken the Sancharo and Klukhor passes and secured the southern flank of Elbruz, but List was unwilling to risk a direct thrust on the port of Sukhum unless this could be assured of some support from the west along the coast. The *Führer* had other views and was very dissatisfied with the way in which List had conducted the campaign.[58]

On 31 August List had been called to Vinnitsa, where he scandalized Hitler by arriving at the conference table with an unmarked small scale map, the *Führer* unmindful of the fact that it was he who had forbidden the carriage of marked maps in aircraft. In front of List, however, he kept his thoughts to himself and heard List out with apparent friendliness and understanding; but no sooner had the Commander-in-Chief of Army Group A taken to the air on his flight back to Stalino, than the *Führer* began again to rage against him.[59]

[56] *Kriegstagebuch des OKW*, Vol. 2, pp. 654 and 658.
[57] All German supplies were coming by road from Rostov, and vehicle fuels were in exceedingly short supply.
[58] The Turks had refused permission for Axis war vessels to pass through the Dardanelles into the Black Sea. The German naval strength in the Black Sea stood at six small U boats, some motor torpedo boats and a number of vessels converted to minesweeping. Soviet naval activity, except for some submarine missions off the Rumanian coast, was negligible.
[59] Halder, *Kriegstagebuch*, Vol. 2, p. 513; Keitel, *Memoirs*, pp. 180–1; Warlimont, *Inside Hitler's Headquarters*, p. 256; and Warlimont's note to *Kriegstagebuch des OKW*, Vol. 2, pp. 662–3.

On 6 September List told the Army High Command (OKH) that he would not be answerable for a further advance and the next day convinced Jodl at his Army Group Headquarters that he was right. There on the 49 Mountain Corps sector the matter rested. Elsewhere this small incident was to have weighty repercussions.

CHAPTER NINETEEN

Advance to Stalingrad

Paulus was a Hessian, the son of a minor civil servant, and had married into the Rumanian nobility.[1] Self-effacing and fastidious, pleasant and with good manners, he tended to be over-deliberate and to lack decisiveness. He was a staff officer by training and experience and his last tour of regimental duty was in 1929 as a captain with an infantry regiment. He was then transferred to the panzer troops and for some months commanded a motorized experimental unit, thereafter having no further experience in command. In 1940 Paulus had been selected by Halder to be his Chief General Staff Officer (*Oberquartiermeister I*) and Deputy Chief of the General Staff, in which appointment he had supervised most of the early planning for *Barbarossa*. In January 1942 came promotion to General and the appointment to the command of 6 German Army, which was to be the largest of the armies in the east.

Paulus was an industrious officer of ability and he carried out much of his work under the eye of the *Führer*, who apparently thought highly of him for he promoted him rapidly during the eleven months of 1942 from lieutenant-general to colonel-general. Of Paulus's personal loyalty Hitler can have had no doubt, since he intended, after the Stalingrad battle had been brought to a successful conclusion, to recall him to the Armed Forces High Command (OKW) to replace Jodl.[2] Paulus's relatively humble origins and his modest appearance and outlook endeared him to the Nazi Party. Although Paulus was not a sycophant, for he retained the respect and friendship of Halder right to the end, he appears to have had a high opinion of the *Führer*'s judgement and military ability. Hitler had been the patron of the panzer arm to which Paulus belonged, and Paulus must have known that he was the *Führer*'s protégé, as well as that of Halder. Paulus was retiring yet ambitious, but lacked the hardness of character to have proved an outstanding commander in times of stress. Although Halder once called him imperturbable (*unbekümmert*), passive might have been a more apt description. Like Jodl, he was a man born to obey, and the *Führer*, who could accurately assess the characters of his

[1] Paulus' father was the book-keeper in a German reform school in Breitenau. Goerlitz, *Paulus and Stalingrad*, p. 4. Paulus himself had married into the Rosetti-Solescu family.

[2] This change appears to have been discussed verbally between Hitler, Schmundt and Keitel. Warlimont, *Inside Hitler's Headquarters*, p. 257; Keitel, *Memoirs*, p. 181. Paulus's post-war testimony, Goerlitz, *Paulus and Stalingrad*, p. 233 and footnote 1.

THE DON BEND AND VOLGA LANDBRIDGE
July–August 1942

subordinates, for this reason selected him as his designate principal executive and military confidant.

As a major-general Paulus had previously been Chief of Staff to 6 Army under von Reichenau for about eight months in 1940, von Reichenau being promoted to field-marshal in July of that year, and there was an enormous gap between them in experience and seniority. After the *Führer* had assumed absolute control over the German Army, seniority and experience counted for nothing, and Paulus was advanced over the heads of dozens of able and battle experienced corps commanders to succeed von Reichenau in the most important command on the whole of the Eastern Front.[3] Ably supported by his

---

[3] Paulus like Rommel was promoted from lieutenant-general to field-marshal in the space of a year.

chiefs of staff, firstly Ferdinand Heim and then Arthur Schmidt, the latter in particular being a strong character and a man of independent views, Paulus proved a very successful commander during the Kharkov and Operation *Blue* battles.[4]

At the beginning of July, 6 Army consisted of five corps with eighteen German divisions, of which two were panzer and one motorized infantry, these forming Stumme's 40 Panzer Corps.[5] 4 Panzer Army, the other army taking part in the advance on Stalingrad, which had reverted to the command of Army Group B at the end of July, had turned sharply north-eastwards after crossing the lower Don and was advancing along the Kotelnikovo-Stalingrad railway, driving before it the five divisions of Trufanov's 51 Soviet Army. Hoth's progress was slow, not because of Soviet resistance, which was in fact weak, but on account of the lack of fuel which immobilized a large part of the force. Hoth's 4 Panzer Army had Kempf's 48 Panzer Corps and one infantry corps, in all four divisions of which only one was panzer and one motorized. Dragalina's 6 Rumanian Corps of six divisions followed in its rear. Both 4 Panzer and 6 German Armies were supported by 8 Air Corps of nine fighter, nine bomber and three *Stuka* groups.

The 6 Army thrust into the Don bend and to the Volga made a slow start since Wagner, the Quartermaster-General, acting on Hitler's Directive of 23 July, had diverted the bulk of the transport capacity from the Army Group B to the Army Group A area. The mistake, once made, could not be readily rectified and in consequence 6 Army was unable to move for ten days.[6]

The Soviet forces had by then fallen back to the far side of the Don except in the large pocket deep in the Don bend, roughly on the line of the Chir and the Tsimla. Timoshenko's Stalingrad Front had formerly stretched 450 miles from Pavlovsk in the north, where it joined Vatutin's Voronezh Front, to the left flank of Trufanov's 51 Army on the Sarpa Lakes in the south. This front-age was so long that the Soviet High Command decided on 5 August to split

---

[4] When hard pressed by Timoshenko in the Kharkov battle, Paulus sided with von Bock, against the advice of his own chief of staff and von Sodenstern, in advocating that the *Fridericus* offensive should be called off. Goerlitz believes that the *Führer*'s decision to leave the plans unaltered left a deep impression on Paulus of the infallibility of the *Führer*, this finding a sequel in the Stalingrad battle. See also Halder, *Kriegstagebuch*, Vol. 3, p. 480. Paulus's Dresden lectures and his post-war evidence after his years of imprisonment are marred by large numbers of inaccuracies.

[5] Stumme handed over command of 40 Panzer Corps to von Schweppenburg on 20 July 1942.

[6] Compare Philippi und Heim, *Der Feldzug gegen Sowjetrussland*, p. 141. The army groups, although they had a Q or administrative staff (*1b*) which operated in an advisory and co-ordinating capacity, were not responsible for their own supply and maintenance. This was undertaken by detachments or outstations (*Befehlstellen*) of Wagner's *Generalquartier-meister* Directorate of the OKH. On 10 September 1942, however, the supply and main-tenance was reorganized and army groups were given their own Quartermaster-General Departments (*O Qu Abteilungen*). Keilig, *Das Deutsche Heer*, Vol. 3, Sect. 205.

the Stalingrad Front into two fronts, a new Stalingrad Front under Timoshenko's successor Gordov, this front stretching from Pavlovsk to the Volga
and not in fact covering Stalingrad at all, and a South-East Front under
Eremenko opposite Stalingrad and the exposed southern flank towards the
Kalmuck Steppe.[7] This decision was later to be regretted when the fighting
became concentrated about the city, since the divided command led to a lack
of co-ordination.[8]

Eremenko, who like many of his fellow Generals had once been a junior
non-commissioned officer of cavalry, had commanded West Front for a few
days at the end of June 1941 after Pavlov's removal, then Bryansk Front and,
at the end of 1941, 4 Shock Army in the Moscow-Kalinin area. Leaving a
Moscow hospital when his wound was not yet healed, he was dispatched by
Stalin to the South-East Front. There he met Khrushchev and Gordov, and
soon established himself on good terms with the one and on bad terms with the
other. Gordov had formerly been the Commander of 21 and then 64 Armies
before taking over the Stalingrad Front from Timoshenko and, if Eremenko is
to be believed, was at the time nervous, highly strung and in low spirits. This
description is at variance with another unfriendly one given by Chuikov,
Gordov's subordinate, who portrayed his chief as autocratic and exuding a
confidence which the situation did not justify. There is evidence, however, that
Gordov's chief crime may have been that he did not approve of commissars,
political members or collective responsibility, and, as Khrushchev was the
political member for the Stalingrad Front, Khrushchev and Eremenko together
determined to unseat him.[9] This in itself could hardly have improved the
efficiency and co-ordination of the two fronts.

In the last two weeks in July Paulus began to close in on the Soviet bridgehead west of the Don bend, which was held by Kolpakchy's 62 Army in the
north and 64 Army in the south (temporarily under Chuikov's command),
together with 1 and 4 Tank Armies which were being formed from Moskalenko's 38 Army and Kryuchenkin's 28 Army.[10] 62 and 64 Armies each had

---

[7] The military council of the Stalingrad Front was Gordov, Khrushchev and Bodin (from
24 July Nikishev) and of the South-East Front Eremenko, Laiok and G. F. Zakharov.

[8] *Istoriya*, Vol. 3, p. 431. The headquarters of South-East Front was actually in Stalingrad.

[9] Zhukov in reply to Stalin's questioning said that Gordov's principal fault was that he
was difficult and did not get on well with people. Zhukov, *Stalingradskaya Epopeya*, pp.
39–40. Konev appears to have had quite a different opinion of Gordov, who was one of his
army commanders right through to the battle of Berlin. He describes him as a very strong
character, experienced and able but a little unbalanced. Konev, *Sorok Pyatyi God, Novyi
Mir* May–July 1965. In June 1943, when Commander of 33 Army, Gordov wrote to Stalin
proposing the liquidation of military councils as he thought them to be 'unnecessary and a
waste of time'. Stalin did not forget the incident and in 1946 Gordov, then Commander of
the Volga Military District, was himself liquidated. Petrov, *Partiinoe Stroitelstvo v Sovetskoi
Armii i Flote*, Chapter 3. For indication of a Khrushchev-Eremenko conspiracy see Eremenko, *Stalingrad*, pp. 55–6 and 209–10.

[10] Kolpakchy was shortly afterwards succeeded as Commander of 62 Army by Lopatin.
64 Army was originally commanded by Gordov with Chuikov as his deputy, by Chuikov
(temporarily) and then by Shumilov, Chuikov eventually becoming Commander of 62

the equivalent of about six rifle divisions and a number of tank battalions; but the two tank armies, still in the process of re-equipping, were disorganized and untrained and did not have their full complement of tanks.[11] In accordance with Stalin's Soviet High Command Order of 28 July Red Army troops had to stand their ground west of the Don, further withdrawal being forbidden. The 6 German Army attack, made in a double envelopment by two flanking thrusts each of a panzer and an infantry corps, isolated Kolpakchy's 62 Soviet Army together with 1 Tank Army and pinned them against the river west of Kalach, the isolated pocket then being attacked from the rear flanks by von Wietersheim's 14 and von Langerman's 24 Panzer Corps and cut off from the river.[12] The tank army's counter-attacks were ineffective. Fighting continued for several days more, and although the enemy managed to demolish the bridge at Kalach he was to surrender with an estimated loss of 35,000 dead and prisoners, nearly 270 tanks and 600 guns.[13] This promising beginning to the German offensive resulted from the Soviet order to stand firm forward of the Don. The next phase of the attack was to clear the enemy, mainly Kryuchenkin's 4 Tank Army and part of Moskalenko's 1 Guards Army, from the area further to the north near Sirotinskaya, and on 15 August these elements were driven over the Don with a loss of a further 13,000 Red Army prisoners.[14] All attempts to take the Soviet bridgehead on the west bank of the Don south of Kremensk failed, however, and this small bridgehead was to form a springboard to be used in the subsequent German defeat. Elsewhere the Soviet

---

Army in place of Lopatin. The old 28 Army in process of being reformed as the new 4 Tank Army should be distinguished from the new 28 Army being raised in Astrakhan by Gerasimenko. See Samsonov, *Stalingradskaya Bitva*, pp. 527–8 and footnote.

[11] Rokossovsky, *Velikaya Pobeda na Volge*, pp. 34–6. Soviet accounts say that the two tank armies had only 240 tanks between them, possibly an understatement in view of the large number of Soviet tanks subsequently destroyed or captured in the Don bend.

[12] 6 Army had lost 40 Panzer Corps firstly to Hoth (for the Millerovo encirclement) after which it was transferred to Army Group A and 1 Panzer Army in the Caucasus. In return Paulus had received 14 and 24 Panzer Corps. For this battle they had only one panzer division each. Von Wietersheim was replaced by Hube on 15 September and von Langerman und Erlenkamp was killed on 3 October and was replaced by von Knobelsdorff.

[13] Halder at the time noted that eight enemy rifle divisions and ten tank brigades had been encircled. Halder, *Kriegstagebuch*, Vol. 3, p. 501, 7 August; also *Kriegstagebuch des OKW*, Vol. 2, p. 577. Soviet sources do not give the detail of the loss although Chuikov says that 62 Army was encircled and suffered heavy losses. Chuikov, *The Beginning of the Road*, p. 43. At the end of July the Stalingrad Front was said to be down to thirty-eight divisions, of which half numbered from 6,000–8,000 men while the remainder were down to as little as a thousand men. Only 360 tanks and 330 aircraft remained. Zhukov, *Vospominaniya i Razmyshleniya*, p. 403.

[14] The designation Guards was awarded to formations as a battle honour, the formations so distinguished being enrolled on a separate list and given a new number. Moskalenko's 1 Tank Army disappeared from the Soviet order of battle at this time, being absorbed into 4 Tank Army, and a newly formed 1 Guards Army (under Moskalenko) took its place, a reformed army under the same headquarters. According to Eremenko, 1 Guards Army contained a large number of airborne units and its commander designate had been Golikov. Eremenko, *Stalingrad*, p. 35.

troops held the east bank in strength and this, in the hot, dry and bare Don Steppe, foretold the necessity for a well prepared assault over a major river obstacle.

Meanwhile, south of the Don, Hoth's 4 Panzer Army had driven Trufanov's 51 Soviet Army, the resistance of which was by then feeble, out into the Kalmuck Steppe, where its presence remained a threat to the German flank, and the Axis troops proceeded to cross the Aksai River which was held by three rifle divisions of 64 Army acting as a flank guard under Chuikov. These divisions counter-attacked with vigour, in vain against the Germans, but with success against 6 Rumanian Corps which was in danger of breaking until rallied by its German liaison officers. 4 Panzer Army then attacked on to Tinguta within fifty miles of Stalingrad, preparatory to moving up the west bank of the Volga to the city. This thrust fell on both 64 Soviet Army and part of Tolbukhin's 57 Army deployed against the Volga, and on 5 August Hoth breached the outer defence line surrounding Stalingrad. A fierce tank battle developed around Tinguta railway station and the strength of the Soviet resistance was such that it became obvious that 4 Panzer Army could advance no further until 6 German Army, still held up about sixty miles to the west, could cross the Don.

The Soviet High Command was thoroughly alarmed by the weight of the German thrusts and intended to hold firm in the south-east. On 28 July it had issued its 'no step backwards' Order Number 227 in which Stalin in moderate, even comradely terms, warned all troops of the consequences to the Soviet Union of further withdrawal. On 12 August, following the great defeat in the Don bend west of Kalach, Vasilevsky, the Soviet Chief of General Staff, visited Stalingrad as the representative of the Soviet High Command and only a week or so after the splitting of the old South-West Front into two separate fronts, took action to recommend the restoration of some form of unified command. The Stalingrad Front (63, 21, 1 Guards, 4 Tank, 24 and 66 Armies) was put under the command of Eremenko, the former commander of the South-East Front (62, 64, 57 and 51 Armies), for better co-ordination. Gordov remained with Stalingrad Front and Golikov, who had arrived from the Voronezh Front, took over South-East Front. Gordov and Golikov became Eremenko's deputies, and the ubiquitous Khrushchev assumed the duties as the political member for both fronts.[15] In the two weeks after 17 August a new 62 Army was built out of the remnant, and 1 Guards Army, 21 and 63 Armies and 4 Tank Army were reorganized and heavily reinforced.

[15] Soviet front and army commanders, particularly those who showed energy and ability, were removed from their posts and almost overnight took over other formations at times of crisis, without necessarily being the travelling representatives of the *Stavka*. They appeared, disappeared and reappeared with confusing suddenness. Golikov, for example, in the space of a few weeks commanded the Bryansk and Voronezh Fronts and was a Deputy Commander in South-East Front and was yet to return to the Bryansk Front. Malinovsky in a short period commanded South Front, Don Group, 66 Army (at Stalingrad) and was then to move on to 2 Guards Army and South Front.

The immediate aim of the new Army Group B attack was to destroy the three Soviet armies in the landbridge between the Don and the Volga and to prevent the enemy reinforcing this area. A concentric attack was to be made by Paulus's 6 Army which, after throwing four bridges across the Don at Vertyachi, was to advance eastwards on the city of Stalingrad on a fairly narrow front with a panzer corps on each flank and an infantry corps in the centre. Hoth's 4 Panzer Army was to break through from the area of the high ground north of Tinguta and was to reach the Volga to the south of Stalingrad. The Soviet troops thus encircled would then be destroyed. Shortly before this German offensive could be launched, the Stalingrad Front on 20 August attacked the German north flank in strength from the Kremensk bridgehead gaining some ground and pinning down a German corps of one panzer and three infantry divisions. Further to the west, however, Gariboldi's 8 Italian Army started to arrive, having been moved over from Group Ruoff in the south in order to take up its new position facing northwards against the Don, so releasing some German troops. This sector was not to be a sinecure for the Italians, since from 20 August onwards Kolpakchy's 63 and Danilov's 21 Soviet Armies north of the river started probing the sector and secured yet another bridgehead south of the Don between Yelansk and Serafimovich.

Crossing the Don at daybreak on 23 August, von Wietersheim's 14 Panzer Corps, heavily supported by von Richthofen's 4 Air Fleet, speedily overcame Lopatin's 62 Army's defences and by nightfall had advanced over fifty miles, 16 Panzer Division reaching the Volga immediately to the north of Stalingrad at Rynok. On 23 and 24 August Stalingrad was heavily bombed and left in a great sea of flame, and fighting started on the northern outskirts of the town.[16] All the Red Army communication networks broke down and Soviet resistance was weak and uncoordinated until the troops had recovered from their shock, and the officers and commissars had re-established their authority. When a radio link was opened with Moscow Vasilevsky, who happened to be in the city at the time, had a very painful telephonic conversation with an angry Stalin who had assumed by the radio silence that the city had fallen, this talk remaining, according to Vasilevsky, for ever indelibly printed on his mind.[17] By 25 August, however, 14 Panzer Corps was making no further progress and was suffering heavy casualties, being stretched out in a long corridor nearly thirty miles long and only two miles wide, and assailed on all sides. Fuel and supplies had to be brought up nightly by armoured convoy. 6 Army awaited the relief from the Soviet pressure which would be occasioned by the expected thrust of Hoth's 4 Panzer Army from the south. Hoth, however, was sorely troubled by the defended and heavily mined area to the north of Tinguta, which formed a part of the inner defence belt of the city, and he had to break

[16] Halder recorded in his diary on 31 August 1942 what were presumably Hitler's thoughts: 'Stalingrad: male population to be destroyed, female to be transported'. Halder, *Kriegstagebuch,,* Vol. 3, p. 514.

[17] Vasilevsky, *Voenno Istoricheskii Zhurnal* No. 10, October 1965.

off the attack in favour of a new thrust some twenty miles further to the west. Regrouping took time, and it was not before 31 August that von Schwedler's 4 Corps and Kempf's 48 Panzer Corps, headed by 24 Panzer Division, cut the railway line south of Pitomnik at a point less than twenty miles west of Stalingrad. 62 and 64 Soviet Armies, which hitherto had resisted desperately, suddenly and unexpectedly withdrew eastwards, having been ordered to retire within the inner defensive belt. 4 Panzer Army and 6 Army then joined hands near Pitomnik on 3 September. Army Group B, wrongly interpreting the Soviet withdrawal as evidence of intention to cross to the east bank of the Volga, tried to press into the city from the west; but 4 Panzer Army's attempt failed because of the enemy strength on the flanking high ground at Beketovka, and 6 Army lacked the necessary strength to make the final effort. 4 Panzer and 6 Armies' enveloping attacks had failed to encircle the enemy between the Don and the Volga because of lack of momentum, for too many German troops had been pinned far to the west of Stalingrad by enemy flank attacks across the Don.

The evacuation of the civilian population of Stalingrad, which numbered 600,000, continued. The city itself had not been fortified at this time, but the demolition by fire, bombing and shelling was to block the routes far more effectively than man-made barricades. One of the main difficulties suffered by the defenders of the city was that the Germans soon had the town and the river under observation, both from the air and from the high ground of the Kurgan Hills and the sand dunes to the south. Movement and supply across the river by day was under enemy observation and fire, and was soon brought to a standstill.

At the end of August Zhukov was attached by the Soviet High Command to the Stalingrad Front Headquarters, which had just been moved out of Stalingrad northwards to Malaya Ivanovka on the landbridge halfway between the Volga and the Don.[18] 1 Guards Army, commanded by Moskalenko, was brought eastwards from the Kremensk bridgehead and concentrated together with Malinovsky's 66 Army and D. T. Kozlov's 24 Army on the west bank of the Don immediately to the north of Stalingrad. 66 and 24 Armies were both poorly trained and had been hastily formed from elderly age groups.[19] 62 Army, which had been reduced by casualties to about 50,000 men, was on 11 September taken over by Chuikov from Krylov, the chief of staff and temporary commander. The defensive perimeter around Stalingrad had shrunk to a long and narrow strip on the west bank of the Volga, at the widest part

---

[18] According to his own account Zhukov returned from West Front on 27 August being appointed as military deputy to Stalin, and from 29 August onwards he was with the Stalingrad Front, being continually driven on by Stalin to attack from the north across the German corridor, so taking the pressure off the Stalingrad defenders. On 12 September he returned to Moscow and there with Vasilevsky presented to Stalin an outline plan for the November counter-offensive. The following day, in response to Eremenko's urgent telephoning, Zhukov and Vasilevsky returned to Stalingrad. Zhukov, *Vospominaniya i Razmyshleniya*, pp. 406–17.

[19] Eremenko, *Stalingrad*, p. 163.

not more than ten miles across, at the narrowest about four. To the north of the town the Germans held about five miles of the Volga west bank, so separating Malinovsky's 66 Army in the north from Chuikov's 62 Army in the city.[20] Immediately to the south of the city, side by side with 62 Army, lay Shumilov's 64 Army. Inside the city itself with 62 Army was a NKVD division, commanded by Saraev who had the additional appointment of city garrison commander. This division had as its primary task police action against the Red Army formations which, under the German hammer blows, were rapidly breaking up and streaming to the rear; but it was itself soon to be drawn into the battle, having been put under the command of 62 Army. This step was apparently resented by Saraev who, as a NKVD officer, at first attempted to disregard the orders issued to him by Krylov, Chuikov's chief of staff.[21]

During July and August there were scenes of the greatest disorder between the Don and the Volga reminiscent of those of the summer of 1941. Many formations disintegrated and many of the Red Army officers and troops deserted or ran away or found pretexts to go to the rear. Long columns of refugees, taking cattle and agricultural equipment with them, moved slowly eastwards towards the Volga ferries and bridges, continually bombed and machine-gunned by *Luftwaffe* fighters and dive-bombers. When Chuikov arrived at his new command post on the Mamaev-Kurgan to take over 62 Army, he found that his armour had withdrawn without orders east of the Volga and that his principal artillery, anti-tank, engineer and armoured commanders and advisers, some of them ranking as Generals, had disappeared. Lopatin, Chuikov's predecessor as commander of 62 Army and a former cavalry non-commissioned officer with a good record of service, was in a state of despair and nervous collapse and was listed by Eremenko as a casualty.[22]

One of the characteristics of Red Army troops was that their fighting capacity could rarely be anticipated with certainty. Formations which ran away on one day were capable, without obvious cause, of putting up the most desperate resistance on the second, and the reason for this cannot be ascribed merely to the volatile and mercurial trait in the Russian character. Other factors must be taken into account such as changes in command, with a resultant improvement in leadership, draconian punishments of defaulting officers and non-commissioned officers, and the presence of NKVD troops. A large proportion of Soviet troops at this time, and this applied particularly to the infantry, were committed with little or no training and broke under the first shock of battle. Within forty-eight hours, this fear had been overcome. The morale of German troops, as usual, was very high and this, Eremenko admitted, was apparent even among German prisoners.

[20] For this reason 62 Army was transferred from the Stalingrad to the South-East Front at the beginning of September.

[21] Saraev commanded 10 NKVD Rifle Division, a formation without artillery.

[22] See Chuikov, *The Beginning of the Road*, pp. 85 and 105; Eremenko, *Stalingrad*, pp. 177–8.

Although the Germans had no intelligence of any new armies being concentrated on the east bank of the Volga opposite Stalingrad – there were in fact none – there was irrefutable evidence that both 62 and 64 Armies were being heavily reinforced across the river at night by the Volga Flotilla. Both armies were estimated to total eight complete rifle divisions, but to these were added numerous detachments and remnants and a large number of home guard and workers battalions. The Army Group B Commander, von Weichs, considered that an early resumption of the attack was essential before the enemy should become too strong; on 7 September von Seydlitz-Kurzbach's 51 Corps of 6 Army attacked with two infantry divisions eastwards from the area of Gumrak on to the Mamaev-Kurgan hill and the city centre, advancing on a very narrow front and systematically fighting its way forward over the four remaining miles to the Volga. On 14 September the Germans had seized the main railway station and detachments had reached the water front, having cut the defending 62 Army into two parts. About five miles further to the south, Kempf's 48 Panzer Corps on 10 September attacked north-eastwards along the boundary between 62 and 64 Armies, and the ferocity of the fighting reached a pitch which German troops had not hitherto experienced during the course of the war. Every street, every block of houses and every bunker had to be fought for. On the city's south-west outskirts in the area of Minina, 24 Panzer Division (of 48 Panzer Corps) was attacking along the boundary between 62 and 64 Armies, through scattered buildings and settlements, and clearings of bush and scrub, across deep *balka* ravines. T34 and T60 tanks, together with artillery pieces, had been dug in and cleverly camouflaged, but German infantry crossing the steep-sided gullies which the panzers could not cross got into the thickets and begasn to make short work of the gun crews. In the close terrain numbers of T34 tanks were destroyed by anti-tank grenades, but eventually 24 Panzer Division was counter-attacked with vigour by Red Army infantry coming out of the scrub, and forced back.[23] By 14 September, however, the old town of Tsaritsyn south of the Tsaritsa stream was in German hands and 48 Panzer Corps was on the banks of the Volga from the area east of the main railway station to Kuporosnoye lower down the river. There it joined hands with 51 Corps. Chuikov's 62 Army was by then completely separated from Shumilov's 64 Army, which lay to the south of the city.

The 14 September was the nadir of Soviet fortunes. German aircraft were mining the Volga; the old town, the city centre and the main railway station had fallen, and groups of German sub-machine-gunners roamed throughout the dock area. The German divisions were yet to experience, however, the real difficulties of fighting in heavily built-up areas. This type of close-range fighting favoured the defence and caused very heavy casualties to the attacking

[23] Von Senger und Etterlin, *Die 24. Panzer-Division*, pp. 118–20. Deserters told 24 Panzer Division at this time that a secret order had been received to evacuate all administrative installations, transport and artillery to the east bank.

troops. Because of the limited observation the fire support of German tanks, artillery and mortars could not always be used with effect, and there was the greatest of difficulty in pinpointing air bombing targets, particularly as the Soviet defenders soon learned that their own safety depended on hugging the German positions. The German numbers were so inadequate that they were forced to attack on very narrow fronts and they were unable to cope with the greatest difficulty of all, the holding of their gains against the swarms of infiltrators which seeped nightly into the rear. On that night of 14 September 13 Guards Rifle Division was ferried over the river and was joined over the next few days by two other rifle divisions, a rifle brigade and a tank brigade. On 15 September the main railway station was being fought over once more, changing hands several times on the following day. Red Army detachments were attacking towards Mamaev-Kurgan. The Germans then changed their tactics and instead of obstinately defending all their gains they narrowed their sectors of attack even further and, maintaining some flexibility, they continually varied the direction of their thrusts. This, however, brought little further success and in the second half of September the fighting died down with the German 48 Panzer and 51 Corps holding on to the southern end of the city.

On 20 September Paulus, whom von Richthofen reported to be in an anxious state of mind, said that without further troops he could do no more, and both he and von Weichs were to have doubts as to the security of the flanks of Army Group B, since 6 German Army and 4 Panzer Army were at the head of a long exposed salient.[24] To the south the flank was uncovered except by 16 German Motorized Division far off in the Kalmuck Steppe, and when 6 Rumanian Corps took up a flanking position near the chain of lakes near Tsatsa it suffered a sharp defeat by comparatively small Red Army forces. This was merely confirmation of what the Germans already knew, that Rumanian troops were unreliable unless organized within a German command framework and supervised and supported by German detachments. This was equally obvious to the Soviet enemy. In spite of this the German plan intended that General Constantinescu's 4 Rumanian Army Headquarters should take over the command of 6 and 7 Rumanian Corps and should become responsible to 4 Panzer Army for the defence of the south. The northern flank of the salient from Stalingrad westwards to the Kremensk bridgehead was covered by three German corps, none of which could be spared to force a decision in the city as they were being attacked by superior numbers down the landbridge between the Volga and the Don and from the Kremensk bridgehead itself.[25] West of Kremensk the protection of the northern Don flank was entrusted to three armies of Germany's allies, Dumitrescu's 3 Rumanian Army, which

[24] Compare von Richthofen *Tagebuch*, 20 August to 22 September 1942; *Kriegstagebuch des OKW*, Vol. 2, p. 750.

[25] 8, 11 and 17 Corps faced the enemy north of the Don bend and the Don-Volga landbridge. On 22 September von Richthofen had noted in his diary that 6 Army was suffering from what he called a blockage, primarily because such a large proportion of its strength was being pinned from the north.

was just moving into place, Gariboldi's 8 Italian Army and Jany's 2 Hungarian Army. 8 Italian Army had already given ground in face of a Soviet probing attack across the river and, although German troops had halted the Red Army advance, they were unable to eliminate this new bridgehead between Yelansk and Serafimovich.

Hitler was intent, however, on securing the whole of the rubble of the former city of Stalingrad before he would agree to clearing up the danger spots on the flanks.[26] Meanwhile Army Group B, like Army Group A and the *Luftwaffe*, lived a hand to mouth existence at the end of a long and insecure railway line which ran back for over 1,200 miles before it entered Silesia. Ammunition and vehicle and aircraft fuel were severely rationed. Both Army Group B and the Army High Command (OKH) were without effective troop reserves and by the end of September Army Group A had become bogged down in the Caucasus. The first heavy frosts heralding the approach of winter were shortly due and, bearing in mind the German experiences of the previous year when winter had found Army Group Centre over-extended and still short of Moscow, it would have been wiser to have withdrawn Army Group A immediately from the Caucasus to Rostov and to have made emergency plans, should the situation so demand, to evacuate Stalingrad and fall back to the line of the Kalitva and Donets. This would have shortened the frontages and would have allowed for the establishing of substantial reserves. The *Führer*, however, was still convinced of the invincibility of German arms and believed, on the basis of intuition rather than of intelligence, that the Red Army and the Soviet Union were in their death throes. In view of the effect such a massive withdrawal would have had on his own personal prestige and the attitude of Turkey and Germany's allies, such a solution, even if of only a temporary nature, was unthinkable. On 6 October an Army Group B order stressed that the complete occupation of Stalingrad had been laid down by the *Führer* as the most important mission of the army group and that this would require the employment of all available forces. All other tasks were secondary. On 14 October the *Führer* issued an order in which he described the Red enemy as being severely weakened and the October 1942 line as the basis or springboard for the new 1943 German offensive.[27] No withdrawal of any kind was to be permitted from this line and army group commanders were made personally responsible to the *Führer* that the orders were carried out in every detail.

In the area of Stalingrad the Soviet High Command had ordered another reorganization and redesignation of its forces. On 28 September the Stalin-

[26] Compare *Führerbefehl vom 13 September 1942, OKH Gen St d H Op Abt I (S/B) Nr. 420710/42 g. Kdos Chefs.*
[27] *Operationsbefehl Nr. 1 vom 14 Oktober OKH Gen St d H Op Abt I Nr. 420817/42 g. Kdos Chefs.*

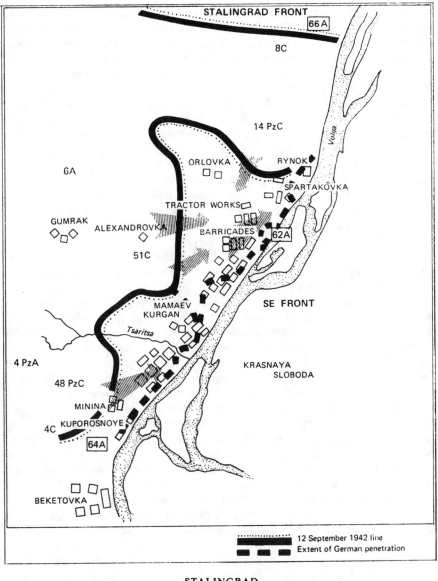

STALINGRAD
September 1942

grad Front, covering the north bank of the Don and the Don-Volga landbridge, was redesignated as the Don Front and Rokossovsky was appointed as its commander with Zheltov as his political member of the military council. The South-East Front was renamed the Stalingrad Front, Eremenko continuing as its front commander and Khrushchev as political member.[28] Both fronts came directly under the Soviet High Command. Troops continued to be put across the Volga, six rifle divisions and a tank brigade joining Chuikov's 62 Army by the beginning of October. The Stalingrad defenders had been supported by 8 Air Army which, during the month of fighting, received no fewer than a thousand replacement aircraft, mainly La 5, Yak 7, Pe 2 and Il 2. At the beginning of September 8 Air Army was joined by a newly formed 16 Air Army. Yet Fiebig's 8 German Air Corps, in spite of unreplaced losses in men and equipment and shortages in aviation fuels, continued to control the air space by day as it pounded the enemy gun positions on the east bank of the Volga. This was the limit of its exertions and at night the Red Air Force took over and returned the bombing in measure.

The end of September and the first half of October saw the final German effort in Stalingrad. In order to strengthen as far as he dared the formations fighting inside Stalingrad, Paulus began to move the fresher and better organized German divisions from the Kremensk bridgehead and Don-Volga landbridge into Stalingrad, relieving them by the badly mauled formations which had been fought to a standstill in the rubble of the city. In this way yet a further dozen divisions were burned out, and the German force holding part of the north flank from Kremensk to Stalingrad became weaker still. On 26 September the final German offensive began in spite of the shortage of artillery and mortar ammunition, the direction of the main attack being changed on to the northern half of 62 Army and being made once again by von Seydlitz-Kurzbach's 51 Corps. In the first few days of fighting the Germans advanced only 400 yards, but during October 51 Corps penetrated into the north of the town as far as the Tractor Works and Spartakovka, making very substantial gains. After a lull of a few days Paulus renewed the attack, and by the night of 15 October had reached the river and began to roll up the northern part of 62 Army, the fighting being of the most bitter kind. The German strength, particularly in infantry, had been drastically depleted. On the other hand, many Soviet divisions were so low in fighting strength that they fought in improvised battle groups, reinforcing themselves as best they could by taking in stragglers, workers' detachments and civilians. On the night of 17 October a further division, 138 Soviet Rifle Division, came across the water and was used to counter-attack towards the Barricades Settlement where it outran its support and was cut off by the Germans. This was the last German success. So senseless had the German effort become that in the first week in November five engineer battalions trained in assault techniques and any troops which could be thrown together, were fighting

[28] *Istoriya*, Vol. 2, p. 444.

desperately for the local government buildings. Although fighting was to continue intermittently, this was the final effort made by Paulus and his exhausted troops.[29]

Although the territorial gains made by Army Groups A and B since midsummer were enormous, the *Führer* was dissatisfied with progress, and the relationship between himself and his army staffs and leaders had become embittered. When von Brauchitsch had been dismissed, Halder had been permitted, and had chosen, to remain as Chief of General Staff. During 1942 Hitler was in direct command and in sole charge of all planning and operations on the Eastern Front and elsewhere, and Halder became little more than his doubting and often unwilling executive. Intelligence, the life's blood of operations, meant nothing to the *Führer* since he only accepted what he wanted to believe and he made his strategic and tactical plans in a vacuum. Nor had he any understanding of the basis of logical appreciations and plans, relative strengths, time and space and logistics. With the departure of von Brauchitsch and Paulus from the OKH, war games and paper exercises ceased to form any part of the planning procedure to test the feasibility of projects, and *Führer* planning was reduced to the study of maps, a meeting or a conference or, more often, to a sudden impulse and a telephone call. The *Führer*'s time was split between Rastenburg or Vinnitsa, Berlin and the Berghof, and in his periods of absence his Chief of General Staff had to manage the Eastern Front as best he might, without being empowered to make any decisions. *Führer* missives to army group commanders were orders and not directives, and were so detailed and so binding as deliberately to stifle all initiative. Hitler was no longer amenable to advice, certainly not to criticism, and his pathological suspicion of military leaders and the General Staff was already beyond reason. Important, even vital decisions were too frequently made in a background of haste, excitement, recrimination, rage, insults and interminable repetitive monologues, and leadership had become the fleeting reaction to momentary impressions and a total ignorance of the function of command.[30] For, as Speer said, Hitler would only take advice from someone who had an even more optimistic appraisal of the situation than himself, and such a man could rarely be found.[31]

Hitler was subsequently to blame von Bock's three-day delay at Voronezh for the failure of the whole campaign. Yet Hitler himself, interfering in detail, detached two of von Bock's panzer divisions to Army Group Centre, while the southward movement down the Don was actually in progress. Hitler's insistence on the concentration of 1 and 4 Panzer Armies near Rostov was to

---

[29] Von Richthofen as an airman was very free in his criticism of Paulus and the German Army, and he laid the blame on commanders who did not go into sufficient detail and ensure that the necessary preparations were made before going into battle. Von Richthofen *Tagebuch*, 1 November 1942. This was unfair criticism since army groups were not responsible for their own maintenance until September 1942. Moreover operational matters were dictated by Hitler irrespective of the supply position.

[30] Halder, *Kriegstagebuch*, Vol. 3, p. 489.

[31] *Speer Interrogation Reports, F. D. C. 1*, Report 19.

1.

widen the breach between himself and Halder, and the movement of the rump of von Manstein's 11 Army to the Leningrad area was, as it transpired, without purpose.[32] List's movement into the Caucasus should never have been made until the Don Basin and lower Volga had been cleared.

Meanwhile the situation had not stood still on the other army group sectors. On 5 July three armies of the Soviet West Front attacked from the area of Sukhinichi towards Bryansk, and at the end of the month the right wing of West Front and the left wing of Kalinin Front attacked towards Rzhev, both of these offensives falling on von Kluge's Army Group Centre. Von Kluge's intention to use his borrowed panzer divisions to clear up the situation at Rzhev was negatived by Hitler, who demanded that they should be used at Sukhinichi. On 24 August Halder, in conference with the *Führer*, tried to insist that 9 Army, threatened on three sides in the north of the Rzhev salient, should withdraw to shorten the line, and this resulted in a stormy scene which presaged the final break between the two men. In the Leningrad area von Küchler, the Commander of Army Group North, had momentarily lost Hitler's confidence and von Manstein, fresh from his Crimean victories, was the man of the moment, and was entrusted with the reduction of Leningrad, although the *Führer* did not hesitate to tell him exactly how it should be done.[33] At the end of August, however, the Soviet Volkhov Front mounted heavy attacks south of Lake Ladoga and Hitler, ignoring von Küchler and forgetting Leningrad, made a personal telephone call to von Manstein on 4 September, telling him to take charge of operations south of Ladoga. Draft Directive 47, the attack on Leningrad, was already in the *Führer*'s pending tray and there it stayed.[34]

Von Bock had gone and then it was List's turn. The OKW diary entry of 30 August had noted that the *Führer* was very dissatisfied with the situation in Army Group A and the next day List had been ordered to report to Vinnitsa where he had been treated with charm and courtesy. In reality the brooding and suspicious *Führer* was anything but satisfied and in the next few days became more determined than ever to pursue his witchhunt. Part of the Black Sea base of Novorossisk had been taken, but otherwise little further progress had been made in the Caucasus towards the Black Sea, and on 7 September Jodl had been sent to Army Group A to see List and Konrad, the Commander of 49 Mountain Corps. On his return the same night Jodl reported his agreement with List's appreciation that the tasks given to Army Group A were impossible to execute. Hitler became maddened with rage and this disastrous flight caused a permanent breach between him and the Armed Forces High

---

[32] Doerr has put forward the view, which he said was supported by the post-war testimony of Halder and Heusinger, that 11 Army was moved to Leningrad because the railway and supply situation made it impossible to maintain it in the Don and Kuban areas. This view does not appear to be supported, however, by contemporary documentary evidence.

[33] See Heusinger-Schulz correspondence, *Kriegstagebuch des OKW*, Vol. 2, pp. 1290–2.

[34] Warlimont, *Inside Hitler's Headquarters*, p. 254; von Manstein, *Lost Victories*, pp. 264–5.

Command (OKW) staff. Jodl was thereafter no longer to sit at meals in privilege at the side of the *Führer* who, in his pettiness, henceforth refused to shake hands with either Jodl or Keitel. From this time onwards Hitler took his solitary meals in his dim, depressing quarters and did not appear in public again, the daily briefings taking place in Hitler's own hut, discussion being forbidden, and the cold and formal atmosphere was not improved by the presence of two duty stenographers who recorded every word that was spoken. Hitler from then on refused to see anyone privately.[35]

Jodl, whose subsequent conduct was unworthy of respect in that he believed that the will of dictators should never be crossed, retired to the toil of his desk. Thereafter such influence as Jodl did exert on the direction of the war was malignant in that he merely agreed with and fortified the *Führer*'s extravagances. Field-Marshal List was relieved of his post on 9 September and the *Führer* himself assumed the command of Army Group A, continuing to hold the appointment until the third week in November. There was a marked reaction in Hitler's personal relationship with his army staffs and the situation now called for a clean sweep. Keitel shared Jodl's disgrace and it was rumoured that he was to be replaced by Kesselring. Jodl, it was believed, would give way to Paulus after Stalingrad had been taken. Halder was to go.[36]

Halder's position as Chief of General Staff had deteriorated since the dismissal of von Brauchitsch. Before December 1941 the Army High Command had prepared its own plans for submission to Hitler, and Jodl and the OKW played little or no part in the planning processes of the major campaigns. By the middle of 1941 the OKW had become responsible to Hitler for all theatres except Russia, although it must be remembered that at that time there was no fighting in any of the OKW theatres other than in North Africa and Finland. With the disappearance of von Brauchitsch, Keitel had assumed many of the former Army Commander-in-Chief's functions and Jodl and the OKW tended, in so far as the *Führer* would permit, to meddle and give gratuitous advice in matters which were the concern of the Army High Command (OKH). The personal relationship between Halder and Hitler was bad since they were entirely unsuited to each other and, Jodl and Keitel being what they were, it followed that there was a lack of cordiality between Halder and the senior staff of the Armed Forces High Command (OKW). The competent and toiling Halder, a loyal executive when everything was going well, had become a prey to doubts about the *Führer*'s war leadership shortly after the beginning of the Russo-German war. He appears to have voiced them and was one of the few who dared to do so. Hitler, however, wanted neither advice nor

---

[35] Since 1939 Hitler had refused to attend social gatherings or places of entertainment and from 1942 onwards he became a social recluse, except that during the early hours of the morning he would talk with a few of his Party cronies, and his secretaries. His meals he later was to share with his cook. In this way he became even further removed from the world of reality.

[36] Warlimont, *Inside Hitler's Headquarters*, pp. 256–8; Halder, *Kriegstagebuch*, Vol. 3, pp. 518–9 and 528; Keitel, *Memoirs*, pp. 180–4.

professional competence, but an unquestioning obedience and a fanatical loyalty to his own person. His choice fell on Zeitzler.

Zeitzler, a newly promoted infantry major-general (the equivalent of a brigadier or brigadier-general) with a reputation as a live wire, had formerly been a colonel in the OKW and a subordinate of Jodl's. A great friend of Schmundt, Hitler's military aide, and personally known to the *Führer*, Zeitzler, as Chief of Staff to Army Group D, gained some credit for the repulse of the British-Canadian raid on Dieppe in August 1942.[37] Hitler expressed the wish for a Chief of General Staff who was optimistic and ready for anything, not like Halder, who was condemned as a pessimist and prophet of doom, always infecting the army groups with his wailing. He approved of Zeitzler, and Schmundt and Göring saw to it that Zeitzler replaced Halder.[38] Zeitzler was promoted to General, jumping the rank of lieutenant-general, as Jodl had before him, and on 24 September Halder went out into the wilderness, firstly to retirement, and then after the attempt on Hitler's life, to arrest, prison and a concentration camp.

As a senior and experienced colonel-general, Halder had up to the end of 1941 held his ground against the OKW and the army group commanders. Field-marshals were usually obliged to defer to him. The new Chief of General Staff, a major-general only since 1942, had none of the advantages of seniority, experience or authority in the eyes of the army group commanders. On taking up his post he publicly made it clear to his staff that loyalty to and confidence in the *Führer* was the order of the day. The sun shone brightly on Zeitzler. The rest of the *Führer*'s court followed suit and even Jodl hoped to profit by the popularity of his former subordinate. The effect of Zeitzler's appointment was, not unnaturally, to debase the post of Chief of General Staff since, as the German Army was by then Hitler's personal instrument, Zeitzler tended to be regarded as the *Führer*'s man. Keitel and Jodl were to hope that, as their former colleague in the OKW, Zeitzler would acquiesce to the OKW assuming overall control over the Eastern Front. In this they were doomed to disappointment because Zeitzler promptly disassociated himself from the pair, and, profiting by the weakness of Jodl's personal position, adroitly did away with the overlapping of some of the dual command responsibilities in the East and won back the ground lost by Halder to Jodl in the preceding nine months. As far as he was able he excluded Keitel and Jodl from all discussions and business concerning the Eastern Front. In his relationship with the army group commanders, Zeitzler tended at first to be merely a mouthpiece and telephonic link between them and the *Führer*. Although in his first year of office he enjoyed Hitler's faith and confidence, Zeitzler was to fail as a Chief of General

---

[37] In June 1942 even before the landing Hitler said of Zeitzler '*Holland dürfte für sie eine harte Nuss sein, weil . . . General Zeitzler wie eine Hummel hin und her brause*'. Picker, *Hitlers Tischgespräche*, p. 405.

[38] Zeitzler was replaced as Chief of Staff Army Group D by Blumentritt, the head of *O Qu 1*, who was himself replaced by Heusinger, the head of the Operations Department inside the *O Qu 1* Directorate.

Staff. It is of course certain that no other man would have succeeded under such a Commander-in-Chief and Zeitzler may not have been quite as strong a character as subsequent accounts portrayed him to be. Yet for all that, he was able and, according to Speer, essentially a man of backbone and candour who would defend his views with vigour.[39]

Although Germany's fate had been sealed as early as December 1941 when it declared war against the United States of America, the effect of the Anglo-American Alliance was not to become apparent until November 1942. In the air and at sea their war effort had admittedly been powerful and had tied down substantial air and significant land forces in occupied Western Europe and Scandinavia, but as far as the land fighting was concerned, only the British had taken a very minor part. On 2 November came the news of the British victory of Alamein, where Montgomery defeated a force of four German and eight Italian divisions, the Axis force losing, however, only 40,000 men of which about one-third were German. A few days later came the Anglo-American landing in French North Africa, news of which reached Hitler at the time of his address to his Party Old Comrades at the Munich beer cellar, when he could boast of nothing more than the blocking of the Volga river traffic. Up to November 1942, notwithstanding Hitler's premonitions and nervousness about the Western seaboard of Europe, the ability of the British or the Americans to fight a war by land had not been taken very seriously in Rastenburg, and for this reason the defeat and landing came as unpleasant tidings to the Armed Forces High Command (OKW) and as a surprise to the German public, where the exploits and significance of Rommel and the Afrika Korps had been much exaggerated by the Propaganda Ministry and the press. In this way the propaganda reacted to Germany's disadvantage in the eyes of both the German public and Germany's allies. Propaganda and its consequences by themselves, however, rarely win wars. The true value of the battle at Alamein lay in the fact that it was coupled with the victory at Tunis six months later, a victory almost as great as that of Stalingrad.

[39] The robust and strong line which Zeitzler says that he took in the *Führer*'s presence is not always apparent in the typescript fragments of subsequent meetings (including that of the midday meeting of 1 February 1943 at the time of 6 Army's surrender). Heiber, *Hitlers Lagebesprechungen*, p. 120. Yet Heusinger has confirmed that there were occasions on which Zeitzler rounded on Hitler with force and heat.

CHAPTER TWENTY

Defeat at Stalingrad

Stalin had watched the progress of the Stalingrad battle with no little anxiety and as he gathered information about the conditions in the ruined city, he frequently goaded on Eremenko to support Chuikov more closely by putting troops across the river. From early September onwards the rough outline of a massive counter-offensive was being worked out in Moscow, and Vasilevsky, Voronov and Zhukov had been detached from the High Command to the fronts and armies to study local conditions and formulate the basis for an offensive. Strict security precautions were insisted on and in the early stages the fronts were given no information either of the plan or the intention. Outside the Soviet High Command in Moscow no plans were committed to writing or to maps and no mention was made of them in radio or telephonic communications, all arrangements being made orally during the visits of the representatives of the Soviet High Command, who flew backwards and forwards from Moscow. Not until the beginning of October were the front staffs drawn into the planning.[1]

The main counter-offensive, known by the cover name of *Uranus*, envisaged a double envelopment by two main armoured thrusts, one from the north striking south-eastwards from Kletskaya and the Don bridgehead at Serafimovich, and one from the south of Stalingrad in the Tsatsa area of the Sarpa Lakes driving north-westwards, both pincers meeting in the area of Kalach on the Don. These thrusts were aimed at cutting off the great salient made by 6 Army and 4 Panzer Army. It was intended that the two main blows should fall on 3 Rumanian Army and on the Rumanian corps of 4 Panzer Army, because their fighting capacity was much lower than that of German troops, their morale being low and their desertion rate relatively high. The thrust from the south, which was to penetrate 4 Panzer Army, was to be made by the Stalingrad Front from the bridgehead forward of the Sarpa Lakes, using Trufanov's 51, Tolbukhin's 57 and Shumilov's 64 Soviet Armies, the mobile component being 4 and 13 Mechanized Corps and 4 Cavalry Corps. The thrust in the north was to be made by Rokossovsky's Don Front and a newly formed South-West Front which on 29 October was interposed between the Voronezh

[1] Vasilevsky, *Voenno Istoricheskii Zhurnal* No. 10, October 1965.

and the Don Fronts. This new front headquarters, formed metaphorically out of a rib of the headquarters of Moskalenko's old 1 Guards Army, was commanded by Vatutin, who had been transferred from the Voronezh Front, with Zheltov who had been moved from the Don Front as his political member, further staff being posted in from other fronts.[2] In the thrust to be made from the north the South-West Front had a predominant role over that of the Don Front. The Don Front consisted of Zhadov's 66, Galanin's 24 and Batov's 65 Armies while South-West Front had Lelyushenko's new 1 Guards and Chistyakov's 21 Armies, and a large armoured element consisting of 5 Tank Army, 3 Guards Cavalry Corps and 4 Tank Corps.[3] 5 Tank Army under Romanenko was a mixed army made up of 1 and 26 Tank Corps, 8 Cavalry Corps and six rifle divisions, and had been moved south from the Voronezh sector.[4]

Meanwhile the General Officers flew between Moscow and the Volga and the Don, the preparation of the South-West and Don Front offensives having been assigned to Zhukov and that of the Stalingrad Front to Vasilevsky. Much of the planning took place not in the rarefied atmosphere of a Supreme Headquarters but in the tactical headquarters and observation posts of the armies in those sectors selected for the main attacks, usually only a thousand yards or so from the forward defended localities; it was observed with some satisfaction that the Rumanian defences were poorly developed and were only from three to five miles in depth. No German reserves were noted in the area nor any preparations for regrouping. The Soviet force to be concentrated in the Stalingrad-Don area, including the troops already deployed, was to total more than a million men supported by 13,500 guns and mortars and over a hundred rocket batteries, and was to include more than four tank and three mechanized corps, fourteen tank brigades and a number of independent tank regiments.[5] The movement, concentration and concealment of this force on the bare steppe involved no little effort and ingenuity, particularly since the autumn mud hindered the movement of lorries and the Don and Volga were

[2] In October Golikov was to return to the Voronezh Front, replacing Vatutin.

[3] All these army commanders took up their new appointments between 1 October and 1 November. The original 1 Guards Army had been formed in August in the Don bend with Golikov as commander designate. This army was commanded in August and September by Moskalenko and from 28 September until 15 October by Chistyakov. The headquarters was disbanded but formed the cadre for the newly forming South-West Front Headquarters under Vatutin. On 4 November a second 1 Guards Army was to be formed from V. I. Kuznetsov's 63 Army with Lelyushenko in command but on 8 December this was redesignated 3 Guards Army (still commanded by Lelyushenko). On 8 December the third 1 Guards Army was established with V. I. Kuznetsov in command. See Samsonov, *Stalingradskaya Bitva*, pp. 526 and 528 and footnotes.

[4] In October 1942 the military councils were as follows: Stalingrad Front, Eremenko, Chuyanov and Varennikov; Don Front, Rokossovsky, Kirichenko and Malinin; South-West Front, Vatutin, Zheltov and Stelmakh.

[5] *Istoriya*, Vol. 3, p. 20. Soviet gun strength includes all guns of 76·2 mm and over and all mortars of 82 mm and over. Battalion and regimental infantry weapons are therefore included.

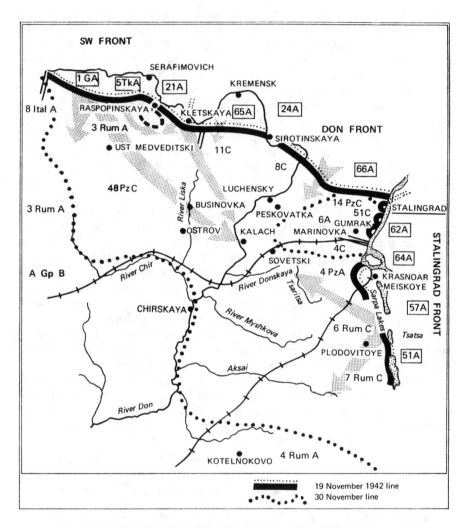

THE SOVIET COUNTER-OFFENSIVE AT STALINGRAD
November 1942

swollen and flooded, so that it took up to four hours to ferry across the Volga
instead of the usual forty minutes. No fewer than fifty new ferry points were
constructed between Saratov and Astrakhan, each using several ferries. The
six air armies allocated to this operation tried as far as they were able to
prevent German air reconnaissance over the Soviet area. All movement was
made by night. Radio silence was imposed and all the formation main radio

networks continued to function in the old areas until after the offensive had commenced, so that the German radio intercept service would remain in ignorance about the redeployment of the Red Army troops. Much use was made of the Volga river transport, but one of the most effective methods by which the troops were concentrated rapidly and by stealth was the unusual use said to have been made of the south-east and Ryazan-Ural railway links. The tracks had for long been used to capacity, but in the final stage of the concentration all troops were moved forward in one great long lift by using one way running for as much rolling stock as could be marshalled. The signalling system was ignored and the frequency of trains speeding south-west towards the front was controlled by railway trackmen equipped with lanterns who let one train through on each track every twelve minutes.[6]

When in October the front commanders had been apprised of the High Command outline plans, their comments on them had been forwarded to Moscow. On 3 November Zhukov and Vatutin, together with Voronov, Novikov, Golovanov and Fedorenko, had attended a presentation and discussion at Headquarters 5 Tank Army at which all the formation commanders, down to division, of South-West Front had been present. The next day the presentation had been repeated for the Don Front and once again on 10 November at Headquarters 57 Army for the benefit of the formation commanders of Stalingrad Front.[7] No orders were, however, to be given to the troops until 18 November, the night before the offensive.

On 11 November Stalin was worrying about the scale of the Red Air Force support for the operation, so high did he rate its importance that he even suggested postponing the whole counter-offensive if Novikov was not satisfied that he could accomplish all his tasks.[8]

On 17 November Zhukov was removed from the Stalingrad area and dispatched to the Kalinin and West Fronts to co-ordinate attacks on the German Army Group Centre in order to pin the enemy mobile reserves. Vasilevsky remained near Stalingrad with the task of co-ordinating the operations of the three fronts. Vasilevsky was surprised during his daily telephone conference with Stalin on 17 November, hardly forty-eight hours before the offensive was due, to be ordered to Moscow to appear before the State Defence Committee (GKO) the next day. The incident, as recounted by Vasilevsky, is illustrative of the way in which the Red Army functioned. Volsky, the Commander of 4 Mechanized Corps, had written to Stalin, so Stalin said, stating that the preparations for the offensive were inadequate and that the attack was doomed to collapse. Stalin and the GKO wanted some reassurance. Vasilevsky affirmed that the offensive should not on any account be postponed, whereupon Stalin there and then had Volsky telephoned and, to Vasilevsky's amazement, addressed a few kind and reassuring words to the Commander of

---

[6] *Ibid*, p. 21.
[7] Zhukov, *Vospominaniya i Razmyshleniya*, pp. 436–7.
[8] *Ibid*, pp. 438–9.

4 Mechanized Corps.[9] Vasilevsky was then briefed to keep a close eye on 4 Mechanized Corps and to make a personal report to Stalin. Thus encouraged to report on each other, the NKVD and the army political departments undoubtedly reported on both.

Within the salient Paulus, faithfully carrying out Hitler's orders of 14 October, fought on near the banks of the Volga. All the twenty German divisions of 4 Panzer Army and 6 Army were to the east of the sector chosen for the Soviet assault, over half being engaged in the area of Stalingrad, and forty per cent of all their battalions were so exhausted as to be considered hardly battleworthy. Moreover, the divisional units lacked the means to move much of their artillery and heavy equipment since many of the horses had been evacuated to the west of the Don because of the difficulty in finding fodder on the bare Volga Steppe.

Soviet historians deride German post-war accounts which maintain that the Red Army counter-offensive was not unexpected, and Moscow prefers to portray the offensive as a complete surprise to the Germans. In truth the offensive was not unexpected, but neither the German High Command nor Paulus had any idea of the strength in which it was to be launched.

Greiner and Warlimont both tell the story of the old civil war map of Tsaritsyn, said to have been produced by Halder, and of Göring's appearance at the briefing conference in Vinnitsa on 28 August when he read out von Richthofen's air reconnaissance reports that there was no evidence of Red Army concentrations north of the Don.[10] Paulus, Halder and even Hitler himself were well aware that the flank to the north of the Don was vulnerable, but it could not be strengthened by German troops unless Army Group A was withdrawn from the Caucasus.[11] At the end of August and the beginning of September Halder had shown some concern because the Italians were having difficulty warding off Soviet attacks on the Don, and a German infantry division was allocated as a reserve behind 8 Italian Army. The *Führer*, too, was particularly concerned about the threat. The three German corps of 6 Army on the Volga-Don landbridge and in the Don bend also came under heavy pressure from Gordov's Stalingrad Front in September and this was noted in detail by Halder; but if he had any great fears concerning the 3 Rumanian Army sector he did not record them in his diary. On 24 September,

[9] Vasilevsky, *Voenno Istoricheskii Zhurnal* No. 10, October 1965. Volsky subsequently had a distinguished career, becoming the Commander of 5 Guards Tank Army.

[10] Greiner, *Die Oberste Wehrmachtführung*, pp. 401–7; Warlimont, *Inside Hitler's Headquarters*, p. 255. Halder makes no reference to the incidents.

[11] Hitler was aware of the vulnerability of the Don flank and from time to time expressed anxiety, although he appears to have been over-confident in the ability of German troops to retrieve the situation. According to Greiner, the OKW diarist, Zeitzler too at this time appeared entirely confident. For the attitudes of both Hitler and Zeitzler, see Greiner, *Die Oberste Wehrmachtführung*, pp. 411–2; also *Kriegstagebuch des OKW*, Vol. 2, p. 597 (16 August 1942). '*Der Führer ist in Sorge, dass Stalin den russischen "Standard Angriff" von 1920 wiederholen könnte, nämlich einen Angriff über den Don etwa bei und überhalb Serafimowitsch in der Stossrichtung auf Rostov . . .*'

the day of his dismissal, he noted the decision that the troops on the Don were to be supported by those elements of 48 Panzer Corps *which would not be needed for the Stalingrad battle*.[12]

Dumitrescu's 3 Rumanian Army, with the German 11 Corps on its right and 8 Italian Army on its left, covered a sector of about a hundred miles with eight infantry and two cavalry divisions, the anti-tank defence being based on discarded German 37 mm guns which were valueless against Soviet KV or T34 tanks.[13] Dumitrescu had noted some strengthening of Soviet troops and had proposed that the Serafimovich bridgehead should be destroyed by a joint German-Rumanian attack to drive the Russian back to the north of the Don. No German troops could be spared, however, until Stalingrad was taken. By the end of October, having collected some intelligence from prisoners and deserters, the Rumanians had become distinctly nervous, without having been able to produce convincing evidence that an offensive was imminent. The winter set in on about 1 November with heavy frosts, snow and sleet showers making aerial visibility poor, and not before the second week of the month did the *Luftwaffe* note the signs of preparations for an attack against 3 Rumanian Army.[14] On 12 November von Richthofen noted that artillery was beginning to make its appearance in the already dug gun emplacements.[15] Another disquieting feature was the sudden strengthening of the Red Air Force to the north of the Don, and during October and early November von Richthofen was obliged to divert his main effort from Stalingrad on to the area opposite Dumitrescu's Rumanians. Air superiority, except in localized sectors, began to pass from the German 8 Air Corps, by then down to 400 aircraft, to the four enemy air armies which were rightly estimated to have a total strength of about 1,200 first line machines.[16]

On 6 November Gehlen of Foreign Armies East had written an inconclusive intelligence report, drawing attention to enemy concentrations which might be directed against either Army Group B or Army Group Centre. On 12 November Gehlen produced another more concrete appreciation, when he noted the build-up in front of 3 Rumanian Army, and came to the conclusion that an attack across the Don with the aim of cutting off Stalingrad was imminent.

[12] Halder, *Kriegstagebuch*, Vol. 3, p. 529.

[13] *OKH Kriegsgliederung*, 5 November 1942.

[14] The *Luftwaffe* noted an increase in bridges and ferry points over the Don on 3 Rumanian Army sector and the presence of formations of 5 Tank Army had been confirmed. Dumitrescu appealed to Marshal Antonescu concerning the vulnerability of his sector and protested at having to take over some of the front previously held by the Italians. These protests found their way back to Hitler; Heim is of opinion that Antonescu's prompting may have been responsible for Hitler's decision to earmark 48 Panzer Corps as a reserve. Philippi und Heim, *Der Feldzug gegen Sowjetrussland*, p. 179.

[15] Von Richthofen, *Tagebuch*, 12 November 1942.

[16] The splitting of Army Group South into Army Groups A and B resulted in 4 Air Fleet being responsible for the support of the two army groups with 4 and 8 Air Corps. In June 1942 the strength of these two air corps stood at 1,600 aircraft but by 20 October it had fallen to 974. Of this total only 594 were airworthy and of these only 141 were first class fighters. *Kriegstagebuch des OKW*, Vol. 2, p. 1321.

Gehlen had some doubts as to whether the Red Army had sufficient strength to do more than threaten the German flank and force a withdrawal from Stalingrad. A threat from the flank to the south of Stalingrad does not appear to have been taken into account.[17]

On the southern flank the Axis position was particularly complicated. It had been Hitler's intention to raise a new Army Group Don under Marshal Antonescu, taking under its command 3 and 4 Rumanian Armies and 6 German Army; a German-Rumanian commission temporarily headed by Hauffe, the Chief of the German Military Mission to Rumania, and Steflea, the Rumanian Chief of General Staff, was already at work in Rostov trying to agree the function and organization of the new headquarters. 3 Rumanian Army was of course in place on the Don, but Constantinescu's 4 Rumanian Army Headquarters had only just arrived in the area of Kotelnikovo and had not yet taken over an active command. The southern approaches to Stalingrad and the southern steppe flank were in fact still covered by Hoth's 4 Panzer Army, a panzer army only in name since it included not a single panzer division and was made up of Jaenecke's 4 German Corps of one Rumanian and two German infantry divisions just south of Stalingrad, and 6 Rumanian Corps covering the southern flank. 7 Rumanian Corps was far to the south on the Sarpa Lakes. In all, Hoth's command included two German and five Rumanian infantry divisions, two Rumanian cavalry divisions and 29 German Motorized Division in army reserve, covering a sector nearly 120 miles in length from the area south of Krasnoarmeiskoye on the Volga, west of the Sarpa Lakes out on to the Kalmuck Steppe, where 16 German Motorized Division tried to maintain contact between Army Groups A and B.

Of army group reserves, von Weichs had very few. 298 German Infantry Division was positioned on the left flank of the army group to the rear of 8 Italian Army and 29 Motorized Infantry Division on the right supported 4 Panzer Army. Heim's 48 Panzer Corps, which on 10 November was ordered to deploy to the rear of the threatened sector of 3 Rumanian Army, consisted of 1 Rumanian Armoured Division equipped with Czech tanks and the much understrength and hitherto unlucky 22 Panzer Division.[18] Heim had some very unpleasant (*unerfreulich*) things to say to von Weichs about the condition of these two formations.[19] 6 Panzer Division and a further two German infantry divisions had been promised by Hitler, but as these were to be withdrawn from France they could not be expected to arrive before December, and their arrival by rail was certain to disrupt the hand to mouth maintenance tonnages received over the overworked railway system. 48 Panzer Corps, also known as Panzer Corps H (Heim), was not really at von Weichs's disposal,

[17] *Ibid*, pp. 1305–7.
[18] 48 Panzer Corps had been stripped of 14 Panzer and 29 Motorized Divisions, which were left in the Stalingrad area.
[19] Von Weichs, *Tagebuch, Band 6*, 1942.

since he had to obtain the *Führer*'s agreement before he could commit it.[20]

It was during November 1942 that it became apparent for the very first time that the initiative, so long held by Germany, was about to change hands. Hitler was Head of the German State, the Commander-in-Chief of all the Armed Forces, the Commander of the German Army in all its overseas theatres and the field commander in Russia. Having successfully held off the enemy on the Volkhov, south of Leningrad, he awaited the next Soviet offensive, but could not make up his mind whether it would fall on 8 Italian Army or on von Kluge's Army Group Centre.[21] He was still acting as the Commander of Army Group A, commanding it from Vinnitsa nearly a thousand miles away, since no replacement had yet been appointed to succeed List. At the end of October the *Führer* left Vinnitsa and went to Germany to prepare his Party speeches to be given in Munich during the second week in November.[22] There, as has already been described, he was to be presented with a succession of crises. Rommel was in full flight from Egypt and on 8 November news reached him of the Anglo-American landings in Morocco and Algeria. Immediate counter action was necessary, firstly to carry out an armed occupation of Vichy France and secondly to build a bridgehead in Tunisia. Meanwhile, Stalingrad and the Eastern Front was left to get on as best it might. When the Soviet offensive was launched, the *Führer* was in Bavaria, and no counter action could be taken without his prior agreement. On 17 November he sent a personal teleprint message to be passed on verbally to all regimental commanders in Stalingrad, telling them that he knew of their low strength but that the position of the Russian was much worse. He expected, therefore, that all commanders would push home their attacks with the greatest of vigour.[23]

On the morning of 19 November Vatutin's South-West and Rokossovsky's Don Fronts, which were estimated by the Germans to have a strength of about forty infantry divisions, opened the offensive on Dumitrescu's 3 Rumanian Army.[24] After heavy artillery preparation, the fire lifted just before 9 a.m.

[20] Zeitzler in Westphal, *The Fatal Decisions*, pp. 128–9.
[21] Von Manstein, *Lost Victories*, pp. 267–71.
[22] The German High Command moved from Vinnitsa back to East Prussia at this time.
[23] *Kriegstagebuch des OKW*, Vol. 2, p. 1307.
[24] The actual strengths were said to be:

South-West Front	18 rifle divisions
	3 tank corps
	2 cavalry corps
	2 tank brigades
Don Front	24 rifle divisions
	1 tank corps
	6 tank brigades
Stalingrad Front	24 rifle divisions
	17 rifle brigades
	1 mechanized corps
	1 tank corps
	7 tank brigades
	1 cavalry corps

Rokossovsky, *Velikaya Pobeda na Volge*, pp. 254–6.

and the infantry began their advance supported by tanks across the hard frozen ground.

Vatutin's South-West Front was to play the principal part in the offensive and the main thrust was to be made by Lelyushenko's 1 Guards Army and Romanenko's 5 Tank Army from the Serafimovich bridgehead. A secondary thrust was to be launched by Chistyakov's 21 Army from the area of the Kletskaya bridgehead about thirty or forty miles to the east, both the main and secondary thrusts of South-West Front being directed towards the Kalach bridge on the Don, which was about a hundred miles from the Soviet start line and about fifty miles due west of Stalingrad. A third subsidiary attack was to be made by Batov's 65 Army on the right wing of Rokossovsky's Don Front, south-eastwards, with the object of isolating the Rumanians from 11 German Corps and cutting off the enemy in the little Don bend.

Dumitrescu's 3 Rumanian Army, attacked by overwhelming strength, began to break up, although many encircled formations continued to fight with great determination. The Soviet armoured thrusts, supported by infantry riding on the tanks, made rapid progress into the rear areas. Army Group B, wrongly believing that the main Soviet attack was being made by Chistyakov's 21 and Batov's 65 Armies from the area of Kletskaya, tried to seal the gap by using part of 6 Army's mobile reserve, a detachment of 14 Panzer Division, against the breakthrough. Permission had been reluctantly given by the *Führer* for Heim's 48 Panzer Corps to be committed to battle, and this, too, was ordered to march north-east in the direction of Kletskaya; but before its attack could be delivered, it was turned away again to the north-west to deal with the more serious thrust by Romanenko's 5 Soviet Tank Army. 48 Panzer Corps ran headlong into 1 Tank Corps of Romanenko's Army on 20 November and after some heavy fighting around Ust Medveditski was swept back, the Rumanian armoured division becoming separated from the panzer corps. The corps was then ordered to retire, but this order was countered by another from the *Führer* directing it north-west to relieve some encircled Rumanian troops under General Lascar near Raspopinskaya.[25] It then ran into more Soviet tanks and became bogged down in the fighting.

On the very first day of the Soviet offensive Army Group B, recognizing the weight of the enemy attacks, had ordered Paulus to break off the engagement in Stalingrad and prepare to turn some of his mobile formations back to meet the threat on his left rear. This order was shortly to be followed by second thoughts as to whether the whole of 6 Army should be withdrawn out of Stalingrad to the west. Hitler, who was directing this battle by telephone from his own faraway Bavarian Berghof home at Berchtesgaden, was angered by the proposal to withdraw 6 Army and told everyone to keep his nerve and

[25] Hitler came under pressure from Antonescu for the German failure to relieve the Lascar Group, and Antonescu and the *Führer* were to make telegraphic proposals and counter proposals between Berlin and Bucharest as to the tactical employment of 22 Panzer Division.

maintain his position until 48 Panzer Corps, on which he apparently pinned great hopes, had fulfilled its task.[26]

Paulus had three panzer divisions, 14, 16 and 24, under his own command, none of which, however, had a fighting strength of more than sixty tanks, and these divisions were turned round and moved westwards across the Don in an effort to hold back the Soviet 5 Tank Army. Hube's 14 Panzer Corps Headquarters was to follow and take command. These panzer formations had been pulled out, some from the Stalingrad area, on the night of 19 November, but the withdrawal was carried out piecemeal and there was great difficulty in finding the fuel to move them. Refuelling in itself was a time consuming process and so the tanks arrived on the west bank of the Don in scattered, incomplete and disorganized sub-units, a large part of the fighting strength remaining in Stalingrad, or still making the approach march to the Don. Part of 14 Panzer Division had already been committed in its luckless thrust towards Kletskaya, when detachments of 24 Panzer Division, crossing the Don by the Kalach bridge, moved towards Businovka to try to join up with it. This they were unable to do. Their own strength was eventually made up to two weak panzer battalions, jointly commanded by a lieutenant-colonel, together with some armoured cars, an artillery detachment, and some anti-tank and anti-aircraft guns. Of infantrymen there were none, as they had been left behind, and to fill this need divisional staffs set to work rounding up any man carrying a weapon from the administrative installations which abounded in the area. A collection of dismounted vehicle drivers, clerks and baggage men could, however, hardly be a substitute for the panzer grenadier battalions.

Early on the morning of 21 November the troops of Romanenko's 5 Tank Army came over the horizon in great columns of tanks, motorized infantry and cavalry. A defended outpost in the tiny hamlet at Mayarov, held by a German field bakery company, was speedily overrun and 24 Panzer Division found itself in battle, its composite tank battalion going forward into an attack. This had some success, in that it caused heavy casualties to Red Army cavalry and destroyed numbers of enemy tanks, but the issue was never in doubt since without infantry the German tanks could not hold their ground, and without a replenishment of vehicle fuels they could not keep moving. Great numbers of the Red Army troops swept on round the flanks, obviously making for the Kalach bridge, and the German tank crews noted with some surprise the practised way in which the Soviet motorized infantry supported their own tanks. This had never happened before in the course of the war. During the five days of fighting this element of 24 Panzer Division, lacking in ammunition and vehicle fuel and already on half rations, as against its own quite heavy loss of 150 men dead and wounded claimed to have destroyed only forty enemy tanks and about 400 cavalry.[27] On 22 November 5 Tank Army had already reached the Liska River about sixty miles from its starting

---

[26] Zeitzler in Westphal, *The Fatal Decisions*, p. 129.
[27] Von Senger und Etterlin, *Die 24. Panzer-Division*, pp. 126–32.

point and was not twenty-five miles from Kalach and that same night a motorized detachment moved from Ostrov to Kalach and seized the German bridge over the Don by a *coup de main*, the detachment commander, a Lieutenant-Colonel Filippov, subsequently being made a Hero of the Soviet Union for his exploit.[28] Hube's 14 Panzer Corps eventually fell back east of the Don using the Luchensky bridge near Peskovatka, although the Don had in fact frozen over by this time.

Meanwhile to the south of Stalingrad the Stalingrad Front had stood by to attack 6 Rumanian Corps on the morning of 20 November. The Red Army system of command and control was very different from that in use in western armies, and instead of commanding the attack by map, radio and liaison officers, all higher commanders, even the front commander himself, would establish battle command posts on prominent ground within sight of the enemy. This meant that in the sectors selected for the main attack within one or two thousand yards of the forward defended localities, regimental, divisional, army and front commanders would be watching the progress of the battle, each commander being accompanied by his personal staff, signallers, orderlies and clerks, and his artillery commander and the commanders of his main arms.[29] The front commander would in addition have a telephonic or short wave radio telephonic rear link to Moscow and Stalin.

It was in such a command post on a hill about 300 feet above the level of the Volga in 57 Army's sector looking out over the barren steppe that Eremenko awaited the 8 a.m. attack. At 7.30 a.m. the heavy mists were so thick that H hour had to be postponed for an hour. An hour later visibility was still less than 200 yards, and there was nothing for it but to put the attack back yet another hour. Meanwhile infantrymen and gunners with weapons loaded lay waiting in the bitter cold in silence; but not so the General Staff officers of the High Command in Moscow, who became increasingly importunate in wanting to know the cause for the delay. At 9.20 a.m. the mists began to lift and the order was given for the artillery to open fire at 10 a.m.

The artillery fire plan and the signals for the start of the offensive were typically Soviet and had been kept purposely very simple and understandable even to the soldier of the meanest intelligence. At 10 a.m. a great salvo of *Katyusha* rockets which could be seen and heard by all would signal the start of the artillery preparatory bombardment. The end of the bombardment was to be marked by a second salvo of rockets, after which infantry and tanks would go into the attack. This, thought Eremenko, would be clear to all. At 10 a.m. the first rocket salvo was fired, when, to Eremenko's horror, he heard a loud hurrah and realised that Colonel Grigorevich Ruskikh had not understood his orders at all, for before his eyes 143 Marine Infantry Brigade

[28] *Istoriya*, Vol. 3, p. 33.
[29] The composition of the commander's tactical group is common to most armies of the world. Some armies, rightly or wrongly, consider it unwise for the higher commander to become involved in the minor detail of the tactical battle.

was clambering out of its weapon pits and streaming away towards the Rumanian trenches. If Eremenko is to be believed, he was able immediately to cancel the artillery bombardment and send in 13 Mechanized Corps after the intrepid Ruskikh. This in itself would appear to indicate a much improved state of Red Army training and communications.[30]

To the south, Trufanov's 51 Army had been untroubled by fog and had attacked 1 and 18 Rumanian Divisions towards Plodovitoye some ninety minutes before. The left wing of Shumilov's 64 Army was not due to attack until midday, when sufficient artillery could be switched to its support. 6 Rumanian Corps had, however, already been broken and, as the Soviet account said, it retreated everywhere as if leaderless. 4 and 13 Mechanized Corps continued to advance rapidly north-westwards in the direction of Kalach, while 51 Army and 4 Cavalry Corps moved south-west towards the Aksai and the lower Don. According to the testimony of a German officer who was an eye witness, the Soviet advance was virtually unopposed. Panic soon spread to the rear areas. Many Rumanian officers deserted their men and made off in motor vehicles, some Rumanian troops took to looting, others threw away their weapons and driving great herds of cattle before them made off across the steppe. Defended localities which had been prepared and stocked in the depth of the position were never used, and only the Rumanian cavalry retained its discipline and showed any fight at all. In the rear areas the Germans, too, came in for some criticism, particularly the civilian supply and ordnance officials. Winter clothing stores were destroyed but weapon stores were left untouched, fuel dumps were set on fire, while vehicles were abandoned nearby for lack of petrol; lorries raced off northwards loaded with personal effects, with officials clinging to the running boards. Soviet troops meanwhile marched steadily along the roads, protected by advanced guards which met with no opposition until, our witness says, they were checked near Marinovka by a field ambulance company fighting for dear life and those of its patients.[31] On 21 November, in this most unpromising situation, the command of 6 and 7 Rumanian Corps was assumed, most unwillingly, by Constantinescu's 4 Rumanian Army.

On 23 November Volsky's 4 Mechanized Corps, the spearhead of the Stalingrad Front, joined with 5 Tank Army near Sovetski on the main railway track running west from Stalingrad, about twelve miles south-east of Kalach, so cutting all land communication of 6 Army and part of 4 Panzer Army, the whole of the encirclement operation having taken less than four days. Only in the north of Rokossovsky's Don Front was progress slow where Batov's 65 Army was opposed by the German troops of Strecker's 11 Corps. Further

---

[30] Eremenko, *Stalingrad*, pp. 347–50. The front and army artillery commanders were by Eremenko's side, and in such a situation much telephone line must have been laid. Even so arms co-ordination was obviously far more efficient than it had been a year before.

[31] Von Senger und Etterlin, *Die 24. Panzer-Division*, pp. 134–6. See also Eremenko, *Stalingrad*, p. 354.

to the west opposite the former Serafimovich bridgehead, where General Lascar and part of 4 and 5 Rumanian Corps were still surrounded, the Rumanians were already surrendering in large numbers. At Hitler's insistence and against the wishes of Army Group B, 48 Panzer Corps had been committed to battle again, this time without the Rumanian armoured division. The attack was unsuccessful and the corps was itself cut off, but on the instructions of Army Group B it broke out of the encirclement and moved to the west of the Chir. Hitler then ordered the arrest of its commander, Lieutenant-General Heim, a former chief of staff to Paulus and Commander of 14 Panzer Division, who was then dismissed in disgrace and flung into prison.[32]

In the Don bend on the line of the Chir, von Weichs, the Commander-in-Chief of Army Group B, was trying to form a reserve to bar any Soviet move to the west. At that time the only troops available were 48 Panzer Corps, consisting of the very weak 22 Panzer Division, and a hastily formed grouping under Hollidt, the Commander of 17 Corps. This was made up of 298 German Infantry Division, the remnants of the retreating divisions of 3 Rumanian Army and a further three intact Rumanian divisions, to which later was to be added 62 German Infantry Division.

On 19 and 20 November the *Führer* Headquarters was in disarray. Hitler himself was nervous and uncertain and did not appear to know what to do. Zeitzler and the OKH came up with no clear proposals. The only logical suggestion, that put forward by Jodl, proposing that the whole battle should be left to von Weichs, was overruled.[33]

At the time of the Soviet breakthrough, Paulus's 6 Army Headquarters was at Golubinskaya on the Don, not far from Kalach, and at midday on 21 November it was obliged to remove itself hurriedly to the south, to an alternative site near the Don bridge of Verkhnaya Chirskaya at the mouth of the Chir. That evening a radio message was received from the *Führer* ordering 6 Army to prepare itself for all round defence and instructing Paulus and his headquarters to get back into the Stalingrad area.[34] Hoth's 4 Panzer Army Headquarters moved back to the Chir on 22 November and Jaenecke's 4 German Corps, still in Stalingrad, passed under command of 6 Army. Hoth himself apparently had little information on the location or condition of the Rumanian troops. Paulus, having seen Hoth, left by air for Gumrak airfield, the site of his new headquarters, on the afternoon of 22 November, and that same evening sent a signal to von Weichs in which he gave warning that the ammunition and vehicle fuel supply position was acute and that 6 Army had rations

[32] Heim's corps was given a succession of contradictory orders. Von Weichs asked the *Führer* for freedom of action on 19 November and this was at first given, then withdrawn. Thereafter Hitler refused Heim freedom to use his judgement and initiative. Compare the Engel diary used by Jacobsen, *Kriegstagebuch des OKW*, Vol. 2, p. 83 and footnote.

[33] *Ibid*, p. 83.

[34] Zeitzler said that the message was sent on the night of 22 November. Presumably he meant 21 November. Greiner, *Die Oberste Wehrmachtführung*, p. 423; *Kriegstagebuch des OKW*, Vol. 2, pp. 83 and 999.

for only six days. He proposed, subject to sufficient supplies being flown in to Stalingrad, to attempt to hold the area between the Volga and Don, but if he could not stabilize the position to the south in the gap left by the Rumanian troops, he asked for freedom to use his own judgement and break out to the south-west.[35]

It has been said that Army Group B failed at first to appreciate the calamity threatening 6 Army, but there can be no doubt that the true situation was fully understood on 23 November when von Weichs sent a signal to Rastenburg, stating that it was not possible to supply a tenth of 6 Army's requirements by air. Since it was unlikely that a relief operation could be mounted before 10 December, and in view of 6 Army's supply situation, he wanted Paulus to break out immediately, although he recognized that such an operation would involve much sacrifice, particularly in equipment. This in any case would, he thought, be preferable to being starved out.[36] Paulus during that day had been in touch with his German corps, only one of which had come under sustained attack, and all the corps commanders were agreed that the situation called for an abandoning of the Stalingrad position and a break-out towards the south-west. That night Paulus, with the agreement of von Weichs, sent a personal radio message to Hitler asking for authority to use his own judgement and initiative, pointing out that only by a concentration and withdrawal of his troops south-westwards could 6 Army survive. Holdings of artillery and anti-tank ammunition were already largely exhausted, many batteries being without ammunition at all, and only immediate action could forestall the early destruction of 6 Army.[37] This message sent on the night of the encirclement was a clear statement of the situation and in no way made light of the gravity of the position.

Zeitzler has subsequently said that he strongly backed the arguments of Paulus and von Weichs and he did in fact do so, although whether he used as strong terms as he has since described is not known.[38] According to Zeitzler, Hitler agreed in principle on 23 November to a break-out and information to that effect was passed verbally to von Sodenstern, the Army Group B Chief of Staff.[39] Zeitzler placed much of the blame for his subsequent failure to convince Hitler on Keitel and Jodl who, he said, told the *Führer* what he wanted to hear, their advice being that Paulus should remain on the Volga ready for the new offensives next spring. That they gave this advice was probable. Yet the *Führer* had already committed himself publicly in bombastic terms to remaining on the Volga, and anything that Paulus, von Weichs or Zeitzler said was unlikely to have had the slightest effect on him.[40]

The fate of 6 Army rested on the decisions of Hitler and on the readiness

[35] Radio message at 1800 hours 22 November.
[36] Signal at 1845 hours 23 November.
[37] Signal at 2130 hours 23 November. *Akte AOK 6-75107/3.*
[38] Warlimont, *Inside Hitler's Headquarters*, p. 284.
[39] Doerr, *Der Feldzug nach Stalingrad*, p. 73. This is confirmed in the *Tagebuch*, von Weichs.
[40] Berlin speech at the Sportpalast 28 September and the Munich speech of 8 November in which Hitler staked his reputation on remaining on the Volga.

of his Generals to obey him. Paulus himself was not an outstandingly strong character nor a man of immediate responses. His relationship with his chief of staff, Arthur Schmidt, was good but not close, and of the two, Schmidt was by far the stronger character, as his behaviour in Soviet captivity was to prove. All the five corps commanders were against Hitler's decision to stay in Stalingrad, but of them four carried out to the letter their orders to remain. The fifth, von Seydlitz-Kurzbach, the Commander of 51 Corps, was an artillery officer, the former commander of 12 Infantry Division, who had come to Hitler's notice when he led the successful relief of the Demyansk encirclement earlier in the year. Von Seydlitz-Kurzbach had apparently been earmarked to replace Paulus as Commander of 6 Army. This officer had the uncanny ability of rapidly evaluating a situation and arriving at the logical and correct course of action. He was moreover a man of independent views, competent and resourceful, and probably somewhat impulsive. Within hours of the Soviet offensive von Seydlitz had come to the conclusion that 6 Army must quit Stalingrad without delay and counter-attack to the south-west, and he urged this course on Paulus with all the vehemence at his command. On 23 November, when 6 Army was still awaiting the *Führer*'s further orders, von Seydlitz informed Paulus that 51 Corps, which held the north-east corner against the Volga, had already begun to withdraw.[41] In such a situation Paulus was justified in ordering the removal, or indeed the arrest, of von Seydlitz, but he did nothing. The sequel, however, was bizarre. When on 23 November Hitler heard that a withdrawal had taken place, Paulus came under immediate suspicion of being about to disobey the *Führer*'s orders and, having great faith in the constancy of von Seydlitz and presumably believing that he was more trustworthy than Paulus, Hitler detached 51 Corps from 6 Army, making von Seydlitz personally responsible to him for the defence of the north-east of the pocket.[42] Thereafter Paulus had no responsibility for the 51 Corps sector (and later the 14 Panzer Corps sector taken over by von Seydlitz) on the banks of the Volga.

Whether or not there was ever any likelihood, as Zeitzler has claimed, that the *Führer* would order an evacuation of Stalingrad on 24 November, the matter was finally settled that morning by Göring who, buoyed by the successful precedent of the Demyansk airlift, guaranteed to the *Führer* that the *Luftwaffe* would keep the encircled troops supplied by air.[43] This assurance

[41] On 25 November von Seydlitz sent a long well-reasoned appreciation to Paulus, coming to the conclusion that if the OKH did not agree to a break-out Paulus owed it to the German people and to the 200,000 men of 6 Army to disobey. There was, said von Seydlitz, no other choice. *51 Korps Nr. 603/43 g. Kdos* of 25 November 1942.

[42] Compare Paulus's own post-war statement, Goerlitz, *Paulus and Stalingrad*, p. 225. Von Seydlitz-Kurzbach has explained to the author that he made the withdrawal on his own initiative purely for tactical reasons.

[43] On 24 November von Richthofen, the Commander of 4 Air Fleet, informed Army Group B, the OKH and the OKL that he did not agree with the *Luftwaffe* opinion, and continued to press for 6 Army to break out. Von Richthofen, *Tagebuch*, 24 November; also Warlimont, *Inside Hitler's Headquarters*, p. 284.

was eagerly seized upon, Stalingrad being declared a fortress, although none could be sure of next week's rations for the beleaguered troops, and 6 Army Headquarters, instead of the expected decision to break out, received a *Führer* order to remain on the Volga.[44] On 26 November at five minutes before midnight the *Führer* addressed a personal message to all soldiers of 6 German Army in which he ordered them to stand fast, assuring them that he would do all in his power to support them.[45]

Among the troops within the Stalingrad pocket there was neither despondency nor alarm. The regimental officers and troops had unshakable confidence and trust in the *Führer* and many had for long lived under threat of encirclement. They were, moreover, ignorant of facts known to Paulus and his staff.

Five corps headquarters, twenty German and two Rumanian divisions had been cut off and their strength on 25 November was believed at the time to be as high as 284,000 men, but this total undoubtedly included a number of Russian auxiliaries.[46] The force had with it about 1,800 guns, 10,000 motor vehicles and 8,000 horses and the daily maintenance requirements reckoned by the standards at that time of about 7 lbs a man a day amounted to about 850 tons, although this would not take into account the building up of stocks required either to break out or assist other troops in breaking in.[47] 6 Army asked originally for an airlift of 750 tons and this would have required 380 sorties a day. With the winter weather and short hours of daylight, and taking into account that the nearby Tatsinskaya airfield had only limited accommodation, it was unrealistic to assume that many aircraft would carry out more than one sortie. Since aircraft availability in the Russian winter was rarely above thirty-five per cent of strength, over a thousand Junker 52 aircraft, each with a two ton airlift, would have been needed for such an operation, assuming that the necessary airfields, ground maintenance and repair organization, packing and dispatch teams and supply and transport system had been available.[48] The success of the airlift depended also on the security of airspace and airfields, good flying weather and on an economical range between dispatching and receiving airfields. The whole of the *Luftwaffe* air transport force at that time amounted to 750 Junker 52 aircraft scattered all over Europe and Africa, and the necessary airfield and transport ground organization was lacking. Of the seven airfields inside the pocket, six were little more than airstrips and only one, Pitomnik, could be used at night. The air situation in the south-west had deteriorated, the Red Air Force being very active, and

[44] This actually laid down the geographical limits Paulus was to hold.

[45] *Akte AOK Ia. 75107/6 Funkspruch 1498* 2355 hours of 26 November 1942.

[46] In addition many troops escaped the encirclement. The figure was probably nearer 250,000.

[47] By a different method of calculation Doerr has estimated the maintenance requirement as 950 tons a day. *Der Feldzug nach Stalingrad*, p. 109.

[48] Morzik und Hümmelchen, *Die Deutschen Transportflieger im Zweiten Weltkrieg*, p. 155.

the Russian winter was about to close in. In the event, Goring was to press bombers into service as transport planes but far from delivering even a so-called minimum requirement of 500 tons, he was to average over the whole period a fly-in of just over ninety tons a day, the best single delivery day being 19 December when 290 tons were landed. Von Weichs was prophetically accurate when he had warned the *Führer* on 23 November that the *Luftwaffe* was not capable of delivering a tenth of 6 Army's actual requirements.

At this time the *Führer* had the highest opinion of von Manstein's capabilities, and 11 Army, which by then had the role of a fire brigade being rushed from one trouble spot to another, was ordered south from Vitebsk to Novocherkassk to deal with the threatening situation which had arisen. Headquarters 11 Army was reinforced by a staff element from the German-Rumanian organization at Rostov and was redesignated Army Group Don, the first time a German army group was to take a territorial designation, and on Hitler's order von Manstein assumed most of von Weichs's responsibilities, just as formerly he had been ordered to usurp those of von Küchler in the Leningrad area. Army Group Don's task was to halt the Soviet advance westwards and throw back the enemy to the positions which he had occupied before the offensive, this involving of course the relief of Stalingrad.

On 27 November Army Group Don took over its new command. 6 Army was part of the new army group, but von Manstein's command function over Paulu was not very real, since the OKH had installed its own liaison detachment at 6 Army Headquarters with direct radio communications to the Army High Command (OKH), which transmitted to Paulus the *Führer*'s wishes and at the same time kept Hitler informed of developments inside the pocket. Besides 6 Army, Army Group Don consisted of Group Hoth, Group Hollidt and 3 Rumanian Army. Group Hoth was based on Headquarters 4 Panzer Army, having under its command Kirchner's 57 Panzer Corps of 23 Panzer Division, removed from Army Group A, to which the up to strength 6 Panzer Division newly arrived from France was added. A third division, 17 Panzer Division, was allotted later. Hoth also commanded as part of Group Hoth 4 Rumanian Army of 6 and 7 Corps, the remnants of four infantry and two cavalry divisions. Group Hollidt consisted of Hollidt's own 17 Corps, part of five German infantry divisions and elements of five Rumanian divisions, to which was to be added von Knobelsdorff's 48 Panzer Corps Headquarters made up of 11 Panzer Division and an infantry and a *Luftwaffe* field division. These forces were not, however, all in position, since 6 Panzer Division had only started to arrive near Kotelnikovo at the end of November, and 11 and 17 Panzer Divisions were still *en route* from Army Group Centre. 17 and 23 Panzer Divisions were very much below establishment, each having a tank fighting strength of about thirty tanks, and 22 Panzer Division had received such a bad mauling from 5 Tank Army that it was withdrawn as no longer

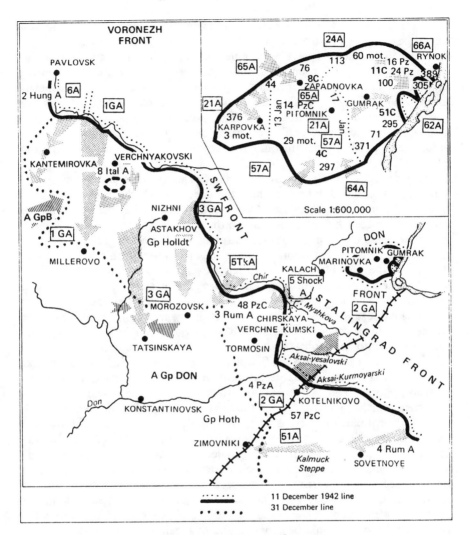

THE DESTRUCTION OF 6 ARMY
December 1942–February 1943

battleworthy.[49] The *Luftwaffe* divisions which were beginning to appear in the field for the first time had only recently been formed. Von Manstein's force, in spite of its grandiloquent designation, was not an army group since its only

[49] 17 Panzer Division had thirty tanks fit for battle and no armoured cars. Of the panzer grenadiers, one company in each battalion had to march behind the division for lack of vehicles. Von Senger und Etterlin, *Neither Fear nor Hope*, p. 64.

offensive element was the under-strength 57 and 48 Panzer Corps. It could not in fact be compared with a 1941 German army. Except for 6 Panzer Division, its German formations were very much under strength and contained in-experienced *Luftwaffe* ground staff, headquarters and supply troops fighting as infantry. The Rumanian troops were disorganized, and they and the newly formed *Luftwaffe* field divisions had no offensive capability. In all it was a makeshift, hastily scraped together force inadequate for its task and in the first week in December, until the arrival of the panzer formations, it was hardly in a position to withstand the Soviet probes across the Chir and Aksai.[50]

The nearest Axis position to the encircled German 6 Army was at Verkhnaya Chirskaya near the Don bridge where the Chir ran into the Don. There Axis troops held small bridgeheads north of the Chir and east of the Don, and the distance from the Chir to Marinovka on the south-west edge of the Stalingrad pocket was less than forty miles in a straight line.[51] Because there were indi-cations of heavy concentrations of Soviet troops to the north of the Chir and because of the possible need for bridging over both the Chir and the Don, von Manstein chose to disregard this direct and shortest approach, and selected the Kotelnikovo-Stalingrad railway east of the Don as the axis for his relief attack. This had to cross over eighty miles of enemy-held bare steppe, devoid of cover or shelter, with numerous small rivers running from east to west into the Don. These frozen streams were not barriers in them-selves, but they had cut into the flat plain deep ravines or *balki* with cliff-like sides, and these made formidable anti-tank obstacles. In selecting this long and unlikely approach von Manstein hoped to gain some surprise, and make rapid movement north-eastwards against the relatively weak 51 Soviet Army, which was rightly estimated to have a strength of not more than five divisions. Von Manstein appreciated that any further delay in attacking towards Stalingrad could only be to the advantage of the Soviet Command, which was tightening and strengthening the belt about the encircled pocket; and on 28 November he proposed that the German relief operation should begin without waiting for the concentration of all the forces which had been allocated to him. His immediate aim was to drive a land corridor to Stalingrad through which the beleaguered 6 Army could be supplied and so regain its mobility, after which he hoped that 6 Army could be withdrawn, and with this in view he had had a large number of vehicles loaded with fuel and supplies for delivery to 6 Army. The relief operation, known as *Winter Storm*, was to consist of a single armoured thrust to be made by Group Hoth, that is to say Kirchner's 57 Panzer

---

[50] Large numbers of extemporized battle groups had appeared taking their names from their commanders. Groups Fiebig and Stahel (8 Air Corps), Group Spang (supply troops), Group Stumpfeld (artillerymen). Returning leave personnel and German railway workers formed other battalions under Group Adam, a staff officer from 6 Army Headquarters.

[51] These bridgeheads were lost on 14 December and the Don bridge was blown by the Germans.

Corps with 6 and 23 Panzer Divisions, from Kotelnikovo north-eastwards along the landbridge between the Volga and Don. The task of Group Hollidt and 3 Rumanian Army, which were in the forward salient along the line of the Chir, was to keep up pressure against the enemy and support the advance by launching 48 Panzer Corps from the area of Verkhnaya Chirskaya against the flank and rear of the Soviet enemy deployed in front of 57 Panzer Corps. 4 Rumanian Army was to protect the exposed right flank of 57 Corps. Paulus, on the receipt of an order from von Manstein, was to use his armoured and mobile elements to attack south-westwards to meet 57 Panzer Corps. Since, however, Hitler was by then insisting that Paulus should at the same time hold on to the whole of his area in the north, no withdrawal by 6 Army could be permitted.[52]

Von Manstein's attack was to be mounted on 3 December but delays in assembling even the minimum force necessary were to lead to repeated postponements. At the beginning of December the enemy began to press heavily on 4 Rumanian Army sector on Hoth's right flank and on 3 Rumanian Army holding the bridgehead pocket between the Chir and Don, and the position could be stabilized only by using German troops required for the later offensive. Von Manstein tried to make good his losses by asking Hitler for 16 Motorized Division, an experienced and strong formation still out on the Kalmuck Steppe, and for the two other panzer formations in Army Group A in the Caucasus. Since von Kleist assured Hitler that this armour could only be given up at the cost of surrendering territory in the south, von Manstein's plea was made in vain.[53]

Moscow had every reason to be satisfied with the Red Army offensive. Before the end of November it claimed that 33,000 Rumanians had been taken prisoner, among them General Lascar. On 3 December the Soviet High Command confirmed a new plan, known as *Saturn*, for the thrust by Vatutin's South-West Front on Rostov, while the Don and Stalingrad Fronts were to destroy the encircled German troops in Stalingrad; but *Saturn* had to be postponed as there were not enough troops available for both tasks, and the presence of the Groups Hollidt and Hoth in the areas of Tormosin and Kotelnikovo was causing some anxiety in Moscow.[54] Rokossovsky's Don Front was given the task of containing the besieged 6 Army in Stalingrad, except for the southern perimeter, which continued to be held by Eremenko. Vatutin's South-West and Eremenko's Stalingrad Front, with the lower Don forming

[52] Von Manstein, *Lost Victories*, pp. 318–24.

[53] The Stalingrad crisis forced Hitler to give up the command of Army Group A (to von Kleist) on 21 November. 1 Panzer Army was taken over by von Mackensen, the former commander of 3 Panzer Corps. Eremenko attempts to magnify von Manstein's strength by claiming that 16 Motorized and the *SS Wiking* Divisions were part of Hoth's force at the beginning of December.

[54] *Istoriya*, Vol. 3, p. 43. According to Zhukov, who was still with Kalinin and West Fronts, Stalin consulted him frequently by telephone as to the next moves to be made. Zhukov *Vospominaniya i Razmyshleniya*, pp. 446–8.

the boundary between them, faced westwards to ward off the German relief force. Stalin and Vasilevsky were apparently certain that the relief thrust, when it came, would be made across the Chir from the area of Tormosin on the shortest and most direct route, and M. M. Popov's 5 Shock Army was allocated to Vatutin in order to support Romanenko's 5 Tank Army on the north bank of the Chir.[55] These two armies then started to probe across the Chir, establishing bridgehead after bridgehead, each bridgehead having to be eliminated by German troops and the precious reserve of armour held by 48 Panzer Corps. Bit by bit the panzer reserve became dissipated, and von Knobelsdorff was forced to move up the Chir away from the Don in his efforts to stop the Chir defences from disintegrating.[56]

To the south of the lower Don, Eremenko's Stalingrad Front faced both Paulus's 6 Army to the north-east and Group Hoth to the south-west. In the south-west, from the Don in front of Kotelnikovo, out on to the Kalmuch Steppe, the front was covered only by Trufanov's 51 Army of three infantry and two cavalry divisions, and it was on this sector that von Manstein's counter-offensive was going to fall. According to Eremenko's post-war account, he and the political member of his military council, Khrushchev, disagreed with Vasilevsky's assessment of the situation and were sure that the offensive would come from Kotelnikovo and not from Tormosin.[57] On 28 November Eremenko's 4 Cavalry Corps had attacked Kotelnikovo, and had suffered very heavy losses when, to its surprise, it was repulsed by the panzer grenadiers and tanks of 6 Panzer Division which were just arriving in the railway sidings.[58] This engagement, which lasted until 3 December, against a new and up to strength German formation just arrived from Brittany, confirmed Eremenko's suspicions that the German offensive was about to fall on him and this intelligence he immediately retailed by radio link to Stalin, asking urgently for reinforcements.[59] In consequence, even as early as the end of November, von Manstein may have already forfeited the benefit of surprise.

Von Manstein meanwhile chafed at the delays which caused the postponement of his relief offensive. A thaw in the Caucasus brought the wheeled movement of troops coming from Army Group A to a halt, and the low capacity of the railways prolonged the build-up still further. At last, on 12 December 57 Panzer Corps, using only two panzer divisions totalling 230 tanks of which most belonged to 6 Panzer Division, began its north-east attack towards Stalingrad and, well supported by 4 Air Corps which had arrived from the Caucasus, moved against Trufanov's 51 Army. On the first day there was some scattered fighting against two rifle divisions and cavalry dug-in to the north of Kotelnikovo but thereafter the advance was made against very little resistance, and

[55] Eremenko, *Stalingrad*, pp. 393–4.
[56] Compare von Mellenthin, *Panzer Battles*, pp. 175–84.
[57] Khrushchev had returned to the Stalingrad Front in November.
[58] Scheibert, *Nach Stalingrad 48 Kilometer*, p. 23.
[59] Eremenko, *Stalingrad*, pp. 395–7.

in some areas the mystified Germans found that the enemy had completely disappeared. Progress was slow, however, and not more than twelve miles were covered on any one day. The ground at first was frozen hard, and this made engineer work difficult at each of the ravine-like *balki*, and Scheibert of 11 Panzer Regiment has told how it took five hours to get his company of tanks over a single gully. During the day the warmth of the sun began to make the frozen surfaces of the southward facing slopes so slippery that even tanks fitted with calks could not climb them. Soon the tanks became separated from infantry and artillery, so that von Manstein's Army Group Don relief thrust was in reality being made by the tanks of 11 Panzer Regiment supported by an armoured assault gun brigade, with the thirty tanks of 23 Panzer Division covering the right flank. Since it was obviously impossible for supply vehicles to keep up with the tanks, fuel was carried on the tank and more than double the usual holding of ammunition was loaded, some long-barrelled 50 mm Mark III tanks each taking as much as 200 rounds for the main armament and 7,000 rounds of machine-gun ammunition. In this fashion the 230 tanks and assault guns struggled on alone.[60]

Eremenko had drawn up 51 Army between the Rivers Myshkova and Aksai-Yesalovski about forty miles to the south of the Stalingrad perimeter, and he started to withdraw troops from the Stalingrad area to reinforce his threatened south flank. 4 and 13 Mechanized Corps and two tank brigades were committed to the area, and on 14 December began a tank battle in the area of Verkhne-Kumski which lasted three days, 11 Panzer Regiment engaging, according to the German estimate, about 400 Soviet tanks.[61] The Germans fought without infantry or artillery, and in the close fighting it was difficult to distinguish friend from foe. Tanks began to run out, first of gun ammunition, and then of fuel, and one by one they were abandoned. The leading elements were about thirty miles from the beleaguered garrison but they could not break the defence. At the end of the engagement the tankmen had come to the conclusion that the German Mark III with the long-barrelled 50 mm, of which they had formerly been so proud (6 Panzer Division had up to shortly before been equipped with Czech tanks) was outclassed by the T34, but that the Russian failure to exploit his advantage was caused by poor optical equipment, inadequate training and a lack of all arms co-ordination.[62]

Eremenko had been pressing Stalin and Vasilevsky for the allocation of Malinovsky's 2 Guards Army from Rokossovsky's Don Front, and this was eventually released to him to support the hard-pressed Trufanov.[63] Meanwhile, however, Stalin and the *Stavka* had been engaged on the preparation

---

[60] Scheibert, *Nach Stalingrad 48 Kilometer*, pp. 59, 60, 109, 110 and 143.

[61] Eremenko says that the Soviet formations were very much under strength and infers that the tank strength was far less than the German estimate.

[62] Scheibert, *Nach Stalingrad 48 Kilometer*, pp. 79, 87 and 131.

[63] On 16 October Malinovsky had given up command of 66 Army to Zhadov and had reformed 2 Guards Army, then part of the High Command Reserve.

of a more effective counter stroke to von Manstein's relief efforts. The original *Saturn* operation, which involved a thrust through Millerovo on Rostov, was altered in favour of an offensive to be mounted both by Vatutin's South-West Front and the left flank of Golikov's Voronezh Front, attacking south-eastwards on Nizhni-Astakhov and Morozovsk, aimed at cutting across von Manstein's lines of communication and capturing the Tatsinskaya and Morozovsk airfields which were being used to supply Stalingrad. The forces had already been concentrated, and on 15 December the decision was taken in Moscow that this thrust would be the most effective method of affording Eremenko the relief he so urgently sought.[64]

Early in the morning of 16 December the left flank of the Voronezh Front and the right and centre of South-West Front attacked Gariboldi's 8 Italian Army, which was still on the banks of the Don between 2 Hungarian Army and Group Hollidt. After a ninety-minute artillery preparation the newly formed 1 Guards Army under V. I. Kuznetsov on the right flank of South-West Front, together with Kharitonov's 6 Army, the left flanking formation of the Voronezh Front, broke through on the left of 8 Italian Army and by 19 December had covered forty miles, reaching the main base of Kantemirovka, capturing munitions, supply trains and dumps. Further to the east, Lelyushenko's 3 Guards Army attacked the Italian right flank. Within a week of the start of the offensive, 8 Italian Army had abandoned its equipment and was in flight. The Soviet tank and motorized forces of 3 Guards, 1 Guards and 6 Armies, which included four tank and one mechanized corps, had reached the open steppe behind the Italians, there being no German mobile reserves to hinder them. About 15,000 Italians were encircled near Verchnyakovski. In five days 24 Tank Corps had advanced 150 miles and on Christmas Eve it carried out a surprise attack on Tatsinskaya, the main Junker 52 airfield for the Stalingrad airlift, fifty miles to the rear of Group Hollidt. This attack, made in thick fog when the airfield staff and crews were asleep, caused heavy German losses in men and aircraft. On the same day the Morozovsk air supply airfield, mainly used by Heinkel 111 aircraft, was threatened by 25 Tank and 1 Guards Mechanized Corps.[65]

Since his left flank was completely uncovered, Hollidt in desperation had tried to halt the Soviet armoured advance by deploying some Rumanian divisions, but these were soon swept away. On 20 December von Manstein sent a teleprinter message to Zeitzler warning him of the danger that both Army Groups A and Don might be cut off by a Soviet thrust on Rostov; but such was the organization of the German High Command that the message could not be delivered to Hitler that day as he was busy in conference with the Italians, and no action was taken until 22 December when a reply was

[64] Vatutin's offensive became known as *Little Saturn* to distinguish it from the earlier planned operation on Rostov, which was known as *Great Saturn*. Zhukov, *Vospominaniya i Razmyshleniya*, p. 447.

[65] Heinkel 111 bombers were being used as transports to augment the supply lift.

dispatched to Army Group Don allotting Group Hollidt a so-called defence line from which the Red Army had already expelled it days before.[66]

Meanwhile Hoth, as yet undeterred by the danger in his rear, was still probing forward towards Stalingrad, every man under his command being grimly aware of what was at stake. By 19 December 6 Panzer Division was on the line of the Myshkova about thirty miles from the beleaguered garrison, but for all that it had achieved it was hardly closer to Stalingrad than the Rumanian troops on the Chir. Yet a break-through was believed to be imminent and on the preceding day, 18 December, von Manstein had dispatched Major Eismann, his intelligence officer, to Gumrak to discuss with Paulus and his senior staff the break-out operation from Stalingrad. Proceedings were conducted as though the little assembly were a war council. Some members were in favour of a break-out. Schmidt, Paulus's chief of staff, on the other hand, according to von Manstein, had no doubts that a break-out was an acknowledgement of disaster and voiced the oft quoted words that 6 Army would still be in position at Easter, provided that it was kept better supplied.[67] Paulus himself appeared to waver, but finally decided that a break-out was an impossibility, and is said to have added, almost as an afterthought, that in any case it was forbidden by the *Führer*.[68] This was the crux of the matter. The weakness of 6 Army, as Schmidt said, was principally one of lack of mobility and supplies of all types, and unless it had been ordered to break out and abandon its positions and the bulk of its equipment, it was unlikely to have been able to give Hoth's Group much assistance. Only 100 tanks remained to Paulus and these were estimated to have fuel for only twelve to twenty miles.

If von Manstein had been hoping to influence Paulus in taking a decision to break out in defiance of the *Führer*'s orders, it would have been better to have made the journey himself instead of sending Eismann. But this does not appear to have been his intention. On 19 December von Manstein informed the *Führer* through Zeitzler that, as 57 Corps could not break in, it was essential that 6 Army should break out, at the same time giving up Stalingrad, sector by sector; that day he sent a directive to 6 Army instructing it to link up with 57 Panzer Corps, for the purpose of getting a supply convoy through into Stalingrad. Paulus was not ordered to give up any part of the Stalingrad enclave but was told that the development of the situation might make such a step necessary.[69] Since, however, Paulus had already made it clear to von Manstein on the teleprinter conversation that same day that if he was required to hold Stalingrad as well as thrust to the south-west towards 57 Panzer Corps, he could only use for the purpose a small tank force without infantry

[66] Von Manstein, *Lost Victories*, p. 344.

[67] Schmidt, who was released from Soviet captivity in 1955, has said, according to Goerlitz, that he was against breaking out in defiance of orders from the High Command, since this seemed to be an act of despair. These, he said, were the words he used at the meeting. *Paulus and Stalingrad*, pp. 254–5 and footnotes.

[68] Von Manstein, *Lost Victories*, p. 334.

[69] Directive *Ia 0369/42* to 6 Army, copy to 4 Panzer Army 1800 hours 19 December 1942.

support, and that with only a limited radius, the Army Group Don directive appeared superfluous.[70] Nor did Paulus consider the directive to be a binding order, because two days later Schulz, von Manstein's chief of staff, when talking to Schmidt on the teleprinter, told him that permission for the breakout and evacuation had not yet been received from the Army High Command (OKH).[71] The *Führer* meanwhile put off making a decision.

To meet the threat caused by the disintegration of 8 Italian Army, von Knobelsdorff's 48 Panzer Corps and one panzer division moved from the lower Chir out towards Group Hollidt's exposed left flank, while Hoth's thrust was weakened yet further by the removal of the strong 6 Panzer Division from 57 Panzer Corps to support the Rumanians on the Chir. Meanwhile the bitter fighting continued on the Myshkova River between Kirchner's 57 Panzer Corps, by then reduced to two skeleton panzer divisions, and Malinovsky's 2 Guards Army.[72] Malinovsky's troops, which consisted of two rifle corps, two mechanized corps and a tank corps had not yet arrived in strength, since tanks and vehicles had momentarily outrun their fuel supplies, and in consequence formations and units were thrown into battle piecemeal as they arrived. The weather was of the most wretched kind with thaw by day and heavy frosts by night, so that the bitterness of the conditions made a lasting impression even on the warmly clad Soviet troops. The wet and soggy felt boots were no longer any protection, the country was open and devoid of any cover from the night cold, and such poor accommodation which could be found was needed to shelter the Red Army wounded. Little vehicle fuel was to be had because of the difficulty of the going, and immobilized Soviet tanks were used as pill boxes.[73] The Germans suffered even more, for they too were out of fuel, since the thaw had undermined the foundations of the roads. They were repeatedly dive bombed by their own *Luftwaffe* and the area of the Myshkova River was swept by heavy Soviet artillery and multiple rocket fire. Soviet resistance was becoming perceptibly stronger day by day as Malinovsky's army arrived, and von Senger und Etterlin, the Commander of 17 Panzer Division, by then down to twenty-three tanks, was to note that his depleted panzer grenadier battalions were losing men steadily, the rate of casualties being such that he would run out of panzer grenadiers long before the division neared the 6 Army pocket. If the Russian had shown more flexibility and initiative he could easily have enveloped this puny panzer corps and von Senger und Etterlin said that he trembled at the prospect of another *Führer* order of last man last round, since this would have meant the complete destruction of his division. The men were exhausted and apathetic, the cold visibly sapping their strength. As usual the infantry were the main sufferers, unable to shelter from

[70] Teleprint conversation 1750 hours 19 December 1942 *Akte AOK 6 75107/2.*

[71] *Ibid.* Teleprint conversation 21 December 1942.

[72] 17 Panzer Division had belatedly joined the corps having been diverted elsewhere on Hitler's orders.

[73] Biryuzov, *Kogda Gremeli Pushki*, p. 108.

the cold and unable to sleep properly for fear, fear of fighting patrols and fear of being left behind asleep should there be a sudden withdrawal. The dead went unburied and the wounded often untended. The worst was the almost entire absence of any accommodation, for villages shown on the map did not exist.[74]

By 24 December, however, the Red Army forces had closed up. M.M. Popov's 5 Shock Army had concentrated west of the Don on the right of Malinovsky's 2 Guards Army and Trufanov's 51 Army was in some strength on the left, and with the re-establishing of the fuel supply the Soviet attack began in earnest. The first to give way were the Rumanians covering Hoth's right flank and in the next three days 57 Panzer Corps was driven back from the Myshkova, first to the Aksai-Yesalovski River, and then to Kotelnikovo, from whence Hoth had begun his offensive on 12 December. 17 Panzer Division strength had fallen to eight tanks and one anti-tank gun. On the broken 4 Rumanian Army flank Soviet tank and mechanized forces of 2 Guards and 51 Armies started to move rapidly westwards towards the lower Don. On 27 December 7 Tank Corps was fighting for Kotelnikovo airfield, while 13 Mechanized Corps and 3 Guards Mechanized Corps swung out from the south taking Sovetnoye and moving on the Zimovniki airfield. Army Group Don was about to be enveloped by double armoured thrusts of Eremenko's three mechanized and one tank corps in the south, and Vatutin's four tank and one mechanized corps in the north; the lines of communication of von Kleist's Army Group A through Rostov were threatened. Late at night on 28 December Hitler was forced to agree to the withdrawal of both Army Group Don and Army Group A to a general line Konstantinovsk-Salsk-Armavir, this new line being about 150 miles west from Stalingrad. Even then the *Führer* still maintained, at least to the outside world, that he intended to relieve Stalingrad.[75]

The reduction of Stalingrad was undertaken by seven armies, 62, 64 and 57 Armies of Eremenko's Stalingrad Front being transferred and added to the four armies of Rokossovsky's Don Front, the Stalingrad Front having been reformed on 1 January as the South Front.[76] No major attack was made against 6 Army until von Manstein's relieving force had been finally repulsed

---

[74] Senger und Etterlin, *Neither Fear nor Hope*, pp. 74–86.

[75] At the end of the year he ordered the SS Panzer Corps to move from France to Kharkov, preparatory to undertaking the relief of Stalingrad. At about this time Hitler or Zeitzler had Hube, the Commander of 14 Panzer Corps, flown out of the pocket in order to present personally to Hitler a picture of the conditions there. Hube apparently spoke out fearlessly and well and yet, according to von Manstein, he returned to Stalingrad fortified and impressed by the *Führer*'s attitude. Hube was later brought out of the pocket by Hitler's order.

[76] *Istoriya*, Vol. 3, p. 56. The decision to give the command to Rokossovsky was that of Stalin and the GKO. Zhukov said that he objected on the grounds of Eremenko's hurt feelings, an argument which understandably failed to make any impression on Stalin. Voronov was the High Command representative attached to the Don Front for this operation, which came to be known as *Ring*.

and Malinovsky's 2 Guards Army could transfer formations to the Don Front. On 8 January Rokossovsky offered the encircled Germans capitulation terms which they rejected. Two days later began the first attack aimed at rolling up the pocket from west to east. Supported by 16 Air Army, which had established an incomplete air superiority over the battle area, and the German language propaganda leaflets and broadcasts edited by Walther Ulbricht, who had been attached to the Political Department of the Don Front, the attack was made at 9 a.m. with a fast-moving rolling barrage and tanks. Despite the many German counter-attacks 65 Soviet Army gained five miles on the first day and by 13 January had taken Karpovka airfield, the most westerly of the seven airstrips by which 6 Army was being supplied. In the north and south of the pocket the other Soviet armies had made smaller gains. In this fierce fighting in bitter wind and snow storms, where the temperature was rarely above minus 30 degrees centigrade, the daily ration for the German troops had sunk to 200 grammes of horsemeat, seventy-five grammes of bread and twelve grammes of margarine or fat. The iron hard ground made digging impossible. The heavy losses to 44 and 76 Infantry and 29 Motorized Infantry Divisions on the first day of the attack were reported to the Army High Command (OKH), but the only reaction was a reply on 11 January laying down a line which 6 Army was not to give up without prior permission. A week later on 17 January the German pocket, which originally stretched forty miles from west to east and twenty miles from north to south, had been reduced to half its former size and a further five airstrips had been lost including Pitomnik, the principal airfield and the only one with night flying facilities. Only one airfield, at Gumrak, remained but as this was frequently out of use because of deep snow and the cratering of the surface by enemy bombing, air supply from this time onwards was continued by loads parachuted or free-dropped from aircraft, this method being relatively inefficient since it required heavy specialist equipment together with trained packers and dispatcher crews. During the dropping operation aircraft were very vulnerable and the delivery was slow and inaccurate, many supplies being scattered or falling to the Red Army. 6 Army was so disorganized and immobile at this time and its troops so weak and apathetic through cold and hunger that it lacked the will and the means to collect and redistribute many of the loads.

When Stalingrad had been under siege for more than eight weeks and had already lost its airfields, the procrastinating *Führer* resolved on a new and more determined effort to keep 6 Army supplied by air. The air-lift operation was removed from the incompetent Göring and placed in the hands of Field-Marshal Milch, an energetic *Luftwaffe* officer, who having been given plenipotentiary powers, arrived in Taganrog on 16 January with his staff.[77] Milch was later to say that if he had been called in earlier he could have increased

[77] *Kriegstagebuch des OKW*, Vol. 3, p. 42. Field-Marshal Milch, said to have been of Jewish origin, had entered the *Luftwaffe* from *Lufthansa*. At this time he was Inspector-General of the *Luftwaffe* and State Secretary for Air.

the rate of supply. In fact such improvements, even if possible, could only have been marginal and would not have prolonged the resistance of 6 Army. Nor was it true that additional aircraft would have improved the position unless these had new airfields and the necessary support organization. In the early days of the air-lift the large numbers of air transport formations arriving at Tatsinskaya choked the airfield organization.[78]

Rudenko's 16 Soviet Air Army, too, took its toll. The German Heinkel 111 bomber had good defensive armament which kept Soviet fighters respectful, but the Junker 52 was more vulnerable. At night German transports operated singly, and in low cloud and poor visibility they risked fighter interception and flew in pairs. In clear weather, however, they flew as squadrons with a fighter escort. Landing and take-off in the pocket were fraught with danger as the airfields were heavily and repeatedly bombed and in due course came under artillery and mortar fire. The airfield staff and labour force on the pocket airfields were so weakened by hunger that great delays occurred in such tasks as aircraft unloading and the filling of the bomb craters on the runways, and towards the end they could not even undertake the rolling down of the thick carpet of soft snow which was preventing aircraft from landing at Gumrak. The scenes on the airfields were particularly unnerving to the younger and more inexperienced aircrews, for the scent of fear was in the air and strict controls were needed to prevent malingerers and deserters from boarding planes. Great numbers of wounded had been collected at the airfields, for the majority of whom there could be no hope of evacuation. In all, the *Luftwaffe* lost 490 transport aircraft during the operation, of which 165 were Heinkel 111 bombers used as transports, and about 1,000 aircrew. Of this aircraft total some were destroyed on the ground, no fewer than seventy transport aircraft being lost when the Red Army took Tatsinskaya airfield.[79]

Because of the success of the Soviet counter-offensive the average flight distance between airfields had increased firstly from 125 miles to 200 miles and finally to nearly 300 miles. The longer the flight the more fuel the aircraft had to carry, with a corresponding reduction in available load capacity; and the longer the aircraft was in the air the less the number of flights which could be made and the greater the maintenance and repair time needed to keep it airworthy. The average daily delivery had fallen from 140 tons in mid December to sixty tons by mid January. As a result of Milch's efforts there was a slight recovery to about eighty tons a day, but this figure bore little relationship to 6 Army's requirements. The end could not be far off. Ammunition and food supplies were exhausted and, although 25,000 wounded had already been flown out, 12,000 wounded lay uncared-for in the bitter cold in the ruins and cellars. On 10 January or shortly thereafter Paulus, unable to feed prisoners of war, ordered them to be sent back to the Red Army; but this

[78] Morzik und Hümmelchen, *Die Deutschen Transportflieger im Zweiten Weltkrieg*, pp. 156–9.
[79] *Ibid*, pp. 161–4.

M

was apparently never done, either because they feared to go, or because they were returned by the encircling Soviet troops. On 17 January the Don Front is said to have sent a second demand to Paulus for a German capitulation, offering terms which it could not and would not keep, these including an offer to care for the German wounded and return all prisoners to their homeland after the war.

On 22 January Rokossovsky began the final phase of his attack and the remaining German defences began to fall apart. By then von Manstein was outside the range of the short wave radio telephone and teleprinter, but Paulus was still in radio communication with the Army High Command (OKH). On the day of Rokossovsky's attack Paulus sent a radio message to Zeitzler to be passed to Hitler, describing the position of the troops and asking how was he to command troops who had neither ammunition nor food.[80] Hitler declined the hint of capitulation and even as late as 24 January refused to allow 6 Army to break out westwards in small groups where, even if they did not succeed in joining Army Group Don, they would sow confusion behind the Soviet lines.

Meanwhile on the upper Don a new great Soviet counter-offensive had been mounted even more threatening than the earlier ones. On 13 January Golikov's Voronezh Front had attacked 2 Hungarian Army further to the north of 8 Italian Army and had swept away what remained of the ill-fated Army Group B. Since the New Year the German public fully appreciated the seriousness of the situation, and few held much hope that the garrison would be relieved. By the middle of January the hopelessness of the situation must have been clearly apparent to Hitler, who could pretend no longer that he had a trick up his sleeve, and the latest offensive against the Hungarians brought Army Group Don and Army Group A in even greater peril. Von Manstein was in favour of 6 Army capitulating, and he had a long argument with the *Führer* on the telephone urging a surrender.[81] Hitler insisted, however, that the fight could still be continued in pockets for some time to come maintaining, not without reason, that capitulation was futile since the Russians would not keep any agreement.

In the city of Stalingrad Chuikov's 62 Army, half encircled to the west by 6 German Army and still cut into two parts, tied down a number of German divisions. Zhadov's 66 and Shumilov's 64 Armies contained the pocket on the north and south, while the other four Soviet armies attacked from the west. On 26 January Chistyakov's 21 Army made contact with 62 Army and 6 German Army was in its turn split into a northern and southern pocket. Immediately before the end, when rations were no longer being issued to the German wounded, Hitler promoted Paulus from colonel-general to field-

---

[80] *Welche Befehle soll ich den Truppen geben, die keine Munition mehr haben?* Signal to Army Group Don and OKH for *Führer*. 1602 hours 22 January 1943, *Akte H. Gr Don 39694/9*.

[81] Von Manstein, *Lost Victories*, p. 360.

marshal on 31 January, apparently hoping that as no German field-marshal had been captured since the inception of Greater Germany in 1871, Paulus would continue to resist, if necessary cheating his would-be captors by suicide. The same day a detachment of 38 Soviet Motor Rifle Brigade entered the great store near Red Square, in the cellars of which were the headquarters of 6 Army, and Paulus and his staff were taken prisoner. Fighting in the southern pocket ceased. The northern group under Strecker, the Commander of 11 Corps, continued to resist until 2 February.

The Soviet High Command claimed the capture of 91,000 prisoners of whom twenty-four were Generals and 2,500 officers. Many of these were sick and wounded. It was said that 147,000 enemy dead were buried.[82] Both von Manstein and Paulus were later to insist that there were no more than 220,000 men there, and the German casualty figure accepted by the German High Command at the time was 200,000 left as dead and prisoners.[83] Moreover, it is very doubtful whether a check was ever made by the Soviet victors of the numbers of prisoners, let alone the German dead on the battlefield, and the Soviet accounts of the prisoners taken vary to a great degree. Zhilin for example, writing in 1956, correctly claims the destruction of twenty German and two Rumanian divisions but states that 130,000 prisoners were taken.[84] However that may be, there can be no doubt at all that about 200,000 German troops met their end inside Stalingrad. Of the 91,000 said to be prisoner of war only a few thousand were ever to return to Germany.

The surrender of Stalingrad was announced from Moscow in the early morning of 1 February but it was not broadcast from Berlin to the German people until two days later in a communiqué which described the end of 6 Army which, under the exemplary leadership of Field-Marshal Paulus, had been overcome by superior numbers of enemy. Three days national mourning were proclaimed for the loss. Hitler's private feelings, however, were very different, and he railed bitterly at Paulus and the General Officers who went into captivity with him, promising to court-martial them after the war. Paulus, he said, would be the last German officer to be promoted to field-marshal; Hitler could not forgive him, that he had lived when so many men had died. The *Führer*'s own responsibility for the disaster appears to have been unacknowledged and he put the blame on his Generals and on his allies.[85]

Within the Stalingrad pocket the German troops had endured terrible

[82] *Istoriya*, Vol. 3, p. 62.

[83] Compare for example, *Berechnungsunterlagen für Schaubild 'Zugänge und Abgänge des Ostheeres vom November 1942–Oktober 1943'*, Gen St d H Org Abt I Nr. 1/10388/43 geh. of 14 December 1943, shown in *Kriegstagebuch des OKW*, Vol. 3, p. 1482. Mueller-Hillebrand has calculated 6 Army German losses from 23 November to 2 February 1943 as 209,500. *Das Heer*, Vol 3, Chapter 12.

[84] Zhilin, *Die Wichtigsten Operationen des Grossen Vaterländischen Krieges*, p. 192.

[85] In fact other German officers did reach field-marshal rank later in the war. Heiber, *Hitlers Lagebesprechungen*, p. 120 *et seq.*; *Goebbels' Diary*, 9 March 1943, p. 220. On the other hand von Manstein says that Hitler accepted responsibility unreservedly in this instance. *Lost Victories*, p. 365.

conditions. When Pitomnik airfield had been taken the main munition and supply dumps had been lost, and panic had begun to spread among the defenders. At first a trickle and then a steady stream of troops had, without orders, left their positions and made their painful way eastwards towards Stalingrad. Many of them were wounded and suffering from severe frost-bite but they had nevertheless been rounded up and driven back to the weapon pits. The parachuted and free-dropped supplies had fallen wide, and many of the loads which dropped on the target had been plundered by German troops, in spite of the fact that they knew the death penalty awaited them for supply looting. At the end of January Headquarters 24 Panzer Division had fallen back on the Tractor Works, joining part of 389 Infantry Division and the Headquarters of Strecker's 11 Corps, and there, in the early hours of the morning of 2 February, the forward troops without orders began to give themselves up. By 9 a.m. the Russians had rounded up the prisoners. They allowed the divisional commander von Lenski to make a final address to his men after which all, the watching Red Army men excluded, had given three cheers for Germany. An unknown Soviet General then addressed the prisoners, praising their courage and promising them good treatment and food, and the right to retain all their private property. They would all, he said, be speedily repatriated after the war.

Then began the long hunger marches. Time and time again the columns were raided for personal belongings, sometimes by Red Army troops but more often by civilians. The prisoners were only lightly guarded but the many men who dropped out through sickness or fatigue were at the mercy of the marauding bands of armed civilians who roamed on the outskirts of the columns. None of those who dropped out was ever seen again. Eventually the columns were loaded on to trains and transported through Saratov, Orenburg and Engels to Tashkent, to the north of Afghanistan. At each stop the dead were unloaded from the cattle trucks and only fifty per cent of those who had been entrained arrived at the destination.[86]

The Red Army counter-offensive and the loss of 6 Army was the greatest defeat which the German Army had suffered up to that time and it had a noticeably dampening effect on the spirits of Germany's allies. The uncommitted nations also took note. Soviet accounts portray the Stalingrad battle as the turning point of the whole of the Second World War as if, by inference, the victory was a major cause of the final overthrow of Hitler's Germany. This it certainly was not. The loss of 6 Army cost Germany twenty divisions and over 200,000 men. In addition six German divisions were virtually destroyed outside the encirclement, the total German casualties, including wounded, amounting to perhaps another 100,000.[87] This was a very grievous

[86] Von Senger und Etterlin, 24. Panzer-Division, pp. 144–6.

[87] In addition to the four armies of their allies, the Germans lost twenty-six divisions and about 300,000 men. Soviet claims for this battle have exaggerated the Axis loss to one and a half million men. Compare Zhukov, Stalingradskaya Epopeya, p. 71; and Rokossovsky, Velikaya Pobeda na Volge, p. 491.

loss but it was fractional compared with the Soviet Union's losses in 1941 and it was a loss which was not going to decide the fate of a nation. Two Rumanian, an Italian and then a Hungarian army had been swept away and henceforth were to have insignificant fighting value; but Germany's future was not to be decided by her relatively weak allies. It is true of course that Stalingrad marked the turning point in the war in the east, in that it cleared the Caucasus and the Lower Volga of the enemy and started to force him back towards the German *Reich*. But seen against the world wide background of the war, Stalingrad represented a landmark along the road to victory over Germany, just as the Battle of Britain, the Greek resistance, the Yugo-Slav defiance, the battle before Moscow, the entry of the United States into the war, and Alamein had done before it. It was a titanic battle and a great victory to which Alamein could hardly be compared, but, like Alamein, far from being a cause of the German defeat in the Second World War, it was rather an effect of the heavy preponderance of Allied resources over those of the Axis powers. By 1942 the balance was heavily weighted against an over-extended Germany, and from then onwards this was to show itself in a series of German losses. Of these Stalingrad was the first, and within three months it was to be followed by another, when at Tunis in May a second Axis force was destroyed, a quarter of a million troops, nearly 100,000 of which were German, being taken in prisoners alone.[88]

The strategic planning and execution of both the *Uranus* and the *Saturn* offensives were of the highest order and demonstrated for the first time in the war the ability of the Soviet High Command and higher headquarters to command and control fast-moving massed tank and motorized formations. Yet the education and tactical ability of the lower field commanders, particularly those of divisions and regiments, was still poor and the training of the air and tank arms remained much inferior to that of the Germans. There was no doubt that the Red Army was learning, yet the real victors at Stalingrad were the front commanders and the whole of the High Command organization, Stalin, the GKO and the *Stavka* pool of General Officers.

The strength of the forces used for the *Uranus* offensive to encircle Stalingrad is given by Soviet sources as one million men. The Soviet figures must, however, be regarded with some reserve since there is a tendency both to exaggerate German and to understate Red Army strengths, in order to prove that the Soviet victory was due not to a preponderance of numbers but to the superiority of the communist system. On the other hand, there exists at the same time an opposite tendency to exaggerate Soviet strengths and production figures in order to vie with those of the United States. Although the total fit tank fighting strength for the three Soviet fronts before the battle has been quoted as only 900 tanks (a figure which was described as sixty per cent of all tanks on the Russo-German front) yet the full organizational tank strength

[88] Platonov's *Vtoraya Mirovaya Voina*, gives details of the Anglo-American victory but these are omitted from the later *Kratkaya Istoriya* and the *Istoriya*.

of the tank formations used at Stalingrad would have been nearer 1,800 tanks. Since the total Soviet production for 1942 is given as 24,700 tanks of all types, the figure of 900 may be an understatement of the true strength or alternatively the tank production may have been exaggerated.[89] The gun strength of the three fronts is said to have been 13,500 pieces, but of these the given artillery organization would account for about 9,000 barrels. Much of the remainder would, however, be made up by regimental and battalion infantry guns and mortars and anti-tank guns. No conclusions can be drawn from these Soviet figures.[90]

The reasons for the German defeat were numerous. The strategy of the *Führer* was over-ambitious and was based on inadequate resources and a wilful underestimate of enemy strength and potential.[91] He undertook the dual and concurrent operations to the Volga and Caucasus when there were barely sufficient troops available to mount one of them. So Hitler called on Rumania, Italy and Hungary to provide formations to fill the gap and did, what the previous year he had said he would never do, entrust the security of German troops to his allies.[92] Great war lord though he considered himself, he had not been able, so he confided to Goebbels, to overcome the problems of movement and supply.[93] In consequence German troops continued, as they had done right from the beginning of the Russo-German War, to live a precarious hand to mouth existence at the end of a long and uncertain supply line with little or no reserves. When 6 German Army was cut off on 23 November it held virtually no maintenance stocks and both Army Group A and Army Group Don were constantly brought to a standstill for lack of vehicle fuel. The *Führer*'s insistence on the capture of the ruins of Stalingrad rather than blocking the Volga elsewhere, played into Soviet hands, in that the Germans engaged in a very costly battle of attrition for which the Red Army was particularly suited by virtue of the ruthless mentality of its commanders and the obstinacy of its troops. Whereas generally Soviet troops were greatly outclassed by the German in the open, in trench warfare and in fighting in built-up areas they became much more formidable. By Hitler's folly the main fight-

[89] *Ibid*, Vol. 3, p. 20. Rokossovsky, *Velikaya Pobeda na Volge*, p. 254; and Samsonov, *Stalingradskaya Bitva*, p. 367 are agreed that the fit tank fighting strength stood at 900 for the Don, South-West and Stalingrad Fronts and allowance must obviously be made for a considerable number of tanks defective or under repair. Zhukov on the other hand produces some very different figures when he gives the total Red Army field army strength of tanks and SUs at the beginning of November as 6,000, to which must be added the tanks in the High Command Reserve, estimated at about 1,500. Zhukov, *Vospominaniya i Razmyshleniya*, p. 430. Notwithstanding these figures even he still maintains that only 900 tanks took part in the battle.

[90] *Istoriya*, Vol. 3, pp. 20 and 171 footnote 1.

[91] Eremenko stated the position correctly when he said that 'the greatest error of the German High Command was to underestimate the power of the Soviet nation and its armed forces, at the same time overestimating its own ability'. Eremenko, *Stalingrad*, p. 336.

[92] Compare Hitler's address to his Generals on 30 March 1941 as recorded in Halder's diary. 'Have no illusions about our allies. The fate of German formations is never to depend on the reliability of the Rumanian.'

[93] *Goebbels' Diary*, 8 May 1943, p. 281.

ing element of Army Group B was pinned in the area of Stalingrad for months on end, like a man with his head in a noose, this giving Moscow ample time to complete plans and preparations for its destruction. Inside Stalingrad all German divisions lost much of their fighting power and mobility and many burned themselves out.

Since the defeat of Germany, numbers of German commanders have blamed Hitler for the succession of defeats which followed his dismissal of von Brauchitsch. The censure is entirely justified. Yet it must be remembered that in 1942 many of these Generals, far from raising objections to Hitler's war leadership, firmly believed in his genius, and were equally guilty of underrating Germany's enemies. On his side, however, Hitler showed an almost pathological dislike and contempt for German Army leaders and the German General Staff.[94]

Through his insistence that Paulus should remain on the Volga, the blame for the German defeat rested primarily on the *Führer*. Of the men around him, Keitel was of no consequence, and Jodl was still very much cowed since the List affair. In any case, neither had any real responsibility for the Russian theatre. The tired Halder had long since departed. Zeitzler, his successor, was without any influence on Hitler or on the army group commanders, and his role at this stage was negative. After Hitler, Göring bore the main responsibility for the disaster because of his assurance that he could keep the pocket supplied by air, an assurance which his own *Luftwaffe* commanders and staff denied immediately he had given it. Von Manstein's part in the tragedy was only minor since he was appointed too late to do too much with too little, and he never exercised real command over Paulus. The extent of von Manstein's responsibility is centred only on the question as to whether he should have given Paulus a categorical order to abandon his positions and break out. In the light of the subsequent events it can be argued that he should have done so, although it is equally certain that the *Führer* would speedily have countermanded such an order.

Von Manstein chose the long approach march from Kotelnikovo to Stalingrad instead of using the Don bridge near the mouth of the Chir which was still in German hands up to 16 December and which was only forty miles from Stalingrad, because he hoped to surprise the Soviet defence, for this reason choosing the axis which was relatively lightly defended by Eremenko's forces. Stalin and Vasilevsky could not bring themselves to believe that the Germans would choose such an unlikely route, and in the event 57 Panzer Corps was beaten, not so much by Trufanov's 51 Army but by the distance, the terrain and the weather. In the circumstances it might have been preferable to have concentrated both 57 and 48 Panzer Corps and attacked across the lower Chir and the Don, the shortest way into Stalingrad, in spite of the Red Army strength on the opposite bank. As it was, both panzer corps were defeated in isolation.

[94] By 1943 this had grown in such measure that even Goebbels was obliged to reflect that the *Führer* was being prejudiced and unfair. *Ibid*, pp. 220–1 and 289.

The role played by Paulus was that destined for him. In some respects Paulus had military qualities and characteristics similar to those of Jodl, whom he was earmarked to replace. He was first and foremost a staff planner, and although not without command ability he was almost entirely without command experience. On the other hand, he was of a much gentler mould than his fellows, a slow thinker and lacking in decisiveness. He can be criticized for not turning his troops about on 23 November or shortly afterwards, and deliberately and without reference to Hitler, fighting his way out. But it is unthinkable that Paulus should have been the man to have reacted so quickly or to have wilfully disobeyed Hitler's intention to have remained on the Volga. Hitler did not select men of independent views for high command nor was Paulus a Hoepner, who did what he wanted and said what he thought, to his own undoing. If Paulus had known that 6 Army was going to be destroyed by remaining on the Volga, he might have disobeyed Hitler, and yet as against this, even as late as 24 January, when the pocket was breaking up before his eyes, when all hope of relief had gone and when he knew that the end was only a few days off, he still asked Hitler's permission for organized groups to fight their way back, and failed to act when his request was unanswered.[95] It must be remembered that on 23 November the German Army had still not suffered a major defeat and Paulus had before him the examples of Hitler's arbitrary treatment of, amongst others, von Sponeck and Heim.

The final point at doubt remains as to whether 6 Army was strong enough on 23 November or again on 19 December, to have fought its way out of the encirclement. This must remain a matter of conjecture. The corps were, however, largely intact and it is probable that in the last week in November, at the cost of the loss of the greater part of its equipment, 6 Army could have done so, since the Soviet forces were disorganized and were not in any great strength.[96] By 19 December the position had changed considerably for the worse, since a large number of the horses remaining to 6 Army had been slaughtered and the German supply position had deteriorated. Yet, as is known, Eremenko was in difficulties at this time and the Soviet tank and motorized troops were out of fuel and supplies. Malinovsky's 2 Guards Army was not due to begin arriving in the area until 19 December.[97] If Eremenko had been attacked in the rear by 6 Army on 19 December when a little more than thirty miles separated Paulus from Hoth's relieving corps, it is possible that, with the prospect of freedom acting as a spur, considerable numbers of men might have got through.

[95] Von Manstein, *Lost Victories*, pp. 358–9; also Paulus's reply to the *Führer* on 23 January when Hitler had forbidden capitulation, *Kriegstagebuch des OKW*, Vol. 3, p. 66.

[96] Von Manstein has given the opinion that by 23 November such action was probably too late. In view of the weather he may have been right, although this opinion is questionable. Later in the war larger German formations (e.g. Hube's 1 Panzer Army) were to fight their way to safety over greater distances in seemingly worse situations by becoming moving pockets.

[97] Eremenko, *Stalingrad*, p. 404.

CHAPTER TWENTY-ONE

German Withdrawal into the Ukraine

The third stage of the great counter-offensive which culminated in the destruction of 6 German Army and the evacuation of the Caucasus was the offensive made by Golikov's Voronezh Front on von Salmuth's 2 German Army and Jany's 2 Hungarian Army. Kharkov and the Donets Basin were the immediate objectives. The assault frontage stretched over 300 miles from Livny to Kantemirovka, and Golikov was to be assisted by the flanking formations of Reiter's Bryansk Front to the north and Vatutin's South-West Front to the south.[1] The main blows were to be struck by Moskalenko's 40 Army together with 18 Independent Rifle Corps against the Hungarians on the right, and Rybalko's 3 Tank Army against the Italians on the left, in order to encircle 2 Hungarian Army by a double envelopment, the two pincers meeting about fifty miles to the rear near the town of Alexeievka. The Soviet forces would then turn outwards and roll up 2 German Army to the north and Gariboldi's 8 Italian Army to the south, by attacking their exposed flanks in conjunction with Chibisov's 38 and Chernyakhovsky's 60 Armies of the Voronezh Front, Pukhov's 13 Army of Bryansk Front and Kharitonov's 6 Army of South-West Front. In this main assault sector 2 German Army had two corps of seven divisions, the Hungarian Army consisting of only nine brigades or light divisions, one armoured division and one German infantry division.[2] The Italian Alpine Corps had three divisions. The Axis forces were outnumbered by the attackers in both tanks and guns, the Voronezh Front alone consisting of nineteen rifle divisions and numerous tank and cavalry formations.[3]

Three weeks were allowed to Golikov for reconnaissance and preparation, and this reconnaissance was carried out from the air and from a series of

---

[1] The military council of the Voronezh Front consisted of Golikov, F. F. Kuznetsov and M. I. Kazakov (chief of staff); that of the Bryansk Front, Reiter, Susaikov and Sandalov.

[2] *OKH Kriegsgliederung* of 1 January 1943. 2 German Army had in all eleven German infantry divisions. The two German corps were 8 and 13 Corps commanded by Heitz and Straube respectively. Soviet estimates put the Axis forces in the Voronezh bend as twelve divisions. Morozov, *Westlich von Woronesh*, p. 89.

[3] Voronezh Front was said to have had fifteen rifle divisions and six rifle brigades, two tank corps and eight tank brigades. *Istoriya*, Vol. 3, p. 102.

observation and command posts constructed close to the Hungarian positions. Reconnaissance by probing attacks and fighting patrols was discouraged in order that the enemy should not be alerted. It soon became apparent that the Hungarian defences consisted of two defensive zones, one about four miles deep and a second about ten to twelve miles to the rear. Because of the passivity of the Hungarians, the Red Army was able to withdraw almost entirely from all secondary sectors, this permitting the concentration of about 200 guns and mortars to the mile on each of the main assault frontages. Guns of all calibres were sited as direct fire weapons, ready to destroy the many identified strong points. The lack of cover on the open steppe made it necessary to bring up troops over the last hundred miles to the front only by night, and Soviet historians claim that these security measures were effective, since the Hungarians believed that the Soviet enemy had expended his strength and that for this reason an attack was unlikely.[4] On 7 January, only seven days before the offensive was due to be launched, Kovacs, the Chief of Staff of 2 Hungarian Army, is said to have sent a report to Budapest in which he excluded the possibility of any Soviet attack on his sector. In fact an attack in this sector was not unexpected by the Germans.[5]

Although the main attack was not due until 14 January, a preliminary reconnaissance probe made in some strength on 12 January threw the enemy into such disarray that Soviet troops were able to make a three-mile deep indentation into the Hungarian defences. The main offensive was then launched without further delay, tank mine rollers being used for the first time to breach the defender's minefields. Soviet accounts claim that the preparatory bombardment and the use of direct fire guns was so effective that the enemy artillery observation posts were knocked out in the first few minutes, Red Army infantry and tanks breaking through almost without loss. By 15 January the field defences which the Axis forces had held for a year but had failed to develop were penetrated, in spite of the repeated counter-attacks by the Hungarian armoured division. The next day the Hungarian communication system broke down and the defence became totally disorganized.[6] By 18 January Rybalko's 3 Tank and Moskalenko's 40 Armies joined hands near Alexeievka and most of 2 Hungarian Army, part of the Italian Alpine Corps and elements of 24 Panzer Corps and Corps Group Cramer were surrounded.[7]

---

[4] *Ibid*, pp. 100–2.

[5] *Kriegstagebuch des OKW*, Vol. 3, pp. 37 and 42.

[6] According to Morozov the breakthrough was not accomplished everywhere so easily. Snow storms and poor visibility restricted air and artillery activity, Soviet arms co-ordination was not good and the enemy often fought with tenacity. Morozov, *Westlich von Woronesh*, p. 94.

[7] Wandel's 24 Panzer Corps was under Gariboldi's command and consisted of one German panzer division and two infantry divisions. Gariboldi had in addition a further panzer and a German infantry division as part of 8 Italian Army. Wandel himself was missing in this battle and was never heard of again. Group Cramer was one German infantry division and part of the Hungarian armoured division with other German elements.

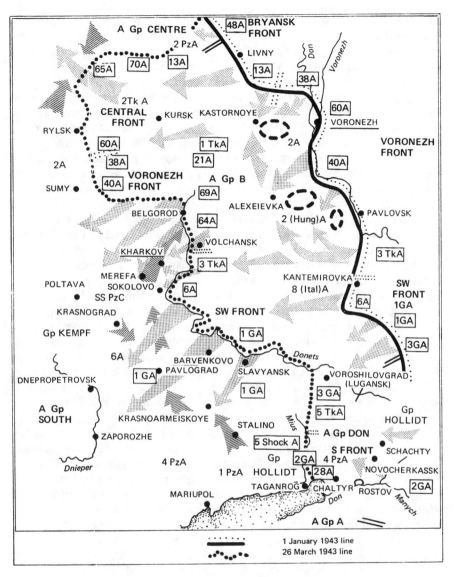

THE SOVIET SPRING OFFENSIVES
January–March 1943

In the heavy snow storms many of the encircled troops escaped, but by 27 January the Soviet command claimed the capture of 86,000 prisoners, mostly Hungarians. The southern flank of von Salmuth's 2 German Army was wide open and on 28 January Moskalenko's 40 Army moved northwards on Kastornoye across the German line of communications to join with Pukhov's 13 Army of the Bryansk Front. Two corps of 2 German Army, totalling about seven divisions, were cut off, Hitler having already shown some reluctance to allow 2 German Army to evacuate Voronezh and withdraw. For these troops, however, there was to be no repetition of Stalingrad. Voronezh was abandoned and set on fire and the many pockets of encircled troops made off to the west fighting as they went, most of them surviving the 120-mile-long march to Rylsk in temperatures of minus 25 degrees centigrade before they joined with their compatriots. Their heavy equipment was almost entirely lost.

On 21 January von Weichs painted a most gloomy picture to the *Führer*. There was a 200-mile gap in the German front where Army Group B had formerly been and he held out little hope of stopping the Soviet troops, particularly as Red Army formations had changed their tactics and simply bypassed all strong points. He feared for the safety of 2 German Army, and could see that the Soviet High Command might be aiming at driving south-west through the gap and cutting off the withdrawal of Army Group Don.[8] There were no available German reserves, except an infantry division being transferred from von Kluge's Army Group Centre and Hausser's 2 SS Panzer Corps which was still arriving from Western Europe. Von Kluge, who had been under heavy Soviet pressure from the Kalinin and West Fronts all the winter, mindful of his danger should the penetrating Soviet forces swing to the north, begged in vain to be allowed to evacuate the great salient near Rzhev and so create reserves to deal with the threat.[9]

Zhukov and Vasilevsky had been attached for a short time during late January to the Voronezh Front to recommend the course of further operations and, following Zhukov's recommendations, a new plan known as *Star* was drawn up to free the area of Kharkov. If Shtemenko is to be believed the General Staff appeared to have some reservations, since the plan involved Golikov thrusting in two divergent directions at the same time, towards Kursk and Kharkov.[10] *Star* began on 1 February. The Soviet forces, not slow in pressing home their advantage, pushed through the gap, Golikov's Voronezh Front moving almost due westwards towards Kursk and Kharkov, while Kharitonov's 6 Army and V. I. Kuznetsov's 1 Guards Army of Vatutin's South-West Front were directed towards Mariupol on the Sea of Azov, in order to cut the communications of both von Manstein's Army Group Don and von Kleist's Army Group A which was still in the Caucasus. On 2 February

[8] *Kriegstagebuch des OKW*, Vol. 3, p. 56.
[9] Orders for the evacuation of the Demyansk salient went out to Army Group North on 31 January. *Ibid*, p. 86.
[10] Shtemenko, *Generalnyi Shtab v Gody Voiny*, p. 97.

Stalingrad fell. Three days later Rybalko's 3 Tank Army reached the frozen Donets but could not cross it in face of determined resistance from the SS motorized division *Leibstandarte* of 2 SS Panzer Corps. Kursk, Belgorod and Kharkov were immediately threatened and von Manstein was in great danger.

Von Kleist's Army Group A was still bogged down in the faraway Caucasus. On 28 December Zeitzler had persuaded the *Führer* to give up part of his oil and Black Sea objectives, but far from agreeing to a complete evacuation of the Caucasus to the safety of the right bank of the Don north of Rostov, Hitler would only permit a partial withdrawal, and this by stages, to the line of the Manych Canal and the Kuban, since he intended to keep the Maikop area and a bridgehead over the Kerch Straits and lower Don as a firm base for a later campaign back towards the Caspian.[11] On 7 January, however, some forward elements of 5 Shock and 2 Guards Armies of Eremenko's South Front were already nearing Army Group Don Headquarters near Novocherkassk, not thirty miles from Rostov, and it seemed that the Rostov bridge which carried the main supplies not only for Army Group A but also for Hoth's 4 Panzer Army and 4 Rumanian Corps was about to be taken.

The Soviet reaction to the German withdrawal on the lower Don and in the Caucasus was very slow.[12] The former Stalingrad Front, since the beginning of January redesignated the South Front, still under Eremenko with Khrushchev as his political member, covered a ninety-mile sector between the Don and Manych and had been forced to give up troops for the reduction of Stalingrad. Eremenko had been ordered to take Rostov and Salsk and so cut the main line of withdrawal of Army Group A; but both Malinovsky's 2 Guards and M. M. Popov's 5 Shock Armies encountered what they reported as fierce resistance from Hoth's 4 Panzer Army. Trufanov's 51 and Gerasimenko's 28 Armies to the south-east had no better fortune against German troops in Zimovniki, 16 Motorized Division and other elements reinforced by the *SS Wiking* Division; and Eremenko and his military council felt obliged to point out to Moscow that they were over 200 miles from their railhead and that their armoured forces were 350 tanks below establishment.[13] Far to the south and the south-east Tyulenev's Transcaucasus Front, still in two isolated groups, Petrov's Black Sea Group in the mountains to the south of the Kuban near Novorossisk, and Maslennikov's North Group covering Grozny and Baku near the Caspian, were operating under great difficulties.[14] There were few roads available and in the frequent periods of thaw the country was

[11] Zeitzler gave himself some of the credit for saving 1 Panzer Army and 17 Army from the fate which was to befall 6 Army. Westphal, *The Fatal Decisions*, p. 156. Only a partial withdrawal had in fact been agreed by Hitler. Compare also von Manstein, *Lost Victories*, pp. 392–3. Even in late January Hitler was still insisting on holding Maikop. See the *Führerbefehl OKW Nr. 552344/42 g. Kdos Chefs WFSt Op.* dated 3 January 1943.

[12] Grechko enumerates the difficulties, including maintaining 80,000 men and 20,000 horses in the waterless Kalmuck Steppe. Grechko, *Bitva za Kavkaz*, p. 226.

[13] *Istoriya*, Vol. 3, pp. 81–4.

[14] North Group became the new North Caucasus Front on 24 January.

almost impassable even to infantry. It was, moreover, difficult to reinforce Petrov's Black Sea Group, which at Stalin's insistence had been given the task of cutting off the German retreat across the Taman Peninsula, since troops and equipment had to be moved by poor roads from the area of the Caspian along the length of the Caucasus range, a distance of nearly 600 miles. The Black Sea Group had started to move forward slowly, using pack transport and building roads as it went; but when it finally emerged from the foothills the Kuban River was in spate and the steppe flooded. As Army Group A moved back by stages the Red Army followed it up but there was never any great danger of the Germans being cut off by the Transcaucasus Front, and both Tyulenev and Maslennikov were later to be accused of timidity, so fearful were they that the Germans might trick them and take Grozny.[15]

The Soviet thrusts during January made it apparent that the threat to Army Group A and Army Group Don was coming in two directions, from Eremenko's South Front on the lower Don and from Vatutin's South-West Front in the East Ukraine. Yet not before 27 January would Hitler give a decision as to the final withdrawal of Army Group A.[16] Von Mackensen's 1 Panzer Army with one panzer and three infantry divisions was ordered to join von Manstein, who was to be allowed to withdraw west of the lower Don, but the remainder of Army Group A totalling about ten German and ten Rumanian divisions, in all more than 350,000 troops, were ordered to withdraw to the Taman bridgehead, where they were to prove of little assistance to von Manstein in the hard battles yet to be fought in the Ukraine. Von Manstein had asked for permission to fall back to the old defensive line of the Mius, but the *Führer's* veto insisted that even this small part of the Donets coal area was essential to Germany's economy. However, the situation was soon taken out of the *Führer's* hands. On 2 February Malinovsky took over command of South Front from Eremenko and on 4 February his troops reached the line Schachty-Novocherkassk. Four days later a cavalry mechanized group of Khomenko's 44 Army arrived near Rostov after its long march from Grozny and crossing the frozen Don, reached Chaltyr between Rostov and Taganrog. Meanwhile further to the north-west in the Ukraine, Golikov's Voronezh Front took Belgorod, Kursk and Volchansk, and crossing the frozen Donets, its 6 Guards Cavalry Corps and M. I. Kazakov's 69 Army reached the outskirts of Kharkov on 11 February, where they were engaged by the *Leibstandarte* of Hausser's SS Panzer Corps.[17] The Voronezh Front's left hand neighbour, South-West Front, using V. I. Kuznetsov's 1 Guards Army, 6 Army under Kharitonov and the Tank Group Popov, crossed the Donets deep in the rear of Army Group Don and, urged on by Stalin, thrust towards the Dnieper crossings of Dnepropetrovsk and Zaporozhe.[18] On 5 February

[15] *Istoriya*, Vol. 3, p. 86; Savyalov and Kalyadin, *Die Schlacht um den Kaukasus*, p. 144.
[16] Von Manstein, *Lost Victories*, p. 398.
[17] M. I. Kazakov formerly Chief of Staff of Voronezh Front.
[18] M. M. Popov's (of 5 Shock Army) tank group consisted of four tank and one rifle corps, a force which at establishment strength would have about 500 tanks.

Lelyushenko's 3 Guards Army of South Front attacked Voroshilovgrad and cleared it after nine days of house to house fighting.

The German position was so serious that von Manstein and von Kluge were called to East Prussia on 6 February, and at this meeting Hitler was unwillingly obliged to agree to their earlier requests to withdraw behind the Mius and give up the Rzhev salient; this was the second large salient to be evacuated, since Hitler had also been forced to agree to give up the Demyansk area in order to stabilize the position near Leningrad, where the Red Army forces had at long last driven a land corridor through to the city.[19] Von Weichs's Army Group B Headquarters was taken out of the chain of command and put into reserve, the remnants of its troops being shared between von Manstein and von Kluge. Von Manstein's Army Group Don was redesignated as Army Group South.

The defeat of 2 German and 2 Hungarian Armies and the sudden withdrawal from Voronezh to Rylsk had partly outflanked von Kluge's Army Group Centre from the south. At the beginning of February Moscow created a new Central Front under Rokossovsky from the old Don Front, which, taking under its command 2 Tank Army and three rifle armies, in an operation personally planned by Stalin attempted on 25 February to envelop von Kluge's Army Group Centre by getting behind the Bryansk-Orel salient from the south.[20] In this Rokossovsky failed, since the retreating 2 German Army, by then under the command of Weiss and forming part of Army Group Centre, had finally secured a stop line from Rylsk to Sumy. The numerous divisions arriving from the evacuated Rzhev area soon contained the Red Army pressure to the north and north-west.[21]

On 17 February Hitler, accompanied by Zeitzler and Jodl, arrived at Army Group South Headquarters at Zaporozhe, where the position was causing alarm. The *Führer* had intended to dismiss von Manstein.[22] The day before, Group Lanz, against Hitler's orders, had evacuated Kharkov and was withdrawing south-west.[23] Group Hollidt, shortly to be reformed as a new 6 German Army, held the line of the Mius against Malinovsky's South Front

---

[19] Von Manstein, *Lost Victories*, pp. 406–13.

[20] *Istoriya*, Vol. 3, p. 117; also Shtemenko, *Generalnyi Shtab v Gody Voiny*, p. 107.

[21] Weiss, the former Commander of 27 Corps, relieved von Salmuth as Commander of 2 Army on 4 February 1943.

[22] *Goebbels' Diary*, 2 March 1943, p. 199.

[23] Group Lanz consisted of the SS panzer corps and Corps Raus. Corps Raus comprised the motorized division *Grossdeutschland* and elements of two German divisions. Lanz, the former Commander of 1 Mountain Division, had commanded the group with distinction and, according to von Manstein, he fell back from Kharkov because the SS corps did the same. No disciplinary action was ever taken against the SS commander. Von Manstein, *Lost Victories*, p. 422. Lanz was replaced by Kempf. The army and SS continued to blame each other for the loss of Kharkov. Meanwhile the SS were taking stories to Berlin of the flight of army supply installations from the area, supplies and munitions being abandoned to the enemy, while carpets, pictures, furniture and Russian typists were speedily evacuated. *Goebbels' Diary*, 20 April, 1943, p. 262.

while von Mackensen's 1 Panzer Army, withdrawn from the Caucasus to von Manstein's left flank, was attempting to hold back part of V. I. Kuznetsov's 1 Guards Army and the Tank Group Popov which were thrusting from Slavyansk towards Krasnoarmeiskoye and Stalino (Donetsk). About seventy miles further to the west, deep in Army Group South's rear, other elements of 1 Guards Army and Kharitonov's 6 Army were only thirty miles from the Dnieper, and having cut the main railway between Dnepropetrovsk and Stalino were within fifty miles of the *Führer*'s conference. To restore the position von Manstein proposed to mount a counter-offensive against the Soviet envelopment, using Hoth's 4 Panzer Army of 57 and 48 Panzer Corps of five divisions, three of which were panzer, and 2 SS Panzer Corps of two, later three, motorized divisions. 4 Panzer Army was to attack from the area between Zaporozhe and Stalino northwards on to the Soviet flank while the SS Panzer Corps attacked southwards from the area of Poltava to meet 4 Panzer Army, so cutting off the forward troops of 1 Guards and 6 Armies. Hoth was in overall command. Hoth's left was to be covered by Group Kempf. On Hoth's right, von Mackensen's 1 Panzer Army of 3 and 40 Panzer Corps and 30 Corps was to hold and destroy Tank Group Popov and the supporting elements of 1 Guards Army. Although Army Group South was dangerously short of vehicle fuel, it was known through radio intercept that the Red Army fuel position was even worse, and the same radio sources indicated that the Soviet field commanders were almost certain that the Germans were about to withdraw behind the Dnieper.[24] Due to the efforts and reinforcement of von Richthofen's 4 Air Fleet the Red Air Force had suffered a sharp tactical defeat.

Hitler, still smarting at the loss of Kharkov, regarded the reoccupation of Kharkov rather than the destruction of the enemy as an immediate aim, and could hardly be persuaded that Army Group South was in any danger. By the second day of the conference, however, he had reluctantly agreed to von Manstein's proposal for a counter-offensive.[25]

Meanwhile Stalin was urging and threatening South-West Front forward to the Dnieper. The Red Army troops had already outrun their support and supplies, and they were beyond the range of effective air support since many of the captured airfields were not yet in use. The supply and reinforcement and maintenance system was functioning badly over the extended line of communications and many formations and units had been reduced by casualties

---

[24] Von Manstein, *Lost Victories*, pp. 429–31. Shtemenko admits this was the case and attributes the Soviet High Command appreciation to erroneous intelligence from Golikov and Vatutin. Shtemenko, *Generalnyi Shtab v Gody Voiny*, p. 99.

[25] Hitler was to use the recurrent argument that although he did not dispute the German intelligence estimate of the Soviet order of battle, the Red Army formations were bled white and were hardly more than skeletons. There was some truth in this. He failed to understand, however, that German formations were similarly weakened and that Germany's military commitments were greater than those of the Soviet Union. Moreover, the German rigid defence played into the hands of the enemy who soon gained the strategic initiative.

to skeleton form.[26] On the morning of 19 February Hausser's 2 SS Panzer Corps attacked the flank of Kharitonov's 6 Soviet Army from the area of Krasnograd, punching a twenty-five mile wide hole, through which the *SS Das Reich* scattered 4 Guards Rifle Corps in disorder. On 22 February von Knobelsdorff's 48 Panzer Corps, moving towards Pavlograd with Kirchner's 57 Panzer Corps on its right, cut off numbers of Soviet troops and joined with the SS Corps. They then changed direction and moved northwards on Kharkov. Only 9,000 prisoners were taken, but Army Group South was to claim 23,000 enemy dead on the battlefield. Von Mackensen, using Henrici's 40 Panzer Corps with two panzer and one SS motorized division, destroyed the forward elements of Popov's Tank Group between Krasnoarmeiskoye and Barvenkovo, some of which had already been stranded for lack of fuel.

The Soviet High Command still believed that the German counter-offensive had been staged to cover the withdrawal of Army Group South from the Mius back behind the Dnieper, and the South-West Front was ordered to attack once more in order to cut off Group Hollidt and 1 Panzer Army. These orders were incapable of being carried out, however, because Hoth's 4 Panzer Army, still moving rapidly northwards and by then about 150 miles north from its original starting point, regrouped between 4 and 6 March and, outflanking South-West Front from the north, launched a heavy attack between Merefa and Sokolovo on the left wing of Voronezh Front near Kharkov. A thirty-mile gap opened between M. I. Kazakov's 69 Army and Rybalko's 3 Tank Army, which the Voronezh Front could not close, and the Germans were fighting in the streets of Kharkov on 12 March and had thrown a ring round the city two days later. The gap continued to grow, no Soviet reserves being available, and the German thrusts were approaching Belgorod, so that Rokossovsky's Central Front appeared to be threatened. Belgorod was taken on 18 March by the motorized division *Grossdeutschland*.[27] By then the Soviet High Command had realized that, far from being faced with a holding operation intended to cover a German withdrawal, the Central and Voronezh Fronts were in danger of being cut off. 3 Tank Army was ordered to break out of encirclement near Kharkov, and the Voronezh and South-West Fronts fell back behind the Donets about forty miles to the east.

Stalin's reaction was typical of the dictator and the Soviet system. He wanted to know what was wrong with the Voronezh Front. The military council needed strengthening from a political as well as a military point of view and Khrushchev was ordered to join it. Zhukov and Vasilevsky were to report there.

Zhukov was with Timoshenko at the North-West Front when he was tele-

[26] Popov's Group and 4 Tank Corps were said to have only 137 tanks between them. Motorized battalions, according to the Soviet historian, were down to the scarcely credible fighting strength of twenty men. *Istoriya*, Vol. 3, pp. 114 and 118.

[27] *Grossdeutschland*, part of Group Kempf, with the *Feldherrnhalle* was the only army formation to be referred to by name instead of by number and was the newest motorized division. Soviet historians, even today, still mistakenly refer to *Grossdeutschland* as a SS division.

phoned by Stalin on 16 March with the news that the *Stavka* had decided to replace Konev, who was at that time commanding West Front, by Soko-lovsky. The position in the Ukraine was discussed, Zhukov, according to his own account, suggesting that Konev should assume command of North-West Front, so freeing Timoshenko to go to the South Ukraine as *Stavka* representative and take the necessary measures to restore the situation. Stalin agreed but ordered Zhukov to return to Moscow where, after discussion and a five o'clock in the morning dinner with the dictator who had spent the night bullying the General Staff, he left by air for the Voronezh Front. Golikov lost his appointment to Vatutin.[28] Zhukov asked for the allocation of a further three armies from the High Command Reserve.[29] Stalin allotted him 1 Tank Army and 21 and 64 Armies.[30] Only the arrival of the three reinforcing Soviet armies from the interior, and the mud following the spring thaw stabilized the position.

Army Group South's limited counter-offensive robbed the Red Army of the initiative which it had held in South Russia and the Ukraine since Vatutin had attacked the Rumanians across the Don in November. It was claimed that von Manstein's daring attack had cost the Soviet troops more than 40,000 casualties and the loss in captured equipment of 600 tanks and 500 guns; the success left the Germans in undisputed control of the area bounded by the Donets and Mius, very much the same line as had been held in the winter of 1941.[31] The defeats inflicted on the Red Army were limited, being temporary and in no way decisive, but they had saved Army Group South from destruc-tion and had earned it some respite. The credit for the German successes belonged to von Manstein and von Kluge who, at long last prevailing upon the *Führer* to permit a shortening of the front and a withdrawal of troops from the line, were able to make use of the initiative which these reserves conferred upon them, rather than continuing to rely on the *Führer* tactics of a rigid defence. Some credit, too, belonged to Hoth. The decisive element, however, was Hausser's panzer corps, consisting of three experienced, well-equipped and rested divisions, *Leibstandarte*, *Das Reich* and *Totenkopf*, all much superior to the scattered, poorly supported and ill-supplied Soviet troops, who had by then outrun their strength.

So ended the successful Soviet offensive of the winter 1942–3. The strongest of the German armies had been totally destroyed and four armies of Germany's allies scattered. Some German critics found fault with the Soviet strategy on two counts. Firstly, that the three offensives against the Rumanians, the Italians and the Hungarians should have been made concurrently rather than consecutively. This criticism can be justified only if the Red Army had suffi-

---

[28] Golikov appears to have taken over the Bryansk Front temporarily, replacing Reiter who had moved to a new Reserve Front. Golikov later made way for M. M. Popov as the Commander of Bryansk Front.

[29] Zhukov, *Vospominaniya i Razmyshleniya*, pp. 464–7.

[30] The commanders were Katukov, Chistyakov and Shumilov. 1 Tank Army had been recently reformed.

[31] The German claim in dead was about 30,000.

cient air power, artillery and motor transport to support all the offensives and this was not the case; the failure of the Soviet counter-offensives of the previous year were caused in part by the dispersing of effort and dissipating of forces. The second point of criticism was that the Soviet High Command failed to make a sufficiently determined thrust to Rostov and the Sea of Azov in order to cut the withdrawal route of Army Group A and part of Army Group Don. This is relevant, since there is no doubt that a successful penetration of this type would have endangered both German army groups. Yet a strong thrust to Azov would have failed if, by so doing, the forces encircling 6 German Army had been weakened. Moreover the Rostov bridges over the lower Don were not the only exits from the Caucasus, since it was proved possible to maintain Army Group A across the Kerch Straits. It was for this reason that Stalin had pressed the Black Sea Group to cut off the withdrawal route across the Taman Peninsula. Unless the Taman Peninsula route could have been blocked by the Red Army, it would have been preferable to have secured the lower Dnieper and the Perekop Isthmus rather than to thrust on Rostov. The taking of Perekop would have blocked the exit from the Crimea and completely cut off both Army Groups A and South. This is what Stalin tried to do.

Due to German folly, the Soviet strategy for the winter of 1942 was probably far more successful than Stalin and the High Command had hoped that it could be. In the post-Stalin era, Stalin has been severely criticized for falling into the same error as that of the winter of 1941, when he overestimated Soviet strength and underestimated that of the enemy, so dispersing Soviet effort by attacking westwards on an over-extended frontage.[32] By the same token it could be argued that if the Voronezh, South-West and South Fronts had concentrated in a south-west drive into the Ukraine on Dnepropetrovsk, Zaporozhe and the Crimean Isthmus, greater successes might have accrued. Even so, these further successes would probably have been marginal. Warfare in Russia continued to be influenced, even decided, by terrain, by distance and by weather. In November the Germans were fully extended, almost at the end of their resources, and the scales became weighted on the side of the Red Army. The successful Soviet counter-offensive threw the Axis troops back nearly 500 miles from Stalingrad and even further from Grozny. The pendulum then swung back again in the German favour. A Red Army, weakened and disorganized by fighting, by distance and by weather, could not hold the tired and under-strength German divisions which were pitted against it.

It was in the beginning of 1943 during the Soviet offensive that a change first became apparent in the composition and relative strength of the German

[32] Compare *Istoriya*, Vol. 3, p. 148:
'The Red Army would have been more successful, but I. V. Stalin's underestimation of the strength and capabilities of the enemy led to grave failures both in the High Command and in the General Staff in the planning of operations. Because of this the Red Army forces were dissipated and the fronts were given impossible tasks to achieve . . .'.
This paragraph has been deleted from some editions.

and Soviet Armies. Germany entered the war with highly efficient and very well equipped panzer and motorized forces, the best in the world, although these represented only a minor part of the German Army as a whole. German tactical air support was excellent. The Red Army at that time did not lack for tanks, aircraft or equipment, but it was in no way a modern motorized army and was not even a match for the German marching infantry divisions with their horse-drawn guns and wagons. By 1943, however, German organization and the quality and scale of equipment, instead of being improved to keep ahead of those of their enemies, had fallen right behind. In March 1943 the Eastern Front was 470,000 men short of establishment and the German High Command tried, through necessity, to make a virtue of going without. Hitler, with his obsession for divisional numbers, was continually raising new formations and he refused to maintain, reinforce or re-equip existing divisions, so that they became little more than cadres, so-called panzer divisions numbering only thirty or forty tanks. The German Army had entered Russia with 3,300 tanks in 1941. On 23 January 1943 it had only 495 tanks fit for battle over the whole of the Eastern Front.[33] Except for a handful of Mark VI Tiger tanks, no new tanks were in service although the Mark III and IV had been improved by the addition of skirting plates, face hardened armour and longer guns with an increase of muzzle velocity. Divisional organizations began to be altered, leaving the divisional title but reducing the number of regiments in the division and the battalions in the regiment, this resulting in a further reduction in the fighting strength of formations. The Red Army's transformation, on the other hand, had been one for the better. The Red Air Force, although still inferior to the *Luftwaffe* in performance, had made great strides in the improvement of the quality of its aircraft. The KV and T34 tanks were superior to the German Mark III and IV and were being manufactured in large numbers, and tank and mechanized corps were, from mid 1942 onwards, being grouped as tank armies. But one of the most significant changes to be observed in the Red Army during 1943 was the rapid motorization which was to enable the Soviet High Command to undertake deep penetration in the depths of winter and at the time of the thaws, and this was achieved largely by the introduction of United States trucks. The German Army, once the best equipped in the world, within a space of two years was relegated to the position of an out-of-date force, indifferently provided with obsolescent equipment. The German equivalent to the Red Army quarter-ton jeep for commander or messenger remained the horse. The counterpart of the Studebaker or Dodge six-wheeled drive truck was the horse-drawn *panje* wagon. The efficiency of German field formation staffs and the quality of the German fighting soldier were still superior to those of the Red Army, yet for all that, the German Army, once the pride of the *Reich*, had become one of the poorer armies of the world.

---

[33] *Kriegstagebuch des OKW*, p. 66. The tank fighting strength was as follows: Army Group A, 34; Army Groups B and Don, 291; Army Group Centre, 167; Army Group North, 3. These figures do not include armoured assault guns.

CHAPTER TWENTY-TWO

The Battle of Kursk

The Axis defeats in Stalingrad and North Africa and the rapidly increasing military strength of the Soviet and Anglo-American Powers gave the first indications that, unless Germany's enemies fell out amongst themselves, the Axis could not win. Japan had shot its bolt and had suffered telling defeats in the Pacific.[1] Italy wanted to end the war against the USSR almost at any price, and Finland was to consider means by which it could safely extricate itself.[2] Antonescu wanted peace with the Western Powers but a continuation of war against the Soviet Union.[3] Hitler and the staffs of the Armed Forces High Command (OKW) and the Army High Command (OKH) were all of opinion that as the danger of an invasion of the Continent of Europe was imminent, it was impossible to force a decision on the Eastern Front in 1943.[4] Jodl and the OKW were generally in favour of removing formations from the East in order to strengthen the German forces in the West and in the Mediterranean.[5] The OKH, on the other hand, had no responsibility and little interest

[1] In May 1942 the Japanese suffered their first check when United States naval aircraft sank a Japanese carrier and turned back an invasion fleet bound for Port Moresby. The next month at Midway the Japanese lost four carriers against a United States loss of one carrier. Thereafter the Japanese rapidly lost all initiative in the Pacific.

[2] Mussolini in a letter to Hitler on 9 March 1943 had come to the conclusion that the Soviet Union was no longer the danger it had been two years before and wanted to come to some sort of terms with it, the better to protect Italy against the Anglo-Americans. *Kriegstagebuch des OKW*, Vol. 3, p. 213. Mussolini was to be overthrown on 25 July 1943. For Finland's attitude compare Mannerheim, *Memoirs*, pp. 460–1.

[3] *Kriegstagebuch des OKW*, Vol. 3, pp. 1531–2.

[4] Von Manstein, *Lost Victories*, p. 443; also Klink, *Das Gesetz des Handelns 'Zitadelle'*, pp. 57–9.

[5] On 1 July 1943 the strength of the army field force (without the Armed SS and *Luftwaffe* divisions) in the East, had risen to 3·1 million. The total strength in the OKW theatres was 1·3 million. The allocation of divisions and tanks on that date was as follows.

	East	Finland	Norway Denmark	West	Italy	Balkans	Total
Army	168	6	15	36	5	13	243
SS	7	1		2		1	12
Lw	12		2	6	1	1	22
Tanks	2,269		59	351	345	118	3,142
Assault guns	997	20	14	113	222	56	1,422

In addition there were over 500 obsolete tanks in the East and about 100 in the West. Mueller-Hillebrand, *Das Heer*, Vol. 3, Tables 48–50.

in any theatres outside Russia and would only willingly accept the removal of formations from the Eastern Front provided that frontages and commitments could be correspondingly reduced. This Hitler refused to do, both for reasons of prestige and because he maintained, quite erroneously, that the war economy of Germany could not sustain the loss of territory and resources. In this way the tug-of-war in the German armed forces between east and west and between OKH and OKW staffs was accentuated. For the moment, however, the OKW, the OKH and the *Führer* were in broad agreement that the German Army must go on to the defensive in Russia.

Hitler was of the opinion, and in this he was supported by Zeitzler, that the best means of defence in Russia was a limited offensive, to be made immediately after the thaw had dried out and before the Americans and the British could mount their attack in Europe. In this belief he had been encouraged by the success of von Manstein's recent Kharkov battle.[6] He had only permitted the earlier evacuation of the Rzhév salient on the understanding that the troops withdrawn, those of Model's 9 Army, would be available for other offensive tasks; and he wanted to attack the Soviet enemy before the Germans were themselves attacked, in order to eliminate if only temporarily and partially the offensive capability of the Red Army. The need was to capture men and equipment, and at the same time restore the reputation of German arms and the faith of his Axis allies by gaining a quick but spectacular victory. This. in his own words, would shine out to the world like a beacon.[7]

It had originally been intended to mount two minor and supplementary enveloping operations to the east of Kharkov, these being known as *Hawk* and *Panther*, but they were finally abandoned in favour of a single offensive on Kursk. The sector chosen was the Soviet Kursk salient, which extended westwards between what were in effect two German salients jutting eastwards. The northern of these German salients included the town of Orel, while that in the south centred round the city of Kharkov. Hitler's and Zeitzler's plan intended that Model's 9 Army of Army Group Centre should attack southwards on Kursk from the area of the Orel salient while Hoth's 4 Panzer Army and Group Kempf of Army Group South should attack northwards from the Kharkov salient to meet Model. The enveloped Soviet enemy in the Kursk salient was then to be destroyed.

Planning for the offensive began in early March, it being intended originally to start the attack in mid April, but the date was postponed, partly because of delays in assembling the troops and partly because Model, to whose

[6] *Operationsbefehl Nr. 5 – OKH/Gen St d H/Op Abt (vorg. St) Nr. 430/163/43 g. Kdos/ Chefs* of 13 March 1943, second sentence.
[7] *Operationsbefehl Nr. 6 – OKH/Gen St d H/Op Abt (1) Nr. 430/246/43 g. Kdos/Chefs* of 15 April 1943.

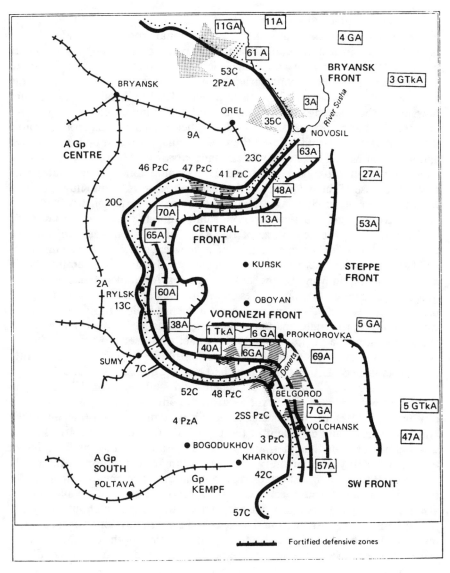

THE BATTLE OF KURSK
July 1943

opinion Hitler attached great importance, had doubts as to the adequacy of his resources, and repeatedly asked for additional troops. On 4 May Hitler held a meeting in Munich to discuss the offensive, to be known by the cover name of *Citadel*, at which von Kluge, von Manstein, Zeitzler and Guderian were present, Guderian having earlier been recalled from retirement to fill the appointment of Inspector General of Mobile Troops. Model, who was not present at the meeting, had raised by letter a number of objections. He maintained that the strength of the Soviet field defences was so formidable that the Red Army could hold off the attack while it brought up new reserves, and although Model did not say in as many words that he disagreed with the plan for the offensive he made it clear by implication that he doubted its success because of the inequality in the relative strengths.[8] Von Kluge and von Manstein were generally in agreement with the plan for the offensive but were not in favour of any further postponement, since they reasoned that delay could only be to the advantage of the Red Army which was known to be bringing up new formations with each new week which passed. Guderian, on the other hand, was vehemently opposed to the *Citadel* operation being mounted at all, in view of the anticipated loss of tanks, tanks which he needed to equip the German forces in Western Europe, and his attitude appeared to have excited the anger of his old enemy Field-Marshal von Kluge, who, according to Guderian, some days afterwards gave way to hysteria and challenged him to a duel, inviting Hitler to act as his second.[9]

Since failure is always an orphan, the responsibility for *Citadel* is not lightly to be established. Hitler apparently had some doubts.[10] Guderian blamed Hitler and Zeitzler, Zeitzler in particular, and said that von Kluge was in agreement with them. Zeitzler subsequently maintained that the army group commanders were not enthusiastic, although according to von Mellenthin, he himself seemed quite confident at the time.[11] Keitel was for the attack, Jodl was against it.[12] Possible alternatives were discussed, such as the breaking in from the 2 Army area in the west rather than from the north and south, as this would have avoided attacking the well developed enemy defences; but this course of action was rejected due to the enforced delay in redeploying the assaulting troops. It was also suggested that the offensive should be postponed until the Red Army should attack, and then be developed as a counter-offensive, but this was too passive to appeal to Hitler. In the end the offensive was postponed once more until more heavy tanks and assault guns could be made available.

The *Führer* was entranced not only by the magic of formation numbers but also by scientific and technological developments which, he hoped, might

[8] Although Guderian says that Speer and Model were present at the meeting, this does not appear to have been the case. Klink, *Das Gesetz des Handelns*, p. 140, footnote 184.

[9] Von Manstein, *Lost Victories*, p. 447; Guderian, *Panzer Leader*, pp. 306–8.

[10] *Ibid*, pp. 308–9.

[11] Von Mellenthin, *Panzer Battles*, pp. 213–6.

[12] Warlimont, *Inside Hitler's Headquarters*, p. 334.

prove Germany's salvation in war. Earlier he had pinned much faith on the hollow charge anti-tank projectile as Germany's counter to the T34 and KV tanks and as this had failed to come up to expectation, he then turned to heavy and super-heavy tanks.[13] The Mark VI, the Tiger tank weighing about fifty-six tons and mounting a 88 mm gun was already in service in small numbers, and a new heavy tank, the Mark V or Panther weighing about forty-five tons, had just been developed. Hitler decided against the advice of his technical staff to commit to *Citadel* all the heavy tanks he could muster, including all the Panthers and the Porsche Tigers and Ferdinands, none of which had completed their acceptance tests.[14]

On 1 July the *Führer* addressed a meeting of the senior commanders taking part in the attack, all leaders down to corps commanders being present. He opened with a preamble of the war situation, in which he roundly blamed the Italians as being the cause of all his misfortunes. Rumania and Hungary were unreliable and Finland was at the end of its resources. At all costs Germany must hold on to the conquered territory – it could not exist without – and the German soldier must be made to understand that where he stood, there he remained. Under no circumstances would he give up the Balkans and he would replace the Italian troops there by Germans. Crete too would be held, rather than give it up to the enemy to become another airfield runway. In Russia he did not doubt that many crises were in store, but he believed that the Red Army would be dormant throughout the summer preparing for another winter offensive. He had no intention of giving up the Orel salient, since it was to Germany's advantage to tie down Soviet troops and in any case he did not believe that the Red Army would again permit an orderly evacuation, since it had learned its lesson from its own supineness during the German withdrawal from the Rzhev salient.[15] The *Führer* rejected any sugges-

[13] Hollow charge anti-tank projectiles had the warhead explosive shaped with an inverted cone, and this, using what was known as the Munroe jet effect, concentrated the explosive energy about a single point. It had excellent penetrative effect, independent of the momentum of the projectile or means of projection, and was therefore an effective close range infantry weapon. It provided the missile for *Panzerfaust*, *Panzerschreck* and *Püppchen* and could be fired by low velocity field guns.

[14] The Mark VI Tiger tanks were developed by both Porsche and Henschel, the Porsche version (Tiger P) being unsatisfactory because of difficulty in manoeuvre and because of the lack of secondary machine-gun armament. Many of the Porsche Tigers were converted to turretless tank destroyers carrying a long L71 88 mm gun, these models being known as Ferdinands. These had no secondary armament at all. The Tiger frontal armour varied from 102 mm at 20 degrees to 62 mm at 80 degrees from the vertical. It was almost invulnerable to frontal attack except at very close range, but it could be penetrated in the sides by normal anti-tank weapons at most combat ranges. The Henschel Tiger had one hull and one turret machine gun and its main armament was originally a L56 88 mm converted flak gun. The Tiger's Maybach engine required very skilled driving and maintenance, without which mechanical troubles soon appeared. The Mark V Panther had excellent sloped armour with a front glacis plate of 80 mm at 55 degrees from vertical and carried a L70 75 mm gun.

[15] When the Germans quitted the Rzhev salient during the early spring (known as the *Buffalo* operation) not only had they removed the dumps and equipment but they had evacuated a large part of the civil population and destroyed anything likely to be of use to the enemy.

tion of awaiting an enemy attack and hitting the Russian on the rebound, that is to say by a counter-offensive, and he was convinced that Germany must seize the initiative and attack. He was prepared to admit that *Citadel* was a gamble, but he himself believed that it would come off and this conviction he based on the events of the past when, against all military advice, he himself had decided to march into Austria, Czecho-Slovakia, Poland and the USSR.[16]

Reason enough, one might have thought, to have abandoned *Citadel* immediately.

Von Manstein's attacking force in the south consisted of Hoth's 4 Panzer Army of Ott's 52 Corps on the far left with three infantry divisions, von Knobelsdorff's 48 Panzer Corps in the centre with one infantry and two panzer divisions and the panzer grenadier division *Grossdeutschland*, which had been brought on to a special establishment and had a larger complement of tanks than a panzer division, and Hausser's 2 SS Panzer Corps with one infantry and three SS panzer grenadier divisions. The far right flank beyond 4 Panzer Army, to the south of Belgorod, was allotted to Group Kempf comprising three corps, Breith's 3 Panzer Corps of one infantry and three panzer divisions, Corps Raus with two infantry divisions and Mattenklott's 42 Corps with three infantry divisions. Nehring's 24 Panzer Corps with 17 Panzer Division and the SS panzer grenadier division *Wiking* was in army group reserve. In all, Army Group South had twenty-two divisions, of which six were panzer and five panzer grenadier, but of the eleven infantry divisions only seven took part in the operation. Von Manstein had under 1,000 tanks and 150 assault guns fit for battle, and of these ninety-four were Tigers and 200 were Panthers. In the north, Model's 9 Army in the Orel salient consisted of 23 Corps on the left and 41, 47 and 46 Panzer Corps with 20 Corps on the right.[17] Group von Esebeck with one panzer grenadier and two panzer divisions formed the army reserve. Model had a total of twenty-one divisions of which six were panzer and one panzer grenadier, and over 900 tanks. Of his fourteen infantry divisions, eight were earmarked for the battle. Air support for *Citadel* was provided by 1 Air Division of 6 Air Fleet in the north totalling 730 aircraft, and 8 Air Corps in the south with 1,100 aircraft. 2 German Army with seven infantry divisions held the west flank of the Kursk bulge.[18] Model's rear to the north of Orel was covered by the infantry divisions of 2 Panzer Army.[19]

[16] Klink, *Das Gesetz des Handelns 'Zitadelle'*, pp. 197–8. Text taken from the notes of Friessner, the Commander of 23 Corps, who was present.

[17] Model's corps commanders were: 20 Corps, Roman; 23 Corps, Friessner; 41 Panzer Corps, Harpe; 46 Panzer Corps, Zorn; 47 Panzer Corps, Lemelsen.

[18] German order of battle from *AOK 9, 1 a Anlage IX KTB Nr. 8; AOK 2, 1 a KTB, Teil 11; AOK 4, 1 a Anlagen 14 zum KTB*. All reproduced from Klink, *Das Gesetz des Handelns 'Zitadelle'*, pp. 331–8.

[19] Of the total German order of battle only twelve panzer, six panzer grenadier and fifteen infantry divisions were brought up to strength for *Citadel*, those formations in fact

The line of Soviet defended localities had not altered since the repulse by von Manstein after the Kharkov battles. The northern half of the Kursk salient was occupied by Rokossovsky's Central Front, while the southern flank was held by the Voronezh Front commanded by Vatutin with Khrushchev as the political member of the military council. To the north of the Central Front lay the Bryansk Front commanded by M. M. Popov, and the West Front commanded by Sokolovsky with Bulganin as the political member of his military council.[20] To the south of the Voronezh Front was the South-West Front. Although the Germans were attempting to divert attention to the area of the Donets south of Volchansk by false radio traffic and dummy vehicle concentrations, from the Soviet side it was obvious that the German blow would fall in the Kursk salient. The Soviet High Command was, as Hitler knew, bringing up its troops in readiness for a major offensive although, contrary to Hitler's forecast, this was to have been launched long before the winter.[21] Following a conference held at Svoboda in the second half of April, the Soviet High Command decided to mount its offensive only after the Germans had committed themselves to an attack, and on Rokossovsky's recommendation the High Command deployed its main strategic reserve, consisting of a Reserve Front, later known as the Steppe Front, in a central position immediately east of the Kursk salient from where it could counter-attack both Model and von Manstein, but where it would not be cut off or be drawn prematurely into the fighting for the salient.[22] The Steppe Front, commanded by Konev, was made up of five armies, including a tank army, and one tank, one mechanized and three cavalry corps.[23] The Central Front comprised six armies, of which one was a tank army, together with two independent tank corps, and the Voronezh Front had four armies deployed forward with a further rifle and a tank army in reserve, together with two tank and one rifle corps.[24] Malenkov, a member of the GKO, Vasilevsky and

---

which had been assigned major tasks. On 30 June there were about 2,700 tanks (including 500 obsolete fighting vehicles) and 1,000 assault guns in the East, making over 3,700 in all. Of this total 2,500 were allocated to *Citadel*. Mueller-Hillebrand, *Das Heer*, Vol. 3, Table 54.

[20] The military councils at this time were as follows: Central Front, Rokossovsky, Telegin and Malinin; Bryansk Front, Popov, Mekhlis and Sandalov; Voronezh Front, Vatutin, Khrushchev and S. P. Ivanov; West Front, Sokolovsky, Bulganin and Pokrovsky.

[21] Shtemenko, *Generalnyi Shtab v Gody Voiny*, pp. 146–68.

[22] *Istoriya*, Vol. 3, pp. 245–8. According to Zhukov, Vatutin and Khrushchev had earlier proposed a preventive offensive on Belgorod, without waiting for the German attack. *Vospominaniya i Razmyshleniya*, p. 483.

[23] The military council of the Steppe Front consisted of Konev, Susaikov and M. V. Zakharov.

[24] The Soviet order of battle:
Rokossovsky's Central Front: On 2 German Army flank, 60 Army Chernyakhovsky and 65 Army Batov;
Facing 9 German Army, 70 Army Galanin, 13 Army Pukhov, 48 Army Romanenko; In reserve, 2 Tank Army Rodin (later Bogdanov).

Zhukov, by then both Marshals of the Soviet Union, were attached to the fronts as representatives of the High Command.[25] The adjoining Bryansk and West Fronts, both of which partially encircled 9 Army in the Orel salient, were ordered to prepare an offensive against Model's rear which was guarded by the infantry formations of 2 Panzer Army.[26]

The Soviet defence system inside the Kursk bend consisted of typical Red Army earthworks, being based on parallel lines of trenches, reminiscent of those used on the Western Front in the First World War. The main forward defensive zone was up to three miles deep and consisted of sets of five lines of trenches, sometimes more, one behind the other, all interconnected and provided with pits and shelters, these having been built with the aid of civil labour. A second defensive zone lay about seven miles behind and resembled the first, and a third zone lay a further twenty miles behind the second. The front reserves, probably forty miles in the rear from the forward defended localities, also dug their miles of linear trenches. So the trenches ran for hundreds of miles, through the cornfields and villages and up the long gradual slopes of the steppe hills. The strength of the defences lay in their formidable anti-tank protection, the whole area being heavily mined and covered with anti-tank strong points, it being claimed that on the Central Front alone nearly half a million mines were laid with a density of 2,400 anti-tank and 2,700 anti-personnel mines a mile.[27] The artillery support allotted to the Central and Voronezh Fronts came largely from the Artillery Reserve of the High Command, 13 Army alone being allotted for its support 4 Breakthrough Artillery

---

Vatutin's Voronezh Front: On 2 German Army flank, 38 Army Moskalenko (vice Chibisov), 40 Army Moskalenko;
Facing 4 Panzer Army and Group Kempf, 6 Guards (formerly 21) Army Chistyakov, 7 Guards (formerly 64) Army Shumilov;
In reserve, 1 Tank Army Katukov, 69 Army Kryuchenkin.
Konev's Steppe Front: 5 Guards (formerly 66) Army Zhadov, 27 Army Trofimenko, 47 Army Ryzhov (then P. M. Kozlov), 53 Army Managarov, 5 Guards Tank Army Rotmistrov.
According to German current estimates the three fronts had a total of thirty-seven tank brigades. If these were at full strength the total tank force would number about 1,500 tanks. Soviet sources maintain however that they had more than double this figure. The fronts had in support and under command Rudenko's 16 Air Army, Krasovsky's 2 Air Army and Goryunov's 5 Air Army (Steppe Front).

[25] The presence of Malenkov is mentioned in Platonov, *Vtoraya Mirovaya Voina* but omitted from *Istoriya*. Zhukov was responsible for the co-ordination of the Central, Bryansk and West Fronts; Vasilevsky for the Voronezh Front.

[26] 2 Panzer Army had been commanded by Rudolf Schmidt since 26 December 1941 when Guderian had been dismissed. Schmidt himself was an unfriendly critic of the Nazi régime, as the Gestapo found when they searched the correspondence of his brother whom they had arrested for treason. *Goebbels' Diary*, 10 May 1943, p. 289. On 10 July just as the Kursk battle was developing, Schmidt was relieved of his duties. After the battle Rendulic took over 2 Panzer Army and at the end of August the headquarters was removed to the Balkans to deal with the defection of the Italian troops there.

[27] The normal density for anti-tank mines at that time was about 1,800 mines a mile frontage.

Corps with 700 guns and mortars. In all, it was said that the two main fronts had 13,000 guns, 6,000 anti-tank guns and 1,000 rocket launchers, much more than the three fronts had had for the Don-Volga attack, and more than the Germans had available to support their break-in. The detail of the formation strength of the forces inside the Kursk bend has not been revealed but according to the German intelligence estimates at the time, the Voronezh Front had thirty-five rifle divisions and twenty-five tank brigades together with a number of independent rifle brigades and tank regiments, and the Central Front had the equivalent of forty rifle divisions and seventeen tank brigades. The Soviet forces were supported by 2 and 16 Air Armies with a probable strength of about 2,500 aircraft.[28]

On the German side no pains were spared in the preparation of the offensive. Reconnaissance and planning were carried out extensively, minute details being taken into account. Air photographs were available for the whole of the Kursk salient. The troops were carefully briefed and rested and units were reinforced and where necessary re-equipped. Only three imponderables remained unsolved. The weather, the location and strength of the Soviet reserves in depth, and the date of the Anglo-American landing in Europe.

According to Soviet reports, it was known on 2 July that an attack was imminent, and it is said that on 4 July a sapper deserted near Belgorod with information that his unit was about to clear the wire and mines on that day. Instead of attacking at the usual dawn hour the offensive in the south began at 3 p.m. on 4 July on a hot, sultry and oppressive afternoon, the cloud being low and thunder threatening. After heavy bombing raids and diversionary probes by Ott's 52 Corps, von Knobelsdorff's 48 Panzer Corps successfully pushed home its attack against moderate resistance by Chistyakov's 6 Guards Army, an experienced formation which, under its former designation of 21 Army, had taken part in the routing of 48 Panzer Corps on the Don.[29] The Germans were of opinion that the defenders had been taken by surprise, an opinion reinforced by the absence of heavy artillery defensive fire. After dark, 2 SS Panzer Corps made some probing attacks to secure observation posts for the next day's fighting, and at about 10.30 p.m. the Soviet artillery opened up with a very heavy fire programme over the whole area.

During that night it rained incessantly, turning roads and tracks into quagmires, but at 5 a.m. the German attack was taken up again by both 48 and the SS Corps, 48 Panzer breaking through the first line of Soviet defences

---

[28] The Central Front figures include the formations of 5 Guards Army and 5 Tank Army which were transferred from the Steppe Front during the early stages of the battle. For the German appreciation of the Soviet detailed order of battle see *Fremde Heere Ost* estimates summarized by Klink. *Das Gesetz des Handelns 'Zitadelle'*, pp. 339–47. According to Zhukov, the Soviet forces had 1,330,000 men, 3,600 tanks and 3,100 aircraft. Zhukov, *Vospominaniya i Razmyshleniya*, p. 492; also *50 Let Vooruzhennykh Sil SSSR*, p. 365.

[29] Although 48 Panzer Corps then had a strength of about 300 tanks, its panzer divisions no longer had more than eighty tanks each and its main numbers came from the *Gross-deutschland* which had a strength of 180 tanks.

and reaching its objective two hours later, against what was described as relatively light opposition. 8 Air Corps, after early morning battles with regiments of Red Air Force bombers trying to reach the German airfields in the Kharkov area, had already established air superiority over the battle area, although this was not to prevent repeated and effective Soviet air attacks throughout the day on 48 Panzer Corps tank concentrations.[30] During the morning of 5 July there was a cloud-burst and the skies opened to let fall a deluge of water which turned the many streams into torrents impassable by tanks, this causing about twelve hours delay before the sappers could bridge them. 48 Panzer Corps reported that the entire area was infested with mines. The Soviet tanks had the advantage of the higher ground and the Soviet artillery, warming to its task, kept up an ever-increasing intensity of fire, hardly affected by the massive bombing attacks made by the *Luftwaffe* on the Soviet gun areas.[31] In the centre, to the right of 48 Panzer Corps, Hausser's SS divisions had breached only the first of the Soviet defence lines by nightfall of 5 July, and Breith's 3 Panzer Corps had secured a small bridgehead over the Donets to the south of Belgorod. At the end of the second day's fighting the Germans had made only three small penetrations, nowhere deeper than six or seven miles, and Hoth came to the conclusion that, contrary to expectation and previous experience, the Soviet infantry were tolerably trained and of good morale.[32] The nature of the ground, although certainly not unsuitable for tanks, was favourable to the defending infantry on account of the mines, gullies and the waterlogged soil, and by virtue of the cover given by the many scattered villages and standing corn. Because of this, the Soviet rifle formations had managed to withdraw men, guns and equipment to the second defensive line.

On 6 July the 4 Panzer Army attack towards Oboyan on the road to distant Kursk continued, and 8 Air Corps flew nearly 1,700 sorties, a half of them being *Stuka* dive bombing attacks, but the weight of German air power was insufficient to support both 48 Panzer and 2 SS Panzer Corps and at the same time cope with the steadily mounting air opposition.[33] During the night of 5 July and in the early hours of the morning of 6 July, Chistyakov's 6 Guards Army had been heavily reinforced by anti-tank formations and Katukov's 1 Tank Army had moved up close behind it into the second defensive zone. According to the Soviet account, of the truth of which there must be some doubt, the military council of the Voronezh Front, in which it is inferred that the genius of Khrushchev again played a leading part, decided to dig in some

[30] 8 Air Corps alone flew 2,400 sorties on 5 July in the southern sector and claimed to have destroyed 260 enemy aircraft.
[31] Von Mellenthin, *Panzer Battles*, pp. 230–9.
[32] Klink, *Das Gesetz des Handelns 'Zitadelle'*, p. 210.
[33] Soviet historians say that on 5 July on the Voronezh Front alone 173 German aircraft were shot down. In fact over the whole of the Kursk salient twenty-six only were lost. The Germans on the other hand claimed 425 Soviet aircraft destroyed on that day, probably also an exaggerated claim.

hundreds of tanks of 1 Tank Army in the area of the rifle formations of 6 Guards Army. This apparently resulted in a cleavage of opinion, Vasilevsky supporting Vatutin and Khrushchev, while Zhukov and Stalin opposed them. In the event the tanks were dug in, in order to thicken up the artillery and anti-tank fire.[34] On 7 July the battle began to develop more favourably for the Germans and it looked momentarily as if they might achieve freedom of manoeuvre and break through the defended area. 48 Panzer and 2 SS Corps began to make ground slowly but steadily, side by side towards Oboyan, and 3 Panzer Corps of Group Kempf, advancing more rapidly north-eastwards along the flank of Shumilov's 7 Guards Army, started to come alongside them. This occasioned some alarm to the Voronezh Front which took the unusual step of ordering Moskalenko's 38 and 40 Armies which were holding the south-west corner of the Kursk salient, a sector which up to now had been quiet, to give up all their artillery, including even the organic regiments of the rifle divisions, to 6 Guards Army.[35] A tank corps and several rifle divisions were moved from these armies to cover Oboyan, and on the same day 2 and 5 Guards Tank Corps counter-attacked on each flank of the 4 Panzer Army thrust.

By 9 July, although 48 Panzer Corps was only sixteen miles from Oboyan, it was still fifty-five miles from Kursk and ninety miles from Model's 9 Army, and the momentum of the German attack had gone. Casualties had been heavy and the troops were already tiring. The Porsche Tiger tanks, the Panther tanks and the Ferdinand assault guns on which Hitler had placed great hopes had not proved a success. The Porsche Tiger had no machine-guns and was unable to provide its own short range defensive fire, and the Panthers and Ferdinands had been provided with insufficient ammunition. The Mark V chassis was still unsuitable because of technical defects and had a tendency to catch fire. The tactical employment of the heavy tanks was at fault for, instead of exploiting the very effective long range guns with which the heavy tanks were fitted by using them to support the medium tanks by fire and for long range sniping tasks, they were put in the forefront of battle.[36] In close combat in the copses and orchards it was soon found that a T34 at point blank range could hole a Tiger as easily as a Tiger could destroy a T34.

Vatutin was unable to launch a counter-attack with Katukov's 1 Tank Army, as this army was already dug in and holding ground and could not be extricated, a difficulty which may presumably have been foreseen by Zhukov when he objected to its use in this role. Voronezh Front was then allotted 5 Guards Tank Army and Zhadov's 5 Guards Army from the Steppe Front.

[34] *Istoriya*, Vol. 3, pp. 268–9. This is probably an attempt by Khrushchev to discredit both Stalin and Zhukov and is made even more curious by the fact that German air photographs had apparently disclosed that eighty-two Soviet tanks had been dug in on 4 Panzer Army sector *before 4 July*. Klink, *Das Gesetz des Handelns 'Zitadelle'*, p. 201.

[35] Both 38 and 40 Armies were small armies without the corps organization, the one having six and the other seven rifle divisions.

[36] Compare Von Mellenthin's description on the *Panzerkeil* and the *Panzerglocke*, *Panzer Battles*, pp. 231–2.

5 Guards Tank Army, commanded by Rotmistrov, who was later to become one of the foremost learned authorities on tank warfare, moved over 200 miles by forced marches to the area of Prokhorovka, where 2 SS Panzer Corps was thrusting eastwards in a new effort to find room for manoeuvre. On 12 July, after a heavy preparatory bombing attack, Rotmistrov's force consisting of four tank and one mechanized corps, in all 850 tanks and SUs, attacked Hausser's 2 SS Panzer Corps.[37] The tank battle of Prokhorovka was one of the largest of the war and was fought in a narrow strip between the River Psiel and the railway embankment, the sloping ground being cut by ravines and covered by copses and orchards. Nearly 1,300 tanks, assault guns and SUs were engaged, while overhead air battles were being fought, and in the close fighting the new heavy German tanks had little advantage over the T34. The fighting continued over the next few days, 5 Guards Tank Army claiming about 300 German tanks destroyed. Meanwhile von Knobelsdorff's 48 Panzer Corps further to the left continued to engage Chistyakov's 6 Guards and Katukov's 1 Tank Armies, and while it reckoned Soviet tank losses to be enormous, it admitted that its own were staggering.[38] Soviet striking power, far from diminishing, seemed to be increasing.

Meanwhile nearly 100 miles to the north, Model's 9 Army had had little success. The German attack began in the early hours of 5 July, twelve hours later than that in the south, with bombing attacks on 13 Soviet Army gun lines, which were answered by a heavy counter-bombardment and harassing fire programme from the Central Front artillery. Shortly after 5 a.m. tanks and armoured infantry attacked Pukhov's 13 Soviet Army and the flanks of the adjoining Romanenko's 48 and Galanin's 70 Armies, the attack being supported by mine gapping tank roller detachments and remote controlled high explosive charges in diminutive Goliath tanks. Three hours later the attack was resumed on a narrower front supported by Tiger tanks and Ferdinand assault guns. At first Soviet resistance was weak and the Red Air Force appeared to lack determination, and by the end of the first day Model's progress was satisfactory in that he had made a penetration about six miles deep on a twenty mile front and had breached the first defence line. That was the extent of his success and he was not to advance much further. On the second day resistance stiffened rapidly and the German infantry clearing the settlements and villages and the numerous copses and woods suffered heavy casualties, over 10,000 men falling within the first two days. On 7 July 9 Army was running out of tank gun ammunition and Model was asking Zeitzler for the immediate dispatch of 100,000 rounds.[39] German tank losses on the minefields were heavy and the Red Army continued to sow mines, thickening up the minefields at the rear

[37] These Soviet figures show that Rotmistrov's tank formations were fully up to their establishment strength. *Istoriya*, Vol. 3, p. 272.

[38] Von Mellenthin, *Panzer Battles*, pp. 226 and 229. 4 Panzer Army claimed to have destroyed 1,032 enemy tanks between 5 and 11 July. *Kriegstagebuch des OKW*, Vol. 3, 12 July 1943, p. 772.

[39] Klink, *Das Gesetz des Handelns 'Zitadelle'*, p. 281.

as the Germans gapped them from the front. Within 48 hours the impetus of Model's offensive had been broken and the attack came to a standstill.

On 10 July an Anglo-American force landed in Sicily and it became immediately obvious that the Italians did not intend to fight any longer. Hitler, fearing that the loss of Italy and the Italian-held Balkans might open up his southern flank, decided to take military action, not merely to contain the enemy landings but also to safeguard Italy and the Balkans against the defection of the Italian Army. On 13 July von Kluge and von Manstein were summoned to East Prussia to be informed of the *Führer*'s decision to break off the *Citadel* offensive and move a number of divisions, including those of the SS panzer corps, to Western Europe. Believing that the Red Army tank reserves were fast running out, von Manstein urged that the offensive should be continued, since failure to do so would, he thought, unleash the Soviet tank forces against Army Group South's long salient down to the Donets Basin and Black Sea.[40] The removal of the SS panzer corps from Army Group South made any form of attrition battle a pointless undertaking.

The 10 July landings marked the beginning of a new stage of the war in that Germany had at long last been forced to fight by land on two European fronts. The time was soon to come when a number of German formations were permanently lost to the war effort as they were shunted throughout Europe in an effort to plug gaps. Hitler may, of course, have used the Anglo-American landings merely as an excuse to extricate himself from an offensive which was not going well and in the success of which he himself had doubts, yet it is more probable that he called off his attacks for the reasons he gave, since he feared for the security of German troops in Italy and the Balkans and the possible loss of those territories to the enemy.[41] He still underrated the Soviet Union and was not to know that the Red Army was about to enter on to a summer offensive. On the other hand, the sudden loss of Italy and the Balkans would have lost Germany economic resources among which was oil, and would have brought the enemy on to Germany's doorstep. Nor was the *Führer* to know then that the Anglo-American invasion of Western Europe was still eleven months away. The Soviet historical account is silent on the reasons given by Hitler for breaking off the offensive but, with the turn of logic common to the communist bloc, states that the Kursk battle forced the German High Command to withdraw strong forces from the Mediterranean thus enabling the Allies to land in Italy, Soviet academicians reasoning that the battle of Kursk thereby finally brought about the defeat of Italy.[42]

[40] Von Manstein, *Lost Victories*, p. 448.
[41] That the OKW knew that the offensive was not going well can be illustrated by the OKW Diary entry of 11 July which questioned whether, since there was no likelihood of quick success, there could be any fortune in a battle of attrition. *Kriegstagebuch des OKW*, Vol. 3, 11 July 1943, p. 769.
[42] *Istoriya*, Vol. 3, p. 296. There is of course some truth in this, although used by Soviet historians so tediously to gain a propaganda point. By the same token it could be argued that the Anglo-American landings were instrumental in winning the victory at Kursk.

N

Sokolovsky's West Front and M. M. Popov's Bryansk Front had been ordered to prepare an offensive, known as Operation *Kutuzov*, against the Orel salient in Model's rear. In the West Front, Bagramyan's 11 Guards Army was ordered to strike directly south to attempt to envelop the Orel salient from the northern shoulder. The Bryansk Front was to drive from the east on to the town of Orel, using 3 and 63 Armies. Gorbatov, recently promoted to lieutenant-general, had just been appointed to the command of 3 Army in June, having some pleasure in serving under the youthful and cheerful Popov, but none at all in meeting with his old enemy Mekhlis, the political member of the military council of the Bryansk Front. Mekhlis, indefatigable, single-minded, severe, fanatical and inflexible, the man who was so mistrustful that he would always draft, write and sign his own messages, was, however, Gorbatov noted, very much subdued since his disgrace in the Crimea.

The Bryansk offensive was to be made from the area of Novosil across the Susha River, near the boundary between Gorbatov's 3 and Kolpakchy's 63 Armies, and was aimed at driving a gap in 2 Panzer Army's defences, through which 3 Tank Army would attempt to gain open country. The offensive was timed for 12 July.[43]

For a week or so before this Rendulic, the Commander of 35 German Corps, had been aware of the Soviet preparations for an attack, and he was particularly well served by radio intercept, aerial reconnaissance and his own intelligence (*Ic*) staff. There was an abundance of information from prisoners and deserters. Appreciating that the offensive would be launched on a narrow frontage against the Austrian 262 Infantry Division, he concentrated the bulk of his resources there so that in the Novosil sector, which was only seven miles wide, were deployed six infantry battalions, eighteen artillery batteries and twenty-four heavy anti-tank guns, so denuding the rest of the corps front that the remaining eighty miles were covered by only eighteen battalions, twenty-four batteries and twenty-six heavy anti-tank guns. The Austrian defences consisted of a single and continuous trench system forming the front line against the River Susha, and a second line 300 yards to the rear, made up of company and battalion localities. Anti-tank guns and artillery pieces were sited in depth with direct fields of fire up to 1,000 yards, and each gun position was wired and mined. Firmly believing that his infantry would hold if it knew what to expect, in the waiting period Rendulic spent much of his time with his fellow Austrians, emphasizing the weight of artillery and tank attack that they must expect, and exhorting them to keep their nerve and let the assaulting tanks roll over their positions. Rendulic, who had no tanks or assault guns to counter the expected tank onslaught, was in a state of nervous tension in case he should have misread Popov's intentions. Early on the morning of 12 July, however, his mind was put at rest when Soviet artillery started

---

[43] Gorbatov, *Gody i Voiny, Novyi Mir*, May 1964.

a very heavy bombardment, the weight of which exceeded anything that had been expected, on the left flank of the Austrian positions.[44]

At six o'clock in the morning Red Army infantry crossed the Susha in tight formation, losing heavily in casualties in the German artillery defensive fire, but successfully establishing a bridgehead. Soviet engineers then began to build a bridge in full observation of the Germans and, although harassed by artillery fire, completed it in six hours. Rendulic was of the opinion that only *Luftwaffe* intervention could have stopped them, but he was unable to obtain any air support at all, and by that afternoon a steady stream of Soviet armour was arriving over the river. Great numbers of heavy KV tanks then came into the attack, unsupported by Red Army riflemen, and, having overrun the Austrian infantry localities, engaged by fire the anti-tank guns in the depth of the position. There for the loss of three German anti-tank guns, tank after tank was destroyed by mines and anti-tank gun fire, so that by evening, when the Soviet armour withdrew, it left behind about sixty disabled tanks on the field of battle. The Austrians had lost their first trench line but they withdrew a few hundred yards and built a second, ready for the next attack, and in this way the Orel battle continued over the next five weeks.[45] Rudolf Schmidt, the 2 Panzer Army Commander, had been removed from his command two days before the opening of the Soviet offensive and from 13 July to 5 August Model acted as the army commander of two armies.

In the Kursk salient the Germans may have been nearer to tactical success than the Soviet accounts will allow. Whereas on 13 July the Germans had only five divisions uncommitted, according to the Soviet account the Central Front had a rifle and two tank corps which had not been in battle. Yet the position of the Voronezh Front facing von Manstein was far less secure. The whole of the Steppe Front was eventually committed to its support and the Soviet command would hardly have accepted the risk of removing the organic artillery from 38 and 40 Armies if the Voronezh Front had not been in some danger. Von Manstein may therefore have been correct in his view that a continuation of the 4 Panzer Army thrusts would have destroyed most of the Soviet armour facing it, and might have gained open country.

Citadel failed because the plan for the offensive was badly conceived. Frequent postponements led to a loss of surprise and after the experiences of fighting in Stalingrad, the concept of attacking a strong enemy in well prepared defensive positions was of doubtful wisdom, however strong the German forces might be. The *Citadel* offensive was undertaken as a gamble, in the hope of snatching an early victory before the Anglo-Americans made a landing in Europe, but Hitler and the German High Command had little idea that the Soviet enemy was by then almost ready to assume the offensive. Hitler and Göring had never been close to the realities of the fighting on the Eastern Front and even Zeitzler had no recent experience of war there. It was notice-

[44] Rendulic estimated it at 120 batteries.
[45] Rendulic, *Gekämpft Gesiegt Geschlagen*, pp. 128–35.

able that the more distant the opinion from the fighting line, the more sanguine it became. Whereas von Kluge was inclined to scepticism, Model had little confidence in the outcome of the attack. This same tendency had become apparent in March in Army Group South when Hoth, the Commander of 4 Panzer Army, had resisted on the grounds of the weather and the exhaustion of his troops the urging of von Manstein and the High Command to renew the Kharkov offensive.[46]

Up to 1943, the Germans usually succeeded tactically but failed strategically. At Kursk they failed strategically because they were unsuccessful tactically. The whole concept of the *Citadel* offensive reflected the bankruptcy of Hitler and the German High Command. After *Citadel* the Axis lost all initiative on the Eastern Front and was never to regain it.

---

[46] The German and Red Army losses during *Citadel* are unknown although they were undoubtedly heavy on both sides. The total German losses in the East from all causes from July to October 1943 were 911,000. Mueller-Hillebrand, *Das Heer*, Vol. 3, Table 55.

CHAPTER TWENTY-THREE

The Soviet 1943 Autumn Offensives

The Soviet offensive against the rear of Model's 9 Army in the Orel salient consisted of concentric thrusts by Sokolovsky's West Front, M. M. Popov's Bryansk Front and later by Rokossovsky's Central Front.[1] The six rifle divisions of Bagramyan's 11 Guards Army of West Front, with a tank corps and four tank brigades supported by two breakthrough artillery corps comprising over sixty artillery regiments, in all nearly 3,000 guns and mortars, made the initial assault, the tactics adopted being those which were to become common throughout the latter part of the war, attacks being made on very narrow assault frontages, rifle divisions being allotted tight boundaries only 2,000 yards apart.[2] After heavy artillery preparation at dawn on 12 July, 11 Guards Army advanced sixteen miles in the first two days. The attack had been taken up from the east of the Orel bend by Gorbatov's 3 Army and Kolpakchy's 63 Army, both part of the Bryansk Front. German resistance was described as bitter and as divisions of Model's 9 Army were turned about to assist 2 Panzer Army in covering the 9 Army rear, the Soviet offensive was slowly brought to a standstill; but not before von Manstein had been compelled to give up to von Kluge the panzer grenadier division *Grossdeutschland*. Although the Red Army progress had been temporarily checked, the pressure was to grow again when the West Front brought up a further two armies, Badanov's 4 Tank Army and Fedyuninsky's 11 Army. In addition the Bryansk Front committed to battle Rybalko's 3 Guards Tank Army.[3]

On 25 July Mussolini, after a last interview with the King of Italy, was deposed and arrested, and the new Italian government formed under Marshal

---

[1] The military council of the West Front was Sokolovsky, Bulganin and Pokrovsky; of the Bryansk Front, Popov, Mekhlis and Sandalov; of the Central Front, Rokossovsky, Telegin and Malinin; of the Voronezh Front, Vatutin, Khrushchev and S. P. Ivanov (later Bogolyubov); of the Steppe Front, Konev, Susaikov and M. V. Zakharov; of the South-West Front, Malinovsky, Zheltov and Korzhenevich; of the South Front, Tolbukhin, Gurov and Biryuzov, the second named in each case being the political member and the third the chief of staff.

[2] *Istoriya*, Vol. 3, p. 277.

[3] 11 Army had been brought up from Kaluga about 100 miles away, where it had been refitted. Fedyuninsky, formerly the Deputy Commander of the Bryansk Front, joined 11 Army immediately before the battle.

Badoglio assured Kesselring that it intended to stay in the war. Hitler, however, was unconvinced and he determined to remove formations, preferably SS divisions, from the Eastern Front to maintain German control over Italy. The Commander of Army Group Centre was sent for the next day, and was told to prepare to evacuate the Orel salient in order to make troops available for Western Europe. The protesting von Kluge enumerated his many difficulties. Neither the Hagen defence line in the rear nor any intermediate line was yet prepared, and all his construction workers were fully employed keeping open roads which were being continually washed away by the heavy rains. The local Russian peasants were busy collecting in the rye harvest and it was impossible to set them to work on the field defences in the rear, because at any hint of withdrawal they would all disappear to the woods. The Red enemy, said von Kluge, had an enormous superiority in numbers of tanks and guns, and to counter it a methodical and gradual evacuation was required, extending over two or three months, since too hasty a withdrawal might lead to the overrunning of the German troops. Partisans, too, were particularly active.[4] The giving up of Orel with its sidings and unloading facilities would reduce the capacity of the railway line from fifty to eighteen trains a day. Hitler listened to these objections with sympathy but remained adamant on the need for the immediate removal of troops, telling von Kluge that he, the *Führer*, was no longer the master of his own decisions. Even von Kluge's suggestion that the evacuation should be spread over a period of three to four weeks instead of the two to three months he had originally proposed did not meet with approval.[5]

At 1 a.m. on 29 July a German radio intercept unit listened in to a radio telephone conversation betweeen Churchill and Roosevelt, in which the intended defection of Italy from the Axis was discussed at length by the two statesmen.[6] This confirmed Hitler's fears and on 1 August he ordered the immediate withdrawal from the Orel salient.

Meanwhile von Manstein of Army Group South was faced with a steadily deteriorating situation in the Ukraine. On 17 July Tolbukhin's South and Malinovsky's South-West Fronts had made probing thrusts in some strength across the Mius and the middle Donets near Izyum, about 300 miles southeast from Orel, the attacks falling on von Mackensen's 1 Panzer Army and on Hollidt's newly formed 6 Army. A substantial weight of German armour, equivalent to two panzer corps, was removed from the left flank of Army Group South near Kharkov and sent to the south-east to restore the position near the Mius and, as von Manstein was subsequently to admit, the decision was a disastrous one, for the Red Army forces were far stronger than either

---

[4] In July alone there were 1,114 partisan attacks on the railway network in Army Group Centre. Teske, *Die Silbernen Spiegel*, p. 192.

[5] Heiber, *Hitlers Lagebesprechungen*, p. 369 et seq.

[6] *Kriegstagebuch des OKW*, Vol. 3, p. 854, 29 July 1943; also Churchill, Vol. 5, *Closing the Ring*, p. 56.

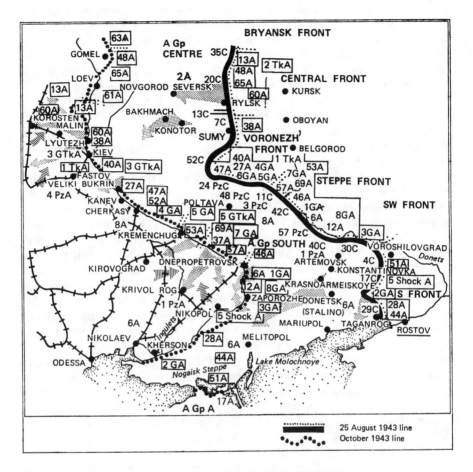

FROM THE DONETS TO THE DNIEPER
August–October 1943

Hitler or von Manstein had imagined that they would be, after the losses which they had undoubtedly suffered during the Kursk battles.[7] The next Soviet blow was to fall in the area of Kharkov, the eastern gateway to the Ukraine.

The Soviet offensive on Belgorod and Kharkov was co-ordinated by Zhukov and was mounted by Vatutin's Voronezh and Konev's Steppe Fronts, together with the right wing of Malinovsky's South-West Front, supported by

[7] Von Manstein, *Lost Victories*, p. 452. The *Führer* had allowed von Manstein to retain temporarily two of the SS divisions earmarked for Italy to restore the situation on the right flank. Hausser's 2 SS Corps Headquarters and the *Leibstandarte* had already left for the West.

their tactical air armies and 200 bombers of the long range bomber force, and artillery of the High Command Reserve removed from the Bryansk Front. A deception operation was undertaken by Chibisov's 38 Army on the extreme right flank of the Voronezh Front, involving radio networks and troop movements, but in the event this deception proved unnecessary since the weight and timing of the attack were unexpected, the German attention having already been diverted to the Mius and middle Donets. On 3 August, while the battle was still being fought inside the Orel salient, the Voronezh and Steppe Fronts, using four rifle armies, thrust towards Belgorod, the attack coming as a complete surprise to the defenders.[8] After three hours the defence was broken and by midday Katukov's 1 Tank Army and Rotmistrov's 5 Guards Tank Army, both of the Voronezh Front, were deep in the German rear. On 5 August Belgorod was taken, the tank troops advancing nearly seventy miles in five days and driving a thirty-mile gap between Hoth's 4 Panzer Army and Group Kempf.[9] Bogodukhov fell on 7 August, the timing of the offensive having been co-ordinated with the activities of partisans who blocked the German railway system for about two days. The Germans were then forced to bring back a panzer corps from the south-east and the panzer grenadier division *Grossdeutschland* and other elements from Army Group Centre to reinforce von Manstein's left. Hitler was still insisting that Kharkov be held at all costs but on 13 August the Steppe Front fought its way into the city, and by 23 August the Germans withdrew to avoid being entrapped there. The arrival of Breith's 3 Panzer Corps and the SS divisions *Das Reich*, *Totenkopf* and *Wiking* and the heavy counter-attacks they made on Katukov's 1 Tank and Chistyakov's 6 Guards Armies near Bogodukhov forced Rotmistrov's 5 Guards Tank Army to come to the rescue of the Red Army formations and the position stabilized itself, the Soviet advance coming to a temporary halt.[10]

Von Manstein, seeking in vain for freedom to make his own decisions, in desperation presented Hitler with two alternatives, the provision of reinforcement formations or the abandoning of the Donets basin. On 27 August the *Führer* arrived at Army Group South Headquarters in Vinnitsa to discuss the situation, and although he made some attempt to be objective, he was evasive and could not be pinned down to giving a major decision. Hitler insisted that the Donets Basin should continue to be held and he made the usual promises of the transfer of troops from Army Groups Centre and North. He showed that he was for the moment almost entirely preoccupied with Italy, the Balkans and with the threat of the Americans and the British in the

---

[8] The armies were Chistyakov's 6 Guards and Zhadov's 5 Guards Armies of Voronezh Front, Kryuchenkin's 69 Army and Shumilov's 7 Guards Army of Steppe Front. Gagen's 57 Army of South-West Front also took part in the thrust on Kharkov. An earlier successful attack made on 23 July had been discontinued with the agreement of the fronts and the Soviet High Command, according to Zhukov, so that a more powerful broad frontal offensive could be prepared.

[9] Group Kempf (formerly Group Lanz) became a new 8 Army in September 1943.

[10] *Istoriya*, Vol. 3, pp. 290–1.

Mediterranean. Von Manstein, beset by his own difficulties in the Ukraine, was later to criticize the *Führer* for being incapable of discerning priorities and for using arguments which events subsequently proved to be irrelevant.[11] They were not, however, irrelevant at the time. Italy had collapsed and was about to throw in its lot with the Anglo-Americans, and the defection of the Italian occupation troops in the Balkans was to leave a great vacuum there. Jodl was to note that the *Führer* was highly perturbed about the danger of an attack from the Mediterranean on South-East Europe which might rapidly win over the Balkan States and even bring Turkey into the war against the Axis, 'such an event giving promise of a quick Allied victory'. The Rumanians were already suspected of putting out peace-feelers to the West through Madrid and Stockholm, and during the month of September 1943 an Allied landing on the coast of France or the Netherlands was expected almost daily.[12] The *Führer*'s difficulties, real as they undoubtedly were, proved cold comfort to von Manstein. Only the day before the Vinnitsa meeting, Rokossovsky's Central Front had opened a new offensive against Army Group Centre, and von Kluge on 28 August hastened to Hitler in East Prussia to resist any transfer of troops from Army Group Centre to Army Group South. Von Manstein therefore got nothing.

On 26 August Rokossovsky, using 60 and 65 Armies against von Kluge's Army Group Centre, had attacked westwards from what had been the west flank of the Kursk bulge onto Weiss's 2 German Army. Batov's 65 Army met with fierce resistance and advanced only twelve miles in five days but on Chernyakhovsky's 60 Army sector the resistance of 13 German Corps was weaker, and Soviet troops moved rapidly forward on a sixty-mile front crossing the Desna near Novgorod Severski on 3 September and threatening the flanks of both Army Group Centre and Army Group South. Meanwhile von Manstein's right flank in the area of the Donets Basin was again under attack. Between 13 and 16 August Malinovsky's South-West Front had taken up the offensive on the middle Donets, and two days later Tolbukhin's South Front attacked in strength across the Mius. Tsvetaev's 5 Shock Army broke through in the centre, and Taganrog together with part of Röpke's 29 German Corps was encircled and cut off.[13] Hollidt's 6 German Army front was by then in danger of collapse and on 31 August Hitler gave von Manstein authority to withdraw 6 Army and the right wing of 1 Panzer Army 'provided there was no other possible alternative'.[14]

A few days afterwards, von Manstein and von Kluge flew to East Prussia to beg the *Führer* to reorganize the German High Command by restoring the

[11] Von Manstein, *Lost Victories*, pp. 459–60.
[12] *Kriegstagebuch des OKW*, Vol. 3, on the Balkans, p. 1394; Rumania, p. 1532; imminence of the Second Front, pp. 956, 961, 976, 1024, 1043, 1065, i.e. 16, 17, 20, 29 August, 2 and 7 September; also *Goebbels' Diary*, 10 September 1943, p. 346.
[13] Röpke's 29 Corps broke out to the west at the end of August.
[14] Von Manstein, *Lost Victories*, p. 460.

responsibility for all theatres of war to the Chief of the General Staff. This would have meant the abolition of the Armed Forces High Command (OKW) and a reversion to the organization which existed when the *Führer* had come to power, except that it lacked an army officer as Defence Minister and Commander-in-Chief. Hitler, who regarded von Manstein as over-ambitious, would have none of this.[15] An earlier letter from von Manstein to Zeitzler, suggesting that the risk be accepted of denuding Western Europe of troops in order to find reserves for Russia, had apparently occasioned a stormy outburst when shown to the *Führer*.[16] On 8 September, the day on which Italy capitulated, Hitler held a meeting at Zaporozhe attended by von Manstein and von Kleist at which von Manstein vainly proposed that he be allowed to withdraw behind the Dnieper. He stressed the danger to von Kleist's Army Group A in the Taman Peninsula and the Crimea should he not be able to hold firm his own right flank. Hitler, who had already agreed to the evacuation of the Taman Peninsula in the Kuban, made the usual promises of reinforcements, but he would not permit von Manstein to shorten the line on his right by falling back from the Donets towards the Dnieper, since this, he said, would result in the loss of the industrial area of the Donets Basin.

Since Army Group Centre and Army Group North lacked the strength to pin the enemy opposing them, the Soviet High Command began to reinforce its formations in the Ukraine by thinning out other sectors. According to Zhukov's post-war account of the situation at that time, Stalin would not agree to the envelopment proposals submitted by himself, Vasilevsky and Antonov, but preferred to attack on a broad front from Velikiye Luki to the Black Sea. The Supreme Commander countered their proposals by maintaining that the Red Army was not yet strong enough to undertake large scale encirclements and that the regrouping necessary for these envelopments would take too much time. At that moment the need, he said, was to evict the invader from Soviet soil and save the industry and agriculture of the Ukraine from being scorched by von Manstein.[17] This may or may not have been true. The Red Army did continue to attack on a very broad front, but this was the Soviet pattern of the offensive throughout the whole war. Hitler's rigid defensive policy certainly played into Soviet hands, but even so there were other indications that Stalin's strategy had a deeper basis than merely driving off the enemy. The closing in on the Sea of Azov and the Perekop Isthmus was to trap Army Group A in the Crimea, this being a repetition of what the Soviet High Command had tried to achieve in the spring of 1942. In fact, the later Red Army operations in the Dnieper bend and the turning of von Manstein's flank by the Central Front gave every indication that envelopment was their object.

[15] *Ibid*, p. 461; for Hitler's views on von Manstein see *Goebbels' Diary*, 2 March and 23 September 1943, pp. 199 and 382.
[16] Von Manstein, *Lost Victories*, p. 461.
[17] Zhukov, *Vospominaniya i Razmyshleniya*, pp. 518 and 522–3.

The South and South-West Fronts, co-ordinated by Vasilevsky, hotly engaged the right flank of Army Group South. Malinovsky's South-West Front started to gain ground south-westwards towards Konstantinovka and Krasnoarmeiskoye, pushing back 1 Panzer Army and threatening the rear of 6 German Army, and willy-nilly von Manstein was forced to evacuate the Donets Basin, destroying such industrial equipment and stocks as he could. At the beginning of August von Mackensen's 1 Panzer Army had been in the Donets while Hollidt's 6 Army was on the Mius, as near as fifty miles to Rostov. During August and September they were both forced back westwards towards the Dnieper. Fretter-Pico's 30 Corps, which was part of 1 Panzer Army and which was made up of four tired and under-strength infantry divisions, withdrew from Artemovsk towards Konstantinovka and Pavlograd across the hot and arid steppe, suffering much hardship as it did so. Previously divisional sectors had been twenty miles or more wide, but the withdrawal was conducted by regimental all arms groups, moving back on foot along the railway lines and the main roads. At the start 30 Corps attempted to carry out a demolition programme, but this was soon given up for lack of manpower, time and resources. The corps headquarters had little control over the operations beyond the laying down of withdrawal routes and timings and in the main the regimental groups operated almost independently. They were continually harassed by detachments of Soviet tanks and motorized infantry which came sweeping over the plain, the Germans fighting by day and making strenuous forced marches by night. As usual there was a shortage of anti-tank guns and, the gun crews being under strength, the heavy 88 mm pak proved a difficult gun to move once it had been unlimbered. German field artillery was inadequate in strength and in design and was outranged by enemy guns and mortars. Infantry casualties mounted steadily and the few replacements lacked training and were often elderly or otherwise physically unsuitable for front line duties, so that Fretter-Pico was to note sourly that, when the Navy, the *Luftwaffe*, the SS and the supporting and technical arms had taken their pick of the annual intake of recruits, what remained went to the infantry divisions. Meanwhile the small groups trudged on, orienting themselves often without maps and compasses as best they might. Every man knew that his safety depended on the group and he took good care not to become separated from his own mob (*Haufen*). Propaganda pamphlets were showered on them from the air and the Soviet loudspeakers were rarely silent. All, however, feared Soviet captivity more than death.[18] Stalino (Donetsk) and Krasnoarmeiskoye were taken by the Red Army on 8 September and Mariupol two days later.

Although Malinovsky was making good progress against the right flank of von Manstein's Army Group South, in the centre Vatutin's Voronezh and Konev's Steppe Fronts were making little headway against the German defence to the south-west of Kharkov. The main threat to von Manstein's left flank

[18] Fretter-Pico, *Missbrauchte Infanterie*, pp. 114–9.

came from the westward movement of Rokossovsky's Central Front towards the Dnieper north of Kiev. Chernyakhovsky's 60 Army had advanced in all over 100 miles, taking Konotop on 6 September and the important railway junction of Bakhmach three days later. The whole of Army Group South appeared to be in danger of being enveloped from the north, but not before 15 September could von Manstein persuade Hitler to agree to pull back behind the Dnieper, and by then there was little time left to carry out an orderly and safe withdrawal.

From a front of about 450 miles in length the German troops had to converge on the five Dnieper crossing places at Dnepropetrovsk, Kremenchug, Cherkasy, Kanev and Kiev, and then redeploy again on the other side of the river, and there was an obvious danger that the Soviet enemy would either block these bridging places or cross the river on a broad front before the German formations had redeployed. In the circumstances, von Manstein was fortunate in being able to withdraw not only his own troops, including about 200,000 wounded, but in addition hundreds of thousands of Ukrainian civilians, in order that the oncoming Red Army should not use them as recruits or for labour.[19] Cattle and industrial equipment were also taken, while attempts were made to devastate a great belt of land in front of the Dnieper in order that the Soviet troops should find neither supplies nor shelter.

Army Group South, although somewhat harassed by partisans, surprised the Red Army by the speed and skill with which it built rear positions and turned towns into strong points; but shortly after 15 September it became obvious to the Soviet High Command that a widespread withdrawal behind the Dnieper was involved.[20] The Central, Voronezh and Steppe Fronts had been strengthened by allotting them a further six armies, and the Central and Voronezh Fronts were ordered to advance on Kiev while the Steppe Front was to converge on Kremenchug.[21] In the third week in September the tank and mechanized troops were moving rapidly as they followed up the German withdrawal, even the rifle formations averaging fifteen miles a day. The long advance inevitably led to disorganization, and much of the artillery had been left behind for lack of fuel; but by the evening of 21 September Soviet troops first reached the Dnieper and by the end of the month had closed up to the

---

[19] According to contemporary evidence the proportion of Ukrainians who were unwillingly evacuees was probably high. A German paper prepared for the *Wehrmacht* Propaganda Department *Brf B Nr. 144/43 g.* of 1 April 1943 ended:

Freeing from Bolshevism is no ideal for the Ukrainian if he does not know what is to follow. For him Bolshevism and Nazism are much one and the same. The surprisingly high count of 70 per cent who avoid evacuation and prefer to await the Soviets, shows in fact that the Bolshevists have the advantage, since they are at least linked (to the Ukrainian) by race and psychology.

Kriegstagebuch des OKW, Vol. 3, pp. 1424–5.

[20] *Istoriya*, Vol. 3, pp. 310–1.

[21] The Central and Voronezh Fronts were allotted Rybalko's 3 Guards Tank Army, Koroteev's 52 Army and P. A. Belov's 61 Army. The Steppe Front was reinforced by Zhadov's 5 Guards Army, P. M. Kozlov's 37 Army and Glagolev's 46 Army.

river on a 400 mile frontage from Loev in Belorussia to Dnepropetrovsk in the Central Ukraine. The Germans continued to hold bridgeheads forward of the river both at Dnepropetrovsk and in the great triangular area east of the Dnieper from Zaporozhe to Melitopol and the Molochnoye Lake near the Sea of Azov, this being their only land link with von Kleist's Army Group A and 17 Army in the Crimea. Hollidt's 6 Army, which held this triangle, was removed from von Manstein's Army Group South and put under the command of von Kleist's Army Group A.

Although Army Group South had avoided disaster the withdrawal did not go smoothly. Von Choltitz was critical of the behaviour of German base and supply troops, who during this withdrawal often gave way to panic.[22] Fretter-Pico, too, described how 30 Corps arrived at the great city of Dnepropetrovsk on the Dnieper to find the German civil administration officials in the process of evacuating equipment; but this, in his view, did not extend beyond materials and supplies required for their own comfort. These officials disposed of fleets of lorries full of beds, furniture and food, while 30 Corps bridging columns could not move for lack of transport. This deficiency Fretter-Pico promptly rectified by requisitioning the vehicles he required.[23]

The Soviet High Command, in a directive to all fronts on 9 September, had offered orders, medals and awards to all ranks who achieved a quick and decisive crossing of the Desna and Dnieper, and because much of the pontoon bridging and ferry equipment had been left behind in the approach march, full use had to be made of local resources. Soviet historians have exaggerated the feats performed in the crossing by describing the river as having a depth of up to thirty feet, a rate of flow of six feet a second, and a width of up to 3,500 yards. This obstacle, they say, was crossed by troops in fishing boats and on locally constructed rafts, and even by Red Army men who kept themselves afloat by straw-filled rain capes.[24] The river was in fact wide and deep in places, but for some of its length it was very shallow and broken by numerous sand banks and islands. Its middle reaches in 1943 varied from 200 to 1,300 yards in width and for some of its length scrub and woodland came right down to the water's edge, the thick beds of reeds giving good cover for small boats.[25] The Red Army did what any other army would have done in the circumstances and, in addition to starting the construction of bridging, it searched for boats and materials to build rafts and ferries, and with no little ingenuity between 22 and 30 September the Central, Voronezh, Steppe and South-West Fronts made numerous crossings of the river over a 300-mile

[22] Von Choltitz, *Un Soldat parmi des Soldats*, p. 172.
[23] Fretter-Pico, *Missbrauchte Infanterie*, p. 121.
[24] *Istoriya*, Vol. 3, pp. 324–5.
[25] In 1943 the widths of the Dnieper were as follows. At Smolensk, 150 yards; at the mouth of the Pripet, 470 yards; below Kiev, between 200 and 1,300 yards; at Dnepropetrovsk, 2,000 yards. The fall was 1 in 10,000. The Germans had found no difficulty in crossing it from west to east in 1941.

front between the Pripet and the area to the north of Zaporozhe. The Voronezh Front alone secured nine bridgeheads.[26]

Since the failure of *Citadel* Zeitzler, the Chief of the German General Staff, had been advising the fortification of a new line running from the Narva and Lake Peipus to Belorussia down the course of the Sozh to Gomel, then along the Dnieper to just north of Zaporozhe and finally on to Melitopol and the Sea of Azov. This line, known as the Panther Line or East Wall, was to hold the Red Army in check. The *Führer* had refused earlier requests to fortify it, partly because he was in principle opposed to rear defences which might encourage his field commanders to withdraw, and partly because all available fortification materials were required for the construction of the Atlantic Wall. Some work had been carried out after the failure of *Citadel* by the army groups themselves using civilian labour, but since they lacked concrete, steel, barbed wire and mines, the defences consisted merely of earthworks. Not until 12 August, in the (OKH) *Führer* Order 10, were the four army groups ordered to begin work on the fortifications. The order gave them no authority to fall back on the line. Jodl, lamenting in the OKW diary on 21 August on the likely effect of the withdrawal, listed the usual political and economic arguments so near to the *Führer*'s heart; Finland and Sweden, Germany's use of the Baltic for sea-borne supplies and U boat training, the loss of thirty-two developed airfields and the industry and ores of the Donets Basin and Krivoi Rog.[27] By the end of September, however, von Manstein's Army Group South had already been driven back onto the East Wall.

Such tactical defences as were in being had been constructed by the labour organization or by rearward troops, and, as Fretter-Pico complained, were often so poorly sited as to be useless.[28] The Dnieper itself was a water obstacle of tactical value only if its entire length could be covered by observation and fire, and then only until it froze. The fighting strength of German formations had sunk so low that they bore little relationship to their designation, and the bayonet strength of many infantry divisions was as low as 1,000 men. Since Army Group South had thirty-seven such infantry divisions to cover about 450 miles of front, the divisions, which were in fact no more than under-

---

[26] In order to take the bridgehead near Lyutezh tanks of the Voronezh Front had to cross both the Desna and the Dnieper, the Desna being crossed so it is claimed by underwater fording. Why the Red Army should have used an assault technique to cross the Desna is not clear. Von Mellenthin, who was with 48 Panzer Corps in the area of Kremenchug, stated that the Red Army crossed the Dnieper by means of underwater bridges. Von Tippelskirch makes a similar statement for the crossing of the Oder near Küstrin in January 1945. There are of course great difficulties in constructing bridges of this type and the reason for doing so is not apparent. Soviet accounts do not claim that such bridges were constructed but they reproduce von Mellenthin's statement without comment. This in itself is possibly indicative that such bridges were never in fact built.

[27] *Kriegstagebuch des OKW*, Vol. 3, pp. 933 and 983. To these was added the surprising argument that from the East Wall the *Luftwaffe* 'would no longer be able to bomb Grozny, Saratov, Gorki and the Urals'.

[28] Fretter-Pico, *Missbrauchte Infanterie*, p. 117.

strength regiments, were each required to cover about twelve miles of front and this allowed no deployment in depth. Seventeen panzer and panzer grenadier divisions remained to von Manstein, but these lacked fire and shock power, the panzer divisions often being reduced to forty or fifty tanks while the panzer grenadier divisions were deficient of both tanks and infantry.[29] On 7 September von Manstein's tank strength, as recorded in the OKW diary, was given as 257 tanks and 220 assault guns.[30]

The *Führer* had formerly decided on keeping the Donets Basin because he considered that the industrial area and the coal were essential to the German war effort. In order to hold this salient he had so extended the German formations that they could no longer withstand Soviet attack. But no sooner had he lost the Donets Basin than he insisted that the iron and manganese deposits just inside the Dnieper bend at Krivoi Rog and Nikopol were likewise indispensable and could not be given up at any cost. Moreover, unless the Crimea was going to be evacuated the Dnieper bend would have to be held. Hitler, using the well-worn objections of the previous year, would not hear of the evacuation of the Crimea since its loss would, he thought, endanger the Rumanian Ploesti oil supplies and would have a decisive effect on the attitudes of Turkey, Rumania and Bulgaria to the war.[31]

Von Kleist's Army Group A consisted of only 17 Army in the Taman Peninsula and a static organization in the Crimea. 17 Army, originally nearly 350,000 strong, had given up over 100,000 troops in the way of drafts to von Manstein, but even so no fewer than fourteen German infantry divisions and seven Rumanian divisions were still locked up holding the so-called Goth's Head bridgehead, awaiting the change in Germany's fortunes which would enable them to reoccupy the Caucasian oilfields. 17 Army, commanded since July by Jaenecke instead of Ruoff, was contained by I. E. Petrov's North Caucasus Front consisting of Grechkin's 9 Army, Leselidze's 18 Army and Grechko's 56 Army.[32]

The *Führer* had only grudgingly agreed to the evacuation of Taman and had delayed giving the executive order for nearly a month.[33] The withdrawal began in the second week of September and was carried out in good order, although Red Army troops landed from the sea behind Allmendinger's 5 and Konrad's 49 Corps in an attempt to pin them. The Red Air Force was very active but the

---

[29] Von Manstein, *Lost Victories*, p. 473. *OKH Kriegsgliederung* 5 September 1943 shows the strength (not including 6 Army) as only ten panzer and panzer grenadier divisions and thirty-four infantry divisions.

[30] *Kriegstagebuch des OKW*, Vol. 3, p. 1083.

[31] *Ibid*, pp. 1263 and 1356; von Manstein, *Lost Victories*, p. 503.

[32] I. E. Petrov's military council included Fominykh as political member and Laskin as chief of staff.

[33] The *Führer* had agreed with Zeitzler's evacuation proposals on 14 August. The executive order demanded the complete demolition of all facilities on the Kuban bridgehead to be carried out ruthlessly, using forced civil labour including that of women's battalions. *OKH/Gen StdH/Op. Abt(1S/A) Nr. 430586/43 g. Kdos Chefsache* of 4 September 1943.

Soviet Black Sea Fleet was inert. The Soviet account has tended to exaggerate the withdrawal into a Red Army victory, claiming the defeat of ten Axis divisions and the sinking of 140 vessels, but in fact the bridgehead force withdrew without much loss. However, as Pickert, the Commander of 9 Flak Division who was present at the time commented, if the Soviet Navy had shown any determination to interrupt the passage over the Kerch Straits the situation might have been otherwise. Not one surface attack was made against the ferrying operations.[34] The evacuation was completed by 9 October, but by the end of the same month Soviet troops closely following up 17 Army were already crossing the Kerch Straits and disembarking on the eastern tip of the Crimea.

On 20 October 1943 the designations of the Soviet fronts were changed once more, those in the south for the last time until the end of the war. All the fronts in the Ukraine became known as Ukrainian Fronts, numbered consecutively from north to south so that the Voronezh Front became the First, the Steppe Front the Second, the South-West Front the Third and the South Front the Fourth Ukrainian Front. At the same time the Central Front became the Belorussian Front. Zhukov remained responsible for the co-ordination of the First and Second and Vasilevsky for the Third and Fourth Ukrainian Fronts.

Vatutin's 1 Ukrainian Front had been ordered by the Soviet High Command to take Kiev on the west bank of the Dnieper. On 22 September Rybalko's 3 Guards Tank Army had obtained a foothold in the loop of the Dnieper near Veliki Bukrin about fifty miles to the south of Kiev, and this was speedily reinforced by parachuted troops and elements of Trofimenko's 27 and Moskalenko's 40 Armies, this attack being made against the new German 8 Army commanded by Wöhler, the headquarters of which had been formed from the former Group Kempf.[35] Wöhler ordered von Knobelsdorff's 48 Panzer Corps to destroy the Soviet bridgehead, and on 27 September the advancing Red Army troops were caught in the open as they moved westwards and were driven back with heavy loss into the bridgehead loop from which they had come. The bridgehead itself, however, could be contained, but not destroyed, by 48 Panzer Corps.

Vatutin still intended in accordance with his orders to make his main thrust from the Bukrin bridgehead to the south of Kiev, using 27 and 40 Armies and 3 Guards Tank Army. At the same time a subsidiary thrust was to be mounted from the Lyutezh bridgehead about twenty miles to the north of Kiev. The Bukrin attack was made against the containing 48 Panzer Corps at 6.30 a.m. on 16 October when, after a two-hour bombardment which reached back as far as divisional headquarters and left the ground looking like a freshly

---

[34] Pickert, *Vom Kuban-Brückenkopf bis Sewastopol*, p. 57.

[35] Wöhler at the beginning of the war had been chief operations officer (*Ia*) to 14 Army, then successively chief of staff to 17 Corps, 11 Army (von Manstein) and Army Group Centre (von Kluge). There he had commanded the Group Wöhler.

ploughed field, Soviet infantry attacked in closely serried ranks behind a barrage with tanks in support, one wave following another, screaming and hurrahing as they came forward. The attack failed. It was renewed in the afternoon. The next day it was repeated with undiminished vigour, and again and again on the two following days, all the attacks being inflexible and unimaginative and, in the German view, causing appalling Red Army losses. 48 Panzer Corps' casualties were by comparison relatively light and yet it was itself near breaking point. Its acting commander, von Choltitz, an officer with a very distinguished record, caused much surprise to his staff by his outspoken and seemingly eccentric views, in which he foresaw the Soviet masses closing in on Germany and submerging it like a great flood. To save his troops unnecessary bloodshed this remarkable officer departed westwards to seek a personal interview with Hitler in order to resign and persuade the *Führer* of the futility of the war.[36]

The bloody failure of the attacks from the Bukrin bridgehead caused Vatutin to change his plans. New proposals were submitted through Zhukov and the General Staff to Stalin, the Supreme Commander, and these, after examination and co-ordination with Rokossovsky's Belorussian Front, were approved.[37] Vatutin's 1 Ukrainian Front then changed its main thrust to the Lyutezh bridgehead to the north of Kiev, although this involved the northwards movement of 3 Guards Tank Army and the bulk of the supporting artillery from one bridgehead to another over a hundred miles away, using a route parallel to the river and the German forward defended localities. The Dnieper had to be crossed twice and the Desna once, the transfer taking place mainly by night, although the concealment of the movement was in fact made easier by the dull and cloudy autumn weather. Eventually so many troops were massed in the Lyutezh bridgehead which according to contemporary accounts was no bigger than a five kopeck piece, that only a few dozen paces from Vatutin's tactical headquarters and observation post were Moskalenko's 38 Army and Rybalko's 3 Guards Tank Army Headquarters, while Kravchenko's 5 Guards Tank Corps was only a stone's throw distant.[38] 7 Breakthrough Artillery Division was in support of the attack, and artillery and mortars had been concentrated in this sector to a density of 480 barrels a mile.[39]

On the early morning of 3 November the Red Army troops attacked out of

[36] For description of the battle and the von Choltitz incident see von Mellenthin, *Panzer Battles*, pp. 247–8; also von Choltitz. *Un Soldat parmi des Soldats*, pp. 172–3. It was apparently with von Manstein's agreement that von Choltitz went to see the *Führer* but got no further than 'the unfortunate Chief of General Staff who, pale and saddened, listened to the report with a helpless shrug of the shoulders'. It was then, von Choltitz said, that he realized that the war was lost.

[37] Zhukov, *Vospominaniya i Razmyshleniya*, p. 529.

[38] Moskalenko gave up command of 40 Army to Zhmachenko, probably at the end of September, he himself relieving Chibisov of command of 38 Army.

[39] *Istoriya*, Vol. 3, pp. 335–8.

the Lyutezh bridgehead, and were supported by a parallel attack by Cherny-akhovsky's 60 Army immediately to the north from the area of the Belorussian Front.[40] In spite of the low cloud and fine rain there was some air fighting over the bridgehead but the poor visibility restricted the use of the heavy Red Army artillery resources. The rain soon changed the roads to bogs, but the attack made steady progress through the thickly wooded area along the banks of the Dnieper, falling on Hoth's 4 Panzer Army, the left flanking formation of Army Group South. His fourteen under-strength infantry and two panzer divisions were engaged by about seventeen rifle divisions and three tank corps, and by evening on 4 November the German defences broke, as the tanks of Rybalko's 3 Guards Tank Army drove throughout the night with blazing headlights into the open country.[41] Moskalenko's 38 Army entered Kiev on 6 November and the main railway junction of Fastov, with its connections to Krivoi Rog and Kirovograd, was taken the next day. By then 4 Panzer Army had been broken into three widely separated groups. On 12 November Zhitomir was taken and as the remaining formations of 1 Ukrainian Front and the Belorussian Front crossed the Dnieper, the Kiev bridgehead was soon ninety-five miles deep by 150 miles wide. Korosten, the railway junction to the north of Zhitomir bordering on the Pripet Marshes, was entered by Chernyakhovsky's 60 Army on 17 November. Colonel-General Hoth, the Commander of 4 Panzer Army, who had fought with distinction throughout the whole war, was regarded by Hitler as being tired and in part responsible for the defeat. He was placed on the reserve and not further re-employed, his replacement being Raus, an Austrian, the former Commander of 47 Panzer Corps and 6 Panzer Division, the division which at the beginning of the year had fought its way to within thirty miles of the beleaguered Stalingrad.

48 Panzer Corps, by then commanded by Balck, was the only readily avail-able armoured headquarters and had become the fire brigade formation for both 8 Army and 4 Panzer Army.[42] It was ordered to the Zhitomir-Fastov area to take command of three strong panzer divisions and two weak ones including the newly arrived 25 Panzer Division which, in battle for the first time, had been scattered on first meeting advanced Red Army elements. A counter-attack was speedily mounted by 48 Panzer Corps against the great Kiev bridgehead but at the insistence of Raus the aim had been limited in the first

[40] Both Chernyakhovsky's 60 Army and Pukhov's 13 Army had been transferred from the command of the Central (Belorussian) Front to the Voronezh (1 Ukrainian) Front on 5 October for better co-ordination.

[41] *OKH Kriegsgliederung* 4 October and 8 November 1943. By 8 November Hoth had been reinforced by Nehring's 24 Panzer Corps and von Knobelsdorff's 48 Panzer Corps, bringing his strength up to twenty-six divisions, of which six were panzer and one panzer grenadier.

[42] Balck relieved von Knobelsdorff in the second week in November. He had been a tank formation commander throughout the war, commanding successively a panzer regiment and brigade, 11 Panzer Division and *Grossdeutschland*.

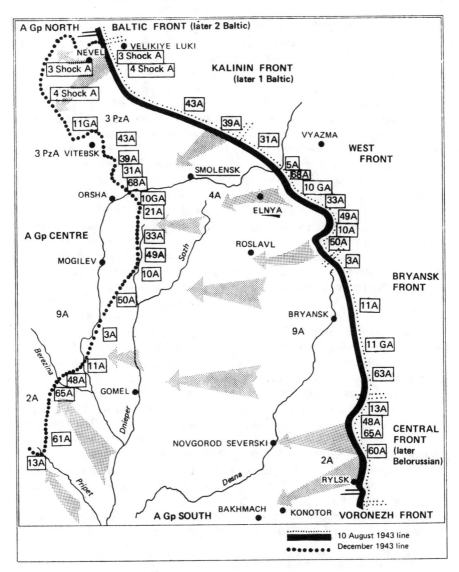

VITEBSK AND THE WITHDRAWAL OF ARMY GROUP CENTRE
August–December 1943

instance to the destruction of the enemy in the area of Zhitomir. By 18 November the town had been retaken with some losses to the Red Army, and in another panzer thrust towards Malin and Korosten part of Chernyak-hovsky's 60 Army was overrun. On 26 November the weather broke completely and the mud and slush stopped most movement. This ended the German relief attack on Kiev.[43]

Experienced German formations, although tired and under strength and inferior in equipment to the Red Army troops, were still tactically their superior. Yet the weakness in numbers and in mobility were such that German formations lacked the momentum and endurance to achieve anything but minor tactical successes. The Red Army noted that German standards had declined and that German troops without adequate training and battle experience were unable to stand their ground against superior numbers of Red Army troops, and this was as true of the inexperienced 25 Panzer Division as of the *Luftwaffe* field divisions.[44] Within the Red Army itself there had been a great improvement in the standard of efficiency of staffs and of regimental officers, but an examination of the rank and file prisoners being taken by the Germans lent weight to the view that the Soviet Union was coming to the end of its manpower. Many of the prisoners appeared to be children in their early teens or old men conscripted only weeks before. Even tank crews were sometimes tractor drivers or factory workers sent into battle with little training. In the event of encirclement, Soviet officers and specialists were extricated in order to form the cadres for new formations and units, and the dispensable other ranks were abandoned to their fate.[45]

To the south-east in the Dnieper bend and the approaches to the Crimea more crises had occurred within von Manstein's Army Group South, where three further Soviet offensives had been mounted. Malinovsky's 3 Ukrainian Front had been ordered to take the German Zaporozhe bridgehead east of the Dnieper and clear the enemy off the left bank, since this bridgehead covered both Nikopol and Krivoi Rog and the only German rail link to the Crimea. The preliminary attack made against part of von Mackensen's 1 Panzer Army by Chuikov's 8 Guards, Lelyushenko's 3 Guards and Danilov's 12 Army was entirely successful, and by 14 October after a four-day battle had taken Zaporozhe and opened the north flank of Hollidt's 6 German Army

[43] Von Mellenthin, as Balck's chief of staff, considered that the counter-offensive would have been more successful if Raus had been less cautious. It is doubtful whether von Mellenthin took full account of the decline in German infantry strength and resources. The retaking of Kiev was in no way possible.

[44] Soviet sources noted that Germans continued to fight obstinately and with stamina 'because of the fairy tales spread about the horrors of Soviet captivity' but that notwithstanding this, most experienced elements were dead or disabled and that replacements had been too quickly and incompletely trained. Above all, said the Soviet account, the German forces suffered from a chronic strength deficiency and a shortage of heavy weapons, bombers and tracked and towing vehicles. *Istoriya*, Vol. 4, pp. 23–4; also Zhukov, *Vospominaniya i Razmyshleniya*, p. 522.

[45] Compare von Mellenthin, *Panzer Battles*, pp. 265–6.

positions against the Sea of Azov and the Crimea. Malinovsky's offensive was then taken up by Tolbukhin's 4 Ukrainian Front which put pressure on 6 German Army, and its first success was measured when Gerasimenko's 28 Army reached Melitopol on 13 October and after ten days' further fighting, took the town against repeated and bitter counter-attacks. Since 6 German Army was deficient in tanks and anti-tank guns, it found the open Nogaisk Steppe most difficult country to defend as it fell back rapidly towards Nikolayev, losing all contact with 17 Army and Army Group A in the Crimea. By the beginning of November Soviet troops were on the lower Dnieper ninety miles west of Melitopol, while further to the south G. F. Zakharov's 2 Guards Army had entered the Perekop Peninsula, and Kreizer's 51 Army crossed the brackish and shallow Lazy Sea to form a bridgehead on the north coast of the Crimea.

Having cut off Army Group A in the Crimea and closed up to the mouth of the Dnieper, the Soviet High Command ordered the third offensive, the destruction of the two German armies in the Dnieper bend. Malinovsky's 3 Ukrainian Front was to resume its attacks westwards between Dnepropetrovsk and Zaporozhe in order to pin 1 Panzer Army, while Konev's 2 Ukrainian Front, heavily reinforced for the purpose, thrust southwards from the line of the Dnieper between Dnepropetrovsk and Kremenchug towards Kirovograd and Krivoi Rog, taking 1 Panzer Army in the flank and cutting its rearward communications. Konev's offensive was to be made by four rifle armies, one of which, 5 Guards Army, had been moved eastwards from the Kremenchug bridgehead, and a tank army transported from the area of Kharkov.[46] The attack by the two fronts began on 16 October.

Von Mackensen's 1 Panzer Army was made up of five corps, but consisted of only two panzer divisions, one panzer grenadier division and eighteen infantry divisions.[47] The four infantry divisions of Fretter-Pico's 30 Corps were deployed on the Dnieper on both sides of Dnepropetrovsk, hoping desperately for a break in the fine autumn weather and the arrival of the rain and mud which must bring the enemy offensives to a halt. Frontages were extended and it was impossible to cover the vast built-up area of Dnepropetrovsk. No help could be expected from army or army group. As there were no mobile or anti-tank reserves, Fretter-Pico had ordered each division to mount one infantry battalion in lorries and every fourth piece in the artillery field batteries had been removed from artillery control to be sited and dug-in in the forward areas as an anti-tank gun. Neither tank nor air support was to

[46] Konev's armies were as follows. Concentrated for the offensive in the small bridgehead between Dereevka and Verchne Dneprovsk, Zhadov's 5 Guards Army, Shumilov's 7 Guards Army, Sharokhin's 37 Army, Gagen's 57 Army and Rotmistrov's 5 Guards Tank Army. Of these, Zhadov, Sharokhin and Rotmistrov had the main roles. Between Kremenchug and Cherkasy the Dnieper line was held by Managarov's 53 Army, Galanin's 4 Guards Army and Koroteev's 52 Army.

[47] OKH Kriegsgliederung 4 October 1943. The corps were 40 and 57 Panzer, 17, 30 and 52 Corps.

be had. Yet, Fretter-Pico noted, the German infantry was still better in the attack than the enemy, since Red Army riflemen lacked determination in the assault unless closely supported by tanks. It was a desperate time, however, for German leaders of all ranks, and the divisional commanders themselves were to be seen daily in battalion areas, many of them saving the defence in moments of crisis by their presence.[48] On 30 October von Mackensen was replaced by Hube as the Commander of 1 Panzer Army.[49]

The main weight of Konev's attack had fallen further to the north-west of Fretter-Pico's positions on Kirchner's 57 Panzer Corps near the boundary between 8 Army and 1 Panzer Army, and on 16 October, after a day of bitter fighting, Rotmistrov's 5 Guards Tank, Zhadov's 5 Guards and Sharokhin's 37 Armies made a breakthrough into open country. On 23 October Rotmistrov's tanks were already outside Krivoi Rog, forty miles in the German rear. On the same day Malinovsky's 3 Ukrainian Front took Dnepropetrovsk. The rain had begun to fall heavily and the ground became waterlogged, but von Manstein was unable to await the arrival of the panzer divisions which the OKH had promised him. A German counter-attack by Schörner's 40 Panzer Corps, with only two panzer divisions and one infantry division but with heavy *Luftwaffe* support, retook Krivoi Rog and drove Konev's 2 Ukrainian Front back twenty miles. This sharp reverse, minor though it was, brought Zhukov hurrying to the worried Konev's forward command post, where both of them observed the battle through the stereo-periscopes. 2 Ukrainian Front fell back to the line of the Ingulets.[50] 40 Panzer Corps claimed 5,000 prisoners and the destruction or capture of 300 tanks.[51]

By the beginning of December 1943 the line of von Manstein's Army Group South still bent eastwards in a salient, but this was very much reduced in size from what it had been six months before, the whole front having fallen back westwards a distance of about 250 miles. The Crimea was isolated and the northern half of the Dnieper bend was in Red Army hands. Only part of the Western Ukraine remained to Germany and the 1941 Rumanian frontier was only 150 miles away. The thrust of Vatutin's 1 Ukrainian Front and Rokossovsky's Belorussian Front eastwards from the area of Kiev formed a wedge which threatened to separate the German Army Groups Centre and South, and to turn von Manstein's left flank and drive Army Group South into Rumania. There were signs that Vatutin's 1 Ukrainian Front was about to

[48] Fretter-Pico, *Missbrauchte Infanterie*, pp. 123–5.
[49] Hube, highly esteemed by Hitler, was the former commander of 16 Panzer Division and 14 Panzer Corps (in Stalingrad). He had just returned to the Eastern Front from the unsuccessful defence of Sicily.
[50] Zhukov, *Vospominaniya i Razmyshleniya*, p. 533.
[51] Von Manstein, *Lost Victories*, p. 483. The OKW Diary entry for 30 October shows 40 Panzer Corps to have destroyed or captured 159 tanks and taken 1,000 prisoners. *Kriegstagebuch des OKW*, Vol. 3, p. 1232. Schörner, a Bavarian, had taken over 40 Panzer Corps from Henrici only three weeks before. As a General of Mountain Troops he had no previous experience of the command of armour.

resume its offensive towards Zhitomir, and von Manstein, unable to obtain the procrastinating *Führer*'s agreement, on 29 December on his own responsibility ordered Hube's 1 Panzer Army out of the Dnieper bend northwards to join Raus's 4 Panzer Army on the threatened left flank.[52] Only Hollidt's 6 German Army, restored to the command of Army Group South, remained in the Dnieper bend. On 4 January von Manstein flew to East Prussia to try once more to persuade Hitler to abandon what was left of the Dnieper bend and pull back the right wing of Army Group South, even if this meant evacuating the Crimea. The *Führer* countered with his usual arguments concerning the effect this would have on Turkey, Rumania and Bulgaria, and refused to move any troops from Western Europe until the Anglo-American landings had been beaten off, or until the British did as he forecast and tied themselves down in Portugal. He said that he expected that before summer the submarine warfare in the Atlantic would begin to make its effect felt, and he was in any case convinced that the Soviet-Anglo-American coalition would fall apart one day. Because private meetings were an anathema to him, associated with unpleasant tidings and views which he would rather not hear expressed, the *Führer* agreed only with great reluctance to a private meeting with von Manstein and Zeitzler, the stenographers and the service and ministerial aides who were usually present having been sent away. Von Manstein, according to his own account, suggested once more that Hitler should give up the command on the Eastern Front to a professional soldier, and that the Chief of the General Staff should be the *Führer*'s only army adviser and executive.[53] This proposal Hitler rejected. There, in Army Group South, the matter rested, awaiting the next move by the Soviet High Command.

Army Group South was not the only army group which was seriously threatened. At his Army Group Centre headquarters in Orsha von Kluge had been beset by difficulties hardly less grievous than those suffered by von Manstein in the Ukraine. After repelling the German *Citadel* offensive at Kursk the Soviet High Command had become much more confident and daring, while von Kluge himself, worried about his sinking fighting strength, became reluctant to make any counter-attack which might involve him in casualties. For this reason he was to forbid the mounting of counter-attacks other than those of a very localized nature without his personal authority. Army Group Centre had been under continuous pressure throughout the summer, firstly at Orel and after that from the Kursk salient, when Rokossovsky's Central and Vatutin's Voronezh Fronts had driven back Weiss's 2 Army and Model's 9 Army of von Kluge's right flank, as well as the formations of von Manstein's left. After July, on von Kluge's left and centre, Reinhardt's 3 Panzer Army and Heinrici's 4 Army came under heavy attack.

Reinhardt complained repeatedly to von Kluge that his troops were stretched beyond their limit. He regarded a frontage of 15,000 yards as the

---

[52] Von Manstein, *Lost Victories*, p. 499.
[53] *Ibid*, pp. 502–5.

maximum that any division could cover, but his under-strength divisions were each defending 25,000 yards, and fighting strengths were so low that a simple arithmetical calculation showed that some divisions had only one man in the forward defended localities to every eighty yards of front. The two divisions which Reinhardt had in reserve had become fully committed in anti-partisan operations to the north-east of Vitebsk. In May the feeding strength of the Panzer Army had dropped to 292,000 men and by September it was reduced to 230,000, since no reinforcements or replacements were being received. There were some doubts, too, as to how long the 20,000 non-German *Osttruppen* on the strength of 3 Panzer Army would remain loyal, as desertion was on the increase. On 17 June Reinhardt expressed misgivings to von Kluge as to the state of training of the four *Luftwaffe* field divisions forming part of Schlemm's 2 *Luftwaffe* Field Corps, and he was to have continual difficulty with this corps because of the intricacies of the *Luftwaffe* command and administrative channels.[54] Reinhardt's fears were not unfounded.

The Soviet High Command had ordered Eremenko's Kalinin Front and Sokolovsky's West Front to attack on Smolensk and Roslavl, and had attached Voronov to them to co-ordinate their activities.[55] Fighting went on during the whole of August without much Soviet success until the axis of the main attack was altered from Roslavl to Elnya. Elnya, the gateway to Smolensk, was taken on 30 August. By the middle of September the West and Kalinin Fronts were attacking with vigour on a 150-mile frontage, and by 24 September West Front had advanced sixty miles to the south of Smolensk while the Kalinin Front outflanked it from the north. The next day both Smolensk and Roslavl were taken. Meanwhile immediately to the south the Bryansk Front, ordered to move on Gomel, attacked Model's 9 German Army as it retired from the Desna towards the new Panther line on the Sozh. On the Soviet side use was made of partisan brigades, but experience soon showed that to be fully effective in the main operations these had to be controlled by, and affiliated to, regular formations.[56] The Bryansk offensive came to a halt between the Desna and the Sozh.

In early October the Bryansk Front was broken up and four of its armies and a cavalry corps were transferred to the command of the Central Front. M. M. Popov's Bryansk Front Headquarters and the remaining troops were then moved northwards to the area of Velikiye Luki between the North-West

[54] Heidkämper, *Witebsk*, pp. 13–18. Heidkämper was Reinhardt's chief of staff. By 6 October 3 Panzer Army strength was down to 200,000 men.

[55] The military council of the Kalinin Front was Eremenko, Leonov (political member) and Kurasov (chief of staff).

[56] The partisan strength and activity in the Ukraine, although not negligible, were small compared with that in the western regions of Russia, where the forest gave refuge to the many bands. According to the Soviet account it was claimed that 45,000 partisans had been enrolled in the area of Vitebsk, Smolensk and Mogilev. Although the activities of these partisans may have lacked co-ordination, they were extremely troublesome to 3 Panzer Army. Heidkämper, *Witebsk*, p. 12; also *Istoriya*, Vol. 3, p. 363.

and the Kalinin Fronts, where they formed a new Baltic Front later renamed 2 Baltic Front.

The Soviet High Command was intent on securing the whole of the Orsha landbridge as well as Vitebsk which was regarded as the gateway to the Baltic States. Eremenko's Kalinin Front and Popov's Baltic Front were ordered to resume the offensive against 3 Panzer Army towards Nevel near the German army group boundary, in order to envelop Vitebsk and drive a deep wedge between Army Groups North and Centre. Subsidiary thrusts were to be made by Sokolovsky's West Front on Orsha and Mogilev, and by Rokossovsky's Central (later Belorussian) Front on Gomel and Bobruisk. At 10 a.m. on 6 October the offensive opened with an attack by 3 and 4 Shock Armies both of the Kalinin Front side by side, supported by tanks and bombers. The half trained and inexperienced 2 *Luftwaffe* Field Division of Schlemm's *Luftwaffe* Field Corps broke up almost immediately, some of the troops giving way to panic, and within a matter of hours Soviet forces were pouring through a ten-mile gap. Nevel was taken and the next day the lateral railway connecting the two army groups was broken. The 3 Panzer Army situation was brought temporarily under control by the intervention of Clössner's 9 Corps with 20 Panzer Division and a battalion of Tiger tanks under command. Göring, whose honour was involved by the failure of the *Luftwaffe* field divisions, immediately allotted reinforcement *Luftwaffe* flak batteries and 600 aircraft to the area. It was obvious to 3 Panzer Army that the Red Army troops had been surprised at the ease with which they had taken Nevel and were regrouping, and Reinhardt, fearing a resumption of Eremenko's offensive, begged von Kluge in vain for permission to counter-attack in conjunction with the neighbouring 16 Army of Army Group North and retake the Nevel area.[57]

Von Kluge's hands were tied at this time by the fighting on the 4 Army front in the area of Orsha and Mogilev, and he was apparently to refer Reinhardt's request for permission to counter-attack back to the Army High Command (OKH). He himself had much less confidence in the OKH than formerly, for he told his staff on 18 October that Zeitzler was very tired and had no further influence, and that in his (von Kluge's) opinion the days of the Chief of General Staff were numbered.[58] Four days before, von Kluge had written a long personal letter direct to the *Führer*, pointing out that although the morale of his fighting men remained good, they were beset by a feeling of isolation and neglect, facing as they did the massed numbers of Red Army infantry. Army Group Centre was 200,000 men deficient of establishment, and the recent losses had been so great that the drop in fighting strength of the formations which had borne the brunt of the attacks was frightening. The standard of such replacements as had been received, said von Kluge, left much to be desired, many of them lacking training and inner soldierly quali-

---

[57] Heidkämper, *Witebsk*, pp. 27–28.
[58] *Ibid*, p. 34.

ties.[59] Without troops, weapons and reserves, no commander could function, however skilful he might be. Von Kluge assured the *Führer* of his own loyalty but stressed that the danger of the trend had to be clearly faced, and he ended his letter by saying that although it was commonly assumed that the Russian had the same losses and problems, this was in reality not the case, because the Red Army could always obtain numerical superiority by concentrating its forces at the point of attack.[60] No answer was received to this letter, and on 27 October, as the result of a motor vehicle accident, von Kluge was invalided from his post, being replaced by Field-Marshal Busch, the former Commander of 16 Army.

On 20 October Eremenko's Kalinin Front had been redesignated as 1 Baltic Front, Popov's Baltic Front becoming 2 Baltic Front and Rokossovsky's Central Front being renamed the Belorussian Front. On 8 November Eremenko resumed the offensive with 3 and 4 Shock Armies against 3 Panzer Army, and speedily broke through the enemy defences into the German rear. Reinhardt was in danger of losing two of his corps, and asked Busch repeatedly for permission to withdraw. Busch merely transmitted these requests to the *Führer*, who replied by ordering the formations to stay where they were.[61] 1 Baltic Front continued to expand the breach until it was nearly fifty miles wide, but although it succeeded in cutting the railway westwards out of Vitebsk on Christmas Eve, the Germans managed to stabilize the position and retain their hold on the town. In this sector, for the first time during the war, a perceptible lowering in German morale was noted. There were a few cases of desertion, hitherto almost unknown, and some indications of panic-stricken flight.[62] During 25 and 26 November Rokossovsky's Belorussian Front had cleared Gomel, and by the end of the month had put detachments over the Berezina.

During the last six months of 1943 the situation opposite von Küchler's German Army Group North had changed little. Leningrad had been connected to the Soviet Union by a narrow neck of land to the south of Lake Ladoga, but otherwise the battle area had not moved from the line of the Volkhov-Lake Ilmen-Lovat. The Soviet Fronts deployed against von Küchler remained as before, Govorov's Leningrad, Meretskov's Volkhov and Timoshenko's North-West Fronts. It was apparent to von Küchler that a big Soviet offensive was about to break on him, but the *Führer*, although in agreement that the position of Army Group North was likely to be critical, could not find even the

---

[59] This applied particularly to German infantry replacements. On 22 June Hitler had himself issued *Führer* Order 15 pointing out the decrease in the fighting value of infantry, but he had required the army groups to remedy this by improving training.

[60] Heidkämper, *Witebsk*, pp. 34–6.

[61] *Ibid*, pp. 50–4. All that the *Führer* could offer Busch was the return of 20 Panzer Division which had just been removed from Reinhardt and the allocation of an armoured assault gun battalion.

[62] *Istoriya*, Vol. 3, p. 375.

six infantry divisions for which von Küchler asked.[63] The Army Group North request on 20 November that 16 Army be allowed to withdraw to the Panther Line was similarly refused.

During the months following *Citadel* Germany had lost all initiative in the Eastern theatre. The army group commanders made competing demands to Zeitzler for reinforcement formations, but any question of reinforcing the Russian front at the expense of Western Europe brought Jodl out in protection of his area of responsibility. Any proposal made by the army group commanders that they should withdraw to shorten their fronts was rejected and the commanders were fobbed off by promises. The *Führer*, whose nervous system was deteriorating, at times appeared to be under severe mental stress. The underlying theme of his strategy was to stand firm and keep one's nerve and he was likely to vent his spite on commanders whom he suspected of giving ground too easily.

[63] *Kriegstagebuch des OKW*, Vol. 3, p. 1243.

CHAPTER TWENTY-FOUR

Germany at Bay

During 1943 the fortunes of the Axis had undergone a fundamental change and by December Germany stood almost alone in its determination to fight on regardless of the cost. An exhausted Finland regarded the war as already lost and was reacting nervously to any proposal that Army Group North should retire to the Panther Line. The Italian Kingdom had been split between two occupying powers and its troops had been withdrawn from Russia and the Balkans. Hungary had watched Italy's desertion with envy. Japan, militarily the strongest of Germany's allies, was already losing its newly-won ocean empire and was faltering under the hammer blows of the United States Navy; and by 1944 it was obvious in Berlin that Tokyo was becoming increasingly anxious about German losses in Europe, and was concealing the extent of its own defeats in the Far East.[1]

In 1943 there had been a crisis of confidence between Rumania and Germany. At the beginning of the year, on 10 January, Hitler had bitterly reproached Antonescu in a three-hour tirade for what he had called the Rumanian failure at Stalingrad. Antonescu in his turn had called attention to the eighteen Rumanian divisions destroyed on the Don and Volga, to 200,000 Rumanian war dead and the fact that of the four Rumanian Generals killed, three had met their death in hand to hand combat. These cavalier reproaches and the abuse of Rumanians by German commanders and troops were not forgotten and on 25 January Rumania formally asked that all its troops be withdrawn from the battle area to west of the Bug and stated that it did not intend to provide the German Command with any further formations.[2] In February the *Führer* was obliged to have an order circulated among German troops warning them against the unworthy treatment of allies, but at the same time he addressed a long written complaint to Antonescu charging the Rumanian troops with poor discipline and bad morale. This note was accepted, but its contents were afterwards rebutted by the findings of a joint German-Rumanian commission of investigation which reported that the

---

[1] Heiber, *Hitlers Lagebesprechungen*, p. 169; *Kriegstagebuch des OKW*, Vol. 3, pp. 1512–3.
[2] *Ibid*, pp. 68 and 1508. By November the number of Rumanian dead had risen to 250,000.

morale of the Rumanian troops was in fact good.[3] Hitler was forced to take back his words and Antonescu began to address to the *Führer* a series of complaints about the German war direction.[4] In October Dumitrescu, the Commander of 3 Rumanian Army, reported to Steflea, the Chief of Rumanian General Staff, that Hollidt's 6 German Army was in reality weak and extended, and he rightly appreciated that it could not hold the approaches to the Crimea against Soviet attack. On 25 October Steflea expressed these fears to Zeitzler and three days later an Antonescu missive arrived in the *Führer*'s headquarters, pointing out that there were only two German divisions in the peninsula as against seven Rumanian, and inferring that if Germany was determined to hold the Crimea it was welcome to do so alone. He, Antonescu, irrespective of the strategic implications that it might entail, wanted the Rumanian troops withdrawn from the Crimea, as he did not propose to be answerable for another Stalingrad.[5]

Nearer home there were other difficulties which destroyed any remaining vestige of German-Rumanian mutual understanding and confidence. The relationship between Hungary and Rumania was bad, particularly since the loss of Rumanian territory through the 1940 Vienna Award, and Bucharest regarded as a threat the Hungarian troops concentrated near the Rumanian frontier. After July 1941 Bessarabia had been returned to Rumania, but Transdniester, the territory between the Dniester and the Bug, had passed only to Rumanian administration. The Rumanians, however, had come to regard this territory as their own by right of conquest, promised to them by the *Führer*; but as the relationship between Berlin and Bucharest deteriorated and as the Red Army swept westwards, the status of the territory was called into question. Army Group South was soon to rely on the Rumanian controlled communications running through Transdniester, and Berlin made an attempt to regain some measure of control by appointing a German officer, Lieutenant-General Auleb, to Transdniester to organize the rear.[6] No sooner, however, had the Rumanians come to realize that Transdniester was slipping from their grasp than they began to strip the territory of all equipment which could be removed to Rumania.

Germany's relationship with its other allies and the neutral states deteriorated sharply during 1943. In the autumn Hungarian formations in Russia began to move very much as they pleased without consulting the Germans, and on 14 November Szombathelyi, the Hungarian Chief of Staff, asked Zeitzler to keep the three Hungarian corps away from the battle area. Only two

[3] The only point on which the German members expressed uneasiness was that Rumanian troops, unlike the Germans, were freely permitted to listen to enemy radio broadcasts.

[4] Antonescu's letters were presumably little to the *Führer*'s liking since he was to comment to Zeitzler 'you must see the letters he writes me'. Heiber, *Hitlers Lagebesprechungen*, p. 480.

[5] *Kriegstagebuch des OKW*, Vol. 3, 29 October, pp. 1228–9.

[6] Auleb had formerly been responsible for the security of the communications and rear areas of Army Group A in the Caucasus and Crimea.

months before, on 6 September, the Defence Ministry of the puppet Slovakia had caused considerable surprise in Berlin by requesting that the two Slovak field divisions should in future not be committed to battle without first obtaining the agreement of the Slovakian Government, and that no task should be given them without first ascertaining that the necessary means were available to fulfil it. The German OKW war diarist was to comment that the reason underlying the request was, presumably, doubt as to a German victory.[7] In October Spain had asked for the return of the Blue Division, and Portugal had followed its true inclinations in allowing the Anglo-Americans the use of the Azores as an Atlantic base. The attitude of Sweden had changed from benevolent to strict neutrality and it was refusing Germany overland facilities to Norway. Ankara was under Anglo-American pressure to enter the war and the *Führer*, disturbed by the coolness of the Turkish attitude to Germany, was holding mobile troop reserves ready to make a demonstration of force against the Turkish frontier, this reserve amounting to nothing more than a single panzer grenadier division, all that he had available.[8]

During 1943 it was apparent to the world that Germany's fortunes were on the wane. The German Navy was beginning to lose the submarine war in the Atlantic and, due largely to the introduction of United States long range fighters, the *Luftwaffe* had already lost daylight air superiority over the territory of the *Reich*. German cities were being devastated with a terrible loss of life by day and by night bombing. Not only had the German Army lost its old offensive power, but it no longer disposed of sufficient formations to defend and garrison occupied Europe, and German manpower was to prove inadequate even to maintain the number of field formations in existence.

In October Gehlen, of the Foreign Armies East Department of the OKH, had prepared a table of comparative strengths on the Eastern Front in which he estimated that the two and a half million German troops in Russia were opposed by five and a half million Red Army men, 177 German divisions defending a front which was being attacked by the equivalent of 860 Soviet formations of divisional and brigade size. The Red Army tank and gun strength he estimated to be superior to that of the defenders by at least three to one.[9] Gehlen's figures, although based on incomplete information, gave a fairly true portrayal of the situation which, if anything, underestimated the Soviet enemy and did not bring out the disparity in the numerical strengths. The German Army had entered the Soviet Union with 153 divisions in June 1941 and at that time had an approximate strength in the East of 3,200,000 German troops. By November 1943 the total strength, including 20 Army in Finland, had sunk to 2,850,000 men although the count of German formations had increased to about 195 divisions. The total number of German ground troops of all types with the army groups, excluding base

---

[7] *Kriegstagebuch des OKW*, Vol. 3, pp. 247 and 1059.
[8] 60 Panzer Grenadier Division (*Feldherrnhalle*).
[9] *Org-Abt Gen StdH H 1/527 Fr. Heere Ost 81/43 g. Kdos.* Situation at 14 October 1943.

troops and the 176,000 troops of 20 Army, was as low as 2,026,000. The allies still under German control, and these did not of course include the Finns, had dropped to only 136,000 men. In addition there were 52,000 foreign troops of somewhat doubtful reliability.[10]

The Eastern Front was only one of the fronts which Germany was committed to defend, and the relative importance which the German High Command placed on each cannot necessarily be judged by the number of divisions deployed, since many of the formations had been reduced by losses to mere shells. For this reason the actual manpower strength of the theatre must at the same time be taken into account.

The Anglo-Americans had undertaken no land fighting in Europe of any great value except in Italy and, as Zhukov was subsequently to remark, these operations on the Italian mainland did not cause any significant redistribution in Germany's fighting strength.[11] On the other hand the defection of Italy and the vacuum in the Balkans gave rise in the autumn of 1943 to the very real German fear that the Anglo-Americans would land not only in France and the Netherlands, but also in South-East Europe, in this way threatening the rear of von Manstein's Army Group South and depriving Germany of one of its sources of oil and raw materials. In the German view the landing in France would, as Hitler forecast, decide the outcome of the whole war.[12] On 2 September, when Jodl was resisting any further troop withdrawals from the west for Russia, Warlimont recorded a minute summarizing the policy of the Armed Forces High Command (OKW), when he said that according to all the indications an attack was imminent in the West, an attack which, contrary to the position in the East, directly threatened the very borders of the *Reich*.[13] This fear was stressed again eight weeks later by the *Führer* in Directive 51, when he said that the danger in the East remained but that a greater existed in the West, for whereas there was sufficient room for manoeuvre in Eastern Europe without danger to Germany's vitals, the position would be very different in the event of a successful Anglo-American landing.[14]

It may be argued with justification that Hitler underestimated the Soviet Union and took exaggerated counsel of his fears of landings in the West and the Balkans in the autumn of 1943, but to do so is merely being wise after the event. The fear was real and was well-founded, and was made even more acute by partisan and resistance activities. Although only eighty-four divisions were deployed in Western Europe outside the *Reich*, the German Army

---

[10] *Gen StdH (Organisationsabteilung I) Nr. 1/10388/43 geh.* of 14 December 1943; *Kriegstagebuch des OKW*, Vol. 3, p. 1484.

[11] Zhukov, *Vospominaniya i Razmyshleniya*, p. 522.

[12] Hitler's briefing conference 20 December 1943. Heiber, *Hitlers Lagebesprechungen*, p. 444.

[13] *Kriegstagebuch des OKW*, Vol. 3, 2 September 1943, p. 1043.

[14] *Führer/OKW/WF St/Op. Nr. 662656/43 g. K. Chefs* of 3 November 1943. Hubatsch, *Hitlers Weisungen für die Kriegführung*, p. 233.

strength in the West outside the homeland in the autumn of 1943 totalled no fewer than 2,440,000 men compared with the figure of 2,800,000 in Russia.[15]

Zeitzler and the army group commanders on the Eastern Front struggled incessantly to draw on the formations from the West, while Jodl insisted that the formation strength of the OKW theatres was insufficient for the attack which they had to meet. On 11 September Blumentritt, the Chief of Staff to the Commander-in-Chief West, brought the attention of the OKW to the fact that in the twelve months since the previous October he had been obliged to find six panzer or panzer grenadier and twenty-two infantry divisions for Russia, mostly against an exchange for worn-out divisions much reduced by casualties, and ten panzer or panzer grenadier and nine infantry divisions for Tunis, Italy and the Balkans. That same day the *Führer*, tired of the incessant complaining, ruled that he would no longer listen to the requests of the competing factions without all interested parties being present, these to include Keitel, Jodl and Zeitzler. That autumn Jodl made a short strategic survey to investigate the possibility of a reduction of commitments and a saving of troops, but could come to no conclusion. The loss of Finland, he argued, would lose Germany both nickel and the Baltic. The evacuation of Norway would bring Sweden into the war. Like Hitler, he reasoned that the underlying aim was to keep the enemy as far away as possible from the frontiers of Germany and because of that, Italy, France and the Netherlands had to be held in strength. Denmark, too, was important as a landbridge to Norway. As for the Balkans and the South-East, the German High Command believed that the coast could be defended more successfully with fewer troops than a line further inland.[16]

Such was the *Führer's* obsession with the raising of new divisions that he had abandoned in the late autumn of 1942 the established German Army system of training and reinforcement. The home replacement organization forming part of Fromm's Replacement Army had been based on a number of replacement battalions, each of which was affiliated to a regiment in the field, these being responsible for the induction and training of recruits who were then forwarded, together with convalescents and leave personnel, as part of march battalions to the field army. These replacement battalions were grouped for control and administration into replacement regiments and replacement divisions, coming under the *Wehrkreise* which formed part of Fromm's command. Towards the end of 1942 the replacement and the training functions were separated, the induction being carried out in Germany by the replacement battalions, regiments and divisions as before, while the training function was carried out by newly formed but affiliated reserve battalions, reserve divisions and corps which were moved out of Germany to train in occupied Europe. In the East some of these were converted to field training divisions under the army groups. In October 1943, therefore, the German Army order

---

[15] *Kriegstagebuch des OKW*, Vol. 3, 31 December 1943, pp. 1393–4.
[16] *Ibid*, pp. 832, 1073 and 1091.

of battle contained thirty-one replacement (*Ersatz*) divisions in Germany, which had an administrative rather than a tactical significance, and four field training and seventeen reserve divisions. Such was the pressing need for German formations of any sort that sooner or later a number of these divisions were either converted to field or static defence divisions or were willy-nilly drawn into the fighting. In 1944 the old established German training and reinforcement system was to break down completely and a new training organization had to be built up again in the German homeland.

According to the estimates issued at the time, 200,000 men had been lost at Stalingrad at the beginning of the year. In addition, the other losses on the Eastern Front alone in the twelve months between November 1942 and October 1943 were 1,686,000 men and of these only 1,260,000 had been replaced. Of the loss, 240,000 were killed, 993,000 wounded, 106,000 missing and 447,000 sick. Of the whole total of the year's casualties in Russia over 900,000 men were entirely lost to the German Army.[17] Although the total strength of all the German armed forces in 1943 stood at over nine million, such was the difficulty in finding replacements that the conscription law which exempted from call-up the youngest or only son of each family had to be suspended, and fifty-year-old men, veterans of the First World War, became eligible for service.[18]

Germany had been at war for three whole years before the *Führer* could bring himself to realize the seriousness of the situation. On 13 January, when it was obvious that Stalingrad could not be relieved, a decree was issued committing Germany to total war, authorizing similar measures to those which had been taken in the Soviet Union and in Britain at the start of hostilities. Goebbels was appointed special plenipotentiary for total war measures. Men between the ages of sixteen and sixty-five and women between seventeen and fifty had to register for war work, and the working hours in administration and industry were increased.[19] The shortage of German manpower was acute everywhere. In the first thirty months of the war since 1939, 7,500,000 German males had left industry for military service, replacements being found by recruiting foreigners from the occupied territories, from prisoners of war and sometimes from concentration camps; but as this was done haphazardly, the six million foreign workers who had been brought into Germany by 1943 formed an unskilled, inefficient and often hostile source of labour.[20] It was intended to employ a further million foreign workers in German industry, and although there were in fact already over 300,000 *Hiwi*

[17] *Ibid*, pp. 1481–2; also *Gen StdH (Organisationsabteilung I) Nr. 1/10388/43 geh.* of 14 December 1943.

[18] *Kriegstagebuch des OKW*, Vol. 3, pp. 1572–3. In 1943 there were more than 5,000,000 German males between the ages of eighteen and forty-eight in reserved occupations.

[19] Janssen, *Das Ministerium Speer*, pp. 119–20.

[20] On 31 May 1943 in addition to 1,620,000 prisoners of war there were 4,640,000 foreign civilians in Germany. *FD 2690/45* Vol. 5, Speer to Hitler, 20 July 1944, pp. 2–3, reproduced from Milward, *The German Economy at War*, p. 113.

O

former Soviet prisoner of war volunteers on the army ration strength in Russia, it was proposed that more recruits should be found from this source. The strength and functions of the Labour Service were extended, and this para-military and partially armed force was ordered to find the gun crews to man the *Luftwaffe* light anti-aircraft defences. Keitel was to undertake a re-examination of all reserved categories, and special field teams under the direction of the OKW were employed to comb out rear military establishments for young able-bodied men. An attempt was made to subject ten annual classes of Lithuanians and Latvians to the German conscription law, and the SS widened its field of recruiting to include many non-German nationalities.

No action was taken to direct German women into industry and this most reliable source of labour was left untapped. When Milch suggested to the *Führer* that it was high time that Germany should follow the Soviet lead, the proposal was abruptly rejected with the retort that as far as work was concerned the slightly built and long-limbed German woman could not be compared to the strong, squat and primitive Russian female.[21] In July 1939 the count of the native born German industrial labour force stood at just under ten and a half million of which 2,620,000 were women. The number of women employed remained constant at about this figure, although the total German labour force had dropped by the end of 1943 to about seven and three-quarter million.[22]

Field formations, particularly those in Russia, bore the brunt of the shortage of manpower and equipment. All panzer grenadier, mountain and light divisions had an establishment of only two infantry regiments and some of the infantry divisions had already lost their third regiment. During 1943 most infantry divisions lost a battalion from each infantry regiment. Divisions were rarely maintained at establishment strength. There had been some slight improvement in fire power by introducing the heavier 75 mm anti-tank gun into the anti-tank companies and by the addition of a Hunter assault gun company to a number of infantry divisions.[23] The new 42 machine-gun was a much better weapon than the old 34 pattern which it had replaced on an improved scale, but German artillery remained very weak and the heavy mortar was beginning to replace the gun. There was only one artillery division on the whole order of battle, and artillery ammunition was in very short supply. Soviet, Czech, French and even Yugo-Slav equipment had begun to make its appearance as the authorized equipment of German formations.[24] German armoured losses in the East from June 1941 to June 1943 had totalled 8,105 tanks and there was increasing difficulty in maintenance and repair.

[21] Janssen, *Das Ministerium Speer*, p. 130.
[22] Milward, *The German Economy at War*, p. 47.
[23] The Hunter (*Hetzer*) was a T38 Czech Skoda tank chassis mounting a L48 75 mm German gun. It weighed about 16 tons.
[24] *Kriegstagebuch des OKW*, Vol. 3, p. 1577.

Of the total October holding of 2,300 tanks a little over one-third were fit for battle.[25]

Although the standard of training had declined, morale remained good and for the most part all ranks continued to have an unshakeable faith in the *Führer*.

The loyalty and the fighting spirit of the *Luftwaffe*, too, were in no way diminished. Göring had admittedly suffered an eclipse after Stalingrad due to his failure to safeguard the skies above the German homeland and, having lost all his former drive, was devoted to idle pleasure. He was, however, ably supported by the tireless Milch, the Inspector General of the *Luftwaffe* and Secretary for Air, and by Jeschonnek, his Chief of Air Staff.[26] In Western Europe the *Luftwaffe* was both qualitatively and numerically inferior to the enemy and by the end of 1943 the long range P51 Mustang fighter could roam over the *Reich* at will. In Russia German airmen could still obtain local air superiority, but Red Air Force bombers had started to raid German territory in the East. *Luftwaffe* air training was severely curtailed by lack of fuel. Losses were mounting. In July over 1,700 aircrew were killed; in September 1,600 planes were lost, of which sixty per cent were destroyed by the Anglo-Americans. During the whole of 1943, against a production figure of 25,000 military aircraft of all types, 17,400 were destroyed, of this total 10,600 being fighters.[27]

After October many of the *Luftwaffe* field divisions had been broken up and incorporated into the Army, but anti-aircraft artillery and parachute formations remained a part of the air arm. On 1 November the strength of the *Luftwaffe* stood at 119,000 officers, 1,970,000 men, 430,000 auxiliaries of all types (including *Hiwis*) and 475,000 civilians, in all just under three million.[28] Yet, in spite of this strength, the *Luftwaffe*, like the German Navy, had ceased to have any strategic significance.

The Red Army and Air Force in Russia at the end of 1943, according to the Soviet account, stood at 6,500,000 men and included the equivalent of about 530 rifle divisions and probably about 140 tank brigades. The artillery order of battle was said to total 90,000 guns and mortars and to have had eighty artillery divisions and seventy-three independent artillery brigades.[29] The armoured strength was put at 5,600 tanks and SUs, and the Red Air

[25] *Ibid*, 5 July 1943, p. 750; also *Org-Abt Gen StdH, H 1/527 Fr. Heere Ost 81/43 g. Kdos* of 14 October 1943.

[26] Jeschonnek committed suicide on 18 August 1943 and was succeeded by Korten as Chief of Air Staff.

[27] *Kriegstagebuch des OKW*, Vol. 3, pp. 1595 and 1597.

[28] *Ibid*, p. 1597.

[29] Of the total of 6,736,000, 266,000 belonged to the Soviet Navy and 483,000 to the Red Air Force. The formations included 480 rifle and cavalry divisions, fifty-five rifle brigades and thirty-two static divisions, thirty-five tank and mechanized corps and forty-six independent tank brigades (not included in a corps organization) and eighty artillery divisions and seventy-three independent artillery brigades. *Istoriya*, Vol. 4, p. 20. These figures are in accordance with subsequent entries in the same work. Zhukov on the other hand gives somewhat different figures, particularly for tank and artillery formations, although these could be explained by different command grouping. Zhukov, *Vospominaniya i Razmyshleniya*, p. 535.

Force at 8,800 military aircraft. These Soviet figures comprised only those forces within the fronts deployed against the Germans and the Finns, together with the formations forming the field reserve of the High Command. They did not include the troops in the Far East or those in the military districts in the interior.[30] By 20 November 1943, the Red Army had lost just over five million prisoners to the Germans.[31]

There is no means of telling whether the Soviet figures accurately portray the position at the time. The count of field formations is lower than that estimated by Gehlen in October of that year, but the total personnel strength is a little greater. The USSR is sensitive to what it calls the denigration of Soviet achievements in the emphasis given by Western historians to the numerical superiority of the Red Army, and Moscow goes to some lengths to point out that Soviet rifle divisions had an establishment of about 9,000 men, these establishments being about seventy per cent of those of German infantry divisions. It also stresses the point that a German army might comprise seventeen divisions whereas a Soviet army averaged about eight. All this is, of course, true. On the other hand these arguments are irrelevant in a comparison of the opposing strengths in Russia, and the Soviet historical account does in fact attempt to minimise the Red Army numerical superiority by exaggerating the strength of the Axis force deployed in the East. Soviet historians estimate the German strength in Russia and the Ukraine at the end of 1943 as 198 divisions, this figure being reasonably accurate, but they give the German strength as 4,200,000 men and credit their enemies with having 3,000 aircraft, 5,400 tanks and assault guns and 54,000 guns and mortars. Yet, at the same time, they affirm that one of the main causes of German weakness was a chronic deficiency in strength and a lack of heavy weapons.[32]

It is possible that the Soviet figure of 6,000,000 ground troops is an accurate one although it appears low, since by a simple calculation it can be seen that at least 4,200,000 men were needed to maintain the 530 infantry formations, even at a reduced strength of 8,000 men to a division. In addition to these infantry formations there were very powerful tank and artillery forces and the rail and road transport troops and rearward services to be provided for. The figure of 6,500,000 on the Russo-German Front was, of course, only a part of the total strength of the Red Army and Air Force, just as the 2,800,000 Germans there formed only a fraction of the *Wehrmacht*. According to Zhukov, the gross output of all the military academies and schools in the USSR in 1944 amounted to half a million officers a year, and 200,000 officers were in reserve.[33]

[30] Compare Zhukov, *Ibid*, p. 539. Zhukov gives an exaggerated estimate of the Germans opposing this Soviet force as 5,000,000 troops, 54,000 guns and 3,000 aircraft.

[31] *Gen Qu Abt Kriegsverwaltung Nr. 11/12115/43 (Qu 5)* of 30 November. The total was 5,078,230 prisoners of which 30,041 were officers.

[32] *Istoriya*, Vol. 4, pp. 20–4.

[33] The annual output of half a million refers to the numbers of officers who underwent courses, not to the output of new officers. Zhukov, *Vospominaniya i Razmyshleniya*, p. 535.

The Soviet armament manufactured output had continued to rise. In 1941 the USSR had produced only 6,000 tanks, this figure increasing in 1942 to 24,700. This 1942 production total was repeated in 1943, but during that year most light pattern tanks went out of production in favour of the medium T34, so that the breakdown of the 1943 production was 3,500 light tanks, 4,000 medium SUs, 14,000 medium T34 and 2,500 heavy KV1, KV2 and KV85 tanks. In 1944 the total tank production was to rise again from 24,000 to 29,000. Military aircraft production in 1943 stood at a total of 30,000 aircraft, but a number of planes, like the U2 biplane, were of a pattern which would scarcely qualify in the West as military aircraft, even of the training or communication type. This production total was increased in 1944 to 32,200. In addition to 23,000 tank guns and 3,700 anti-aircraft guns, 45,000 field and anti-tank guns were produced in 1943, this field and anti-tank gun figure rising again in 1944 to a total of 56,000.[34]

Before 1943 the USSR armament industry was turning out many more guns, tanks and aircraft than were being produced by Germany, and qualitatively the standard of gun and tank was equal and sometimes superior to that of its German equivalent. From 1942 onwards, however, the German armament production began rapidly to overtake that of the USSR.

The German economy and industry had suffered from a complexity of organization, an overlapping of directional responsibilities and a lack of skilled scientific control and research. The economic Minister was Funk, but his main responsibilities had been assumed by Göring as head of the Four Year Plan Office. Göring in his turn was to lose ground to the able Todt, the head of the large para-military labour organization, who in 1940 had become the Minister for Armaments and Munitions. Todt and Göring, and to a much lesser extent Funk, all had some responsibility for Germany's war production, yet they shared it with Thomas, the head of the *Wi Rü Amt* of the OKW and Milch of the OKL. The OKM, too, had some voice in naval production matters. Ninety per cent of the armament industry in 1942 was still working on a single shift basis and, due to the Party's emphasis on the maintenance of relatively high German standards of living, much of industry and the industrial labour force was employed on the production of consumer goods.[35] On 10 January 1942 a great increase was ordered in the manufacture of heavy equipment and this may, as Professor Milward considers, have implied an abandoning by the *Führer* and Todt of the *blitzkrieg* armament policies and the preparation for a war of attrition and armament in depth.[36] However this might be, Todt died a month later in an aircraft crash, and he was succeeded as Armaments Minister by Speer, a young architect and subordinate of Todt's, and a firm friend of Hitler. The *Führer* had never made a happier choice of minister.

The energetic Speer, one of the very few men who had direct access to

[34] *Istoriya*, Vol. 2, p. 158; Vol. 3, pp. 167–72; Vol. 5, pp. 10–16.
[35] Milward, *The German Economy at War*, p. 93.
[36] *Ibid*, pp. 56–67.

Hitler, soon used his position and gifts to rationalize and reorganize German industry. Funk was never really a rival. Göring and the Four Year Plan Office were edged aside. In May 1942 Thomas and the *Wi Rü Amt* were removed from the OKW and Keitel's and Göring's control and were incorporated into Speer's organization. Milch and Saur, Speer's deputy, formed a single executive body to concentrate on fighter production, and the independence of the German Navy was severely restricted. The labour force under Sauckel remained, however, outside Speer's influence.

Motivated by the spur of total war, although many of the measures were in fact much less than total, German war production began to show an immediate and most remarkable improvement. In 1941 the German aircraft industry made only 11,000 military aircraft of which about ten per cent were trainers. In 1942 the military aircraft figure had risen to only 14,700, but in 1943 it jumped suddenly to 25,200 of which ten per cent were training aircraft. The 1944 aircraft production outstripped that of the Soviet Union, reaching 34,300 military and 3,200 training planes, although it must be remembered that fighters were being produced at the expense of bombers. The graph of tank production showed a similar rise. 2,875 medium tanks and assault guns were produced in 1941 in addition to 2,200 lightly armoured vehicles of all types. In 1942 4,300 medium assault guns and tanks and 1,200 SP guns on tank chassis were produced. In 1943 there were some difficulties in increasing the total by much, because the Mark III tank went out of production and the Marks V and VI were being introduced, but even so the medium tank and assault gun total for the year was 6,700, together with 2,500 heavy tanks and 2,600 SP guns on tank chassis. In 1944 production approached that of the Soviet Union and was made up of 11,000 medium tanks and assault guns, 1,600 tank destroyers and 5,200 heavy tanks, in all 17,800 medium and heavy tanks and assault guns. To this total was added 1,250 SP guns on tank chassis and 10,000 lightly armoured vehicles of all types. Even more significant was the improvement in the design of German armour which had done much to redress the inferiority of 1942 and 1943, since the Tiger and King Tiger were superior to the Soviet KV tanks, while the improved Mark V and the upgunned Mark IV and assault guns were to prove a match for the T34.[37] In 1942 German gun production (75 mm and above) stood at 12,000 artillery and 2,400 tank guns, and by 1944 these figures had risen to 40,600 artillery and 15,300 tank guns a year.[38]

[37] The King or Model B Tiger which appeared in 1944 had armour of improved design and slope and carried 150 mm at 50 degrees front armour and a L71 88 mm gun compared with 102 mm at 20 degrees and a L56 88 mm gun on the Tiger. The *Jagdpanther* which had a Panther chassis mounting a L71 88 mm gun (the same gun as the King Tiger) at their weight were eventually to become the most formidable tanks on the battlefield. The new Soviet Joseph Stalin heavy tanks had by this time gone into production but did not come into service until mid-1944.

[38] *Speer Papers, FD 2690/45 Vol. 10 (Flensburg Collection) Statistische Schnellberichte zu Kriegsproduktion*; also Janssen, *Das Ministerium Speer*, pp. 332–9.

Hitler and his advisers through ignorance and wilfulness had until too late failed to face the seriousness of Germany's position. Three years which might have been used better to equip the German forces had been largely wasted. Yet in spite of this, Germany's armament position *vis-à-vis* the Soviet Union had greatly improved in 1943 and showed every indication of continuing to do so. The key raw materials needed for armaments still caused some anxiety, however, since forty-seven per cent of Germany's iron ore requirement had to be imported, mainly from Sweden and France, together with a hundred per cent of its needs of manganese and bauxite, mainly from Russia and the Balkans, forty-five per cent of its copper requirement from Sweden, seventy-five per cent of its wolfram from Portugal and all its chrome from Turkey.[39] Only about thirty per cent of Germany's consumption of oil was imported from Rumania, this import total being restricted by transportation difficulties.[40] Germany's manpower losses during 1943 had been serious, the more so since the casualties had been high among the experienced junior leaders, but the loss was as yet by no means crippling and, as a percentage of population, was much lighter than that suffered by the Soviet Union.

When Stalin returned from Teheran he is reported to have told his war leaders that if Roosevelt did not keep his promise and open a Second Front in Western Europe in 1944, then the USSR had sufficient strength itself to finish off Hitlerite Germany.[41] If he did make this statement, it is doubtful whether it reflected his considered and sober judgement at that time. By the end of 1943 the USSR had extricated itself from a perilous position and could henceforth face the future with confidence. It was no longer struggling for survival and the battles of attrition and the Russian winters had robbed the German Army of much of its offensive power. Yet Germany was still very strong and, given sufficient respite, would revitalize its armed forces as it had done its industry. The Red Army was opposed by only part of the might of the *Reich* and an analysis of the deployment of German forces and manpower makes it difficult to believe that the USSR could in fact have undertaken the destruction of Germany by its own efforts. The Soviet Union needed Anglo-American intervention on the mainland of Europe just as acutely as the British and Americans wanted the Red Army to pin German forces in Russia; for without a First there could not have been a Second Front. The fear of the members of this strange alliance was that German intrigue should break them asunder.

Whereas Soviet production during 1944 stood at 32,000 aircraft and 29,000 tanks, the production of the Anglo-American bloc stood at over 120,000 military aircraft and over 22,000 tanks.[42] The quantitative superiority of arma-

[39] Janssen, *Das Ministerium Speer*, p. 374, Note 74; Medlicott, *The Economic Blockade*, Vol. 2. Appendix I, pp. 665-8.
[40] German home and synthetic oil production in 1943 reached nearly seven million tons. Rumanian imports mainly by Danube water traffic were less than three million tons.
[41] Zhukov, *Vospominaniya i Razmyshleniya*, p. 538.
[42] Production 1944: Britain, 26,000 aircraft, and about 5,000 tanks; USA, 96,300 aircraft and 17,500 tanks. In 1943 USA produced 29,500 tanks. *United States in World War II – The*

ment of the USA, the British Commonwealth and Empire and the USSR combined over Germany has been estimated by one source as about nine to two.[43]

Meanwhile the two Western Allies had put strong diplomatic, economic and military pressure on those neutrals which had been forced to supply the requirements of strategic raw materials so vital for Germany's war industries. The measures they undertook extended even to buying up raw materials for which they had no use, and as a result of this pressure supplies from Spain, Portugal, Sweden and Turkey were to be reduced and in some cases stopped.[44]

Hitler, brought down to reality, was finally forced to admit that a Second Front on the Atlantic or English Channel coast of France was imminent, but he put his hopes on German ability to throw the Anglo-Americans back into the sea, which success would then allow him to concentrate all his resources against the Soviet Union.[45] On 3 November he had issued Directive 51, giving absolute priority to the German forces in Western Europe for the supply of reinforcements and equipment, this meaning that the Eastern Front would for the next few months receive nothing.

If an Anglo-American invasion of France was likely from February 1944 onwards, a Soviet winter offensive into the Baltic States and Belorussia was certain even before February. During the whole of 1943 Hitler and many of his senior commanders and staffs had believed that the Red Army was near exhaustion and time after time they had continued to be surprised by the rapidity and the strength with which the Soviet fronts had returned to the offensive. The causes of German failure during 1943 were identical to those which gave rise to the defeats in 1942, an inadequacy of resources, particularly motor vehicles and motor fuels, and the insistence by the *Führer* on a rigid defensive strategy. Together, these lost the Germans both the strategic and tactical initiative. Hitler has been rightly blamed by his leading commanders on the grounds that he who defends everything defends nothing, for his demand that every yard of territory be held secure. Von Kluge sounded the note of truth when he told the *Führer* on 14 October that the Soviet success was due not so much to overwhelming strength, but to Soviet mobility and a preponderance of troops and equipment at the decisive points of the battle. This view is shared by the Soviet historian.[46]

Ordnance Department – Procurement and Supply, p. 263; *Buying Aircraft – Material Procurement for the Army Air Forces*, p. 555. *Statistical Digest of the War*, HMSO 1951.

[43] Milward, *The German Economy at War*, p. 102.

[44] The supplies of wolfram from Portugal were stopped entirely and Swedish iron ore was reduced from 10,262,000 tons in 1943 to 4,500,000 tons in 1944. Even stocks of near worthless goatskins were bought up to prevent them being acquired by the *Wehrmacht* for winter clothing. Medlicott, *The Economic Blockade*, Vol. 2, pp. 607 and 658.

[45] Heiber, *Hitlers Lagebesprechungen* 20 December 1943, p. 444. '*Wenn dieser Angriff abgeschlagen wird, ist die Geschichte vorbei. Dann kann man auch in kürzester Frist wieder Kräfte wegnehmen*'.

[46] *Istoriya*, Vol. 4, p. 21.

Germany had arrived at an impasse. It was impossible that Germany could be victorious against the three power coalition, and the time had arrived to extricate itself as best it might by making peace. After its great victory at Stalingrad an arrogant Soviet Union was deaf to such overtures, and it may be that Stalin had in sight yet another goal, the extension of communist influence and Soviet power into Central and South-East Europe. When Japan, possibly on its own initiative, in 1943 suggested a peace between the USSR and Germany, the proposal was immediately rebuffed by Moscow.[47] Goebbels, when visiting Rastenburg in the autumn, had found the atmosphere at Supreme Headquarters downcast by the general war situation, and he began to cast around as to which side Germany should first address its peace overtures, to the Russian or to the Anglo-American. Goebbels himself urged Hitler to try Stalin but the *Führer* appeared to think that some arrangement with the English would be easier. At the beginning of 1944 Goebbels was again pressing with greater urgency for peace with the USSR.[48] These proposals the *Führer* rejected.

It was unthinkable that the United States or Britain would have treated with Hitler or any members of his régime or political party or have agreed to negotiations from which the Soviet Union was excluded. Although Hitler awaited and would have encouraged and profited from any dissension between the three allies who opposed him, it is doubtful whether he really ever considered that a separate peace was possible with the Anglo-Americans. He had behind him a grisly record of the treatment of occupied Europe and all bridges to a settlement had long ago been burned. For him it was all or nothing, victory or annihilation, and he could be in no doubt of the treatment which was to be reserved for him and a defeated Germany. Convinced of his mission, resignation or suicide was out of the question. The German Army might of course have deposed him and his government, and, with its own nominee as the head of state, sought peace. Hitler had, however, safeguarded himself against a *coup d'état* by centralizing the police and counter-intelligence organization under Himmler and by raising the numerous SS formations which were independent of the German Army. The loyalty of the *Luftwaffe* and the German Navy to the régime was never in doubt and an attempt by the German Army to overthrow the *Führer* might have led to civil war. The Army Generals in senior appointments were most unlikely as a class to take such action since most of them owed to the *Führer* their high position and rank, and any strong-minded dissidents among them had long since been retired by Hitler's order. Goebbels, commenting in his diary after Mussolini's downfall, was firmly of the opinion that a military uprising was impossible 'considering the mentality of the German Generals'.[49] The Generals were in the main Hitler's men, yet

[47] Account given by Mamora Shigemitsu, the Japanese Foreign Minister. *Kriegstagebuch des OKW*, Vol. 3, p. 1521.

[48] *Goebbels' Diary*, 10 September 1943, pp. 341 and 347; *Kriegstagebuch des OKW*, Vol. 4, p. 57.

[49] *Goebbels' Diary*, 23 September 1943, pp. 382-3.

in spite of this the *Führer* had for some time past been dissatisfied with the resolution and political conviction of his senior commanders, and had come to the conclusion that armies which had their basis on a firm spiritual and ideological foundation were superior to those of the bourgeois states. He believed that the introduction of political commissars into the Red Army had made it formidable, and during the last eighteen months he had introduced his own form of commissar organization into the armed forces. The German Army as a whole had been penetrated by National Socialist Guidance Officers, although its loyalty, like that of the great majority of the German people at this time, lay with Hitler.[50]

Even if the Army had forcibly removed Hitler and the Nazi governmental system and at the same time won over the German people to its side, a military government would have been no more trusted abroad than a Hitlerite one, and it is most unlikely that after the 1943 Casablanca declaration of unconditional surrender any of Germany's enemies would have agreed to peace without a complete occupation of Germany. The idea of Soviet troops entering German territory filled both the Army and the civil population with terror, because they were well aware of the dreadful barbarities which partisans, Red Army troops and the NKVD had inflicted on prisoners and on civilians of all nationalities. In these circumstances the German people had no alternative but to continue the fight to the very end.

Hitler would have acted in Germany's interest if he had accepted the advice given to him by von Manstein and von Kluge and had given up the leadership of the Armed Forces and the German Army. If he had done so, however, he would in the final outcome of the war probably have been deposed and possibly handed over to his enemies. A Defence Minister and Commander-in-Chief should have been appointed from among the General Officers to command the Army and the *Luftwaffe*. To fill these key appointments there was a dearth of senior commanders of both up to date knowledge and independent thought, but von Rundstedt, von Bock or von Manstein would have been much preferable to the newer school typified by Guderian and Rommel, both of whom were tacticians of too limited education and too restricted an outlook to be fitted for the highest command. An immediate withdrawal would have been necessary from the Baltic States, Belorussia, the Ukraine and the Crimea, and from Italy, France, Scandinavia and the Balkans in order to have shortened the strategic frontages and accumulated reserves. Such measures might possibly, even at this late hour, have brought the war

---

[50] For Hitler's views on commissars see his address to the *Reichsleiter* and *Gauleiter* conference reproduced in *Goebbels' Diary*, 8 May 1943, p. 277. National Socialist Guidance Officers had no command or veto function comparable with those of Red Army commissars. Their tasks, like those of the commissars, were to promote political awareness and, as the Party representatives with the Army, to provide the Party with an additional information network as to the activities of commanders down to divisions. These Guidance Officers were later appointed down to the level of battalions, although at the lower levels they normally carried out some additional military function.

in the East to a stalemate, provided that Germany was not engaged in fighting a war on two fronts. Anglo-American intervention on the mainland of Europe was likely, however, to be the final decisive factor in the outcome of Germany's fate, as Hitler himself said it would. In the circumstances which existed at the time, even if General Officers and the German General Staff had once more assumed their rightful tasks of conducting all operations, at the best they could have achieved little more than the prolongation of the war without change to Germany's fortunes.

CHAPTER TWENTY-FIVE

Defeat at Leningrad and in the Ukraine

The strategy of the Soviet High Command was based on the immediate resumption of a general winter offensive in the hope that this would be unexpected by the enemy, and it was intended to attack both in the Leningrad area and in the Ukraine in order to clear Soviet territory as far west as the old border with the Baltic States and Rumania. Pressure was to be maintained in the centre of the Eastern Front in order that the Germans might not reinforce their flanks.

In the north the offensive which had taken two and a half months to prepare was to be launched by Govorov's Leningrad Front on the left of the exposed 18 German Army, both from the Oranienbaum bridgehead and from the area south of Leningrad, while Meretskov's Volkhov Front penetrated 18 Army's right flank, making its main thrust from the area north of Lake Ilmen near Novgorod.[1] The immediate aim of the Leningrad and Volkhov offensives was the double envelopment and destruction of Lindemann's 18 Army. Further to the south Popov's 2 Baltic Front was to engage and pin 16 German Army.[2] In all, the three fronts disposed of the equivalent of 105 rifle divisions and twelve tank brigades, and the Leningrad and Volkhov Fronts alone claimed a numerical superiority over 18 German Army in tanks and aircraft of at least six to one.[3] On the German side von Küchler, the Commander of Army Group North, having lost over the past few months a number of divisions to von Manstein, had a strength of forty infantry divisions, a single panzer grenadier and two mountain divisions to hold a 500-mile long front in heavily

---

[1] The military councils of the Leningrad and Volkhov Fronts were: Govorov, Zhdanov and Gusev; Meretskov, Shtykov and Ozerov. The second and third named in each council were the political member and chief of staff.

[2] The military council of 2 Baltic Front was M. M. Popov, Bulganin and Sandalov, Bulganin having replaced Mekhlis.

[3] The Leningrad Front had thirty-three rifle divisions and three rifle brigades, five static divisions and four tank brigades. The Volkhov Front had twenty-two rifle divisions and six rifle brigades and four tank brigades; the Baltic Front had forty-five rifle divisions, three rifle brigades and four tank brigades. Together the Leningrad and Volkhov Fronts were said to have 1,200 tanks and SUs, 14,300 guns and 375,000 men. *Istoriya*, Vol. 4, pp. 33–4.

wooded and marshy country.[4] 18 Army had twenty-one infantry divisions, of which five were *Luftwaffe* field divisions. There were no reserves and very little armour, and divisional frontages were as much as 25,000 yards wide.

During the autumn von Küchler had been making preparations for the withdrawal to the Panther Line near the 1940 frontier between the Baltic States and the Soviet Union, since it was intended to evacuate the area systematically and thoroughly before the actual troop withdrawal took place. An earlier and unsuccessful attempt to remove the civilian population had been modified to the compulsory evacuation of all adult males and the removal or destruction of all equipment, shelter and food supplies. It was known that a Soviet attack was likely, although Hitler had some doubt as to whether it was as imminent as von Küchler believed it to be. On 30 December von Küchler presented the situation at the midday *Führer* conference and protested at having had to find formations for the other army groups.[5] Von Küchler was in favour of beginning the withdrawal to the Panther Line before the Soviet offensive should break, but the request was refused by Hitler, who would never give up territory voluntarily, on the grounds that this would make Finland's exit from the war certain. It became obvious, too, that Lindemann was in disagreement with von Küchler and took a more optimistic approach, considering that he could hold his present positions against a Soviet offensive.[6] The *Führer* always accepted the opinion which coincided with his own, and von Küchler lost the day.

On 14 January Fedyuninsky's 2 Shock Army attacked out of the Oranienbaum bridgehead, the perimeter of which was held by two *Luftwaffe* field divisions, the SS panzer grenadier division *Nordland* and other elements, all under the command of Steiner's 3 SS Panzer Corps. After heavy fighting the German defenders began to give ground. A day later Maslennikov's 42 Army attacked across the Neva from the area south of Leningrad while Sviridov's 67 Army made a diversion in the area of Mga, and by 19 January Maslennikov had joined up with Fedyuninsky's forces, cutting off some German troops in Peterhof. Further to the east, Meretskov's Volkhov Front was to pin Lindemann's centre (54 and 26 Corps) and at the same time penetrate 18 German Army's south flank. The pinning operation undertaken by Starikov's 8 Army and Roginsky's 54 Army was so successful that Roginsky's troops began to envelop 26 German Corps. The Volkhov Front enveloping attack by Korovnikov's 59 Army further to the south near Novgorod also fell on a *Luftwaffe* field division near the boundary between 16 and 18 German Armies; but after some initial success made a very slow advance, since bad weather and lack of visibility made air and artillery support difficult, and the tanks became

---

[4] *OKH Kriegsgliederung* 26 December 1943. In addition von Küchler had a field training division and three security divisions.

[5] 1, 96 and 254 Infantry Divisions.

[6] Heiber, *Hitlers Lagebesprechungen*, pp. 516–25. Von Küchler wanted to begin the withdrawal on 6 January to have it completed by 20 January.

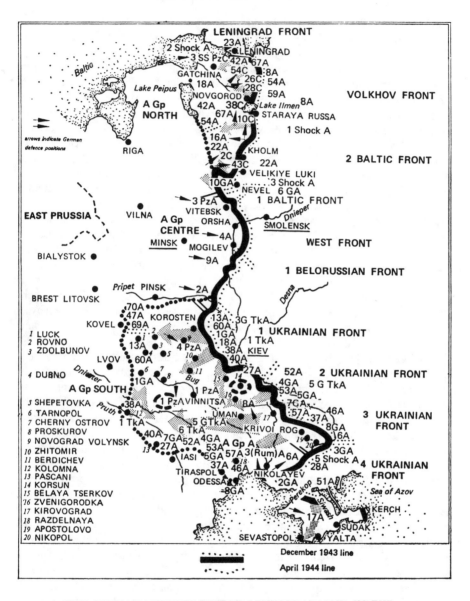

THE GERMAN DEFEATS BEFORE LENINGRAD AND IN THE
WEST UKRAINE
January–April 1944

410

bogged down in the marshes. To the south of Novgorod, however, Soviet troops had more success when they crossed the frozen Ilmen in a snow-storm, cutting off German troops in the area of the city. Von Küchler, being well aware of the Soviet intention to envelop 18 Army from both flanks, pressed the *Führer* in vain for permission to withdraw the exposed 26 and 28 Corps to an intermediate *Rollbahn* position on the line of the Leningrad-Chudovo railway. On 22 January he personally explained the difficulty of the situation to Hitler, since by then 54 Corps was threatened by envelopment as well as 26 Corps in the area of Mga and Tosno; but for all his efforts he received in return only the promise of a panzer division from Army Group Centre. The *Führer* was opposed to sanctioning the break-out of the encircled troops in the Novgorod area and when he reversed his decision the order was given too late. The same difficulty arose in the withdrawal to the *Rollbahn* intermediate line, for when the agreement was given the German defenders were already too closely pressed and the *Rollbahn* could not be held.

Conditions had always been bitter in the Volkhov sector for both German and Soviet troops. There had been relatively little movement over the last two years and in many places the fighting had taken the character of trench warfare in heavily wooded marshes. Inured to hardship though the German defenders undoubtedly were, the Soviet offensive burst on them with a fury which none had expected, amid scenes which none had ever experienced before. On the night of 19 January those troops of 28 Light Division encircled in Novgorod received the order to break out. The seriously wounded had to be abandoned in the ruins, the medical staff volunteering to remain behind with them, and all who could carry weapons, including the walking wounded, tried to withdraw under cover of darkness. Elsewhere to the north-east, troops fell back under heavy enemy artillery fire while the Red Air Force bombed and machine-gunned all movement. German formations and units became mixed and confused and fighting units included in their number stragglers and leave and baggage men. All suffered from the wet and lack of sleep and food, and unless supply column commanders took most energetic action to maintain contact, replenishment failed. *Luftwaffe* divisions disintegrated, and in some of the infantry divisions nearly all the regimental and battalion commanders were killed or wounded. Divisional infantry strengths fell to only 500 men. Scaremonger rumours ran up and down the front and there were some cases of panic and flight. Gatchina, the main German railhead, where countless German soldiers had begun and ended their home leave, came under an intense fire from the heavy calibre guns of the Soviet warships in the Gulf of Finland and was soon made unusable.[7]

On 28 January von Küchler on his own responsibility ordered 18 Army to fall back to the line of the River Luga, although he could offer Hitler no assurance that even this could be defended. Hitler, choosing to ignore that if 18 Army had held its original positions it would have been encircled, used the

[7] Pohlmann, *Wolchow*, pp. 112–25.

events to argue that the fault lay with von Küchler for having advised withdrawal in the first place. That same day he remarked bitterly to Zeitzler at the midday conference that the experience of the last three years, if it had shown anything, had proved that when one retired from a position in order to shorten the front or to build a firmer defence line, the new position could never be held.[8] On 29 January von Küchler was retired and replaced by Model, who had acquired a reputation as a lion of the defence.

Model had been given, together with his appointment, two further divisions from Army Group Centre, and although the commitment of a panzer division near the town of Luga caused some check to the Soviet advance, it was far too late to hold the line of the river, the situation in the German rear being confused as the Leningrad partisans derailed trains and demolished railway track and bridges. At first the main Soviet effort appeared to be developing on the 18 German Army north-west flank where 2 Shock and 42 Armies were already on the lower Luga threatening the narrow neck of land to the north of Lake Peipus; but as Model started to move troops over to this left flank 16 German Army on the right came under increasingly heavy attack from Popov's 2 Baltic Front, and from this time onwards the whole of Army Group North appeared to be in danger of envelopment. On 15 February Hitler was forced to agree to the withdrawal of Army Group North out of Russia to the Panther Line. Finland then asked Moscow for armistice terms.

The long period of static defence by the Leningrad and Volkhov Fronts had resulted in defects in the training of staffs and troops, and attacks were, according to the Soviet account, particularly badly co-ordinated and supported. Army Group North was said to have owed its salvation to this and to the bitter weather conditions, snow, fog, thaw and rain, and to the difficult marsh and forest terrain, all of which slowed up the advance of the Red Army. In mid-February the Volkhov Front was broken up and its formations shared between the Leningrad and 2 Baltic Fronts. By 1 March all operations ceased in the Baltic theatre as both sides went over to the defensive.[9]

In the Ukraine the situation of the German Army Group South had fast deteriorated. Von Manstein's troops were still stretched precariously right across the South Ukraine from above Korosten down to the Dnieper bend, presenting the enemy with a vulnerable salient. Nikopol and Krivoi Rog were held at Hitler's insistence, despite the fact that the ores were no longer mined and that the loss of the area would not have presented the German economy with an insoluble problem.[10] Meanwhile another threat had developed on the left flank of Army Group South, where the Soviet salient to the south-west of

[8] Heiber, *Hitlers Lagebesprechungen*, p. 532.

[9] *Istoriya*, Vol. 4, pp. 39–41.

[10] Speer said subsequently that the loss of Krivoi Rog and Nikopol would have presented no great problem as twelve months' supply of ore was already assured and this by economic reorganization could have been extended to eighteen months. *Speer Papers, FD 2690/45 Vol. 12 (Flensburg Collection)*.

Kiev made by 1 Ukrainian Front appeared likely to separate von Manstein from Busch's Army Group Centre.

The Red Army fronts in the Ukraine were not without their difficulties. The winter had been very mild in the south, and the spring thaw with rain and mud began exceptionally early at the end of December. The lines of communication to the Red Army bases stretched over 300 miles to the rear and there were consequent difficulties in supply, maintenance and repair. In 2 Ukrainian Front only fifty per cent of the motor vehicles were roadworthy, and of the 168 rifle divisions in the West Ukraine most were much under strength in spite of the energetic measures taken to make good the deficiencies by rounding up the local Ukrainian population. Airfields were particularly badly affected by the rain and flooding.[11] Undeterred by these problems, the Soviet High Command relentlessly renewed its offensive along the whole of the line, Zhukov remaining with 1 and 2 Ukrainian Fronts while Vasilevsky co-ordinated 3 and 4 Ukrainian Fronts.[12] 1 and 2 Ukrainian Fronts were to make parallel thrusts in a south-westerly direction on the axes Vinnitsa-Mogilev-Podolskiy and Kirovograd-Pervomaysk, while 3 and 4 Ukrainian Fronts made concentric blows on Nikopol and Krivoi Rog. The first phase of the offensive was to be undertaken by the sixty-three rifle divisions of Vatutin's 1 Ukrainian Front.[13] On the morning of 24 December the attack began against Raus's 4 Panzer Army and as it developed the frontage of Vatutin's assault broadened to 200 miles, the main thrusts being made by V. I. Kuznetsov's (later Grechko's) 1 Guards Army, Rybalko's 3 Guard Tank Army and Leselidze's 18 Army on Zhitomir, and by Moskalenko's 38 Army and Katukov's 1 Tank Army towards Vinnitsa.[14] Vatutin's main thrust, therefore, was to come in the centre with two tank and three rifle armies striking south-west while the two rifle armies on each flank fanned out westwards and southwards.

At the end of 1943 von Manstein's Army Group South consisted of 1 and 4 Panzer Armies and 8 Army, in all the equivalent of forty-three infantry, fifteen panzer and seven panzer grenadier divisions. Von Kleist's Army Group A was made up of 17 Army in the Crimea and 3 Rumanian Army and Hollidt's 6 Army in the Dnieper bend, the army group totalling eight German infantry and ten allied divisions.[15]

[11] *Istoriya*, Vol. 4, pp. 57–8. Soviet order of battle was said to include nine cavalry and 168 rifle divisions with strengths as low as 2,500 (probably cavalry) to 6,500 men to a division.

[12] Military councils of the Ukrainian Fronts in sequence from 1 to 4 were: Vatutin, Grechko (deputy commander), Khrushchev and Krainyukov (both political members) and Bogolyubov; Konev, Susaikov and M. V. Zakharov (second and third named political member and chief of staff); Malinovsky, Zheltov and Korzhenevich; Tolbukhin, Subbotin and Biryuzov.

[13] 1 Ukrainian Front was said to comprise sixty-three rifle and three cavalry divisions, six tank and two mechanized corps. Zhukov, *Vospominaniya i Razmyshleniya*, p. 542.

[14] The other formations of 1 Ukrainian Front which attacked were on the north flank Pukhov's 13 Army and Chernyakhovsky's 60 Army, and on the south flank Zhmachenko's 40 Army and Trofimenko's 27 Army.

[15] *OKH Kriegsgliederung* 26 December 1943. In addition von Manstein had two security and two reserve divisions and von Kleist one field training division.

Although the *Führer* maintained the semblance of good relations with von Manstein he was in fact very hostile to him, and von Manstein's proposals to evacuate the Dnieper bend and move his own army group headquarters from Vinnitsa to Lvov were discussed by the *Führer* with Zeitzler, Jodl and others and subjected to mockery and bitter sarcasm.[16] Von Manstein had appealed earlier to Hitler for permission to move 1 Panzer Army over to his left flank and evacuate the Dnieper bend, but the *Führer* had countered this proposal by promising the dispatch by rail of three divisions, one division each to come from Army Groups A, Centre and North. Since these divisions could not arrive in time to be of use, von Manstein, five days after the start of Vatutin's offensive, had on his own responsibility moved 1 Panzer Army Headquarters with one infantry and three panzer divisions from the Dnieper bend to his left wing. He conformed, however, to Hitler's strategy in that Wöhler's 8 Army continued to hold part of the area of the Dnieper bend to the west of Hollidt's 6 Army, which was deep in the Nikopol pocket.[17] Although Hube's 1 Panzer Army Headquarters had come to organize the relief of the assailed 4 Panzer Army, taking over its right-hand sector while Raus took over more ground to the left, both had to give way before Vatutin's attack which threatened the German railway link from Lvov to Odessa, vital to both the right wing of Army Group South and Army Group A. 1 Ukrainian Front continued to fight its way forward, at first steadily and then rapidly, Korosten, Novograd Volynsk, Zhitomir, Berdichev and Belaya Tserkov being taken in the first two weeks of the attack. On 5 January, the day after von Manstein had returned from East Prussia, having asked once more that the Dnieper bend be evacuated and that he be given 17 Army from the Crimea, Konev's 2 Ukrainian Front began its offensive in a thick fog, the attack this time falling on Wöhler's 8 German Army further to the east.[18]

Konev's 2 Ukrainian Front offensive consisted of a single thrust on a fairly narrow sixty-mile frontage between Cherkasy and Starodub well to the east of Vatutin's sector, the main axis being in a south-west direction towards Kirovograd. The main attack was to be mounted by Managarov's 53 Army, at this time under the temporary command of Galanin, and Rotmistrov's 5 Guards Tank Army. Subsidiary flanking attacks were to be made by Ryzhov's (later I. K. Smirnov's) 4 Guards Army, Zhadov's 5 Guards and Shumilov's 7 Guards Armies, while Koroteev's 52 Army took the far north flank. By attacking eastwards on Kirovograd and towards Malaya Viska it was hoped to outflank part of 8 Army defending the south bank of the Dnieper,

---

[16] Heiber, *Hitlers Lagebesprechungen*, pp. 486–7 and 493.

[17] Hollidt's 6 Army was placed under the command of Army Group A in mid-September 1943 (von Manstein, *Lost Victories*, p. 475) and according to the *OKH Kriegsgliederung* was still under von Kleist on 26 December. Von Manstein says that 6 Army reverted to him temporarily again in December and was returned to Army Group A on 6 February (pp. 498 and 512). The point is of minor importance since on 26 December 6 Army consisted of only one corps (44 Corps).

[18] Von Manstein, *Lost Victories*, pp. 501–3.

roughly between Cherkasy and Korsun, and complete a double envelopment by joining with Vatutin's forces in the German rear.[19]

Konev's offensive opened on 52 German Corps and 47 Panzer Corps. Von Vormann, who had arrived from Germany only a few days earlier to take over the command of 47 Panzer Corps, has told of the condition in which he found his three panzer, one panzer grenadier and four infantry divisions. The panzer divisions were hardly more than panzer groups and the infantry divisions no stronger than reinforced regiments. Ramcke's 2 Parachute Division had a fighting strength of 3,200 men and a frontage of thirteen miles, and 10 Panzer Grenadier Division with a strength of 3,700 men covered a sector ten miles wide. Deep snow lay everywhere and the temperature was minus twenty degrees centigrade. Any change of battle position on the infantryman's part, even of only a few hundred yards, meant that he had to find himself new fire trenches and fresh shelter from artillery fire and from the cold, often an impossible task in the iron hard ground. The morale of the German troops remained good but, according to von Vormann, many were already a prey to doubts as to the future and the outcome of the war. Letters from home told of the devastating bombing and of the increasingly heavy police controls. Few could understand the seemingly senseless orders which came from above, apparently from the highest. Most knew that there could be no hope of terms with East or West, and the *Führer* remained their only salvation. To the soldier in the field Hitler was the Commander-in-Chief of the Army and in their eyes there was no other army leader of sufficient stature who could replace him.[20]

Radio intercept had provided numerous indications that an offensive was imminent, particularly as Russian wireless traffic made little effort to conceal the preparations for the attack. The offensive opened in the usual fashion with a half hour of devastating artillery bombardment followed by heavy tank and infantry attacks. Von Vormann noted that although the higher Soviet plans were well laid, the Red Army still suffered from its earlier weaknesses, a want of flexibility and co-ordination in its artillery fire, some lack of initiative on the part of the lower commanders and a poor performance by its untrained infantry which, outnumbering the German defenders by eight to one, was made up largely of locally raised and often unwilling levies, known to the German soldiers as booty troops (*Beutesoldaten*). On 5 and 6 January alone, 47 Panzer Corps artillery fired off 177,000 rounds, trying to cover the many gaps in the front by fire. No corps or army troop reserves were available and the corps fronts were in danger of falling apart. On 8 January Kirovograd was lost. On the night of 9 January 47 Panzer Corps Headquarters was dispersed with losses in men and equipment by a Soviet tank brigade carrying infantry

---

[19] *Istoriya*, Vol. 4, p. 61. According to Zhukov the detailed plan for the encirclement was not put to Stalin until 11 January and was agreed the next day. Zhukov, *Vospominaniya i Razmyshleniya*, p. 546.

[20] Von Vormann, *Tscherkassy*, pp. 46–51.

on its tanks, and the German divisions were repeatedly encircled as they fought their way back.[21]

Konev's advance continued in the face of the fierce opposition of a German enemy who, in the words of the Soviet account, used the many villages and gullies in a skilful defence. Further to the west Vatutin's 1 Ukrainian Front continued to force apart 1 and 4 Panzer Armies until the gap between them was forty miles wide; but in the second half of January Army Group South mounted two powerful counter-attacks on 1 Ukrainian Front in the area between Uman and Vinnitsa using two panzer corps and one infantry corps.[22] The first of these forced back Zhmachenko's 40 and Zhadov's 5 Guards Armies north of Uman, while the second cut off part of Moskalenko's 38 Army and Katukov's 1 Tank Army and inflicted heavy casualties, particularly in tanks. Here 1 Ukrainian Front temporarily lost ground and fell back some twenty miles.[23]

The penetration by 1 and 2 Ukrainian Fronts to the east and west of the area of Korsun had already left an exposed German salient south-west of Cherkasy, held by troops of both 1 Panzer and 8 Armies. The offensive was renewed by the flank formations of both 1 and 2 Ukrainian Fronts aimed at the double envelopment of this salient. 2 Ukrainian Front attacked first on 25 January taking Shpola on 27 January and the next day Zvenigorodka, deep in the German rear, in spite of strong counter-attacks by German armour which enveloped and cut off the attackers for a space of three days. During this fighting von Vormann noted that the heavy pak anti-tank gun and the gun of the Panther could slice through a T34 at any battle range.[24] 1 Ukrainian Front then took up the attack from the west on 26 January, and on 28 January, the same day that Hitler had called all his army group and army commanders to East Prussia to hear a lecture on the virtues of National Socialism within the German Army, elements of Kravchenko's 6 Tank Army joined Rotmistrov's 5 Tank Army of 2 Ukrainian Front near Zvenigorodka, this double envelopment cutting off Lieb's 42 and Stemmerman's 11 Corps. Four infantry divisions, one SS panzer division, a SS brigade and other elements, in all about 60,000 men, were in the pocket sealed off by a Soviet force of about twenty-seven rifle divisions, four tank and one mechanized corps.[25]

In Army Group South there was an immediate flurry to collect a relieving force, as it was known by experience that the longer the attack was delayed the more difficult the task of relief would be. But all major decisions were reserved for the *Führer*. He was informed of the encirclement by a telephone

[21] *Ibid*, pp. 27, 29–31, 35–8.
[22] Hell's 7 Corps, Breith's 3 Panzer Corps and 46 Panzer Corps (commander unknown).
[23] Von Manstein, *Lost Victories*, pp. 508–9; *Istoriya*, Vol. 4, p. 60.
[24] Von Vormann, *Tscherkassy*, p. 58.
[25] 389, 57, 72 and 88 Infantry Divisions. SS panzer grenadier division *Wiking* was in the process of being reformed as a panzer division. The Soviet account has quoted the encircled force as ten divisions. *Istoriya*, Vol. 4, p. 65.

call from Zeitzler at five o'clock that evening and having described the situation as a crying shame (*ein reiner Jammer*) he set to work pulling out a division here and a battle group there. Infantry, he suddenly told Zeitzler, were no longer any use in battle unless they had tanks or assault guns behind them.[26] Hube's 1 Panzer Army was to end its battle against Katukov's 1 Tank Army on the far left, and 8 Army had to make available von Vormann's 47 Panzer Corps. Von Manstein ordered 24 Panzer Division over from Hollidt's 6 Army sector in the Dnieper bend; but Hitler, conducting the war on all fronts from his desk, had it sent back again, after it had actually begun to attack at Cherkasy, because the Nikopol area was threatened. After a round march of about 500 miles it arrived there too late, having been of no use to either sector.[27]

The encircling Soviet troops formed their usual pattern, the inner infantry cordon being found by the infantry divisions of I. K. Smirnov's 4 Guards and Trofimenko's 27 Armies, while Rotmistrov's 5 Guards Tank and Kravchenko's 6 Tank Armies provided the outer cordon, ready to repel the awaited panzer attacks of the relieving forces. On 8 February the encircled German enemy was invited to surrender, promise being made of humane conditions together with the guarantee of life and safety. By 10 February the whole of the pocket was within range of Soviet artillery as the two encircled corps were compressed and crowded into an area about ten miles by twenty under the pressure of Red Army attacks. Lieb's 42 Corps had been placed under the command of Stemmermann, the Commander of 11 Corps, and all troops in the pocket were put under command of Wöhler's 8 Army. A skeleton airlift organization already existed at Korsun airfield to supply those forward elements of 8 Army cut off by the muddy weather, and this organization was expanded to airlift eighty tons a day to the encircled troops. The visibility and flying conditions were poor, due to heavy snow and rain showers.

Wöhler chafed at the delay in assembling the relief force and at having the method of relief, an ambitious, unrealistic encirclement aimed at destroying the enemy rather than extricating his own troops, imposed on him from above. The first relief thrust made by the left pincer, Breith's 3 Panzer Corps, started on 4 February but was directed too far to the west and came to a standstill in blood and mud and, having lost five days and many casualties, the troops were withdrawn to their starting point. With no time for further delay formations were committed on a direct new axis piecemeal as they arrived. Von Vormann's 47 Panzer Corps took up the attack further to the east. Seas of mud made movement difficult and vehicles ran out of fuel, and the air supply of the relieving troops was not really effective.[28] The change of 3 Panzer Corps axis surprised the enemy and a temporary drop in the temperature assisted movement,

---

[26] Heiber, *Hitlers Lagebesprechungen*, 28 January, pp. 545–7.

[27] Von Manstein, *Lost Victories*, p. 515; von Senger und Etterlin, *24 Panzer-Division*, p. 191.

[28] Von Vormann, *Tscherkassy*, pp. 79–82.

but resistance stiffened as Bogdanov's 2 Tank Army, allotted to 1 Ukrainian Front by the Soviet High Command, joined the battle. On 12 February 3 Panzer Corps had reached a hamlet called Lysyanka within ten miles of the pocket and the Soviet High Command then made desperate efforts to prevent the German relief. The command of the area of break-in was given to 2 Ukrainian Front and Trofimenko's 27 Army was transferred from 1 to 2 Ukrainian Fronts.[29] The losses of infantry were rapidly made good when formations such as 180 Rifle Division descended on the village of Kvitki in the narrow strip of land between the pocket and 3 Panzer Corps, prevailing upon its male population, about five hundred men, to enter its ranks. These so-called volunteers must have seen their first action shortly afterwards. Although the Soviet tanks with their wide tracks had superior tactical mobility to those of the Germans, and the Red Army was better provided with tracked vehicles, the Soviet troops also had their difficulties in the sea of mud, and before long bombers were flown as transport planes and all formations were using teams of oxen and horses to move guns and vehicles and the local peasantry to move supplies.[30] On the German side 3 Panzer Corps in its advanced position could no longer be supplied by land due to the state of the ground and was already on air supply.

The German air supply operation was carried out under the direction of Seidemann's 8 Air Corps direct to Korsun airfield. Supplies were originally airlanded and wounded flown out until the ground conditions made the airfield unusable. The parachuting of supplies did not prove satisfactory as this slow and inefficient method caused an increase in aircraft losses, and in the final outcome supplies, including forty gallon petrol drums, were free dropped at heights as low as thirty feet. The air transport force suffered some losses due to anti-aircraft fire and Red Air Force interception, but enemy aircraft kept their distance, although the lack of German fighters reduced the escorts to a scale of three Me 109 to thirty-six transport planes. In all, 2,000 tons of supplies were flown in, in 1,500 sorties; 2,400 wounded were flown out and thirty-two transports were lost.[31]

On 5 February 8 German Army had ordered Stemmermann to be ready to break out at any time after 10 February; but not before 15 February, on the same day on which he authorized Model to withdraw to the Panther Line, did the *Führer* agree that the encircled troops should fight their way out. The pocket then started to move southwards, sometimes in a sea of mud, sometimes in a

---

[29] Zhukov has told a long and involved story of how he was awakened on the night of 12 February by a long distance call from Stalin who had been informed (presumably by Konev or the NKVD or commissar network) that the German pocket had started to move southwards, Zhukov himself being ignorant of the matter. Stalin, against Zhukov's advice, thereupon transferred the troops and the responsibility for liquidation to Konev. Zhukov, *Vospominaniya i Razmyshleniya*, p. 553.

[30] *Istoriya*, Vol. 4, pp. 66–8.

[31] Morzik und Hümmelchen, *Die Deutschen Transportflieger im Zweiten Weltkrieg*, pp. 176–81.

blizzard as the weather altered day by day. Some units and formations had kept their organization and were in cohesive groups, but many of the troops were a mass of stragglers put under the command of the nearest officers. Guns, tanks and vehicles were left behind and the troops had nothing but small arms to defend themselves against almost incessant tank and infantry assault, the *SS Wiking* Division distinguishing itself in repelling the attacks. In addition the pocket had to run the gauntlet of artillery fire and the casualties mounted steadily. On 17 February the advanced elements joined up with 3 Panzer Corps and a large part of the encircled troops came out of the pocket. All the sick and wounded had been abandoned to their fate, all heavy equipment had been left behind and General Stemmermann was himself killed on 18 February. The Germans' claim that 30,000 men got through to safety has to be weighed against that of the Red Army that 18,000 wounded and unwounded prisoners and 50,000 dead remained in the pocket.[32] However many men escaped from Cherkasy, the truth was that Army Group South had suffered a significant tactical defeat. Many of the survivors of the pocket were physically and mentally unfit for immediate service and two experienced corps had been destroyed as fighting formations. Their loss was to be sorely felt in the battles which were to follow.

To the north of Raus's 4 Panzer Army, the left flanking formation of Army Group South, a great gap had appeared between Army Groups South and Centre since Hitler had been unwilling and unable to form another army in the Rovno area as von Manstein had requested. Some troops of Hauffe's 13 Corps were detached to cover the land approach from Rovno to Lvov, while some SS and police battalions covered the railway line in the area of the Pripet Marshes. No immediate Soviet attack was expected in this area as it was believed that 1 Ukrainian Front was preoccupied both at Cherkasy and in the wedge between 4 and 1 Panzer Armies. On 27 January, however, Pukhov's 13 and Chernyakhovsky's 60 Soviet Armies, the right flanking formations of Vatutin's 1 Ukrainian Front, attacked eastwards, being helped through the marsh and woodland by partisans. Using 1 and 6 Guards Cavalry Corps on the extreme flank, two days later they reached the River Styr well inside the 1939 borders of Poland. Rovno, Luck and the Zdolbunov railway junction were soon taken and on 10 February Shepetovka fell. Koch, the *Reich* Commissioner for the Ukraine, fled from his headquarters at Rovno on the approach of Red Army troops, and the loss of the town led to the usual recriminations by the *Führer* against the German Army and the threat of the death sentence on officers in command.[33]

---

[32] Soviet accounts speak of the encirclement as a second Stalingrad claiming that 80,000 were in the pocket and that only small groups escaped. On 18 February 1944 Stalin issued an Order of the Day claiming the destruction of 90,000 men. Two days later the *Führer* issued a communiqué saying that the encircled formations had broken out, and claiming to have inflicted significant losses (720 tanks and 800 guns) on the enemy. Of the undoubtedly heavy German losses nothing was said. Compare also von Manstein, *Lost Victories*, p. 517.

[33] *Ibid*, pp. 518–19.

Four weeks earlier on 10 and 11 January, far to the east in the Dnieper bend, Malinovsky's 3 Ukrainian Front and Tolbukhin's 4 Ukrainian Front attacked Hollidt's 6 German Army; but the attack was called off after only five days, fighting as it had made little progress. The two fronts were then regrouped and reinforced preparatory to mounting a new attack on 30 January. Glagolev's 46 Army and Chuikov's 8 Guards Army made the main attack in the centre of 3 Ukrainian Front, while Sharokhin's 37 and Shlemin's 6 Armies held the flanks. 4 Ukrainian Front, using Tsvetaev's 5 Shock, Lelyushenko's 3 Guards and Grechkin's 28 Armies, attacked the bridgehead forward of Nikopol on the Dnieper. 6 German Army had some weeks before taken over that corps which was left earlier by 1 Panzer Army when it was removed to the left flank of Army Group South, and at the end of January 6 Army consisted of 4, 17, 29 and 30 Corps and 57 Panzer Corps, in all three panzer and eighteen infantry divisions.[34] At about this time, in the middle of the battle, Hitler removed 6 Army from the command of Army Group South and put it under von Kleist's Army Group A which had removed from the Crimea to its new headquarters on the mainland at Nikolayev.[35] 3 Ukrainian Front attack fell on Fretter-Pico's 30 Corps, an understrength formation, which broke under the strain.[36] The left bank of the Dnieper was cleared and Nikopol taken by 7 February, and the German troops in the Dnieper bend, abandoning all their baggage as they went, were soon in retreat, as their line of withdrawal was threatened by Chuikov's 8 Guards and Glagolev's 46 Armies to their rear. On 17 February the attack began on Krivoi Rog and five days later the town was taken.

The Red Army then began to regroup in order to complete the conquest of the Ukraine. In the north the Ukraine is bound by the Pripet Marshes and these began to influence the course of operations. The eastern end of the marshes barred the progress of Rokossovsky's Belorussian Front from the area of Gomel, but to the south of the Pripet Vatutin's 1 Ukrainian Front was making rapid progress westwards leaving the Belorussian Front behind it, and a vacuum was appearing between the two fronts. Since Vatutin was about to make a left-angled turn to the south to envelop von Manstein, another formation was required to plug the gap. For this purpose a new 2 Belorussian Front was formed under Kurochkin on 24 February in the area of Kovel, made up of P. A. Belov's 61 Army and Gusev's 47 and V. S. Popov's 70 Armies from the High Command Reserve.[37] Rokossovsky's Belorussian

[34] *OKH Kriegsgliederung* 1 February 1944.

[35] According to Zeitzler, 6 Army was removed from von Manstein by Hitler to overcome von Manstein's resistance to the transfer of divisions from 6 Army to Army Group A. Von Manstein, *Lost Victories*, p. 513.

[36] Fretter-Pico said that the bayonet strength of his battalions was down to sixty to eighty men. Only one panzer grenadier division had battalion strengths of about 250 men. Fretter-Pico, *Missbrauchte Infanterie*, pp. 128–9.

[37] The military council of the new 2 Belorussian Front was Kurochkin, Bokov and Kolpakchy as chief of staff. For redesignation Rokossovsky's Front, see *Istoriya*, Vol. 4, p. 98.

Front was at the same time redesignated as 1 Belorussian Front. Although the East Ukraine had been relatively free from partisan activity, the West Ukraine with its woods and forests and its mixed Polish-Ukrainian population formed a hotbed of partisan movements, the Poles being antagonistic to German, Russian and Ukrainian, while the Ukrainian partisans were often against the Pole and either for or against the Red Army, depending on whether or not their sympathies were communist or nationalist. The nationalist Ukrainian partisans ambushed Red Army troops and vehicles and in one of these attacks on 29 February Vatutin, the Commander of 1 Ukrainian Front, on a motor tour with Khrushchev in 60 Army area, is said to have received severe wounds from which he shortly died.[38] The Red Army lost one of its most able soldiers, a commander who, according to Zhukov, was an excellent staff officer able to express himself well verbally and in writing, a most conscientious man who was at the same time a confirmed worrier, reluctant to delegate authority.[39] Vatutin's vacant command was taken by Zhukov.

Soviet strategy in South Russia and the Ukraine was based on a westwards movement of Kurochkin's 2 Belorussian Front along the edge of the Pripet Marshes in the direction of Kovel and Brest, while Zhukov's 1 Ukrainian Front struck south in von Manstein's rear towards the Dniester. Konev's 2 and Malinovsky's 3 Ukrainian Fronts were to move on parallel axes in a south-westerly direction on Iasi and Odessa while Tolbukhin's 4 Ukrainian Front prepared to take the Crimea. The coming offensive was not unexpected by Army Group South, for whereas Hitler was still relying on the mud and Soviet exhaustion to give him some respite, the troops in the field were well aware that the opposing Red Army troops possessed far greater mobility than they did themselves. The Soviet tank and motorized formations were better mechanized than their German counterparts, and whereas the German motorized formations were tied to the roads, the Soviet troops, using great numbers of American four-wheeled and six-wheeled drive trucks, were able to operate across country in all but the very worst weathers. All German formations, whether motorized or infantry, suffered from a lack of motorization and a deficiency of tracks and tractors and were being worsted at the hands of a more numerous and more mobile enemy. The retreats in the Ukraine had caused great losses in tanks and in motor vehicles, these being abandoned for lack of fuel or because they were awaiting repair and could not be moved. Many were lost simply because they could not be extricated from the mud. The protracted movement by road of the panzer divisions, much of it needless, caused heavy vehicle casualties, so that 24 Panzer Division lost at this period 1,958 vehicles of all types, over fifty per cent of its establishment, and like many other panzer divisions was forced to reorganize its supply and baggage transport as horse-drawn *panje* columns. On 8 February, just after it had been

[38] Earlier accounts (e.g. Platonov) do not describe the manner of Vatutin's death. The attack is described in detail by Zhukov, *Vospominaniya i Razmyshleniya*, pp. 557–8.
[39] *Ibid*, p. 541.

turned back from Cherkasy, this division had 335 otherwise fit vehicles, which were non-runners because they were stuck in the mud.[40]

Army Group South had 8 Army still in the general area of Zvenigorodka and Uman, 1 Panzer Army about Vinnitsa and 4 Panzer Army on the extreme left flank in the area of Dubno and Tarnopol. Von Manstein had to decide whether the next Soviet blow would be a frontal one aimed at securing the crossing places over the Bug at Vinnitsa and Voznesensk, or an envelopment of his exposed left wing. Fearing envelopment from the north in the gap between himself and Busch, he continued to urge on Zeitzler that fresh formations be found to occupy this area and meanwhile, believing the envelopment on the left flank to be the greater danger, he moved all his formation boundaries to the left. Breith's 3 and Balck's 48 Panzer Corps were withdrawn over to the left flank in the area of Tarnopol and Proskurov, and von Manstein moved his own headquarters to Lvov behind what he believed to be the decisive sector. 4 Panzer Army had taken over the Rovno area but Raus commanded only 13 Corps, of two infantry divisions, and 48 Panzer Corps, of two panzer divisions; immediately to his south Hube's 1 Panzer Army between Shepetovka and Vinnitsa commanded 59 Corps and 3, 24 and 46 Panzer Corps, in all sixteen divisions, including six panzer divisions.[41] The Soviet offensive when it came was neither in the left nor in the centre, but over the whole of the Ukraine. Zhukov's heavy Soviet thrust on von Manstein's left fell on Raus's weak 4 Panzer Army.

Zhukov's 1 Ukrainian Front had six rifle armies of about forty divisions, two tank armies with a strength of 520 tanks and SUs and a further tank army in reserve.[42] On 4 March Zhukov attacked von Manstein's left wing to the north of 1 Panzer Army using Grechko's 1 Guards and Chernyakhovsky's 60 Armies, and the initial attack was so successful that 4 Panzer Army and Schulz's 59 German Corps near Shepetovka which formed part of 1 Panzer Army, were almost overrun. Two of the Soviet tank armies in reserve, Rybalko's 3 Guards Tank and Badanov's 4 Tank Armies, were committed to battle the same day. A week later the attack had penetrated to the area of Cherny Ostrov, sixty miles to the German rear, where it was brought to a temporary standstill by the counter-attacks of Breith's 3 and Balck's 48 Panzer Corps in a battle which, according to Zhukov, matched that of Kursk in its bitterness.[43] On 5 March Konev's 2 Ukrainian Front attacked from Zvenigorodka to Uman to the south of 1 Panzer Army on the left wing of Wöhler's 8 Army, using in its main thrust I. K. Smirnov's 4 Guards, Trofimenko's 27 and Koroteev's 52 Armies, together with Bogdanov's 2 Tank, Rotmistrov's 5 Guards Tank and Kravchenko's 6 Guards Tank Armies, these tank armies totalling, however, only 650 tanks and SUs.[44] N. I. Krylov's 5

[40] Von Senger und Etterlin, *24 Panzer-Division*, pp. 193–4.
[41] *OKH Kriegsgliederung* 3 March 1944.
[42] *Istoriya*, Vol. 4, pp. 77–8. Zhukov's other armies were Pukhov's 13, Zhuravlev's 18 and Moskalenko's 38 Armies.
[43] Zhukov, *Vospominaniya i Razmyshleniya*, p. 558.
[44] *Istoriya*, Vol. 4, pp. 80–1.

Army and Shumilov's 7 Guards Armies were to make subsidiary flanking attacks. The five extended infantry divisions of Hell's 7 German Corps which lay in Konev's path were rapidly scattered, and by 10 March Uman had been taken on the way to the Bug and the Dniester. Further east, troops of Malinovsky's 3 Ukrainian Front had started to build bridgeheads over the flooded Ingul River, putting heavy pressure on von Kleist.

Hube's strong 1 Panzer Army was already in a very dangerous position, being threatened by encirclement. On its right flank Konev was sweeping by, moving south-west towards Rumania. Zhukov was about to envelop its left flank. On 21 March Katukov's 1 Tank Army of 1 Ukrainian Front took up the attack again near Cherny Ostrov over the heavily flooded ground, and in three days reached the Dniester at Zaleshchiki, crossing the river and nearing Kolomna on the Pruth near the Czecho-Slovakian border. Its neighbouring formation, Lelyushenko's 4 Tank Army, said by then to be reduced to a tank strength of sixty tanks, took Kamenets Podolskiy in Hube's rear. Meanwhile Zhmachenko's 40 Army from Konev's 2 Ukrainian Front had turned Hube's right flank from the south, and by 28 March Hube's 1 Panzer Army was completely encircled.

Further to the south-east Konev's Front had reached the River Bug on a broad sixty-mile frontage without meeting resistance and, crossing it without deploying from the line of march, had raced on to cross the Dniester two days later. On 26 March 2 Ukrainian Front reached the Pruth on a fifty-mile front, and a week later Konev advanced into Rumania as far as Pascani. Wöhler's 8 Army and von Kleist's Army Group A in the South Ukraine were threatened with destruction by this deep encirclement in their rear.

Von Kleist, however, faced a danger nearer at hand. Army Group A on the Black Sea coast consisted of 17 Army in the Crimea, Dumitrescu's 3 Rumanian Army, mainly in Transdniester, comprising four Rumanian, a Slovak and elements of four German divisions and Hollidt's 6 German Army of twenty-one divisions.[45] 3 Ukrainian Front had taken Apostolovo to the west of Nikopol on 5 February and two days later Nikopol and the remaining German positions on the left bank of the Dnieper had fallen to 4 Ukrainian Front. On 22 February Malinovsky had taken Krivoi Rog, pushing 6 German Army back to the line of the River Ingul. At the beginning of March 3 Ukrainian Front had secured bridgeheads over the flooded river just to the south of Krivoi Rog preparatory to pinning 6 Army frontally and making a main armoured enveloping thrust through Novy Bug behind Army Group A down to the Black Sea coast to the east of Nikolayev. This main encircling thrust was to be made by Chuikov's 8 Guards and Glagolev's 46 Armies together with a cavalry mechanized group, while Gagen's 57, Sharokhin's 37, Shlemin's 6 and Luchinsky's 28 Armies, together with Tsvetaev's 5 Shock Army, pinned von Kleist's troops frontally on the line of the Ingul.

The attack began on the morning of 6 March, and by the same evening

[45] *OKH Kriegsgliederung* 1 February and 3 March 1944.

the infantry divisions had made a breakthrough and the cavalry mechanized group had been committed to battle. Although Novy Bug was taken on 8 March the mobile troops were not strong enough to envelop the defenders. The pinning formations advanced rapidly, however, and on 24 March elements were across the Bug. The Soviet High Command orders to 3 Ukrainian Front were then altered to include the seizure of the Black Sea coast from Nikolayev to Odessa and from Odessa to the Danube; the axis of the main mechanized thrust was changed from Chuikov's and Glagolev's armies to that of Sharokhin's 37 and Gagen's 57 Armies towards Tiraspol and Razdelnaya in the Odessa area, since these two armies had broken into the enemy rear and were making the fastest progress westwards.[46]

On 19 March von Manstein and von Kleist had been called from their theatres of operations to Obersalzberg in Bavaria, merely to attend the presentation to Hitler of a declaration of loyalty, intended as an answer to the propaganda being put out through Moscow by von Seydlitz-Kurzbach and the communist-sponsored Free Germany Committee.[47] Admittedly the seriousness of the situation in the Ukraine was as yet apparent to neither of the army group commanders, but the *Führer* was entirely out of touch with reality. He declined to allow 6 Army to withdraw from the lower Bug, partly because the German Navy were insisting that Odessa was essential to supply the Crimea and partly, so he said, to sustain the morale of Rumania. He was disinclined to discuss future strategic regrouping which would be necessary should Army Groups Centre and South become separated, and busied himself with tactical details which took little account of the situation.[48] Since the Volga defeat of early 1943 it had been German policy to keep Rumanian and Hungarian troops out of the fighting zones, but in 1944 Hitler was obliged to press Horthy and Antonescu to provide him with new formations, even though he knew that the Hungarians were becoming increasingly reluctant to continue the war. There were six Rumanian divisions in the Crimea and 3 Rumanian Army already formed part of Army Group A. A newly formed 4 Rumanian Army had been brought up to the Iasi area on the old Rumanian frontier and the Hungarians had promised to mobilize an army of two corps to hold the Carpathian passes.

The speed of the Soviet advance took the Germans entirely by surprise and great quantities of munitions and equipment were lost. It had originally been intended to fortify and hold the line of the Bug, but the Red Army reached it in places in advance of the withdrawing German troops. Even when 6 Army had retired across the river it found itself still threatened by encirclement by 23 Tank Corps, the right flanking formation of 3 Ukrainian Front, which was moving towards Tiraspol and Odessa, while further to the west Konev's 2 Ukrainian Front was making an even deeper outflanking penetration towards

[46] *Istoriya*, Vol. 4, pp. 85–6.

[47] Although von Seydlitz-Kurzbach was to be subjected, even after the war, to attack from some quarters in Germany, it must be emphasized that he was an honest and honourable man and a true German patriot.

[48] Von Manstein, *Lost Victories*, pp. 532–6.

Iasi. The Ukrainian railtracks maintaining Army Group A and the right wing of Army Group South were already in Soviet hands, and henceforth reliance would have to be placed on the relatively inefficient Rumanian railways. Von Kleist, together with Wöhler's 8 Army which had just been transferred to the command of Army Group A, was almost completely cut off from von Manstein, so that von Kleist had to turn about to face the enemy to his north-west. On 26 March von Kleist informed the *Führer* that he would have to with-draw westwards from the Bug towards Rumania, and was called to account to explain his temerity. When finally forced to agree with the withdrawal proposal, Hitler insisted on the defence of the line of the Tiligul, a small river between the Dniester and the Bug, in order to cover the sea communication between Odessa and the Crimea. This was the last opportunity to evacuate the Crimea, a course which had been advised by Antonescu long before.

Hitler had agreed to Hube's proposal that the encircled 1 Panzer Army should break out to the south, moving down the valley of the Dniester towards Tiraspol and the Black Sea. Von Manstein, who intended that Hube should break out westwards in the general direction of Lvov to meet 4 Panzer Army and together with Raus provide the force to cover the gap to the north of the Carpathians, flew to Hitler at the Berghof on 25 March in order to get the order rescinded. To this the *Führer* reluctantly agreed but not before he had heaped on von Manstein charges that the German Army was running away without a fight.[49] A SS panzer corps of two divisions was to be withdrawn from France to assist Hube in the break-out.

On 2 April an ultimatum timed 1000 hours bearing Zhukov's signature was delivered to Hube's headquarters, promising that if all armed resistance did not cease by nightfall one-third of all German troops subsequently surrender-ing would be shot out of hand. A second ultimatum followed, stating that all German officers failing to surrender immediately would be shot on capture.[50]

The encircled 1 Panzer Army in the area of Kamenets Podolskiy consisted of 3, 24 and 36 Panzer Corps and 59 Corps with six panzer, one panzer grenadier, one artillery and ten infantry divisions. The formations were in fact very much under strength, 8 Panzer Division, for example, on 14 March having only thirty-two battleworthy tanks; but even so the panzer army numbered between two and three hundred thousand men. As it was impossible to ration so large a force by air supply, the formation was ordered to obtain its own food by foraging, and only ammunition, vehicle fuel, tank spares and medical supplies were flown in from airfields near Lvov by a transport force of Junker 52 and Heinkel 111 aircraft, diverted from its primary task of assisting in the supply of 17 Army in the Crimea. An air supply organization was set up under Morzik, Dessloch's 4 Air Fleet being responsible for the overall control of the operation. No German fighters could be allocated as escorts, and, as the Red Air Force was very active by day, most supply sorties were flown unescor-

[49] *Ibid*, pp. 539–41.
[50] *Kriegstagebuch 13/Pz AOK1/Ia*, 2 April 1944.

ted by night. As the encircled pocket was continually on the move, frequent problems were to arise as to the selection and preparation of landing strips and dropping zones. Although landings were in fact made, most of the supplies were air dropped, this meaning that very few wounded could be evacuated so that the hospital cases had to be transported with the moving pocket. Although Soviet anti-aircraft artillery was used most skilfully there were few German aircraft casualties, and once again the Red Air Force failed to undertake the destruction of the German air supply airfields.[51] Eventually by 9 April the whole of the force, after a march of about a hundred and fifty miles, joined up with 4 Panzer Army to the south of Tarnopol, but its heavy equipment and many heavy weapons were lost. For the failure to destroy the German force Zhukov, who subsequent to 1957 fell into political disfavour, has since been blamed, yet 1 Ukrainian Front in its march from the Dnieper to the Carpathians had advanced over 200 miles in six weeks and it was by then strung out and lacked both support and supplies.[52]

Hitler's more recent contribution to the direction of the fighting was the selection off the map of nodal points of road or rail traffic, which were declared strongholds and which were to serve as breakwaters to slow down the Red flood. Each was stocked with ammunition and supplies and a commander was appointed who had to answer with his life for the holding of the place; but they had little effect on the course of the fighting since they were usually in the first instance bypassed by Soviet troops, and too many men were wastefully deployed and locked up in these garrisons. In one of these Major-General von Neindorff held out in the *Führer*-designated fortress of Tarnopol, where he soon became a liability for the *Luftwaffe* transport force which had to maintain him. This resulted in the Tarnopol ring becoming a collecting point for Soviet anti-aircraft units, and so intense was their fire that they had to be engaged by *Luftwaffe* fighter and bomber formations before the transport aircraft could drop their loads. Transport gliders were flown in at dawn and dusk to supplement the air drops. On 15 April, however, the fortress was taken by 1 Ukrainian Front, von Neindorff falling in the fighting. Only part of the garrison escaped and reached the German lines.

On 30 March von Manstein was awakened at his Lvov headquarters by the surprising news that Hitler's Condor aircraft was about to land, with von Kleist already on board, in order to take the two field-marshals to Obersalzberg, there to be removed from their commands. Neither was re-employed.

[51] On an average over 200 tons were delivered daily over the fifteen-day period. Two Heinkel 111 only were lost and there were forty-four aircrew casualties. Morzik und Hümmelchen, *Die Deutschen Transportflieger im Zweiten Weltkrieg*. pp. 193–205.

[52] *Istoriya*, Vol. 4, p. 79. Zhukov has since written his own apologia which lists a number of difficulties, the shortage of support of all kinds, the attack by the SS Corps and, most important of all, the fact that Hube moved off westwards and not southwards, contrary to the Soviet intelligence forecast 'from an unimpeachable source'. On the question of German losses, Zhukov says, quite accurately, that most heavy equipment was lost. On personnel losses he makes no claim but hints that they were probably heavy. Zhukov, *Vospominaniya i Razmyshleniya*, p. 560.

Their replacements, Colonel-General Model and General Schörner, were both temporarily in the *Führer*'s favour, Model having gained some credit by the energy with which he had waged his defence in Army Group North and Schörner having come to Hitler's attention for his part as Commander of 40 Panzer Corps in the Krivoi Rog and Nikopol battles.[53] For the last month Schörner, who was a fervent supporter of the régime, had been Chief of National Socialist Guidance in the OKH. Both army groups were re-designated, Army Group South becoming Army Group North Ukraine, while Schörner's Army Group A became Army Group South Ukraine. For the second time during the war in Russia the Germans followed the Soviet practice of giving army groups territorial designations, but since neither was in the Ukraine, their designation was intended to imply that their mission was one of reconquest of the lost territories.

At the beginning of April the seasonal muddy period and floods began, and it was hoped that the Soviet offensive would cease entirely as the Red Army fronts had already outrun their supply and transport organization; and so it transpired, except that Hitler was not to be so fortunate as to retain his bridgehead forward of the Dniester covering Odessa. Sharokhin's 37 Army of 3 Ukrainian Front crossed the Tiligul and on 4 April, having taken Razdelnaya, started to break up part of Hollidt's 6 Army, encircling German and Rumanian troops against the coast.[54] Chuikov's 8 Guards Army and Glagolev's 46 Army began to press on Odessa which was finally evacuated by Axis troops after a protracted signal argument between Army Group South Ukraine and the Army High Command (OKH). Soviet troops entered the port on 10 April, the German naval support base having been moved to Constanta in Rumania.

Except in the Crimea there then followed a lull in operations over the whole of the Eastern Front, save for local activity where the Soviet troops set about establishing and improving bridgeheads south of the Dniester, the Pruth and the Sereth. Model's Army Group North Ukraine and Busch's Army Group Centre gained some small tactical successes in the Carpathian foothills near Kolomna and in counter-attacks against Belov's 61 Army of 2 Belorussian Front south of the Pripet Marshes. Although it encircled Kovel, 2 Belorussian Front failed to take the town. On 4 April Kurochkin's 2 Belorussian Front was disbanded and its armies transferred to 1 Belorussian Front or the High Command Reserve.

The final in the succession of German defeats in the Ukraine was probably the greatest. The Crimea continued to be garrisoned at Hitler's insistence out of political and prestige considerations by 17 Army, the commander of which, Jaenecke, had inspired much confidence by the able and orderly way in which he had evacuated the Kuban. By April, 17 Army had been reduced in strength to two corps, 49 Mountain and 5 Corps, and five German infantry and six

---

[53] Model was replaced by Lindemann as Commander Army Group North.
[54] Hollidt was replaced a few days later by Angelis, appointed temporary commander of 6 Army.

Rumanian divisions and one flak division.[55] It had no armoured formations and only two assault artillery brigades. Konrad's 49 Corps held the north shore of the peninsula, including the Perekop Isthmus, and Allmendinger's 5 Corps was on the Kerch Peninsula containing a small Red Army bridgehead. It was reckoned that eighty days would be needed for a systematic and complete withdrawal from the Crimea, and that it would take at least twenty-three days even to ship the 270,000 personnel; but because of Hitler's order that the Crimea was to be held, no joint planning covering evacuation arrangements had taken place with the Black Sea Naval Command. Jaenecke and Deichmann on their own responsibility had, however, begun parallel planning inside 17 Army and 1 Air Corps for the withdrawal to Sevastopol and a possible emergency evacuation. 17 Army had for some time been maintained by air and sea without any significant interference by the Soviet Fleet or Red Air Force, but it continued to pin its hopes on the reopening of the land link through the Perekop Isthmus rather than on giving up the Crimea.

The German troops in the Crimea had long been conscious of a feeling of isolation and even the simplest soldier was well aware of the vulnerability of the peninsula. After the evacuation of the Kuban bridgehead the previous autumn they had fully expected that the Crimea would be given up; all the necessary arrangements had been made to withdraw from the Kerch Peninsula. At 1830 hours on 29 October 1943 the order had been given out from Headquarters 98 Infantry Division for the withdrawal to start the next day, but a few hours later the divisional commander had been called to 5 Corps to receive counter orders. The *Führer* had decreed that the Crimea would not be given up. It was, commented the divisional commander, like the 1941 winter before Moscow all over again, stop and go, backwards and forwards, uncertainty and doubt.[56] So 5 Corps was drawn into the winter fighting as the Soviet troops reinforced their bridgehead about Kerch.

Schörner, who at that time enjoyed the *Führer*'s fullest confidence, had replaced von Kleist, and Wenck had taken over from Röttiger as Chief of Staff of Army Group A. It was known that Red Army troops were concentrating to attack the Crimea, but Schörner, having paid 17 Army a fleeting visit, reported to the OKH on 7 April that everything was in the best of order in the peninsula. Wenck too, took an optimistic view, which was not shared either by Jaenecke or even by Zeitzler. By the evening of 9 April, however, Schörner had changed his views entirely, and, expressing full confidence in the Commander of 17 Army, he asked that Jaenecke should be given the fullest freedom to act as he thought fit, even if this were to result in the evacuation of the Crimea, as Schörner thought that it would. Hitler refused, but said that he would send Zeitzler down to Galicia. The next afternoon Schörner reported that Jaenecke had already on his own responsibility ordered 5 Corps to fall back some distance to the narrows, a decision which he, Schörner, supported

[55] Pickert, *Vom Kuban-Brückenkopf bis Sewastopol*, pp. 142–3.
[56] Gareis, *Kampf und Ende der Fränkisch-Sudetendeutsch-98 Division*, p. 316.

to the full. Hitler was obliged to accept this withdrawal but he ordered that 49 Corps was to remain on the Perekop Isthmus, come what may. That same day, on 10 April, Schörner was pressing for the evacuation of the Crimea.[57]

Stormy weather in the Sea of Azov and the delay in the capture of the port of Odessa slowed the mounting of the Soviet offensive against the Crimea, but on 8 April the main attack began, this being mounted from the north by Tolbukhin's 4 Ukrainian Front with G. F. Zakharov's 2 Guards and Kreizer's 51 Armies across the Perekop Isthmus and Lazy Sea bridgehead, while Eremenko's Independent Coast Army thrust eastwards from the Kerch Straits. Vasilevsky and Voroshilov were entrusted with the co-ordination of the operations. The Soviet force was made up of just under half a million men and included the equivalent of thirty-two divisions with 560 tanks and SUs and 1,200 aircraft.[58] The main thrust was not made from Perekop but from the Siwash coast against a Rumanian division which soon broke under the 51 Army attack. 19 Tank Corps was committed to battle on 11 April and, making open country, streamed off across the steppe towards Simferopol. Meanwhile the *Führer*, from his distant retreat in the Berghof, was still forbidding any withdrawal in the north, but as a concession had eventually sanctioned 5 Corps in the east to withdraw a few miles to the Theodosia narrows. He can have had no conception as to the effects of his war direction on the troops in battle.

Withdrawals could not, of course, be carried out successfully on snap decisions by the High Command, for a decision given too late led almost inevitably to the loss of heavy equipment and guns and the dispersal or routing of the fighting troops who, without artillery support, ammunition or anti-tank guns, broke and ran under Soviet tank attack. To call German formations in the East divisions, regiments and battalions was simply a form of self-deception. 290 Grenadier Regiment of 98 Division had 200 men in the line, hardly one-tenth of what it had in 1941. Experienced infantry were getting fewer in number, and many of the German troops manning the forward positions were not infantrymen by arm of service or by training. Before these fighting men could break contact, the *Hiwis*, the wounded, the Rumanians, the baggage and the flak had to go, together with every other unit not vital to the forward area, and when on that Easter Monday on 10 April 98 Division was suddenly told that it was to withdraw that night, the horses, without which nothing could be moved, were still twenty miles to the rear. Since there was little motor transport available for the withdrawal, the division was to move back on foot, closely pursued by tanks and a fully motorized enemy. At seven o'clock that same night the regimental gun and heavy weapons companies destroyed their infantry and anti-tank guns and mortars, since they lacked the means to move them; this, their commander emphasized, on the very first night of the withdrawal. Shortly afterwards units and sub-units lost contact as many of

[57] Hillgruber, *Die Räumung der Krim 1944*, p. 32.
[58] *Istoriya*, Vol. 4, p. 104.

P

them were routed and broken up. On 13 April I Battalion of 290 Grenadier Regiment numbered fewer than thirty men to whom another thirty stragglers from other units had attached themselves, and the regimental heavy support company had nothing but one heavy and three light machine-guns.[59]

The defence had by then fallen apart and Jaenecke ordered a general withdrawal to Sevastopol, an order which Hitler tried to countermand, saying that Jaenecke had lost his nerve. Konrad, the Commander of 49 Corps, was dismissed his command, a *Führer* order which was disregarded as Konrad continued in his attempts to rally his broken troops. On 12 April Hitler finally agreed to the withdrawal to Sevastopol and even to the shipping away of those elements not required for battle. Sevastopol, however, was to be held 'for the time being'. Zeitzler was openly telling everyone his opinion that Sevastopol could not be held and was warning Schörner of the danger that 'Russian tanks might be in Sevastopol before 17 Army'. In the Crimea the *Führer*'s agreement was no longer relevant to the position of the Axis troops as there was already a deadly race to get to Sevastopol before the Russian did, and the German Navy ferried back some of 5 Corps by sea. No reliance could be place on the Rumanians, and the five German divisions were entirely disorganized with a broken fighting strength and a lack of heavy weapons. By 16 April the Red Army had occupied most of the strategic points including Yalta and Sudak, and two days later the Independent Coast Army under its new commander, Melnik, was incorporated into 4 Ukrainian Front.

On 21 April Schörner was forced to follow the path which so many of his predecessors had trod before him, when he made the painful flight to the Berghof to persuade Hitler that the Crimea should be evacuated, but he was put off with the persuasive charm reserved for newcomers to high command who were temporarily in favour. Sevastopol had to be held for eight weeks until the Anglo-Americans had made their attempt to land in Europe. In any case the holding of Sevastopol was of paramount importance in keeping Turkey out of the war, since the Turks were already submitting to Western pressure to cut off German supplies of chrome. The usual empty promises of equipment and reinforcements followed, and Schörner came back empty-handed. Hitler was obliged, however, in response to a request from Antonescu, to begin the evacuation of Rumanian troops from the peninsula.[60]

[59] Gareis, *Kampf und Ende der Fränkisch-Sudetendeutsch-98 Division*, pp. 364–7, 373–5.

[60] On 10 February Antonescu told E. Hansen of his wish to evacuate the Crimea and this was repeated to Hitler by Steflea five days later. On 28 February Antonescu again brought up the matter when visiting Hitler at Klessheim, and on 27 March he warned the *Führer* that the Crimea must be evacuated before Odessa was given up. See also Hillgruber, *Die Räumung der Krim 1944*, pp. 30–1; Heusinger has told how, before Antonescu saw the *Führer*, the Rumanian told the OKH General Staff of his strong views and these gave birth to the hope that the German troops would also be withdrawn. Heusinger was astounded by Antonescu's declaration after the meeting that Hitler was right and that Rumanian troops would remain in the Crimea. Such apparently were the *Führer*'s persuasive powers. As soon as Antonescu had returned to Bucharest however, he saw the matter in an entirely different light and demanded once more the evacuation of the Crimea.

In Sevastopol the disorganized remnants of the divisions had been set to work on the defences. Morale was surprisingly good, even optimistic. The men were certain that when the German naval, *Luftwaffe* and administrative organization had been shipped off after the Rumanians, the German fighting troops would follow. Fourteen days should see the last man away. The troops were not particularly worried about likely enemy interference with shipping by air or by water, since they were confident that the *Luftwaffe* and German Navy would not leave them in the lurch. On 24 April they were informed of the *Führer* order that Sevastopol would be held to the last, and all of them knew that it was their death sentence.[61] That same day Jaenecke, the Commander of 17 Army and a survivor of Stalingrad, being unwilling to sacrifice his troops, flew to Hitler with whom he had two painful and stormy meetings. An angry and vindictive *Führer* removed him from his command, replacing him by Allmendinger.

The Soviet attack was not long delayed. The Red Air Force had become very active and before the final offensive 2,000 tons of bombs were dropped on the fortress. On 5 May G. F. Zakharov's 2 Guards Army began the attack to draw the defenders off to the north, while Kreizer's 51 and Melnik's Coast Army made the main thrust in the south on the Sapun Hill above the British War Cemetery. On the evening of 7 May the Sapun Hill was taken and the next day the attackers penetrated the town. German troops did what the Red Army defenders had done two years before, and in their tens of thousands withdrew covered by rearguards, the 98 Infantry Division among them, to the open Khersones Peninsula to make a last stand in the hope of being picked up from the sea. On 9 May the *Führer* changed his mind once more and ordered the German troops to be brought off, but by then nothing more could be done.[62] On 10 May a dozen *Luftwaffe* fighters took off for the last time and disappeared towards the mainland. That same day, as an exaggerated version of the latest *Führer* order reached the disorganized masses on the heavily bombed and shelled beaches, it was rumoured that a *Luftwaffe* group and a great fleet of ships were being sent to their rescue. Nothing came.

In the final days very few men got away from the Khersones Peninsula and the losses in Axis shipping caused by the Red Air Forces had been heavy. 29,000 German and 7,000 Rumanian troops went into captivity, although the total Axis losses were very much higher, probably nearly 80,000 men.[63] Nearly all the equipment had been lost.

[61] Gareis, *Kampf und Ende der Fränkisch-Sudetendeutsch-98 Division*, pp. 385–7.

[62] Compare *Kriegstagebuch des OKW*, Vol. 4, p. 858.

[63] On 12 April the ration strength of 17 Army totalled 230,000 men. 130,000 were evacuated by sea and 21,000 by air and 77,500 remained, dead or missing. The majority of these were German. In Sevastopol on 3 May the strength had stood at 64,700, of which 10,000 wounded and 16,700 unwounded were withdrawn. The fate of the other 38,000 was unknown. Hillgruber, *Die Räumung der Krim 1944*, p. 72.

CHAPTER TWENTY-SIX

Belorussia and East Poland

The German defeat in the Ukraine in the winter and spring of 1944 had resulted in the retreat of the Axis forces to the area of Galicia and the Rumanian and Czecho-Slovak borders, and by April of that year Red Army forces were within fifty miles of the Russo-German frontier line of the upper Bug across which Hitler had launched the 1941 *Barbarossa* campaign.[1] The German withdrawal from the Ukraine had completely uncovered the right flank of Army Group Centre.

Field-Marshal Busch's Army Group Centre stretched forward into Belorussia in a great 650-mile long salient from the area of Brest-Litovsk, eastwards along the southern edge of the Pripet Marshes to Bobruisk and then northwards to Vitebsk where it joined with Army Group North. Although the Pripet gave some protection along the newly exposed southern flank, Busch was threatened on his right rear by Soviet forces which, moving along the edge of the swamps, reached the firmer and more open ground opposite German Army Group North Ukraine in the area of Kovel.[2] Busch's Army Group Centre consisted of Weiss's 2 Army covering the southern flank along the Pripet, Jordan's 9 Army in the area of Bobruisk, Heinrici's 4 Army to the south of Orsha, and Reinhardt's 3 Panzer Army near Vitebsk. Busch had a total strength of thirty-eight German infantry and two panzer divisions.[3] The German troops were over-extended, but the average divisional strength of about 2,000 infantry (300 men to each of the six battalions) was probably higher than elsewhere on the Eastern Front. The morale of the Soviet enemy in Belorussia appeared to have been distinctly better than that in the Ukraine and might have been accounted for by lighter casualties and better organized formations, for the Germans reported that Red Army infantry was willing and able to attack without the support of tanks and that it defended its own positions to the very end. In spite of good camouflage and deception measures and

---

[1] Galicia had some economic importance in that its oilfields produced about five per cent of Germany's fuel consumption in June 1944.

[2] In March and April the Soviet troops had made desperate attempts to take Kovel, having encircled it for over two weeks. Under its SS commander Gille the garrison had held out successfully until relieved.

[3] *OKH Kriegsgliederung* 15 June 1944. In addition 2 Army had some cavalry and Hungarian formations in the Pripet.

a shut-down of Soviet radio traffic, the arrival of new formations from the Crimea had been noted and, a sure indication of the imminence of an offensive, the reinforcing of all Red Army formations to bring them up to establishment. There was a feeling of tenseness in both commanders and troops on the German side which had never been experienced before, and from about 10 June onwards Busch expressed his anxiety to the Army High Command (OKH).[4] His intelligence appreciation was to some extent supported by the views of Army Group North Ukraine, where Model believed that no further attack was to be expected from the West Ukraine.

Hitler and the OKH had other opinions, however, and disagreed with Busch. The Anglo-American invasion of Western Europe was overdue, and there was some speculation as to whether the next Red Army offensive would be co-ordinated in timing with the landings in the West. None could be sure of the axis of the next Soviet offensive, whether it would be directed against Army Groups Centre and North in order to break through to the Baltic or whether the main impetus would continue to come from the Ukraine, thrusting south-westwards to occupy the Balkans. Political and economic considerations and his own preconceptions always took precedence in Hitler's mind over military intelligence, and he became convinced that the Kremlin would not fail to seize the source of Rumanian oil, so valuable to Germany, and to extend its hold over the whole of the Balkans, thus securing a military and political advantage over its Anglo-American allies. The preponderance of Soviet forces in the Ukraine and the Crimea appeared to lend weight to this view and in consequence the deployment of German forces followed the same pattern as the Soviet, with its centre of gravity situated in the south, heavily weighted by the eighteen panzer and panzer grenadier divisions in Army Groups North Ukraine and South Ukraine.[5] The OKH attempted to allay Busch's anxieties by dismissing reports of the reinforcing of the Soviet centre as part of a Moscow cover plan to divert attention from the area in the south where the main offensive was intended. It was also probable, the OKH thought, that some reinforcing would take place in the Soviet centre in order to pin Busch while the main attack was launched from the West Ukraine. The forty divisions available to Busch were reduced by a further six when the *Führer* began to take a hand by deploying detachments to garrison the fortresses of Bobruisk, Mogilev, Orsha and Vitebsk; the further construction of the rearward defences on the line of the Berezina was forbidden.

From the middle of February the Finns had been attempting to negotiate a peace with the USSR, but since the Soviet terms were unacceptable the talks had been broken off. On 9 June the Soviet Union opened a heavy attack in the north in order to put Finland out of the war, and this continued with growing intensity throughout the month. On 18 June Helsinki appealed in vain to Berlin for the dispatch of six German divisions to Finland.

[4] Heidkämper, *Witebsk*, pp. 144–5 and 147.
[5] *OKH Kriegsgliederung* 15 June 1944.

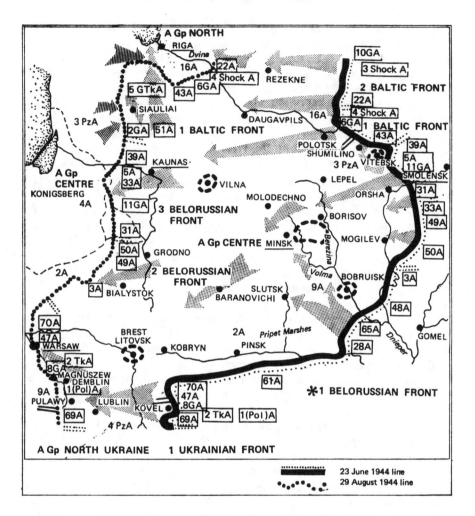

THE DESTRUCTION OF ARMY GROUP CENTRE
June–August 1944

The organization and deployment of the Red Army fronts in North and West Russia had undergone some change in the spring of 1944. The Volkhov Front had disappeared, its commander, Meretskov, having been transferred to take over the command of the Karelian Front opposite the Finns. Govorov's Leningrad Front was responsible only for the Narva sector to the north of Lake Peipus. A new 3 Baltic Front to the south of Lake Peipus under Maslennikov had been formed in April from the left wing of the Leningrad Front.

434

2 Baltic Front remained to the north of Nevel, with 1 Baltic Front to the south, 2 Baltic Front being commanded at the beginning of the year by M. M. Popov, followed by Eremenko, and 1 Baltic Front by Bagramyan. A new 3 Belorussian Front had been formed in April in the area of Smolensk from Sokolovsky's West Front under a new commander, Chernyakhovsky, Sokolovsky being transferred to Zhukov's 1 Ukrainian Front as chief of staff. Rokossovsky's 1 Belorussian Front was still in the area of Gomel. Kurochkin's 2 Belorussian Front along the edge of the Pripet Marshes to the south of Rokossovsky, after a short life of only seven weeks, had been disbanded at the beginning of April to be resuscitated again two weeks later near Mogilev immediately to the north of Rokossovsky's 1 Belorussian Front. This revived 2 Belorussian Front was commanded by G. F. Zakharov.[6]

In the middle of May Zhukov, Vasilevsky and Antonov, the deputy to the Chief of General Staff, began to work on the outline of a new operation known as *Bagration*, which was intended to envelop the salient occupied by Army Group Centre within a space of fifty days, and penetrate the rear to a depth of 160 miles. On 20 May a draft was ready for presentation to Stalin and for dispatch to the fronts concerned. On 22 May Rokossovsky was called on a visit to Moscow and a day later Bagramyan and Chernyakhovsky arrived, bringing with them members of their staff, situation reports and their own outline plans. More detailed work then began both by the General Staff in the Defence Ministry and by the front staffs at the front headquarters, the planning proceeding in parallel as heads of supporting arms and services were brought into the operation. Frequent consultation and close contact soon ironed out all difficulties and queries before a final version of the outline directive was sanctioned by Stalin and confirmed to the fronts on 31 May. On 4 and 5 June Vasilevsky and Zhukov left for their respective groups of fronts to continue more detailed planning in conjunction with front, army and corps commanders and staff, Shtemenko, the head of the operations directorate within the General Staff, having been allotted to Zhukov to assist him. Much of the planning took place at army and corps command posts and if Zhukov is to be believed, Zakharov made his own decision as to which of his armies was to make the main thrust, while Gorbatov disagreed with the axis allotted to the tank corps which was to break out in his sector. Stalin was phoned at frequent intervals and at Zhukov's request Novikov and Golovanov arrived to assist in planning the employment of the air support allocated to the operation. All corps, divisional and supporting arm commanders then attended what was in effect a central presentation and war game.[7]

[6] The military councils of the respective fronts *circa* June 1944 were as follows. Leningrad – Govorov, Zhdanov and Gusev (later M. M. Popov); 3 Baltic – Maslennikov, Rudakov and Vashkevich; 2 Baltic – Eremenko, Bogatkin and Sandalov; 1 Baltic – Bagramyan, Leonov and Kurasov; 3 Belorussian – Chernyakhovsky, Makarov and Pokrovsky; 2 Belorussian – Rokossovsky, Bulganin and Malinin. The second named in each front was the political member and the third the chief of staff.

[7] Zhukov, *Vospominaniya i Razmyshleniya*, pp. 569–70, 573–6.

The offensive was to begin over a 450-mile-wide sector with six main assault thrusts, all widely dispersed so as to cause the enemy to separate and dissipate his reserves. The first phase of the main attack was to be made in the north by Bagramyan's 1 Baltic and Chernyakhovsky's 3 Belorussian Fronts on 3 Panzer Army in the area of Vitebsk, while Rokossovsky's 1 Belorussian Front attacked 9 Army near Bobruisk. When a lodgement had been made in these two areas 3 and 1 Belorussian Fronts would envelop Minsk from north and south, destroying 4 and a part of 9 German Armies. Zakharov's 2 Belorussian Front served as the connecting link between 1 and 3 Belorussian Fronts. All the fronts were heavily reinforced, the greater part of the reinforcing formations going to Rokossovsky and Chernyakhovsky, whose fronts were to play the principal parts in the attack, and by early June the overall ground force had been brought up to a strength of 166 divisions. Of this total 124 divisions were to be used in the offensive. 1,200,000 men were said to be involved, not including administrative troops of the rear services, and the armoured and air force component of the fronts numbered 5,200 tanks and SUs and 6,000 aircraft.[8] The Soviet preponderance over the Germans in tanks was reckoned at ten to one and in aircraft seven to one, but in fact it was much more than this. Five lines of ammunition, twenty refills of vehicle fuel and thirty days rations were brought up within reach of formations. Energetic and aggressive ground reconnaissance began all along the line from Pskov to the Carpathians by fighting patrols or by company and battalion probing attacks.[9]

Marshals of the Soviet Union Vasilevsky and Zhukov had been transferred from the Ukraine to Belorussia, Vasilevsky being made responsible for the direction and co-ordination of Bagramyan's 1 Baltic Front and Chernyakhovsky's 3 Belorussian Front, the northern pincer of the Minsk enveloping force, while Zhukov was attached to Zakharov's 2 and Rokossovsky's 1 Belorussian Fronts which were to form the southern pincer, although he still retained responsibility for Konev's 1 Ukrainian Front. In addition two marshals of the Red Air Force were detached from the High Command to co-ordinate air support.

In the south Rokossovsky, whose headquarters were just outside Gomel, had a sector which ran for 190 miles in a west-east direction along the southern edge of the Pripet swamp before opening up into the partially wooded and drier country near Bobruisk, and this long Pripet frontage was covered only by P. A. Belov's 61 Army in a holding role, Rokossovsky's main attack being made on the comparatively narrow ninety-mile long Bobruisk sector where Batov's 65 and Luchinsky's 28 Armies were to attack in the south, and Gorbatov's 3 and Romanenko's 48 Armies in the north, in order to carry out a short tactical

---

[8] In addition about 1,000 bombers of the long range air force under Golovanov were allotted to the offensive. The artillery strength was said to number 31,000 guns and mortars, the artillery density being between 240 and 320 barrels a mile. Each front had about 12,000 three-ton motor vehicles as third line transport and over a quarter of a million hospital beds had been made ready before the offensive.

[9] *Istoriya*, Vol. 4, pp. 158–67.

double envelopment to encircle Bobruisk. Both the north and south groups included a tank and a mechanized cavalry corps and had the support of craft of the Soviet Navy Dnieper Flotilla which was to move up the Berezina towards Bobruisk. Having taken Bobruisk, Rokossovsky was to move west and north-west to envelop Minsk from the south. Zakharov's 2 Belorussian Front with three rifle armies, Boldin's 50, Grishin's 49 and Kryuchenkin's 33 Armies, had an important yet subsidiary role as the connecting link between the two powerful armoured pincers provided by Rokossovsky in the south and Chernyakhovsky in the north. Zakharov's immediate task was to take Mogilev. Chernyakhovsky's 3 Belorussian Front with its headquarters near Smolensk was the most mobile and heavily armoured of all the fronts having four rifle armies, Galitsky's 11 Guards, Lyudnikov's 39, Krylov's 5 and Glagolev's 31 Armies together with Rotmistrov's 5 Guards Tank Army and a tank and a mechanized cavalry group, and its task was to envelop Vitebsk in conjunction with its right-hand neighbour, 1 Baltic Front. Bagramyan's 1 Baltic Front consisted of Beloborodov's 43 and Chistayakov's 6 Guards Army, Maly-shev's 4 Shock Army and a tank corps. Having seized Vitebsk, Chernyakhov-sky was to envelop Minsk from the north.

The Soviet offensive began two weeks after the opening of the Anglo-American landings on the Normandy beaches, having been purposely timed for 22 June, the third anniversary of the start of the war. The offensive opened in the usual Soviet fashion with the front and army reconnaissance elements making preliminary probing thrusts. When resistance was light the rifle divisions immediately took up the attack in earnest, but where the recon-naissance units made little headway a heavy preparatory artillery bombard-ment was called for, and the attack was resumed under cover of a fast moving rolling barrage in conjunction with timed artillery concentrations. The partisans in occupied Belorussia had apparently done their work well, tying down the few German reserves, and they claimed to have derailed no fewer than 147 trains in three days.[10] Soviet success was both widespread and immediate. Bagramyan's 1 Baltic Front, intent on enveloping Vitebsk from the north, by 23 June had penetrated to a depth of ten miles on a thirty-five mile front against the left flank of Reinhardt's 3 Panzer Army, in spite of bitter resistance in the area of Shumilino and the heavy rain which washed away the roads.

Reinhardt's panzer army had three infantry corps of nine infantry divisions forward and two in reserve, of which total four divisions were committed by the order of the *Führer* to the defence of the general area of Vitebsk. Its only armoured reserve was a *Hornisse* 88 mm tank destroyer battalion and an assault gun brigade. To the north of Vitebsk and in the lake-studded area of Shum-ilino, Wuthmann's 9 Corps fought desperately as both sides put in counter-attack after counter-attack. 6 Corps to the south of Vitebsk was also hard

---

[10] Such is the Soviet claim. Heidkämper on the other hand has said that due to previous German anti-partisan operations, partisan activity in the rear of 3 Panzer Army was negligible.

pressed. In spite of bad flying weather, low cloud and rain storms the Red Air Force bombing and machine-gun attacks were so violent as to be described as murderous.[11] Heidkämper, Reinhardt's chief of staff, was aghast at the unexpectedly rapid successes of the Red Army troops, and on the evening of 23 June there began the first of a number of difficult and outspoken meetings, when Reinhardt demanded from Busch that Vitebsk be evacuated immediately. Busch refused point blank. Nor would he allow Reinhardt to withdraw troops from the inactive 53 Corps in Vitebsk to reinforce 9 and 6 Corps on the threatened flanks until he had received the agreement of the OKH.[12]

Early in the morning of 24 June Zeitzler arrived in Minsk to be briefed by Busch on the situation, after which he flew directly to the *Führer* in Bavaria. At 1500 hours Zeitzler telephoned Reinhardt from Obersalzberg, to be told that Vitebsk was in danger of being encircled and that the last opportunity had arrived to withdraw 53 Corps from the town. When Zeitzler explained that Hitler was against giving up Vitebsk because of the loss of equipment which it would entail, the Commander of 3 Panzer Army replied bluntly that the loss of five divisions was at stake. Reinhardt was told to hold the line while Zeitzler scurried off to talk again to the *Führer*, but after a very anxious seemingly long ten-minute delay Zeitzler returned to the telephone with the curt message that 'the *Führer* has decided that Vitebsk will be held'. A few minutes later a radio message received by 3 Panzer Army from 53 Corps in Vitebsk told of the road west from Vitebsk being directly threatened. This message was passed on to Army Group Centre with the request for permission to withdraw. Within the hour Busch repeated the request to Hitler and was told that Vitebsk would be held and that, should it be necessary, the road into the town was to be reopened by counter-attack. Two hours later at 1830 hours, to the surprise and consternation of 3 Panzer Army, a radio message was received from the *Führer* that 53 Corps should fight its way out of the encircled Vitebsk, but that one division should be nominated to remain and hold the fortress. Heidkämper was unable to understand the logic of the order, since if a corps could not hold, then the sacrifice of a division availed nothing; but, thankful for the opportunity to save any of the encircled troops, the order was transmitted, Lieutenant-General Hitter's 206 Infantry Division being ordered to remain in the town.

During the next day, on 25 June, Gollwitzer's 53 Corps attempted to fight its way out of Vitebsk, but its formations found difficulty in disengaging from the surrounding 39 Soviet Army which was actually forcing its way into the town from a number of directions. During that afternoon Reinhardt, anxiously watching Gollwitzer's efforts to break out, was surprised and irritated to receive an order from the suspicious *Führer* that he should have an officer of

[11] Von Greim, the commander of the supporting air fleet, when visiting 3 Panzer Army Headquarters on 25 June had said that with his limited resources there was nothing which he could do at that time to reverse the air situation.

[12] Heidkämper, *Witebsk*, pp. 150 and 152.

the General Staff parachuted into Vitebsk solely to hand personally a written order to Hitter, ordering him to fight to the end. A bizarre situation then resulted when Reinhardt told Busch that since the radio order to 53 Corps had been acknowledged, he refused to waste even one more life in Vitebsk. Busch in return reminded Reinhardt of the nature and origin of the order and said that the *Führer* awaited the name of the officer and the time of his dispatch. To this an angry Reinhardt could only reply that if the *Führer* really insisted on the order being carried out, he, Reinhardt, would go himself. Within an hour the order was withdrawn. Over the next few days, however, Busch frequently demanded that repeated orders be sent to 206 Infantry Division telling it to fight to the end.[13]

At 9 a.m. on 27 June a last radio message was received from 53 Corps, saying that progress was being made in the break-out about ten miles south-west of Vitebsk, but complaining of the lack of ammunition and the heaviness of the Red Air Force attacks. Thereafter there was silence and 53 Corps and about 35,000 men disappeared.[14]

From the Soviet side the battle was progressing very satisfactorily. Bagramyan's 1 Baltic Front had enveloped Vitebsk from the north and on 25 June its 43 Army, commanded by Beloborodov, had joined with Lyudnikov's 39 Army of 3 Belorussian Front and Vitebsk was encircled. Chernyakhovsky's 3 Belorussian Front had attacked Reinhardt's right flank on 23 June, one day later than Bagramyan, and although its right, 39 Army, had made good progress in encircling Vitebsk, its left at first made little headway along the Minsk highway. After three days of heavy fighting Galitsky's 11 Guards Army broke out, however, and together with Glagolev's 31 Army took Orsha. Thereafter the battle became fluid. The tank corps in front reserve had already been committed, the Berezina was crossed north of Borisov on 28 June and Rotmistrov's 5 Guards Tank Army entered the battle, attacking along 11 Guards Army axis through open country down the Minsk road, so separating Reinhardt's 3 Panzer Army from Heinrici's 4 German Army. Yet further to the south, Rokossovsky's 1 Belorussian Front began the offensive on 24 June. Heavy morning rain and low cloud again made air support difficult, but by late afternoon and evening the supporting 16 Air Army had flown 3,200 sorties and the weather began to clear. To the south of Bobruisk Batov's 65 Army made swift progress, committing its tank corps to battle that same afternoon, and as this reached open country in the rear it encountered no serious resistance. To the north of Bobruisk, however, Gorbatov's 3 and Romanenko's 48 Armies made only slow headway until 9 Tank Corps was committed to their support.[15] By 27

---

[13] *Ibid*, pp. 153–6 and 159–61.

[14] Gollwitzer and 10,000 men were taken prisoner.

[15] Gorbatov and Romanenko received some blame for inadequate reconnaissance and underestimating the task. Gorbatov, however, had correctly warned Zhukov that 9 Tank Corps was being committed in the wrong place. During the battle Gorbatov obtained Zhukov's consent to altering its axis and thereafter progress was rapid. Zhukov, *Vospominaniya i Razmyshleniya*, p. 579.

June Bobruisk, like Vitebsk, had been encircled, while Mogilev was already under close attack by 2 Belorussian Front. The Dnieper Flotilla supported the troops on the Berezina by preventing the enemy using the bridges and by ferrying men, guns, horses and lorries across the river. By then Soviet tank and cavalry forces were thrusting deep into the enemy rear.[16]

Reinhardt had lost a second corps when 6 Corps had been shattered; he was left with two of his original eleven divisions. The larger part of 9 German Army had been encircled near Bobruisk in the south. In the centre, Heinrici's 4 German Army, temporarily under the command of von Tippelskirch, was retiring under pressure from Zakharov's 2 Belorussian Front, and it was also in danger of being cut off by the Soviet tank columns directed on Minsk coming from the north-east and south-east. Hitler's views did not change. All that was required was to hold firm up front. He had not agreed to Busch withdrawing from Vitebsk or anywhere else, because of the appalling impression it would make on the Finns, who, he said, were fighting desperately near Ladoga for their lives and their very existence as a nation. On 26 June, the day before the destruction of 53 Corps, Busch made the long journey to the Berghof to plead the seriousness of the situation, but he received little understanding. Orsha and Mogilev had to be held as bastions to the end, and so another two German divisions were destroyed. The next day, however, the *Führer*, probably realizing for the first time that Army Group Centre had been torn open, removed his attention from the fighting in France and, leaving his Berghof retreat, he flew to his East Prussian General Headquarters. That same night he attempted to solve the difficulty by drawing a *ne plus ultra* line across the map from Polotsk to Lepel and the Berezina, and ordering Army Group Centre to hold it. Busch, in his turn, planned counter-offensives in the grand style. Where the troops were to come from none knew.[17] The *Führer* ordered each of the neighbouring army groups to give up a division, although the total of the four divisions to be transferred, even if they had been readily and promptly available, which they were not, could not have had any effect on the situation. He reluctantly sanctioned the withdrawal of 4 and 9 Armies to the new line, although by then it was in fact doubtful whether they could disengage or escape the enveloping armoured pincers. None of the three armies existed as cohesive formations, and the fighting was being waged by parts of divisions, engineer and police battalions, rear echelons and baggage men, alarm units and the para-military labour organization. On 28 June it was apparent that Soviet tanks were already over the Berezina and to the west of Lepel.

The crisis pattern of the reshuffle of commanders followed. It was inevitable that Field-Marshal Busch should be removed from his command, although like his predecessors and fellows, being allowed no initiative he had done only what the *Führer* had instructed him to do. Model, by then a field-marshal

[16] *Istoriya*, Vol. 4, pp. 171–6.
[17] Heidkämper, *Witebsk*, p. 163.

and still in Hitler's favour, replaced him, but still retained his post as Commander of Army Group North Ukraine, Harpe, the Commander of 4 Panzer Army, deputizing for Model in his absence. Nor was the *Führer* satisfied with Army Group North which, under pressure from Bagramyan's 1 Baltic Front and fearful of the developments on its south flank, wanted to pull back its south wing. Zeitzler, supporting this request and trying to meet the demand for new formations, went so far as to advise the evacuation of Estonia and the withdrawal of Army Group North to the line Riga-Daugavpils (Dünaburg). Hitler was so far from agreeing that he ordered Army Group North not only to hold on to Polotsk but also to attack south-eastwards in support of Army Group Centre. Lindemann, the Commander of Army Group North, was unable to do so and was immediately replaced by Friessner, the Commander of the Narva Group.

Field-Marshal Model was in command of two army groups and, unwilling to await the divisions promised by Hitler, he began to move panzer divisions from Army Group North Ukraine to Army Group Centre, and the loss of this reserve was to be sorely felt when the Army Group North Ukraine itself came under heavy attack a few weeks later. By the end of the month Model realized that the Soviet objectives were far deeper than had hitherto been imagined, and included the landbridge gaps carrying road and railway through the Nalibocka forest belt and marsh near Molodechno and Baranovichi. There was never any question of holding Hitler's Polotsk-Lepel-Berezina-Slutsk line. On 2 July Model had to admit that he could not even hold Minsk or save many of the encircled troops of 4 and 9 Armies, and he told the Army High Command (OKH) that he must have more formations to bring the enemy to a halt to the west of Molodechno and Baranovichi. Vilna itself appeared to be threatened and Model joined forces with Zeitzler in advising the *Führer* to withdraw Army Group North to the west of Riga.

The committal of the few German reserves which could be scraped together had little impact on the Soviet advance. 14 and 95 Infantry Divisions and 60 Panzer Grenadier Division were thrown into the battle, and as the performance of 20 Panzer Division failed to transform the situation its commander was summarily removed from his post. The motorized troops were suffering from a serious shortage of fuel, this precluding any long road moves, and rail communications were both slow and uncertain because of Red Air Force and partisan attack. The great woods and marshes were the homes of irregulars and brigands, and since German movement was restricted to roads the main highways were beset by partisans. The three corps of von Tippelskirch's 4 German Army, engaged frontally by 2 Belorussian Front, fell back westwards, and at the same time tried to protect their flanks and keep the rearward communications open. Endless columns of heavy artillery, anti-aircraft guns and motor and horse transport crawled slowly back over the winding highway towards the Berezina bridge. Few German aircraft were to be seen and continuous Red Air Force attacks caused many casualties, including the deaths of three Generals, and the Berezina bridge was put out of action. While German engineers tried to repair the bridge a vast collection of men and transport remained halted on the east bank, heavily bombed and machine-gunned by the Red Air Force.[18]

On 1 July Rotmistrov's 5 Guards Tank Army crossed the Berezina further to the north at Borisov and three days later, together with elements of 11 Guards and 31 Armies, took Minsk, the capital of Belorussia. Most of 4 German Army and a large part of 9 Army, in all, it is claimed, 100,000 men, had been cut off in a great pocket to the east of Minsk, and between 5 and 11 July the Soviet High Command began the destruction of these forces, without halting the rapid movement of their tank formations to the west. The 4 German Army pocket lay between the Volma and the Berezina and was split into two main segments, one under Traut, the Commander of 78 Assault Division, and the other under Müller, the Commander of 12 Corps. Similar scenes were enacted to those which had taken place in Belorussia in 1941, except that the positions were reversed. Zhukov reported enormous destruction, with artillery and *Katyushi* pouring in a deluge of shells and rockets while waves of bombers dropped their loads on to the encircled enemy. For the most, where they could, the German troops ran. Where they could not run, they died. Some escaped singly or in small parties, but resistance was not protracted. On 8 July Müller surrendered with his men, and nine days later the 57,000 prisoners were paraded through the Moscow streets. Part of 9 Army succeeded in escaping westwards to Baranovichi, due to the valiant efforts of a panzer division which fought its way eastwards to meet them. Of the whole of Army Group Centre only the wings remained. 2 Army was still in the south in the Pripet Marshes and a skeleton 3 Panzer Army was in the north. About twenty-eight divisions of Army Group Centre had been lost as fighting formations, and the total casualties were put as high as 300,000 men.[19] A gigantic 250 mile breach gaped in the German line and, as the route to the Baltic States and East Prussia seemed to be open, border guards and training regiments from East Prussia, even the *Führer*'s own guard battalion, were rushed eastwards towards the battle area to fill the gap. For Germany the defeat was of dimensions as great as that of Stalingrad.

The Soviet High Command determined to exploit this situation by clearing Belorussia and entering the Baltic States and Poland before the enemy could plug the breach. Bagramyan's 1 Baltic Front on the right flank was to move on Daugavpils and the area north of Vilna, while Chernyakhovsky's 3 Belorussian Front took Vilna and the area to its south. Zakharov's 2 Belorussian Front on the far south flank attacked towards Brest. This new series of advances developed rapidly, 1 Baltic Front reaching the Daugavpils-Vilna railway without difficulty, although German resistance stiffened thereafter. The Daugavpils-Kaunas road was cut, but Chistyakov's 6 Guards Army was

---

[18] Von Tippelskirch, *Die Geschichte des Zweiten Weltkriegs*, pp. 535–8.
[19] *Kriegstagebuch des OKW*, Vol. 4, p. 858.

unable to take the town of Daugavpils. The 3 Belorussian Front advanced to Vilna, where 3 Panzer Army had collected a motley array of its own units and stragglers. Rotmistrov's 5 Guards Tank and Krylov's 5 Armies took the town on 13 July and held it against German counter-attacks. Rotmistrov's armoured thrust then began to force the remnants of 3 Panzer Army north-westwards into Lithuania, and a great gap had already appeared between Army Groups Centre and North. Further to the south Zakharov's 2 Belorussian Front had advanced 160 miles in ten days, having crossed the Niemen south of Grodno, and was less than fifty miles from the East Prussian border, while Rokossovsky's 1 Belorussian Front, supported by a force of 500 bombers, advanced over 100 miles in twelve days, taking Baranovichi and outflanking Pinsk as it moved towards Brest.

On 9 July Model, who had been in command of Army Group Centre for only twelve harassing days, flew with Friessner, who was himself only in his fifth day of office as Commander Army Group North, to persuade the dictator to give up Estonia and provide formations to plug the many gaps. Their request was refused once more, partly because of the effect that this would have on the Finns and partly because the German Navy opposed it. On 12 July Friessner sent a personal memorandum to the *Führer* explaining the seriousness of the position, a letter which Hitler was afterwards to reject as a threat.[20] During the next few days the position of Model's and Friessner's army groups continued to worsen. On 10 July Eremenko's 2 Baltic Front attacked C. Hansen's 16 Army, thrusting westwards towards Rezekne, and a week later Maslennikov's 3 Baltic Front further to the north began an attack to the south of Lake Peipus. On the Narva a further offensive was expected daily from Govorov's Leningrad Front. On 15 July Chanchibadze's 2 Guards and Kreizer's 51 Armies, both from the Crimea, had joined Bagramyan's 1 Baltic Front from the High Command Reserve, and within a matter of days they went over to the offensive, thrusting north-eastwards into the gap between Army Groups Centre and North through Lithuania into Latvia. On 18 July Model and Friessner returned once more to the *Führer*, Model begging that the Lithuanian gap be closed and as he himself had not the troops to do it, suggesting, much to Friessner's indignation, that Army Group North might find the necessary forces.[21] Friessner, too, had his difficulties. The threatened separation from Army Group Centre would result in encirclement if the Red Army should break through to the Gulf of Riga, but the extension of his southern frontage and the growing Soviet pressure in the east meant that he needed every man to prevent himself being driven into the Baltic. Friessner had taken over his army group with energy and enthusiasm, being determined to mount a rapid counter-offensive to the south-east in support of Army Group Centre in accordance with Hitler's directions, but a few days of the

---

[20] Friessner, *Verratene Schlachten*, pp. 18–22.

[21] *Ibid*, p. 27. The meeting was attended by Göring and Koch, then Gauleiter of East Prussia.

realities of command had persuaded him of the correctness of his predecessor Lindemann's views. Friessner, too, had asked the *Führer* for freedom to use his initiative or for dismissal.

A further Soviet blow was about to fall further to the south in Galicia and Southern Poland. When Vatutin had been mortally wounded, he had been replaced in command of 1 Ukrainian Front, as a temporary measure, by Zhukov. At the conclusion of the successful Ukraine operation, Zhukov had given up this command in order to take over the co-ordination of Zakharov's 2 and Rokossovsky's 1 Belorussian Fronts during the offensive against Busch's Army Group Centre. Zhukov was succeeded as Commander 1 Ukrainian Front in early May by Konev, who came from 2 Ukrainian Front.[22] Konev's place was filled by Malinovsky from 3 Ukrainian Front, who was himself replaced by Tolbukhin from 4 Ukrainian Front. After the victory in the Crimea 4 Ukrainian Front became temporarily inoperative and was withdrawn to the High Command Reserve.[23]

The second Soviet offensive was to be made against Army Group North Ukraine, and the main attacks were to be mounted by Konev's 1 Ukrainian Front and the left wing of Rokossovsky's 1 Belorussian Front which was to be specially reinforced for the purpose. Konev was to launch what was to become known as the Lvov-Sandomierz operation against Army Group North Ukraine, in order to overrun Galicia and Southern Poland. Rokossovsky was to thrust against the left flank of Army Group North Ukraine into Central Poland towards Lublin and Warsaw.

The German Army Group North Ukraine and Army Group Centre were at this time still under the command of Model, who kept up a display of energy as he toured the battle area, livening up his divisions and often leaving a trail of disorder behind him, losing some of the confidence and respect of his subordinate commanders by a wanton interference in details which were not his concern.[24] Army Group North Ukraine under its acting deputy commander Harpe comprised 4 and 1 Panzer Armies and 1 Hungarian Army (on the Carpathian south flank) and was spread over South Poland and part of Czecho-Slovakia and Galicia; it consisted of thirty-one German divisions of which four were panzer, and twelve Hungarian light divisions or brigades.[25] The Hungarian Army was grouped with 1 Panzer Army to form Group Raus, Raus having been transferred from 4 to 1 Panzer Army in April on the death of Hube in an air crash. Raus in his turn had been replaced in 4 Panzer Army by Harpe from 9 Army, but Harpe was at the beginning of July also acting as the deputy commander of the army group. Eventually, at the beginning of

---

[22] Zhukov was relieved at his own request, Stalin's agreement being conditional on Zhukov remaining responsible for the co-ordination of 1 Ukrainian Front in addition to the two Belorussian Fronts. Zhukov, *Vospominaniya i Razmyshleniya*, p. 566.

[23] *Istoriya*, Vol. 4, p. 102.

[24] Lange, *Korpsabteilung C*, p. 90; also von Mellenthin, *Panzer Battles*, p. 281.

[25] *OKH Kriegsgliederung*, 15 July 1944.

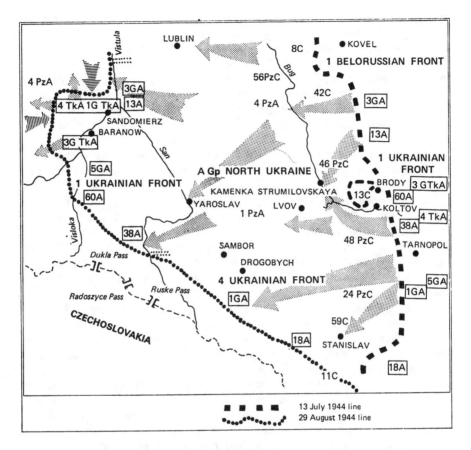

THE DEFEAT OF ARMY GROUP NORTH UKRAINE
July–August 1944

August Balck, the former Commander of 48 Panzer Corps, became Commander of 4 Panzer Army. At the time of Konev's next offensive, however, both Army Group North Ukraine and 4 Panzer Army were controlled by absent commanders.

When in May Konev had taken over the command of 1 Ukrainian Front, Khrushchev and Krainyukov were the joint political members of the military council and Sokolovsky was the chief of staff. No action was taken to concentrate the assault force until after the start of the Belorussian offensive further to the north, but between 24 June and 7 July half of the rifle divisions and all the three tank armies had been assembled, the troops having to travel mainly

445

by night distances of up to 250 miles to the concentration areas, the tank formations going by rail and the artillery and rifle formations by road. In all, 1 Ukrainian Front disposed of six rifle armies in the first echelon and one rifle army, three tank armies and several independent tank, cavalry and rifle corps in the second echelon. The force totalled eighty divisions, of which six were cavalry, ten tank or mechanized corps and a number of brigades, and had a total of 840,000 men, 14,000 guns, 1,600 tanks and SUs and 2,800 aircraft.[26] The front was ready to attack Model's Army Group North Ukraine by 12 July.

The attack took the customary form used by the Red Army at that time. The rifle army and all the tank and cavalry formations were held back in depth, ready to be committed as soon as the six rifle armies in the first echelon had made some penetration. On the night of 12 July the armies carried out strong fighting reconnaissance and probing attacks in company and battalion strength, and any yielding on the enemy's part was followed through by the rifle divisions without waiting for artillery preparation. Strong and determined enemy resistance, on the other hand, called for heavy air and artillery preparatory bombardment. The offensive by the whole front was fully launched by 14 July.

On the German side the attack was not unexpected and there had already been a general stand-to on 6 and 7 July. What was found surprising, however, was the overwhelming power of the Red Air Force which for the first time in the experience of many of the troops who took part obtained an absolute air supremacy over the battlefield.[27] 4 Panzer Army had ordered the withdrawal of its forward elements to escape the fury of the Soviet artillery bombardment and this movement being observed, Gordov's 3 Guards Army and Pukhov's 13 Army on the right flank of 1 Ukrainian Front immediately took up the attack. By evening they had penetrated up to ten miles in depth and by the morning of the next day had reached the second enemy defensive zone. Recknagel's 42 German Corps together with 46 Panzer Corps started to fall back although 16 and 17 Panzer Divisions counter-attacked repeatedly and the *Luftwaffe* made some sorties over the area. By the evening of 15 July the penetration had been increased by a few more miles, enveloping the left flank of Hauffe's 13 Corps to the south, and a Soviet mechanized cavalry group was thrust into the German rear dispersing 20 Panzer Grenadier Division and reaching the Bug near Kamenka-Strumilovskaya about twenty-five miles from Lvov, the headquarters of Army Group North Ukraine. The progress of this thrust was, however, still uncertain and hesitant. On 13 July Kurochkin's 60 Army and Moskalenko's 38 Army had taken up the attack in the centre to the south of 13 Corps, and after two days' fighting had advanced only ten miles in the face of counter-attacks by two panzer divisions, the armoured reserve of Balck's 48 Panzer Corps. On 15 July both Rybalko's 3 Guards Tank and

[26] *Istoriya*, Vol. 4, p. 207.
[27] Von Mellenthin, *Panzer Battles*, p. 285.

Lelyushenko's 4 Tank Armies were committed to support 60 and 38 Armies, with orders to punch their own way through the enemy defences, and the next day near Koltov they pierced a narrow corridor less than three miles wide and ten miles long. Through this narrow gap poured a column of men and vehicles as the two tank armies emerged into the open. Part of 3 Guards Tank Army turned north to join hands with the mechanized cavalry group south of Kamenka-Strumilovskaya, so encircling 13 German Corps near Brody. Meanwhile the remainder of the Soviet forces, together with 4 Tank Army, neared Lvov on 18 July, the same day that Rokossovsky's 1 Belorussian Front attacked from Kovel towards Lublin.

Inside the Brody pocket Hauffe's 13 Corps was made up of Lasch's 349 and G. Lindemann's 361 Infantry Divisions, Nedtwig's 454 Security Division, Freitag's 14 SS (Galician) Grenadier Division and Lange's Corps Formation C, consisting of 183, 217 and 339 Cadre Infantry Divisions much reduced by casualties. The whole of 13 Corps totalled about 40,000 men. The SS division had been formed from Galician Ukrainians who, although well armed and equipped, were poorly trained and had never been in action before. Lange and von Mellenthin are agreed that this SS formation was worthless, and was no more than an undisciplined rabble over whom their officers had little control.[28] Lange's formation, like the other so-called corps formations (*Korpsabteilungen*), had the equivalent fighting strength of an infantry division, the retention of all the divisional titles within the formation being partly a deception measure intended to portray to the Soviet High Command a large number of divisions in the German order of battle.[29] 13 Corps had been very recently transferred from the command of 4 Panzer to 1 Panzer Army.

The decision and orders to break out and join with Balck's 48 Panzer Corps to the south were not given until the afternoon of 18 July, it being understood that 1 and 8 Panzer Divisions would attack northwards to meet 13 Corps as it broke out southwards. The West Bug and about fifteen to twenty miles of enemy-held territory had to be crossed, some of it being swampland and much of it heavily wooded. The corps could expect to be attacked from the front and on both sides as it moved southwards, and for this reason one German division was put on each of the east and west flanks. Lange's and Lasch's formations were both entrusted with the break-out while the Galician SS brought up the rear. The pocket was already becoming compressed in size, and vehicles and baggage lay everywhere, blocking the tracks and exits and adding to the chaos so that Lange, with the benefit of hindsight, was subse-

[28] Lange, *Korpsabteilung C*, p. 104; von Mellenthin, *Panzer Battles*, p. 285.
[29] There were in all six *Korpsabteilungen*. Since reinforcements had not been forthcoming the original intention had been to fuse three divisions into one thereby making supporting arms and services available to form other divisions. The retention of the original divisional numbers was both a deception device to deceive Moscow as to the true German strength and a means by which divisions retained their identities until reinforcements became available to expand them again. Mueller-Hillebrand, *Das Heer*, Vol. 3, p. 75; Lange, *Korpsabteilung C*, p. 9.

quently and ruefully to say that it would have improved the chances of survival if at an early stage all vehicles and equipment had been pushed clear of the tracks and abandoned.[30] At the time, however, 13 Corps was intent on salvaging everything it could.

With Lange's and Lasch's troops at their head, the pocket started to move with its wounded, transport and baggage on its hazardous journey southwards; but the Soviet reaction was immediate, and heavy tank and infantry attacks were mounted against the moving flanks. Lange had formed an armoured infantry group from his assault gun brigade and a company of captured T34 tanks on which he mounted all the remaining sappers of his engineer battalions as supporting infantry. This force, together with the marching infantry, made slow but steady progress, knocking out some Soviet tanks and capturing intact some American tank destroyers which were added to the armoured group. No contact was made, however, with 48 Panzer Corps, which due to Red Air Force interference and a series of accidents had in fact made little progress. Finally, partly owing to the difficult broken ground and the indescribable traffic blockage, all radio communications failed between 13 Corps and 48 Panzer Corps and between Hauffe's corps and the divisional units. Liaison officers and runners were the only means of communication.[31] Casualties and the difficulties of the going soon thinned out the vehicles of the armoured group, but at midday on 21 July the members of the group, by then on foot, together with elements of Lange's 217 Group, had fought their way south and found 1 Panzer Division. Because of the failure of communications none of this was known to Lange, or apparently to Hauffe and the remainder of the encircled corps. The Soviet attacks on the pocket were becoming so heavy that the perimeter was becoming tighter, and immediate action was required to complete the break-out. Having that same afternoon found a mood of depression at 13 Corps Headquarters, Lange issued orders for his command to break out southwards after dark that night. Lange and Lasch, with much of Corps Formation C and 349 Infantry Division, after heavy close-quarter fighting forced their way through to the south and over the Lvov-Tarnopol railway embankment.[32]

The remainder of 13 Corps was doomed. The next morning on 22 July Bader, the Roman Catholic padre of 454 Security Division, met Hauffe wandering with one of his staff in the woods. Hauffe said that the odds were too great and that the position was hopeless, although perhaps that next night, he thought, a break-out might be attempted again. They left each other without a word. During that afternoon Soviet bombers and fighter bombers kept up an incessant attack, while a torrent of shells, bombs and rockets poured in from all sides. The German artillery had been long silent and no German aircraft were to be seen. Ammunition and petrol were bursting every-

[30] *Ibid*, p. 106.
[31] *Ibid*, pp. 107 and 109; see also von Mellenthin, *Panzer Battles*, p. 286.
[32] Lange, *Korpsabteilung C*, pp. 110–13.

where amid the cries and groans of the hit and the dying. Many men kept their wits about them to the end, but many were numbed and dazed and many took their own lives. On that fine summer's evening the blood-red sun going down over the pall of smoke that hung over the pocket showed the end of 13 Corps. About 25,000 Germans lay dead and 17,000, including Nedtwig and G. Lindemann, went into captivity.[33]

There was an absence of co-ordination between 13 and 48 Corps. Yet the remarkable aspect of this defeat, if Lange is correct, is that even after the encirclement, Hauffe had a direct (radio) telephonic link to Raus.[34] If this was in fact the case, much of the command and control organization of 1 Panzer Army must have broken down under the shock of battle.

Meanwhile the Soviet armoured advance continued westwards in spite of the protracted resistance in the town of Lvov which had tied down both Rybalko's 3 Guards and Lelyushenko's 4 Tank Armies. Katukov's 1 Guards Tank Army then took up the pursuit with Baranov's mechanized cavalry group, moving south-west towards Yaroslav at a rate of about twenty miles a day in company with Gordov's 3 Guards and Pukhov's 13 Armies which moved due west, the Sokolov mechanized cavalry group keeping contact between them. The heavy rain and poor roads made supply almost impossible and the Soviet thrusts were losing momentum as the frontage spread. Although the Red Army had reached the San on 23 July, the Germans still fighting in Lvov many miles to the east began the evacuation of the town on 24 July and marched off without undue difficulty to Sambor to the south-west. Not until 27 July did the Red Army occupy Lvov, the same day that the Germans gave up the great town of Stanislav about eighty miles to the south-east.[35]

The third and final stage of the summer campaign was to be made by the left wing of Rokossovsky's 1 Belorussian Front just to the north of Konev's offensive, which it was to follow by only five days.

Rokossovsky's long flank along the edge of the Pripet Marshes had been covered only lightly by P. A. Belov's 61 Army during the Belorussian offensive, but a strong force had subsequently been assembled on the extreme left tip of his front south of the marshes near Kovel, consisting of Chuikov's 8 Guards Army, Gusev's 47, Kolpakchy's 69 and V. S. Popov's 70 Armies, Berling's 1 Polish Army and Bogdanov's 2 Tank Army, many of these troops having been allocated from the reserve. The usual deception and camouflage measures were taken, none of the new arrivals being allowed to approach the forward defended localities; radio sets were sealed, vehicle tracks were obliterated and the troops were kept under the cover of the woods, bathing or drying of clothes in the open near the streams being strictly forbidden. The customary

---

[33] *Ibid*, pp. 115–16. Hauffe was killed later that day.

[34] *Ibid*, p. 112.

[35] Khrushchev telephoned Stalin to say that he did not agree with the tasks given to Rybalko's tank army. Stalin then instructed Zhukov to forget about further movement westwards until Lvov had been taken. Zhukov, *Vospominaniya i Razmyshleniya*, p. 591.

higher commander and staff planning rehearsals were held immediately before the attack, these being attended by Zhukov, Rokossovsky, Novikov and Peresypkin.[36] The movement of this force to the area of Kovel resulted in Rokossovsky's front being split between the areas to the north and to the south of the Pripet, but the concentration appeared to come as a surprise to the Germans when on 18 July, only a few days after 1 Ukrainian Front had attacked to its south, Rokossovsky's left wing supported by 1,400 aircraft of its own 6 Air Army moved westwards on a broad front, crossing the Bug at three places in its thrust into Poland and driving in the left flank of 4 Panzer Army. Model's Army Group North Ukraine was already fully extended by the 1 Ukrainian Front offensive to the south and it had lost its reserve of panzer divisions which Model had transferred to Army Group Centre.[37] The Soviet 2 Tank Army, commanded by Bogdanov, was then committed in Chuikov's 8 Guards Army sector and it thrust forward, taking Lublin on 23 July.

The *Führer* had forbidden the withdrawal of 4 Panzer Army to the Vistula, but the course of events made his orders of no consequence when 2 Tank Army reached the Vistula near Demblin on 25 July, being joined by 1 Polish Army two days later. Army Group North Ukraine forward of the Vistula had been separated by these Soviet thrusts from Army Group Centre, and the Army Group Centre right flank was dangerously threatened. Rokossovsky, on the other hand, had already left the Pripet Marshes behind him and his 1 Belorussian Front was no longer covering an enormous frontage divided by the belt of the swampland. Weiss's 2 German Army in the area Brest Kobryn was threatened on three sides, by V. S. Popov's 70 Army from the south, P. A. Belov's 61 Army from the Pripet in the east, and Batov's 65 and Luchinsky's 28 Armies which had advanced westwards along the north of the Pripet swampland belt. An attempt was made to stand at Brest-Litovsk, but this fell on 28 July. 2 Tank Army under the temporary command of Radzievsky, who had replaced the wounded Bogdanov, moved on Warsaw, reaching the Praga suburbs east of the Vistula on the last day of the month. That same day Bagramyan's 1 Baltic Front broke through to the Baltic coast a few miles west of Riga and cut off Army Group North from Army Group Centre.

On 20 July Count von Stauffenberg, the chief of staff designate to Fromm's Replacement Army, made the bomb attempt on Hitler's life in the East Prussian General Headquarters at Rastenburg, and there followed the abortive attempt to take over the government in Berlin. The bomb wrecked the army hut which was being used temporarily as a conference room, but failed to destroy him for whom it was intended. Schmundt, Korten, Brandt and a stenographer received injuries from which they died and others of those present received lesser hurt. Hitler himself escaped almost unscathed. Then began a purge to liquidate not only the conspirators, but all who had knowledge of

[36] Chuikov, *The End of the Third Reich*, pp. 27 and 33.
[37] According to Zhukov this transfer had already been noted in Moscow. *Vospominaniya i Razmyshleniya*, p. 585.

the existence of a plot. The German Army and the General Staff were to suffer heavily and many of the senior serving and retired officers were arrested and executed because of real, or suspected, implication, while others escaped arrest by suicide. The fatalities included Beck, Canaris, Hoepner, Rommel, von der Schulenburg, Fromm, von Kluge, Wagner and many others. Halder, the former Chief of General Staff was arrested, together with Heusinger, the Deputy Chief of General Staff and Chief of Operations, and Stieff, the Chief of Operations-Organization; the purge spread throughout the High Command and General Staff with the arrest or removal of even junior officers. The command of the Replacement Army was given to Himmler, and Canaris's *Abwehr* was abolished, its functions being taken over by Himmler's SS organization which from this time onwards became responsible for all but tactical intelligence activities. The purge was carried out with a vindictiveness intended to crush not only any vestige of resistance but the independence and initiative of commanders and staff. Military courts were assembled to try suspected senior officers and dismiss them from the Army so that they could be thrown to the Peoples' Courts for trial, and some of the members of these military courts were hardly less implicated than those on whom they passed judgement.

Friessner, who apparently had no knowledge at all of the existence of the plot, has described how he first became aware that something untoward was happening on 20 July when Kinzel, formerly of Foreign Armies East and then Chief of Staff to Army Group North, was telephoned by von Stauffenberg to say that Hitler was dead and that Beck had taken over the Government.[38] Friessner's reactions to the plot and its failure were those of the great majority of the German people and the German Army. Except for some of those higher commanders and senior government officials who were near him, and therefore had opportunity to observe at close quarters the peculiarities of his character, most Germans were solidly behind Adolf Hitler, and the news of the assassination attempt was received throughout the *Reich* with anger and horror. Among the conspirators there were, as has been subsequently recognized in Germany, many brave and honourable men and women, but in 1944 even that section of the population which had doubts as to the wisdom and honesty of Hitler's leadership saw national unity and the solidarity of the Nazi régime as the only hope against the great flood of Red terror, barbarity and bestiality that threatened to submerge the eastern territories of Germany. They were to remain behind Hitler to the very end and only when he fell did the population almost to a man denounce him.

Politically, the bomb attack confirmed to Germany's allies what they already knew, that Germany's defeat was certain. The assassination attempt and the purge which followed it shook the German Army to its foundations. The German Army hierarchy lost much of the respect and confidence of the German public and the formations in the field. The whisper of treachery, already widespread since the disastrous defeat of Army Group Centre, was

[38] Friessner, *Verratene Schlachten*, pp. 30–2.

listened to and accepted.[39] Within the Army there was often friction and mistrust between military leaders and their National Socialist Guidance Officers, who henceforth were on their mettle to closely observe their commanders. Cases were to occur of officers being imprisoned or reduced to the ranks because of anonymous complaints sent in by their own men.[40] The High Command and military organization were in this way partially destroyed from the inside at what was the greatest moment of crisis in the war when the German armies in France were already defeated and the whole of Army Group Centre in the East was in the throes of collapse. In addition Hitler had abruptly rid himself of Zeitzler, who although, as far as is known, was not implicated in the conspiracy, in his master's eyes bore the responsibility for the guilt of the OKH and General Staff.[41] For some time past Zeitzler had been sick, and he left in disgrace, making way for Guderian, formerly the Inspector General of Mobile Troops, who was no more fitted for the responsibilities of the Chief of General Staff than Zeitzler, except that Hitler had eroded the status of the appointment to that of an executive who acted as the intermediary and telephonist between the Commander-in-Chief and the army group commanders. There remained to the Chief of General Staff not a vestige of authority or initiative.

When Guderian arrived in Rastenburg he found the General Staff offices of the OKH almost deserted. Zeitzler had already gone. Heusinger and Stieff had been removed. Many of the department heads had been hauled off by the Gestapo and part of the OKH had transferred itself from East Prussia to its old main headquarters in Zossen, in the suburbs of Berlin. Nothing daunted, Guderian set to work in a flurry of energy, exactly as Zeitzler had done before him, in spite of the fact that the *Führer* had only just before categorically and forcefully refused to allow him to issue any orders on his own authority.[42] Differences appear to have arisen immediately between Guderian on the one hand and Model and Friessner on the other. Friessner was still pressing to evacuate Estonia, and Model wanted to cover his open south flank offensively by withdrawing Weiss's 2 Army from the area of Brest and concentrating the reserves behind the Vistula. Guderian entered the unreal world of the *Führer* when he professed to believe that the situation would be restored by two or three divisions removed from Rumania. On 24 July Hitler issued an order committing Army Groups North and Centre to remain where they were and ordering Friessner to exchange his command with Schörner, the Commander of Army Group South Ukraine and the firm favourite of the National Socialist régime. Friessner, by way of consolation,

---

[39] *Kriegstagebuch des OKW*, Vol. 4, p. 858.

[40] Guderian, *Panzer Leader*, p. 408.

[41] There was some suspicion that Zeitzler may have had some knowledge of the plot.

[42] Guderian, *Panzer Leader*, pp. 342–3 and 351. Jodl, in supporting Hitler's decision, is reported to have told Guderian that the General Staff (of which Guderian was temporarily the most illustrious member) ought to be disbanded.

was advanced to the rank of colonel-general, and was sent off to what was considered to be a quiet theatre of operations.[43]

The Soviet High Command then directed Rokossovsky's 1 Belorussian and Konev's 1 Ukrainian Front to advance westwards and cross the Vistula on a broad 130 mile wide front from south of Warsaw to the mouth of the Visloka. The Vistula, although a broad river about 200 yards wide, had in places a depth of not more than six feet and was only a minor obstacle compared with many of the great Russian rivers which the Red Army had already crossed. On 28 and 29 July, Gordov's 3 Guards and Pukhov's 13 Armies and Katukov's 1 Guards Tank Army of 1 Ukrainian Front closed up to the Vistula and began to cross, using heavy fifty-ton ferries in addition to the normal lighter sixteen-ton pontoons. At first 1 Ukrainian Front made good progress against light opposition, consolidating a bridgehead west of the river to a depth of nearly twenty-five miles, but on 10 August Balck's 4 Panzer Army, reinforced with three panzer divisions withdrawn from 1 Panzer Army further to the south-east, counter-attacked the bridgehead and, driving the Soviet forces back several miles, brought the situation temporarily under control. By then Konev's 1 Ukrainian Front had outrun its strength.

Further to the north Radzievsky's 2 Tank Army was still in the Praga suburbs of Warsaw and had already attempted to cross the railway bridge into the capital when the Warsaw uprising began on 1 August. The exiled Polish Government in London which was, not without cause, suspicious of the Soviet Union's intentions with regard to a liberated Poland, had supported and directed a Polish patriotic underground army known as the AK or *Armia Krajova*. This patriotic Home Army, having intercepted radio messages from 4 Panzer Army which made clear the German intention to withdraw behind the Vistula, came out into the open and attempted to seize Warsaw before the Red Army should do so, in order to drive out the Germans and impress on the Soviet Union that it was dealing with real Polish military and political strength. The rising may, as the Soviet Union claimed, have been timed to coincide with the visit to Moscow of Mikolajzcyk, the Prime Minister of the Government-in-Exile, in order to strengthen his hand in the negotiations in the Kremlin. The Soviet Government was to complain, with justification, that it was informed of the rising only after it had begun, yet it is also true that the Soviet High Command itself had already been dropping manifesto leaflets from the air, inciting the Polish people to take up arms against the Germans, and that on 29 July Moscow radio was calling on Warsaw to do the same.[44] The USSR intended, however, that such a rising should be entirely subor-

[43] *Ibid*, p. 354; and Friessner, *Verratene Schlachten*, pp. 28–9.
[44] Bor-Komorowski, *The Secret Army*, p. 212; Feis, *Churchill Roosevelt Stalin*, p. 380; Churchill, Vol. 6, *Triumph and Tragedy*, p. 114. Zhukov, who met the puppet Polish Committee of Liberation at Stalin's dacha on 8 July, tells of the intention to issue the manifesto on 20 July. Zhukov, *Vospominaniya i Razmyshleniya*, p. 585; and *Istoriya*, Vol. 4, pp. 238–9. Bulganin was removed from 1 Belorussian Front at this time to become Stalin's representative with the Committee of Liberation, and was replaced as political member by Telegin.

dinate to communist and Soviet interests and not directed by a nationalist and capitalist émigré organization supported by the British, an organization which was as rabidly anti-communist and anti-Russian as it was anti-German, the Poles having suffered most barbarous treatment at the hands of both German Fascists and Soviet Communists in the course of the previous four years. The Kremlin had, with its usual forethought, raised and trained a Polish Army, suitably indoctrinated and kept under surveillance by its attached Soviet officers and political workers. These troops under Berling, a former officer of the old Polish Army, were to have a dual role in that they were to provide the cadre for new Polish forces to be conscripted on Polish soil to fight in the Soviet cause and were also to provide the necessary overt police support for the puppet communist Polish régime which Moscow intended to establish in Lublin in opposition to the London Government. By doing this the Kremlin hoped to give the appearance of reality to what was not, of course, true, that liberated Poland was governed by Poles and not by Russians. Berling's Army had been recruited from the prisons, prisoner of war and concentration camps and, as there was no lack of incarcerated foreigners in the Soviet Union, Czecho-Slovak and Baltic formations were raised in exactly the same way.

On 1 August Bor-Komorowski, the Polish patriotic Commander-in-Chief of the Home Army, began his insurrection which threatened the rearward communications of part of von Vormann's 9 German Army, an army head-quarters which after its defeat near Bobruisk had been withdrawn to reserve and recently reintroduced into the battle area. The Polish rising, lacking weapons and ammunition, was at first poorly organized, and yet it spread almost spontaneously, the people showing great heroism as they fought not only to rid themselves of the old invader but to safeguard their future as a nation against the coming of the new.[45] For its part the Soviet Government, well understanding the mentality and aspirations of the exiled Polish Government in London, and being mistrustful of the British, hardly wished the uprising well. If it had supported the insurgents with all the means in its power and had succeeded in occupying Warsaw during August, it would have been faced with the existence of a patriot army estimated at about 35,000 strong, armed mainly with German weapons, a citizen force which would have been an embarrassment to the new Lublin Government. At this time the Krem-lin was unwilling to involve the Red Army in fighting Polish patriots, nor was it yet ready for a trial of strength with the West as to the future of the Polish State. Moscow therefore pretended at first that there was no rising, then that the Home Army was friendly to the Germans, and finally that its leaders were both criminal and irresponsible in needlessly sacrificing Polish lives. Stalin used these arguments as excuses for inaction.

[45] This heroism is freely acknowledged in the Soviet histories, even if only as a political gesture to present day Poland. Chuikov, the arch-propagandist, maintains however that the AK did not fight the Germans at all but 'were there just for the sake of appearance'. Chuikov, *The End of the Third Reich*, p. 43.

Soviet sources have maintained that both 1 Belorussian and 1 Ukrainian Fronts had outrun their supplies and had the Vistula in front of them, and this statement was undoubtedly true, except that the Vistula itself was no great obstacle. 2 Tank Army was said to have met determined German resistance in the Praga suburbs on the east bank of the Vistula and to have lost 500 tanks and SUs since it entered Polish territory.[46] This is in part borne out by Model's claim that his army group reserve of three panzer divisions, formed by thinning out 2 and 4 Armies, had encircled and destroyed a tank corps to the northeast of Warsaw.[47] On the other hand at Magnuszew, about twenty-five miles south of Warsaw, 8 Guards Army mounted strong attacks across the Vistula and on 2 August, the day after the Warsaw rising, three Polish divisions of Berling's Army together with part of 69 Soviet Army were put across the Vistula, not into Warsaw but about forty miles south of the city near Pulawy and Demblin.[48] These Poles suffered heavy casualties but managed to hold on to their bridgehead. They and the Soviet troops at Magnuszew might have been better used attacking over the Vistula near Praga to aid the insurgent Poles. The demeanour of the Soviet Government and the field commanders at that time lends weight to the charge that it was the Kremlin's intention to let the Germans destroy the patriots. On 16 August Moscow informed the British Government that it proposed to have nothing to do with the uprising, and on 19 August a British and United States request for air landing facilities on Soviet soil so that the insurgents might be supplied by air with arms, ammunition and medical supplies was refused. On 22 August in a message to Churchill and Roosevelt, Stalin referred to the AK as a group of criminals.[49] Not before 10 September, when the rising was already dying down, did the Soviet High Command make some pretence of affording assistance. Between 10 and 14 September Gusev's 47 Soviet Army cleared Praga and 1 Polish Army was ordered to support the uprising and enter Warsaw by crossing the Vistula. On 16 September Berling's troops secured bridgeheads across the river, but the raw Polish peasant levies forcibly enlisted into 1 Polish Army were no match for the German Army and SS defenders and on 23 September they were driven back again across the Vistula. Not before 14 September did the Soviet Union start to drop food and ammunition to the hard-pressed Poles, and even then much of it was valueless since Red Army ammunition was dropped to a force which was fighting mainly with captured German rifles and machine-guns. Two Red Army liaison officers equipped with radio were parachuted into the city to act as Bor-Komorowski's liaison link with Rokossovsky, but this served little purpose as no replies were received to outgoing radio messages.[50] It is likely that the liaison officers were intended to act as Soviet spies on the

[46] *Istoriya*, Vol. 4, pp. 244–5.
[47] Guderian, *Panzer Leader*, p. 359.
[48] *Istoriya*, Vol. 4, p. 246.
[49] *Ibid*, p. 274. Churchill, Vol. 6, *Triumph and Tragedy*, pp. 118–20.
[50] Bor-Komorowski, *The Secret Army*, pp. 342–6.

patriot organization, since a little earlier on 17 July near Vilna, after many Soviet protestations of friendliness and gratitude, all the local leaders and staff of the Home Army were invited to a staff conference with Chernyakhovsky, the Commander of 3 Belorussian Front; none of them came back. The Soviet attitude was what might have been expected in the circumstances, and its intentions were confirmed when Poland was occupied and the Lublin Government came into being. Those who had taken a leading part in the insurrection or were connected in any way with the London émigrés either disappeared or were dispatched in railway trucks to the Russian interior, most of them never to be seen again.[51]

It is said that Hitler refused to entrust to the German Army the quelling of the uprising, but gave the task to Himmler who delegated it to von dem Bach-Zelewski. Twelve SS police companies, Dirlewanger's regiment of convicted German criminals, and Kaminski's White Russian brigade formed for the most part of Red Army prisoners of war, committed under their German masters indescribable atrocities on the Polish population.[52] German troops sheltered behind crowds of women and children who were herded towards the Polish lines. Polish sick and wounded, irrespective of sex, were taken out of hospitals and shot in masses. Rape and the cutting of throats were commonplace. Guderian, according to what he himself said, protested to Hitler that the units should be withdrawn, and in his subsequent account he attempted to deny the responsibility of both the Army and Armed SS.[53] Meanwhile the patriot Home Army continued to fight on in the cellars and sewers through the whole of August and September, the remnants not surrendering until 2 October.

During July and August the Soviet High Command attempted to improve its position in the Carpathians and the Baltic, preparatory to launching a new offensive into the Balkans. Konev's 1 Ukrainian Front had been brought to a standstill in its bridgehead beyond the Vistula in the Sandomierz-Baronow area, a bridgehead which threatened German Upper Silesia. Konev was left, however, with a long and exposed southern flank along the line of the Carpathians and in order to relieve him of its protection so that he might concentrate on his next mission, the resumption of the advance eastwards, 4 Ukrainian Front Headquarters, with I. E. Petrov and Mekhlis, was allocated to the area from the High Command Reserve. Petrov arrived in Stanislav to take command of Konev's left wing, Grechko's 1 Guards and Zhuravlev's 18 Armies passing to the command of 4 Ukrainian Front.[54] Petrov's task was to clear the industrial area of Drogobych and, taking the Carpathian passes, move into the Danube plain.

[51] Churchill, Vol. 6, *Triumph and Tragedy*, pp. 434–6.

[52] Of these SS, Fegelein said '*Mein Führer, das sind wirkliche Strolche*'.

[53] Guderian, *Panzer Leader*, pp. 355–6; also Bor-Komorowski, *The Secret Army*, pp. 234–5 and 331.

[54] The military council of 4 Ukrainian Front consisted of Petrov, Mekhlis and Korzhenevich as chief of staff.

In the area of the Baltic, German Army Group North remained cut off from Army Group Centre just to the west of Riga where Bagramyan's 1 Baltic Front had reached the shore of the Baltic. Schörner, the new Commander of Army Group North, was having no greater success than his predecessors Friessner and Lindemann, and like them he advised the immediate evacuation of Estonia. Hitler continued to insist that every inch of Baltic territory was to be held, in spite of the fact that Finland was about to leave the war. Schörner was at this time under heavy attack from Govorov's Leningrad Front across the Narva and from Maslennikov's 3 Baltic Front which was thrusting vigorously from the area to the south of Lake Peipus towards Dorpat (Tartu) and Valga (Walki), with the obvious intention of reaching the Gulf of Riga and cutting Army Group North in half. To the south of Riga Bagramyan's 1 Baltic Front appeared to be about to attack 16 Army positions south of the Dvina, in order to widen its hold on the tongue of land which separated Army Groups North and Centre.

The *Führer* had carried out yet a further reorganization and a reposting of many of his senior commanders. In France the German front had collapsed and Model was transferred to the West, his Army Group Centre command being taken over by Reinhardt on 16 August. Reinhardt's post in 3 Panzer Army was taken by Raus, whose appointment as Commander of 1 Panzer Army was filled by Heinrici, formerly of 4 Army. In early September Harpe was confirmed in his post as Commander of Army Group North Ukraine.

At this point Hitler launched a new counter-attack, devised by himself, to be made by two panzer corps of 3 Panzer Army with one panzer grenadier and four panzer divisions, two of which were still on their way from Rumania where they had provided the last reserves available to Army Group South Ukraine. This force was to attack north-eastwards from its concentration area in West Lithuania and restore the land communication between Army Groups Centre and North. Then, in conjunction with the infantry divisions of Army Group North, it was to strike south-east on Kaunas in a raid across the rear of 1 Baltic and 3 Belorussian Fronts. The attack began on 16 August but after some initial success quickly came to a halt in the area of Siauliai (Schaulen). It did however have some small benefit in that it halted the 1 Baltic Front attack against the German troops south of the Dvina, since these Soviet forces had to be turned about westwards to face Raus's 3 Panzer Army in their rear. On 21 August German troops with the aid of naval forces managed to drive a narrow corridor through to Army Group North along the coast, this offering the last chance of evacuating by land Army Group North from the North Baltic States. Hitler had, however, found a substitute for Finland, when he maintained that an evacuation would have a disastrous effect on the attitude of Sweden, and he moved a further two divisions from Army Group Centre to Army Group North.

By then Red Army offensive power was synonomous with tank armies and tank and mechanized corps. Where tank and motorized forces were concentrated, together with the means to keep them supplied, the Soviet High Command could be sure of some success. Red Army infantry formations had suffered so severely in casualties and their infantry were often so poorly trained that they had only limited offensive capability. The same applied to some extent to the German troops in the East. Panzer and panzer grenadier divisions were the most effective counter to Soviet tank formations, and German infantry divisions were only a shadow of their former selves. Reduced by casualties below the size of regiments, their training and performance, superior though it might have been to that of their Red Army counterpart, was hardly to be compared with that of German infantry of 1941 and 1942. Much of the benefit of the increase in armament and equipment brought about by Speer's reorganization of the armament industry had been lost in the great encirclements in the Ukraine, in Belorussia and in France. Yet the industrial and economic power of Germany and the potential of the German Army remained formidable and, allowed time for reorganization and given good strategic and higher tactical leadership, it might have fought on for a long time to come.

During the winter of 1943 and the spring of 1944 German strength on the Eastern Front had declined due to the transfer of formations and reinforcements to the West and the Mediterranean theatre. On 1 June 1944, at the time of the Normandy invasion and the fall of Rome, there were the equivalent of 164 German Army, *Luftwaffe* and SS field divisions in the East, some of which were hardly more than regiments, as against 121 German divisions in the West and the Mediterranean.[55] The German panzer force in France and the Netherlands which in December 1943 numbered only 650 tanks and 220 assault guns, by June 1944 had increased to 1,550 tanks and 300 assault guns.

Zhukov, in commenting on the German failures in 1943 and 1944, has laid part of the blame on the German High Command and on the commanders of the army groups, since the quality of the leadership suffered, in his view, a sharp decline. In contrast with the first period of the war the German command had lost its resourcefulness, particularly when it ran into difficulties, and there was a marked ignorance of the true appreciation of its own capabilities and that of its enemies. Hitler's Generals, who have tried to blame their own deficiencies on the *Führer*, come in for some criticism by Zhukov, who, while grudgingly admitting that Hitler was in part responsible for the catastrophes, feels that the main reason for the defeats was German failure to

[55] Deployment of German divisions on 1 June 1944.

	East	Finland	Norway Denmark	West	Italy	Balkans
Army	149	6	15	47	23	18
Lw	—	—	—	3	3	—
SS	8	1	—	4	1	7
	157	7	15	54	27	25

Mueller-Hillebrand, *Das Heer*, Vol. 3, Table 62.

understand the very real improvement in the performance of the Soviet armed forces.[56] All of which is, of course, true.

On the other hand, Zhukov professes to be surprised at the German conduct of the battle in Belorussia. He argues that as soon as defeat threatened, Busch should have acted as the Red Army would have done and retired rapidly to a defence line in the rear and meanwhile have used mobile formations to engage the flanks of the attacking force, instead of doing what he did, contracting his line and trying to defend the area east of Minsk.[57] Zhukov's criticism is to the point. Yet there is little cause for surprise and Zhukov must know why Busch acted as he did. He should remember, too, that the Red Army in 1941 and 1942 had also been ordered by a menacing dictator to hold its ground and had suffered grievously in consequence.

On 25 August the Anglo-Americans were in Paris and rapidly advancing on the western frontiers of Germany. The *Führer* then came to the conclusion that the main war effort should be made in the West and decided to collect within the *Reich* a striking force which would deal the Western Allies a crippling blow west of Germany's frontiers. He would then turn eastwards to face the oncoming Red Army. Meanwhile he turned a deaf ear to Guderian's pleadings to evacuate the Balkans, Norway and part of Italy, all of which were in fact Jodl's responsibility. Guderian himself had turned his energies towards the raising of home defence units to protect the German frontier areas in the east. The building of fortifications began around Königsberg, Danzig, Glogau and Breslau, the construction being mainly of earthworks and being built by volunteers, women and children and old men, the only readily available labour source. Guderian gave orders for a hundred infantry battalions and the same number of artillery batteries to be raised from convalescents and low medical category soldiers to protect the eastern frontier, but most of these, Guderian complained, were seized by Jodl and dispatched to the West, followed by the reserve of guns and heavy equipment which the Chief of General Staff had hoped to deploy in the East. Even the last drafts of combat troops which Himmler's Replacement Army produced were destined not for the defence of the East but for an offensive in the West.[58] The responsibility for the raising of German volunteer part-time citizen units for regional defence was removed by the *Führer* from the state and defence machinery to the Party organization, just as he had transferred that for the collection of winter clothing three years before. The measures taken were dilatory and ill-considered, but eventually the Volkssturm was born. The new organization had been publicized and recruited to such an extent, however, that insufficient leaders, instructors or arms were available to make it in any way an effective force.

[56] Zhukov, *Vospominaniya i Razmyshleniya*, pp. 561–2.
[57] *Ibid*, p. 580.
[58] Guderian, *Panzer Leader*, pp. 360–4.

CHAPTER TWENTY-SEVEN

Finland Leaves the War

As early as November 1941 Finland had lost its enthusiasm for the war. In December the Germans had received their severe check before Moscow, the United States was in the war, and Helsinki could no longer count on the Soviet Union being overcome in a short campaign. When Heinrichs visited Halder in East Prussia the next spring he noted that the German Chief of General Staff was tired and depressed and considered that the war had been too costly for the Germans.[1] Yet the Finns disregarded a Soviet peace feeler received through the Swedish Foreign Office at the end of 1941. During 1942 Finland was under German pressure to undertake another operation to cut the Murmansk railway and under counterpressure from the United States, with whom Finland was not at war, to refrain from doing so. Germany's war position deteriorated rapidly from the latter part of 1942. The Anglo-American landings and victories in Africa, the surrender of Italy, the heavy defeats at Stalingrad and Kursk, and the Allied bombing offensive were anxiously noted in Helsinki, and the correct conclusions drawn that Germany had already lost the war. The Finnish Government decided to make peace as soon as it could. Mannerheim, the seventy-five year old Commander-in-Chief, relied very much on capable lieutenants such as Heinrichs, Oesch and Siilasvuo, but he himself was in complete control of the Finnish armed forces and had a powerful voice in the affairs of State. He was up to a point pro-German and on good terms with Hitler, but first and foremost he was a patriot. Hitler and the OKW went to great lengths to charm and humour the ageing marshal and keep Finland in the war; but although they succeeded in making a good personal impression, their fortune did not extend to promoting Germany's cause. Whereas in the middle of 1941 Mannerheim had good grounds for optimism, by December of that year he had already been assailed by doubts. Erfurth, the German military representative accredited to Mannerheim, was of the opinion that none of his staff had any influence with him. Above all, Finnish interests as Mannerheim saw them were paramount and so he determined upon a policy of obstruction and inactivity. By the autumn of 1943 Finland still had more than 350,000 men under arms, but these were opposing about 180,000 Soviet troops, while 20 German Mountain Army

[1] Mannerheim, *Memoirs*, p. 442.

with a strength of more than 180,000 combat troops outnumbered the Red Army facing it by two to one. Fret as they might against Mannerheim's indecision, the Germans could not attack without Finnish agreement and support. Erfurth and Dietl, the Commander of 20 Army, were to report that Helsinki's reluctance to cut the Murmansk railway and destroy the Soviet armies facing them was due to Finnish fear of alienating the United States. This was partly true. It must also be taken into account, however, that the Murmansk railroad was not absolutely vital to the Soviet war effort, and that even if the 7 and 23 Soviet Armies had been destroyed, this could only have been done at a cost of heavy Finnish casualties without contributing in any way to the final outcome of the war, since Germany was already doomed. The conditions of a Soviet-dictated peace, however, were likely to be intolerable, and in July 1943 Finland rejected yet another proposal from Moscow. On the other hand the presence in the country of Dietl's 20 Mountain Army was threatening to become an embarrassment.

On 28 September 1943 Hitler ordered 20 Mountain Army to prepare to hold North Finland and the Petsamo nickel mines in case the Finns should go out of the war. Dietl objected in vain to Jodl that these orders were unrealistic, since he was sure that he could not hold North Finland for a protracted period and as the neutrality of Sweden could no longer be relied upon, he feared that his troops would be stranded.[2]

In January 1944 the Soviet offensive to the south of Leningrad forced back Army Group North towards the Baltic States, leaving the Finns isolated and nervous. In mid-February the Finns at last sent delegates to Moscow, but the Soviet peace conditions were so harsh that they were rejected. Hitler retaliated by restricting arms and grain shipments to Finland.

Stalin had already agreed at Teheran in December 1943, in response to pressure by Roosevelt and Churchill, that Finland should retain its national independence, but he had made up his mind to put Finland finally out of the war. Gusev's 21 Soviet Army of six rifle divisions and a breakthrough artillery corps were moved by sea from Oranienbaum to the area north of Leningrad, and a further nine rifle divisions and a breakthrough artillery division were added to Krutikov's 7 Army on the left wing of the Karelian Front. The Leningrad Front, commanded by Govorov with Zhdanov as the political member of his military council, was concentrated on the narrow Karelian Isthmus to the north of Leningrad and consisted of Gusev's newly arrived 21 Army of ten divisions on the left, and Cherepanov's 23 Army of eight divisions on the right. The left wing of Meretskov's Karelian Front consisted of Krutikov's 7 Army of fourteen rifle divisions on the Svir between Lakes Ladoga and Onega, and Gorelenko's 32 Army of only three divisions to the north of Onega. For this offensive the Leningrad and Karelian Fronts were to use about forty-five divisions and a number of tank and marine brigades, in all nearly

[2] Hubatsch, *Hitlers Weisungen für die Kriegführung*, p. 231, *Weisung* Nr. 50; *Kriegstagebuch des OKW*, pp. 1148–9, 28 September 1943.

Q

half a million men, 800 tanks and SUs, and about 1,500 aircraft. 10,000 guns and mortars were said to be available for the attack, together with some heavy calibre guns of the Baltic Fleet.[3]

The Soviet plan was to make the main thrust on the Karelian Isthmus on 21 Army sector onto Viborg, while 23 Army would attempt to pin the bulk of the enemy against Lake Ladoga and the small lakes to the Finnish rear. Govorov failed, however, to make provision for securing the neck of the isthmus to the east of Viborg in order to cut off the only line of withdrawal of the Finnish troops.

The Finnish troops defending the thirty-mile wide Karelian Isthmus were grouped under Siilasvuo's 3 Corps and Laatikainen's 4 Corps and consisted of three infantry divisions and a brigade deployed forward in the line, with two further divisions and a cavalry brigade in the rear working on the defences. The Finnish defences were made up of two main defensive zones, the forward zone comprising a forward line with a second VT line about ten miles to the rear, the rear zone consisting of a third VET line across the narrow neck of the isthmus, thirty miles back immediately to the east of Viborg. A fourth incomplete defence line on the old 1940 frontier, and for this reason known as the Moscow line, stood further to the rear. The forward three lines were well sited and organized, although they consisted mainly of earthworks thickened up with concrete and steel emplacements. The Soviet High Command had no illusions as to the toughness of the fight and current Soviet historical accounts still stress the skill and experience of Finnish troops in forest and marsh and the bravery and fortitude with which they fought this last pitched battle.[4]

The Anglo-Americans had just landed in Normandy and the Soviet High Command was shortly to launch its great offensive in Belorussia. The USSR intended to eliminate Finland from the war, but, according to its own account, it had other subsidiary aims in that it wanted to divert German attention from the Belorussian Front and at the same time improve the security of Leningrad and bring the Kirov route and the White Sea Baltic Canal into use once more.

For some time before the attack there was the usual radio silence on the Soviet side, and the Finns appeared to have been surprised by the scale of the attack rather than by its timing, and by the fact that 10 Finnish Division was so speedily overcome.[5] On 9 June there was heavy bombing, and the next day, after a massive artillery bombardment more intense than the Finns had ever experienced before, 21 Soviet Army crossed the Sestra and penetrated ten

---

[3] *Istoriya*, Vol. 4, p. 157. According to Erfurth, Finnish sources put the Soviet strength at no higher than twenty-nine rifle and two artillery divisions, four tank brigades and other detachments. Erfurth, *Der Finnische Krieg 1941–1944*, pp. 242–3.

[4] *Istoriya*, Vol. 4, p. 156.

[5] 23 Soviet Army went off the air as early as 10 May. Erfurth says that the timing of the attack came as a complete surprise to the Finns and on 11 June made an entry to that effect in his war diary. Oesch on the other hand disputes this. Erfurth, *Der Finnische Krieg 1941–1944*, p. 227; Oesch, *Finnlands Entscheidungskampf 1944*, p. 67.

miles into the Finnish defences. Twenty-four hours later, 23 Soviet Army on the right joined in the attack, and on 13 June the second VT line was reached. Here the Finns wrongly deduced that the main Soviet thrust was coming in the centre, whereas in fact it was delivered in the west on the coast road. There, with the support of 3 Breakthrough Artillery Corps, an eight-mile wide gap was driven through the line on 14 June. On 18 June Soviet troops were approaching Viborg. The Finns had a few days before appealed to the Germans to lift the embargo on arms (imposed when Helsinki had begun peace overtures) and provide six German divisions to relieve Finnish troops on the quiet sector in Karelia, so that more Finnish formations could be moved west to the Viborg area. Soviet tanks in particular were proving a great threat. Of German troops Hitler had none to spare, but he did make available 122 Infantry Division and a brigade of about thirty self-propelled armoured assault guns. The *Luftwaffe* air support was increased and an air and fast sea lift was begun to bring in 9,000 *Panzerfaust* and 5,000 *Panzerschreck* short range anti-tank weapons. A more unwelcome consignment was von Ribbentrop, who arrived by air to insist on a *quid pro quo* in the form of a signed undertaking by President Ryti that Finland would not make a separate peace.[6] This was a contributory cause occasioning the breaking-off by the United States of diplomatic relations with Finland.

The Finns had already committed their only armoured division and they were beginning to transfer formations from Karelia east of Lake Ladoga to the Viborg area. In order to co-ordinate 3 and 4 Corps, Oesch was given overall command of both, and the continuous and furious fighting was, according to the Finnish account, the most violent of the whole war. Although 10 Finnish Division, which had borne the brunt of the initial offensive, was no onger effective, the other divisions managed to withdraw in fighting order to ihe north of Viborg, their success being partly due to the Soviet failure to close the narrow land exit of the isthmus. The town of Viborg was lost on 20 June, but shortly afterwards the Soviet offensive was brought to a standstill.

On 21 June Meretskov launched his attack in Eastern Karelia against the weakened Finnish positions on the Svir to the east of Lake Ladoga and to the north of Lake Onega, positions from which the Finns had already begun to withdraw. 5 Finnish Corps had been transferred to the Karelian Isthmus to help stem Govorov's offensive and so the rearguard action against 7 Army on the Svir was carried out by 6 Corps and Group Olenez (Aunus), while 2 Corps defended the area of Velikaya Guba to the north of Lake Onega against 32 Soviet Army. The Finns mined and demolished the area as they withdrew, but they were in continuous contact with the enemy and fighting was at times heavy. Most of the area conquered in 1941 was given up in the space of about six weeks. Towards the end of July the Red Army pressure fell off as Soviet formations were removed and sent to the south into the Baltic States where the German line was being torn open by the Belorussian offensive. Because

[6] Mannerheim, *Memoirs*, pp. 481–3; Erfurth, *Der Finnische Krieg 1941–1944*, pp. 241–2.

of this, German assistance to Finland dried up entirely and on 29 July Hitler asked for the return of 122 Infantry Division.

Germany's defeat in Belorussia and the Baltic and the failure to repel the Normandy landings confirmed the belief that German military power was waning fast, and there was some bitterness that Germany was failing to keep its part of the Ryti-Ribbentrop agreement. On 4 August Ryti resigned and was succeeded as President by Mannerheim, this permitting the Finns to repudiate the agreement made with the Germans by the former President. The Germans sent first Schörner, the Commander of Army Group North who had at one time commanded 6 Mountain Division and 19 Mountain Corps in North Finland, and then Keitel to convey the Oak Leaf Cluster to Mannerheim and the Knight's Cross of the Iron Cross to Heinrichs. They had nothing more to offer. Mannerheim took the opportunity of the presentation to inform a surprised and slightly shocked Keitel that Finland had suffered 60,000 casualties during the fighting in the summer and could not afford more. The Ryti undertaking not to end the war, said Mannerheim, was no longer valid. Immediately after receiving news that fighting had broken out between German and Rumanian troops when Rumania had sued for peace, Finland asked the Soviet Union on 25 August for peace terms. Moscow agreed to receive a Finnish delegation on the prior understanding that Finland should break off all relations with Germany and that all foreign troops should have quitted Finland by 15 September.

Dietl, the German Commander in Finland, had been killed on 23 June in an air accident and had been succeeded by Rendulic, an able Austrian whom Guderian has described as being on good terms with Hitler. Rendulic was a man of courteous but hard exterior and when he called on Mannerheim to urge him not to submit to Soviet pressure to take up arms against the Germans, Mannerheim, rightly or wrongly, regarded the urging as a threatening hint.[7] Germany had frightened Europe in 1940 and 1941 and could count on a respectful audience in Italy and Rumania in 1943, but in Finland any suspicion of heavy-handedness had a hollow ring since the isolated 20 Mountain Army could not be reinforced and was outnumbered by Finns by two to one.

The Germans began to withdraw stores and munitions from the first week in September but it was obvious that they could not be out of the country by the middle of the month without abandoning most of their heavy equipment. The Soviet High Command meanwhile showed little interest in pinning the Germans by the use of Red Army troops. The relationship between German and Finn remained quite good, however, until the German naval staff persuaded Hitler to agree to the seizure of the Finnish naval base at Suursaari. The attack was made on the morning of 15 September. The Finnish garrison, contrary to expectation, opened fire and the Red Air Force took a hand, so that

---

[7] Mannerheim, *Memoirs*, pp. 495–6. Rendulic, *Gekämpft Gesiegt Geschlagen*, p. 284. Rendulic has subsequently affirmed that no threat was intended.

the Germans were driven off with heavy loss. By attacking Suursaari Hitler played into Soviet hands and let the Finns out of an embarrassing situation. Mannerheim was not slow to take advantage of the position; he ordered all Finnish vessels back to port and requested Rendulic's immediate withdrawal. Even so, there was as yet no question of hostilities. Rendulic noted that the Finns were under heavy Moscow pressure to take a more active part in expelling 20 Mountain Army, but he tended to regard the activity of the Finns who followed up the German withdrawal into Norway merely as show to satisfy the Soviet demands. The withdrawal took place without incident until the German troops were pressed by the competent and individualistic Siilasvuo who was in command of the Finnish troops following up 20 German Army. Fighting broke out near the Baltic coast town of Tornio with all the destruction to the countryside which war entails. The town of Rovaniemi was gutted when an ammunition train blew up. The Soviet High Command showed little interest in entering Finland or undertaking pursuit operations against Rendulic's troops; not until 15 October did they move troops forward to occupy the Petsamo area.

So ended the Finnish War, a war which cost Finland about 200,000 casualties, of which 55,000 were killed. In addition it lost heavily in territory and economic resources and was oppressed with a near-crippling reparations debt. Finland took up arms in order to regain the territories lost in the Winter War. In the final outcome it probably hoped for more. Yet the USSR was in no small way responsible for forcing this tiny nation to join the German anti-Comintern crusade, since in the period of peace after the Winter War Moscow bullied, blackmailed and menaced Finland with extinction. The Finns were desperate men who remembered Stalin's words in 1939 when, showing a mocking sympathy for Finland's desire to stay out of any war between Germany and the Soviet Union, he gave his opinion that geography alone made this out of the question. For Finland, Germany was the lesser of two evils. Finland was fortunate to have remained an independent nation and for this it had to thank its own courage and sturdy resolution, its closeness to the sea and the deep emotional interest taken in its future by the United States and Britain.

Although the Finnish War was of little account to Hitler's life and death struggle with his three principal enemies, it must be viewed as part of Germany's strategy in Scandinavia. Hitler believed, not incorrectly, that the occupation of Denmark and Norway safeguarded the Baltic Sea and Germany's northern flank, together with Swedish iron ore and Finnish nickel. Iron and nickel were necessary to Germany's war economy but could be obtained elsewhere; whether these ores justified keeping nearly half a million German troops idle in Norway and Finland for the whole of the war is more than questionable. Norway had been conquered by a corps, but could only be held by an army, such were the *Führer*'s exaggerated fears of an Anglo-American landing and so difficult was the lateral movement of troops along the Norwegian coast. The occupation of Norway did admittedly give Germany air bases from which to raid the convoys to Russia and naval anchorages with easy exits into the North Atlantic, but neither of these was of any decisive importance to the outcome of the war. In Finland during 1942–4 half a million high grade Finnish and German troops stood idle, facing less than half their number of low category Soviet formations.

Finland's entry into the war was an embarrassment to the Soviet Union only in so far as it tied down Red Army troops; but when it became obvious that Helsinki did not intend to aid the Germans to take Leningrad and that it was disinterested in crossing the Svir, the Soviet High Command thinned out its troops accordingly. 20 German Mountain Army, which eventually reached a strength of three corps and nearly 200,000 men, attempted little and achieved nothing more than the defence of Petsamo, which was in any case never seriously threatened. Hitler's insistence on the cutting of the Murmansk railway was not entirely logical if the Archangel route continued to function. The Murmansk and Archangel areas could have been occupied in 1941 with fairly serious consequences to the USSR, but this northern sea flank could only have been seized after Leningrad had fallen. Hitler could have taken Leningrad quickly and easily, but not with the number of divisions he had allotted to von Leeb's Army Group North. Hitler failed because he would not decide on priorities and tailor his strategy according to his resources.

CHAPTER TWENTY-EIGHT

Rumania

Rumanian oil was not vital to Germany's war effort but it provided a very necessary part of the *Reich*'s war supplies, and in 1943 about 2·4 million tons of mineral oil and petroleum products had been exported to the German homeland or direct to German troops in the field.[1] On 5 April, shortly before the Soviet attack on the Crimea, Mediterranean based United States bombers began a series of attacks on the Ploesti oilfields and the river traffic on the Danube, so that by 20 May Rumanian oil production had been halved.[2] On 21 April Turkey had stopped its deliveries of chrome to Germany.

At the beginning of that month the Soviet Foreign Minister Molotov speaking, he said, with the agreement of the Anglo-American Powers, had broadcast assuring the Rumanians that the Soviet Union had no territorial claims against Rumania other than the return of Bessarabia, and that it had no intention of interfering in any way with the social order in the capitalist state. Unknown to Germany, peace talks began in Cairo on 12 April with United States, British and Soviet representatives, the Soviet Ambassador Novikov presenting the Rumanian Prince Stirbey with his six-point conditions, copies of which Novikov had caused to be given to Maniu, the Rumanian leader of the opposition and head of the National Smallholders' Party. Rumania wanted peace but asked for an airlift of Anglo-American formations into the country as security for its future. On 19 April Maniu made some counter-proposals, but after protracted delays negotiations were finally broken off by Antonescu on 15 May, since the conditions were unacceptable to him. Talks are said to have continued, however, in Stockholm, these being kept secret from both Germany and the Western Powers.[3]

Rumanian nobility, intelligentsia and other opposition elements were

---

[1] Hillgruber. *Hitler, König Carol und Marschall Antonescu*, pp. 200–1, 249–50 (*Klugkist*). In 1942 German synthetic production rose to its peak of 6·3 million tons, Galicia and Hungary producing only ·34 and ·15 million tons respectively. By 1944 however Hungarian production had risen to ·8 million tons and Austrian production to 1·3 million tons. See also June 1944 production figures in the *Dereser* paper (*Abt Qu des W F Stabs*) of 12 June 1944 reproduced in *Kriegstagebuch des OKW*, Vol. 4, p. 942.

[2] Hillgruber, *Hitler, König Carol und Marschall Antonescu*, p. 189.

[3] *Ibid*, pp. 194–5.

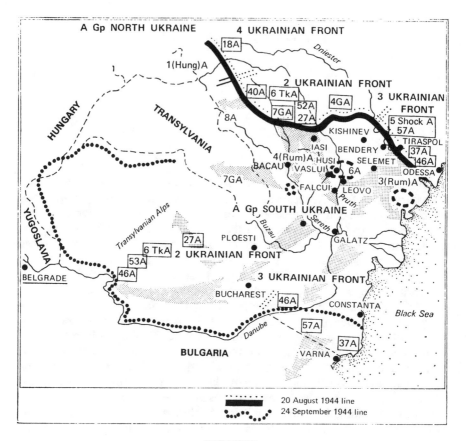

RUMANIA
August–September 1944

determined to get out of the war, whether Antonescu agreed or not. Reassured by Moscow promises, they began to plot Antonescu's removal and the break with Germany, although for many of them liquidation or the slow death of the Soviet concentration camp was to be their fate.

The German-Rumanian relationship which had deteriorated so much during 1943 had shown no improvement in 1944. Antonescu had insisted on equality of command between Rumanian and German troops and would not allow German detachments to be interposed in the Rumanian deployment unless these troops were put under Rumanian command. The presence of the German troops of Army Group South Ukraine on Rumanian soil gave rise to numerous difficulties of supply, maintenance and finance, these creating a

468

balance of payments problem and a strain on the Rumanian economy. Moreover, Rumania wanted German equipment for which it could not pay and which Germany was unwilling or unable to provide. Assistance with air defence was one of Rumania's most pressing needs. Friction was not lessened by the presence on Rumanian soil of large numbers of *Osttruppen, Hiwis* and the 125,000 *Volksdeutsch* refugees from Transdniester. German commanders and troops, by then acclimatized to the full rigours of total war, were becoming increasingly impatient of Rumanian temperament and ways, particularly the apparent indifference and apathy as to the course and outcome of the struggle. The *Führer* refused, however, to let Schörner take more energetic measures to prepare his command for war, in case further injury should result to Germany's foreign relations.

The German political and military organization in Rumania was complicated and confusing. The German Ambassador in Bucharest, von Killinger, was directly responsible to von Ribbentrop's Foreign Ministry; but his duties had become so onerous that a second and additional ambassador, Clodius, had been appointed to undertake all the more important negotiations with Antonescu and the Rumanian Foreign Minister, while von Killinger saw to day to day matters. The German Ambassador had his own Military Attaché, Spalcke. E. Hansen headed the German Army Mission and commanded all German base troops in Rumania, receiving his orders from the German Armed Forces High Command (OKW) through Jodl or Keitel. Gerstenberg, who was Air Attaché and head of the Air Mission, was responsible to both the Embassy and to Göring; he commanded all *Luftwaffe* air and ground troops including the two flak divisions, and was charged with the air and ground defence of Ploesti. Schörner's Army Group South Ukraine on the other hand was not responsible to Bucharest or to the OKW at all, but to the *Führer*, either direct or through Guderian in the Army High Command (OKH). Because of Antonescu's insistence on equality in command, higher Rumanian formations could no longer be coupled with and put under command of relatively subordinate German headquarters, and Schörner was obliged to accept that a Rumanian army commander should exercise real command over two armies on the right, one of them German, in order that a German should have tactical control over a Rumanian army on the left. For the first time in the war German corps and divisions were under real instead of nominal Rumanian command.

This division of responsibility, with the advantage to the Rumanian host, was extended throughout the rear areas. Antonescu maintained governmental control over the whole of the country except to the east of a line Ploesti-Bucharest, this being designated a military controlled area under a Rumanian Commander-in-Chief to whom was accredited Auleb, formerly the German administrative and lines of communication commander to Army Group A and Transdniester. Auleb was responsible to Schörner and not to Hansen.[4]

[4] *Ibid*, pp. 186–7.

The German supply channel depended on the Rumanian and Hungarian railway systems, both of which had a limited capacity, the more so since they were inefficiently operated. Because of the deep-rooted enmity between Rumanian and Hungarian, great difficulties were made by both sides in the transfer of rolling stock across the frontiers, and it was not unknown for the *Luftwaffe* to carry out air reconnaissance sorties over hundreds of miles of track in search of German trains which had become lost in the system. It took from two to three weeks for goods to arrive from Germany, and the railways were so uncertain that German formations and reinforcements found it quicker to move between Hungary and Bessarabia by the road route, marching from one staging camp to another.[5]

When Friessner was exchanged with Schörner and sent to Rumania to what was described as a quiet front, he was to find that the officers under his command had feelings of grave disquiet concerning the new and strange attitude of their Rumanian comrades in arms. Bessarabia and Moldavia were untouched by war, and the Rumanian authorities, even after due allowance had been made for corruption and incompetence, were taking no steps to bring the country onto a war footing. The effect of Antonescu's earlier mobilization measures were half-hearted, and it was becoming obvious that his orders were no longer being obeyed. The German Army was frequently ignored, and key Rumanian commanders and staffs, sometimes even those integrated within the German field organization, were removed by Bucharest without notice and without consultation, events which would have been considered impossible two years before. Many of the newly appointed Rumanians were hostile to the régime, and there were grounds for suspicion that some were preparing to come to terms with the Soviet invaders while others, preferring the West to the East, were hoping to secure Anglo-American support. These fears and suspicions were relayed by Friessner to Rastenburg.[6]

The *Führer*, however, had received entirely contrary intelligence through the OKW. On 2 April, only fourteen days before the Rumanians attended the secret peace talks in Cairo, Hansen had emphasized that a spirit of determination to continue the war existed among the Rumanian leaders and people, and this was confirmed by Jodl's representative Poleck, who visited Bucharest two days later.[7] Gerstenberg took very much the same view in his reports to Göring and, according to Friessner, was to say that he was confident that he could quell a *coup d'état* in Bucharest with a *Luftwaffe* flak battery. Although the young King Michael and his mother were British in their sympathies, and the royal palace was known as a centre of anti-Axis intrigue, Antonescu was believed to be entirely Hitler's man and throughout the war he had shown himself to be understanding of Germany's problems at the expense of Rumanian interests. Von Killinger regarded Friessner's misgivings as baseless, being

[5] Rehm, *Jassy*, p. 14; Friessner, *Verratene Schlachten*, p. 48.
[6] *Ibid*, pp. 53–6.
Hillgruber, *Hitler, König Carol und Marschall Antonescu*, p. 186.

convinced that the whole country was entirely behind Antonescu, and he reported in this vein to the German Foreign Office. Yet he failed to convince von Ribbentrop, who requested the *Führer* to station a panzer division in the capital as a pledge for the security of Antonescu and his government. Guderian had not one to spare, but as he and Jodl freely offered each other's formations and as the Chief of General Staff regarded Bucharest as a OKW responsibility, he suggested that a SS police division from Yugo-Slavia might be suitable. Jodl demurred and there the position was left.[8]

It is probable that Hitler still had some doubts as to Antonescu's intentions because when the Rumanian statesman visited Rastenburg on 5 August in company with Mihai Antonescu, the Foreign Minister, and Steflea, the Rumanian Chief of General Staff, Hitler put to him the direct question as to whether Rumania would stay in the war to the end. Whatever Antonescu's true intentions, the *Führer* appears to have been satisfied with the outcome of the meeting. Antonescu gave an impression of honesty to both Guderian and Friessner.[9]

In Bulgaria, too, the Germans experienced a feeling of disquiet. At war with the United States and Britain, but not with the USSR, Bulgaria was in occupation of part of Greece and Yugo-Slavia and had been firmly in the German camp, although by origin, language and culture the Bulgarian has many affinities with the Russian. Von Jungenfeldt, with the Military Mission in Bulgaria, reported to Guderian that the morale and general behaviour of the Bulgarian troops indicated that something was going on beneath the surface.[10] Boris, the King of Bulgaria, a staunch adherent to the Axis and no friend of communism, had died some time before under what the Germans considered to be mysterious circumstances. On 2 August Turkey had broken off diplomatic relations with Germany and there was a possibility that Rumania might be attacked in the rear.

When Friessner arrived in Rumania he found that his new command was being used by Hitler, Göring and Guderian as a pool from which other army groups were reinforced. A *Luftwaffe* Group (*Geschwader*) was removed to Latvia. Of the nine panzer divisions originally available to Schörner some had already been transferred to Army Group Centre, and a further three panzer, one panzer grenadier and two infantry divisions were under orders to move. Only one panzer and one panzer grenadier division and one Rumanian armoured division remained. Friessner's new command consisted of two German and two Rumanian armies and these were tactically organized into two groupings. The Dumitrescu Group in East Bessarabia commanded by Dumitrescu, the Commander of 3 Rumanian Army, was formed of 3 Rumanian Army and Fretter-Pico's 6 German Army and held the line of the lower Dniester, except where the Red Army had already gained some bridge-

[8] Guderian, *Panzer Leader*, pp. 365–6.
[9] *Ibid*, p. 365; Friessner, *Verratene Schlachten*, p. 72.
[10] Guderian, *Panzer Leader*, p. 366.

heads over that river.[11] The Wöhler Group was further to the west in Buko-vina and Moldavia and consisted of Wöhler's 8 German and Racovitza's 4 Rumanian Armies. The total strength of Friessner's force was the equivalent of twenty-three German and twenty-three Rumanian divisions numbering over 800,000 men, of which 360,000 were German.[12]

The battle readiness of the German formations of Army Group South Ukraine was by no means satisfactory. The Commander-in-Chief, Friessner, had taken over on 25 July to find that his chief of staff, Wenck, had been re-moved by Guderian to replace Heusinger in the OKH. The new chief of staff, von Grolman, did not arrive until 31 July. Fretter-Pico had taken over command of 6 German Army only at the end of July and 6 Army had also lost its chief of staff as a casualty, the replacement, Gaedcke, not arriving until 17 August. Two key commanders and chiefs of staff had therefore been at their new posts only weeks or days before the Red Army invaded Rumania. On paper the German divisional personnel strengths appeared very satisfactory. Although the services and transport of 79 Infantry Division were manned largely by *Hiwis*, the German element numbered 10,000, with infantry company fighting strengths standing at between sixty and eighty men. 15 Infantry Division had nearly 13,000 officers and men. On the other hand although many of the grenadier regiments had a strength of over 2,000 in July, of these no more than 300 men had been with the regiments in the previous May. The infantry divisions were up to strength only because most of them had been heavily reinforced in the previous two months; but not more than about fifteen per cent of the old battle experienced infantry remained, and the standard of the reinforcements was not at all satisfactory. Quite a number were over age for front line duty and many of the others had been combed out from the adminis-trative services and rearward depots; although these in due course might have made useful infantry, in August too many of them, officers included, were newly arrived and without any experience of action. Infantry divisions still had up to 6,000 horses but only 400 motor vehicles and on the march they still looked like endless *panje* columns. Shortages of guns, mortars and ammunition were widespread, and obsolete German and captured Red Army artillery and mortars had been taken into use. Although these Soviet guns had a very good performance, they lacked tractors and ammunition.[13]

The most serious of Friessner's deficiencies were in tanks and aircraft. Army Group South Ukraine had only 10 Panzer Grenadier Division and 13 Panzer Division and the latter was reduced to less than forty tanks. Of the total of 120 tanks fit for battle on 19 August more than half belonged to the Rumanian armoured division. In addition, however, the Germans did have an

[11] Fretter-Pico, formerly of 30 Corps, took over command of 6 Army from Angelis at the end of July.
[12] *OKH Kriegsgliederung* 15 July 1944; Friessner, *Verratene Schlachten*, p. 48. Friessner had twenty-one German divisions and *Korpsabteilungen* A and F, each the equivalent of a division.
[13] Rehm, *Jassy*, p. 24; Kissel, *Die Katastrophe in Rumänien 1944*, p. 29.

armoured force of 280 assault guns. Dessloch's 4 Air Fleet was responsible for the air support of Army Group South Ukraine and comprised two flak divisions and 1 Air Corps, which had a strength of less than 300 battleworthy aircraft on 19 August. Of these about fifty were first class day fighters (Me 109). Of the two flak divisions one had no experience at all in engaging tanks or other ground targets and half its gun crews were made up of Rumanians.[14]

The army group front stretched for about 400 miles, and of this sixty per cent was manned by the German divisions. Dumitrescu's 3 Rumanian Army was on the extreme right near the Black Sea on the lower Dniester, with Fetter-Pico's 6 German Army to its left covering the area of Kishinev, the capital of Bessarabia. Further to the west was Racovitza's 4 Rumanian Army in the area of Iasi and on the extreme left Wöhler's 8 German Army held the lower slopes of the Eastern Carpathians. 3 Rumanian Army had one German corps and a total of three German divisions, and of the fourteen divisions in 6 German Army all but one were German. Group Wöhler had six German divisions including the two in the flanking 17 Corps which acted as the link with Army Group North Ukraine. The grain of the country ran from north-west to south-east along the line of the many rivers and marshes, and the German supply channel and the line of communications and withdrawal ran almost due westwards, parallel to the front and across the line of the rivers, swamps and forested ridges.

Antonescu had suggested some time before that the Axis forces should evacuate Bessarabia and withdraw southwards into Transylvania onto the line of the Carpathians, lower Sereth, Focsani, Galatz and the Danube estuary. In his view, the existing line was long and vulnerable because of the grain of the country, and because, in particular, the valleys of the Sereth and Pruth ran south-eastwards from the Soviet positions north of Iasi through 4 Rumanian Army area, so offering to the enemy easy access to the rear of 6 German Army and 3 Rumanian Army on the lower Dniester. This proposal, although supported in turn by both Schörner and Friessner, had been rejected by Hitler. Failure to act on the recommendation was to cost the Germans dearly.[15] Friessner, more disturbed by the political and internal security position in Rumania than by the immediate Red Army threat to his front, proposed to Hitler that he should be given command of all the armed services and henceforth should not be called upon to provide formations to reinforce other army groups. Hitler, apparently reassured by Antonescu's visit to East Prussia on 5 and 6 August and by the tone of dispatches received from the German Ambassador in Bucharest, gave Friessner's fears little credence and caused Keitel to tell von Trotha, Friessner's chief operations officer, that the

---

[14] *Ibid*, pp. 35–7.

[15] Friessner, *Verratene Schlachten*, pp. 56–9 and 70; Guderian, *Panzer Leader*, pp. 365–6. Guderian's statement that the *Führer* said that no withdrawal should take place until the enemy attacked is rejected by Friessner, who has said that if Hitler did in fact agree with his proposals, he (Friessner) was not informed.

task of Army Group South Ukraine was to hold the front without concerning itself about the rear.[16] At the beginning of the summer the German High Command had believed that the main Soviet offensive would be made in the Balkans rather than in Belorussia, but when events proved it wrong and the attack had fallen on Busch's Army Group Centre and run its course, it was generally assumed that the Red Army had temporarily exhausted its strength and that some respite was to be expected. A fresh and major attack in the Balkans hard on the heels of the Belorussian offensive was certainly not anticipated.

By July Rumania was in close touch with the Soviet Union, and during August some elements in the Rumanian armies were already in contact with the Red Army north of the Dniester by means of nightly line crossers. As a first step to breaking with Germany came the removal of key Rumanian commanders who might put old loyalties before new ones, and preparatory measures to isolate German commanders from the control of Rumanian formations. Racovitza, the Commander of 4 Rumanian Army, who appears to have been privy to the plot, was suddenly replaced by Avramescu only a few days before the Soviet offensive started, and he returned to Bucharest to become head of the operations department of the General Staff. Neither Friessner nor Wöhler was informed. On 22 August, immediately after the Soviet attack, Avramescu was replaced by Steflea, the Rumanian Chief of Staff. Aldea, a confidant of the young King Michael, was in contact with Malinovsky's 2 Ukrainian Front from 21 August onwards.[17]

The Soviet offensive into Rumania was to be made by Tolbukhin's 3 Ukrainian Front on the left nearest the Black Sea and Malinovsky's 2 Ukrainian Front further inland, attacking jointly on a 250 mile frontage.[18] 3 Ukrainian Front had a mechanized corps and four rifle armies, Shlemin's 46, Sharokhin's 37, Gagen's 57 Armies and Berzarin's 5 Shock Army, while 2 Ukrainian Front had Kravchenko's 6 Tank Army and six rifle armies, Galanin's 4 Guards, Koroteev's 52, Trofimenko's 27, Shumilov's 7 Guards and Zhmachenko's 40 Armies, together with three independent corps. The total Red Army strength was ninety rifle divisions, six tank and mechanized corps, 1,400 tanks and SUs and 1,700 aircraft. The force was said to total 900,000 men of whom more than a third were Ukrainian recruits collected from town and homestead in the three months before June of that year. Timoshenko, whose light by then lacked lustre compared with that of Zhukov and Vasilevsky, was detached as the representative of the High Command to co-ordinate the two fronts.[19]

Malinovsky's 2 Ukrainian Front was to break through to the north-west of Iasi and thrust towards Vaslui-Falciu along the west bank of the Pruth,

[16] Friessner, *Verratene Schlachten*, p. 57.

[17] Hillgruber, *Hitler, König Carol und Marschall Antonescu*, p. 221.

[18] The military councils were: of 2 Ukrainian Front, Malinovsky, Susaikov and M. V. Zakharov as chief of staff; of 3 Ukrainian Front, Tolbukhin, Zheltov and Biryuzov.

[19] *Istoriya*, Vol. 4, pp. 260–6.

joining with Tolbukhin's 3 Ukrainian Front which was to strike from its bridgehead over the lower Dniester south of Bendery and Tiraspol to Selemet and Husi.[20] This double envelopment would encircle 6 German Army in the area of Kishinev. Thereafter 3 Ukrainian Front was to advance to the south, crossing the Danube into Dobrudja, while 2 Ukrainian Front covering its right flank moved south-west to Ploesti and Bucharest and westwards to the passes in the Carpathians and Transylvanian Alps.

The offensive was to follow the usual pattern, in that the areas held by the Rumanian formations were selected for the initial penetration in order to envelop 6 German Army which was sandwiched between the Rumanian 3 and 4 Armies. The design of the battle was in some respects similar to that which had destroyed 6 German Army at Stalingrad, but there was no intention that the Rumanians should fight. On the night of 19 August there were German reports of light signals and flares on the Soviet side being answered by the Rumanians and of an increase in the number of line crossers.

In the Soviet historical accounts of the battle there is no mention of the Soviet-Rumanian conspiracy, and there is an obvious intention to depict the campaign as a well planned and ably executed operation, a model of a victory of Soviet arms over the joint German and Rumanian armies.[21] There is a tendency, too, to overstress the comprehensiveness of Red Army deception and camouflage measures, this being taken to such lengths as to quote the number of square yards of screen sacking erected.[22] In fact the two main Soviet concentrations in the Iasi and Tiraspol areas were detected by German air reconnaissance, and in the tactical area many Soviet commanders scarcely bothered to conceal their intentions. Nightly between 18 and 20 August seemingly endless columns of Red Army trucks with lights blazing moved across the front of 79 Infantry Division sector towards the area of 5 Rumanian Cavalry Division, this movement, as it so transpired, being no deception measure.[23] Timoshenko did, however, succeed in some degree, in that he caused Friessner to believe quite erroneously that the main offensive would be made by Malinovsky between the Pruth and the Sereth, while Tolbukhin would merely pin the Axis forces across the lower Dniester.[24]

The day of Saturday 19 August was cloudless and very hot and there had been numerous Red Army company and battalion probing attacks along the whole front. During that evening the chiefs of staff of 6 and 8 Armies and 4 Air Fleet had attended a meeting at Friessner's headquarters at Slanic, and all were agreed that the main Soviet offensive was to be expected on the morrow. A staff examination had been made of a planned withdrawal known

[20] Mazulenko, *Die Zerschlagung der Heeresgruppe Südukraine*, pp. 22–3.

[21] Compare both Mazulenko, and Zhilin, *Die Wichtigsten Operationen des Grossen Vaterländischen Krieges*, pp. 461–83.

[22] Mazulenko, *Die Zerschlagung der Heeresgruppe Südukraine*, p. 43.

[23] Rehm, *Jassy*, p. 33.

[24] Friessner, *Verratene Schlachten*, p. 63; Rehm, *Jassy*, p. 33. Soviet accounts stress the activity of Berzarin's 5 Shock Army to strengthen this deception. *Istoriya*, Vol. 4, pp. 267–8.

as Operation *Bear*, but no knowledge of this could be passed on to units as the decision to implement was reserved for the *Führer*. It was felt, moreover, that the troops would fight with easier minds if kept in ignorance of plans for a possible withdrawal.

On the morning of 20 August, after a short but heavy artillery preparation, Berzarin's 5 Shock Army of 3 Ukrainian Front attempted to pin Buschenhagen's 52 Corps of 6 Army forward of Kishinev, while the left flanking Gagen's 57 and Sharokhin's 37 Armies penetrated 3 Rumanian Army. Two Rumanian divisions of von Bechtoldsheim's 29 Corps (part of 3 Rumanian Army) disappeared and Postel's 39 Corps, which was the right flanking formation of 6 Army, came under heavy attack. Much further to the west, to the left of 6 German Army, Malinovsky's 2 Ukrainian Front rapidly broke through 4 Rumanian Army defensive system north-west of Iasi. Several Rumanian divisions quitted the field, leaving German troops isolated. By the afternoon of the first day Trofimenko's 27 and Koroteev's 52 Armies had advanced twelve miles. Kravchenko's 6 Tank Army was then committed, taking Iasi and reaching open country the next day. The Germans were still convinced that the 3 Ukrainian Front attack in the east was subsidiary, but by the evening of 21 August 3 Ukrainian Front had separated 6 German from 3 Rumanian Army and the next day Shlemin's 46 Army, the left flanking formation of 3 Ukrainian Front, had encircled Dumitrescu's Rumanians and pinned them against the coast. The air onslaught by the Red Air Force was massive and overwhelming.[25]

By then it was obvious that most of the Rumanian formations were giving way without a fight, as Antonescu had to admit when he met Friessner on the second day of the attack.[26] Yet there were worse reports of the disarming or arrest of German liaison staffs and detachments by Rumanian troops, the cutting of German telephone communications and the refusal to obey any instructions unless they came from Bucharest, which meant that German orders were ignored with varying degrees of politeness. German formations were entirely unaware that the enemy was already many miles to their rear. On 21 August the men of 5 Rumanian Cavalry Division said that they had been demobilized and left the battlefield without their weapons, and 79 German Infantry Division near Iasi first became aware of the true situation by the sounds of battle and Soviet air strikes twelve miles to its rear. 3 German Mountain Division was attacked by several hundred troops in Rumanian uniforms who showed such resolution that they were suspected of being Red Army men.[27]

The Axis defence had disintegrated and on 21 August Friessner, knowing the danger to 6 Army if it did not cross to the west bank of the Pruth, has said

[25] An Army Group South Ukraine War Diary entry for 21 August reads *'Unerhört stark sei die feindliche Luftwaffe. Sie mache, was sie wolle'.*
[26] Friessner, *Verratene Schlachten*, p. 72.
[27] Rehm, *Jassy*, pp. 45–6; Klatt, *Die 3. Gebirgs-Division 1939–1945*, pp. 283–7.

that on his own responsibility he issued the withdrawal order.[28] Motorized elements with heavy flak guns, to be used in a ground role, were sent back to protect the Pruth crossings, and the next day the Rumanians were cut out of the command system when 6 Army reverted to army group control; 29 Corps was taken back from the Rumanians by 6 Army and an attempt was made to bring under command the scattered German divisions which had formerly been part of the Rumanian corps. The German 6 and 8 Armies were already falling back when the *Führer* order to begin the withdrawal arrived at Headquarters Army Group South Ukraine.[29]

On the evening of 21 August the Soviet fronts had been ordered to complete the encirclement of both 6 German Army and the German formations on the right flank of Group Wöhler, by carrying out the pincer movement directed on Husi just west of the Pruth.[30] Tank and motorized groups moved rapidly south-eastwards down the few good roads which ran along the river valleys, and they occupied much of the west bank of the Pruth about forty miles in 6 Army rear before the German withdrawal was really under way. By 23 August six corps headquarters and the main element of twenty German divisions were almost encircled in a great pocket between the Dniester and the Pruth, 6 Army Headquarters, like that of Paulus two years before, being outside the pincers. On 24 August Malinovsky's and Tolbukhin's troops joined up in the area Husi–Leovo. Since the Red Army troops continued to move rapidly both southwards and south-westwards, Friessner was faced with the triple task of defending and evacuating the numerous German military and civilian organizations in Rumania and of creating a new front to impede the Soviet advance westwards into Hungary. At the same time he had to extricate 6 Army from the pocket to the east of the Pruth. Only seventy-eight assault guns and forty-five tanks remained to him.[31]

On the evening of 23 August, having reported to the King to brief him on the war situation, Antonescu was arrested, together with Pantazi the Minister for War and Vasiliu the Minister for the Interior. The Chief of the Rumanian Secret Police, Christescu, alarmed by Antonescu's failure to return from his audience, reported his suspicions immediately to the German Embassy; von Killinger dismissed the intelligence as mischief. At ten o'clock that night, however, the King announced the formation of a new Government under Sanatescu, and broadcast to the people that the war was at an end and that Rumanian troops should cease hostilities. It was intended that German troops should be allowed fourteen days to quit the country.[32]

---

[28] Friessner, *Verratene Schlachten*, p. 69. Friessner in fact ordered the withdrawal at 1430 hours on 21 August in response to a request from 6 Army. By 1730 hours Wenck at OKH agreed with Friessner's assessment that a withdrawal to the Carpathians would be needed. *Kriegstagebuch des Oberkommandos der Heeresgruppe Südukraine, Band 4, Teil 1*, pp. 17–22.

[29] Hitler's sanction was not received until midnight 21 August. *Ibid*, p. 23.

[30] *Kratkaya Istoriya*, p. 390.

[31] *Kriegstagebuch des Oberkommandos der Heeresgruppe Südukraine, Band 4, Teil 1*, p. 27.

[32] Hillgruber, *Hitler, König Carol und Marschall Antonescu*, p. 216. Army Group South

That night was one of orders and counter-orders from the *Führer* and his two headquarters, the OKW and OKH. The two Rumanian army commanders, Steflea and Dumitrescu, appeared to be surprised by the news from Bucharest, but Friessner came to the conclusion that no further reliance could be placed on them. At 11 p.m. Friessner telephoned Hitler to inform him that Army Group South Ukraine had taken over command of all German troops in Rumania, and this action the *Führer* readily confirmed. When Friessner advised the immediate evacuation of all German troops and installations to Hungary, Hitler countered with a proposal that Friessner should arrest the King and what he called his traitor clique, and set up a suitable Rumanian General as Head of the Rumanian State. Friessner declined this course of action as impossible to carry out and was told to await the receipt of further orders in an hour. The *Führer*'s air of detachment left an impression on Friessner that the urgency and seriousness of the situation was not at all understood. Meanwhile communications from the German Embassy had been cut, but Gerstenberg could still talk on the night of 23 August on a military signal link to Kreipe, the *Luftwaffe* Chief of Air Staff, to whom apparently he made light of the affair and to whom he suggested a *Stuka* bombing attack on the capital and its occupation by the flak division from Ploesti. This conversation was relayed by the mouth of Göring to the *Führer*. During the course of that night Jodl instructed Hansen, the Commander of the German Military Mission in Rumania, to occupy Bucharest by using 5 Flak Division, and at the same time safeguard the oil pipe lines and railway. There was, said Jodl, to be no parleying with dissident Rumanians. Von Weichs, the Commander-in-Chief of Army Group F in Yugo-Slavia, who happened at that time to be with the *Führer*, was to direct a mobile group from the area of Belgrade to Bucharest. Meanwhile Friessner, the newly designated commander of all forces in Rumania, awaited further orders which, when they arrived early on the morning of 24 August, were little to his liking.[33]

On the morning of 24 August the Embassy and German buildings in the capital were ringed by Rumanian troops and at 10.30 a.m. fire was opened on buildings occupied by the *Luftwaffe*. Gerstenberg was permitted after a parley to leave the capital on the understanding that he would turn back 5 Flak Division which, under *SS Brigadeführer* Hoffmeyer, was advancing south from Ploesti.[34] This formation was eventually deterred from entering the capital by the deterioration of the situation elsewhere in the country, and by the presence in Bucharest of numbers of Rumanian tanks, including some

---

Ukraine rang Gerstenberg's office at 2050 hours that night for clarification of the position, but was told quite erroneously that Antonescu had returned. *Kriegstagebuch des Oberkommandos der Heeresgruppe Südukraine, Band 4, Teil 1*, pp. 49–50.

[33] Hillgruber, *Hitler, König Carol und Marschall Antonescu*, p. 218; Friessner, *Verratene Schlachten*, pp. 87–90.

[34] Even on his release on parole, Gerstenberg was still counselling an attack on Bucharest, saying that only a small clique were involved '*die, die Hosen voll Angst habe*'.

Tiger Mark VI. The plight of the numerous and scattered German detachments, airfields, depots and hospitals became precarious, because these relied almost entirely on Rumanian communications, labour, transport, supplies and goodwill in order to exist. There were reports of some scattered incidents of fighting between German and Rumanian troops in the rear areas. On 25 August a 150 sortie bombing attack was made on Bucharest, and this gave the Rumanians the pretext that they were awaiting when immediately following the attack the new Rumanian Government declared war on Germany.

Friessner was faced with momentous and difficult decisions. With the Rumanians in the war as enemies, the withdrawal was likely to be even more difficult. He had neither aircraft nor tanks nor reserves of troops to extricate 6 Army and 4 Corps of 8 Army from the pocket, and in this helpless situation he made the decision to abandon the encircled formations to make their own efforts to break out. He forbade Fretter-Pico, the Commander of 6 Army, to rejoin his beleaguered troops.[35] Friessner then set to work to scrape together a new force for the defence of Hungary. The army group and army headquarters were rapidly pushed westwards and soon lost radio touch with the pocket. The *Führer* meanwhile tried to control the situation from his desk. On 26 August he instructed Army Group South Ukraine to take up a new defence line from the mouth of the Danube to Galatz, Focsani and the Carpathians, the same line which had been urged on him earlier by Schörner, Friessner and Antonescu.

Inside the pocket the withdrawal had begun in good order, except that the flanking corps could not disengage. 79 Division left its positions which had taken months to prepare with great reluctance in the early hours of the morning of 21 August. Other divisions followed the next night, although a number of guns had to be destroyed on the first day as the horses could not move them in the deep mud. The pattern of the withdrawal varied according to the sector, some formations remaining as cohesive fighting groups, others losing their order and in some cases their discipline at a very early stage.

Mieth's 4 Corps, originally consisting of 79 and 376 Infantry Division and 11 Rumanian Division, all belonging to Wöhler's Group, was deployed to the west of the Pruth near Iasi and was to be driven back to the south on an axis parallel to the river. Malinovsky's southward thrusts soon outflanked the corps to the west so that Mieth became separated from 8 Army and was encircled together with 6 Army.

On 21 August 79 Division had already evacuated its original positions, taking with it the two battalions in Iasi which had been earmarked to remain in the town and hold it as a fortress. A new temporary and unsatisfactory defensive line was occupied to the south of the Bahliu stream and was held for too long in the face of Soviet probing attacks. Meanwhile the order was awaited to retire to the prepared Trajan position to the rear. In the cool clear morn-

---

[35] Friessner, *Verratene Schlachten*, p. 82; Fretter-Pico, *Missbrauchte Infanterie*, p. 135.

ing air the Carpathians could be seen nearly a hundred miles to the west, but as the sun rose in a cloudless sky the day became, like those to follow, one of scorching tropical heat. Dust and heat haze arose and observation became difficult. Although Mieth managed to keep his corps together, there was little or no contact with the flanks, and on 22 August the corps was forced back to the Trajan position, still in good order, in spite of continuous fighting with mounting casualties. Soviet infantry was showing reluctance to push home its attacks. Like other infantry divisions, 79 Division had only two grenadier regiments, and this grouping made for difficulties in the withdrawal, the lack of the third regiment being made good by the fusilier and engineer battalions fighting as infantry of the line. During that long hot day reports were received that enemy tanks were attacking vehicle columns some twenty miles back near Trestiana on the corps withdrawal axis to Husi, and enemy aircraft bombed and machine gunned all movement on roads and tracks. From 21 August onwards, except for an occasional reconnaissance plane, there was to be no *Luftwaffe* activity at all.

Since the beginning of the Soviet offensive, no German radio speech and key frequencies had been issued, and radio intercommunication was to become a haphazard affair, increasingly unreliable as distances extended. Centralized control was entirely lacking. Divisional commanders had to gain their intelligence by listening to the sounds of battle around them and by visiting their neighbours, if they could be found.[36]

11 Rumanian Division was still in existence, although it was failing to conform with 4 Corps plans, and on 22 August on Mieth's instructions, Weinknecht, the Commander of 79 Infantry Division, visited the Rumanian commander in order to co-ordinate and bring the Rumanians back into the battle. When engaged in this task the two divisional commanders were surprised by hordes of Rumanian troops, officers among them, streaming to the rear in panic-stricken flight, saying that they had been attacked by tanks, although not a single vehicle motor could be heard. The enraged Rumanian divisional commander, a holder of the German Iron Cross, laid about him with his whip in his efforts to restore the situation, but the next day he was to appear at Weinknecht's headquarters, tears in his eyes, with the news that his division had disappeared.[37]

On 23 August, in another long day of sweltering heat, the withdrawal continued, the division still having no idea that it was in the encircled pocket. During the short darkness of the previous night the flashes and the rumble and growl of artillery in the east and south-east indicated heavy fighting, but to the west there was darkness and absolute silence. To the front, however, the enemy was much bolder and he made determined attacks with tanks and lorried infantry, these being driven off by the direct fire of field guns. The

[36] Descriptions from Rehm, the second General Staff Officer (*Ib*), of 79 Infantry Division. Rehm, *Jassy*, pp. 47–55 and 130.

[37] *Ibid*, pp. 56 and 65.

obvious requirement was for 4 Corps to move south-westwards, but all roads and tracks went south-east along the valley of the Pruth. The roads were largely blocked by destroyed or abandoned vehicles, and deployment or movement off the roads was very difficult because of the wooded ridges. On 24 August the German troops were suffering badly from exhaustion and the heat, and the plight of the wounded was pitiful as they were carried for the most part untended in Rumanian farm carts, many of them delirious and many unconscious or dying. Morale, however, was still not bad, but on that day a radio message picked up by chance told them that the rear divisional headquarters and the supply and B echelons had been attacked and dispersed by Soviet armour at Husi. Thereafter any possibility of ammunition resupply ceased. For some time past the main diet for the troops had been the maize they collected from the fields.

On 25 August an order was received from corps to burn all carts and shoot unwanted horses, but this was not obeyed because of the 600 wounded with the divisional column. Elements of five infantry divisions had by then collected just to the north of Husi, almost immobile because of the blocked roads and surrounding swampland, and unable to wrest the town of Husi and the main road to the south from the Red Army troops who held them.[38]

Late on the night of 27 August, the same day that all organized German resistance ceased to the east of the Pruth, Mieth decided that his three formations, 79, 370 and 376 Infantry Divisions, should change direction and attack westwards over the Berlad River. Once over the river, all remaining equipment was to be destroyed and the divisions were to break up, small parties of troops making their way independently as best they could to the Carpathians about seventy miles away. Mieth himself had been without orders for days, there was no contact with the neighbouring corps and no knowledge of the German or enemy situation. No reconnaissance was possible. Four remaining assault guns with the two engineer companies, these being the freshest troops, were to spearhead the attack. Most of the infantry were completely exhausted and lay in stupefied sleep; if the men could only be aroused, the best that could be hoped was that they would follow the spearhead through on a broad front. The vehicles with the wounded were to follow the first wave. That same night in the early hours of 28 August Mieth's 4 Corps Headquarters was overrun by Soviet troops.

Weinknecht determined to carry out the crossing as ordered, but as it proved almost impossible to arouse the men and get them to move, this led to delays and enforced postponements so that it was daylight before any number of the troops were ready. During that night Mieth appeared entirely alone at Weinknecht's headquarters in a Rumanian farmhouse, tiredness and frayed nerves leading to a sharp dispute between the commanders. That morning the remnants of 79 Infantry Division with elements of other divisions crossed the

[38] *Ibid*, pp. 57–84 and 98–108.

Berlad under Soviet artillery and mortar fire, Mieth dying, it is thought of a heart attack, in the close quarter fighting.[39] There on the west bank of the river near a village called Chitcani on the evening of 29 August, 79 Infantry Division ceased to exist.[40] Only one man of the encircled 79 Infantry Division reached Hungary twelve days later.[41]

Elsewhere in the pocket east of the Pruth the withdrawal and attempted break-out was not so orderly. Once the movement had begun, troops converged on the routes and formations and detachments became mixed as they flooded westwards towards the crossings over the Pruth. All form of higher control was gradually lost as the mass of troops moved on, most of them still with personal weapons, the wounded carried in *panje* carts, artillery drivers and gunners mounted on artillery horses with cut traces, the few towed guns in the columns being drawn aside from time to time at the order of senior officers to engage marauding Soviet tanks. Corps commanders were to be seen but could have little control over the retreat. There were some heavy air attacks, and the increasing intensity of Soviet artillery and massed rocket fire finally drove the great body of men away from roads and tracks into the forests for shelter. Any remaining cohesion of units or detachments was broken up in the woods and the marshes and men arrived at the Pruth in scattered, often leaderless parties, only to find that Red Army detachments were on the other side of the water. Soon there were tens of thousands of German troops thronging the east bank. Buschenhagen, the Commander of 52 Corps, made some attempt to reorganize troops in small detachments under officers and non-commissioned officers and Müller, the Commander of 44 Corps, himself addressed a collection of 200 officers shortly before the break-out across the river.[42] Frequently Red Army parlementaries appeared under cover of white flags but these were usually sent back unheard or frightened off with rifle shots; but the parlementary from Tolbukhin's 3 Ukrainian Front who had come in search of the German Commanding General was to complain that he could find no one in command or with any authority.[43] By then any wounded unable to walk had been abandoned together with the heavy equipment. Some troops threw away their personal weapons and surrendered, but most were still determined on escape. Where the Red enemy attempted to

[39] Mieth had formerly in 1940 been the head of the Operations Department (*O Qu 1*) in the OKH.

[40] Army Group South Ukraine did not know what was happening inside the pocket and relied for its information on intercepted Red Army radio traffic which told them that Mieth was south-west of Husi on 29 August with about 20,000 men. Group Mieth did not disintegrate with the death of the corps commander and the destruction of 79 Division; the *Luftwaffe* reported 700 men and seventy vehicles west of the Sereth and twenty-five miles south-west of Bacau on 31 August. *Kriegstagebuch des Oberkommandos der Heeresgruppe Südukraine, Band 4, Teil 1*, pp. 102–6.

[41] Rehm, *Jassy*, pp. 96 and 115–29.

[42] Evidence of Steinmeyer (162 Infantry Division). Kissel, *Die Katastrophe in Rumänien 1944*, pp. 256–61.

[43] *Istoriya*, Vol. 4, p. 272.

bar their progress waves of desperate men, fully understanding that this was their final chance of freedom, ran down the Soviet troops through artillery and small arms fire, and crossing the Pruth, made off to the cover of the woods. For those that escaped, captured Soviet maps and Red Army weapons with their plentiful supply of ammunition became prized booty.

Many parties of troops, several General Officers among them, starting twenty or thirty men strong but being reduced as the weeks went by to groups of two or three, made their long and perilous journeys through the Carpathians to Hungary and the safety of the new German lines more than 300 miles away. Harried and hunted by the Red Army, they were sometimes assisted and sometimes betrayed by the Rumanian population, the Soviet High Command going to extraordinary lengths to net the stragglers. Aircraft were used in large numbers, road blocks were established at all focal points and woods were frequently and thoroughly swept. The civil population had been threatened with draconian punishments for withholding information, and propaganda leaflets in German were scattered from the air giving the entirely false news that Germany was already being occupied and that the war was nearly at an end, and promising fair treatment and early repatriation to all who gave themselves up. Very few men escaped to safety.[44]

When by 29 August the two pockets on both sides of the Pruth were finally cleared, the Soviet High Command was to claim 106,000 German prisoners and 150,000 German dead.[45] The actual German loss is unlikely ever to be known but it was probably not less than 180,000. The majority of these men disappeared without trace and were never heard of again. Only 29 Corps with elements of 13 Panzer and 10 Panzer Grenadier Divisions escaped.[46]

The loss of 6 Army and part of 8 Army in Rumania was in some respects a greater catastrophe than the disaster to the earlier 6 Army at Stalingrad. Paulus's army had fought for two and a half months in bitter Asiatic cold, whereas Fretter-Pico's force lasted only nine days in the hot Rumanian summer. There were many reasons for the defeat. The political, strategic and indeed the real tactical direction lay with Hitler, who on 25 August was ordering *Luftwaffe* forces, so badly needed to support the encircled troops, to bomb Bucharest. A day later, when more than three-quarters of the troops of the army group had been encircled, he was to instruct Friessner to establish

---

[44] Evidence of F. Platz (258 Artillery Regiment), Baron (44 Corps) and others. Also *Der Untergang der 15. Infanterie-Division (aus dem Entwurf einer Geschichte der 15. Inf. Div. von W. Willemer)*. Kissel, *Die Katastrophe in Rumänien 1944*, pp. 262–6, 233–9 and 267–79.

[45] Mazulenko, *Die Zerschlagung der Heeresgruppe Südukraine*, p. 103. Biryuzov quotes a figure for Axis casualties, which presumably includes the Rumanian, as 300,000, but it is significant that the enemy tanks destroyed and captured is given as only 350, and aircraft as only 400. This indicates the weakness of Army Group South Ukraine. Biryuzov, *Surovye Gody*, p. 423.

[46] The Commander of 29 Corps with his chief of staff and 'some other members' of his headquarters reached the safety of the Carpathians on 1 September on foot.

a new defensive line which had already been lost. It is doubtful whether Guderian was better informed.[47] Nearly all panzer and air reserves had previously been removed from the theatre. German political and strategic intelligence was never good and the *Abwehr* organization had been broken up or transferred to the SS after the attempt on Hitler's life. The Rumanian conspiracy appears to have been entirely unexpected except to the commanders and troops on the spot, and Army Group South Ukraine was unprepared to cope with both Soviet attack and Rumanian defection, its frontage being too long and the German troops being too widely dispersed. The joint Rumanian-German command organization was in reality unworkable, but a sufficient number of Rumanians were in control so that through defection or paralysis of will they wrecked much of the command system when the crisis arose. It is possible that the Soviet High Command was given detailed intelligence on the German order of battle and deployment before the offensive started. Fretter-Pico's 6 Army might of course have chosen to remain where it was instead of withdrawing, but this would have entailed the redeployment of many of its divisions to fill the gaps left by the Rumanians, and in the circumstances this redeployment would have been impossible to carry out. If 6 Army had stayed in its original positions it might have held out much longer and it would certainly have pinned a number of Soviet formations and inflicted on them more casualties, but the final outcome would have been the same in that the German force would have been totally destroyed. As it was, the alternative of withdrawal was chosen in an attempt to save some troops, but it was not appreciated at the time that the marching German infantry with its horse-drawn transport and guns could not possibly escape the fast moving motorized Soviet pincers, and that Malinovsky's and Tolbukhin's highly mobile tank and mechanized forces would join up west of the Pruth before the withdrawing Germans had reached the river. Only elements of the two motorized divisions escaped the net.

The decision to order Fretter-Pico, the Commander of 6 Army, to stay outside the pocket and direct the withdrawal of his army by radio may have been the wrong one. Although with some exceptions a degree of self-discipline was maintained among the encircled troops almost to the end, centralized command and control broke down in the early stages of the withdrawal. This certainly did not happen at Stalingrad. The German troops were admittedly much less experienced than those of two years before and there had been a falling off of standards, while those of the Soviet enemy, particularly in the tank and air arm, had much improved. Yet German troops were not lacking in determination and the cause of failure did not lie with the men or with their

---

[47] Guderian writing subsequent to the war was to imply, somewhat surprisingly, that a cause of the encirclement was Friessner's failure to disengage quickly and (says Guderian) retire immediately south of the Danube. *Panzer Leader*, p. 366. The Danube at Georgiu is nearly 330 miles from Kishinev in a straight line and all Friessner's troops marched on their feet.

regimental leaders. The intervention of the Red Air Force and the scale of its support were the final decisive factors in the annihilation of 6 Army.

Elsewhere in Rumania the plight of the German rear installations, the supply and service units, airfield ground staffs and the hospitals with their sick and wounded was serious, since they were threatened not only by the rapidly advancing tank and mechanized columns of the Red Army but also by the uncertainty of the attitude of the local population with whom Germany was by then at war. Long columns of fleeing vehicles crawled slowly nose to tail up the long winding single tracked roadways towards the passes of the Transylvanian Alps, crammed with wounded and German female auxiliaries and staffs, while *Luftwaffe* flak units and artillerymen and drivers formed rear and flank guards. Soviet sources claim that fourteen General Officers and 53,000 Germans, amongst whom there must have been many female nursing staff and auxiliaries, were taken prisoner during the occupation of Rumania.[48] For the Soviet troops the campaign in Rumania had become merely an occupation of east and south Rumania as far west as the Carpathians, an exercise in rapid movement to the accompaniment of a spate of horrifyingly violent excesses, including murder, rape and robbery, committed on the civil population by a capricious and often drunken soldiery. The Red Army was accompanied by 1 Rumanian Tudor Vladimirescu Division, recruited during 1943 from communist trusties and Rumanian prisoner of war camps inside the Soviet Union, and although the Soviet historians were to claim that the Royalist Rumanian troops were re-employed against the Germans and Hungarians, this rarely happened except in the initial stages of the occupation. For the most part officers were marked down for arrest and the men either transported to the USSR or disarmed and dispersed.[49] New units were raised by the usual method of the forcible recruitment of male civilians who were sent off eastwards to fight the Hungarian for the return of the Transylvanian territories removed from Rumania by von Ribbentrop's Vienna Award of 1940, the communists using what was left of Rumanian nationalist sentiment for the benefit of the Soviet Union.[50]

Constanta had been evacuated, and part of the German Black Sea naval force tried to sail up the Danube. The remainder transferred to Bulgarian ports from which about 16,000 men made their way westwards overland.

On 30 August Soviet troops took Ploesti and the next day entered the Rumanian capital, only fifty miles from the Bulgarian border. In the shelter of the German Embassy gardens about 600 Germans had assembled, including many women and children, but on 1 September the Ambassador was told to vacate the buildings. Von Killinger then shot himself. The more prominent

[48] *Istoriya*, Vol. 4, p. 279.
[49] Friessner, *Verratene Schlachten*, pp. 98–9.
[50] The Rumanian troops redeployed under the command of the Red Army included 5 Army under Racovitza, 4 Army under Avramescu (later arrested) and 1 Army under Anastasiu.

of the staff, including Gerstenberg, E. Hansen and Spalcke were handed over to the Soviet authorities and this was the fate of nearly all German troops who were taken prisoner by the Rumanians. Of the 200,000 Transylvanian Saxons and 240,000 Swabians in Rumania, only 60,000 Volksdeutsch made their way to Austria.

CHAPTER TWENTY-NINE

Hungary

When Sharokhin's 37 Army, together with 4 Guards and 7 Mechanized Corps of Tolbukhin's 3 Ukrainian Front, had reached the area of Leovo, and Koroteev's 52 Army and 18 Tank Corps had taken Husi, the railway terminus and German supply rail head, the German 6 Army was doomed. The task of the destruction of the great thirty-mile wide pocket between Kishinev and Husi was undertaken by both Soviet fronts, 3 Ukrainian Front making concentric attacks from the east and south-east, with Berzarin's 5 Shock, Gagen's 57 and Sharokhin's 37 Armies, while 2 Ukrainian Front with Galanin's 4 Guards and Koroteev's 52 Armies tried to hold and destroy the pocket as it moved to the west. By 27 August all organized resistance had ceased east of the Pruth but large numbers of the troops of 6 Army in addition to Mieth's 4 Corps were already across the river and approaching the Berlad. On 29 August the Berlad was crossed not only by 4 Corps but by a great number of men from other German divisions. The moving pocket, scattered groups totalling in all more than 10,000, moved on another forty miles crossing the Sereth south of Bacau on 31 August. These men were both desperate and dangerous, and could only be destroyed or dispersed by the intervention of Galanin's 4 Guards Army and 23 Tank Corps.[1] Even so, fighting continued until 3 September.

Meanwhile Zhmachenko's 40, Shumilov's 7 Guards, Kravchenko's 6 Guards Tank, Trofimenko's 27 and Managarov's 53 Armies, all from 2 Ukrainian Front, and elements of Shlemin's 46 Army from 3 Ukrainian Front, had no responsibility at all for the encirclement operations or for the liquidation of the pockets. These formations moved out on fan-like axes westwards and south-westwards over Rumania.

On 23 August Zhukov had been recalled to Moscow to prepare for a campaign against Bulgaria, with which country the Soviet Union was not yet at war; after a political and military briefing, he was dispatched at the end of the month to Tolbukhin's 3 Ukrainian Front Headquarters.[2] Bulgaria was directly threatened. On 26 August, fearing invasion by Russian and Turk, the Bulgarian Government ordered the disarming of the Germans withdrawing

---

[1] Mazulenko, *Die Zerschlagung der Heeresgruppe Südukraine*, p. 93.
[2] Zhukov, *Vospominaniya i Razmyshleniya*, pp. 596–7.

from Rumania; it evacuated occupied Thrace, affirming its neutrality towards the USSR and asking the USA and Britain for an armistice. This, however, did not save it. Tolbukhin's 3 Ukrainian Front, by then reduced to three rifle armies and a mechanized corps, crossed the frontier in the Dobrudja area between the lower Danube and the Black Sea and speedily occupied the whole of the country without being opposed by the Bulgarians.[3] Bulgaria declared war against Germany on 8 September and the Bulgarian armed forces, estimated to number about 450,000 men, were taken under Soviet command. Three Bulgarian armies were provided for the campaign in the Balkans.

Transylvania and the Hungarian plains are protected from the north-east and south-east by two mountain ridges which join in the form of an arrowhead facing east. The northern of these two ridges, the Carpathians, which are up to 8,000 feet in height, start as the Tatra to the south of Cracow, and run south-eastwards almost to the valley of the Sereth in Central Rumania. The southern ridge forming part of this massif, the Southern Carpathians or Transylvanian Alps, run from west to east. The mountains are steep and heavily wooded, being accessible only to mountain troops except through the twelve main passes in the north and the six main passes in the south. For this reason the ridges could be easily defended by relatively few troops, and the nature of the terrain made it generally unsuitable for the use of tank formations.

Hitler had come to the conclusion that the Red Army occupation of Bulgaria and the strong thrusts south-west over the Yugo-Slav border could presage only a Soviet main thrust to the Aegean or to the Dardanelles, and in the second week in September he explained to senior German and Hungarian officers how the moment of crisis was imminent in the Anglo-American-Soviet coalition. Soviet ambitions in the Balkans and Mediterranean would be challenged by Great Britain, and he confidently awaited the turning point in the whole war.[4] Meanwhile he believed that Hungary was safe. He had in any case decided to hold both Hungary and the Transylvanian plateau and safeguard Hungarian oil, manganese and bauxite for Germany's needs. Friessner's north wing was temporarily secure, since Wöhler's still unbroken 8 Army had fallen back on to the Carpathians facing north-east, its German mountain and Hungarian troops successfully defending the passes against Zhmachenko's 40 Army. On 30 August Friessner was ordered to secure the south flank of the Transylvania plateau and establish a new defensive line from the Iron Gate near the Danube along the ridge of the Transylvanian Alps to Brasov (Kronstadt). Hitler allocated to Friessner 2 Hungarian Army which consisted of only four divisions and some German formations which were still on the long march route from Army Group E in Greece.

---

[3] Tolbukhin's force consisted of 17 Air Army, Sharokhin's 37 Army, Gagen's 57 Army and Shlemin's 46 Army together with 4 Guards Mechanized Corps.

[4] Friessner, *Verratene Schlachten*, pp. 122–5.

HUNGARY
October 1944–February 1945

After the destruction of 6 Army this action was entirely beyond Friessner's capabilities. Long lines of vehicles, refugees and stragglers were still making their way over the Buzau Pass, while the battle group von Scotti consisting of detachments and part of 15 Flak Division tried to protect the columns. By 2 September Red Army troops were already through the exits of the Buzau passes, overcoming the resistance of the von Scotti group while cavalry and other troops had infiltrated on to the plateau by the lesser mountain paths to the north. Further to the west even the main passes could not be covered by German troops. The new 6 German Army consisted of nothing but twenty battalions, mainly detachments and stragglers hastily thrown together, and elements of 13 Panzer and 10 Panzer Grenadier Divisions. There was an acute shortage of all armament and supplies and particularly of radio equipment and motor fuels, and the railways were no longer working.[5] 6 Army's right wing was entirely unsupported and out of contact with von Weichs's Army Group F in Yugo-Slavia beyond the Danube.[6]

The Bulgarian declaration of war and the approach of Tolbukhin's 3 Ukrainian Front to Yugo-Slavia put in jeopardy the existence of Loehr's Army Group E in Greece. On the night of 8 September there were widespread partisan uprisings, and Army Group E with its headquarters in Salonika, which was in fact subordinate to von Weichs's Army Group F in Belgrade, began to evacuate the Greek islands by air preparatory to withdrawing from Greece; this air evacuation from the islands was brought to a halt by Western fighter aircraft operating from the Mediterranean and was never completed. By the end of September the withdrawal from the mainland started, and in the first week in October British troops landed in Southern Greece to become involved in a civil war as the communist ELAS and anti-communist EDES fought each other with the same bitterness and cruelty that they had shown during the Axis occupation. Army Group E then withdrew from Greece in good order to join Army Group F in Yugo-Slavia, the last troops crossing over the border on 2 November.

In Hungary Friessner was faced with a political and military situation similar to that which he had formerly experienced in Rumania. In the previous March Hungary had showed an inclination to leave the war and the Regent, Horthy, had been invited to Germany for discussions with Hitler. This was normal *Führer* diplomacy, since the absence of the Head of State simplified the armed occupation of the country. Hungary was occupied by German troops and its Minister of the Interior and many prominent citizens and members of parliament were arrested. Hungary was then treated as a German vassal; Horthy was forced to take Sztojay as his Prime Minister, the Social Democrat and Smallholders Parties were banned and the round-up and liquidation of the Hungarian Jews began. The Hungarians were caught between the barbarities of a German or a Soviet occupation. Like the Rumanians, they hoped for better terms by negotiating with the Anglo-Americans, but with the Red Army at its frontiers a crisis arose, and Sztojay's Cabinet fell on 29 August to be replaced by a Government headed by Colonel-General Lakatos.

In September there was to be further friction between German and Hungarian military leaders. The Hungarian formations which were being received by Friessner made a poor impression on him, although they were

[5] *Ibid*, p. 107; Fretter-Pico, *Missbrauchte Infanterie*, p. 137.
[6] At this time von Weichs was journeying to and from Rastenburg impressing on the *Führer* that he held a frontage of 5,000 kilometers with only ten divisions and he asked for the German withdrawal from the Balkans. Hitler, however, would come to no decision. Von Weichs. *Tagebuch*, 24 September 1944.

certainly willing and able to drive off those Rumanian troops who were making their appearance with the Red Army. Once again the Hungarians tried to insist that their own Hungarian national formations be kept separated from, and independent of, German formations, and subject to the orders of their own General Staff. After his experiences in Rumania, Friessner would not tolerate this and the new 3 Hungarian Army which was being formed under Heszlenyi was allotted a complement of German troops. Meanwhile Hungary was demanding the dispatch of five panzer divisions to the theatre as its price for staying in the war. On 20 September a German ultimatum was sent to Hungary because of Hungarian unwillingness to put its troops at Germany's disposal. Following this ultimatum, it appeared that Budapest had bent to superior force, but in fact there were other indications that much else was going on behind the scenes. On 23 September von Greiffenberg, the OKW representative with the Hungarian Government, reported to Friessner a situation which he judged to have been caused by a loss of nerve, in which the Hungarian General Staff had begun to order the withdrawal of formations and the removal of officers, often without informing the German commanders. There were reports, too, of meetings of Hungarian officers to which Germans were not admitted, these meetings often being held in the vicinity of German headquarters.[7] In fact, although Friessner did not know it, Horthy was by then in touch with the Russians, and at the end of September was to send an armistice mission to Moscow. Horthy had already aroused Guderian's suspicions, so Guderian said, at the end of August.[8]

Friessner's Army Group South Ukraine stretched south-eastwards in a long horse's head-shaped salient known as the Szekler tip, covering what was at that time Hungarian Transylvania. The salient was assailed on three sides by enemy forces. The north-east edge was held by six divisions of Wöhler's 8 Army, its frontage running along the line of the East Carpathians from near Krasnoilsk, where the army group boundary joined with 1 Hungarian Army which was the right hand formation of Army Group North Ukraine.[9] Facing Wöhler were I. E. Petrov's 4 Ukrainian Front on the extreme left and Malinovsky's 2 Ukrainian Front in the centre. The remnants of Fretter-Pico's 6 Army held the south side of the salient to the north of the Transylvanian Alps.[10] Verres's 2 Hungarian Army was concentrated about Cluj (Klausenburg) and Heszlenyi's 3 Hungarian Army was in process of forming on the far west flank. Further German formations were about to arrive. Von Weichs had been ordered to hand over Schmedes's 4 SS Police Division, a panzer

---

[7] Friessner, *Verratene Schlachten*, p. 140.

[8] Guderian, *Panzer Leader*, p. 368.

[9] In September Wöhler had a further two Hungarian divisions. *OKH Kriegsliederung* of 31 August and 16 September 1944.

[10] At the end of August 6 Army consisted of only those elements which had escaped the encirclement in Rumania, 29 Corps with part of 13 Panzer and 10 Panzer Grenadier Divisions, 153 Field Training Division and 306 Division. *OKH Kriegsgliederung* of 31 August 1944.

grenadier formation in Yugo-Slavia, and Rumohr's 8 SS Cavalry Division had been in Hungary since the beginning of the year forming another division, a *Volksdeutsch* and Hungarian 22 SS Cavalry Division. Kirchner's 57 Panzer Corps had been allocated to the theatre without having any panzer formations under command, but 23 Panzer Division was already in transit to Hungary and 24 Panzer Division was to follow.[11] By 7 September, however, Malinovsky's 2 Ukrainian Front had already crossed the South Carpathians and was in Transylvania. On 5 September an attack by 2 Hungarian Army and 8 SS Cavalry Division had had some success and had driven back 4 Rumanian Army for a short distance until the arrival of Soviet troops of Kravchenko's 6 Tank Army brought the Axis counter-attack to a standstill.

Friessner feared that his army group would suffer a double envelopment by Petrov's 4 Ukrainian Front from the north and Malinovsky's 2 Ukrainian Front from the south, using the upper and lower Theiss (Tisza) as their axes, and he ordered Wöhler to make some minor withdrawals from the south-east tip of the salient. He then visited Horthy on 9 September to propose the evacuation of Hungarian Transylvania. To this Horthy assented in general terms. Armed with this agreement in principle, Friessner flew on the next day to ask for Hitler's sanction. This was declined, partly because the *Führer* was of opinion that Hungary would not be attacked by the Red Army and partly because he insisted on keeping the manganese area of Vatra Dornei, although ores were in fact no longer mined there since the *Reich* labour organization had been withdrawn.[12] Henceforth requests by Friessner to be given freedom to use his own initiative were to be refused, and he was to suffer continual interference from both the *Führer* and Guderian in the actual conduct of operations.[13] To add to his already heavy load, as political conditions deteriorated in Budapest Friessner was to be ordered to take his panzer and panzer grenadier formations out of the line and station them in the capital.[14]

By the end of September the position of Army Group South Ukraine was unchanged except that 6 Army had been moved westwards from the area south of Cluj to the area of Oradea (Grosswardein) south-east of Debrecen. Because of the removal of his motorized formations, Wöhler was down to a strength of three German and three Hungarian divisions and Fretter-Pico had four German and six Hungarian divisions. In these circumstances, unless he were allotted a further panzer corps, Friessner did not see how a Soviet attack could be held and gave the detail of this information to Guderian in a teleprint

[11] *OKH Kriegsgliederung*, 16 September and 13 October 1944; and Friessner, *Verratene Schlachten*, pp. 259–60.

[12] *Ibid*, pp. 119–26.

[13] *Ibid*, pp. 130–1. Von Weichs was to make a similar complaint on 20 September against Guderian. Von Weichs, *Tagebuch*.

[14] Friessner, *Verratene Schlachten*, pp. 132–3 and 139.

message on 27 September. During September he had only lost 4,000 men but this was a quarter of his infantry strength.[15]

The position on both of Friessner's flanks continued to give him cause for concern. From 6 September onwards Zhmachenko's 40 Army and Shumilov's 7 Guards Army on the right flank of 2 Ukrainian Front started their slow advance against 8 German Army in the East Carpathians and as soon as the fighting started many of the Hungarian troops ran away. Meanwhile Malinovsky began to transfer his main weight from his right to his left in order to outflank the German positions from the west, so that the attack of Kravchenko's 6 Guards Tank and Managarov's 53 Armies should fall on the inexperienced and newly formed formations of 3 Hungarian Army.[16] Further to the south-west, von Weichs's Army Group F against the Adriatic appeared threatened with permanent separation from Army Group South Ukraine by the thrusts of Tolbukhin's 3 Ukrainian Front which had crossed the Bulgarian frontier into Yugo-Slavia. When Kravchenko's 6 Guards Tank and Managarov's 53 Armies changed their main axes from the area of Cluj further to the west and started to move on Szolnok and Debrecen, scattering 3 Hungarian Army before them, Army Group South Ukraine was in danger of being rolled up from the south. Meanwhile a further danger had developed on Friessner's left flank further to the north in Army Group North Ukraine sector. Following a popular uprising in Slovakia in September, officers of the two Slovak divisions forming part of the Axis forces sent word across the line at the beginning of September to Konev that they were ready to take up arms against their German masters. They were thereupon ordered to assist the Red Army in an attack on the town of Krosno and the Dukla Pass which connected South Poland with Slovakia. The attack on Dukla was made near the junction point between 1 and 4 Ukrainian Fronts by Moskalenko's 38 Army, 1 Communist Czecho-Slovak Corps which had been raised in the USSR, and Grechko's 1 Guards Army of 4 Ukrainian Front. Both fronts were exhausted and had no experienced mountain troops, but in spite of this the attack started on 8 September and three days later Krosno was captured, the defecting Slovaks taking little part as they were speedily disarmed by the Germans. The attacks were maintained against fierce German resistance, the Red Army and Czech troops moving slowly up the high ridges.[17] Army Group South Ukraine was directly threatened on both flanks and Guderian ordered it on 24 September to prepare to fall back firstly to the line of the railway Debrecen–Uzhorod and then behind the River Theiss covering Budapest. On 6 October, the same day that 1 Ukrainian Front seized the Dukla Pass in the north, the Soviet High Command launched a major offensive from the south into Hungary.

On 24 September Army Group North Ukraine had been redesignated as

[15] Teleprint 0250 hours of 27 September *1a Nr. 3723/44 g. Kdos.*
[16] *Istoriya*, Vol. 4, p. 283.
[17] *Ibid*, pp. 320–6.

R

Army Group A while Friessner's Army Group South Ukraine became Army Group South.

The Soviet offensive which started on 6 October was co-ordinated by Timoshenko and mounted by Malinovsky's 2 Ukrainian Front between Oradea and Arad, supported in the north by Petrov's 4 Ukrainian Front in the Carpathians. Malinovsky's task was to envelop and destroy Army Group South, making his main thrust in the area of Debrecen and Nyiregyhaza. 2 Ukrainian Front consisted of six armies of which one was a tank army, and two Rumanian armies, in all forty-two Soviet rifle divisions, twenty-two Rumanian divisions, 750 tanks and SUs and 1,100 aircraft.[18] On the left, the initial attack by Managarov's 53 Soviet Army and the Pliev Mechanized Cavalry Group penetrated 3 Hungarian Army to a depth of fifty miles in the first three days. On the other hand Kravchenko's 6 Guards Tank Army further to the north near Oradea was stopped almost immediately by 23 Panzer Division, and held until the Pliev Group turned back to assist it. On 8 October, Friessner warned Guderian of the danger to Wöhler's 8 Army, stating that six days would be needed to withdraw it to the Theiss.[19] Hitler could not be prevailed upon to give a decision, and meanwhile on 12 October Oradea was lost, and 76 Infantry Division which held it was almost destroyed. Finally, said Friessner, the order to withdraw was given on his own responsibility.[20] Cluj and all towns to the east were given up. On 17 October, when Malinovsky tried once more to drive northwards east of the Theiss across the Hungarian plain in order to cut Wöhler's withdrawal to the river, it became obvious that the Germans intended to hold Debrecen, Nyiregyhaza and Cop (Csap) in order to safeguard the withdrawal of 8 German and 1 and 2 Hungarian Armies. Debrecen, the third largest city in Hungary, was taken on 20 October, however, and the Pliev Mechanized Cavalry Group consisting of 1 Tank Corps and 2 Guards Cavalry Corps struck northwards to Nyiregyhaza in Wöhler's rear. The town was taken on 22 October, and the Soviet troops then pressed on to the upper Theiss having cut Wöhler's line of communications. From 23 to 29 October Breith's 3 Panzer Corps, newly arrived in the theatre, using 23 Panzer Division attacked from the west while Wöhler, with part of Tiemann's 17 and Roepke's 29 Corps, thrust westwards to meet it. This concentric attack succeeded and cut off the Soviet tanks and cavalry which had outrun their infantry support, the Germans claiming to have inflicted 25,000 casualties and destroyed 600 tanks.[21] Nyiregyhaza was retaken and Wöhler's troops, who were already under great pressure from Petrov's 4 Ukrainian Front which was advancing across the Carpathians westwards on Uzhorod, were withdrawn safely to the west bank of the upper Theiss. 4 Ukrainian Front took Uzhorod on 26 October and joined up with 2 Ukrain-

---

[18] *Ibid*, p. 380.
[19] Teleprint 2045 hours of 8 October *Ia Nr. 3899/44 g. Kdos.*
[20] Friessner, *Verratene Schlachten*, p. 136.
[21] *Ibid*, p. 153.

ian Front to the east of Wöhler's positions. Although on 27 October 6 Army consisted of four panzer and two panzer grenadier divisions, it had a tank fighting strength of only 67 tanks and 58 assault guns.[22]

The German troops who retook Nyiregyhaza and parts of the *puszta* had ample opportunity to observe the behaviour of the Soviet troops towards the Hungarian population. Women of all ages were raped and sometimes murdered. Parents were nailed to doorposts while their children were mutilated.[23] The sights seemed to have steeled the resolution of German troops in their efforts to keep the enemy out of Germany, because in Hungary German troops put up the most desperate resistance yet encountered by the Red Army.[24] The Hungarian population, on the other hand, was either apathetic or had been penetrated by communist agitators. In any event, the Hungarians had had enough of their German masters. Friessner complained with some bitterness that it was beyond his power to make the Hungarian rulers or people face up to the seriousness of the situation. Budapest itself, like the Rumanian town of Iasi shortly before the Soviet offensive of 20 August, seemed entirely at peace.

On 1 October the Hungarian delegation had arrived in Moscow to sign an armistice, but three days later the Germans became aware of the negotiations and seized all Hungarian communication centres, Hitler being better prepared in Budapest than he had been in Bucharest.[25] On 15 October Horthy broadcast to the Hungarian people that Germany was on its way to defeat and that for Hungary the war was at an end; the next day he was removed to Germany under arrest and a puppet government set up in his place. German police and panzer formations were held in readiness in the capital and in the Hungarian rear areas. These energetic measures assured German communications but they destroyed any remaining vestige of the will to fight in the Hungarian commanders and men who began to desert in large numbers, Miklos, the Commander of 1 Hungarian Army, going over to the Red Army on 18 October, having first issued a proclamation instructing all Hungarians to treat the Germans as enemies. Verres, the Commander of 2 Hungarian Army, was arrested on Friessner's orders.

It had not escaped the Soviet High Command that the Axis defences on the Theiss ran from north to south and that these, far from being strongly developed, consisted of a linear trench system lacking in any depth. There were some scattered earthworks on the line of the Danube, these also running from

[22] The divisions were 1, 13, 23 and 24 Panzer Divisions, 4 SS Police Panzer Grenadier Division and *Feldherrnhalle*.

[23] Friessner, *Verratene Schlachten*, p. 151.

[24] *Istoriya*, Vol. 4, p. 407.

[25] On 14 October 57 Panzer Corps reported that a Hungarian officer friendly to the Germans had warned that the day of crisis would come on 16 October. On 15 October the *Führer*, in spite of Friessner's protests, ordered 24 Panzer Division to return to Budapest. *Kriegstagebuch des Oberkommandos der Heeresgruppe Süd, Band 4, Teil 3, (Entwürfe)*, 1–16 October 1944.

north to south, and some attempt had been made to turn the eastern outskirts of Budapest into a defensive ring. The German formations were on the left of Army Group South, while the open right flank to the south continued to be entrusted to the very weak 3 Hungarian Army.[26] Friessner still had no firm contact with von Weichs's Army Group F in Yugo-Slavia, and the southern flank was very exposed since 2 Ukrainian Front had already crossed the lower Theiss and had secured much of the Hungarian plain between the Theiss and the Danube. Hitler, still insisting that no withdrawal should take place without a battle, commanded Friessner to fight for every foot of soil.[27] Army Group South, however, was overtaken by events. The Soviet High Command had ordered Malinovsky to attack northwards into the area between the Danube and the Theiss towards Budapest using Shlemin's 46 Army and a number of mechanized corps. On the afternoon of 29 October 3 Hungarian Army was scattered once again near Kecskemet, and 2 and 4 Mechanized Corps raced northwards behind 6 German Army positions on the Theiss. The Red Army troops had learned from their earlier losses near Debrecen and Nyiregyhaza, and their tanks and infantry were in well co-ordinated all arms groupings; notwithstanding the determined counter-attacks by 23 and 24 Panzer and 4 SS Police Panzer Grenadier Divisions, 46 Army fought its way forward to within a few miles of the outskirts of Budapest. There it was stopped.

2 Ukrainian Front regrouped and withdrew 46 Soviet Army from the outskirts of Budapest so that 8 and 22 SS Cavalry Divisions were able to follow and take possession of the ditches surrounding the capital. Budapest breathed again. The shops reopened, the tramcars started running and life returned to normal, and it was possible for the troops to leave their weapon pits and, after a short walk, climb on a tram and rattle into the city centre, just as once before they had done in Iasi. Friessner learnt, to his indignation and disgust, that Hungarian officers were leaving their troops in the line and going off home to their private houses for the night.[28] Meanwhile 20,000 workers in Miskolc, including many who were employed in armament factories, were on strike, many of the strikers adopting a surly and sometimes threatening attitude to German troops. At night Germans were fired on from the factory areas and tenements, and the Hungarian police and gendarmerie were entirely passive.[29]

After the repulse of 46 Army in the southern outskirts of the capital,

[26] In mid-October 3 Hungarian Army consisted of 8 Hungarian Corps of one armoured and two reserve divisions and 57 German Panzer Corps of one German SS panzer grenadier division and a Hungarian infantry and cavalry division. *OKH Kriegsgliederung* of 13 October 1944.

[27] At the time of the Debrecen tank battles Hitler gave Friessner freedom of manoeuvre. On 17 October however he was ordering the holding of a line in the enemy's rear before falling back on the Theiss. Friessner, *Verratene Schlachten*, p. 150.

[28] *Ibid*, p. 168.

[29] *Ibid*, p. 177.

Malinovsky regrouped his forces preparatory to resuming the offensive on a much broader front, this time to the north of Budapest, using for the purpose Shumilov's 7 Guards Army, Managarov's 53 Army, Trofimenko's 27 Army and Zhmachenko's 40 Army. The new attack began on 11 November against Wöhler's 8 Army and the left flank of Fretter-Pico's 6 Army, driving them back from the Theiss beyond Miskolc. By 26 November, when Red Army troops were already to the north of Budapest, the attacks became bogged down in the Matra Hills to the north-east of the capital, and the offensive was temporarily discontinued. It was then determined to try again to the south of Budapest, this time to the west of the Danube.

At the beginning of November, Tolbukhin's 3 Ukrainian Front, having taken Belgrade ten days before, crossed the Yugo-Slav frontier into Hungary with Gagen's 57 and G. F. Zakharov's 4 Guards Armies and 18 Tank Corps, and on 7 November began to cross to the west bank of the Danube near Mohacs, Batina and Apatin. The area was heavily flooded, and Tolbukhin did not reach Lake Balaton about sixty miles south-west of Budapest until 9 December. Meanwhile Shlemin's 46 Army had moved westwards across the Danube just to the south of Budapest, suffering heavy losses as it did so, and was transferred from Malinovsky's to Tolbukhin's command. It then took up a position on the right of 3 Ukrainian Front against what was known as the German Margareten line between Balaton and Erd, a defensive line being built to prevent the encirclement of Budapest from the south-west. On 12 December the Soviet High Command issued its directive for the encirclement of the Hungarian capital. Malinovsky's 2 Ukrainian Front with its thirty-nine rifle divisions, two tank, two mechanized and two cavalry corps, together with fourteen Rumanian divisions, was to pin the German defenders in Pest on the east bank of the river and at the same time continue the encirclement of the capital from the north. Tolbukhin's 3 Ukrainian Front with thirty-one rifle divisions, a cavalry, a tank and two mechanized corps was to attack north-wards in the area between Balaton and Budapest and, leaving the city to its right, would join hands with 2 Ukrainian Front about thirty miles to the north-west of the capital.[30] Meanwhile 40 and 27 Armies of 2 Ukrainian Front together with 4 Rumanian Army would take no part in this battle, but would outflank Budapest from the north and would enter Slovakia.

Friessner had redeployed his force to meet the new threat. Angelis's 2 Panzer Army, part of Army Group F, in an OKW theatre which received its orders through Jodl and not through Guderian and the OKH, was on 2 December put under the tactical control of Army Group South, this command arrangement resulting in difficulties and misunderstandings.[31] 2 Panzer Army held a defensive position covering the south of Lake Balaton and was primarily responsible for the security of the Hungarian oilfields in the area of Nagykanizsa. Fretter-Pico's 6 Army held the Margareten line from the Balaton to Hatvan,

[30] *Istoriya*, Vol. 4, pp. 393–4.
[31] Friessner, *Verratene Schlachten*, p. 183.

about twenty-five miles north-east of Budapest, with Breith's 3 Panzer Corps and August Schmidt's 72 Corps, Pfeffer-Wildenbruch's 9 SS Mountain Corps being inside the capital and Kirchner's 57 Panzer Corps on the extreme left. Wöhler's 8 Army with Kleemann's 4 Panzer and Roepke's 29 Corps held the area to the north-east of Budapest, with 1 Hungarian Army and Tiemann's 17 German Corps on its left flank. Friessner had the equivalent of fifteen German divisions of which four were panzer, two panzer grenadier and two cavalry.[32] A further three panzer divisions were yet to be transferred to him from other army groups.

On 5 December Malinovsky's 2 Ukrainian Front made a short but powerful attack from the area of Hatvan north-east of Budapest, using Kravchenko's 6 Guards Tank and Shumilov's 7 Guards Armies against the junction point of 6 and 8 German Armies, and in eight days made an insertion sixty miles deep, outflanking Budapest from the north and creating an excellent jumping-off position for the new Soviet offensive.

Hitler demanded not only that Budapest should be defended house by house, but the mounting of a new offensive to the west of the Danube. For this reason he had ordered the transfer to Friessner of three panzer and two infantry divisions from the army groups in the north.[33] The *Führer*, who was at this time busily engaged in preparing the Ardennes offensive, had decided on an armoured counter thrust in Hungary to be made from the area between Lakes Balaton and Velencze south-east to the Danube. Three panzer divisions, 3, 6 and 8, and two Panther battalions had been allotted for the purpose and the offensive was to be mounted by Breith's 3 Panzer Corps of 6 Army. Much of the ground across which the attack was to be launched, however, was covered by marsh, ditch and canal, and Friessner on 14 December refused to be responsible for ordering such an operation until the arrival of the frosts which would harden the ground.[34]

Meanwhile the Soviet offensive by Kravchenko's 6 Guards Tank Army and Shumilov's 7 Guards Army to the north of Budapest from the area of Hatvan along the boundary between 6 and 8 Armies continued to make progress, and on 14 December Ipolysag was taken. In an air of crisis Friessner journeyed out to see 357 Infantry Division and the Dirlewanger SS Brigade, both of which had given ground. When he arrived at Dirlewanger's formation, the same brigade which had been responsible for many of the terrible atrocities in Warsaw a few months before, he was amazed at the situation with which he was confronted. Dirlewanger himself, whom Friessner describes as an arrant adventurer, was calmly sitting at a desk with a monkey on his shoulder. Neither he nor his staff could throw much light on the battle situation. The SS troops, in Friessner's words, were nothing but an indisciplined and unruly mob.

---

[32] *Ibid*, p. 260; also *OKH Kriegsgliederung* 26 November 1944. This does not include 2 Panzer Army which on 26 November commanded motley Croat and SS formations.
[33] Friessner, *Verratene Schlachten*, pp. 185 and 193.
[34] Friessner, *Verratene Schlachten*, p. 193.

Hearing that Dirlewanger was proposing to withdraw, Friessner ordered him to remain. Later that evening, returning from a visit to 24 Panzer Division, Friessner called again on the Dirlewanger Brigade to see that his orders were being carried out and found that it had gone. Only narrowly did he himself escape falling into enemy hands.[35]

One of the panzer divisions earmarked for the offensive in the area of Balaton was committed to the north of Budapest in an effort to check the Soviet offensive, but Friessner then came under continuous and heavy pressure from Guderian, who was in fact merely the *Führer*'s mouthpiece, to begin the 3 Panzer Corps operation to the south of Budapest. Guderian was so persistent that the exchanges became heated, and Friessner flew to Zossen on 18 December to explain personally why the attack should await the coming of the frost, Friessner using as an argument Breith's experience in the mud of the earlier Cherkasy battles. Guderian and von Bonin, the Chief of the Operations Department, appeared to be in full agreement with him. Friessner also raised the matter of the *Führer* order commanding the house by house defence of the city of Budapest, most of which lay on the east bank of the Danube, the defence of this bridgehead requiring no fewer than four divisions. The city was not ready for a siege, the shops were open, life went on as usual, with preparations being made for Christmas, and there had been little bombing and shelling. If the city had to be held, the civilian population should, in Friessner's view, be evacuated. All this Guderian promised to represent to the *Führer*.[36] Friessner returned to Hungary tolerably satisfied.

The next day, however, brought a further decline in German fortunes. The 8 Panzer Division counter-attack against Kravchenko's 6 Tank Army to the north of Budapest had failed and the men of Dirlewanger's Brigade had run away or given themselves up. The *Führer*, Guderian and the OKH took over the conduct of the tactical battle. 3 and 6 Panzer Divisions (part of Breith's 3 Panzer Corps to the south of Budapest) were ordered to leave all tanks, assault guns, armoured personnel carriers and self-propelled artillery in the Balaton Margareten line area, while the dismounted infantry, separated from their tanks, vehicles and gun support, were to be committed to the north of Budapest against Kravchenko's tank army, this remarkable order coming, as Friessner said, by word of mouth of Guderian, the expert on armoured warfare. So it came about that when 4 Guards Army and 46 Army attacked 3 Panzer Corps a few days afterwards, using large numbers of infantry formations to cross the wet and ditch-intercoursed ground, they had no difficulty in sweeping round the flanks to the rear. 3 Panzer Corps, without infantry, could not stop them.[37]

On 20 December the joint offensive by 2 and 3 Ukrainian Fronts to encircle Budapest was resumed. On the first day, 6 Guards Tank Army attacked to the

[35] *Ibid*, pp. 194–5.
[35] *Ibid*, pp. 196–7.
[37] *Ibid*, pp. 198–201; Fretter-Pico, *Missbrauchte Infanterie*, pp. 141–3.

north of Budapest and penetrated twenty miles. There was some delay there-after due to German counter-attacks between the Ipel and Hron, but by 24 December 2 Ukrainian Front reached the Danube north of Esztergom (Gran). To the south-west of Budapest, 3 Ukrainian Front had been engaged in heavy fighting against 6 German Army when Fretter-Pico committed his reserves in the area of Szekesfehervar on the second day. The Soviet armoured force, 7 Mechanized and 18 Tank Corps, were put into action on this and the following day, and on 23 December achieved a breakthrough sixty miles wide. By 26 December 18 Tank Corps reached Esztergom and joined up with 2 Ukrainian Front. Meanwhile Friessner had been forbidden to withdraw troops from Budapest or from 2 Panzer Army to restore his broken line. Four German divisions and one Hungarian division were entrapped inside Budapest.[38] On 21 December Friessner and Fretter-Pico were relieved of their commands and replaced by Wöhler and Balck.

The *Führer* then ordered 4 SS Panzer Corps under Gille to move from Army Group Centre to Budapest.[39] Gille's corps, coming by rail from Bratislava, detrained near Komarno about sixty miles north-west of Budapest and together with 96 Infantry Division went straight into action with little artillery support, and on 2 January drove back 31 Guards Rifle Corps of 4 Guards Army about twenty miles.[40] Shumilov's 7 Guards Army and Kravchenko's 6 Guards Tank Army counter-attacked in the SS corps flank but were them-selves brought to a halt. Gille finally broke off the attack near Perbal, not more than fifteen miles from the outskirts of Budapest. Further to the south an attack by Breith's 3 Panzer Corps from the area of Mor towards Budapest had little success and advanced only four miles in four days fighting, Breith losing sixty-eight of his eighty fit tanks.[41] Meanwhile 4 SS Corps withdrew, and marching back to Komarno it entrained once more and was shunted off westwards. This apparently deceived the Red Army scouts, and when a few days later the SS Corps suddenly reappeared about forty miles to the south near Lake Balaton, it attacked 135 Rifle Corps on the night of 17 January and nearly destroyed it. The SS tanks then advanced rapidly eastwards, reaching the Danube at Dunapentele on 19 January and cutting off most of 3 Ukrainian Front from its rearward support. Although 4 SS Corps was still a long way from Budapest, Tolbukhin was, as the Soviet historian has admitted, in a serious situation.[42] The SS Corps was yet to improve its position, when, turn-ing northwards, it moved up the west bank of the Danube reaching a point only twelve miles from the encircled garrison. Pfeffer-Wildenbruch com-manding 9 SS Mountain Corps inside Budapest, if he had been ordered to do

---

[38] 13 Panzer Division and *Feldherrnhalle* (panzer grenadier) and 8 SS and 22 SS Cavalry Divisions.
[39] Gille's corps consisted of *Totenkopf* and *Wiking*.
[40] *Kriegstagebuch des OKW*, Vol. 4, p. 977; *Istoriya*, Vol. 4, pp. 398–9.
[41] *Kriegstagebuch des OKW*, Vol. 4, p. 1004.
[42] *Istoriya*, Vol. 4, p. 401.

so, could have broken out, but this solution was of no interest to Hitler, who wanted only the recapture of the capital. By then 4 SS Panzer Corps had lost momentum and its flanks were insecure; from 27 January onwards it was attacked by 2 Ukrainian Front which had deployed 23 Tank, 1 Guards Mechanized and 5 Guards Cavalry Corps covering the south-west approaches to Budapest, and by 3 Ukrainian Front which had been given Skvirsky's 26 Army Headquarters to concentrate and command the various scattered formations between the Balaton and the Danube. On 2 February 26 Army, by then commanded by Gagen, attacking northwards, restored contact with 4 Guards Army to the west of Budapest near Adony. By 7 February 4 SS Panzer Corps had withdrawn.

Hope had gone for the German force inside the capital. Some attempt at air supply had been kept up over the period of the encirclement and the German Navy had run a supply vessel down the Danube only to beach it in the shallows. The Hungarians had deserted in large numbers but the Germans fought grimly on from the buildings and sewers. From 1 February the ration was down to seventy-five grammes of bread a day, and Red Army parlementaries who came to offer surrender terms were, according to the Soviet account, shot down.[43] On the night of 11 February a force of about 16,000 Germans who were still fit to fight and walk, leaving their wounded with the Papal Nuncio, attacked in a north-westerly direction towards Vienna. Making some progress, they quitted the built-up area and advanced about twelve miles, reaching the township of Perbal, close to where Gille's 4 SS Panzer Corps had been stopped in its first attempt to get into the capital. There the German force was almost totally destroyed, three divisional commanders being among the killed. Only a few hundred men reached the safety of the German lines.[44]

[43] *Ibid*, pp. 403–4; *Kriegstagebuch des OKW*, Vol. 4, p. 977.
[44] *Istoriya* says that 33,000 prisoners were taken inside Budapest. The *Kratkaya Istoriya*, p. 417, claims that 138,000 'Hitlerites' were taken prisoner, this term presumably covering Hungarians.

CHAPTER THIRTY

War at Sea

The Soviet Navy took second place to the Red Army and in comparison was rated of very minor importance. Up to 1935 little naval construction had been carried out as the requirements of the army and air force were given priority over those of the fleet. From 1935 onwards large numbers of submarines and light torpedo craft were constructed, so that by 1941 the Soviet Fleet consisted of three battleships (two of which had been launched prior to the First World War), seven cruisers, fifty-nine destroyers, 269 torpedo-boats and 218 submarines, together with a large number of minelayers, minesweepers and auxiliary vessels.[1] Imposing though the Soviet Navy was in terms of numbers, the standard of its equipment, training and efficiency was very much below that of the German Navy.

The designation of the ranks of Soviet officers and ratings was similar to that used by the navies of other sea powers, but the naval commissars had been seconded from the Red Army and used army commissar ranks.[2] The naval air arm, numbering over 2,500 aircraft, was in reality a detached branch of the Red Army Air Force based on airfields ashore, its personnel holding Red Army ranks and wearing Red Army uniform. Marines did not form an integral part of the Soviet Navy, although large numbers of officers and ratings were later to be formed into the marine infantry brigades which took a prominent part in the land fighting.

In 1941 the Soviet Navy was divided into four widely separated commands. The three largest were the Baltic Red Banner Fleet based on Tallinn (Reval), the Black Sea Fleet based on Sevastopol, and the Pacific Fleet based on Vladivostok. The fourth, the Northern Fleet, centred on the ice-free port of Polyarny (near Murmansk), was much smaller than the other three. In addition to the White Sea Fleet based on Archangel, which was later downgraded to a flotilla, there was the inland water Pinsk Flotilla operating in the Pripet Marshes and on the Dnieper, this being based on Pinsk and Kiev, and the Danube Flotilla centred on Ismail.[3]

In June 1941 the Northern Fleet under Golovko consisted of only eight

---

[1] *50 Let Vooruzhennykh Sil SSSR*, p. 240.
[2] From 1942 onwards the commissars adopted naval officers' ranks.
[3] *Istoriya*, Vol. 3, p. 472. There was also a Dvina Flotilla.

destroyers, fifteen submarines and fewer than twenty other light vessels, supported by over a hundred aircraft.[4] Later in the summer a further five submarines arrived from the Far East Fleet. The White Sea Flotilla, which was based on Archangel and which was later put under the command of the Northern Fleet, consisted of about twenty torpedo-boats and minesweepers.[5] In the autumn and early winter of 1941 the Northern Fleet had some freedom of operational movement in the coastal waters off North Norway and Finland, since Hitler's strategy was based on the taking of Murmansk and the cutting of the Murmansk railway by ground operations from Finnish territory, and for this reason insignificant *Luftwaffe* and German naval forces had been allocated to the theatre.[6] The Northern Fleet bombarded coastal areas behind the German mountain corps and landed detachments from the sea.[7] Some attacks were made on the German coastal shipping operating off the Norwegian and Finnish shores, but the attacking submarines operated without enterprise or skill and achieved little success.[8]

In 1941 and early 1942 Murmansk and Archangel were to assume a special importance as the ports of destination for incoming Anglo-American material aid, and were to hold this importance until the Japanese Fleet withdrew from the Indian Ocean after Easter 1942.[9] The clearing of the southern waters allowed the opening and development of the overland entry into the USSR through Iran, and the volume of traffic through Iran increased when the Mediterranean and Suez Canal were opened to British and United States shipping; eventually the Persian corridor became as important as the northern sea route.[10] The third point of entry, that into the Soviet Far East Maritime Provinces by the Pacific sea route, could not be used by United States vessels after December 1941 when Japan first came into the war. Soviet cargo ships

[4] Soviet figures given in Pitersky, *Die Sowjet-Flotte im Zweiten Weltkrieg*, p. 109.

[5] The military council of the Northern Fleet was Golovko, Nikolaev and Kucherov (after February 1943, Fedorov) the second and third named being the political member and the chief of staff respectively. Stepanov was the Commander of the White Sea Flotilla (there being no military councils below the level of fleet).

[6] The *Fliegerführer Lofoten und Kirkenes* had under command thirty-three *Stuka* Junker 87, twenty-one Junker 88 twin-engined bombers and twelve Messerschmitt fighters. The German Admiral Polar Coast on 22 June had only a dozen light and auxiliary vessels, and until July and August no destroyers and no U-boats.

[7] Vainer, *Severnyi Flot v Velikoi Otechestvennoi Voine*, p. 42.

[8] The Soviet claims for the Northern Fleet submarine sinkings for the whole of 1941 total 95,000 tons of shipping. Dmitriev, *Atakuyut Podvodniki*, p. 48. Rohwer says that only 28,000 tons of Axis shipping were lost in 1941 off these coasts of which 6,000 tons were sunk by Soviet submarines, the remainder falling to British submarines. In 1941 a total of only 52,000 tons of shipping were sunk by the forces of the USSR of which 5,000 tons were sunk by submarine and 34,000 tons by mine. Roskill, *The War at Sea*, Vol. 3, Part 3, p. 474.

[9] Murmansk was the preferable port to use since it was ice-free throughout the year and was a shorter sea run with a quicker turn round than Archangel, which had to be kept open in winter by ice-breakers. On the other hand it was close to German-occupied Norway and Finland and was very vulnerable to air and sea attack.

[10] The southern route was of particular importance as the main point of entry of the great number of United States motor trucks dispatched to the Soviet Union.

and United States freighters sailing under the Red Flag continued to use the Pacific link, but the route was slow, particularly since all supplies had to be sent by rail across the breadth of Siberia and Central Russia. Not until 1943 did the volume of supplies flowing into Vladivostok exceed that unloaded at Murmansk and Archangel.

In 1941 and 1942, however, the northern sea route was the major route into the Soviet Union. The sea transports were brought in by convoys controlled and protected by the British Navy, United States warships forming part of some of the covering forces. The contribution of the USSR to the protection of these convoys was very small, although theoretically the operational area of responsibilities of the Northern Fleet was to be extended to the western half of the northern sea route. Red Air Force aircraft operated intermittently above the estuaries. Few Soviet cargo ships formed part of the convoys, although a number did sail independently until, eventually in 1942 and 1943, they were transferred to the Pacific route. The early convoys to Russia arrived without loss or major damage.

In the late autumn of 1941 Hitler's attention was drawn to the area as the fear of a British landing in Norway took hold in his mind, and during the winter of 1941–2 he determined to interrupt the northern supply route to Russia.[11] The *Luftwaffe* was to strengthen its forces in North Norway so that by mid February they stood at 175 aircraft, and the German Navy was to concentrate both underwater and surface vessels in the area. In January the new German battleship *Tirpitz* arrived in Trondheim and was joined a little later by the pocket battleship *Admiral Scheer* and the heavy cruiser *Admiral Hipper*, this force being further increased by light cruisers and a complement of destroyers and submarines.[12] Thereafter the convoys came under attack from both the *Luftwaffe* and the German Navy, and the losses in Allied warships and transports became heavy in the period of full daylight in the summer of 1942.[13] The greatest destruction was caused by air and submarine attack.

A British Military Mission, including a naval section, had been sent to Moscow, with naval detachments at Murmansk, Archangel and in the Black Sea, and these, together with the Royal Navy escorts which brought in the convoys, had opportunities closely to observe the Soviet Navy in action. There were, however, fundamental differences between the British and Soviet Navies, and difficulties arose in establishing a basis for co-operation and mutual understanding. The Soviet officers, and particularly the commissars, were suspicious and on occasion deliberately obstructive. Soviet officers understood no English and very few of the British naval mission spoke Russian.

[11] Hubatsch, *Hitlers Weisungen für die Kriegführung*, pp. 156 and 163 (Directives 36 and 37); Doenitz, *Memoirs*, pp. 206–11.
[12] Roskill, *The War at Sea*, Vol. 2, Chapter 5.
[13] Churchill, Vol. 4, *The Hinge of Fate*, pp. 228–247. Of the 300 vessels which were dispatched in 1941 and 1942 fifty-three were lost at sea and eight warships sunk. Roskill, *The War at Sea*, Vol. 3, Part 2, pp. 432–3.

It is doubtful whether many of the British understood or could make allowances for the peculiarities of the Soviet military-political system or of the Slav temperament. Nor did the protests which these British officers made to London concerning the Soviet attitudes and actions always receive the support which they deserved from the British Government or Foreign Office. In consequence, it is understandable that British observers had a low opinion of the Soviet Navy and that Soviet sailors were perhaps not always given sufficient credit for making good use of their inadequate resources.

In the British view the Soviet Northern Fleet played a very minor role, since only five Soviet destroyers sailed with the convoys compared with the participation of 203 British, United States and Polish warships. The Soviet historical account of the activities and achievements of the Northern Fleet, on the other hand, is far removed from the contemporary descriptions given by the British Admiral Miles and his staff and liaison officers; Soviet historians go as far as saying that the Soviet Navy fought this war in Arctic waters *together with the navies of the Anglo-Americans*, the impression being given that the success of the reception of the convoys was due largely to the efficiency of the Soviet air and sea support.[14]

Admiral Miles, who headed the British Military Mission after the departure of General Macfarlane, was to say that the Soviet Navy had an inefficient hydrophone submarine detecting gear, no magnetic mines, no concept of degaussing, no radar and no idea how to sweep magnetic or acoustic mines. Soviet naval personnel appeared to suffer from an inferiority complex or alternatively to have a completely misplaced confidence in their own technical ability. They disliked monotonous and routine work and soon became bored with minesweeping and escort tasks.[15] According to another British account, unlike some of the crews of the Soviet cargo vessels who showed great fortitude on the Arctic convoys, many of the naval complements who took part in escort duties seemed to be happier in harbour than at sea. Their sea-going efficiency was said to be poor. On occasions a few Soviet warships met the convoys outside the Kola estuary but Soviet escorts were usually sent on with that part of the convoy which was destined for Archangel, since the British felt that Soviet warships would benefit by a spell at sea, and on such occasions the senior Soviet officer, regardless of his rank, was always put under British naval command.[16] The British could place little reliance on Soviet efforts.

[14] For example, *Istoriya*, Vol. 3, p. 414; Golovko, *With the Red Fleet*, pp. 94 and 103. Golovko made many extravagant claims, including the torpedoing of the *Tirpitz* by the submarine K21 and the sinking between June 1941 and June 1942 of 135 enemy ships of 583,000 tons displacement. During this year he also gave the Northern Fleet the credit for the safe arrival in convoy of 177 transport ships *with their 133 Anglo-American escorting warships*. In eighteen months of war until the end of 1942, all Soviet fleets and airforces sank in fact a total of 120,000 tons. Roskill, *The War at Sea*, Vol. 3, Part 2, p. 474. It is not improbable that in time all mention of Anglo-American naval activity will be omitted from Soviet accounts.

[15] Saunders, *The Soviet Navy*, pp. 76–7.

[16] *Ibid*, pp. 77–8.

German submarines lay in wait off the estuary of the Kola and one-fifth of the Anglo-American shipping losses occurred off these North Russian coasts; according to the British accounts, the Soviet Navy and its air arm achieved little against the enemy submarine and bomber force, in spite of constant Allied pressure to keep the area clear.[17]

By 1943 the Soviet Northern Fleet was said to include nine destroyers, twenty-two submarines, sixteen minesweepers, twenty submarine-chasers and six torpedo-boats, together with no fewer than 300 aircraft.[18]

The Baltic Red Banner Fleet had been based originally on Kronstadt, but in 1940 the main base was moved forward to Tallinn (Reval), Kronstadt being retained as a rear support base. Lighter squadrons were deployed forward outside the Gulf of Finland at Leepaja (Libau), Windau and Ust-Dvinsk (Dünamünde).[19] The Baltic Fleet was commanded by Tributs and is said to have consisted of two old battleships, two cruisers, forty destroyers, six torpedo-boats, over 100 motor torpedo-boats and ninety-three submarines.[20] In June 1941 the German Navy was almost fully committed in the war against Great Britain and had only five U-boats, forty motor torpedo-boats and ten minelayers available for operations in the Baltic.[21] The German naval forces originally formed part of the Baltic Command under Guse, but two further Naval Headquarters C and D were established to take over static organizations and the coastal defence of the occupied Baltic coast. In November 1941 Headquarters C was disbanded and D took over its tasks, becoming a sea-operational command with the new designation *Ostland*; its commander was Burchardi, with his headquarters at Tallinn.[22] The West Baltic and later the whole Baltic command eventually became the responsibility firstly of Schmundt and then of Kummetz, the Commander-in-Chief Baltic, with his headquarters at Kiel.

The supremacy of the *Luftwaffe* and the bold handling of the German naval craft caused considerable Soviet casualties, and the German Navy, with the assistance of the Finns, laid a mine barrage system and a steel net across the mouth of the Gulf of Finland in order to prevent the enemy emerging into the more open waters of the Baltic Sea. In September and October the Red Army garrisons on the Baltic islands were cleared, and the Soviet Union withdrew from its bases on Hanko and Odensholm at the entrance to the Gulf of

[17] See also Roskill, *The War at Sea*, Vol. 2, pp. 119, 127–8 and 134.

[18] *Istoriya*, Vol. 3, p. 407.

[19] *Ibid*, Vol. 1, p. 472.

[20] The military council of the Baltic Fleet was originally Tributs, Yakovenko and Panteleev and later Tributs, N. K. Smirnov and Rall (after February 1943, Arapov), the second named being the political member of the council.

[21] An indication of the relative importance in the German mind of the naval war against the Soviet Union can be drawn from Doenitz's *Memoirs*. Of the 490 pages in the English translation two and a half pages are allocated to the Baltic and four and a half pages to the Black Sea.

[22] In November 1941 the Baltic Station comprised four commands; West Baltic, Pomerania, East Baltic and Ostland.

Finland. Kronstadt and Leningrad became the main naval bases with a forward base on the Island of Lavansaari. In December the Gulf of Finland froze, and Finnish troops crossed the ice to attack the island naval bases and the warships lying off Kronstadt, the crews of which were obliged to defend themselves with small arms, wire and counter patrols.[23]

In April 1942, after the ice had broken up, the Soviet Navy swept mine channels from Leningrad to Kronstadt and then on to the forward base of Lavansaari, and began submarine training in the restricted waters to the east of the barrier. From June onwards, determined efforts were made to penetrate the German-Finnish mine barrage, and numbers of Soviet submarines broke out into open Baltic waters. However, due to the poor standard of crew training and equipment, they achieved little and of the 1,738 Axis vessels which sailed in Baltic convoys in 1942 only twenty-six were sunk, the Germans claiming the destruction of ten Soviet submarines during this period.[24] The Royal Air Force, and in particular the operations of Bomber Command, caused more disruption to German shipping and U-boat training in the Gulf of Danzig than did the Soviet Baltic Fleet.[25]

During 1943, however, the situation in the Eastern Baltic began to change radically. The Soviet naval strength stood at two battleships, two cruisers, eleven destroyers, thirty-three submarines, fifty-seven minesweepers, twenty-nine large and seventy-five small motor torpedo-boats; the naval air arm was increased from 280 to a total of about 880 aircraft.[26] This addition of air power was decisive. German patrol vessels and minelayers, many of which were converted fishing vessels, lacked both armament and speed and could no longer patrol the mined and netted areas in daylight because of the heavy air attacks. Soviet craft began to sweep and penetrate the mine barrage. In 1944 the increasing Red Air Force activity, the capitulation of Finland, and the Red Army offensives in the Baltic States created the situation which forced the German Navy to abandon the Gulf of Finland and the Eastern Baltic. The bulk of the Soviet Baltic Fleet remained in Kronstadt and Leningrad supporting the land operations by gun fire, while the Germans used such heavy ships as were still in commission, together with destroyers and torpedo-boats, to form off-shore battle groups under Thiele and Rogge to give artillery support to the German ground forces in the Baltic States.[27]

In the late winter and early spring of 1945 Germany still controlled the Baltic waters off Kurland and East Prussia, and unescorted German transports plied in home waters with only minor interference from Soviet submarines. It is possible that the main Baltic Red Banner Fleet was still immobile in the ice-covered Gulf of Finland, and it is probable that in any case it could not

[23] *Istoriya*, Vol. 3, pp. 418–9; Malaparte, *The Volga Rises in Europe*, pp. 212–3.
[24] Saunders, *The Soviet Navy*, p. 62 (Rohwer).
[25] *Ibid*, p. 66; Roskill, *The War at Sea*, Vol. 2, p. 393; Vol. 3, Part 1, p. 96; Part 2, pp. 140 and 269.
[26] *Istoriya*, Vol. 3, pp. 416–7.
[27] Doenitz, *Memoirs*, p. 399.

have put to sea because its warships lacked crews since great numbers of officers and ratings had been transferred to the Red Army. Whatever the reason, the main fleet remained inactive in the Gulf of Finland. Soviet air acitivity, however, was formidable in the Baltic area by 1945. In the last eight months of the war thirty-three German ships (102,000 tons) were destroyed in the Baltic by submarine, whereas fifty-seven merchantmen and thirty-four warships were sunk by aerial bomb or torpedo.[28] In spite of this, between January and May more than a million and a half German troops and civilians were safely evacuated by sea from Kurland, East and West Prussia and Pomerania.[29]

In 1941 the Black Sea Fleet commanded by Oktyabrsky was said to consist of one old battleship, five cruisers, fifteen destroyers, possibly as many as fifty submarines and numerous motor torpedo-boats and light craft.[30] Against this formidable force the Rumanians could deploy only four destroyers, three torpedo-boats, one submarine and some coastal vessels.[31] In the early days of the war the Black Sea Fleet enjoyed such naval superiority as the *Luftwaffe* would allow, and it did in fact carry out operations against enemy sea traffic besides bombarding German and Rumanian positions and installations on the Black Sea coast; it also covered the successful evacuation of the Red Army garrison and some of the civilian population from Odessa, and took off a number of troops from the Crimea. During 1942 the Soviet Union lost the naval base of Sevastopol and the use of Novorossisk so that all vessels had to be based on the Caucasian ports of Tuapse, Poti and Batum. The possession of the air and naval bases in the Crimea gave the Germans almost undisputed naval supremacy in the Black Sea.

The German Navy brought about 500 small cargo craft and light war vessels, including six small Type IIB submarines of about 250 tons displacement, up the Elbe to Dresden from where they were transported by road and refloated at Ingolstadt on the Danube. They then made their way down to the Black Sea to complete their 1,500 mile inland journey. In all twenty-three minesweepers, sixteen motor torpedo-boats, fifty landing craft and twenty-six submarine-chasers were transported by this route.[32] The Axis naval forces from 1943 onwards were under Fricke, the Commander-in-Chief Naval Group South in Sofia with a subordinate Admiral Black Sea, Kieseritzky (from November 1943, Brinkmann). The naval organization consisted of four main commands, Caucasus at Kerch, Crimea at Yalta (later Sevastopol), Ukraine at Mariupol (later Odessa) and the Rumanian Training Command at Constanta. In 1943 the German naval force was made up of six U-boats, a motor torpedo-boat

[28] Saunders, *The Soviet Navy*, p. 65 (Rohwer).

[29] Doenitz, *Memoirs*, p. 465. Doenitz puts the figure at over two million.

[30] The military council of the Black Sea Fleet was Oktyabrsky (after May 1943, Vladimirsky), Kulakov and Eliseev.

[31] See also Pitersky, *Die Sowjet-Flotte im Zweiten Weltkrieg*, p. 296.

[32] Meister, *Der Seekrieg in den Osteuropäischen Gewässern*, p. 232; Doenitz, *Memoirs*, p. 388.

flotilla of thirteen motor torpedo-boats, two minesweeping flotillas of twenty-two minesweepers, a boom flotilla, three flotillas of submarine-chasers and some landing craft and convoy flotillas. The Rumanians had four destroyers, three torpedo-boats, three U-boats, three gun-boats, three minelayers, seven monitors and fifteen fast motor boats.[33]

Among the duties of the British liaison officer with the Black Sea Fleet was that of providing intelligence as to the movement of Axis shipping and the notification of Mediterranean meteorological forecasts. In vain did he urge the Soviet commanders to take more offensive action against the German and Rumanian shipping plying along the coastal waters off the Ukraine, and he was invariably told that Soviet war vessels would not put to sea without air cover.[34] The opinion of these British naval officers was that the Black Sea Fleet was inadequately equipped and trained.[35] By 1943 the Black Sea Fleet had four cruisers, eight destroyers, twenty-nine submarines and sixty-seven motor torpedo-boats, with an air arm of about 280 aircraft.[36] Yet at this time von Kleist evacuated the Kuban, and 17 German Army was brought back across the Straits of Kerch, the passage being made without disruption by the Soviet Navy. In the following April the larger part of the Axis troops in the Crimea were evacuated by sea, once again without serious interference, except by aerial bombing in the closing stages of the withdrawal.

There were many reasons for the lack of enterprise shown by the Soviet Navy, and these are by no means attributable to lack of marine experience or naval tradition. In the Second World War the equipment of the Soviet Navy was obsolete and of poor quality, and the standard of command, the seamanship and the technical training were very much below that of the German Navy. Successful commanders of warships, particularly of submarines and smaller craft, must necessarily possess both initiative and self-reliance as well as determination, since they operate for long periods on their own. These qualities were certainly not markedly apparent in Soviet naval officers at that time. Too often they were passive and avoided responsibility, and sometimes, according to the description of the British naval officers who worked with them, they appeared to be overshadowed by their commissar colleagues. Decisions of even minor importance were referred back to Moscow.

Some German sources, in noting the lack of offensive spirit shown by Soviet naval commanders in the Second World War, have speculated as to whether it was Stalin's intention to husband his warships in order to be in a better position to challenge the naval supremacy of the Anglo-Americans after the war.[37] This was certainly not the case. It is more probable that the

[33] Hillgruber, *Die Räumung der Krim*, p. 119.

[34] *Istoriya*, Vol. 3, pp. 426–7; Saunders, *The Soviet Navy*, pp. 79–82 (from Garwood, the British Liaison Officer in the Black Sea).

[35] *Ibid*, p. 82.

[36] *Istoriya*, Vol. 3, p. 425.

[37] For example Pickert, *Vom Kuban-Brückenkopf bis Sevastopol*, pp. 57–8.

sea war was of no interest to the dictator, except that he wanted war supplies delivered to Murmansk and Archangel. Since the Soviet Union was shouldering nearly all the land fighting in 1941 and 1942, it is more likely that, even if the Soviet Navy had the ability and means to undertake the task, which it had not, he saw no reason why the USSR should exert itself to sweep the Arctic Sea of German bombers and U-boats for the benefit of allies whom he deemed to be well provided with both warships and aircraft. In the Arctic, the Baltic and in the Black Sea the key to the control of the surface waters lay in air power, and the Soviet Union did not achieve a decisive air superiority in the Baltic and Black Sea until early in 1944.

If Stalin had intended that the Soviet fleets should put to sea to engage the German Navy, they would have done so, irrespective of loss. It is doubtful, however, whether Stalin's interest went beyond using the Soviet Navy as a reserve of manpower to provide bayonets for the land fighting. Between June and September 1941 six marine infantry brigades, each about 5,000 men strong, were formed from the Baltic Fleet to fight at Leningrad. This was later increased to nine, and in all the Baltic Red Banner Fleet gave up 130,000 officers and ratings for the land campaigns. In October 1941, by the decision of the GKO, a further twenty-three marine infantry brigades were formed, and a total of 390,000 sailors were transferred to the Red Army over and above the 100,000 officers and ratings in marine infantry brigades who remained under naval command. Eventually, thinned by casualties, many of these marine infantry brigades were marine only in name, since they were often commanded by Red Army officers and received their reinforcements from Central Siberia, from men who had never even seen the sea.[38]

[38] Pitersky, *Die Sowjet-Flotte im Zweiten Weltkrieg*, pp. 428–9.

CHAPTER THIRTY-ONE

The Balance of Power in Europe

In 1941, at the time when Eden made his winter visit to Moscow, it had been noted that Stalin was already demanding to know what the USSR was to have as its share after the war. Stalin wanted his 1941 frontiers recognized by Great Britain and the United States and the boundary between Poland and the Soviet Union to be based on what had formerly been known as the Curzon line.[1] Molotov had even hinted that the Soviet Union's post-war frontiers should be moved westwards into East Prussia.[2] In July of that year, partly as a result of British prompting, General Sikorsky, the Prime Minister of the Polish Government-in-Exile, had begun talks with Maisky, the Soviet Ambassador in London, who acted as the spokesman for the USSR. On 14 August 1941 some agreement was reached between them as to the formation and equipping of a Polish Army on Soviet soil, but the solution of the dispute as to the post-war Russo-Polish frontier was deferred. The attitude of the British and United States Governments with regard to the Polish frontiers was not entirely clear, but appeared to be based on the view that while they would not recognize the Soviet annexation of what was formerly East Poland, neither would they guarantee, nor necessarily support, the restoration of the August 1939 Polish frontiers, frontiers which encompassed White Russian and Ukrainian populations.[3] In December 1941 Sikorsky went to Moscow to sign a Polish-Soviet Declaration of Friendship and Mutual Aid, but declined to enter into any discussions as to a realignment of the frontier.

On 8 January 1942 Churchill had written to Eden saying that the transfer to the Soviet Union of the peoples of the Baltic States, Bessarabia and North Bukovina against their will would be contrary to all the principles for which the British were fighting the war. Such a transfer would dishonour Britain's cause. There could be no question, Churchill thought, of settling frontiers until the post-war peace conference should take place.[4] On 20 May 1942, when

---

[1] Eden, *The Reckoning*, pp. 289–91. The Curzon line ran from Grodno, Vapovka, Nemirov, Brest-Litovsk, Dorogusk, Ustilug, east of Grubeshov, Krilov, east of Rava Ruska and east of Przemysl to the Carpathians.

[2] Feis, *Churchill Roosevelt Stalin*, p. 26.

[3] Churchill, Vol. 3, *The Grand Alliance*, pp. 348–50.

[4] *Ibid*, pp. 615–6.

Molotov came to London, Churchill's Government rejected as incompatible with the Anglo-Polish Agreement of 1939 a demand that Britain should agree to the Soviet occupation of what had formerly been Eastern Poland.[5] These-views were different from those said to have been subsequently expressed by the British Government in 1944.

On 6 January 1943, after the successful encirclement at Stalingrad, the Soviet Government made an open and blunt pronouncement that it regarded as Soviet territory the former occupied area of East Poland. The Polish Government-in-Exile in London appealed against this announcement to both the United States and British Governments. Roosevelt was non-committal in his reply and he too professed to believe that the frontiers of Eastern and Central Europe would be decided at the peace conference after the war; he appeared to be opposed to displeasing the Soviet Union which was at that time engaged in heavy battles, in marked contrast with the United States which had as yet taken little part in the land fighting against Germany.[6] In London a note of impatience, even irritation, is said to have crept into the Foreign Office dealings with the Polish Government-in-Exile, and Sikorsky was even charged with being troublesome about his aspirations, the retention of those same frontiers which the British Government had guaranteed in 1939, the violation of which had been the *casus belli* with Germany. The Polish desire to return to its pre-war territories was regarded in London as being unrealistic.[7] Meanwhile Stalin had begun to form from among Polish trusties in the Soviet Union what was eventually to become the puppet Polish communist government.

In April 1943 the mass graves were found near Katyn of about 12,000 murdered Polish officers, who were last known to have been alive in 1939 in that part of Poland occupied by the Red Army. It has not been established whether these Poles were murdered by NKVD troops or by the *SS Einsatz-kommandos*. Both were equally capable of such an atrocity, but much of the evidence, together with the attitude adopted by the USSR at the unearthing of the crime, suggests that the Soviet Government was probably responsible.[8] However, the disquiet and anger expressed by members of the Polish Government-in-Exile, who demanded an independent inquiry, provided the long awaited opportunity for Moscow to cast off the London Poles. Stalin denounced them bitterly for acting on what he called the German slander before giving the Soviet Government a chance to refute the charges. Undeterred by Roosevelt's and Churchill's appeals not to do so, Stalin, on 26 April, broke

---

[5] *Ibid*, Vol. 4, *The Hinge of Fate*, p. 296; Eden, *The Reckoning*, pp. 326–8.
[6] Feis, *Churchill Roosevelt Stalin*, p. 191.
[7] *Ibid*, p. 192.
[8] See Churchill, Vol. 4, *The Hinge of Fate*, pp. 679–81; *Goebbels' Diary*, pp. 253 *et seq.* Some indication of the Soviet attitude to officer prisoners of war can be drawn from Stalin's statement in Teheran to a shocked Churchill 'that 50,000 at least, perhaps 100,000, of the German commanding staff ought to be liquidated'.

off diplomatic relations with the. Poles and the way was then clear for the Soviet Union to set up its own communist régime as soon as Red Army troops entered Polish territory. On 6 October 1943 the Polish Ambassador in Washington warned Hull, the United States Secretary of State, that the Soviet Union intended to rule Poland through its own Polish communists, and he pressed that the United States and Britain should jointly guarantee the integrity of Poland, taking such action as might be necessary to station United States and British troops in Poland as earnest of their intention.[9]

In the middle of the summer of that year Sikorsky was killed in an air accident, and Mikolajczyk, the leader of the Polish Peasant Party, became the Prime Minister of the Government-in-Exile in his stead. Mikolajczyk's views were moderate and yet when he met Eden shortly before the British Foreign Secretary left for the Moscow meeting of Foreign Ministers, he was, according to his own account, flabbergasted to hear Eden say that unless the Polish Government agreed to give up the eastern areas of the former Poland there was little chance that the Soviet Union would renew relations with it or agree to entrust it with the rule of the liberated Polish territories. Mikolajczyk is said to have replied that the giving up of this territory would only be the beginning of the Russian demands.[10] At the meeting of the Foreign Ministers there was little discussion on Poland and nothing was settled. Hull did not at that time want to be drawn into the matter, but Molotov made it clear that the Polish question was one for the Soviet Union to settle, although it might listen to what others had to say. According to Eden, on his return from Russia he asked the Foreign Office to draw up for him the possible lines of a plan for a Polish-Russian settlement. The British Foreign Office, said Eden, recommended to him the adoption of the Curzon line, except that Lvov should go to the Poles, Poland being given East Prussia, Danzig and Upper Silesia in compensation for the loss of the Eastern territories.[11]

In November 1943 at the Teheran meeting, Roosevelt and Churchill elaborated their proposals for the post-war peace organization connected with the Atlantic Charter. The inclination of Roosevelt and the United States Government at this time, according to the judgement of one American historian, was virtuous and ineffectual. That of the British, pliant.[12] Stalin and Molotov agreed in general terms with the Anglo-American views on post-war security but at the same time expressed quite clearly their own territorial demands: the retention of all lands occupied by the Red Army before June 1941 and part of East Prussia, including Königsberg. Churchill and Roosevelt were in disarray, particularly as Roosevelt seemed anxious to secure Stalin's goodwill and esteem. Roosevelt was to explain to the dictator that the time was not yet opportune for him to come to any firm decision with regard to Poland, as

[9] Feis, *Churchill Roosevelt Stalin*, p. 195.
[10] Mikolajczyk, *The Rape of Poland*, p. 45, reproduced from Feis, p. 196.
[11] Eden, *The Reckoning*, pp. 421–2.
[12] Feis, *Churchill Roosevelt Stalin*, p. 272.

there were between six and seven million Americans of Polish extraction in the United States and he did not want to lose their votes. By default, therefore, the Polish question was for the moment left to Churchill and Stalin, Stalin saying that he would be satisfied with the Curzon or the 1939 Ribbentrop-Molotov line provided that he was given part of East Prussia; the Poles in compensation should take German territory as far west as the Oder. Churchill agreed to recommend this proposal to the London Poles, and went so far as to say that he believed that the Poles had a duty to the Powers of Europe, who had twice *rescued* Poland, to agree to the transfer of territory and *accept the duty of guarding the bulwark of the Oder against further German aggression upon Russia.*[13]

The London Poles, however, were not easily convinced by these grandiose words and the crudest pressure was put on them by the British Government, Churchill informing Mikolajczyk that Great Britain and the United States would not go to war with the Soviet Union over Polish frontiers.[14] Roosevelt meanwhile deliberately kept himself aloof. Stalin hinted that he might renew diplomatic relations with the London Poles if they rid themselves of those elements which were displeasing to him, but on 3 March he told Harriman that by the time Poland was free a government other than that of the London Poles would have emerged inside the country.[15]

Between 7 and 14 June 1944 when the Normandy landings had just taken place, Mikolajczyk saw Roosevelt in Washington. The President was re-assuring but non-committal and describing Stalin as 'a realist but no imperialist', he advised the Poles to come to an understanding with Russia as 'the British and Americans have no intention of fighting Russia'. Roosevelt recommended Mikolajczyk to visit Stalin, and on 17 July he sent a communication to Moscow asking that the Polish Prime Minister should be received.[16] The deferential message which he sent, and that of Churchill which followed three days later, indicated to Moscow the Anglo-American view that the fate of Poland was in Stalin's hands. Stalin's reaction was immediate. The next day, on 21 July, the Polish National Council was reformed as the Committee of National Liberation with Bierut as President, and four days later Lublin was declared to be the capital of Poland; the Soviet Government hastened to sign an agreement by which the puppet committee was to administer the liberated Polish territory, this being done at the time when Mikolajczyk was *en route* to Moscow. During Mikolajczyk's stay in Moscow the Warsaw uprising broke out. Because of Stalin's insistence that Mikolajczyk should deal with the Lublin government, meetings with the Polish communists took place in Moscow from 6 August onwards. These failed to produce any form of agreement.

[13] Churchill, Vol. 5, *Closing the Ring*, p. 400.
[14] Mikolajczyk, *The Rape of Poland*, p. 51, from Feis, pp. 294–5.
[15] Feis, *Churchill Roosevelt Stalin*, p. 298.
[16] *Ibid*, pp. 373–5.

Later in the year in October 1944 when Churchill and Eden were in Moscow, Mikolajczyk and two of his associates acceptable to Stalin were invited to join them. To the Western statesmen Stalin had by then become Uncle Joe, and Churchill, displaying what Feis has called a curious streak of optimism, was supporting the Soviet proposals, according to Mikolajczyk's account, not because the USSR was strong but because it was right. However, Mikolajczyk would not agree either to the acceptance of the Curzon line or to the fusion of the London and Lublin Governments on the terms offered by Stalin, and consistently and adamantly maintained that even if Poland gave up the territory in the east, it still would have no guarantee of independence from Moscow.[17] Lvov, too, was claimed by both Russian and Pole. In all these negotiations only Stalin and Mikolajczyk showed realism and a true understanding of what was involved. For all his good intentions Churchill, regrettably, was the *lishnyi chelovek.*

On returning to London Mikolajczyk put a number of questions to Churchill and Roosevelt concerning post-war Poland, the most pertinent of which was whether Great Britain and the United States intended to guarantee the territories and independence of the new Poland. Roosevelt replied in courteous tones but promising nothing, since he considered the guarantee of Polish frontiers to be the responsibility of the new post-war security organization when it was formed. Churchill was willing to give the required guarantee, but only jointly with the Soviet Union. Since, in Mikolajczyk's view, the guarantee was required as protection from the USSR, the British reply was worthless. Mikolajczyk then resigned. On 31 December 1944, in spite of Roosevelt's urging not to do so, Stalin recognized the Lublin committee as the Provisional Government of Poland. Soon afterwards it became apparent that Stalin intended that Poland should be yet further enlarged at Germany's expense by siting its western frontier along the Oder and the Western, not the Eastern, Neisse.

When Roosevelt, Stalin and Churchill met at Yalta in February 1945 nothing further was decided concerning Poland. The three participants had publicly bound themselves that the Polish Government should be consulted as to its frontiers and that the final settlement should be made at the peace conference after the war. American and British Government observers were not allowed entry into Poland, however, and in reality Stalin was bound by nothing.

In April 1945, immediately after the death of Roosevelt, Vishinsky, the Deputy Foreign Minister of the USSR, hinted that the Soviet Union was about to sign a treaty of mutual assistance with the Warsaw Poles and in spite of United States and British protests and requests to defer action, did so on 22 April. The Soviet Government were then to make over to the Warsaw Government Danzig, Silesia and German territory as far west as the Western Neisse on the pretext that the Poles were administering part of the Soviet Occupied Zone of Germany on behalf of the USSR.

[17] *Ibid*, pp. 453–8.

Churchill's attitude in the war years towards Stalin, the Soviet Union and communism, far from being consistent, was subject to great change. Early in the war he had cast out any doubts concerning the wisdom of allying himself with communism by the simple logic that Hitler's enemies were Britain's friends. His dealings with the USSR and his views at that time seemed to have been tinged with optimism and comradely trust. In August 1943 Churchill was telling Harriman that he foresaw bloody consequences in the future and that he thought Stalin an unnatural man with whom there would be grave trouble. Yet amid these bouts of gloomy realism Churchill appears to have attached an exaggerated importance to the effect of his own personality in his dealings with Stalin. Even as late as the autumn of 1944 Churchill still spoke with some pride of the cordiality of his talks with Stalin, and went so far as to state his belief that Stalin was not a free agent, in that the dictator was subjected to strong pressures from party and military extremists.[18] This statement in itself is indicative of Churchill's lack of understanding of the mentality of Stalin and the nature of his government. At the beginning of May 1945, however, even before the war had ended, Churchill, in a message to Eden in San Francisco, was noting the terrible things which had happened during the Russian advance to the Elbe, and was trying to urge on the Americans the adoption of a hardening of attitude in their dealings with the Kremlin until some satisfaction could be obtained from Moscow as to the solution of the Polish question and Soviet occupation policies in the Balkans and Central Europe.[19] These wise words were four years too late, and they went unheeded in the United States.

The Soviet Government had lured out from hiding the leaders of the Polish Underground under a written guarantee of safe conduct, only to have them arrested and sentenced to long terms of imprisonment. In May 1945 President Truman sent Hopkins to Stalin to attempt to solve the difficulties concerning Poland and to effect the release of the arrested Poles. In both of these aims he was unsuccessful.[20] On 5 July, at Truman's request, Britain recognized the new Polish Provisional Government, which was in effect the former Lublin puppet communist administration, and shortly afterwards recognition was withdrawn from the Polish Government-in-Exile in London. The new Poland and its government were entirely in Stalin's power.

As in Poland, so elsewhere in Central and Eastern Europe. Benes, the optimistic Russophil, against the advice of Eden, had gone to Moscow in December 1943 to sign a Czecho-Slovak Treaty with the USSR. One-fifth of his Cabinet posts were to be given to Moscow-trained Czecho-Slovak

[18] Churchill, Vol. 6, *Triumph and Tragedy*, pp. 207–8.

[19] Feis, *Churchill Roosevelt Stalin*, p. 635; Churchill, Vol. 6, *Triumph and Tragedy*, pp. 449–52. Yet at Potsdam in July 1945 the emotional Churchill, whom Eden described as under Stalin's spell, kept repeating 'I like that man'. Eden's comment was to the point when he said that he was full of admiration for Stalin's handling of Churchill. Eden, *The Reckoning*, p. 545.

[20] *Ibid*, pp. 505–7; Sherwood, *The White House Papers*, pp. 888–90.

communists, and so Benes gave entry to that element which was one day to destroy Masaryk and Free Czecho-Slovakia. At the time, however, Benes told Harriman in Moscow that he was wholly satisfied and that Soviet intentions could be trusted. Stalin and Molotov had time and time again assured him that no matter what might arise they would not interfere in Czecho-Slovakian internal affairs.[21]

The overrunning of Rumania in August 1944 has already been described. Molotov had promised in his broadcast in the previous April that the Soviet Union had no intention of interfering in internal Rumanian affairs, but following the arrest of Antonescu on the orders of the Rumanian King, the communists began to conspire and agitate against the moderate and inefficient Sanatescu Government. This agitation was directed from Moscow through Anna Pauker and the communist National Democratic Front. The Sanatescu Government gave way to a coalition under Radescu, but Moscow did not intend that this should survive either. The country was being stripped for reparations, and Vinogradov, the Soviet Chairman of the Allied Control Commission in Bucharest, gave orders to the Rumanian Government without consulting his British or United States colleagues. On 6 March Vishinsky visited Bucharest and in a violent scene dismissed the Radescu Government, replacing it by one headed by Groza, a *de facto* government which Washington and London refused to recognize.

In Bulgaria and Hungary the political developments took on a similar pattern. United States and British representatives formed part of the Allied Control Commissions but had no influence at all, remaining uninformed and unconsulted. Yugo-Slavia had been spared a Soviet occupation because of the participation of the partisan forces of the Moscow-trained communist Tito, and Tito was believed to be firmly in the Soviet camp. In Czecho-Slovakia and in Austria Western representatives were deliberately excluded at the time of the Soviet occupation. Only in Greece had popular freedom not been extinguished, and this solely because of the presence of British troops.

Admiral Leahy, the Chief of Staff to the President of the United States, was to subscribe to Joseph E. Davies' assessment of Churchill, when he described him as a very great man, but first and foremost a great Englishman, basically more concerned over maintaining England's position in Europe than in preserving peace.[22] Hopkins, too, was to interpret to Truman Churchill's actions in terms of British-Russian rivalry for power. Both of these judgements will be questioned by history. None can doubt that Churchill was a great man, and this was shown by his early recognition of the dangers of German and Italian Fascism and by the energetic and able manner in which he directed the British war effort. Yet in 1940 he took over the government of a country which was still very powerful in resources, independent and free, but he left it in 1945 impoverished and under United States' tutelage. Britain's

[21] Feis, *Churchill Roosevelt Stalin*, pp. 198 and 290.
[22] *Ibid*, p. 652.

losses in shipping and income had been great and by 1945 the Commonwealth, and in particular the United Kingdom, was economically much dependent on United States' aid and trade. Yet Great Britain's sudden decline as a World and European Power during the war years cannot be explained merely by this loss of wealth and resources, since militarily and potentially it was in 1945 still very strong indeed, and its economic losses were only fractional compared with those of the Soviet Union.[23] The USSR, too, during the war years had depended to an appreciable extent on United States material aid.[24]

From the earliest days of the Russo-German War, Churchill and his Coalition Government allied themselves with the Soviet Union and, in the circumstances, no alternative was open to them. Churchilll, however, had one simplified aim, the defeat of Hitlerite Germany, and he allowed no other factor to enter into his calculations. Because of this overriding mission, and since he feared that the Soviet Union might fall out of the war, he accepted almost without rebuke Stalin's calumny and insult. Thereafter he found himself coerced by tactics akin to blackmail. Unlike Stalin, he failed from the earliest days of the struggle to project himself into the post-war world in order to win not only the war but the peace which was to follow. It has been said that the confirmed anti-Bolshevist Churchill held in check his suspicions, forcing himself to co-operate with the Soviet Union for the better prosecution of the war. This may be true. Yet the testimony of his writings shows that, at least in the early war years, he was not well informed as to the nature of communism and the aspirations and methods of the Soviet Union; in his dealings with Moscow, even as late as 1944, he appears at times to have been guided by a spirit of optimism and faith which past experience and events did not justify.

[23] At sea Britain had already taken second place to the American Navy and the United States Air Force was by 1945 numerically three to four times as strong as the Royal Air Force. The Soviet Navy was a negligible factor but the Red Air Force was more powerful in 1945 than was generally assumed in the West and was possibly comparable in numbers of first line fighter and light bombers with the Royal Air Force. Whereas the Red Air Force had no heavy bomber force, the British bomber strength was formidable. In general Soviet figures must be regarded with reserve as the formation and equipment figures do not relate to the personnel figures. An indication of comparative strengths at the end of the war is given below:

	US	Soviet	British (UK only)
Army	5,574,000	6,289,000	2,930,000
Marines	467,000		
Air Force	2,290,000	467,000	963,000
Navy	3,315,000	329,000	790,000
Field divisions	89	488	27
First line aircraft	40,000		8,400
All aircraft		15,800	

Of the Soviet aircraft possibly not more than half were first line military warplanes.

[24] The detail of Anglo-American aid to the Soviet Union is shown at Appendix C to this book.

Britain, the free world and the. Soviet Union owed to the United States a great debt for the part it played in the Second World War, for without American intervention the war would have lasted for decades. But as far as Britain was concerned, the price of this intervention became a negation of British interests in favour of a benevolent policy directed by Washington towards European or World Commonwealth. For this Britain, rather than the United States, was to blame.

From 1941 onwards it became apparent, even in Moscow, that Churchill's Government was unwilling to commit itself to action or indeed to a firm statement of policy in Europe or elsewhere without consultation with, and often the prior agreement of, the Roosevelt Administration. In consequence, by degrees London lost its freedom of action and appeared content to follow the United States lead, where this lead was given. Often, however, the United States deliberately avoided committing itself to an initiative since Roosevelt declined at the time to entangle himself in European affairs. In consequence the Anglo-American war strategy was based mainly on military rather than on political aims.

If the British Government was not well informed as to Soviet aspirations and methods, the United States Government and many of its political and military advisers were distinctly ill-informed. Roosevelt himself was determined on a good neighbour policy which would enable the United States to live in harmony with the USSR after the war, and he was sure that by patience, friendship and generosity, he could allay and finally remove what he believed to be Soviet suspicions and mistrust. Personally, he wished to stand well with Stalin. As has been said, he saw nothing incongruous in the dictator's régime subscribing on paper to the Atlantic Charter or to the basic freedoms, and he and many of his circle were inclined to be more suspicious of British imperialism than of the USSR. Some of his close personal advisers and representatives had a pro-Soviet bias.

The fact that Great Britain had lost its freedom of political and military action, and the extent to which it was already dependent on the United States, were entirely unknown in war-time Germany.[25] Even until late in 1942 Britain was still regarded as the principal of Germany's enemies. Nor was there any appreciation of Churchill's anxiety that Soviet demands should be met. Hitler firmly believed that the overrunning by the Red Army of the Balkans and Central Europe would be a grave danger not only to the nations of continental Europe but also to Britain, and he confidently forecast that Great Britain at least would oppose Stalin's pretensions. As Germany's fortunes declined, the *Führer* promised that the coalition of his enemies would soon break up, as of course it did shortly after Hitler's death. But it was not until May 1945 that Churchill told in violent terms President Truman's representative, a startled Davies, of the threat of Soviet domination and the spread of communism in Europe, revealing what Davies termed a lack of confidence in

[25] Hubatsch, *Kriegswende 1943*, p. 34.

the good faith of Soviet leadership.[26] But during the war years Churchill and the Coalition Government had in fact failed to plot an independent course for Great Britain, a course aimed not only at the destruction of Nazi Germany but also at the attaining of security against Soviet domination for itself and for its European allies.

Great Britain's record in the Second World War, notwithstanding the determination and self-sacrifice of its people, had not been as impressive as that in the war years of 1914 to 1918. Its Royal Navy and mercantile marine had admittedly acquitted themselves well, in spite of being overshadowed in the early war years by enemy air superiority. The U-boat menace had been overcome after a bitter and costly struggle, although the economic sea blockade of Germany was without effect until very late in the war. The Royal Air Force was efficient and powerful, but the wisdom of using the great resources of Bomber Command nightly to lay waste the German cities, without obvious strategic or military benefit, was open to doubt. The British Army took third place in priority in the allocation of resources, and although it was fully mechanized and its morale and training were good, it had often lacked tactical air support and its fighting equipment did not match the ability of its soldiers.[27] In Europe, even in 1944, only thirty British field divisions were in combat, and of this total some were from Canada and New Zealand. The weakness of the British position in Europe was partly attributable to the lack of ground troops, since the manpower and resources of the British Army had been dispersed over most of the globe. Indian and colonial divisions all had a United Kingdom element. British Army garrison, administrative and headquarters troops, together with numbers of field divisions, were scattered throughout Africa, in the Middle East from Suez to Iran, and in India from Afghanistan to China. Only in Burma were British and Indian divisions engaged in heavy fighting. Even in 1943 Britain was faced with the alternative of being a European or an Imperial Power. To be effective, it could not be both.

The United States and Britain in 1943 were already joint by far the greatest air and sea powers the world has ever known. If they had wished to bring about the defeat of Hitler's Germany and at the same time safeguard Europe from Soviet domination, the way into Europe lay not across the Normandy beaches but from Italy into the Balkans, from the Bosporus into the Black Sea and from Jutland and Norway into the Baltic. These were the landings which Hitler forecast and feared. The invasions of France, although they had everything to recommend them tactically, were irrelevant both politically and strategically. The politics and strategy of campaigns into the Baltic and Balkans would have been quite foreign to Roosevelt, however.

[26] Feis, *Churchill Roosevelt Stalin*, pp. 651–2.
[27] The British Army was not provided with a really efficient anti-tank gun until 1943, and throughout the whole war no British tank was produced comparable with the best of those of its allies or its German enemy.

British resources alone, even if its land armies had been concentrated, would have been inadequate for such a strategy; yet they were sufficiently powerful to have attacked into the Balkans without United States participation or support. Von Weichs, the Commander-in-Chief Army Group F, visited the *Führer* in Rastenburg on 24 September 1943 to warn him that he held 5,000 kilometres of frontage with only ten divisions, some of which were of poor quality. If attacked, von Weichs was certain that he could not defend, and he advised the evacuation of the Balkans without delay.[28] The British, and Churchill personally, were popular in both Rumania and in Hungary, both of which wanted to get out of the war; Yugo-Slavia and Greece were a cauldron of partisans. There appears little doubt that if the British had concentrated their forces to overrun the Balkans and South-East Europe, regardless of the attitude of allies and at the expense of participation in the Normandy landings, success must have attended their efforts. Britain's failure to undertake this campaign was one of its most costly errors.[29]

As it was, because of the acceptance by the British Government of the United States lead, Great Britain had already ceased to play any real part in the affairs of Europe. Churchill's urging of a reluctant Roosevelt was not enough. Initiative and action were required.

[28] Von Weichs, *Tagebuch*, 24 September 1943.
[29] Hubatsch, *Kriegswende 1943*, p. 34.

CHAPTER THIRTY-TWO

Vistula to the Oder

The strategic intention of the Soviet High Command at the end of 1944 was to advance in East Prussia, Poland, Czecho-Slovakia, Hungary and Austria on a broad front, the thrusts being made towards four main areas, the Baltic, Berlin, Prague and Vienna. Before the offensive could be mounted in Central Europe, however, the clearing of the Baltic States was considered to be an essential preliminary to the resumption of the advance in Poland.[1]

At the beginning of September Schörner's Army Group North held a front nearly 500 miles long stretching from the Gulf of Finland near the Narva to the area of Dobele to the south-west of Riga, a frontage which was to be extended southwards to the Niemen when eventually Army Group North took 3 Panzer Army under command. In the north of Estonia Group Narva held the line of the Narva and the northern shores of Lake Peipus, but was threatened in the south by the Soviet penetration in the province of Tartu (Dorpat) between Lakes Peipus and Vorts (Wirts-Järw). Boege's 18 Army was to the east of the Gulf of Riga while Hilpert's 16 Army was to the south.[2] Schörner, like his predecessor Friessner, wanted to evacuate Estonia and without Hitler's knowledge had made secret preparations to do so, building rings of earthworks in 16 Army area to the east of Riga through which he planned to withdraw 18 Army.[3] Following Finland's acceptance of the Soviet peace terms which allowed the USSR to use Finnish waters and naval bases on the south-west coast of Finland, the Red Fleet was free to enter the middle Baltic and as a precautionary measure Hitler had a German division put on the islands covering the Gulf of Riga.

The Soviet offensive into the Baltic States was made by Bagramyan's 1 Baltic Front, Eremenko's 2 Baltic Front and Maslennikov's 3 Baltic Front co-ordinated by Vasilevsky as the Soviet High Command representative. Supporting operations were mounted on the flanks by Govorov's Leningrad

[1] *Istoriya*, Vol. 4, p. 345.
[2] In September Boege replaced Loch and Hilpert replaced Laux.
[3] Guderian appears to have been privy to these plans. Guderian, *Panzer Leader*, p. 354.

and Chernyakhovsky's 3 Belorussian Fronts.[4] In the far north the Leningrad Front had to engage the German Group Narva across the isthmus to the north of Lake Peipus and clear the Estonian shore on the Gulf of Finland. 3 Baltic and 2 Baltic Fronts were to penetrate 18 Army from the east and, reaching the Baltic, cut off the withdrawal route of both 18 Army and Group Narva. 1 Baltic Front was to attempt to reach the sea near Riga and cut once more the narrow German corridor south of the town. 3 Belorussian Front was not given a task during this first offensive. The Leningrad and the three Baltic Fronts had 133 rifle divisions, six tank and one mechanized corps with a total strength of 900,000 men, 3,000 tanks and SUs and 2,600 aircraft.[5] The offensive was to start on 14 September. Army Group North consisted of thirty-two divisions, of which one was panzer and two panzer grenadier, and three SS brigades.[6]

Immediately to the south of the town of Riga the upper reaches of the Memele (Nyemenek) and Lielupe (Ada) Rivers had been dammed so that the level of the water fell rapidly below the obstruction, and tanks and infantry crossed the obstacle with ease. At first Bagramyan's 1 Baltic Front made good progress but by 16 September it was brought to a halt a few miles to the south of Riga. The next day, however, Fedyuninsky's 2 Shock Army of Maslennikov's 3 Baltic Front broke through Hasse's 2 Corps defences near Tartu. This thrust threatened only the safety of the Narva Group, but the existence of the whole of Army Group North was imperilled by the narrowing corridor south of Riga. The order was given after having been grudgingly agreed by Hitler for the withdrawal of the Narva Group from North Estonia to the ports of Tallinn and Parnu (Pernau) and 18 Army began to fall back on Riga.[7] Meanwhile Army Group Centre had ordered Raus's 3 Panzer Army to thrust against 1 Baltic Front's flank from the area of Siauliai (Schaulen) in support of Army Group North, but these attacks were to have only very limited success. The command of 3 Panzer Army was thereafter transferred from Army Group Centre to Schörner, thus extending his frontage down to the Memel and the East Prussian frontier. In accordance with Hitler's direction, he shifted the weight of the German panzer formations from Siauliai to the area of Jelgava (Mitau) just south of Riga, from where it was planned to launch a counter-offensive.[8] On 24 September, when most of Estonia was already in Soviet hands, all Red Army attacks suddenly and inexplicably ceased.

[4] The military councils were as follows: 1 Baltic Front, Bagramyan, Leonov and Kurasov; 2 Baltic Front, Eremenko, Bogatkin and Sandalov; 3 Baltic Front, Maslennikov, Rydakov and Vashkevich; Leningrad Front, Govorov, Zhdanov and M. M. Popov; 3 Belorussian Front, Chernyakhovsky, Makarov and Pokrovsky.

[5] *Istoriya*, Vol. 4, p. 344.

[6] *OKH Kriegsgliederung*, 16 September 1944.

[7] The order was given by Hitler and not by Guderian on his own responsibility.

[8] Guderian's account appears to have confused this battle with the earlier one on 16 August when the Soviet forces had actually reached the Gulf of Riga. Guderian, *Panzer Leader*, pp. 353-5.

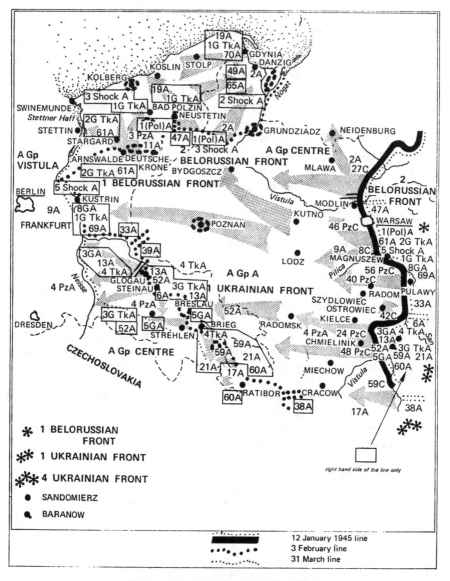

FROM THE VISTULA TO THE ODER
January–March 1945

524

That day a new Soviet High Command directive was issued involving a complete change of plan. Since most of the German forces had been successfully withdrawn from Estonia to the area of Riga and Kurland, Moscow was no longer interested in closing the Riga gap. The new intention was to change the direction of the main offensive from north to west, attacking 3 Panzer Army, to reach the Baltic near the town of Memel and cut off the whole of Army Group North in Kurland. To do this Bagramyan's 1 Baltic Front was to transfer three rifle armies, a tank army and a number of independent corps from its right to its left flank, a distance of a hundred miles, in the space of six days. Two other armies were affected by the movement and in all half a million men and 1,300 tanks and SUs were moved.[9] The transfer of troops was covered by deception measures including overt preparations for the resumption of the attack near Riga. Meanwhile Chernyakhovsky's 3 Belorussian Front to the south of 1 Baltic Front was to support the offensive and pin German reserves by a three-pronged attack into East Prussia towards Tilsit, Gumbinnen and Suwalki. 3 and 2 Baltic Fronts were to continue the attack into Latvia on Riga while the Leningrad Front began to clear the Baltic offshore islands.

Bagramyan's attack started on 5 October with a reconnaissance in force and only twenty minutes' artillery preparation, and since a large part of Raus's 3 Panzer Army's armour had been moved to the north to the area of Jelgava, resistance was found to be light. The terrain made movement difficult, being covered by wood and marsh, but Chistyakov's 6 Guards and Beloborodov's 43 Armies had advanced over ten miles by the end of the day. Low cloud and bad weather had restricted air support and observation and made it impossible to commit the tanks until the second day of the offensive, when Volsky's 5 Guards Tank Army and two tank corps entered the battle. A great gap was soon torn in 3 Panzer Army defences and Bagramyan began to move westwards towards the Lithuanian Baltic coast. On 6 October Schörner started to withdraw troops from the north-east of Riga and throw them in against Bagramyan's 1 Baltic Front right flank; Schörner was unsuccessful and on 10 October Kreizer's 51 Soviet Army arrived on the Baltic coast just north of Palanga while Beloborodov's 43 Army reached the outskirts of the town of Memel, but was unable to take it. Except for 3 Panzer Army, which had been forced southwards into East Prussia, the whole of Army Group North was cut off in Kurland and Riga, and East Prussia was open to an attack across the Niemen. By 12 October, however, 3 Panzer Army, with the assistance of a *Luftwaffe* parachute panzer corps which had been rushed eastwards from the centre of Germany, succeeded in stabilizing the front on the line of the river. To the north in Kurland Schörner, using 18 Army, managed to create an east-west line south of Leepaja (Libau). Riga was evacuated and the Germans fell back to Tukhum. In spite of the urgings of Guderian, Hitler refused to permit

[9] *Istoriya*, Vol. 4, pp. 354–5. The armies transferred were Malyshev's 4 Shock Army, Beloborodov's 43 and Kreizer's 51 Armies, and Volsky's 5 Guards Tank Army.

the evacuation of Kurland, although this could in fact have been carried out from the sea, since he maintained that the bridgehead would fill a useful purpose in pinning down enemy formations.[10] Although Memel was taken by the Red Army in January 1945, the Kurland bridgehead, held by 16 and 18 Armies with twenty-six divisions, was to remain in existence until after the end of the war.

After the taking of Riga Maslennikov's 3 Baltic Front was disbanded.

Further to the south Chernyakhovsky's 3 Belorussian Front with thirty-five rifle divisions and two tank corps attacked Army Group Centre's 4 Army in East Prussia, made up of fifteen infantry divisions and two cavalry brigades, the Germans believing that the attack was directed at Königsberg. With the aid of some reinforcing formations made available by 3 Panzer Army and the High Command, Hossbach's 4 Army counter-attacked and dispersed or destroyed firstly, on 22 October, part of Galitsky's 11 Guards Army at Gumbinnen and then, in the beginning of November, other elements near Goldap. This was the first time that Red Army troops had been on German soil and they left behind them a trail of murder and devastation which was to augur badly for the population of Germany's eastern territories.[11]

Within the German Armed Forces High Command (OKW) Hitler and Jodl lived in a world divorced from reality. Jodl had little interest in the war in the East and much of his time was spent in thwarting any attempt by Guderian to persuade the *Führer* to transfer troops from west to east and in destroying any remaining independence of the OKH and General Staff. His adversary Guderian, shorn of authority, was no less narrow-minded and blinkered than Jodl. He was convinced, not without reason, that it was preferable to lose German territory to the Western Allies rather than to the Red Army, but so limited was his understanding of the relative strength of Germany and its enemies that he could not realize that the shuffling of divisions from west to east or east to west could make no difference to the outcome of the war. By the end of 1944 Germany was a weakened husk held firmly in the powerful jaws of a gigantic nutcracker, and was so enfeebled that it was unable to defend itself from either of the power blocs opposing it. Taking his cue from the *Führer* who was to remark that 'nothing ever went right now', Guderian, harking back to the halcyon summer days of years before, was frequently and mistakenly to bemoan that Germany no longer had commanders or troops of the 1940 quality.[12] The German Army which had been Hitler's pride in 1941 was in 1944 a poorly equipped and obsolete army with little air and artillery support, crippled for lack of vehicles and motor fuel, and was fighting really powerful enemies. There was little cause for wonder that Germany was fast losing the war.

[10] Guderian, *Panzer Leader*, p. 355.
[11] *Documents on the Expulsion of the Germans from Eastern Central Europe*, Vol. 1, pp. 12–3.
[12] Guderian, *Panzer Leader*, p. 327.

Hitler and Jodl were fully occupied with the *Führer's* new brainchild, an offensive to be made in November or December in the area of the Ardennes in the West. This offensive, aimed at enveloping the British 21 Army Group and 1 United States Army and pinning them against the Belgian coast, was to be made by more than twenty-five divisions, nearly the whole of the German strategic reserve, the aim of the operation being to delay the invasion of Germany from the west and gain time. The strategic reserve would then have been switched from west to east to save Budapest or to meet the expected new threat in the area of the Vistula.

Gehlen's Foreign Armies East Department of the Army High Command had forecast the imminence of a Soviet offensive, estimating the Red Army strength opposite East Prussia and the Vistula as 225 rifle divisions and more than twenty-two tank corps. On the basis of these figures Guderian was to calculate that the Soviet superiority was eleven to one in infantry, seven to one in tanks and twenty to one in guns.[13] On Christmas Eve the Chief of the General Staff journeyed to Ziegenberg in Hesse to Hitler's Western Command Post, taking with him Gehlen's intelligence appreciation. This, however, availed him nothing. Mesmerized by figures and numbers of divisions, Hitler had for long been raising new formations rather than reinforcing existing ones. Infantry divisions had been reduced to only six battalions and some of the newest *Volksgrenadier* divisions had only two regiments of two battalions, and at full strength numbered little more than 6,000 officers and men. Many of the divisions in the east retained their divisional titles expressly for the purpose of deceiving the Soviet enemy. The German order of battle on the Eastern Front was becoming a gigantic bluff in which regiments were called divisions, battalions were called brigades and brigades corps, and the time was shortly to come when mobile tank destroyer units were in reality companies of cyclists equipped with anti-tank grenades. Hitler became convinced that the enemy was attempting a similar deception, and after a stormy meeting attended by Keitel, Jodl, Guderian and Burgdorf he rejected Gehlen's appreciation.

At the end of 1944 the Red Army, according to the Soviet account, was made up of fifty-five armies, six tank armies and thirteen air armies commanding 500 rifle divisions, ninety-four artillery divisions and 149 independent artillery brigades. Its total equipment strength was said to total 15,000 tanks and SUs and 15,000 military aircraft of all types.[14] It also had the assistance of twenty-nine Polish, Czech, Rumanian and Bulgarian divisions. By 1944 the corps organization had been taken into use again almost everywhere, and armies usually consisted of three rifle corps each of three divisions. A front might have from five to seven armies, one or two tank armies and several tank, mechanized and cavalry corps. During 1944 equipment was said to be becoming so plentiful that each front was reinforced by several breakthrough

---

[13] *Ibid*, p. 382. This estimate was no exaggeration. 1 Ukrainian and 1 Belorussian Fronts together had 163 divisions. *Istoriya*, Vol. 5, pp. 27 and 57.

[14] *Istoriya*, Vol. 5, p. 27. The total personnel strength was given as only 6,800,000.

artillery divisions and a rocket (*Katyusha*) division and a number of anti-aircraft divisions and artillery brigades. Tank armies still did not use the divisional organization but usually consisted of two tank and one mechanized corps, each of three to four brigades. Guards rifle divisions had additional scales of equipment in that each had been allotted an artillery brigade instead of a three battery regiment, the brigade consisting of a gun, a howitzer and a mortar regiment.[15] A proportion of the cavalry had been remounted in American quarter-ton vehicles and according to German contemporary estimates half of all the motor vehicles used by the Red Army were of United States origin.[16]

The Ardennes offensive starting on 16 December had come as a complete surprise to the Anglo-Americans and the German troops had initially gained notable success. By Christmas Eve, the day on which Hitler held his meeting with Guderian, it was obvious that the zenith had been reached and that the strategic objectives of the offensive would never be reached. Guderian was in favour of calling off the offensive and transferring troops eastwards to form a new army in the area to the north of Lodz covering Brandenburg. The *Führer*, on the other hand, refused to take Soviet intentions seriously and did not believe a major offensive probable. In any case it was easier, he thought, to give up territory in the east than in the west where the Ruhr was directly threatened. The only areas in the east in which he felt himself directly concerned were in the defence of Budapest and the Hungarian oil area of Nagykanizsa.

The Chief of General Staff had asked in vain for the evacuation of the troops locked up in Kurland in order that these might form a reserve, and begged for the German divisions returning from Finland (an OKW theatre). These were denied to him with the retort that the German Army in the East must take care of itself. On 31 December and 9 January he tried yet again to bring the urgency of the situation to the attention of the *Führer*.[17] Hitler had lived, however, too long in his own shadowy world and, still convinced of his own genius, he was pathologically suspicious of his military subordinates who, he was sure, wrecked his plans by failing to obey his orders in the minutest detail. Commanders and staff officers continued to be arrested. The enemy's capabilities or intentions never had any place in the *Führer*'s appreciations. At the end of November he issued an order which was to be made known to every soldier in which it was stated that the commander of any fortress, garrison or strong point should, before retiring or breaking out from his defences, offer his command to any officer or soldier. Any officer or soldier who thought that he could continue the defence should be given full command regardless of rank.[18] In the middle of January, after the great Soviet offensive predicted

[15] *Ibid*, pp. 39–40.
[16] *Kriegstagebuch des OKW*, Vol. 4, pp. 1155 *et seq.*
[17] Guderian, *Panzer Leader*, pp. 384–8.
[18] Hubatsch, *Hitlers Weisungen für die Kriegführung*, p. 299. *Führerbefehl über die Befehlsführung WF St/Qu 2 Nr. 1409/44 of 28 November 1944.*

by Guderian and Gehlen had started and the eastern defences had already been torn apart, Hitler was sure that the leaders in the field were retreating through lack of will power and cowardice, and he issued a *Führer* order which was remarkable even by the German standards at the time. No commander of any formation from division upwards was to attack or counter-attack or withdraw without first notifying his intention through the normal channels to the German High Command, in sufficient time to allow the *Führer*'s intervention.[19] The *Führer*'s intervention usually meant a countermand. Hitler was by then ready to conduct his war from his bunker, the master of every move down to divisional level.

The population in the eastern territories, including the many evacuees from the bombed areas of West Germany, were under no illusions as to their fate should they be caught up in a Soviet invasion and, gripped with terror, most of them wanted to quit their homesteads and flee to the west. The army commanders, knowing that the flight of civilian refugees after the Soviet offensive had started would impede their operations, urged that the forward areas should be evacuated immediately. This proposal was denounced by Hitler as another manifestation of defeatism, and the Party *Gauleiter* were ordered to see that the population remained firmly in place. This order was to have terrible consequences in the early months of 1945. Since the war was about to be fought on German soil, the depth of the combat zone for an army group in which the German Army held undisputed sway was reduced to six miles, hardly a sufficient depth to deploy a division. Behind this line operations and even the deployment of troops were subject to the permission and interference of the Party and state administrative machine, a machine over which the German Army had none of the powers of requisition or enforcement which it had enjoyed in Russia and the *General Gouvernement* of Poland.

At the beginning of January the German forces in the east were made up of five army groups. Schörner's Army Group North of 16 and 18 Armies, encircled in Kurland, henceforth played little significant part in the war. Reinhardt's Army Group Centre of 3 Panzer, 4 and 2 Armies held East Prussia and Northern Poland along the Narew to its junction with the Vistula north of Warsaw. Harpe's Army Group A of 9, 4 Panzer, 17 and 1 Panzer Armies held a north-south line from north of Warsaw along the middle Vistula to the Carpathians in Czecho-Slovakia. Wöhler's Army Group South was in Hungary and von Weichs's Army Group F held the far southern flank. The new Soviet winter offensive which was to take the Red Army in one great bound from the middle Vistula to the Oder hardly fifty miles from Berlin was to fall on the seventy divisions of Reinhardt's Army Group Centre and Harpe's Army Group A.[20] The main Soviet thrust, based on tank and mechanized

[19] *Ibid*, p. 300. *OKW/WF St/Op (H) Nr. 00688/45 g. Kdos* of 19 January 1945. Commanders, staffs and signal officers were threatened that they were personally answerable to the *Führer* not only in event of disobedience of the order, but also in event of signal failure or untruthful reports.
[20] *OKH Kriegsgliederung*, 31 December 1944.

forces, was to be made on the axis Warsaw-Berlin and it was here that the German panzer and panzer grenadier forces were at their weakest. Of the total of eighteen panzer divisions in the east seven were in Hungary, two in Kurland, four in East Prussia and only five in the centre covering Branden-burg.[21]

The Soviet offensive, rightly regarded as one of the greatest strategic operations of the war, was based on two parallel and mighty armoured thrusts; the southern one made by 1 Ukrainian Front from the Baranow bridgehead on the Vistula to Breslau in Silesia; and the northern thrust made by 1 Belorussian Front from the Pulawy and Magnuszew bridgeheads on to Poznan (Posen). The axes of both of these formations converged on Berlin. The immediate and primary aim of the offensive was to reach the Oder preparatory to plunging into the heart of Germany.

At the end of September, so Zhukov has said, he and Rokossovsky had been ordered to Moscow to be cross-examined as to the lack of success of Perk-horovich's 47 Army attacks immediately to the north of Warsaw. Stalin was nervous and excitable and he was at first unwilling to agree with Zhukov's and Rokossovsky's recommendation that all offensives should be broken off.[22] Following, and possibly as a result of this meeting, Stalin decided to bring 1 Belorussian and 1 Ukrainian Fronts directly under his own control. Zhukov gave up his co-ordinating appointment as *Stavka* representative and was appointed to take over the command of 1 Belorussian Front in the middle of November from Rokossovsky, Rokossovsky going to 2 Belorussian Front, replacing G. F. Zakharov who took over 4 Guards Army. Zhukov, according to his own story, remained in effect the senior member of the *Stavka*, being Stalin's principal military deputy.

During October Zhukov and Antonov began work on the staff preparation for the new offensive. Zhukov appears to have been preoccupied with the flank threat posed by the German Army Group Centre in East Prussia and blamed Stalin for failing to accept his recommendation that 2 Belorussian Front be reinforced by an additional army to eliminate this danger. On 1 or 2 November the plans were presented to Stalin; by the middle of the month planning was continued in a series of exercises and war games at the head-quarters of the two fronts and the armies which were to take part in the offensive. No firm date had been given for the offensive, but formations were to be in a state of readiness by 15–20 January. Zhukov has stressed the new

---

[21] Army Group North had 4 and 14 Panzer Divisions; Army Group Centre, 5 and 7 Panzer, 1 *Hermann Göring* and Panzer Brigade 102; Army Group A, 16, 17, 19, 20 and 25 Panzer Divisions; Army Group South had 1, 3, 6, 8, 13, 23, 24 Panzer Divisions. Soviet sources credit the Germans with twenty-four panzer divisions in the east, but this is not borne out by the order of battle of 31 December 1944 unless the panzer grenadier divisions are counted as panzer divisions. Compare *Istoriya*, Vol. 5, p. 34.

[22] Zhukov, *Vospominaniya i Razmyshleniya*, pp. 600–2. This may be true or may be a be-lated attempt to justify lack of Soviet action at the time of the Warsaw uprising.

difficulties that faced the Soviet troops, since railways and lines of communication ran through Polish territory and for this reason might be vulnerable to disruption; there were greater difficulties, too, than had existed before in obtaining information and intelligence from enemy rear areas. The existence of both of these problems gives an indication of the strained relationship between the occupying Red Army troops and the local Polish population.[23]

Konev's 1 Ukrainian and Zhukov's 1 Belorussian Fronts each had ten armies, including two tank armies and several other corps, and their joint strength was said to number 163 divisions, 6,400 tanks and SUs (forty-three per cent of all the armour on the east front), 4,700 aircraft, and 2,200,000 men.[24] The total frontage of the offensive on both fronts was over 300 miles in width.

The 1 Belorussian Front offensive was to consist of three separate operations. In the most northerly of these, Warsaw was to be doubly enveloped by Perkhorovich's 47 Army to the north of the capital while Berling's 1 Polish Army and P. A. Belov's 61 Army, attacking from the north corner of the tiny Magnuszew bridgehead, outflanked the city from the south. The centre operation, also from the Magnuszew bridgehead, was the main thrust westwards direct on Kutno and Lodz and then on to Bydgoszcz (Bromberg) and Poznan, the break-out frontage being less than ten miles wide. This westwards thrust was to be made by Berzarin's 5 Shock and Chuikov's 8 Guards Armies with Katukov's 1 Guards Tank and Bogdanov's 2 Guards Tank Armies committed in the second echelon on the flanks. The third operation was a subsidiary thrust from the Pulawy bridgehead towards Radom made by Tsvetaev's 33 Army and Kolpakchy's 69 Army and three tank corps, cooperating with the right flank of 1 Ukrainian Front.

Konev's 1 Ukrainian Front was to advance from the Baranow bridgehead and destroying the enemy at Kielce, in twelve days reach the line Radomsk-Czestochowa-Miechow. It was then to move on Breslau, the capital of Silesia. The break-out from the Baranow bridgehead was to be made on a narrow nineteen mile frontage using the six break-through artillery divisions and three armies, Pukhov's 13 Army, Koroteev's 52 Army and Zhadov's 5 Guards Army. Gusev's 21 and Korovnikov's 59 Armies, Rybalko's 3 Guards Tank and Lelyushenko's 4 Guards Tank Armies were to follow in the second echelon. Subsidiary attacks were to be made to the flanks, one in the north of Szydlowiec and Ostrowiec by Gordov's 3 Guards and Gluzdovsky's 6 Armies to assist in the attack on Radom, and one to the south on Cracow by Kurochkin's 60 Army in conjunction with Moskalenko's 38 Army of Petrov's 4 Ukrainian Front.[25] Meanwhile Rokossovsky's 2 Belorussian

---

[23] *Ibid*, pp. 609–11.
[24] *Istoriya*, Vol. 5, p. 57.
[25] *Ibid*, pp. 58–61.

Front to the north-east of Warsaw was to strike north-west and, clearing the right bank of the Vistula and taking Marienburg, close in on the Baltic near Danzig, so cutting off East Prussia from the remainder of Germany and at the same time giving some protection to Zhukov's right flank.[26]

Although preparations for a Soviet offensive had been ready since early December the Red Army lay inactive, and in German quarters the erroneous view was expressed that the delay was deliberate in that the Kremlin was attempting to bring pressure on the Western Powers to recognize the Lublin Polish Government.[27] Winter was in fact late that year and the Soviet High Command was unwilling to begin an offensive in the heavy mud since this would make it impossible to exploit armoured and mechanized superiority. Good visibility, too, was required for the employment of artillery and air power.[28] As early as 14 December Stalin had told Harriman that he was awaiting a spell of fine weather before starting any major action.[29] The fact that the Red Army had long been ready and was waiting for clear and frosty weather was known, too, on the German side and had been noted in the war diary entries at the time.[30]

On 6 January Churchill sent a personal communication to Stalin asking whether a renewal of the offensive on the Vistula could be counted on during January, the Ardennes battle being, in Churchill's words, 'very heavy'.[31] In his reply to Churchill on 7 January Stalin explained that he was awaiting a change in the weather and promised an offensive not later than the second half of January, which was promising nothing that he had not already arranged since the provisional date had been set at between 15–20 January.[32] Although Churchill, forgetful of Stalin's intransigence at the time of the Warsaw uprising and of Soviet duplicity in the closing stages of the war, was later to quote the incident and what he called Stalin's thrilling reply as an example of the speed with which he could settle business with Moscow, the true nature of the Soviet

---

[26] The military councils were as follows: 2 Belorussian Front, Rokossovsky, Subbotin and Bogolyubov; 1 Belorussian Front, Zhukov, Telegin and Malinin; 1 Ukrainian Front, Konev, Krainyukov and Sokolovsky; 4 Ukrainian Front, I. E. Petrov, Mekhlis and Korzhenevich.

[27] *Kriegstagebuch des OKW*, Vol. 4, p. 993.

[28] Konev, *Sorok Pyatyi God, Novyi Mir*, No. 5, 1965.

[29] Feis, *Churchill Roosevelt Stalin*, p. 478.

[30] *Kriegstagebuch des OKW*, Vol. 4, p. 1002, 9 January 1945. '*Ausser Ungarn zeichnen sich Schwerpunkte als bei Baranow, Pulawy, Magnuszew und Ostpreussen. Dass der Gegner . . . sich bereits seit 2 Monaten bereithält, aber noch nicht angreift, ist zum Teil bedingt durch das Wetter, da der Gegner Frost braucht und ausserdem geeignete Sicht, um seine Luftwaffe voll ausnutzen zu können.*'

[31] Churchill, Vol. 6, *Triumph and Tragedy*, p. 243. In fact by this time the German attack had lost all impetus.

[32] Earlier historical accounts say the offensive was not to be mounted earlier than 20 January (e.g. Platonov, *Vtoraya Mirovaya Voina*, pp. 675–6) although Konev and Zhukov appear agreed that the date was bracketed between 15–20 January. Compare Zhukov, *Vospominaniya i Razmyshleniya*, p. 610.

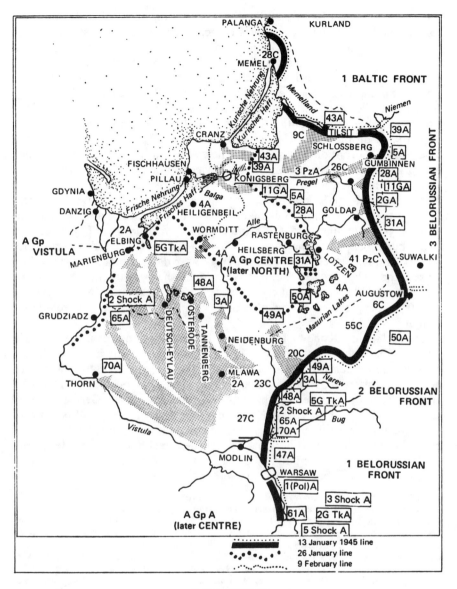

EAST PRUSSIA
January–February 1945

intentions remains obscure. Stalin did in fact bring the date of his offensive forward and he may have done this in a genuine attempt to assist his Western Allies. On the other hand it is remotely possible that he may have done so out of self-interest, in order to get his blow in before the German strategic reserve should be turned eastwards once more against the Red Army. Further doubts remain. Stalin, who was in personal touch with his front commanders by high frequency radio sometimes several times a day, did not give Konev any intimation of a change of date until 9 January when 1 Ukrainian Front was ordered by Antonov on the radio telephone to begin the offensive on 12 January and 1 Belorussian Front on 14 January.[33] The two lost days remain a mystery and out of keeping with the pattern of the Soviet conduct of higher operations at that time. However, an examination of the daily weather records of European Russia and Western Siberia in the first ten days of January throws some fresh light on the affair. Before 6 January the weather was mild and wet and the outlook generally unsettled. On 7 and 8 January a large area of high pressure began building up to the north of the Caspian and moving steadily northwards into Central Russia. On the 8 January there e were definite indications that West Russia and Poland were about to have cold and hard weather, but not before 9 January could this be definitely confirmed.[34] Prisoners taken by the Germans on 10 January said that the offensive would be launched between 11–16 January.[35]

On 12 January Konev's 1 Ukrainian Front began the offensive from the Baranow bridgehead against Graeser's 4 Panzer Army, the attacking troops seizing the German forward defended localities around the Baranow bridgehead by surprise. At 10 a.m. the artillery preparatory bombardment began, and this lasted just under two hours during which time the German control and communication system broke down. At 11.47 a.m. the fire lifted and the storm battalions, some of which were punishment units, attacked supported by tanks and a double artillery barrage.[36] The attack fell on von Edelsheim's 48 Panzer Corps of three infantry divisions and Recknagel's 42 Corps of four infantry divisions, both of which were powerless to move their forward

[33] Konev, *Sorok Pyatyi God, Novyi Mir*, No. 5, 1965.

[34] From contemporary daily weather charts drawn by the RAF Meteorological Office during the month of January 1945 from data from Soviet weather stations. For the interpretation of these contemporary charts I am indebted to the London Weather Centre. A short sharp hard spell of weather followed sufficient to take Red Army troops to the Oder. On 12 January when the 1 Ukrainian Front offensive started it was cold with snow, no wind and poor visibility. On 14 January when 1 Belorussian Front attacked it was colder but visibility was still poor. The next day visibility was better and on 16 January the weather was clear, fine and cold. By 21 January, however, when Red Army troops reached the Oder the thaw had set in again, the ground was again marshy and the river could not be crossed. All weather descriptions from *Istoriya*, Vol. 5.

[35] *Kriegstagebuch des OKW*, Vol. 4, pp. 1006–7.

[36] According to the contemporary German account there was one hour's artillery preparation from 3 a.m. to 4 a.m. and a further hour from 7 a.m. to 8 a.m. after which the probing began. *Ibid*, p. 1010. The variation in timings may be accounted for by the difference in Moscow and Berlin time.

formations since they were pinned both by Hitler's orders and the over-whelming weight of the artillery fire.[37] Part of 24 Panzer Corps which had been moved close up to the front by Hitler's express order was sucked into the battle and dispersed by the bombardment; even Konev was subsequently to admit that under the new system of *Führer* control the German tactical defence was paralysed.[38] Bad weather restricted the Red Air Force tactical support to a few hundred sorties, but by the end of the first day the armies in the first echelon had penetrated up to a depth of twelve miles. The next day, however, German resistance stiffened, particularly in the area Kielce-Chmiel-nik, and the tempo of the Soviet attack slackened. Konev therefore committed Korovnikov's 59 Army and a tank corps from his second echelon in a thrust southwards towards Cracow. Progress became faster again on 14 January, and the next day Nehring's 24 Panzer Corps was finally defeated and the Soviet troops were in open country, having advanced over sixty miles in four days. All German communications had broken down and the troops were in disorder. The partially encircled 42 German Corps tried to withdraw but its corps headquarters was attacked by tank troops and its commander, Recknagel, killed. Meanwhile the German shoulders of the break-through area had given way. The good weather had so improved the flying conditions that the daily Soviet sorties increased from 300 to 1,700. On 17 January the Warthe was crossed, and after six days Soviet troops had penetrated a hundred miles on a 160-mile front.

Hitler, still at Ziegenberg and attempting to control the Ardennes operation and mount an attack into Alsace, could do nothing to remedy the situation, but on 15 January he had resorted to his usual strategy of robbing one sector to reinforce another. This frequently resulted in two sectors going without, while the reserves were shunted about in railway sidings. Against Guderian's advice he ordered von Saucken's panzer corps *Grossdeutschland* from Army Group Centre in East Prussia to Lodz in order to assist in the defence of Kielce, a town that had already been taken by Konev.[39] When von Saucken detrained in Lodz this town was already under fire and he was fortunate to have been able to fight his way clear to join Nehring's 24 Panzer Corps.

Zhukov's 1 Belorussian Front attacked from the Pulawy and Magnuszew bridgeheads on 14 January, two days after Konev's offensive. The tiny Magnuszew bridgehead which was only fifteen miles wide by about seven deep was, according to the Soviet account, to contain on the day of the offensive no fewer than 400,000 men and 1,700 tanks and SUs; but by then the Soviet front commanders hardly bothered to conceal their actions or intentions. Flying weather here was poor at first as it had been to the south, and reliance was to

[37] 4 Panzer Army consisted of only two corps. *OKH Kriegsgliederung*, 31 December 1944.

[38] Konev, *Sorok Pyatyi God, Novyi Mir*, No.5, 1965; see also Guderian, *Panzer Leader*, p. 390.

[39] *Ibid*, pp. 392–3. The designations of *Grossdeutschland* and *Feldherrnhalle* had been assumed by two corps headquarters. In this operation von Saucken was in command of the panzer grenadier divisions *Grossdeutschland* and *Hermann Göring*.

be placed on artillery and tanks for fire support. The forward battalions attacked after a relatively short artillery bombardment against Block's 56 Panzer and Hartmann's 8 Corps, both part of von Lüttwitz's 9 German Army which consisted in all of only seven infantry divisions and the Warsaw garrison.[40] Success was immediate and both of these corps were scattered, the two divisions of Henrici's 40 Panzer Corps held in 9 Army reserve suffering the same fate. On 15 January the Pilica was forced and Radom fell on 16 January. 16 Air Army supporting Zhukov's Front in the newly arrived fine weather flew 3,400 sorties against a reported forty-two *Luftwaffe* sorties. On 1 Belorussian Front's right flank Warsaw was being steadily enveloped from the north and the south, the main weight of the attack coming from the southern pincer made up of Bogdanov's 2 Guards Tank and Belov's 61 Armies. Fries's 46 Panzer Corps which had the task of blocking the route to Poznan was forced to withdraw westwards from the Warsaw area to avoid the pincers, but such was the pressure of 2 Guards Tank Army from the south that 46 Panzer Corps was forced back northwards over the Vistula thus leaving the axis to Poznan and the Oder uncovered. By 17 January Warsaw, a *Führer* selected fortress, was evacuated by the Germans and occupied by 1 Polish Army.

On 16 January Hitler returned to Berlin having ordered the removal eastwards of Sepp Dietrich's 6 SS Panzer Army from the area of the Ardennes. Undeterred by the ruin of Army Group A and the plight of Army Group Centre, with the frightening consequences for scores of millions of Germans, he sent the greater part of the forces being removed from the Ardennes to Hungary to protect the oilfields and refineries.[41] The evacuation of Warsaw against his orders fed the flames of his fury, and he busied himself over the next few days in conducting an inquiry and ordering the arrest of a number of General Staff officers who appeared blameworthy.[42] On 16 January Harpe was removed from his command of Army Group A and replaced by the *Führer*'s favourite, Schörner, from Army Group North, Schörner's place being taken by the Austrian Rendulic. Von Lüttwitz, too, had to go. Schörner, however, could do nothing to influence the battle situation. Such reinforcements as he received from Himmler's Replacement Army were a few poorly trained and half equipped *Volksgrenadier* divisions, the staff and students at military schools and some police and SS. Meanwhile the troops of 1 Ukrainian and 1 Belorussian Fronts poured westwards and the pursuit continued by day and night, the tanks moving along the roads in great columns against negligible opposition. On 19 January, only seven days after the start of the offensive, Red Army troops crossed the 1938 Polish-Silesian frontier to the east of Breslau, encouraged by the promise of rewards and honours for

[40] *OKH Kriegsgliederung* 31 December 1944.
[41] The main Hungarian oilfield area was in Nagykanizsa and the oil refineries were in Budapest and Komarno.
[42] Guderian, *Panzer Leader*, pp. 393–4.

crossing the Oder, and the approach to the river developed into a race.[43] What remained of 4 Panzer and 9 Armies had been left miles behind, a great pocket moving slowly westwards towards Glogau on the Oder. Only Schulz's 17 Army, which had not been closely engaged, had managed to retire in some semblance of order, giving up Cracow on 19 January and falling back to the upper Oder in the south-east of Silesia.

Reinhardt, commanding Army Group Centre in East Prussia, was also in the gravest danger. His command was made up of 3 Panzer and 4 and 2 Armies, and he was also supported by a motley German force of armed police and *Volkssturm* believed to number about 200,000. Reinhardt had pressed Hitler without success to permit the evacuation of Kurland and the withdrawal of 4 Army which stretched out to the south-east in a salient towards Suwalki and Augustow back to the chain of the Masurian Lakes near Lötzen. The Soviet armies had a mobility and preponderance in strength which enabled them to attack in the north and south, with the Masurian Lakes between them, in two great pincer movements directed on Königsberg and Marienburg aimed at enveloping the whole of East Prussia. The Soviet fronts had an abundance of equipment and very strong tank and artillery forces, but there existed the customary dearth of infantry caused by high casualties. At this time Rokossovsky's 2 Belorussian Front received 120,000 replacements, but none of these came from the Soviet Union's home reinforcement organization. Just under 40,000 were wounded and sick returned to duty and 20,000 were troops combed out from the rear and supply services. 10,000 were former Soviet prisoners in German hands who had been retaken, and 53,000 were conscripts, mainly Poles, Ukrainians and Balts, forced into the Red Army.[44]

Rokossovsky's 2 Belorussian Front was to attack northwards from the Narew bridgehead. The main thrust was to be made almost due northwards against Weiss's 2 German Army on Mlawa, Deutsch-Eylau, Osterode and Marienburg by four armies and a tank army with another army in reserve. Two other armies and a tank corps were to make subsidiary thrusts north-west towards Thorn and Pomerania.[45] Chernyakhovsky's 3 Belorussian Front further to the north was to attack westwards into East Prussia against Raus's 3 Panzer Army, moving along the line of the Pregel to Königsberg and cutting off the German troops in Memelland. Four armies and two tank corps were to be used in the main sector of the attack and Beloborodov's 43 Army from 1 Baltic Front was to support the north flank by attacking across the Niemen.[46]

---

[43] *Istoriya*, Vol. 5, pp. 81–2.

[44] *Ibid*, pp. 103–4.

[45] 2 Belorussian Front consisted of V. S. Popov's 70 Army, Batov's 65 Army, Fedyuninsky's 2 Shock Army, Gusev's 48 Army, Gorbatov's 3 Army, Grishin's 49 Army, Boldin's 50 Army and Volsky's 5 Tank Army.

[46] 3 Belorussian Front consisted of Shafranov's 31 Army, Chanchibadze's 2 Guards Army, Luchinsky's 28 Army, Krylov's 5 Army, Lyudnikov's 39 Army and Galitsky's 11 Guards Army.

Five lines of ammunition were allotted to the attack, two of which were to be used on the first day of the fighting.

Rokossovsky's offensive began on 14 January amid heavy snow which cut the visibility to only 200 yards, the forward battalions attacking with such success that the artillery fire programme was cancelled. In the first few hours resistance was insignificant but then, bit by bit, company and battalion strength counter-attacks were mounted and the German enemy began to fight bitterly with all his old vigour. On 15 January Reinhardt committed to battle his army group reserves, 7 Panzer Division and the panzer grenadier division *Grossdeutschland*, and these inflicted losses and delays on 2 Belorussian Front. It was at this time, however, that Hitler removed von Saucken's panzer corps *Grossdeutschland* from Reinhardt and dispatched it by rail to Army Group A at Lodz to stem the 1 Belorussian Front offensive further to the south, and when Rokossovsky committed a further two tank corps against Reinhardt his offensive started to move once more. On that day the weather became fine everywhere and Vershinin's 4 Air Army made 2,500 sorties. The two Hitler designated fortresses of Mlawa and Modlin were taken, and by 19 January Rokossovsky had broken through on a seventy-mile front and had penetrated to a depth of forty miles. That same day Red Army troops crossed the 1938 East Prussian frontier from the south near Neidenburg, 2 German Army retiring before them, abandoning depots and supplies and mining the roads as it went. Tannenberg was taken on 21 January, the Germans before they withdrew removing the remains of Hindenburg and his wife and destroying the great memorial.

Chernyakhovsky's 3 Belorussian Front had moved due westwards into East Prussia to the north of Rokossovsky, attacking Raus's 3 Panzer Army on 13 January, using the fog, low cloud and the noise of low level aircraft to conceal the presence of the forces being concentrated for the attack. The attack began at 6 a.m. but in spite of the heavy weight of supporting fire Soviet progress was very slow, Schlossberg and Kattenau changing hands several times in the fighting. Tilsit was taken on 18 January. 3 Panzer Army although under heavy pressure continued to present an unbroken front. Hossbach's 4 German Army in the exposed salient forward of the Masurian Lakes had not yet come under attack, but Weiss's 2 German Army in front of Rokossovsky's 2 Belorussian Front was in danger of disintegration. Although reinforced by sailors, *Luftwaffe* ground staff and *Volkssturm*, many fled and many gave up the fight. Some strong points when surrounded did not fight on and some of the commanders of these garrisons were to be shot out of hand for their failure. On the evening of 23 January a detachment of 29 Tank Corps of Volsky's 5 Guards Tank Army reached Elbing near the Baltic. The shops were open and the factories were still at work as the tanks drove down the main street with their headlights on. Thorn and Marienburg were taken and by 26 January 3 Panzer Army, 4 Army and part of 2 German Army had been cut off in East Prussia. Rokossovsky's forces had advanced 125 miles in twelve days.

The German war diarist noted at the time that the Soviet troops made good use of maps and bypassed all centres of resistance, and he was particularly impressed by the flexibility of the Red Army leadership.[47]

Reinhardt had pressed for the early withdrawal of Hossbach's 4 Army behind the Masurian Lakes, but not until 21 January would Hitler agree to this. By then it was required to form a new front to the rear of 3 Panzer Army near Wormditt facing westwards to cover the gap caused by the breaking of 2 Army. On 22 January the *Führer* further agreed to the evacuation of Memel, but the following day he was insisting that the Lötzen line in the Masurian Lakes was to be held at all costs. This position was already outflanked by the Soviet advance. Reinhardt was convinced that he should withdraw, taking with him many of the East Prussian population in a bid to rejoin the German positions on the Vistula and Nogat to the west of Danzig; Hossbach, the commander of 4 German Army, shared his views and retired on Heilsberg behind the Masurian Lakes preparatory to mounting an attack to the west. On 26 January a suspicious Hitler began to rage against Reinhardt and Hossbach, ordering their removal, Reinhardt being replaced by Rendulic from Army Group North and Hossbach by F. W. Müller. Rendulic was expressly ordered to hold Königsberg, the East Prussian capital, to the very end. The same day Hitler instigated another reorganization and redesignation of formations, Army Group North becoming Army Group Kurland, Army Group Centre becoming the new Army Group North while Army Group A became Army Group Centre. A new Army Group Vistula had been formed covering Danzig and Pomerania, this taking under command Weiss's 2 Army and Busse's 9 Army composed largely of part formations and detachments, the command being entrusted to Himmler (who held in addition the posts of Commander of the Replacement Army and Chief of Police and the SS), since Hitler was of the conviction that loyalty, reliability and fanaticism outweighed military ability and experience. Of these two latter qualities Himmler had none. Since Army Groups Kurland and North were already cut off from the *Reich*, the defence in the east was to depend on Army Group Vistula covering the approaches to North Germany, while Army Group Centre covered Saxony, Sudetenland and the whole of Czecho-Slovakia. Army Group South was still in Hungary and German troops continued to hold the greater part of Yugo-Slavia and Northern Italy. Hitler still considered that the strategic areas most important for the survival of Germany were the oil districts of Hungary and the Vienna basin and the deep water U-boat training grounds in the Gulf of Danzig. Twenty-six divisions were in Kurland and twenty-seven divisions had been cut off in East Prussia.

The battle for East Prussia was almost at an end, although Rendulic was to hold on grimly to the city of Königsberg, Samland and part of the south bank of Frisches Haff for some months yet. Meanwhile the battle for Pomerania was about to begin. The Soviet forces were having difficulty with ammunition

[47] *Kriegstagebuch des OKW*, Vol. 4, p. 1022–3.

and motor fuel supply as railway construction and repair lagged far behind the advance. Good airfields and food supplies there were in abundance. It had originally been intended to destroy Army Group Vistula's 2 Army under Weiss and the newly formed 11 Army under Steiner by the use of Rokossovsky's 2 Belorussian Front, but in the event the attack towards Neustettin mounted on 10 February was brought to a standstill after ten days' fighting, many of the Soviet divisions being very tired and reduced to a strength as low as 4,000 men.[48] 2 Belorussian Front's fighting strength at this time was about 300 tanks and forty-five rifle divisions.[49] Zhukov's 1 Belorussian Front which was closing up to the Oder had meanwhile probed northwards into West Pomerania in order to improve the security of its flanks and, meeting with little resistance, advanced over thirty miles, destroying enemy groupings at Deutsche-Krone and Arnswalde. A new plan for a Soviet offensive into Pomerania was therefore drawn up, involving both 1 and 2 Belorussian Fronts. Rokossovsky's 2 Belorussian Front was to resume its attack northwards into the centre and east of Pomerania, its main thrust being made initially on Koslin. Zhukov's 1 Belorussian Front was to take up the attack one week later, attacking northwards from Arnswalde into West Pomerania, the main axis being from Arnswalde to Kolberg on the Baltic.

Raus, the Commander of 3 Panzer Army, had meanwhile arrived back in Pomerania from East Prussia, since it was intended that his headquarters should take over from the newly formed 11 Army headquarters later that month. Having seen some of the troops available for the defence, in particular those of the so-called Pomeranian Division, a motley force of engineers, *Luftwaffe* ground staff, naval survey units and *Volkssturm* battalions, without artillery, anti-tank guns, signal equipment or supply services, in some cases without even regimental and battalion commanders, Raus doubted whether Pomerania could be held. On the *Führer*'s orders Himmler was about to mount the Stargard counter-offensive on which Guderian had set such hopes, and Himmler told Raus that both he and the *Führer* were convinced that the Stargard offensive would decide the whole outcome of the war in favour of Germany. Then began the selection of officers to fill the vacant regimental and battalion commanders posts, and these were simply selected by Himmler from a list of officers about to return from leave to Army Group Kurland. Many of these were rushed off to their stations in one of Himmler's cars after the battle had actually started. The Stargard counter-offensive which had begun on 15 February was a failure and was halted almost immediately.[50]

On 20 February, to all Germans except the *Führer* and his immediate circle, the situation appeared very serious. Speer repeatedly affirmed that the war was lost, but the *Führer* had long since refused to give him an audience. Guderian

---

[48] 11 Army had been formed in Pomerania at the end of November as a joint Army-SS headquarters.
[49] *Istoriya*, Vol. 5, p. 140.
[50] Documentary evidence of Raus, the Commander of 3 Panzer Army.

had informed von Ribbentrop that an armistice must be sought on at least one front. To the more enlightened and critical the German position seemed hopeless. In the centre on the Oder Berlin was directly threatened by 1 Ukrainian and 1 Belorussian Fronts; on the lower Vistula Red Army troops around Elbing and Marienburg were trying to break through to Danzig and Gdynia. On 21 February Hitler issued a series of unrealistic orders. 17 Army in Upper Silesia was to prepare to operate offensively against the left flank of 1 Ukrainian Front. The Oder-Neisse line was to be defended while the Pomeranian railway from Stettin to Danzig, so necessary, according to Hitler, for the German Navy in the Baltic, was to be held at all costs. The true situation, as the Chief of General Staff and the Commander of 2 Army advocated, demanded the evacuation of Kurland, East Prussia and the whole of Pomerania. 11 Army which had attacked on 15 February with such limited success from Stargard towards Arnswalde had been forced back again by the enemy.[51] A week later, when Rokossovsky began the offensive from the area between Danzig and Bydgoszcz, the fate of the German troops in Pomerania was sealed.

Red Army progress was slow at first but Neustettin was taken on 28 February, and on 1 March part of Zhukov's 1 Belorussian Front joined the offensive from the area of Arnswalde. Zhukov had left only three armies on the Oder and used four rifle armies and two tank armies with other corps in his thrust from Arnswalde.[52] The presence of so many formations to the north had not been suspected by the German High Command. G. K. Kozlov's 19 Army reached Koslin near the Baltic on 5 March and 2 German Army was cut off. The Soviet troops then fanned out west towards Kolberg and east on Gdynia.

The *Führer*'s reaction was predictable. Kolberg became a fortress and he made a clarion call for the reconquest of Pomerania. Five panzer and panzer grenadier divisions were ordered up from Army Group Centre to Stettin, but the shortage of vehicle fuel was such that only sufficient was available for battle; all moves had to be carried out by rail, and the formations arrived at Stettin only shortly before the bridgehead came under attack from east of the Oder and the Stettiner Haff by Belov's 61 Soviet Army and Bogdanov's 2 Guards Tank Army. All reinforcing German formations were swallowed up in this battle. Meanwhile hordes of refugees from the Baltic States, East Prussia and Pomerania, mainly women and children, the young and the very old, blocked all roads and tracks, as they made their way with farm carts and on foot through the bitter weather westwards away from the Soviet and

---

[51] On 25 February 3 Panzer Army Headquarters (removed from East Prussia) took over the functions of 11 Army.

[52] The armies taking part in the Pomeranian battle were as follows:
   1 Belorussian Front: Perkhorovich's 47 Army, P. A. Belov's 61 Army, Bogdanov's 2 Guards Tank Army, Simonyak's 3 Shock Army, Katukov's 1 Guards Tank Army and 1 Polish Army.
   2 Belorussian Front: G. K. Kozlov's 19 Army, V. S. Popov's 70 Army, Grishin's 49 Army, Batov's 65 Army and Fedyuninsky's 2 Shock Army.

Polish terror. Many of them had fled their homes in the Baltic States and East Prussia by crossing the Kurische Nehrung and Frische Nehrung, narrow strips of land more than fifty miles long and barely a mile or two wide connecting Memel with Königsberg and Königsberg with Danzig. Dying from exposure and under frequent attack from the air, they tramped on in the wake of prisoners and slave labourers who were being moved under escort from the east to the west. Sometimes they came under fire and on at least one occasion a refugee column was ground under the tracks of Red Army tanks which deliberately ran over it. 2 German Army and 3 Panzer Army were broken apart into isolated formations and detachments and these continued to fight on during the next few weeks. Part of 10 SS Corps and Corps Group Tettau were encircled near Bad Polzin. Stargard was taken on 5 March and the encircled garrison at Grudziadz was destroyed the next day.

The German anti-tank defence relied mainly on the anti-tank grenade and the short range hollow charge missile, and of the 580 enemy tanks destroyed during the battle two-thirds were disabled by courageous men and youths in close combat. Anti-tank companies consisted of men of the supply services on motorcycles or bicycles kept in readiness for mobile action. In Baldenburg there was a surprise break-through of about fifteen tanks, but a handful of men all over fifty years of age kept their nerve and drove them off with losses, this being the first time that any of these men had ever seen enemy tanks. At noon the same day a telephone message was received from a forestry station which was part of the warning system that a number of Soviet tanks were concentrating nearby, and immediately a bicycle company from Baldenburg pedalled off furiously in pursuit, destroying six of the enemy tanks that same afternoon. Although the action of these brave irregulars could have proved of valuable assistance to the field forces, without a field army framework the German resistance could not be long protracted. The Latvian and French SS Divisions, which had become separated from 2 Army during the break-through, flooded back, many of them in panic-stricken flight, and their conduct threatened to demoralize the hitherto staunch *Volkssturm*. Enemy soldiers disguised as Baltic or Polish refugees hid their weapons in carts and joined the wagon trek into the rear and then occupied communication centres by *coup de main* attack. In the overrun areas there was an orgy of murder and rape.

On the afternoon of 25 February when 3 Panzer Army was told of the *Führer* order that Kolberg was to be a fortress, Raus objected on the grounds that the town was full of hospitals and wounded and overcrowded with refugees; he lacked the means to defend the town or the command staff to control the defence. He was told from the OKH that a colonel would arrive by air to take command of the fortress and that twelve new anti-tank guns would be dispatched from Spandau, this in spite of the fact that all rail communication to Kolberg was known to be blocked by hospital and refugee trains. Within two days the refugees and inhabitants had thrown up a ring of earthworks and fortifications and commandos were organized both inside and outside the town to press men and equipment into service. Nobody raised any objections to the instructions of the fortress commander who in his domain was master over life and death.[53] In Kolberg the *Volkssturm* was to fight desperately until 18 March, covering the evacuation by sea of the wounded and refugees. On 20 March Himmler was removed from the command of Army Group Vistula and replaced by Heinrici, the former Commander of 1 Panzer Army, but by then the campaign in Pomerania was nearly over. Gdynia fell on 28 March and Danzig was taken two days later, 2 Belorussian Front claiming to have captured there 10,000 prisoners with 140 tanks and forty-five U-boats. The German troops defending Gdynia and Danzig, with great masses of refugees who clung to them for protection, in spite of contrary orders from the High Command had risen up and moved off eastwards into the delta of the Vistula where they held out between that river and the Nogat until after the end of the war.

Between 10 February and 4 April 2 Belorussian Front was said to have taken 63,000 prisoners while 1 Belorussian Front claimed 28,000. This short campaign removed the danger, such as it was, of a German attack from the north flank, although by then the half-trained and disorganized German troops, lacking aircraft and vehicle fuel, had since the Ardennes offensive been in no condition to mount a powerful and co-ordinated offensive anywhere. The short campaign in Pomerania enabled the Red Air Force to threaten the sea communications to Kurland and East Prussia and resulted in a further ten Soviet armies becoming available for the attack on Berlin.[54]

The outrages and atrocities perpetrated against the German civil population by the Red Army in some respects were little removed from those committed by the German *SS Einsatzkommandos* in Russia. They were probably the more terrifying because they were committed not just by the NKVD but by the officers and the rank and file of the Soviet Army, atrocities occurring wherever German territory was overrun. Some apologists for the Red Army associate this behaviour with looting and the raping of German women in the intoxication of victory, and this is sometimes accounted for by race hatred, poor discipline and the conditions of war. There is an element of truth in this. Red Army discipline was poor and it had certainly not been improved by the enlistment of convicted criminals and the conscription of peasants whose military service was measured in weeks. On the other hand Red Army commanders had no difficulty in keeping a tight rein on their troops when they were in the USSR and serious offences against the Soviet civil population carried the death penalty, a penalty which was speedily enforced. Outside the Soviet Union, however, these codes appear no longer to have applied. The Rumanian and the Hungarian civil population suffered badly also, and yet such treatment was not reserved for enemy nationals since the Poles and the Yugo-Slavs, the allies of the USSR, did not escape entirely. The Red Army

[53] Documentary evidence of Raus.
[54] *Istoriya*, Vol. 5, p. 148.

only crossed the north-east corner of Yugo-Slavia yet in that short time there were reported 1,200 cases of looting with assault and 121 cases of rape in which all but ten of the rapists accompanied the rape with murder.[55]

The record of the Germans in Eastern Europe, particularly that of the SS and the civil administration, was admittedly vile, especially their treatment of Jews, gypsies, Poles and Red Army prisoners of war. This treatment was a deliberate act of policy on the part of the German Government. Yet the Soviet record in Germany in 1945, in the Baltic States in 1940 and in Poland in 1939, was in every way as terrible. The Red Army soldier was often primitive, barbaric and cruel and he needed the restraint of the threat of draconian punishment to keep him under control. Outside the Soviet Union this restraint was lifted, since such was the arrogance of the Soviet rulers and system that non-Soviet citizens were regarded as a lesser breed, often without protection or rights. Bitter hatred against Germans had been instilled into all ranks throughout the course of the war, this being the particular task of the commissar or political deputy. Some of this propaganda was based on truth and some of it on lies. As the Red Army approached the borders of Germany the propaganda was intensified and as an act of policy the troops were told that personal property and German women were theirs by right and that they were not accountable by law for civil crime committed in Germany. The writer Ilya Ehrenburg devoted his talents to preaching this race hatred, and the military and national press exhorted the Soviet soldier not to spare the German population. The underlying reason for this policy cannot be stated with certainty. It has been suggested that the Soviet intention was to create such terror that the German population east of the Oder-Neisse line, in what was to become the new Poland, should flee, leaving their towns and farmlands to the Pole. Such an aim and such methods are at least logical, but the assertion cannot be supported since Soviet outrages continued right to the banks of the Elbe weeks, even months, after the war had ended. It is more likely that this evil and horrific policy, which was in some respects similar to that preached by Hitler, was based on emotional as well as material factors, and was characteristic of the dictatorship which ordered it. Stalin's primary aim was to wreak Soviet revenge not on the German state or economy but on the German people as a whole.

Churchill at about this time had apparently begun to have serious doubts about the true nature of his Soviet ally. He noted a conversation with Stalin in which the dictator had said that the USSR would require a labour force of four million Germans to be kept in the Soviet Union indefinitely. Stalin had talked to him of the mass liquidation of 50,000 German officer prisoners of war and the dictator's attitude was sufficiently grim for Churchill, on reflection, to doubt whether Stalin had meant to joke. Churchill noted, too, what he described as the dreadful things committed by Red Army troops in Europe.[56]

[55] Djilas, *Conversations with Stalin*, p. 82.
[56] Feis, *Churchill Roosevelt Stalin*, p. 635.

Much of the German population of Pomerania remained where it was because it was unable to flee or because, being rooted to the soil, it hoped that reports of Soviet excesses were exaggerated and that conditions might return to normal after the first few days of occupation. If they had known the terror to which they were to be subjected, followed by an enforced deportation both eastwards and westwards, none of them would have stayed. Until the NKVD had firmly established its own form of control, there was to be no uniformity or pattern in the behaviour of the Red Army troops or the communist Poles who followed, except that they looted and raped indiscriminately. The German communists, real or professed, and hardy members of the proletariat who, armed with red flags, went out to greet their Soviet brothers were to receive the rudest of treatment. Many were relieved of their valuables and their boots, after which they were beaten to the ground with rifle butts. Hospitals were raided, the doctors murdered and the nurses raped. The wounded were sometimes dispatched by a shot in the head or were flung out of high windows. In some towns everyone in uniform and anyone in office, the burgomaster, his staff, the police, postmen, railway officials and foresters were murdered out of hand, in some cases the killings extending even to Party members; in other towns all officials were spared. The nobility, the landed gentry and clergymen were sometimes hunted down and killed with great savagery, cases having been reported of the victims being blinded, mutilated or hacked to pieces. Men and women were dragged to their deaths behind horses. Victims of rape were sometimes murdered and this extended to children not yet in their teens. Nor was rape left to the private enterprise of soldiers but was sometimes an organized business, women being rounded up in droves and imprisoned in barracks or public buildings for a week at a time after which they were flung out into the street to make room for more. Those Red Army men who had little taste for murder, sadism or rape were often unstable and would sometimes shoot down German men and women for little or no reason.[57]

Before long the deportations began. Notices were posted instructing all males to report as labour for the repair of bridges and the railway track destroyed by the retreating *Wehrmacht*. They were to bring with them two changes of clothing and fourteen days food; this was the invitation to Siberia. Many Germans went on that long journey; many others declined and went into hiding. When invitations no longer produced recruits the round-ups began both of men and of women, but these were conducted in a most haphazard fashion. People were sometimes collected from the streets without warning and were marched off in columns, presumably to the labour camps inside the Soviet Union, since they were never seen or heard of again. Others were marched from one end of Pomerania to the other, those who fell out being shot on the spot. Then, for some unaccountable reason, the survivors were marched back again and set free until the next round-up should occur.

[57] *Documents on the Expulsion of the Germans from Eastern Central Europe*, pp. 48–68.

There appeared to be little logic in the actions of Soviet troops, who were both wilful and capricious. A Pomeranian family is said to have returned to their hometown in Stolp to find their house occupied by Red Army troops. These were correct and remarkably civil, telling the family that they could have their house back as soon as the troops had vacated it. When the family moved in some days later they found three Germans had been done to death in the cellar and another in an outhouse.[58] There were cases where Soviet troops behaved themselves perfectly correctly and others where they defended Germans against the revengeful Pole and Russian. There were other cases where Poles defended Germans against Red Army men. Meanwhile in Berlin Keitel, well informed of what was afoot in the occupied territory, was bemoaning that the leaderless and terrorized German civil population had lost its valour and that the heroes of the hour were the much despised Polish slave workers who, without ties and without property and having nothing but their lives to lose, were soon fighting with the marauding Russians.[59]

The Soviet historian has subsequently attempted to gloss over these crimes by claiming that they never happened except in isolated cases, or by drawing attention to the fearful loss of life caused to the innocent by the Anglo-American bombing over Germany.[60] There can be no point in moralizing or attempting to allocate relative responsibility for war crimes whether allegedly committed by German, Russian or Anglo-American. The true facts of the Soviet occupation must, however, be recorded.

[58] Jahn, *Pommersche Passion*, p. 113.

[59] Minute in file *OKH Gen St d H Op Abt IV, Fremde Heere Ost*, of 20 January 1945.

[60] 'The Red Army came as a deliverer from the Fascist yoke. However there were individual acts of revenge by Soviet soldiers against *resisting* Germans.' *Istoriya*, Vol. 5, pp. 85–6; 'Not all Soviet soldiers knew how to conduct themselves towards the inhabitants but 2 Belorussian Front took firm measures to deal with these.' *Ibid*, p. 113.

CHAPTER THIRTY-THREE

East Prussia, Austria and Silesia

In the early summer of 1944 the *Wehrmacht* had had over a million and a half troops in France and the Low Countries, but of these only 900,000 belonged to the field formations of the German Army and Armed SS.[1] The field strength of the Army and SS on the Eastern Front at that time stood at 2,160,000. Between June and November 1944 the German Army in Russia, Rumania and Hungary lost 214,000 dead and 626,000 missing; in France the loss stood at 54,000 dead and 339,000 missing. This total of 1·2 million men permanently lost equalled the total German casualty rate for all theatres from August 1939 to February 1943 including the defeat at Stalingrad, and the figure did not cover the wounded, who were reckoned to be three times as numerous as the dead. Throughout the whole year of 1944, 106 divisions were destroyed or had to be disbanded, the same number of divisions that Germany had in 1939 at the beginning of the war.[2] The losses in army equipment in the east and the west were no less serious, and with such blood-letting the end could not be far off. On the day of the Normandy landings the *Luftwaffe* first line strength *for all theatres* stood at 2,300 fighters and 700 night fighters, of which a little more than half were serviceable, whereas the Anglo-Americans alone on that day had 5,400 fighters and over 5,000 bombers in the air.[3]

During the second half of 1944 following the attempt on Hitler's life there had been some fundamental changes in the structure of the German Army. The growth of the National Socialist Leadership Organization was accelerated, with elements to be found as low as battalion level, and although it was impressed on these Party representatives that they were not to take on the appearance of commissars, in fact that is what they were.[4] On 1 August 1944 it was decreed that in Germany, as had long been the practice in the Soviet Union, relatives of officers or soldiers judged guilty of treasonable conduct should share the responsibility and the punishment for the crime. The military

---

[1] This does not include the German forces in Italy or the Mediterranean.
[2] Mueller-Hillebrand, *Das Heer*, Vol. 3, Table 65 *et seq.*
[3] *Ibid*, p. 110, quoting *Unterlagen des Gen Qu 6 Abt/OKL.*
[4] The OKW instructions regarding the duties of the NSFO contained the sentence '*So wird auch nur der Anschein eines Politruks vermieden*'.

salute was replaced by the outstretched arm and the Hitler greeting. The political reliability and religion of General Officers and that of their wives became a factor of importance to be taken into account if they were to remain in positions of authority. On 20 July when Himmler, the *Reichsführer SS*, had been appointed to the command of the Replacement Army, infantry divisions gave way to *Volksgrenadier* divisions, closely associated with the people and the Party, and the responsibility for the raising, control and political reliability of these formations was given to the Armed SS. Foreign volunteer formations were transferred to the SS, and the Armed SS was authorized to form an SS army headquarters and more SS corps headquarters, army officers being compulsorily transferred to the Armed SS in order to provide the staffs for the new formations. The Party and the Armed SS had in fact taken over the German Army. The *Volkssturm* was neither part of the German Army nor of the *Wehrmacht* but belonged to the Party, and was composed of males between the ages of sixteen and sixty. The Party *Gauleiter* was responsible for the raising and control of the *Volkssturm* units, sharing this responsibility with the *Reichsführer SS* who, as Commander of the Replacement Army, controlled their military organization, equipment and training.[5]

It has already been related how during January 1945 the commanders of the German army groups were changed and most of the designations of the army groups were altered. Harpe, the Commander of Army Group A, lost his appointment to Schörner, the former Commander of Army Group North. Army Group North was taken over at this time by Rendulic, formerly Commander of 20 Mountain Army in Finland. On 25 January Rendulic's Army Group North, cut off in the Baltic States, was redesignated Army Group Kurland; Reinhardt's Army Group Centre became the new Army Group North based on East Prussia; and Schörner's Army Group A on the Oder became the new Army Group Centre. The title of Wöhler's Army Group South in Hungary remained unchanged. A new Army Group Vistula, firstly under Himmler and then Heinrici, had been interposed on the lower Vistula covering Danzig and Pomerania.

On 26 January, when Rendulic had been in Kurland for exactly twelve hours, he was ordered by the OKW to East Prussia to take over command of Army Group Centre from Reinhardt, who had been dismissed. When Rendulic arrived at his new place of duty he was given verbal instructions from the *Führer* that under no circumstances should Königsberg be lost, as Hitler feared that it was the Russian intention to set up a puppet German government in that ancient capital.[6]

[5] Many members of the *Volkssturm* wore civilian clothing with a *Volkssturm* armband. It was equipped with weapons mostly of foreign pattern, and the ammunition supply was limited to that carried on the man, in some cases only five rounds. The *Volkssturm* had some value, however, in the east, particularly in close-quarter fighting against tanks where the close range hollow charge weapons took a toll of the Soviet armoured force.

[6] Rendulic, *Gekämpft Gesiegt Geschlagen*, p. 338.

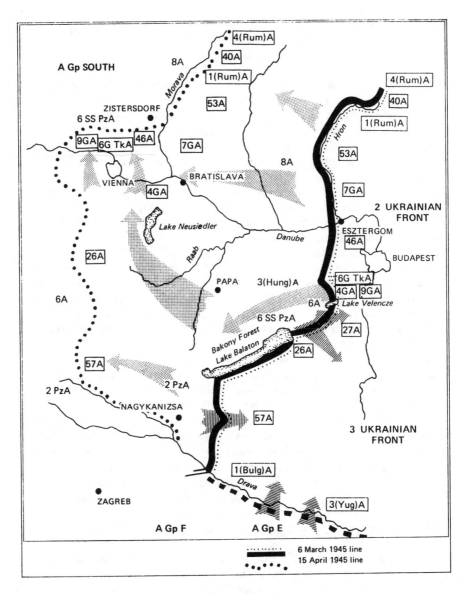

THE END IN HUNGARY AND AUSTRIA
March–April 1945

In East Prussia the battle which had begun in the middle of January was still raging. In the north, Bagramyan's 1 Baltic Front in Lithuania followed up Gollnick's 28 German Corps and occupied Memel on 27 January. To the south of 1 Baltic Front, Chernyakhovsky's 3 Belorussian Front had advanced due west and by the end of January was on the eastern outskirts of Königsberg. Yet further to the south the right flank of Rokossovsky's 2 Belorussian Front had overrun the whole of the south-west of East Prussia and was closing in on Königsberg from the south. In the first week in February it appeared that Königsberg would fall quickly when Beloborodov's 43 Soviet Army encircled the town from the north, taking Cranz at the exit of the Kurische Nehrung, and moving down to the Frisches Haff, cut off the city both from Samland and from Pillau, its only port. Meanwhile Galitsky's 11 Guards Army crossed the Pregel and cut Königsberg off from the German troops fighting to the south of the Frisches Haff. This Soviet gain had been diminished, however, when the panzer grenadier division *Grossdeutschland*, the *Hermann Göring* Division and other elements attacked 11 Guards Army in the flank, drove it off and re-established contact with Königsberg from the south. Rokossovsky's left flanking force, Romanenko's 48 Army, had temporarily found itself in great difficulties when Hossbach, the Commander of 4 German Army, had attacked westwards on the night of 26 January, in order to break out to the Nogat. This operation had cost Hossbach his appointment and he had been replaced by F. W. Müller.[7]

Rendulic's Army Group North consisted of Raus's 3 Panzer Army to the east of Königsberg until the headquarters was withdrawn in February to organize the defence of Pomerania, and Müller's 4 Army to the south-west and south of Königsberg. Weiss's 2 Army, which had formerly been part of Reinhardt's command, had been driven off westwards when the Red Army had reached the Frisches Haff, and had been put under command of Army Group Vistula. After the withdrawal of 3 Panzer Army Headquarters, 4 Army held an area to the south of the Frisches Haff nowhere deeper than twelve miles and about forty miles in breadth, including at its northern end the city of Königsberg, with elements of about twenty-three divisions.[8] Gollnick's Group Samland was separated from 4 Army by an eight mile strip of Soviet-held territory to the west of Königsberg, and consisted of detachments and elements of about nine divisions.

By this time Rokossovsky's 2 Belorussian Front had become committed to the offensive in Pomerania, and the destruction of the enemy forces in Königsberg and Samland was entrusted to Bagramyan's 1 Baltic Front, while Chernyakhovsky's 3 Belorussian Front was to destroy 4 German Army south of the Frisches Haff. 2 Baltic Front took over from 1 Baltic Front the responsibility for containing Army Group Kurland further to the north, and there

[7] Dieckert und Grossmann, *Der Kampf um Ostpreussen*, pp. 115-7; Guderian, *Panzer Leader*, p. 400.
[8] *OKH Kriegsgliederung* of 19 February 1945.

was some redistribution of formations between Chernyakhovsky's and Bagramyan's commands. In the third week of February, however, the Red Army met with further reverses and misfortunes which delayed the final offensive. On 19 February, a day before 1 Baltic Front was due to attack Königsberg, the Germans themselves attacked from the city and from Samland in order to reestablish a ground corridor into the city. Supported by the guns of the German Navy, the attack succeeded and a firm corridor was established three days later, this giving Königsberg a lease of life for another two months. On 18 February, only two days before the proposed offensive, Chernyakhovsky, the Commander of 3 Belorussian Front, was killed near Mehlsack, and it became necessary to delay operations and reorganize the Soviet forces yet again. Vasilevsky who, as the representative of the High Command, was to have controlled the two fronts, took over the command of 3 Belorussian Front on 21 February. Bagramyan, who was temporarily in disfavour due to his failure to prevent the enemy relieving Königsberg, had his command downgraded, 1 Baltic Front being redesignated as the Samland Group of 3 Belorussian Front, Bagramyan coming under Vasilevsky's command. The offensive itself was put off until 13 March.[9]

Rendulic, the Commander-in-Chief of Army Group North, was ordered by Hitler on 11 March to return to the command of Army Group Kurland where a new Soviet offensive was expected. Rendulic's replacement was Weiss, the former Commander of 2 Army.

By that time there was a build-up of supplies in Königsberg through the newly reopened corridor, and, although Vasilevsky estimated that there were nineteen German divisions to the south of the bridgehead and only eleven in Samland and Königsberg, he decided with Stalin's agreement to alter the priorities and attack the southern grouping before opening the offensive on Samland and Königsberg.[10] The attack started in bad weather in poor flying conditions and was directed on Heiligenbeil in the centre. The German defences had been well constructed, the pumping stations having been destroyed and much of the area flooded from the sea. 4 Army resisted bitterly and fought for every yard. By 19 March the bridgehead had been reduced to an area twenty miles in length by six in depth and as it shrunk stili further, 4 Army was forced back and compressed on to the narrow Balga Peninsula jutting into the Frisches Haff towards Pillau. There were many cases of desertion and flight. On 18 March the weather had cleared and this led to an intensification of bombing attacks on the promontory. A representative of 6 German Corps was sent to the *Führer* to request permission to evacuate the beaches, but this was refused. On 26 March, however, Hitler sanctioned the withdrawal 'after all the artillery, tanks and vehicles had been shipped off'.[11] By then it was too late even to save all the troops and their personal weapons. Many did escape

[9] *Istoriya*, Vol. 5, pp. 163–8.
[10] *Ibid*, p. 169.
[11] Dieckert und Grossmann, *Der Kampf um Ostpreussen*, p. 149.

across the Frisches Haff to the Frische Nehrung and Pillau, but Vasilevsky claimed to have captured 46,000 prisoners, 600 tanks and assault guns and to have inflicted in addition 93,000 casualties.[12]

Vasilevsky then turned his attention to Königsberg and Samland. Bagramyan's Samland Group Headquarters was disbanded and its staff and plans incorporated into the Headquarters of 3 Belorussian Front, Bagramyan's formations being taken under direct command. According to Soviet estimates there were four infantry divisions in Königsberg and eleven in Samland, the *Luftwaffe* tactical support being down to about 170 aircraft operating from the airfields in Samland and on the main boulevards in Königsberg. The sluices of the Pregel had been opened and the surrounding area was flooded.

The final assault on Königsberg involved detailed preparation, and, if the Soviet historian is to be believed, maps of Königsberg were issued down to platoon commander level with all blocks, roads and reference points numbered, while a 1:3000 model of the city was built for the briefing of the higher commanders. The air support was provided by a concentration of air armies, 18 Long Range Army and air formations of the Leningrad and 2 Belorussian Fronts together with aircraft of the Baltic Fleet being added to the two organic air armies of 3 Belorussian Front, making a total of 2,400 aircraft in all, co-ordinated and controlled by Novikov, the Commander-in-Chief of the Air Forces. River gunboats were brought overland to the Pregel from Oranienbaum on the Gulf of Finland and railway artillery was hauled up from the area of Leningrad, together with 203 mm and 305 mm heavy artillery. Four armies, totalling 137,000 men with 530 tanks and SUs, were detailed for the assault into Königsberg.[13]

Meanwhile the position inside Königsberg appeared hopeless. Headquarters Army Group North had been removed from East Prussia and the command of Group Samland and the Königsberg Fortress devolved upon Müller and Headquarters 4 Army. This officer, who after the war was to meet his death before a Greek firing squad, arrived in Königsberg on 2 April on a one-day visit, and there was an immediate and heated exchange between him and Lasch, the Commander of the Königsberg Fortress, after which he threatened to report Lasch to the *Führer* on account of his pessimism. Müller then addressed all formation commanders and Party leaders in the cellar of the University buildings in buoyant tones, assuring them that not only would Königsberg be held, but that he, Müller, would drive the enemy out of East Prussia. Meanwhile, however, Group Samland had removed from Lasch an infantry and his remaining panzer division, so that he was left with four infantry divisions and eight battalions of *Volkssturm*, in all about 35,000 men. *Luftwaffe* support was virtually non-existent. The Red Army by this time was making good use of its Free Germany Committee organization adherents

---

[12] *Istoriya*, Vol. 5, p. 170.
[13] The armies were Beloborodov's 43, Ozerov's 50, Lyudnikov's 39 and Galitsky's 11 Guards Armies.

and was tapping telephone conversations inside the city, and sending in numerous German spies dressed as soldiers or as civilians. At the end of March 561 Volksgrenadier Division was attacked by a number of Germans in army uniform who, having introduced themselves as stragglers, produced machine-carbines and disappeared over to the Soviet lines with twenty prisoners.[14] Treachery was suspected everywhere. In the 100,000 strong civilian population there was a feeling of great terror, and the presence of so many civilians can only have reduced the battle efficiency and morale of the defending troops. Koch, the *Gauleiter* of East Prussia, had carried out the *Führer*'s instructions faithfully in that he had prevented any evacuation. These city dwellers, lacking even farm transport, had been unable to disobey him.

After heavy air and artillery preparation the assault began at midday on 6 April and by evening Soviet infantry had already fought their way into the town. Lasch, the Commander of the fortress, asked Müller for permission to withdraw to Samland. This was refused. The next day, however, the city was cut off from Group Samland and Müller ordered Lasch to break out, by which time this was no longer possible. On the evening of 9 April the wounded Lasch asked in vain for authority to capitulate; Lasch then surrendered and except in some isolated pockets fighting stopped on 10 April. On 12 April the angry *Führer* had Lasch sentenced to death in his absence and without trial, and his family was arrested by the SS as hostages.[15] Müller, too, lost his command, being replaced by von Saucken, the Commander of the rump of 2 Army encircled in the delta of the Vistula. At about the time when *Gauleiter* Koch was fleeing to Denmark on an ice breaker, the city of Königsberg was entered by the Red Army and became the scene of the most fearful barbarity and atrocity.[16]

On the morning of 13 April began the final stage of the attack against the German Group Samland. The German force, reckoned at eight infantry divisions and one panzer division with a strength of about 65,000 men, began to fall back the next day on the Fischhausen Pillau Peninsula to prevent Soviet penetration, and about 20,000 men managed to reach Pillau where they organized a hasty defence.[17] The resistance there was fanatical and desperate and took six days to overcome. Meanwhile headquarters and troop detachments with a great mass of civilians had been evacuated by sea from the port, movement which the Baltic Red Fleet made no attempt to interrupt. Between

[14] Lasch, *So Fiel Königsberg*, pp. 84–5.

[15] *Ibid*, p. 117. Among the arrested were his wife and daughters and his son-in-law, who was at that time commanding a battalion at the front. They were fortunate to escape with their lives.

[16] Dieckert und Grossmann, *Der Kampf um Ostpreussen*, p. 181. About a quarter of the 100,000 population are estimated to have died, either during the fighting or in the excesses which followed. *Documents on the Expulsion of the Germans from Eastern Central Europe*, p. 32.

[17] There were three corps headquarters in Samland, Matzky's 26, Wuthmann's 9 and Chill's 55 Corps (in Pillau).

13 and 26 April 3 Belorussian Front claimed to have taken 30,000 prisoners. The campaign in East Prussia had lasted 105 days and the endurance of Army Group North, the German Navy and *Luftwaffe* had been remarkable. Soviet casualties were heavy, 3 Belorussian Front losing twenty-two and 2 Belorussian Front fifteen per cent of its strength in the four weeks before 10 February.[18] Soviet historians give the credit for the German success in prolonging the struggle to the fact that the enemy was able to make good use of sea communications.

At this time there were 135 weak German divisions on the Eastern Front and seventy-seven disorganized divisions on the Rhine.

Meanwhile Hitler, undeterred by the Soviet forces massing on the Oder preparatory for the attack on Berlin, had ordered a German offensive on his far distant southern flank in Hungary. The *Führer*'s intention was to envelop part of 3 Ukrainian Front between the Danube and the Drava and, establishing new bridgeheads over the Danube, retake Budapest and eastern Hungary. His aims, so he persuaded himself, were mainly economic, since the Hungarian and Austrian oilfields were together producing eighty per cent of Germany's oil, and nothing that Guderian said would persuade him to transfer troops to the Oder. For this reason he was to commit to Hungary Sepp Dietrich's 6 SS Panzer Army, recently withdrawn from the Ardennes.[19]

The new offensive was to be made by Wöhler's Army Group South together with a subsidiary attack from the south by Loehr's Army Group E in Yugo-Slavia. Balck's 6 Army together with 8 Hungarian Corps and Dietrich's 6 SS Panzer Army, having in all ten panzer and five infantry divisions, was to attack between Lakes Balaton and Velencze and split Tolbukhin's 3 Ukrainian Front into two parts. 2 Panzer Army, commanded by Angelis, with four infantry divisions was to attack eastwards from the south of Lake Balaton while three divisions of Army Group E crossed the Drava from the south.[20] Tolbukhin's Front was made up of five armies with thirty-seven Soviet and six Bulgarian rifle divisions, two tank and one mechanized corps and a cavalry corps, totalling in all over 400,000 men, 400 tanks and SUs and 1,000 aircraft.[21] The Soviet formations were being prepared for an offensive and for this reason were in great depth; Tolbukhin knew that a major German offensive was imminent to the south-west of Budapest and this was confirmed by Hungarian deserters at the beginning of March. The Soviet High Command intended that the launching of the Soviet offensive should be delayed until the German attack had spent itself, and for this reason Red Army troops were ordered to hold and not to counter-attack.

---

[18] *Istoriya*, Vol. 5, pp. 179–80. It is most unusual for Soviet accounts to make any mention of Soviet losses.

[19] Guderian, *Panzer Leader*, pp. 412–3.

[20] *OKH Kriegsgliederung* 1 March 1945. There is a doubt about the accuracy of these totals since no firm figure is available for 6 SS Panzer Army.

[21] *Istoriya*, Vol. 5, p. 195. The four Soviet armies were Gagen's 26, Sharokhin's 57, Trofimenko's 27 and Zakhvataev's 4 Guards Armies.

3 Ukrainian Front was in some difficulty because of the low-lying ground and the network of rivers and canals to its front and rear. Moreover the Danube formed a great obstacle right across the Soviet line of communications. In the forward area these water obstacles were of assistance in the defence, but in the rear they complicated the problems of movement and supply; the Danube, too, was full of ice floes which threatened the eight pontoon bridges and ferry points, some of which had capacities of up to sixty tons, in operation below Budapest. To overcome this difficulty an overhead cable track had been constructed capable of delivering 1,200 tons of stores daily across the river, while for the first time in the Red Army forward area a pipeline was used to deliver fuel.[22]

On the night of 5 March Loehr's Army Group E attacked 1 Bulgarian and 3 Yugo-Slav Armies across the Drava while Angelis's 2 Panzer Army attacked Sharokhin's 57 Soviet Army south of Lake Balaton. These attacks were, however, only subsidiary, and the main offensive began the next day between Lakes Balaton and Velencze, with 6 SS Panzer Army on the right and 6 Army on the left, the attack falling on Gagen's 26 Army and Zakhvataev's 4 Guards Army. The German offensive was preceded by a short thirty-minute artillery bombardment, but air support was restricted by the availability of aircraft and the poor flying weather. The thrust began to make ground slowly, four miles in the first two days and sixteen miles after four days, the SS making the better progress against 26 Army; but the German offensive was slowed and halted by the reserves of artillery deployed under Nedelin, the Chief of Artillery of 3 Ukrainian Front, and by the bringing forward of formations of Trofimenko's 27 Army to plug the gap. Casualties were very heavy on both sides. On 10 March the position gave Tolbukhin some anxiety since most of the Soviet reserves had been committed, and for this reason he asked to be allotted Glagolev's 9 Guards Army which was still east of the Danube and held as part of the High Command Reserve. This request was refused, as by 13 March the German attack was observed to be losing its momentum. On 14 March, however, Wöhler committed his remaining panzer reserve based on 6 Panzer Division, and a mixed grouping of 200 tanks and assault guns continued to battle with Trofimenko's 27 Army for the next few days. The 2 Panzer Army attack to the south of Lake Balaton, although it changed the direction of its thrusts several times, became bogged down under the weight of the artillery fire of Sharokhin's 57 Army, and the Yugo-Slavs and Bulgarians on the Drava, with some assistance by Soviet troops, successfully contained the German bridgeheads.

When it was obvious to the Soviet High Command that Wöhler had shot his bolt, the Soviet counter-offensive was ordered. Malinovsky's 2 Ukrainian Front had taken no part in the battle and 9 Guards Army was still uncommitted in reserve. The counter-offensive was to be made by both 2 and 3 Ukrainian Fronts, co-ordinated by Timoshenko as the representative of the

[22] *Ibid*, p. 196-7.

High Command, but whereas it had originally been intended that Malinovsky should make the main thrust towards Vienna, the Soviet High Command changed its plan on 9 March by earmarking Kravchenko's 6 Guards Tank Army for Tolbukhin, in order that he should use it to envelop and destroy both Balck's 6 Army and Dietrich's 6 SS Panzer Army between the Lakes Velencze and Balaton.[23]

On 16 March Zakhvataev's 4 and Glagolev's 9 Guards Armies, with Kravchenko's 6 Guards Tank Army in reserve, attacked the left flank of Balck's 6 German Army to the north-west of Lake Velencze, and struck south-west to seize the area between Lakes Velencze and Balaton and so cut off part of Balck's 6 Army and the whole of Dietrich's 6 SS Panzer Army, which Gagen's 26 and Trofimenko's 27 Soviet Armies were to attempt to pin frontally. A proposal by Wöhler to use Dietrich's force offensively against the Soviet flank was not sanctioned by Hitler until some days afterwards, by which time it was too late. The SS troops started to withdraw, sometimes without orders, and the enraged Führer repudiated the former pride of the Party by ordering a personal representative to Hungary to ensure that the members of the SS, including the Leibstandarte Adolf Hitler, were stripped of their armbands.[24]

At the beginning of the offensive 3 Ukrainian Front was said to be down to one and a half lines of ammunition, although this presumably could not have applied to 6 Guards Tank Army which was fresh from 2 Ukrainian Front. With heavy air support from 17 and 18 Air Armies, 4 and 9 Guards Armies fought their way slowly forward against bitter resistance as the Germans strove to keep their line of withdrawal open; not until 19 March was Kravchenko's 6 Guards Tank Army committed to battle. The German escape corridor was eventually reduced to less than two miles in width, and through this gap most of the German troops escaped, leaving much of their heavy equipment behind them. The operation developed into a pursuit as the Germans retreated in disorder westwards through the Bakony Forest, unable to make a stand since no intermediate defensive positions had been prepared. On 25 March Papa was taken, and Soviet armour started moving north-west towards the River Raab and the Austrian border. That same day Wöhler was removed as Commander of Army Group South to be replaced by Rendulic, who was considered by Hitler to be an expert in defence. Meanwhile Malinovsky's 2 Ukrainian Front to the north had cleared Esztergom and the Hron valley, and was moving on Bratislava. This city it took on 4 April.

German resistance in Hungary was at an end. Kreysing's 8 German Army in the north fell back rapidly before Malinovsky's 2 Ukrainian Front into Austria. Elements of 6 Army and 6 SS Panzer Army made some effort to defend the line of the Raab, but they were bypassed by 3 Ukrainian Front

---

[23] *Ibid*, pp. 203–5. Malinovsky's 2 Ukrainian Front at this time consisted of Kravchenko's 6 Guards Tank Army, Petrushevsky's 46 and Shumilov's 7 Guards Armies, Managarov's 53 and Zhmachenko's 40 Armies.

[24] Guderian, *Panzer Leader*, p. 419.

which swept on into Austria. On the south flank Sharokhin's 57 Soviet Army and 1 Bulgarian Army had on 2 April, after the hardest of fighting against Angelis's 2 Panzer Army, taken the oil producing region of Nagykanizsa. As the Austrian border was reached the Hungarians, whose morale and enthusiasm for the Axis cause had always been low, began to give up in large numbers, no fewer than 45,000 surrendering in the two days before the end of the month.

Rendulic did not arrive at his new post until the second week in April. On 6 April, when *en route* from Army Group Kurland to Austria, he was seen by the *Führer* to be briefed and receive his orders. He has described how he motored through the ruined Berlin streets to the Chancellery, the outside and the entrance hall of which appeared to be undamaged. Inside, however, he noted a great deal of damage to the mosaic hall. Below the Chancellery, in the bunker in which he lived and worked. Hitler personally briefed his new army group commander on the battle situation. He had changed much since Rendulic had last seen him about three months before, insofar as his physical appearance was concerned. He was bent and stooping, dragged his left leg while continually holding his left arm with his right and yet, Rendulic maintained, the deterioration of his body had not affected the state of his mind. His speech, his eye and his manner appeared, said Rendulic, as clear and as purposeful as ever. The *Führer* said that it appeared impossible to bring the Russian to a standstill and Rendulic's task was to hold Vienna and to prevent the enemy from getting into the Alps or north up the Danube valley. The main enemy, Hitler had decided, was the Russian, and the Anglo-American forces were merely to be held back or delayed. The German Oder line defences, the *Führer* was convinced, were very strong and he said that he was supremely confident. Rendulic, suspecting that the quiet in the centre on the Eastern Front was the prelude before the storm, would have liked to have known more about the factors on which this optimism was based, but Hitler volunteered nothing. When Rendulic looked questioningly at Jodl, Jodl merely shrugged his shoulders.

So Rendulic went on his way, while the *Führer* returned to poring over his out-of-date battle maps. The new Commander of Army Group South, shortly to be redesignated Army Group *Ostmark*, was not even to be allowed to demolish the Vienna Danube bridges without the express authority of the *Führer*, and the detail of his subsequent actions and troop movements within the city of Vienna were to be questioned from Berlin.[25]

On 1 April the Soviet High Command had issued its orders for the early capture of Vienna, since the capital was of great strategic importance as a communication centre for German-occupied Europe. The city was to be encircled from the east by Petrushevsky's 46 Army with a tank and mechanized corps, all part of Malinovsky's 2 Ukrainian Front, while Zakhvataev's 4 and Glagolev's 9 Guards Armies and Kravchenko's 6 Guards Tank Army of 3 Ukrainian Front attacked from the south and west. In order to transfer 46

---

[25] Rendulic, *Gekämpft Gesiegt Geschlagen*, pp. 367–73.

T

Army to the east bank of the Danube, 72,000 men and 500 guns were ferried across the Danube and Morava by the Danube flotilla near Bratislava in the space of five days.[26] On 6 April street fighting developed in the Vienna out-skirts which were defended by elements of 6 SS Panzer Army; but the double encirclement of the town meant that fighting was not protracted, particularly since Rendulic needed troops to cover both the oil producing area of Zisters-dorf in the north-west of Austria and the open country to the west of Vienna between the city and the foothills. The centre of the city was evacuated on 10 April and the remainder was occupied by Soviet troops three days later. Meanwhile fierce fighting continued, as Rendulic tried to hold the Soviet forces as far east as possible while he withdrew his wounded to the west.

On the northern flank Heinrici, who had succeeded Himmler as the Commander of Army Group Vistula, held the line of the lower Oder. On 19 March Hitler had been obliged to agree to 3 Panzer Army, commanded by von Manteuffel who had succeeded Raus, evacuating its Stettin bridgehead east of the Oder. Heinrici's alternatives, that the 3 Panzer Army troops on the east bank could either be saved during the night or lost in the morning, were to the point and not without effect. German troops still held out in an enclave in Danzig, Gdynia and the Vistula estuary and Hitler refused to evacuate these forces or 16 and 18 Armies from Kurland by sea.[27]

Meanwhile Guderian, the Chief of the General Staff, was in difficulties and his days in office were numbered. His principal operations officer, Wenck, had been injured in a motoring accident and had been replaced by Krebs, the former Chief of Staff to Model's Army Group B in the West. Krebs's war service had been spent on the staff except for a short period of some weeks duration when he deputized for Köstring, the Military Attaché in Moscow, during the latter's absence on leave. Krebs was a friend of Burgdorf, who since Schmundt's death had been Hitler's military aide and Chief of the Army Personnel Department. Burgdorf was responsible to Hitler for all the main army appointments and, living in the tightly knit circle about Hitler together with Bormann and Fegelein, he was much closer to the *Führer* than Guderian or even Jodl and Keitel. According to Guderian, Krebs was drawn into this inner circle. Guderian, far from enjoying Hitler's confidence at this time, merely excited his anger, and it was inevitable that the *Führer* and Burgdorf should be looking about them for a suitable successor as Chief of the General Staff. Krebs had occupied the principal operations appointment under Guderian for the previous few weeks and was therefore *au fait* with current

---

[26] *Istoriya*, Vol. 5, p. 213.

[27] Guderian, *Panzer Leader*, p. 413; Doenitz, *Memoirs*, pp. 399–400. Of Hitler's many reasons for holding the Baltic coast had been the Baltic sea trade, the political attitudes of Sweden and Finland and the covering of the U-boat training area in the Gulf of Danzig. On 17 March 1945 Guderian reproached Doenitz that the German Army was being retained in Kurland partly on naval considerations. Doenitz says he protested that Kurland was of no importance to the German Navy but that Hitler told him that Kurland was being held because of the land situation.

operational matters, and his personality was such that Hitler saw in him an obedient and malleable executive. Just as Zeitzler, the personal friend of Schmundt, had been brought in to oust Halder, so did Krebs, through the prompting of Burgdorf, displace Guderian. On 1 April Guderian was dismissed from an appointment for which he was not suited and in which, like Zeitzler, he had achieved nothing. The occasion chosen for Guderian's dismissal was the failure of five divisions of Busse's 9 Army to destroy the Soviet bridgehead on the west bank of the Oder near Küstrin and throw back the encircling enemy troops. This check was all the more galling to Hitler as it forced him to give up an ambitious and unrealistic plan to mount an Army Group Vistula counter-offensive from Frankfurt-on-Oder into the rear of 1 Belorussian Front.[28]

Meanwhile in Silesia events had not stood still. The fanatical Schörner had taken over Army Group Centre (formerly Army Group A) on 20 January at a time when his three major formations, 4 Panzer Army, 17 Army and 1 Panzer Army, were retreating in disorder before Konev's 1 Ukrainian Front from the area of the Upper Vistula east of Cracow and from Eastern Czecho-Slovakia. Schulz's 17 Army and Heinrici's 1 Panzer Army had contrived to maintain cohesion and organization, but Graeser's 4 Panzer Army was so greatly under strength that it became necessary to reinforce it heavily by *Volkssturm* and police units. Schörner's right wing had suffered a further weakening by the loss of 1 Hungarian Army, which had disbanded itself during the withdrawal. Army Group Centre had fallen back on to the line of the Oder on a very extended front over 300 miles in length, reaching from the mouth of the Neisse, which was the boundary with Army Group Vistula, to the area just north of Vienna where Army Group Centre joined with Army Group South. 4 Panzer Army stood before South Brandenburg, and together with 17 Army covered the great industrial area of Silesia in front of Glogau, Breslau and Oppeln, and 1 Panzer Army stretched away in a great salient to the south in Czecho-Slovakia. The Silesian industrial region was still working at full production and was the main armament complex remaining to Germany. Schörner had the equivalent of eighteen infantry divisions and elements of six panzer and panzer grenadier divisions and these were insufficient to cover his frontage. Of reserves he had none.

Konev's 1 Ukrainian Front had reached the Oder on 23 January and had secured two large bridgeheads over the river, one to the south near Brieg between Breslau and Oppeln, and one to the north between Breslau and Glogau in the area of Steinau. Nehring's 24 Panzer Corps and von Saucken's panzer corps *Grossdeutschland*, both under strength and nearly exhausted, had completed the long march back to the Oder to the area of Glogau, where a German bridgehead was maintained on the east bank. Despite the opposition of the corps commanders, Hitler and Schörner ordered both panzer corps to destroy the Red Army Steinau bridgehead. This attempt failed.

[28] Guderian, *Panzer Leader*, pp. 427–9.

In the second week of February Konev reopened the offensive, in spite of his lack of reinforcements and supplies and the tiredness of his troops. The Soviet intention was to occupy Silesia west of the Oder and close up to the line of the River Neisse in Brandenburg thus bringing Konev's troops alongside Zhukov's 1 Belorussian Front ready for the final offensive on Berlin, Brandenburg and Saxony. On 8 February Konev broke out of the Steinau bridgehead north of Breslau with four rifle and two tank armies against Graeser's 4 Panzer Army and after three days had extended his breakthrough to a depth of forty and a width of ninety-five miles, closing up to the Neisse and encircling about 18,000 German troops in the fortress of Glogau. On 14 February Zhadov's 5 Guards Army attacked north-west from the Brieg bridgehead south of Breslau, and in conjunction with Gluzdovsky's 6 Army from the Steinau bridgehead, encircled Breslau. Since the railway between Berlin and Silesia had been cut on 3 March, Graeser's 4 Panzer Army counter-attacked in order to regain the control of the railroad and to relieve the garrison at Glogau. The German formations were by then without offensive capability, consisting as they did of stragglers and detachments thrown together with unknown commanders and staffs to form alarm units and improvised regiments. Many of the *Volkssturm* units were of doubtful military value. Willpower and fanaticism could not compensate for the lack of air and artillery support, for tanks and vehicles without fuel, and the absence of signal communications. On 15 March Konev moved yet again, this time on his left flank in order to occupy Upper Silesia as far as the Czecho-Slovakian frontier. The attack was made on both sides of the town of Oppeln, a number of troops having been withdrawn for this purpose from the earlier attack grouping which had reached the Neisse. One army, a tank army and a mechanized corps attacked from the area of Grottkau while two armies, a mechanized corps and a tank corps moved westwards from the area north of Ratibor, all the thrusts being concentric on Neustadt. By 31 March Upper Silesia had been occupied.[29]

The Red Army approach and entry into Silesia caused a mass exodus of the German population. Of the 4,700,000 inhabitants listed in February 1944 only 620,000 remined in occupied Silesia by mid-April the next year.[30] Breslau, like Glogau and Neisse, had been designated a fortress, its first commander being von Ahlfen and its second Niehoff. When the Soviet troops encircled Breslau, 17 and 269 German Infantry Divisions were ordered to break out of the encirclement and rejoin the main forces, leaving only 609 Infantry Division together with a miscellany of units and detachments inside the fortress.[31] 609 Division had been raised in Dresden only a few weeks earlier and of all the officers in its headquarters only one, other than the divisional

[29] *Istoriya*, Vol. 5, p. 149–52. The armies were Gusev's 21 Army and Lelyushenko's 4 Tank Army from the area of Grottkau and Korovnikov's 59 and Kurochkin's 60 Armies from the area of Ratibor.

[30] See also *Documents on the Expulsion of the Germans from Eastern Central Europe*, p. 92.

[31] Von Ahlfen und Niehoff, *So Kämpfte Breslau*, pp. 30–1.

commander, had ever served on a divisional staff before. Its three regiments were made up of various detachments, some troops from 269 Infantry Division, army and SS stragglers, police and the staff and students of military schools. In addition there was an improvised SS regiment formed from training establishments, a *Luftwaffe* regiment of ground staffs and three regiments of army troops made up of miscellaneous elements. The fortress artillery consisted of thirty-two batteries equipped with German, Soviet, Polish, Yugo-Slav and Italian guns. There were no tanks in the garrison except for a company of fifteen assault guns, mostly of different pattern with a variety of main armament. The ill-assorted force was supported by thirty-eight *Volkssturm* battalions, each about 400 strong.[32]

This most unpromising material continued to defend Breslau against all attack until the end of the war and laid down its weapons only after the remainder of Germany had capitulated. The city fought on desperately, buoyed by propaganda and rumour and encouraged by Hitler, Goebbels and the *Gauleiter* Hanke, the garrison purposely being fed with false news by the German propaganda machine. Convinced that Breslau was like a bulwark or a breakwater in a Red Sea, and that help would eventually come, the soldiers and inhabitants repulsed all attacks. In truth, even if Hitler had had the means, it was doubtful whether he would have relieved it.[33] Some still pinned their faith in the *Führer*, others in the new wonder weapons on which Hitler placed such hopes. Rumours were rife. Some of the defenders expected to be relieved by German troops, others by American forces once the enemy coalition had broken down. The 17 Army main front between Striegau and Strehlen remained static for some weeks and the inhabitants could hear nightly the distant rumble of artillery fire. This not unnaturally kept up their spirits. The Kaiserstrasse on the north bank of the river was cleared and used as an airstrip to fly in supplies, and part of two infantry battalions of parachute troops were sent into the city. So they fought on for nearly three months, and of the garrison of 35,000 troops, 15,000 *Volkssturm* and 80,000 inhabitants, 29,000 became casualties.[34] Mostly without training or experience they learned among the ruins and rubble to fight by fighting, and by so doing it is estimated that they tied down seven besieging Red Army divisions. On 6 May Gluzdovsky, the Commander of 6 Soviet Army, sent an offer of terms to the besieged garrison over his signature and that of his chief of staff Panov (but omitting that of the political member of the military council), guaranteeing safety, medical care, and the retention of personal property to the garrison and civil population and the immediate repatriation of prisoners at the end of the war.[35]

None of the conditions of the offer was kept by the Soviet Union.

[32] *Ibid*, pp. 36 and 120–7.
[33] Von Ahlfen, *Der Kampf um Schlesien*, p. 219.
[34] The figures are in doubt. *Documents on the Expulsion of the Germans from Eastern Central Europe*, p. 44, puts the loss of lives of civilians as high as 40,000.
[35] Von Ahlfen und Niehoff, *So Kämpfte Breslau*, pp. 109–10.

CHAPTER THIRTY-FOUR

Berlin

On the night of 23 March Montgomery's 21 Army Group established a firm foothold over the lower Rhine and started to move eastwards. Further to the south Bradley's 12 Army Group extended its bridgeheads at Remagen and Mainz, and 1 United States and 9 United States Armies began the rapid double envelopment which ended on 1 April in the encirclement of Field-Marshal Model's 325,000 strong Army Group B in a great eighty-mile pocket in the Ruhr.

On 28 March, when the Anglo-American troops were already advancing into Germany with great rapidity, the Supreme Allied Commander in the West, General Eisenhower, without consulting the Combined Chiefs of Staff or his British Deputy Commander, sent a telegram for delivery to Stalin direct to Major-General Deane, the Head of the United States Military Mission in Moscow. Eisenhower explained to Stalin that his primary mission after he had destroyed the pocket in the Ruhr would be to split the enemy forces by making a junction with the Soviet armies in the east, and that the main axis to be taken by the Anglo-American forces would be from west to south-east to the area of Erfurt, Leipzig and Dresden. In addition, Eisenhower intended to advance into the Regensberg-Linz area of Austria in order to forestall any German plans for the setting up of a Bavarian Austrian redoubt. The Allied Supreme Commander asked to be informed of Soviet plans in order that action might be co-ordinated between the Western and Eastern Allies. This telegram was handed to Stalin in Moscow on 28 March.[1]

Although Germany and Europe had been politically dissected at Yalta by Roosevelt, Churchill and Stalin, there had been no previous consultation or agreement on the co-ordination of military strategy between the Red Army on the one hand and the Anglo-American forces on the other. In the previous September Montgomery had pressed Eisenhower to continue his advance into Germany and although this proposal had been resisted, Eisenhower and Montgomery had apparently been agreed at that time that the main political

[1] Message FWD – 18264 (SCAF 252) General Eisenhower to Military Mission in Moscow, personal to Marshal Stalin, 28 March 1945.

and military objective was the capture of Berlin.[2] Even as late as 27 March, the day before Eisenhower sent his telegram to Moscow, Montgomery in his report on operations had informed Churchill that he was thrusting for the Elbe and Berlin, and both Churchill and Montgomery were greatly surprised when they were acquainted with the contents of Eisenhower's telegram. Churchill felt that Eisenhower had overstepped the bounds of his responsibilities in that he had taken it upon himself to decide his own objectives, political as well as military. Moreover, Churchill disagreed with the Supreme Allied Commander's decision, believing that the Western Allies would be in a better position to bargain with the Soviet Union, which since Yalta had become increasingly arrogant, by taking Berlin before the Red Army.[3] Churchill's protests, however, were of little avail. Montgomery remonstrated with Eisenhower when his 21 Army Group lost the control of 9 United States Army and was allocated objectives on the North Sea and Baltic Coast, but Eisenhower felt that Berlin was no longer a particularly important objective. 9 United States Army was ordered to advance towards Berlin as far as Magdeburg on the Elbe, while the remainder of the United States forces turned southeast into South Germany and Austria, where, it was wrongly believed, Hitler was planning to continue the war.

Whether or not Eisenhower could have or should have taken Berlin as his primary strategic objective is outside the scope of this history. He had his reasons for declining to do so, reasons which at the time he considered to be cogent. A thrust on Berlin would, he believed, have cost him 100,000 casualties, and he was misled by an intelligence appreciation which drew its false deductions from the strong grouping of German forces in South Germany, Austria and Czecho-Slovakia.[4] The remarkable aspect of this sudden change of strategic aim is that Roosevelt and the United States Chiefs of Staff should have left this final stage of the war to the discretion of a single individual who, although a soldier of distinction, may at that time have been lacking in political acumen and an understanding of the aims and methods of the Soviet Union.[5] Military objectives should of necessity have been related to post-war political strategy.[6]

When Stalin received Eisenhower's communication from General Deane he sent off an immediate reply in which he stated that he was in general agreement with the American proposals. Stalin affirmed that Berlin had no longer its former strategic significance and for this reason agreed that the Soviet main thrust should be made towards Dresden and Leipzig, subsidiary

---

[2] *Command Decisions*, pp. 377–8.

[3] Churchill, Vol. 6, *Triumph and Tragedy*, pp. 399–409; Eisenhower, *Crusade in Europe*, pp. 433–40.

[4] *Command Decisions*, p. 378.

[5] Even as late as 1948 Eisenhower was to describe the Soviet Union as 'being free of the stigma of empire building by force'. Eisenhower, *Crusade in Europe*, p. 499.

[6] Pogue, *The Supreme Command*, p. 440. The United States President and the United States Chief of Staff left the final stages of the battle to the Supreme Commander.

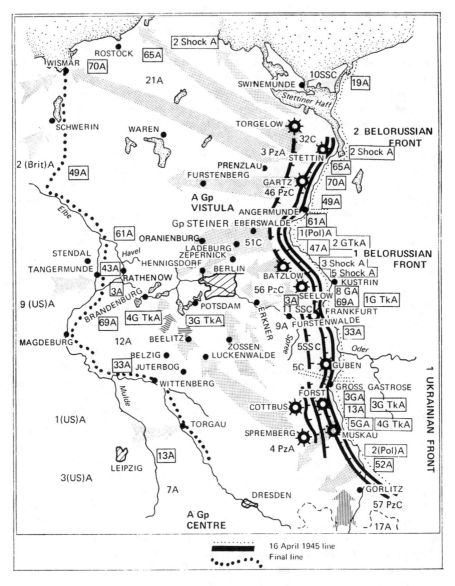

FROM THE ODER TO THE ELBE
April–May 1945

forces only being allocated to the Berlin sector. The Soviet offensive would, he said, be opened in the second half of May, this date being subject to alteration.[7]

Zhukov and Konev were ordered to report to Moscow with their principal staff planning officers. They arrived by air in the late afternoon of Easter Sunday, 1 April, and were received by Stalin in his office at the Kremlin, the other members of the State Defence Committee (GKO) being present, together with Antonov, by then Chief of the General Staff, and Shtemenko, the head of the Operational Planning Directorate. This preliminary meeting is of interest because, if Konev is to be believed, Shtemenko at Stalin's order read out a telegram from an undisclosed source giving intelligence of an Anglo-American plan to capture Berlin before the Red Army should get there. This plan, so the telegram read, involved the rapid movement of an assault force commanded by Montgomery across the North German Plain from the area north of the Ruhr. This incident may in fact have occurred or the account may be a post-war attempt to justify Soviet duplicity.[8] Zhukov and Konev were ordered to prepare their offensives to start on 16 April, Zhukov being given the primary task and the bulk of the forces necessary to capture Berlin and advance on the Elbe, while Konev was to share the primary task, in that he was to support Zhukov in the Berlin operation and was also to undertake the subsidiary one of advancing on Dresden and Leipzig. Not before 15 April were the Western Allies informed of the new date of the offensive and then only because they had become aware of its imminence through the monitoring of German radio.[9] The information was given in answer to a direct question from the United States Embassy in Moscow, Stalin still insisting even at this late hour that the main thrust was to be made in the south-west on Leipzig.

By 3 April Zhukov and Konev had completed their plans and these were agreed by Stalin. Konev had the problem of transferring troops from his strong left flank, where the operations in Upper Silesia had just been completed, to his weakened right in Brandenburg on the Neisse, a task all the more essential since the additional two armies offered to him from the area of the Baltic could not arrive before the beginning of the offensive. Time, however, could not be lost, particularly since 9 United States Army was on 11 April already on the Elbe south of Magdeburg about sixty-five miles from Berlin.[10]

The main attack into Brandenburg and Berlin, to be made by Zhukov's 1

[7] *Istoriya*, Vol. 5, p. 257.

[8] Konev, *Sorok Pyatyi God, Novyi Mir* May 1965; Zhukov has a more elaborate version, in which Stalin is said to have shown him reports of contacts between the Germans and elements of the Western Allies who intended to make a separate peace. Zhukov, *Vospominaniya i Razmyshleniya*, pp. 640–3; also Shtemenko, *Generalnyi Shtab v Gody Voiny*, pp. 329–30.

[9] For German knowledge of the imminence of the offensive see *Kriegstagebuch des OKW*, 14 and 15 April, Vol. 4, pp. 1240 and 1242.

[10] Simpson, the Commanding General of 9 Army, asked permission to thrust on Berlin from the Elbe. This was refused by Eisenhower on the grounds that his centre of gravity was too far to the rear. *Command Decisions*, p. 382.

Belorussian Front in the centre from the line of the Oder, had four rifle armies and two tank armies forming the main thrust, with other subsidiary thrusts to the north and south of the capital. Zhukov's task was to take Berlin and reach the Elbe by the fifteenth day. Konev's 1 Ukrainian Front, further to the south, was to cross the Neisse and seizing the area of Cottbus and Spremberg, was to advance north-west to Wittenberg on the Elbe and to Beelitz to the south-west of Berlin near Potsdam, this line to be reached within twelve days. A subsidiary thrust was to be made on Dresden. In all, Konev's front consisted of five infantry and two tank armies. Rokossovsky's 2 Belorussian Front on the Baltic, with three rifle armies and three tank and one mechanized corps, was to destroy the enemy grouping near Stettin and drive west and north-west into Mecklenburg.[11] Since the main thrust of the whole offensive was to be made by Zhukov's 1 Belorussian Front, there was a re-arrangement of the boundaries to allow the contraction of Zhukov's frontage from a breadth of 200 to 120 miles, so that his front ran from Angermünde in the north to Gross Gastrose in the south. Within his overall boundaries the width of the actual assault frontage was reduced further to only twenty-eight miles, so that each of the four first echelon armies in the area of the breakthrough had a frontage of little more than 12,000 yards.[12]

By then the three fronts had been reinforced and according to the Soviet figures comprised 2,500,000 men, 41,000 guns and mortars, 6,200 tanks and SUs and 7,500 aircraft of all types.[13] In the area of the main assault the gun density was said to vary from 300 to 400 barrels to the mile. This concentration of troops involved much movement and ammunition dumping, the digging of gun positions and communication trenches, and the construction and operation of no fewer than twenty-five bridges and forty ferries over the Oder, of capacities of up to sixty tons.[14] Since 1 Belorussian Front was firmly

[11] The military councils of the fronts were: 1 Belorussian Front, Zhukov, Telegin and Malinin (chief of staff), with Sokolovsky as deputy commander; 2 Belorussian Front, Rokossovsky, Subbotin and Bogolyubov; 1 Ukrainian Front, Konev, Krainyukov and Sokolovsky (from 9 April, I. E. Petrov). The second named in each council was the political member.

[12] There has been much protracted debate in the Soviet military press subsequent to the war as to whether Zhukov should have crossed the Oder at the beginning of February instead of waiting for the clearing of East Prussia and Pomerania. This is irrelevant since Stalin decided that the northern flank should be dealt with first, and Zhukov's opinions were of secondary importance. There has been a similar controversy as to the rivalry between Zhukov and Konev in the taking of Berlin, and this is touched upon by Shtemenko in *Generalnyi Shtab v Gody Voiny*, pp. 329–30. Stalin himself laid down the inter-front boundary between Zhukov and Konev, but this extended for only fifteen miles. Thereafter there were no boundaries.

[13] *Kratkaya Istoriya*, p. 487. These enormous figures have a propaganda rather than a military historical value since they are likely to be exaggerated and in any case include all types of gun and mortar. The contemporary record made by Busse's 9 Army showed that according to its own estimate it came under the fire on 16 April, on the first day of the offensive, of 2,500 guns and 450 tanks, (Zhukov's 1 Belorussian Front). *Kriegstagebuch des OKW*, Vol. 4, p. 1249.

[14] *Istoriya*, Vol. 5, pp. 260–1.

established to the west of the Oder on the Küstrin bridgehead, Zhukov's offensive was to start with only thirty minutes' preparatory artillery bombardment whereas Konev, who had to carry out an assault crossing of the Neisse from its eastern bank, was to be supported by no less than two and a half hours' artillery preparation. Konev had only the air support of his own 2 Air Army whereas Zhukov had his own organic 16 Air Army together with 18 Air Army and, until 20 April when Rokossovsky began his attack, the additional support of 4 Air Army, the air formation organic to 2 Belorussian Front.

It was intended that 4, 2 and 3 Ukrainian Fronts further to the south should keep up their pressure against the enemy to prevent the movement of strategic reserves from Schörner's Army Group Centre or Rendulic's Army Group South to the Brandenburg area; in fact the Germans were stronger in the Berlin area than had previously been supposed and it was subsequently recognized that the whole of 1 Belorussian and 1 Ukrainian Fronts should have been directed on to Berlin. Zhukov's task was not made easier by the fact that Rokossovsky was still engaged in the fighting in the area of Gdynia and Danzig and was not in a position to begin an attack until four days later than the other two fronts. Zhukov was to launch his main forces from the Küstrin bridgehead before first light and, at the conclusion of the short artillery preparation, was to attack by the light of a great concentration of anti-aircraft searchlights. Four armies were to make the initial attack and when the breakout had been achieved, Bogdanov's 2 Guards Tank Army was to envelop Berlin from the north supported by Perkhorovich's 47 and V. I. Kuznetsov's 3 Shock Armies, while Berzarin's 5 Shock and Chuikov's 8 Guards Armies thrust in towards the Berlin suburbs from the east. A little further to the north P. A. Belov's 61 Soviet Army and Poplavsky's 1 Polish Army were to cover Zhukov's right flank and move through North Brandenburg to the Havel and the Elbe. Katukov's 1 Guards Tank Army was to envelop Berlin from the south supported by the two left flanking rifle armies, Kolpakchy's 69 Army and Tsvetaev's 33 Army.

The task confronting Zhukov was not without difficulties, notwithstanding that the Küstrin bridgehead put the Oder behind him. The terrain to his front was low and marshy being intersected by numerous minor tributaries of the Oder, waterways and ditches, many of which were in flood. The German defences in his area were well developed and the enemy had a good view over his bridgehead from the slopes of the heavily defended area of the Seelow redoubt. Zhukov's plan was to concentrate his first echelon armies into the tiny bridgehead and break out by the use of overwhelming artillery fire which was to be used in a short but intense preparatory bombardment. The 140 searchlights which were to illuminate the battlefield before dawn were not to be used as movement light, reflecting their rays from the low cloud, but were to direct their beams close to the ground in order to blind the German defenders. Gorbatov, the Commander of 3 Army, which had just arrived from the Baltic into 1 Belorussian Front reserve, had the plan of attack outlined to him by Zhukov on 15 April, and has said that he had his own reservations about its soundness. He did not care to see so many troops and tanks packed into such a tiny bridgehead and doubted the wisdom of attacking before dawn and trying to turn the night into day, but probably having learned something from his earlier exchanges with Chernyakhovsky, he forebore to comment as he himself was only involved in guarding part of the southern flank between Küstrin and Frankfurt.[15] His doubts appear to have been justified since the use of the searchlights proved to be a failure, as the light was unable to penetrate the dust and smoke of the artillery bombardment which reflected the beams as glare and silhouetted the attacking troops as they advanced. The troop commanders called for them to be extinguished, but this no sooner happened than someone else countermanded the order and the confusion became even worse as they were repeatedly switched on and off so that the troops became night-blind. Chuikov, who was no friend of Zhukov, has added his own biting criticism of the confusion as a multitude of troops, vehicles and tanks choked the roads and tracks so that formations were unable to move, forwards or to the rear.[16]

From 19 January the German High Command had been established in Berlin. The *Wehrmachtführungstab* had moved from Friedberg to Zossen in Camp Maybach, the old OKH headquarters, although Keitel and Jodl established themselves in Berlin Dahlem.[17] The *Führer* had taken up residence in the deep underground bunker under the Chancellery in the centre of the city. If, living beneath the ruins of his new Chancellery, he knew that the end was not far off, he gave little sign of it. He had admittedly caused two orders to be issued demanding the total destruction of resources likely to be of use to the enemy.[18] The thrust of 9 United States Army to Magdeburg, with 1 and 3 United States Armies close behind and further to the south, indicated that Germany was about to be cut into two, and the *Führer* made such arrangements as were possible for the struggle to be continued from both the north and the south of Germany.[19] It has been said that Hitler at this time began to voice the opinions which had been pressed on him in vain by Guderian during the previous year and determined to transfer all available forces to the east against the Russians. It was in any case too late for this. The forces in the west for which Guderian had bickered with Jodl had been destroyed. Further

---

[15] Gorbatov, *Gody i Voiny, Novyi Mir*, May 1964. When the youthful Chernyakhovsky had described a divisional commander of forty-five as 'fairly old' Gorbatov, who was fifty-four at the time, had retorted that forty-five might be old to be playing with dolls, but was not old to be commanding a division. Chernyakhovsky had taken offence at the reply.

[16] Chuikov, *The End of the Third Reich*, pp. 143–50.

[17] *Kriegstagebuch des OKW*, Vol. 4, pp. 1021 and 1289.

[18] *OKW/WFSt/Qu II Nr. 002711/45 g. K* of 20 March and *Nr. 003132/45 g. Kdos* of 4 April 1945. Hubatsch, *Hitlers Weisungen für die Kriegführung*, pp. 303–4.

[19] *Ibid*, pp. 308–10. The *Führer* order dated 15 April made Doenitz responsible for the command in the north of Germany and Kesselring for that in the south.

afield good divisions, many of them battle experienced, lay idle or committed to lost ventures from the Channel Islands to Yugo-Slavia and from the Arctic Circle to Crete, in Norway, Kurland, Italy and the Balkans. There is little evidence that the *Führer* understood the situation so clearly as to appreciate Germany's true position, and for a long time past he had been unable to face facts or order priorities; his ideas were becoming increasingly illusory. The German people as a whole, ignorant that Germany had in any case already been partitioned at Yalta, realized only too well that occupation by the Western Allies was preferable to the severity of the Soviet régime and the dreadful barbarities which were being inflicted on the populations of the eastern territories. Yet it is doubtful whether even considerations of humanity entered Hitler's reasoning at this time. Instead of bolstering the east at the expense of the west, he raised a new 12 Army under Wenck at the end of March made up of about eight newly-formed divisions, in order to relieve Model's Army Group B in the Ruhr pocket and throw back the Anglo-Americans across the Rhine.

Wenck's 12 Army was of relatively minor fighting value. It had been allocated four experienced corps headquarters, but of these two were not able to function in a tactical capacity due to lack of transport and radio. Some of the newly raised divisions were designated panzer divisions and panzer grenadier divisions and had been given factory-new tanks, assault guns, armoured personnel carriers and artillery together with stirring and resonant names such as *Scharnhorst*, *Potsdam* and *Clausewitz*. Their ranks, however, were filled largely by recruits and members of the *Reichsarbeitsdienst*. Many of the formations and units did contain cadres of experienced officers and non-commissioned officers and to these were due the successes which attended Wenck's endeavours.[20]

Model's Army Group was quickly destroyed by American forces, Model himself committing suicide. On the receipt of changed and more realistic orders to relieve the encircled 1 German Army in the area of the Harz, Wenck moved south-west with two of his best equipped panzer divisions as his spearhead, enjoying at first a local success against the British, whom he caught unawares. He was counter-attacked by both British and Americans and shortly afterwards both panzer divisions were almost destroyed. Wenck fell back to the line of the Elbe and the Mulde where, somewhat to his surprise, he found that he was free from Anglo-American air attack. The American forces showed no inclination to follow him up across the Elbe.

The disposition of the German troops on the Oder had undergone little change. In the north Heinrici's Army Group Vistula, consisting of 3 Panzer Army and 9 Army, covered the Oder from the Baltic to the mouth of the

[20] Wenck, Guderian's former chief of operations, was still convalescent from a motor accident at the time of his appointment. He was given Decker's 39 Panzer Corps, Holste's 41 Panzer Corps, Köhler's 20 Corps and von Edelsheim's 48 Panzer Corps, all battle experienced and from the Eastern Front.

Neisse, von Manteuffel's 3 Panzer Army in Mecklenburg standing opposite Rokossovsky's 2 Belorussian Front in Pomerania, while Busse's 9 Army faced Zhukov's 1 Belorussian Front in East Brandenburg. Against Konev's 1 Ukrainian Front stood Graeser's 4 Panzer Army forming the left wing of Schörner's Army Group Centre. Von Manteuffel had ten, Busse had fifteen and Graeser had fourteen divisions. Of this total each army had only one panzer or panzer grenadier division. Behind von Manteuffel and Busse stood Weidling's 56 Panzer Corps in army group reserve consisting of three panzer and three panzer grenadier divisions. The German regular troops covering Mecklenburg and Brandenburg between the Baltic and Görlitz amounted in all to about forty-five field divisions of which five were panzer and three panzer grenadier; but Graeser could, however, be reinforced by Schörner, and during the battle a further four divisions were so committed on the German southern flank.[21] Roughly, therefore, there were fifty weak field divisions deployed against the Soviet offensive of 193 divisions. There were no German strategic reserves and the only tactical reserve, Weidling's 56 Panzer Corps, was already split up between von Manteuffel and Busse.[22]

The *Führer* was sure, once again on the basis of intuition, that the main Soviet offensive when it came would not be directed against Berlin at all but would be made in the south into Czecho-Slovakia, and on 6 April he had removed three panzer grenadier divisions from Army Group Vistula and sent them to the south. Heinrici's protests against the weakening of his sector were countered with the retort that the Red Army was at the end of its resources and that its troops consisted of nothing more than recruits and released prisoners of war. The *Führer* made promises of replacements, offering Heinrici 137,000 armed troops from the SS, *Luftwaffe* and Navy, troops which existed only in his imagination. About 30,000 were eventually produced.

Between January and March sixteen- and seventeen-year-old German youths had been called to the colours and these formed a substantial part of all reinforcements and of the newly raised formations. In addition to the forty-five regular divisions on the Oder and Neisse there was a great miscellany of units, detachments and makeshift formations together with a large *Volkssturm* element. The *Volkssturm* battalions possibly numbered more than a hundred; there were estimated to be thirty in the Forst and Muskau areas on the Neisse and another thirty in Berlin, and although these were poorly equipped with a variety of small arms mostly of obsolete foreign pattern, they had

---

[21] *OKH Kriegsgliederung* dated 12 April 1945.
[22] The Soviet account exaggerates the German strength and includes 17 German Army which was far to the south. *Istoriya*, Vol. 5, pp. 253–4, gives the German strength as four armies and the *equivalent* of eighty-five divisions, listing four panzer, ten motorized and forty-eight infantry divisions and no fewer than 200 *Volkssturm* battalions, 1,500 tanks and 3,300 aircraft. Zhukov in *Vospominaniya i Razmyshleniya*, p. 641, gives an even higher figure of ninety divisions, of which fourteen were panzer and panzer grenadier, thirty-seven independent regiments and ninety-eight independent battalions.

panzerfaust anti-tank weapons in abundance, and the *Volkssturm* were to show sufficient determination to use them at close quarters.[23] In addition to the *Volkssturm* battalions there were armed police units and a large number of Hitler Youth detachments hastily collected and commanded by SS or SA officers. Whether motivated by fear or by devotion to duty, these youths, who were mostly in their very early teens, were often to prove more effective than the *Volkssturm*.[24]

Torgelow, Stettin, Gartz, Batzlow, Seelow, Frankfurt, Guben, Cottbus, Forst, Muskau, Zossen and Spremberg had been developed either as fortresses or as strong points, and the field defences behind the Oder had been well constructed by the use of civilian volunteers. Although these earthworks had some depth they were linear, running from north to south parallel to the river. There were in addition a few poorly developed peripheral defences in the out-skirts and suburbs of Berlin. There were no mobile panzer forces capable of destroying or even checking the enemy tank armies once they had gained a breakthrough; there was no plan of defence for the capital nor had troops been earmarked for the task. German artillery support was inadequate and in the air barely three hundred aircraft remained to support Army Group Vistula.

On 15 April, the day before the Soviet offensive, Hitler issued his last order of the day. It foretold to the fighters on the Eastern Front the fate in store for their families if they lost this battle and the Bolsheviks overran Germany. Old people and children would be murdered, women and girls would become barrack room whores and everybody else would be marched off to Siberia. Hitler promised the support of massive artillery which he did not possess and assured his troops that the Red Army would be destroyed before the capital of the *Reich*, choking in a bath of blood. All ranks were warned against obeying orders of unknown German officers, a precaution in view of the previous Soviet activity of this type in East Prussia and Pomerania.[25] The order was issued too late, however, to reach the troops for whom it was intended.

On the morning of 14 April each division of Zhukov's front had mounted a reconnaissance in force by a battalion attack and had found that the German defenders had withdrawn up to a mile or more as soon as the preparatory bombardment had started. The Soviet troops closed up once more but they did not follow the usual practice of developing the probing attack to a full scale offensive.

The 1 Belorussian Front main offensive opened two days later, before dawn on 16 April, Zhukov moving into Chuikov's 8 Guards Army observation and command post near Reitwein where he was a most unwelcome guest. After three hours of heavy fighting, assaulting divisions reached the second

[23] Kissel, *Der Deutsche Volkssturm 1944–1945*, pp. 75–8.
[24] Konev, *Sorok Pyatyi God, Novyi Mir*, May 1965.
[25] Hubatsch, *Hitlers Weisungen für die Kriegführung*, pp. 310–1.

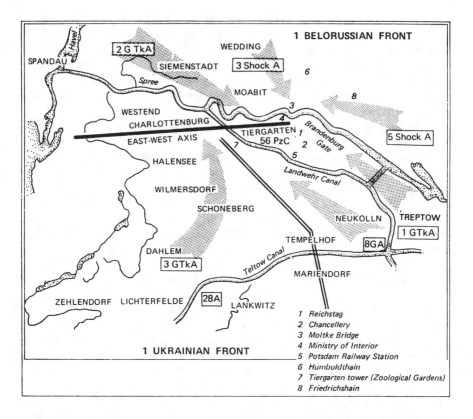

BERLIN
April 1945

line of the German defences where resistance stiffened, particularly in front of the Seelow position. Busse's 9 German Army defences there were based on steep slopes and well constructed anti-tank ditches covered by 88 mm flak guns. To overcome this obstacle, Zhukov at midday committed Katukov's 1 Tank Army to the breakthrough battle rather than wait until the infantry armies had penetrated into the open, and the three tank corps slowly worked their way forward over the few roads and tracks already crammed with 8 Guards Army troops and vehicles.[26] The prisoners who fell into Soviet hands said that orders had been given that any German who retreated without orders was to be shot on the spot, so the Red Army leaders assumed that they would have to fight for every yard of the route to Berlin. So it transpired.[27]

[26] Zhukov, *Vospominaniya i Razmyshleniya*, p. 659. Bogdanov's 2 Tank Army was also committed at this time.
[27] On the morning of 17 April the battle situation of Army Group Vistula was regarded in Berlin as satisfactory. *Kriegstagebuch des OKW*, Vol. 4, p. 1246.

Soviet frontal attacks became too costly and troops were broken up into small detachments to infiltrate through to the German rear. After a very heavy bombing attack on 17 April the Seelow redoubt was taken by Chuikov's 8 Guards Army, supported by a concentric armoured thrust by Katukov's formations; on 18 April the second defensive zone was breached. The staunch resolution of the German defenders, many of them *Luftwaffe* and *Volkssturm*, had come as a surprise to the Soviet High Command, and Zhukov was already two days late in his ordered programme.[28] Some of the flanking Soviet formations had hardly advanced a step.

Further to the south, on the other hand, Konev's 1 Ukrainian Front was making excellent progress in spite of the fact that his support was weaker than that allotted to Zhukov. On the eve of the offensive he had even had to give up his chief of staff, Sokolovsky, to 1 Belorussian Front and received in return I. E. Petrov, the former Commander of 4 Ukrainian Front, a man who was at home with troops but not with paper.

Konev's infantry assault across the Neisse was made on a comparatively narrow frontage between Forst and Muskau by Gordov's 3 Guards Army, Pukhov's 13 Army and Zhadov's 5 Guards Army. As was the Soviet custom, army commanders had their own observation and command posts overlooking the battle area, and Konev took up temporary residence on the night of the attack in Pukhov's command post. Unlike the 1 Belorussian attack, Konev did not attempt to move his troops up to the water line until it was broad daylight, but he covered his activity from German observation by the smoke laid by guns and aircraft. Despite the earlier plans for a long preparatory bombardment, after only forty minutes of artillery preparation the forward troops began to cross in boats, the 85 mm anti-tank guns, according to Konev, being hauled across the bed of the river by cable. Pontoon and fixed bridges followed, twenty fixed and seventeen pontoon bridges and a number of ferries being in operation by the night of 16 April. All the tanks of Rybalko's 3 and Lelyushenko's 4 Guards Tank Armies crossed the Neisse by ferry, it having been ordered that they should use their own river crossing fording equipment when they reached the Spree.[29] Both tank armies were over the Neisse by 17 April. By 18 April, notwithstanding determined resistance and some fierce counter-attacks by Graeser's 4 Panzer Army, Konev reached the two strongholds of Cottbus and Spremberg, neither of which he could take. Cottbus remained the strong southern shoulder of the German defence line. Spremberg he bypassed from north and south and moved rapidly into the enemy's rear, cutting off Schörner's Army Group Centre from Army Group Vistula. The terrain over which Konev moved differed from that met by Zhukov to the east of Berlin, and although watered by a number of rivers and

[28] Chuikov, *The End of the Third Reich*, pp. 150–8.
[29] Presumably Konev means the use of deep or underwater fording tank equipment. Why 85 mm anti-tank guns, which weighed at the most 1¾ tons, should be dragged across the river bed is not clear.

streams it was in the main sandy and less marshy, and for this reason more suitable for the use of tanks. On the other hand much of it was heavily forested, and nearer Berlin it was intersected by numerous lakes. Yet Konev was to say that movement was easier than he had anticipated, since the great forests and plantations were traversed by broad rides, very strange to one who had been brought up in the Russian forests. Control, however, was difficult. All around was the smoke and noise of battle and yet nothing was to be seen, the fierce fires raging in the woods adding to the perils and difficulties of tank and infantrymen alike. Red Army and German troops were scattered and inter-mingled and one Soviet General, bumping along the forest tracks in his 'Willys', met his death at the hands of German stragglers. The bodies of the dead and dying choked the brooks and streams.

On the evening of 17 April Stalin had spoken to 1 Ukrainian Front on the short wave radio and, explaining that Zhukov's troops were making slow head-way in the face of strong opposition, he proposed that some of the tank formations of 1 Belorussian Front should use the gap made by Konev in order to close in on Berlin from the south. Konev countered by pointing out the delays that this would involve, and so it was agreed that Konev should turn Rybalko's 3 Tank Army and Lelyushenko's 4 Tank Army further northwards on Zossen and Potsdam.[30] Meanwhile Zhukov's 1 Belorussian Front continued to make its slow progress westwards as the tanks had not yet gained open country and their casualties were heavy. After some very hard fighting near Batzlow, V. I. Kuznetsov's 3 Shock and Perkhorovich's 47 Armies on the night of 19 April broke the third line of the defences, while Bogdanov's 2 Tank Army reached open country and the outskirts of north Berlin at Ladeburg and Zepernick.

The 9 German Army defenders had contained the heavy weight of the offen-sive for three days before the Soviet tank forces broke out to the north of Berlin and separated them from von Manteuffel's 3 Panzer Army. To the south they had already been isolated from much of 4 Panzer Army by Konev's thrust towards Zossen and Potsdam which cut across Busse's 9 Army's lines of communications. 9 Army could no longer defend Berlin; nor could the original front be restored. The war, as Jodl was later to say, was finally lost. It only remained to withdraw the remnants of the troops and save them from the Soviet concentration camps; most of the German commanders came to this conclusion. This, however, was not the *Führer*'s appreciation of the situation, and he acted not as though the war was lost, but rather as if the tempo of the battle was rising to a crescendo and reaching its critical point. On 20 April Hitler refused to permit the withdrawal of 9 Army and committed it to remain on the Oder. Heinrici therefore moved Steiner's SS corps head-quarters to the area of Eberswalde, due north of Berlin, to take command of a number of detachments and secure von Manteuffel's exposed southern flank; but when on 21 April the existence of this little formation came to Hitler's

[30] Konev, *Sorok Pyatyi God, Novyi Mir*, May 1965.

ears he ordered Group Steiner, which he magnified to the size of an army, to take command of elements of a panzer grenadier and two infantry divisions. Steiner was to attack south-eastwards to seal off the great gap through which Zhukov's right wing was pouring, and so establish contact with 56 Panzer Corps to the east of Berlin. The troops which he allocated to Steiner were either not available or were divisions only in name and, at the most, Steiner had about 15,000 men without heavy weapons under his command. *Führer* orders had gone out to both Busse's 9 Army and Graeser's 4 Panzer Army ordering them to close the gap in the south through which Konev's troops had already passed.

Inside Berlin there was part of 1 Flak Division manning the anti-aircraft defences, including the great flak towers in the Tiergarten, the Humboldthain and the Friedrichshain. Many of its heavier guns could be used in an anti-tank role. A naval battalion had been flown in by Doenitz together with part of Himmler's personal bodyguard troops, SS battalion Mohnke. In addition there were scattered military units and detachments, two police battalions and about thirty *Volkssturm* battalions and some Hitler Youth detachments. Labour was plentiful. On 6 March Reymann, formerly the Commander of 11 Infantry Division, had been appointed by Hitler to be Commander-in-Chief Berlin Area Defences, but this appointment proved to be a title without substance, authority or resources and subject to petty interference by the *Führer* and *Gauleiter* Goebbels. On 19 April the *Führer* changed his mind and Heinrici's Army Group Vistula was made responsible for the defence of the city. Only three days later Hitler himself took over the direction of the defence of Berlin, Kuntze, an officer of engineers and Kaether, the National Socialist Leadership Officer in the OKH, being selected as his deputies. On 24 April he reverted again to his original idea of appointing a military commander of Berlin area and Weidling, the Commander of 56 Panzer Corps, which was still fighting near the Spree to the south-east of the city, was appointed as the Commander of Berlin acting directly under the *Führer*'s orders. 56 Panzer Corps, which consisted of the remnants of the panzer division *Müncheberg*, 18 Panzer Grenadier Division, 11 SS Panzer Grenadier Division *Nordland* and elements of 9 Parachute Infantry Division, fell back to the southern and eastern outskirts of Berlin, and Weidling, in order to free himself for his new task, handed over his corps to Mummert, who was commanding panzer division *Müncheberg*.

Weidling and the field commanders of 56 Corps were to be plagued by the activities of SS and SA commandos and detachments of military police, the so-called flying field courts martial, of the type which had been so active in other eastern regions of Germany. Some even appear to have been self-appointed, others were detachments of Mohnke's SS battalions. Together they roamed the rear areas looking for army, *Volkssturm* and Hitler Youth stragglers, who on suspicion of withdrawing to the rear without orders were, without evidence or trial, shot or hung in the streets. Mummert is said to have threatened to shoot down any of these detachments which dared to enter his area.

The last Anglo-American air raid to be made on Berlin was a massive one lasting two hours from midday on 20 April, and the city thereafter lay heavily ruined and quiet.[31] Electricity, gas and sanitation had broken down and the only water supply was provided by the street fire hydrants. Little food could be obtained and that only by long hours of queueing.

The 20 April was the *Führer*'s birthday, the day on which Hitler had planned to leave Berlin for Obersalzberg. Ten days earlier his personal servants and part of the OKW had left for Bavaria to set up headquarters preparatory to his arrival. Beneath the new Chancellery the *Führer* and his circle lived and worked in the twenty-eight tiny rooms known collectively as the bunker and there he met all his staff for the last time. Hitler appeared undecided whether or not he would leave Berlin, but he ordered the implementation of the previously agreed plan whereby Doenitz should take over the command in the northern part of the *Reich* while it was generally assumed, but not confirmed, that Kesselring should command all forces in the south. Göring then departed for Bavaria, leaving Koller and Christian to deputize for him on *Luftwaffe* matters, and Himmler made off for Hohenlychen in North Germany. That day Keitel, according to his own account, attempted to persuade Hitler to open surrender negotiations. The next day Field-Marshal Schörner, the Commander of Army Group Centre, arrived in the bunker for a private meeting and restored the *Führer* to good spirits and optimism. Wenck from 12 Army put in an appearance later in the afternoon to brief the *Führer* about his operation to break through the Americans to the Harz, a thrust which, as yet unknown to Wenck, met disaster that very day. All in all, the *Führer* showed such breezy optimism that at last things were beginning to move that even Keitel and Jodl were privately to express surprise as that night they drove back to their OKW Headquarters at Dahlem.[32] Late that night Doenitz left for Ploen in Schleswig Holstein.

When Keitel attended the war conference the next day, however, the *Führer* was back in the depths of despair. Hitler's face was yellow, his twitching was accentuated, he was extremely nervous and his mind kept wandering. Red Army men were already in the eastern suburbs of Berlin, while in the south Konev had reached the Juterbog area which housed the German Army's biggest ammunition dump. No action had apparently been taken by Group Steiner to attack into Berlin from Eberswalde in the north. Hitler announced his intention to remain in Berlin and had already given instructions to have this news broadcast on the radio. If Wenck, he said, could keep the Americans off his back, he (Hitler) would direct the battle for the *Reich* capital. If there had to be any negotiating with the enemy, then Göring was better suited to it than

---

[31] *Kriegstagebuch des OKW*, Vol. 4, pp. 1260–1.
[32] Keitel, *Memoirs*, p. 200.

he was.[33] This statement was repeated verbatim by Jodl to Koller, who was not present at the conference.

It has been said that during that day when the *Führer* became aware that Group Steiner had failed him, he raged against the SS, the German Army and the German people. Such scenes had become very frequent over the past four years but the shock and confusion of those in the bunker had been caused not so much by the *Führer*'s rage as by the sudden realization that Germany was finally defeated. That night the remainder of the *Führer*'s circle including Koller, but not including Goebbels, Bormann, Keitel, Jodl, Burgdorf or Krebs, flew out from Gatow airfield to Bavaria. Hitler's statement regarding peace negotiations was recounted by Koller to Göring, who sent the *Führer* a telegram proposing that he, Göring, should assume plenipotentiary powers. The answer, prompted by Bormann, came swiftly, removing Göring from all his posts and placing him under close arrest. Meanwhile in Lübeck, Himmler was trying to begin peace negotiations with the Western Powers through the Swedish Count Bernadotte.

Keitel and Jodl, after failing to persuade the *Führer* to leave Berlin, undertook to organize a counter-offensive by ordering Wenck's 12 Army to turn about from the Elbe and move eastwards on to Potsdam, where it was to join with Busse's 9 Army. Steiner and von Manteuffel were to attack on to Berlin from the north. The part of the Armed Forces High Command (OKW) staff which had not departed for Bavaria moved out of Berlin to Krampnitz to the north of Potsdam, while Keitel motored south-west through columns of refugees in search of 12 Army. In the early hours of 23 April he arrived at Wenck's tactical headquarters and ordered him to leave the Elbe and move eastwards to Juterbog and Potsdam.

By 21 April Zhukov's right, which consisted of part of Bogdanov's 2 Guards Tank Army, V. I. Kuznetsov's 3 Shock and Perkhorovich's 47 Armies had crossed the main autobahn ring in the north of Berlin; elsewhere 1 Belorussian Front was dogged by lack of success. Chuikov's 8 Guards Army and Katukov's 1 Tank Army were making heavy weather of the fighting in the area of the Fürstenwalde, Erkner and Petershagen immediately to the east of Berlin and were being counter-attacked by infantry elements and *Volkssturm*, losing heavily in tanks.[34] Further to the south Kolpakchy's 69 and Tsvetaev's 33 Armies had still not progressed beyond the area of Frankfurt, while on the northern flank of 1 Belorussian Front, P. A. Belov's 61 Soviet and 1 Polish Army had made little headway westwards against Group Steiner.[35]

The main threat to Berlin came from the remarkable success of Konev's

---

[33] *Ibid*, p. 202.

[34] Zhukov had two radio-telephone conversations with a terse and irritable Stalin, who reproached him for the way in which Bogdanov's tank army had been used and who proposed to use both Konev's and Rokossovsky's fronts to take Berlin. Zhukov has subsequently maintained that he made no errors. Zhukov, *Vospominaniya i Razmyshleniya*, pp. 659–61.

[35] *Istoriya*, Vol. 5, pp. 268, 270–1.

two tank armies under Rybalko and Lelyushenko, sweeping up from the south-east. Konev had been opposed by part of Graeser's 4 Panzer Army, totalling fourteen infantry divisions and one panzer division. Elements of a further four panzer or panzer grenadier divisions were later to be allocated to Graeser, but never at any time was there sufficient armour to counter the breakthrough of the 1 Ukrainian Front tanks.[36] Some fierce fighting took place in the early stages of the battle, but this was waged by infantry and *Luftwaffe* formations and detachments of the *Volkssturm*, whom Konev has described as old men and children who, although they wept, still knocked out Red Army tanks with their short range *panzerfaust* weapons. On the night of 20 April Zossen, the town to the south of Berlin where the High Command of the Army (OKH) had been situated in peace and in war, had been taken by Rybalko's 3 Guards Tank Army, while Lelyushenko's 4 Tank Army had arrived further to the west in the area of Luckenwalde and Juterbog. Meanwhile most of the Red Army rifle formations were still engaged in the heavy fighting round Cottbus and Spremberg, and to fill the fifty-mile gap between the tank and the rifle armies Luchinsky's 28 Soviet Army was brought forward from the second echelon to the area south-east of Berlin. Spremberg fell to Zhadov's 5 Guards Army only after very heavy bombing and artillery fire had neutralized the desperate resistance. The thrust made by Koroteev's 52 Soviet and Swierczewski's 2 Polish Armies towards Dresden made only slow progress because of Graeser's counter-attack into their southern flank from the area of Görlitz, and this caused Konev to send I. E Petrov to the area to put what he euphemistically called some heart into the troops.

On the morning of 20 April Rokossovsky's 2 Belorussian Front, after sixty minutes' artillery preparation, attacked across the Oder into Mecklenburg against von Manteuffel's 3 Panzer Army. Grishin's 49 and Popov's 70 Armies had little success and only Batov's 65 Army managed to secure and extend a bridgehead, the poor visibility and bad flying weather being of great assistance to the Germans.[37] For the time being, therefore, von Manteuffel could maintain his position.

In Berlin Soviet troops were pressing into the suburbs. Perkhorovich's 47 Army from Zhukov's right wing had almost encircled the city from the north and on 22 April it crossed the Havel at Hennigsdorf and moved southwards towards Potsdam; that same evening Pukhov's 13 Army reached the railway running south-west through Juterbog. Two days later 1 Ukrainian and 1 Belorussian Fronts made contact to the south-east of Berlin and on 25 April Lelyushenko's 4 Guards Tank Army joined with Perkhorovich's 47 Army to the west of Berlin. The city and Busse's 9 Army were encircled. That same day Zhadov's 5 Guards Army met patrols of 1 United States Army near Torgau

---

[36] Konev's account exaggerates the German counter-attacking forces thrown against him to six up-to-strength panzer divisions and five infantry divisions.

[37] *Istoriya*, Vol. 5, pp. 271–4.

on the Elbe, about fifty miles below Dresden. Germany was then split across its centre into a northern and southern part.

Wenck had suffered considerable losses in armour in his engagement with the British and American troops west of the Elbe, but he still had some tanks, assault guns and armoured personnel carriers. 12 Army was already in contact with Soviet troops on its southern flank between Wittenberg and Juterbog. Hoping that the American forces would remain passive on the Elbe, Wenck turned his back on the west and started his march towards Potsdam and encircled Berlin. On 29 April he surprised Soviet troops near Belzig, the 5 Guards Mechanized Corps which was taking its ease. Using a mixed force of assault guns and infantry, Wenck soon broke through into the Red Army rear. At Beelitz his troops recaptured a hospital holding over 3,000 German wounded which had been overrun by Soviet troops; Wenck had then arrived at the Potsdam lakes over which he evacuated the encircled Potsdam garrison. By then, however, 12 Army had exhausted its strength and was in no condition to withstand the expected Soviet onslaught on its extended flanks. There Wenck waited to be joined by 9 Army.

Gorbatov's 3 Soviet Army had pushed a wedge south-west in the area between Erkner and Zossen, driving back 56 Panzer Corps into Berlin and cutting it off from the rest of Busse's 9 Army in the south. Gorbatov was of opinion that the resistance put up by Busse's troops at first was less determined than that which he had met in East Prussia, but as soon as 9 Army was encircled the fighting became fierce.[38] Busse's 9 Army together with some elements of 4 Panzer Army which had been driven northwards by Konev's envelopment fell back battered and disorganized. Suffering heavy losses, particularly from air bombing, the encircled troops moved from the Spreewald due west to Luckenwalde. The roads were thick with refugees and stragglers and they came under attack from time to time by elements of 13 Soviet Army and 3 and 4 Guards Tank Armies which made determined efforts to bar their progress towards the west. The German supply and transport system had long since broken down and it was Heinrici's intention to save what he could and get the wounded, the civilians and the troops to the comparative safety of American captivity. In the midst of this carnage an order bearing Jodl's signature was received almost unnoticed, ordering the establishing of a firm front to the south of Berlin against which Army Group Centre was to counter-attack.[39] By 29 April 9 Army lay between Beelitz and Luckenwalde due south of Berlin, being unable to make further movement in daylight because of attacks by Soviet aircraft and tanks. In the following two nights, troops, variously estimated to number between 3,000 and 30,000,

---

[38] Gorbatov, *Gody i Voiny, Novyi Mir*, 1964.
[39] The Eastern Front was an OKH theatre and therefore the responsibility of Krebs. On 28 April Keitel and Jodl prevailed upon Hitler, when he was past caring, to do what they had sought for years, and put the OKH under the command of the OKW. This was effected in an order *OKW/WFSt/Qu Nr. 003857/45 g. Kdos* dated 28 April over Keitel's signature.

together with civilians infiltrated through by night to reach Wenck's 12 Army. Except for 56 Panzer Corps and other scattered elements in Berlin, Busse's 9 Army had ceased to exist. On 1 May Wenck, with the wounded and a great mass of refugees, prepared to fall back towards the Elbe between Stendal and Tangermünde, where one of his corps commanders, von Edelsheim, was attempting to negotiate with 9 United States Army terms of surrender and the reception of the German wounded.

In Mecklenburg to the north of Berlin the position was confused. Group Steiner had been ordered by the *Führer* on 21 April to attack south onto Berlin with four divisions, but in fact Steiner had only the weakened 4 SS Police Panzer Grenadier Division, which had lost much of its heavy equipment in Danzig, and a division of naval ratings. Since the other two divisions had not joined him, he made no move. Steiner was independent of Heinrici, the Commander of Army Group Vistula, who, as 9 Army was on the point of destruction, commanded only von Manteuffel's 3 Panzer Army, which was by then itself in difficulties holding back Rokossovsky on the lower Oder. Jodl had moved his OKW staff detachment to the safety of Fürstenberg to the north of Berlin, and there Keitel arrived to make his last frantic efforts to relieve the *Führer* and the capital. Heinrici wanted to take Group Steiner and Corps Holste, which had been detached from Wenck, under his own command, since these two formations were in a position to keep secure von Manteuffel's south flank in the areas of Rathenow and Oranienburg; but Keitel, still intent on using them to attack into Berlin, would not agree. On 27 April, after a week's hard fighting, Rokossovsky began to break out of his bridgehead over the Oder towards Prenzlau, so threatening to cut 3 Panzer Army in half. Heinrici withdrew from the exposed coastal area of Swinemünde and in order to restore the position committed his last reserve, a panzer grenadier division withdrawn from the west and part of a panzer division. An attack on Berlin from the north was by then entirely out of the question, but Keitel, in the best *Führer* fashion, began to cry treason.

For the first time in seven years Keitel was free from the dominating presence of Hitler. Inexperienced in field command he rushed about the countryside, quizzing the troops and threatening the commanders, and was horrified to find that Heinrici had begun an orderly withdrawal without obtaining permission from the *Führer* or himself. On 28 April Jodl briefed Hitler by radio, and Army Group Vistula was forbidden to retreat further. Later that night Heinrici came on the telephone to say that, in spite of his orders not to do so, he was going to continue to withdraw; for this both he and his chief of staff, von Trotha, were relieved of their appointments. The *Luftwaffe* commander, Student, was appointed by Keitel as Heinrici's successor, but until he should arrive from Holland the command was to devolve upon von Tippelskirch.[40]

[40] Keitel, *Memoirs*, pp. 216–20; von Tippelskirch, *Die Geschichte des Zweiten Weltkriegs*, pp. 662–3.

Von Tippelskirch, who in 1940 had been the Director of Army Intelligence inside the OKH, was in command of 21 Army, a new formation which had been brought into being on 29 April behind 3 Panzer Army in order to bolster the southern flank between Rathenow and Oranienburg. Keitel has described how on a beautiful summer's morning he went to meet von Tippelskirch near Waren, motoring through the forest rides and drives, avoiding roads and villages and the sounds of the battle where Red Army troops were already combing the forests near Fürstenberg. Von Tippelskirch earnestly and repeatedly begged Keitel not to confer on him the command of Army Group Vistula, so that in the end Keitel had to order him to assume the appointment. That done, Keitel and Jodl left the scene of operations for Dobbin, where Himmler gave them a radio message from the *Führer*, dated 28 April and addressed to Keitel, asking for the location of Wenck's, Busse's and Holste's spearheads in the breakthrough to Berlin. On the night of 29 April Keitel replied that a break-in was no longer possible and advised that the *Führer* should break out or fly out. To this telegram Hitler did not deign to reply. Thereafter Keitel and Jodl *en route* to Schleswig Holstein were still going through the daily rituals of war conferences in which they solemnly briefed each other.[41]

On 28 April Hitler was informed by his Propaganda Ministry of a Reuter report concerning Himmler's attempted negotiations with the Western Powers and this threw him into a great rage in which he railed against Himmler, Steiner and the SS. Fegelein, who was Himmler's SS representative at the *Führer*'s Headquarters and Eva Braun's brother-in-law, was suspected of complicity, and as he had been apprehended in civilian clothes in Charlottenburg and was under suspicion of trying to escape, he was speedily cross-examined and shot by Hitler's order. Himmler, who was safely out of the *Führer*'s reach, was disowned, although Bormann on 30 April was to send a radio signal to Doenitz ordering in the *Führer*'s name instant and ruthless action against the *Reichsführer SS*.[42]

In the south-east suburbs of Berlin 56 Panzer Corps had crossed the Spree covered by Ziegler's 11 SS Panzer Grenadier Division *Nordland*, which took up its position in the quarter of Neukölln. Weidling, dissatisfied with the steadfastness of the division, replaced Ziegler by Krukenberg. 18 Panzer Grenadier Division was in the Grunewald, while panzer division *Müncheberg* was in Tempelhof. About a thousand Hitler Youth held the Havel bridges towards Spandau in readiness for the arrival of Wenck. Gatow airfield near the Havel to the south-west of the city was still operating and there was an air ferry service by Fieseler Storch and training aircraft from Gatow to the city centre. The main boulevard between Charlottenburg and the Brandenburg Gate, known as the East-West Axis or the Charlottenburger Chaussée, had been taken into use as an airstrip, originally for three-engined Junker 52

[41] *Kriegstagebuch des OKH*, Vol. 4, pp. 1464–8; Keitel, *Memoirs*, pp. 221–5.
[42] Doenitz, *Memoirs*, p. 440. Bormann had also tried to have Göring shot.

aircraft; but this improvised airstrip was soon closed by air crashes caused by anti-aircraft fire and poor visibility. From 25 April Gatow was no longer usable.

On that day Konev's 1 Ukrainian Front closed in through the southern suburbs of Berlin, with Rybalko's 3 Tank Army on the left and Luchinsky's 28 Army on the right. Zehlendorf, Lichterfelde, Lankwitz and Mariendorf had already been taken, and there was only a brief check on the Teltow Canal which the Germans defended in some strength. Konev's troops were operating in small all arms combat groups, each consisting of a company of infantry, several tanks and guns and an engineer detachment, but they experienced all the difficulties met in fighting in built-up areas. Tank casualties were heavy, Konev giving the loss at about 800, the greater part of which were lost inside Berlin. The defenders kept appearing in the Soviet rear, where they had concealed themselves or made their way through alleyways and sewers. Some Soviet casualties had been caused by the heavy Red Air Force bombing raids carried out on 25 April, and there was the ever-present danger of Red Army troops fighting bloody battles with each other. Numerous casualties occurred during the day of 25 April and both Konev and Zhukov appealed to Stalin to lay down a front boundary. This was established as the line from Tempelhof to the Zoological Gardens in the city centre.[43]

While the southern sector of Berlin was Konev's responsibility, Zhukov's 1 Belorussian Front covered the east, the north and part of the west side of the city. In the east, Chuikov's 8 Guards Army and Katukov's 1 Guards Tank Army were to the south of the Spree, while Berzarin's 5 Shock Army was to the north of the river. The north and north-west suburbs were held by V. I. Kuznetsov's 3 Shock Army and Bogdanov's 2 Guards Tank Army. The hypercritical Chuikov judged it wrong to have employed a tank army for offensive action in a great city and his criticism probably had some merit. Nor did he like the way Zhukov always passed the blame for the slow progress onto his subordinates instead of seeking the fault in himself or in his staff. Moreover, he resented being telephoned on 24 April by a suspicious and glory-seeking Zhukov (the description used by Chuikov) and told to send out patrols to find out whether Konev had really penetrated into Berlin on Chuikov's left flank.[44]

During the next three days both fronts closed in rapidly towards the city centre, and by 28 April the whole of the south and east of Berlin was in Soviet hands almost as far as the Tiergarten. In the south-west, part of Charlottenburg, Halensee and Wilmersdorf remained German, so that it was still possible with difficulty to get to the Havel bridges in the west where the Hitler Youth held out. The north-east suburbs between Humboldthain and Friedrichshain remained German-occupied, but Old Moabit had fallen on the north

---

[43] Stalin had been unwilling that there should be an inter-front boundary after the opening stages of the offensive as he proposed to keep the battle fluid.

[44] Chuikov, *The End of the Third Reich*, pp. 169–70.

edge of the Tiergarten. In the south Chuikov was little more than a thousand yards from the Chancellery, while 2 Tank Army to the north was about a mile away.

The approach of Wenck to Potsdam on 29 April had been used by Goebbels as a clarion call to unite the defenders of Berlin and spur them on to new endeavours; but as the hours ran out it became obvious that no help could be expected from Wenck, from Steiner or from Busse. That morning at four o'clock Adolf Hitler, having already resolved to take his own life, signed his last will and testament. This was witnessed by Bormann and Burgdorf, two of his intimate circle who, since the assassination attempt a year before, had formed a closely knit group about him, a circle which it was almost impossible to penetrate. The third member of the trio, Fegelein, lay dead outside. The two other signatories were Goebbels and Krebs. In this testament for posterity the *Führer* disclaimed all responsibility for the provocation of the 1939 War and made an oblique condemnation of the officers of the German Army with a reference to the surrender of territory. Göring and Himmler were expelled as traitors, and Doenitz was to be President and Commander-in-Chief of the Armed Forces.[45] Hitler continued to interfere from the grave when he appointed the members of the Doenitz Government, these to include Goebbels, Bormann, Seyss-Inquart, Greim, Schörner and von Krosigk.[46] On the afternoon of 30 April he, together with Eva Braun, his newly-wed wife, committed suicide.

On the evening of the same day an officer was sent under cover of a white flag from the SS Division *Nordland* sector to the forward defended localities of Chuikov's 8 Guards Army, asking whether Krebs might be permitted to cross the line. Shortly before 4 a.m. the last Chief of General Staff, accompanied by Duofing, the Chief of Staff of 56 Panzer Corps and a Russian speaking Latvian lieutenant in the German service, appeared at Chuikov's headquarters. Speaking on behalf of Goebbels and Bormann, Krebs asked for a truce, and his requests were relayed by telephone from Chuikov to Zhukov and thence to Moscow. According to the Soviet account, Krebs had been commissioned to negotiate an armistice which would permit the new German Government to assemble and undertake peace negotiations. This led to a protracted argument as to which was to come first, the cease-fire before the surrender or the surrender followed by the cease-fire. After midday the German party returned to the Chancellery without having achieved agreement, and Soviet troops began their final assault on the Tiergarten and the government buildings immediately to its east and south-east.

Inside the bunker Goebbels and Bormann still strove for power within the newly-appointed Doenitz Government, intending to use the Admiral as their tool. Doenitz had been informed by them that he had been appointed to succeed Hitler after the *Führer*'s death, but had not been told that Hitler

---

[45] Jacobsen, *Der Zweite Weltkrieg in Chronik und Dokumenten*, pp. 530–3.
[46] Doenitz, *Memoirs*, pp. 440–7; Keitel, *Memoirs*, pp. 226–7.

was in fact already dead; not until eleven the next morning, when Zhukov and Stalin had been notified of the death six hours before, was it thought politic to inform Doenitz that the testament was in force, by which he might deduce, but not in fact be certain, that the *Führer* was dead. At three o'clock in the afternoon when Krebs had already returned and there was no longer any hope that the Berlin rump might be permitted to join Doenitz, the Grand Admiral was told the truth. Goebbels and his wife destroyed their children and themselves. It is believed that Burgdorf and Krebs shot themselves, while Bormann and the remainder of the *Führer*'s court made their attempted escape from the Chancellery and the city centre through the Soviet lines.

Just after midnight on 2 May a division of Chuikov's army received a Russian language radio message from 56 Panzer Corps asking for a cease fire and the reception of parlementaries on the Potsdam Station railway bridge. On 2 May General Weidling, the Commander of the German troops in Berlin, surrendered and called on all German troops to cease resistance. By that afternoon all fighting had come to an end.

CHAPTER THIRTY-FIVE

Epilogue

The Commander of the German troops in Italy surrendered to Field-Marshal Alexander on 29 April and all hostilities in the Italian theatre ceased on 2 May. This capitulation was followed by that of Army Group G in the South-West and of the German troops in Norway, Denmark and Holland.

In the last week in April Himmler had attempted to communicate with Churchill through the Swede Bernadotte, in order to surrender on the Western, but not on the Eastern, Front. This peace overture was rejected with the reply that any surrender by the German Government must be unconditional and made to the Soviet Union as well as to the Anglo-American Powers. The Soviet Union was informed of the rejection of this approach. Since there was no longer hope of a separate armistice with the West, German army group and army commanders in the field took what measures they could, often in defiance of the orders from Berlin, to make tactical surrenders to the Western Allies in order to save their troops from Soviet capture. For the encircled troops in Kurland and in the Frische Nehrung there could be no withdrawal. Army Group Vistula and Wenck's 12 Army, with accompanying columns of refugees, gave ground rapidly in order to reach the protection of the Anglo-American line near Wismar and to the west of the Elbe. Further to the south Schörner's Army Group Centre, Rendulic's Army Group South and Loehr's South-East Command, which was withdrawing from the Balkans, were all in a dangerously exposed position.

Doenitz, the new head of the German Government, had already instructed all German troops in the West to surrender to the British and Americans and had ordered all U-boats back to port. On 5 May he sent von Friedeburg, the Naval Commander-in-Chief, to Eisenhower at Rheims, and the next day von Friedeburg was joined by Jodl. Eisenhower, sensing that the German delegation was playing for time while it withdrew its troops in the East, threatened the immediate sealing of the Anglo-American boundary against all line crossers unless an immediate and unconditional surrender was signed. This was done by Jodl on 7 May and two days later a second surrender document ratifying the first was signed by Keitel in Berlin. Meanwhile the mass movement westwards of German troops and civilians continued. Whether or not they were permitted to cross the boundary between East and West appeared to vary according to the sector; in Mecklenburg troops and refugees were admitted; in Brandenburg troops were permitted across the Elbe but not civilians. In Bohemia and the south troops and civilians were halted at gun point and in some instances disarmed prisoners of war were handed over to the Red Army. With few exceptions German commanders on the Eastern Front, even though they knew that they had been listed by the USSR as war criminals, remained at their posts and went into Soviet captivity with their men.

So ended what was probably the greatest war in the long history of Germany and Russia. The Soviet losses are not known but the total dead from all causes for both military and civilians was said to total about twenty million.[1] The German troop casualties in the field on the Eastern Front from 22 June 1941 to 31 March 1945 numbered 1,001,000 dead, 3,966,000 wounded and 1,288,000 missing, in all, just over six million.[2] These figures show the magnitude of the German Army's losses in Russia. The Red Army casualties including the six million lost in prisoners probably amounted to more than fourteen million men, of which about ten million were permanently lost.

The outset of the war saw Germany as the master of Europe at the peak of its fortunes having established a New European Order which Hitler boasted was to last a thousand years. In comparison with Germany, the Soviet Union appeared a second-rate power so that Churchill, probably counting on United States support, was to reckon in 1940 and 1941 that even if the USSR should enter the war on the side of Germany, Great Britain with its Commonwealth and Empire would, in the final outcome, be victorious. In 1939 the Soviet Union lacked confidence in its own revolutionary armed forces which had never been put to the test of war. In 1940 Molotov had been fearful of British intervention in the Finnish Winter War, and in 1941 the Soviet Union lived under the great shadow of German military might. Yet the end of the war saw the USSR, although much weakened by its great losses in manpower, victorious and arrogant, while Germany stood totally destroyed as a political and military factor, torn apart by the two great power blocs.

The reasons underlying Soviet success and German failure have already been discussed. Hitler had been responsible for the outbreak of the Second World War and to Hitler was largely due the credit for the early successes in West and South-East Europe. There is little doubt that Hitler alone was the motivating force which turned Germany eastwards in its attack on the Soviet Union. Hitler was solely answerable for the great German defeat at Stalin-

---

[1] *Istoriya*, Vol. 6, p. 30. 'The USSR suffered the greatest loss in people (20 million), of which almost a half were civilians and prisoners of war killed by the Hitlerites in occupied Soviet territory'.

[2] *OKH/Gen St d H/Gen Qu/Az: 1335 0 (IIb) KR. H.A/224/45 g. Kdos* of 5 April 1945. (*Kriegstagebuch des OKW*, Vol. 4, pp. 1515–6). German losses in Western Europe and the Mediterranean (but not including the Balkans) in this period amounted to 1,260,000.

grad, and with his blind insistence on a rigid defence and the holding of ground, lost the initiative by playing into the hands of an enemy who relied for success on the movement and build-up of reserves to achieve a decisive superiority in men and materials in selected theatres and sectors. Yet irrespective of his faulty strategic and tactical handling of the troops in the field, Hitler had already caused Germany's defeat when, by political misjudgement, he entered into a war on two fronts. The odds were weighed too heavily in his enemies' favour and against such a coalition Germany could not be victorious.

Western Aid for the Soviet Union

Great Britain and Canada together dispatched about a million and a half tons of war supplies and food to the USSR between 1941 and 1945 and among the equipment shipped were over 5,000 aircraft and 5,000 tanks and 200,000 tons of wheat and flour. The United States provided by far the greater share of the aid and sent about sixteen million tons of stores under the Lend-Lease and earlier agreements. Of the total 17,500,000 tons of material aid dispatched to the USSR, just under four million tons went by the North Atlantic sea route to Murmansk and Archangel and just over four million tons entered the Soviet Union through Persia. The Pacific route, in spite of the fact that it included a long rail haul across the breadth of Siberia, eventually proved capable of importing as much as the North Atlantic and Persian routes together. Even the entry of Japan into the war against the United States did not seriously check the flow into Vladivostok since all available Soviet freighters were moved over to the Pacific and a large number of United States vessels were transferred to the Soviet flag. The tonnage dispatches of Western material aid to the USSR from the period from 22 June 1941 to 20 September 1945 were as follows.

Year	Totals	Persian Gulf	Pacific	North Atlantic	Black Sea	Arctic
1941	360,778	13,502	193,299	153,977		
1942	2,453,097	705,259	734,020	949,711		64,107
1943	4,794,545	1,606,979	2,388,577	681,043		117,946
1944	6,217,622	1,788,864	2,848,181	1,452,775		127,802
1945	3,673,819	44,513	2,079,320	726,725	680,723	142,538
	17,499,861	4,159,117	8,243,397	3,964,231	680,723	452,393
Percentages		23.8	47.1	22.7	3.9	2.5

Among the goods delivered were 427,000 motor vehicles, 13,000 armoured fighting vehicles (including 10,000 tanks), 35,000 motorcycles, nearly 19,000 aircraft, 1,900 railway locomotives, 11,000 railway trucks (flats), ninety freight ships, 105 submarine-chasers and 197 torpedo-boats, four and a half million tons of foodstuffs and large quantities of raw materials.

During the war Stalin clamoured for this material assistance and protested vehemently when the British proposed to reduce the deliveries by the northern sea route. Yet at the same time, even in the war years, the Government of the USSR attempted to conceal from the Soviet population the extent to which a communist economy relied on the capitalist states. Since 1945 the aid has been deliberately denigrated and made to appear of little account.

According to the Soviet account the 10,000 American and British tanks received by the USSR represented only ten per cent of the USSR tank production, which is said to have totalled 102,000 tanks and SUs over the whole war. Soviet sources complain that the quality of the tanks, which were mainly Shermans, Valentines and Matildas, was inferior to the German and Soviet models; there is some truth in this. Yet it must be remembered that the Sherman was a match for the earlier German Mark III and that the Sherman, Valentine and Matilda, although inferior to the T34, were much superior to the T60 and many other types of Soviet tank which were being produced in large numbers, even in the middle of the war. The 18,700 Western aircraft are said to have represented only twelve per cent of the total Soviet war production, 136,000 planes. The Kremlin was rightly to judge the performance of the Kittyhawks and Hurricanes as below that of the main German fighter (the Me 109); on the other hand, although this is not acknowledged in the Soviet Union, the Kittyhawks and Hurricanes were superior to the Red Air Force fighters in service in 1941 and 1942. However this may be, the numbers of aircraft and tanks shipped to the Soviet Union, although of undoubted benefit, were probably too small to be of decisive importance. The same can be said for the consignments of guns and small arms.

At the end of the war the equipment holding of the Soviet Armed Forces amounted to 665,000 motor vehicles. Of these, 427,000 had been provided mainly from United States sources during the war years; contemporary evidence indicates that over fifty per cent of all vehicles in Red Army service were of American origin. These trucks, together with the thousands of locomotives and railway flats, gave to the Red Army the strategic and tactical mobility required to destroy the German forces. At Teheran Stalin had attributed the Soviet success to the ability to move the High Command Reserve, which he put at no higher than sixty divisions, from theatre to theatre in turn. This mobility could not have been achieved without this United States material aid.

Although Moscow was to compare the 2·6 million tons of imported petroleum products disparagingly with its own output of thirty million tons a year, it does not disclose that the imported petroleum consisted of blending agents and high octane fuels (which were not available in the USSR) to produce aviation gas. In addition numbers of complete oil refineries, tyre factories, electric generator stations, machine tools, explosives and raw materials of all types formed part of the aid. A very large proportion of the food for the Soviet Armed Forces, (estimated at 1 lb a day of concentrated ration for six million men over the whole duration of the war) came from United States and Canadian sources and much of the Red Army's clothing and footwear came from America and Great Britain.

As to whether the Western, and in particular the American material aid, was a decisive factor in the Soviet victory over the German forces on the Eastern Front, no opinion can be expressed without an independent and detailed survey of Soviet economic strength during the war years. It can only be stated with certainty that without United States vehicles and railway equipment some of the great Soviet victories in Belorussia and the Ukraine would not have been possible as early as 1943 and 1944.

It is possible, though by no means certain, that some earlier Western assessments may have overestimated the effect of the material aid afforded to the Soviet Union. Yet at the same time it is probable that insufficient account has been taken of the effect on operations in Russia of the overwhelming economic and military might of the Anglo-American Powers and in particular that of the United States. Japan's fate was decided by American naval and air power, and without the United States presence in the Pacific Japan would have attacked the Soviet Union. Moreover it is now possible to make an accurate assessment of the forces engaged by the USSR and the Anglo-American bloc. Until 1943 the United States and Great Britain took little part in the land operations against Germany and they were not really committed to heavy fighting on the Continent until the middle of 1944. Yet until 1944 they had absorbed nearly all the German naval effort. In June 1941 about forty per cent of the *Luftwaffe* was deployed in the West and in defence of the *Reich* but, with the rapid growth of British and United States offensive air power, by 1944 about sixty-five per cent of the *Luftwaffe* air strength was deployed against the Anglo-Americans. Anglo-Saxon naval power and strategic mobility caused the dispersal of German ground forces. In 1941 and 1942 between twenty and twenty-five per cent of the German field divisions were committed to the defence of the Mediterranean and Western Europe, and as the time of the Second Front approached this figure rose to a peak of forty-two per cent.

If the United States and Great Britain with its Commonwealth and Empire had been strictly neutral during the Russo-German War, the German and Axis military forces so released would have overwhelmed the Soviet Union.

Sources

Istoriya, Vol. 6, pp. 48, 62 and 72; Jacobsen, *Der Zweite Weltkrieg*, p. 568; Deane, *The Strange Alliance*, pp. 86–103; Werth, *Russia at War*, pp. 624–8; *Command Decisions*, pp. 154–81; Stettinius, *Lend-Lease*; Schlauch, *Rüstungshilfe der USA an die Verbündeten im Zweiten Weltkrieg*.

GERMAN ARMY GROUPS IN THE EAST
Showing Changes of Designation and Commanders
June 1941 – May 1945

	North	Centre	South			
1941 June.	von Leeb	von Bock	von Rundstedt			
Dec.		von Kluge	von Reichenau			
1942 Jan.	von Küchler		von Bock			
			B			**A**
Jul.			von Weichs			List
Sep.						Hitler
Nov.				**Don** (*from 11 Army*) von Manstein		von Kleist
1943 Feb.			*disbanded*	**South**		
Oct.		Busch				
1944 Jan.	Model					
				North Ukraine		**South Ukraine**
Mar.	Lindemann			Model		Schörner
June.		Model				
Jul.	Friessner Schörner					Friessner
Aug.		Reinhardt				
				A		**South**
Sep.				Harpe		
Dec.						Wöhler
1945 Jan.	Rendulic					
	Kurland	**North**	**Vistula** (*new*)	**Centre**		
Jan.	von Vietinghoff	Rendulic	Himmler	Schörner		
Mar.	Rendulic	Weiss	Heinrici			
Apr.	Hilpert	*disbanded*				Rendulic
May			Student			**Ostmark**

591

ACTIVE SOVIET FRONTS IN THE WEST
Showing Changes of Designations and Commanders

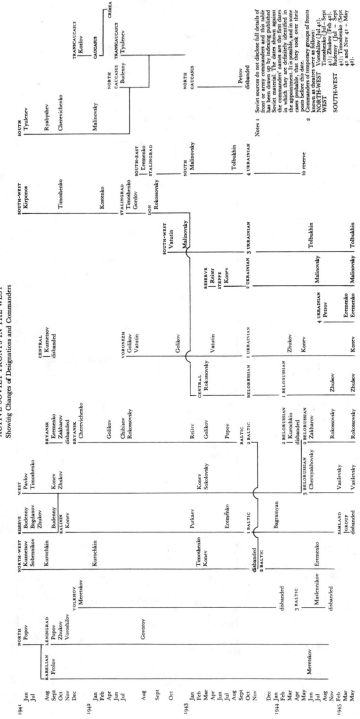

Notes 1 Soviet sources do not disclose full details of
front or army commanders and this table
has been drawn up by indexing published
Soviet material. The dates shown against
the commanders' names are the first dates
in which they are definitely identified in
the appointment. It is possible, and in some
cases probable, that they took over their
posts before this date.

2 Commanders of temporary groups of fronts
known as theatres were as follows:
NORTH-WEST   Voroshilov (Jul – Sept
41).
WEST   Timoshenko (Jul – Sept
41): Zhukov (Feb 42).
SOUTH-WEST   Budenny (Jul – Sept
41): Timoshenko (Sept
41 and Nov 41 – May
42).

Select Bibliography

This list is not intended as a complete bibliography but merely to indicate the principal works to which reference has been made in the writing of this history.

I. Official and Semi-Official Publications

Abwehrkämpfe am Nordflügel der Ostfront 1944–1945. Herausgegeben vom Militärgeschichtlichen Forschungsamt. Deutsche Verlags-Anstalt, Stuttgart 1963.

Command Decisions. Department of the Army. Harcourt Brace, New York 1959.

Documents on the Expulsion of the Germans from Eastern-Central-Europe (Volume 1). Federal Ministry for Expellees, Refugees and War Victims, Bonn.

Documents on German Foreign Policy 1918–1945. HMSO, London.

German Air Force Airlift Operations. (Morzik) Department of the Army 1961. Arno Press, New York.

German Air Force Operations in Support of the Army. (Deichmann) Department of the Army 1962. Arno Press, New York.

German Air Force versus Russia. (Plocher) Department of the Army 1967. Arno Press, New York.

German Campaign in Poland 1939. (Kennedy) Department of the Army Pamphlet No. 20–255.

German Campaign in Russia Planning and Operations 1940–1942. Department of the Army Pamphlet No. 20–261a.

German Northern Theater of Operations 1940–1945. (Ziemke) Department of the Army Pamphlet No. 20–271.

Stalingrad to Berlin. (Ziemke) Department of the Army (Army Historical Series).

Istoriya Velikoi Otechestvennoi Voiny Sovetskovo Soyuza (six volumes). Moscow.

Kratkaya Istoriya Velikaya Otechestvennaya Voina Sovetskovo Soyuza. Moscow 1964.

Nazi Conspiracy and Aggression (eight volumes). US Government Printing Office 1946–1948.

Nazi-Soviet Relations 1939–1941. Department of State Publication 3023.

Official Documents Concerning Polish-German and Polish-Soviet Relations 1933–1939. London 1939.

Operationsgebiet Ostliche Ostsee. Schriftenreihe des Militärgeschichtlichen Forschungsamtes. Deutsche Verlags-Anstalt, Stuttgart 1961.

Russian Air Force in the Eyes of German Commanders. (Schwabedissen) Department of the Army 1960. Arno Press, New York.

Supreme Command. The United States in World War II. (Pogue) Department of the Army 1954.

Ordnance Department Procurement and Supply. The United States Army in World War II. (Thomson and Mayo) Department of the Army 1960.

Buying Aircraft Material Procurement for the Army Air Forces. The United States Army in World War II. (Holley) Department of the Army 1964.

Statistical Digest of the War. HMSO London 1951.

Strength and Casualties of the Armed Forces of the United Kingdom 1939–1945. Cmd. 6832, HMSO London.

50 Let Vooruzhennykh Sil SSSR, Moscow 1968.

II. Edited or collected Works

Anatomy of the SS State. Collins, London 1968.

Bilanz des Zweiten Weltkrieges. Gerhard Stallin Verlag, Hamburg 1953.

Bitva za Moskvu. Moscow 1968.

Kriegstagebuch des Oberkommandos der Wehrmacht (four volumes). Bernard und Graefe Verlag für Wehrwesen, Frankfurt am Main.

III. Books

Ahlfen, H. von, und Niehoff, H. *So Kämpfte Breslau*. Gräfe und Unzer, München 1960.

Ahlfen, H. von. *Der Kampf um Schlesien*. Gräfe und Unzer, München 1961.

Alliluyeva, Svetlana. *Twenty Letters to a Friend*. Hutchinson, London 1967.

Baransky, N. N. *Economic Geography of the USSR*. Moscow 1956.

Baumann, H. *Die 35. Infanterie=Division im Zweiten Weltkrieg*. G. Braun, Karlsruhe 1964.

Beinhauer, E. *Artillerie im Osten*. Wilhelm Limpert, Berlin 1944.

Bekker, C. *Angriffshöhe 4000*. Gerhard Stalling, Oldenburg und Hamburg 1964.

Beloff, M. *The Foreign Policy of Soviet Russia 1929–1941*. Oxford University Press, London 1949.

Benary, A. *Die Berliner Bären Division 257. Infanterie-Division* Podzun, Bad Nauheim 1955.

Bezymensky, L *Sonderakte Barbarossa*. Deutsche Verlags-Anstalt, Stuttgart 1968 (orig. Moscow).

Bidlingmaier, I. *Entstehung und Räumung der Ostseebrückenköpfe 1945*. Kurt Vowinckel, Neckargemünd 1962.

Birkenfeld, W. *Geschichte der deutschen Wehr- und Rüstungwirtschaft (1918–1945)*. Harald Boldt, Boppard am Rhein 1966.

Biryuzov, S. S. *Surovye Gody*. Moscow 1966.

Blumentritt, G. *Von Rundstedt*. Odhams, London 1952.

Bor-Komorowski, T. *The Secret Army*. Gollancz, London 1950.

Bradley, O. N. *A Soldier's Story*. Eyre and Spottiswoode, London 1951.

Butler, J. R. M. *Grand Strategy. History of the Second World War*. (Volumes 2 and 3 (2)). HMSO, London 1957 and 1964.

Chales de Beaulieu, W. *Der Vorstoss der Panzer Gruppe 4 auf Leningrad*. Kurt Vowinckel, Neckargemünd 1961.

Generaloberst Erich Hoepner. Kurt Vowinckel, Neckargemünd 1969.

Choltitz, D. von. *Un Soldat parmi des Soldats*. Aubanel 1964.

Chuikov, V. I. *The Beginning of the Road*. Macgibbon and Kee, London 1963 (orig. Moscow).

The End of the Third Reich. Macgibbon and Kee, London 1967 (orig. Moscow).

Churchill, W. S. *The Second World War* (six volumes). Cassell, London.

Ciano's Diaries 1939–1943. Heinemann, London 1947.

Dallin, A. *German Rule in Russia 1941–1945*. Macmillan, London 1957.

Deane, J. R. *The Strange Alliance*. Murray, London 1947.

Deutscher, I. *Stalin*. Oxford University Press, London 1967.

Dieckert und Grossmann. *Der Kampf um Ostpreussen*. Gräfe und Unzer, München 1960.

Dieckhoff, G. *Die 3. Infanterie-Division*. Erich Börries, Göttingen 1960.

Djilas, M. *Conversations with Stalin*. Rupert Hart-Davis, London 1962.

Dmitriev, V. I. *Atakuyut Podvodniki*. Moscow 1964.

Doenitz, K. *Memoirs*. Weidenfeld and Nicolson, London 1959.

Doerr, H. *Der Feldzug nach Stalingrad*. E. S. Mittler, Darmstadt 1955.

Eden, A. *The Reckoning*. Cassell 1965.

Eisenhower, D. D. *Crusade in Europe*. Heinemann, London 1948.

Eremenko, A. I. *Stalingrad*. Moscow 1961.

Erfurth, W. *Der Finnische Krieg 1941–1944*. Limes, Wiesbaden 1950.

Feiling, K. *The Life of Neville Chamberlain*. Macmillan, London 1947.

Feis, H. *Churchill, Roosevelt, Stalin*. Princeton University Press 1966.

Feuchter, G. W. *Der Luftkrieg*. Athenäum, Frankfurt am Main 1964.

Förster, O. W. *Befestigungswesen*. Kurt Vowinckel, Neckargemünd 1960.

Forstmeier, F. *Odessa 1941*. Rombach, Freiburg im Breisgau 1967.

Fretter-Pico, M. *Missbrauchte Infanterie*. Bernard u. Graefe, Frankfurt am Main 1957.

Friessner, H. *Verratene Schlachten*. Holsten, Hamburg 1956.

Gareis, M. *Kampf und Ende der Fränkish-Sudetendeutschen 98. Infanterie-Division*. Gareis, Tegernsee 1956.

Gilbert, F. *Hitler Directs His War*. Oxford University Press, New York 1950.

Goebbels, J. *The Goebbels Diaries*. Hamish Hamilton, London 1948.

Goerlitz, W. *Paulus and Stalingrad*. Methuen, London 1963.

Golikov, F. I. *V Moskovskoi Bitve*. Moscow 1967.

Golovko, A. *With the Red Fleet*. Putnam, London 1965 (orig. Moscow).

Gorbatov, A. V. *Gody i Voiny*. Novyi Mir, Moscow 1964 (published in English as *Years off my Life*, Constable, London 1964).

Grechko, A. A. *Bitva za Kavkaz*. Moscow 1967.

Greiner, H. *Die Oberste Wehrmachtführung 1939–1943*. Limes, Wiesbaden 1951.

Grossmann, H. *Geschichte der Rheinisch-Westfälischen 6. Infanterie-Division*. Podzun, Bad Nauheim 1958.

Gschöpf, R. *Mein Weg mit der 45. Infanterie-Division*. Oberösterreichischer Landesverlag 1955.

Guderian, H. *Panzer Leader*. Michael Joseph, London 1952.

Gwyer, J. M. A. *Grand Strategy. History of the Second World War*. Volume 3 (1). HMSO, London 1964.

Haferkann, H. *Ostwärts bis Sewastopol*. Deutscher Volksverlag, München 1943.

Halder, F. *Kriegstagebuch* (three volumes). Kohlhammer, Stuttgart 1962.
Hitler as War Lord. Putnam, London 1950.

Haupt, W. *Demjansk*. Podzun, Bad Nauheim 1961.
Baltikum 1941. Vowinckel, Neckargemünd 1963.

Hausser, P. *Soldaten wie Andere Auch*. Munin, Osnabrück 1966.

Heiber, H. von. *Hitlers Lagebesprechungen*. Deutsche Verlags-Anstalt, Stuttgart 1962.

Heidkämper, O. *Witebsk*. Vowinckel, Heidelberg 1954.

Hess, W. *Eismeerfront 1941*. Vowinckel, Heidelberg 1956.

Hillgruber, A. *Hitlers Strategie*. Bernard u. Graefe, Frankfurt am Main 1965.
Hitler König Carol und Marschall Antonescu. Franz Steiner, Wiesbaden 1965.
Die Räumung der Krim 1944. Mittler, Berlin/Frankfurt 1959.
(Ed.) *Probleme des Zweiten Weltkrieges*. Kiepenheuer u. Witsch 1967.
und Hümmelchen, G. *Chronik des Zweiten Weltkrieges*. Bernard u. Graefe, Frankfurt am Main 1966.

Hitler, A. *Mein Kampf*. Hurst & Blackett, London 1939.

Hoth, H. *Panzeroperationen*. Vowinckel, Heidelberg 1956.

Hubatsch, W. *Hitlers Weisungen für die Kriegführung 1939–1945*. Bernard u. Graefe, Frankfurt am Main 1962.
Kriegswende 1943. Wehr u. Wissen Verlagsgesellschaft, Darmstadt 1966.

Jacobsen, H. A. *Der Zweite Weltkrieg in Chronik und Dokumenten*. Wehr u. Wissen Verlagsgesellschaft, Darmstadt 1961.

und Rohwer, J. *Entscheidungsschlachten des Zweiten Weltkrieges.* Bernard u. Graefe, Frankfurt am Main 1960.

Janssen, G. *Das Ministerium Speer.* Ullstein, Berlin 1968.

Jenner, M. *Die 216/272 Niedersächsische Infanterie-Division.* Podzun, Bad Nauheim 1964.

Keilig, W. *Das Deutsche Heer 1939–1945* (three volumes). Podzun, Bad Nauheim.

Keitel, W. *Memoirs.* Kimber, London 1965.

Kesselring, A. *Soldat bis zum letzten Tag.* Athenäum, Bonn 1953. *Gedanken zum Zweiten Weltkrieg.* Athenäum, Bonn 1955.

Kissel, H. *Die Katastrophe in Rumänien 1944.* Wehr u. Wissen Verlagsgesellschaft, Darmstadt 1964.

Der Deutsche Volkssturm 1944–1945. Mittler, Frankfurt am Main 1962.

Klatt, P. *Die 3. Gebirgs-Division 1939–1945.* Podzun, Bad Nauheim 1958.

Klietmann, K. G. *Die Waffen SS.* Der Freiwillige, Osnabrück 1965.

Klink, E. *Das Gesetz des Handelns 'Zitadelle' 1943.* Deutsche Verlags Anstalt, Stuttgart 1966.

Kolganov, K. S. *Razvitie Taktiki Sovetskoi Armii v Gody Velikoi Otechestvennoi Voiny.* Moscow 1958.

Konev, I. S. *Sorok Pyatyi God. Novyi Mir.* Moscow 1965.

Kravchenko, G. S. *Voennaya Ekonomika SSSR 1941–1945.* Moscow 1963.

Kurowski, F. *Armee Wenck.* Vowinckel, Neckargemünd 1967.

Lange, W. *Korpsabteilung C.* Vowinckel, Neckargemünd 1961.

Lasch, O. *So Fiel Königsberg.* Gräfe u. Unzer, München 1959.

Lelyushenko, D. D. *Zarya Pobedy.* Moscow 1966.

Lemelsen, J. *Die 29. Division.* Podzun, Bad Nauheim 1960.

Leverkuehn, P. *German Military Intelligence.* Weidenfeld and Nicolson, London 1954.

Liddell Hart, B. H. *The Other Side of the Hill.* Cassell, London 1951.

Livshits, Ya. L. *Pervaya Gvardeiskaya Tankovaya Brigada v Boyakh za Moskvu.* Moscow 1948.

Lossberg, B. von. *Im Wehrmachtführungsstab.* Nölke, Hamburg 1950.

Lundin, L. *Finland in the Second World War.* Indiana University Press 1957.

Mackensen, E. von. *Vom Bug zum Kaukasus.* Vowinckel, Neckargemünd, 1967.

Maisky, I. *Memoirs of a Soviet Ambassador.* Hutchinson, London 1967. *Who Helped Hitler.* Hutchinson, London 1964 (orig. Moscow).

Malaparte, C. *The Volga Rises in Europe.* Alvin Redman, London 1957.

Malinovsky, R. Ya. *Final.* Moscow 1966.

Mannerheim, C. G. *Memoirs.* Cassell, London 1953.

Manstein, E. von. *Lost Victories.* Methuen, London 1958.

Martel, G. *The Russian Outlook.* Michael Joseph, London 1947.

Mazulenko, W. A. *Die Zerschlagung der Heeresgruppe Südukraine.* Berlin 1959 (orig. Moscow).

597

V

Medlicott, W. N. *The Economic Blockade. History of the Second World War.* (Volumes 1 and 2). HMSO and Longmans Green, London 1959.

Meister, J. *Der Seekrieg in den Osteuropäischen Gewässern 1941–1945.* Lehmanns, München 1958.

Mellenthin, F. W. von. *Panzer Battles.* University of Oklahoma Press, 1956.

Metzsch, F. A. von. *Die Geschichte der 22. Infanterie-Division.* Podzun, Bad Nauheim 1952.

Meyer, K. *Panzergrenadiere.* Schild, München-Lochhausen 1965.

Milward, A. S. *The German Economy at War.* The Athlone Press, London 1965.

Morozov, W. P. *Westlich von Woronesh.* Berlin 1959 (orig. Moscow).

Morzik und Hümmelchen. *Die Deutschen Transportflieger im Zweiten Weltkrieg.* Bernard u. Graefe, Frankfurt am Main 1966.

Mueller-Hillebrand, B. *Das Heer 1939–1945* (three volumes). Mittler, Frankfurt am Main.

Munzel, O. *Die Deutschen Gepanzerten Truppen bis 1945.* Maximilian, Herford 1965.

Nitz, G. *Die 292. Infanterie-Division.* Bernard u. Graefe, Berlin 1957.

Oesch, K. L. *Finnlands Entscheidungskampf 1944.* Huber, Frauenfeld 1964.

O'Neill, R. *The German Army and the Nazi Party.* Cassell, London 1966.

Pavlov, D. V. *Leningrad 1941: The Blockade.* University of Chicago Press 1965. (orig. Moscow).

Petrov, Yu. P. *Partiinoe Stroitelstvo v Sovetskoi Armii i Flote.* Moscow 1964.

Pfahlmann, H. *Fremdarbeiter und Kriegsgefangene in der Deutschen Kriegswirtschaft 1939–1945.* Wehr u. Wissen Verlagsgesellschaft, Darmstadt 1968.

Philippi, A. *Das Pripjetproblem.* Mittler, Frankfurt am Main 1955.

u. Heim, F. *Der Feldzug gegen Sowjetrussland 1941–1945.* Kohlhammer, Stuttgart 1962.

Picker, H. *Hitlers Tischgespräche.* Seewald, Stuttgart 1963.

Pickert, W. *Vom Kuban-Brückenkopf bis Sewastopol.* Vowinckel, Heidelberg 1955.

Pitersky, N. A. *Die Sowjet-Flotte im Zweiten Weltkrieg.* Stalling, Hamburg 1966 (orig. Moscow).

Platonov, S. P. *Vtoraya Mirovaya Voina.* Moscow 1958.

Pohlman, H. *Wolchow 1941–1944.* Podzun, Bad Nauheim 1962.

Pottgiesser, H. *Die Reichsbahn im Ostfeldzug.* Vowinckel, Neckargemünd 1960.

Redelis, V. *Partisanen Krieg.* Vowinckel, Heidelberg 1958.

Rehm, W. *Jassy.* Vowinckel, Neckargemünd 1959.

Rendulic, L. *Gekämpft Gesiegt Geschlagen.* 'Welsermühl' Wels, München 1957.

Röhricht, E. *Probleme der Kesselschlacht.* Condor, Karlsruhe 1958.

Rohwer, J. u. Hümmelchen, G. *Chronik des Seekrieges 1939–1945*. Stalling, Oldenburg and Hamburg 1968.

Rokossovsky, K. K. *Velikaya Pobeda na Volge*. Moscow 1965.

Roskill, S. W. *The War at Sea. The Second World War*. (Volumes 2 and 3). HMSO, London.

Samsonov, A. M. (Ed.). *Stalingradskaya Epopeya*. Moscow 1968.

Stalingradskaya Bitva. Moscow 1960.

Die Grosse Schlacht vor Moskau. Berlin 1959 (orig. Moscow).

Saunders, M. G. (Ed.). *The Soviet Navy*. Weidenfeld and Nicolson, London 1958.

Savyalov, A. S. u. Kalyadin, T. J. *Die Schlacht um den Kaukasus*. Berlin 1959 (orig. Moscow).

Scheibert, H. *Nach Stalingrad 48 Kilometer*. Vowinckel, Heidelberg 1956.

Zwischen Don und Donez. Vowinckel, Neckargemünd 1961.

Schellenberg, W. *The Schellenberg Memoirs*. André Deutsch, London 1956.

Schlauch, W. *Rüstungshilfe der USA an die Verbündeten im Zweiten Weltkrieg*. Wehr u. Wissen Verlagsgesellschaft, Darmstadt 1967.

Schmidt, A. *Geschichte der 10. Division*. Podzun, Bad Nauheim 1963.

Schramm, P. E. *Hitler als militärischer Führer*. Athenäum, Frankfurt am Main 1962.

Senger u. Etterlin, F. M. von. *Die 24. Panzer-Division vormals 1. Kavallerie Division*. Vowinckel, Neckargemünd 1962.

Senger u. Etterlin, F. von. *Neither Fear nor Hope*. Macdonald, London.

Sherwood, R. E. *The White House Papers of Harry L. Hopkins* (two volumes). Eyre and Spottiswoode, London 1948.

Shtemenko, S. M. *Generalnyi Shtab v Gody Voiny*. Moscow 1968.

Sokolovsky, V. D. *Razgrom Nemetsko-Fashistkikh Voisk pod Moskvoi*. Moscow 1964.

Military Strategy. Pall Mall Press, London 1963 (orig. Moscow).

Steets, H. *Gebirgsjäger in der Nogaischen Steppe*. Vowinckel, Heidelberg 1956.

Gebirgsjäger zwischen Dnjepr und Don. Vowinckel, Heidelberg 1957.

Stettinius, E. R. *Lend-Lease*. Macmillan, New York 1944.

Roosevelt and the Russians. Jonathan Cape, London 1950.

Telpukhovsky, B. S. *Die Sowjetische Geschichte des Grossen Vaterländischen Krieges 1941–1945*. Bernard u. Graefe, Frankfurt am Main 1961 (orig. Moscow).

Teske, H. *Die Silbernen Spiegel*. Vowinckel, Heidelberg 1952.

General Ernst Köstring. Mittler, Frankfurt am Main 1966.

Tessin, G. *Verbände und Truppen der deutschen Wehrmacht und Waffen SS 1939–1945*. (Volumes 2 and 3). Mittler, Frankfurt am Main.

Tippelskirch, K. von. *Die Geschichte des Zweiten Weltkriegs*. Athenäum, Bonn 1954.

Tornau, G. u. Korowski, F. *Sturmartillerie Fels in der Brandung*. Maximilian, Herford and Bonn 1965.

Trevor-Roper, H. R. *The Last Days of Hitler*. Macmillan, London 1947.

Vasilevsky, A. *Voenno Istaricheskii Zhurnal 8–10*. Moscow 1965.

Vormann N. von. *Tscherkassy*. Vowinckel, Heidelberg 1954.

Vorobev, F. D. and Kravtsov, V. M. *Pobedy Sovetskikh Vooruzhennykh Sil v Velikoi Otechestvennoi Voine*. Moscow 1953.

Wagener, C. *Moskau 1941*. Podzun, Bad Nauheim 1965.

Wagner, E. *Der Generalquartiermeister*. Günter Olzog, München 1963.

Warlimont, W. *Inside Hitler's Headquarters*. Weidenfeld and Nicolson, London 1964.

Werner-Buxa. *11. Division*. Podzun, Kiel.

Werth, A. *Russia at War 1941–1945*. Barrie and Rockliff, London 1964.

Westphal, S. *The Fatal Decisions*. Michael Joseph, London 1965.

Wheeler-Bennett, J. W. *The Nemesis of Power*. Macmillan, London 1961.

Wollenberg, E. *The Red Army*. Secker and Warburg, London 1940.

Woodward, E. L. *British Foreign Policy. History of the Second World War*. HMSO, London 1962.

Wuorinen, J. H. *Finland and World War II 1939–1944*. The Ronald Press Company, New York 1948.

Zhilin, P. A. *Die Wichtigsten Operationen des Grossen Vaterländischen Krieges 1941–1945*. Berlin 1958 (orig. Moscow).

Zhukov, G. K. *Vospominaniya i Razmyshleniya*. Macdonald, London 1969 (orig. Moscow).

Index

Banzai, J., Lt-Gen., 168
Baranov, V. K., Lt-Gen., 449
Baranovichi, 122, 441–3
Baranow, 456, 530–1, 534
Barbarossa Operation, 59, 63–4, 68–9, 132, 432
Barricades Settlement, 300
Basic Order No. 1, 25, 105n.
Batov, P. I., Lt-Gen. to Col-Gen., 149, 307, 314, 317, 359, 373, 436, 450, 537, 541n.
Batum, 267, 284–5, 508
Bavaria, 313, 424, 438, 562, 576, 577
Bear Operation, 476
Beaverbrook, Lord, 164
Bechtoldsheim, A. R., Freiherr von Mauchenheim, Lt-Gen., 476
Beck, L., Gen., 28n., 49, 451
Belaya Tserkov, 139, 414
Belgorod, 192, 345–6, 349, 358, 361–2, 372
Belgrade, 14, 478, 490, 497
Beloborodov, A. P., Maj.-Gen. to Lt-Gen., 204, 437, 439, 525, 537, 550, 552n.
Belorussia, 1, 24, 52, 55–7, 64, 88, 99, 109, 116, 118, 124, 131, 138, 166n., 377–8, 404, 406, 432, 436–7, 442, 458–9, 462, 464, 474
Belov, P. A., Lt-Gen. to Col-Gen., 376, 420, 427, 436, 449–450, 531, 536, 541, 567, 577
Benes, Dr Eduard, 5, 6n., 516–7
Berdichev, 137–9, 414
Berezina River, 55, 121–2, 126, 390, 433, 437, 439, 440–2
Bergbauernhilfe, 135n.
Berghof, 301, 314, 429, 430, 440
Beria, L. P., 20n., 79, 83
Berlad River, 481–2, 487
Berlin, 7, 10n., 14, 15, 18, 20n., 23, 65–7, 69, 301, 314n., 335, 347n., 392–4, 434, 452, 522, 529, 530, 536, 541, 543, 546, 554, 557, 560, 562–3, 566–8, 570–2, 574–9, 580–5
Berling, S., Gen., 166n., 449, 454, 455, 531
Bernadotte, Count Folke, 577, 585
Berzarin, N. E., Maj.-Gen. to Col-Gen., 104, 109, 243, 245, 474, 475–7, 531, 567, 582
Bessarabia, 9n., 11, 12n., 39, 55–6, 61–3n., 98–9, 133–6, 138, 165, 393, 467, 470–1, 473, 511
Bialystok, 55, 61, 116, 119, 120–5, 131
Bierut, B., 514
Biryuzov, S. S., Maj.-Gen. to Col-Gen., 369n., 413n., 474n.,
Bismarck, Prinz von, 23
Bittrich, W. SS Obergr. führer, 77n.
Black Sea, 55, 60, 130, 134, 140, 147–8, 151, 192–3, 254, 263, 266–7, 277–8, 280–1, 285, 302, 345, 365, 374, 424–5, 473–4, 488, 504, 508, 510, 520
Blaskowitz, J., Col-Gen., 198, 243

Blau, see Blue
Block, J., Lt-Gen., 536
Blomberg, W. von, Col-Gen. to FM, 27, 49
Blücher Operation, see Hitler's Directive, 43
Blue Operation, I, II and III, 258n., 272, 289
Blumentritt, G., Lt-Gen. to Gen., 99n., 207, 248n., 304n., 396
Bobkin, L. V., Maj.-Gen., 260
Bobruisk, 61, 121–2, 127–9, 130, 389, 432–3, 436–7, 439, 449, 454
Bock, F. von, FM, 53, 61, 116–7, 120n., 121, 124, 142, 143–4, 152, 175–8, 184n., 186, 188, 190, 200, 203n., 206—211, 215, 216n., 225, 228, 230, 234, 248, 250, 260, 262, 264, 269, 271, 274, 275, 276, 289, 301–2, 406
Bodin, P. I., Lt-Gen., 250n., 260, 279, 281, 290
Boege, E., Gen., 522
Bogatkin, V. N., Corps Commissar to Lt-Gen., 106n., 235, 435, 522
Bogdanov, I. A., Lt-Gen., 129, 130
Bogdanov, S. I., Col to Col-Gen., 185, 359n., 418, 422, 449, 450, 531, 536, 541, 567, 574, 577, 582
Bogolyubov, A. N., Lt-Gen., 369n., 413, 532n., 566
Bokov, F. E., Lt-Gen., 420
Boldin, I. V., Lt-Gen. to Col-Gen., 20, 119, 123, 180, 183, 184n., 203n., 206–7, 210, 235, 437, 537
Bonin, B. Von, Col, 499
Boris, King of Bulgaria, 471
Borisov, 126, 439, 442
Bor-Komorowski, T., Gen., 454–5
Bormann, M., 558, 577, 581, 583–4
Bosporus, 11, 520
Bradley, O. N., Gen., 562
Brandenburg, 528, 530, 559, 560–1, 567, 570, 586
Brandt, H., Maj.-Gen., 450
Bratislava, 500, 556, 558
Brauchitsch, W. von, FM, 28, 31; character, 32; begins campaign study, 36, 36–8; competence, 50, 54, 56, 58–60, 68, 106–8, 116, 118, 122, 124, 139n., 141n., 143, 144, 148, 156, 186, 192n., 194n., 197–200, 206 208–210; retired, 211, 212, 216–7, 219, 225–7, 229–231, 234, 256, 301, 303, 339
Braun, Eva, 581, 583
Breith, H., Gen., 358, 362, 372, 417, 422, 494, 498–500
Brennecke, K., Gen., 108, 246
Breslau, 459, 530–1, 536, 559–61
Brest (Litovsk), 55–6, 61, 116, 119, 120, 421, 432, 442–3, 450, 452, 511
Brinkmann, H., Vice-Adm., 508
Britain, see Great Britain